Britain ascendant: comparative studies in Franco-British economic history

François Crouzet has devoted much of his life to the study of European industrialisation, and in *Britain ascendant* he draws together a series of essays, written in the course of his career and now thoroughly revised, examining the rise of Britain to the position of dominance in the world economy of the nineteenth century, and the concomitant decline of France. This theme is explored from several angles, and the crucial question of 'why was Britain first?' discussed extensively. Special attention is paid to the problems of capital formation, foreign trade and the consequences of empire, but the political and military vicissitudes of the 'second One Hundred Years War' (1689–1815) and their economic implications are not neglected.

In the concluding chapters of *Britain ascendant* Professor Crouzet examines some more contemporary aspects of Anglo-French economic relations, and throughout the book conventional wisdom is attacked and new views proposed of central issues like the linkages between the Napoleonic Wars and the Industrial Revolution. The approach is systematically comparative, and draws on Professor Crouzet's unparalleled knowledge of the economic structure and organisation of both Britain and France at the onset of industrialisation.

This book is published as part of the joint publishing agreement established in 1977 between the Fondation de la Maison des Sciences de l'Homme and the Press Syndicate of the University of Cambridge. Titles published under the arrangement may appear in any European language or, in the case of volumes of collected essays, in several languages.

New books will appear either as individual titles or in one of the series which the Maison des Sciences de l'Homme and the Cambridge University Press have jointly agreed to publish. All books published jointly by the Maison des Sciences de l'Homme and the Cambridge University Press will be distributed by the Press throughout the world.

Cet ouvrage est publié dans le cadre de l'accord de co-édition passé en 1977 entre la Fondation de la Maison des Sciences de l'Homme et le Press Syndicate de l'Université de Cambridge. Toutes les langues européennes sont admises pour les titres couverts par cet accord, et les ouvrages collectifs peuvent paraître en plusieurs langues.

Les ouvrages paraissent soit isolément, soit dans l'une des séries que la Maison des Sciences de l'Homme et Cambridge University Press ont convenu de publier ensemble. La distribution dans le monde entier des titres ainsi publiés conjointement par les deux établissements est assurée par Cambridge University Press.

Britain ascendant: comparative studies in Franco-British economic history

FRANÇOIS CROUZET
University of Paris-Sorbonne

Translated by MARTIN THOM

The right of the University of Cambridge to print and sell all manner of books was granted by Henry VIII in 1534. The University has printed and published continuously since 1584.

Cambridge University Press
Cambridge New York Port Chester
Melbourne Sydney

Editions de la Maison des Sciences de l'Homme
Paris

CAMBRIDGE UNIVERSITY PRESS
Cambridge, New York, Melbourne, Madrid, Cape Town, Singapore, São Paulo

Cambridge University Press
The Edinburgh Building, Cambridge CB2 8RU, UK

With Editions de la Maison des Sciences de l'Homme
54 Boulevard Raspail, 75270 Paris Cedex 06, France

Published in the United States of America by Cambridge University Press, New York

www.cambridge.org
Information on this title: www.cambridge.org/9780521344340

Originally published in French as *De la supériorité de l'Angleterre sur la France*
by Librairie Académique Perrin 1985

First published in English by Editions de la Maison des Sciences de
l'Homme and Cambridge University Press 1990 as
Britain ascendant: comparative studies in Franco-British economic history

A catalogue record for this publication is available from the British Library

Library of Congress Cataloguing in Publication data
Crouzet, François, *1922–*
(De la supériorité de l'Angleterre sur la France. English)
Britain ascendant: comparative studies in Franco-British economic
history/François Crouzet. translated by Martin Thom.
Translation of De la supériorite de l'Angleterre sur la France.
Includes index.
1. Great Britain – Economic conditions. 2. France – Economic
conditions. I. Title.
HC254.5.C7513 1990
330.941 – dc 20 89-17256 CIP

ISBN 978-0-521-34434-0 hardback

Transferred to digital printing 2008

Contents

Introduction

Why do many historians and social scientists work on foreign countries? Some of them are looking for roots which happen to be abroad. Some are attracted by exoticism, in a broad sense; for instance, some British scholars find in French history a strong and recurrent element of drama, which they feel to have been absent from their own country since the seventeenth century. Some hope to discover abroad a mirror for their motherland, that is some explanations of its development, identity and originality; or, by studying a country which has been or is a leader, they intend to obtain a better understanding of the general course of history. There is also the unreasoned and unreasoning attraction for some foreign culture – including political culture – whether it is close or distant, not to mention the random element of accident in individuals' careers, which has led some historians to become interested in alien lands.

I had no family connection with England, where I did not set foot before the age of twenty three, and I had taken German at school. A combination of several factors was thus needed to make me give up early plans to become a medievalist and to devote most of my research and teaching to Modern British history. I can mention, pell-mell: heavy doses of English novels (from H. Fielding to Agatha Christie – but all in French translation) as a teenager; admiration and gratitude towards Britain during the dark years 1940–4; a course of lectures on England in the eighteenth century, which I took when an *hypokhâgneux*; an interest in economic history, which I shared with a number of would-be historians of my generation (the depression and the war had taught us that economics were 'important'), and the feeling that it could be satisfied in the first industrial country (though the expression had not yet been coined); the opportunity, through a fellowship, to start graduate research in England; and more.

There was rashness in such a reconversion, as 'foreign' historians labour under serious handicaps *vis-à-vis* those who work on the history of their own country. Whatever their efforts, there will be gaps in their knowledge of the country which they study and of its history, there will be failings in their understanding. They are like travellers, narrating their experiences, who may remark some significant details, which are too familiar to the local inhabitants to be noticed by them, but who, on the other hand, easily make gross blunders and pass preposterous judgements. There is, however, an area in which 'foreign' historians may hope to enjoy some comparative advantages and which is comparative history, but even this ground is not absolutely safe. Comparatist historians have to be proficient in the history of two countries (or more), but, by extending the scope of their studies, they risk becoming superficial or being ignorant of some crucial aspects; historians whose main interest is abroad also can lose touch with advanced research in their land of origin. There is, moreover, a danger of bias, to which I shall return later.

It must be added that comparative economic history has been dismissed as unscientific by some learned writers.[1] None the less, there are few works on broad problems of economic growth and even few textbooks of 'national' economic history, from which some kind of comparison between the experiences of different countries is absent. Cliometricians rightly argue that all historical explanations imply some counter-factual statements, so that it is better to make them explicit – and to test them. Likewise, I have reacted against the crude, uninformed, out-of-date comparisons with France, which were implicit or semi-implicit in many works – especially those belonging to the 'whig' tradition of economic history, and I have pleaded for serious and systematic comparisons. Though I can claim to have been interested in British economic and social history *per se*, and to have been fascinated by some of its *minutiae*, it has been difficult to keep comparisons with Continental countries, and especially with France, out of my thoughts. I also felt that this was a niche, in which I had an opportunity to make some contribution to scholarship.

This approach also supplies some vindication of the present volume – though the re-publication in book form of articles and essays has become so frequent in recent years that it does not need to be justified at length. This book has a central theme – and thus some unity of

[1] See chapter 2, pp. 55–7.

purpose – which is the ascendancy of Britain, how it was established and maintained, from the late seventeenth century up to the end of the nineteenth. True enough, one chapter looks as though focused on Britain only, but its subject – capital formation – has loomed large in the study of the Industrial Revolution (a misnomer, according to Rondo Cameron, but which I go on using, *faute de mieux*),[2] which, of course, was crucial to Britain's mastery. The other chapters are devoted either to comparisons of development and growth in Britain, France and Western Europe, or to the movements of goods, capital, technologies, ideas and images in and out of Britain, or to the conflicts which have opposed England and France – and to their economic consequences.

Indeed, the Anglo-French couple has to be considered not only with a comparative and economic approach, but also from the conflictual and political point of view. Britain's rise to economic ascendancy was accompanied by a succession of military and political successes, which made her first a great power, then the super-power; those successes were mainly achieved over France. The relationship between those two drives towards ascendancy will be discussed later; even though the Industrial Revolution can not be seen as the product of British victories and conquests overseas, the latter at least helped to destroy the chances which Britain's competitors in the economic race might have had. Anyhow, rivalry and armed struggles between England and France were a constant and major factor in the history of the two countries, not only from the Glorious Revolution to Waterloo, but for almost the whole of their existence as nations. Thus some remarks about this conflict will not be ill-timed here.

Crécy, Poitiers, Agincourt, the siege of Orléans, La Hogue, Blenheim, Fontenoy, Trafalgar, Waterloo, Fashoda, Mers el Kebir, with many other lesser encounters ... one battle after another: such is the record, unparalleled in the history of any other two countries, of the chronic and prolonged bouts of warfare down the centuries between the French and English. Since 1815, apart from a few clashes between the British and the forces of the Vichy government, the sound of battle has died away. But relations between our two countries have still often been stormy: 'ententes cordiales' have become unfriendly misunderstandings; wartime companionship in arms has involved bitter dis-

2 R. Cameron, 'The Industrial Revolution: A Misnomer', in J. Schneider (ed.), *Wirtschaftskräfte und Wirtschaftswege: Festschrift für Hermann Kellenbenz* (Stuttgart, 1981), vol. 5, pp. 367–76.

agreement. General de Gaulle therefore had some grounds for thinking that the Anglo-French conflict was much more deep-seated and long-standing than the enmity between France and Germany.[3]

The memory of these conflicts has been part of the folk memory of generations of British and French, and is still vivid today – particularly in Great Britain, where a feeling for the historic past, sustained as it is by education and the media, is far more acute than in France. The French, preoccupied by their earlier wars of religion and impulses towards general fratricide, mainly retain of their past whatever may serve to nourish their hatred of each other. The memory of ancient feuds with their neighbours is relegated to the lumber room.[4] Of course, for the English, the memory of past feats of arms simply means victories over the French, while the French have fought many other enemies. Anyhow, the cult of Joan of Arc, once pushed to a height of hysteria, is now almost non-existent, whereas at Windsor the Waterloo Banquet is still an annual event at which the Duke of Wellington ceremoniously presents the Queen with a replica of a French eagle captured on the great day.

This endless strife has deeply affected the economic, social, political and even cultural evolution of the two countries. The awakening of national feeling on both sides of the Channel was undoubtedly due to the Hundred Years' War. Later, the wars against Louis XIV forced England into abandoning an archaic system of public finance and brought about the creation of the Bank of England (1694). While on the other side, the war of American independence destroyed the finances of the French monarchy and helped to spark off the Revolution.

But these interactions were not the result of war only. Over the centuries there have been incessant cross-Channel contacts and exchanges in both directions in various spheres of activity. Some of these – in the realm of culture and the arts – are not touched on in this book, despite their importance. But who is not aware of the influence of French art in England – from Norman churches to Post-Impressionism – or of English literature, notably Shakespeare and Walter Scott, on the French romantics? Not to mention the occasional waves of

[3] I am grateful to M. Alain Peyrefitte, to whom General de Gaulle had made this remark, for authorising me to mention it here.

[4] This paragraph and those which follow, up to p. 7, are reprinted, with a number of changes and cuts, from D. Johnson, F. Bédarida, F. Crouzet (eds.), *Britain and France. Ten Centuries* (Folkestone, 1980), pp. 13–15.

anglomania and gallomania in fashions: after all, mini-skirts and long hair came from the English side of the Channel. The most chauvinist Frenchman has to admit that from the seventeenth century onwards France, however unwillingly, has absorbed more in the way of technology, ideas, political and economic knowhow from England than she has offered in return, in spite of having, up to the late nineteenth century, a larger population.

So, in spite of, perhaps even because of the quarrels and the hates that have divided them, there is a true symbiosis between England and France. Even more, one can find parallels in their histories. A narrow view, of short periods only, inevitably produces violent contrasts of the sort favoured by generations of nineteenth- and early twentieth-century historians: for Michelet England was the 'anti-France', France's exact opposite. English historians used to make a facile comparison between England's steady and progressive *evolution* with the violent *revolutions* that have characterised French history since 1789; forgetting that in the seventeenth and eighteenth centuries it was the English who were reputed to be turbulent and ungovernable.

In a recent book about the eighteenth century, Jeremy Black has written: 'Those who argued that the British and the French were both different and rivals were not fools'; and he makes a plea for the xenophobes, zealots and bigots of the time, who 'were more realistic assessors of their circumstances and predictors of the future than the intellectuals who wrote of the brotherhood of man. Britain and France were competing states, rival cultures and antagonistic people'.[5]

But on a longer view, and taking into account the historic experience of other European and (*a fortiori*) non-European peoples one is struck rather by the similarities and convergences. Whatever, for instance, the gap between British and French incomes per capita and its variations during the last forty years, it fades into insignificance when it is compared with incomes in the Third World. Historians, of course, enjoy minutely analysing small differences, but to the danger of short-sightedness.

England and France were the first 'nation states', with centralised monarchical government, and populations imbued with the feeling of belonging to one community.

England and France were the first large states to experience violent

[5] J. Black, *Natural and Necessary Enemies. Anglo-French Relations in the Eighteenth Century* (London, 1986), p. 211.

revolutions, which in the long run (though more slowly in the case of France) led to liberal parliamentary systems pursuing moderate policies.

England and France were, the one the pioneer of industrial revolution and modern economic growth, the other the first to follow suit (though Belgium and Switzerland may be said to share this distinction).

England and France both gained by conquest, and finally lost, great colonial empires – even if that of France was only a smaller scale copy of the majestic British empire; both have left their mark, sometimes a deep one, on their erstwhile subject peoples.

With their countless 'firsts' (in the mountaineering sense) England and France have together, from the seventeenth to the nineteenth century, been the guiding lights of Europe and the world: leaders whose different qualities have complemented each other. Was not the modern world born of the monstrous union of those two great contemporaneous movements, the Industrial and the French Revolution? Is not 'liberty' an English discovery; 'equality' a French invention? With all the differences between their national ways of thought, England and France have originated and diffused the ideas of natural rights, the rights of man, liberty, toleration and democratic government. Alas, it is symbolic that in the same year, 1798, between them they also invented two great afflictions of the world today – France, compulsory military service; England, income tax! A more sombre remark is that the French Terror of 1793–4 was the harbinger and, in many respects, the inspirer of the mass murders and massacres which have prevailed in the twentieth century. Several recent writers have seen the repression by Republican troops of the Royalist insurrection in the Vendée as the precursor of ideological genocides. The British record of the time is not as bad, but the crushing of the 1798 Irish rebellion is not terribly different from what happened in the Vendée.[6]

In 1843 the socialist, Cabet, was to write: 'France and England are marching together in the forefront of humankind; if one looks more closely at the progress of these two peoples in the vanguard one sees that they endlessly react upon one another, each guiding or being

[6] The hulks on which French prisoners of war were detained were forerunners of modern extermination camps; HM Government indulged in 'State Terrorism', when abetting the Cadoudal plot to kill Bonaparte.

guided by the other; sometimes France is at the head of the column, sometimes England takes the lead.'

It would, of course, be utterly foolish to replace the old devils of nationalism with a chauvinistic 'bi-nationalism', inasmuch as first France, then later England have irretrievably lost their former leadership (so that decline is to be added to their common heritage . . .).

Shared misfortune has not brought our countries closer; on the contrary it has caused sulks and snarls, crocodile tears over the neighbour's problems barely concealing smug satisfaction, indifference or even contempt for the way they do things the other side of the Channel; notwithstanding the fact that their problems of adaptation to the role of lesser powers, and to a stormy *fin de siècle* are broadly identical. The Straits of Dover remain a yawning gulf and the Channel Tunnel is unlikely to close the gap.

This is what can be called the Franco-British paradox: two countries that have hated each other yet have never ceased to borrow ideas, institutions, techniques, works of art from each other; for whom geographical propinquity has only served to increase psychological alienation, each viewing his neighbour as the personification of *foreignness*. Their ancient hates may now be damped down, but so too are the warmly affectionate feelings of the francophile and anglophile minorities.[7]

Admittedly, specificities and differences remain momentous. After all, the history of England is a success story, even in its decline, the history of a people who have played their cards with skill. The history of France, in a sense, is nothing but a preposterous tragi-comedy of lost opportunities, good luck misused, disasters following on achievements. It is odd that so far she has managed to survive, though the end of the road may not be far away; her chances of survival have seriously fallen since 1981 and in the next century she may only be a geographical expression, a territory mainly inhabited by people of Arabic and

[7] The British and the French have even managed to hate each other in different ways. French francophobia was based upon grievances related to events which had actually happened – in the past: for instance the burning of Joan of Arc, the loss of Canada, the ill-treatment of prisoners of war, the peace treaties of 1814 and 1815; it involved charges of insolence, brutality, perfidy, hypocrisy, but, most of the time, was not insulting. Conan Doyle wrote, during the Boer war, that it was normal for the French to hate the British whose Empire was built upon the ruins of French greatness. On the other hand, English Francophobia was, basically, a quasi-physical and racial dislike of the French and their ways; and it also thrived upon phantasms, such as popish plots and invasion scares – or Palmerston's idea that the French hated England from the depth of their hearts and were only dreaming of humiliating her; the British attitude also was, quite often, deliberately offensive.

African origin: *Finis Galliae*. On the other hand, Britain has been confidently expected to become the Japan of the 1990s; though this prediction appears to have soon faded, a British Renaissance has obviously taken place in the 1980s.

A friendly reviewer has defined me as 'a French francophobe anglophile',[8] and there is also the warning, given on the occasion of the reprinting of the francophile John Stuart Mill's *Essays*, about the danger of 'going native in the foreign culture' which one studies, especially 'for the writer who, while nurturing a vivid sense of alienation, remains practically and ... emotionally implicated in his own society'.[9]

It would be difficult to plead not guilty on those counts, except that strict objectivity and complete detachment are not easy when one has known the traumas of 1940, 1968 and 1981 and when living under a régime one abhors. Moreover, the problem of economic growth – and specially of French growth – always has had political undertones; it can not be de-politised and sanitised, because of a constant inter-play between the present and the past. The depression of the 1930s, the collapse of 1940, the difficult recovery of the late 1940s, all threw a dark shadow upon the whole of French economic history; it was natural thus for French writers to denounce the failings of capitalism, for Americans, who discovered in 1944–5 a starving and medieval-looking country, to think that there always had been something seriously wrong with its economy. Unexpectedly, however, came the *Trente Glorieuses*, the thirty years or so of fast economic growth and change from the 1950s to the 1970s. Their prosperity reverberated over views of the past; historians wondered whether, after all, the French people

[8] R. Cameron, 'Was England Really Superior to France?', *Journal of Economic History*, XLVI, 4, December 1986, p. 1037.

[9] *The Times Literary Supplement*, 8 November 1985, p. 1251. At the other extreme, there is the total insularity, displayed in the same weekly (2–8 September 1988, p. 969), in a review of a book on *The Hundred Years War*, whose author was so rebuffed:

> Whether the French 'had the last laugh', as he also maintains, is more debatable. In the sense that the English were driven from France, obviously so. But the long-term legacy of the war which the French won was the institutions of the *ancien régime*: the *gabelle*, the *aides*, the *taille*, a standing army, a privileged nobility and bureaucracy, and an overtaxed peasantry. If the war had any corresponding long-term effect on England, it was to confirm the position of Parliament and the necessity for Parliamentary consent to taxation. In its dual influence on the constitutions and social structures of the two countries, the war helped to create the preconditions for a revolution in France and for its avoidance in England.

The reviewer appears to have forgotten that two revolutions had happened in England well before 1789!

were as unfit for industrialisation as it had been previously maintained; the result was the emergence of 'revisionism', while marxists gave up economic history, in disgust, and turned to social history or to other fields, where they could go on denouncing exploitation and immiseration. Since 1981, there has been a new change of positions. Supporters of the Socialist régime have praised the achievements of capitalism *à la française*, that is, subordinated to the State, controlled and directed by Government. Liberal economists, on the other hand, see France going the way of the Argentine under Peron, of Rumania under Ceausescu, etc., with its economy being irretrievably wrecked by a tyranny; the mere fact that such a disaster can happen demonstrates that the French economy was not sound, but brittle and weak; once again the look at the past has become dim and gloomy, and historians are searching for explanations of *die Französische Katastrophe*. Vice versa, the economic decline of Britain in the post-1945 period and her retreat from Empire have strongly brought out her power and ascendancy before 1914; they have also emphasised how exceptional the latter had been, and that they were man-made and transitory, instead of God-given and permanent as the Victorians had believed. Moreover, in this light, the major question is not 'Why did Britain decline?', but 'Why was she – for a century at least – the dominant economy and the only super-power?' On the other hand, if Britain's Renaissance assumes permanence, economic historians will have to take new view-points.

The author of a book like the present one is faced at the start with a dilemma: will it be a mere reprint, with no changes in the original papers? Or have the latter to be altered and recast, in order to take into account recent research – and also eventual changes in the writer's views? Actually, a compromise solution has been chosen (it may give the worst of both worlds!): articles have been reprinted as they were when published, but for some corrections in the form or the substance – and also some cuts, especially in footnotes. However, in cases when recent research had produced some significant findings, the latter have been summarised, either in footnotes or in appendices to some chapters. I have not, however, tried to be exhaustive and to bring up-to-date the whole of the reprinted articles; sometimes, I only have supplied a short list of 'additional readings'. On the other hand, the first of the articles which are reprinted here was the starting point for a debate – about the British and French economies in the eighteenth century; I have tried, in a new essay (Chapter 2), to strike the balance of those discussions and to give my own afterthoughts on this problem. I have not attempted, however, to iron out the differences or – possibly – contradictions between the hypotheses which I have suggested at various times over the years.

It would be unfair to end this introduction without acknowledging my debt both to individual British colleagues and friends, and, more generally, to the 'school' of British economic historians as a whole. The former often have had the doubtful privilege of being first to hear, in lecture- or seminar-room, early drafts of most of the papers which follow; their comments and criticisms have been invaluable. They and also many past and present British and American writers, who I have never met, but whom I diligently read, have greatly helped me to be freed from the stifling atmosphere which prevailed in French academic and intellectual circles. It is now widely recognised that, for two generations, left-wingers have imposed in France a kind of intellectual terrorism (which, moreover, since 1981, has had the full force of the State apparatus behind it). Most historians have had to pay at least lip-service to a crude and vulgar marxism, to vituperate against feudalism and capitalism and to indulge in an extreme and ridiculous miserabilism (the latter is not absent from British writings, but to a lesser extent); dissidents have been persecuted, abused or at least ignored. Moreover, the centralised and hierarchised system, which prevailed – and still prevails to some extent – in French universities, and also a genuine, but misplaced, devotion to some *pontifes*, have largely crippled discussions among historians. So simplistic, obsolete and even grotesque concepts or views (like Simiand's A and B phases) have enjoyed far too long a lease of life. To make things worse, the various factions into which French historians are divided – for both ideological and institutional reasons – have suffered from inward-looking parochialism; each one of them has often ignored all work coming from a different group.

This is not to deny that, in the last decades, France has had many first-class historians – though a frequent mistake abroad is to believe that they all have been *Annalistes* or devotees of *la nouvelle histoire.* But the British have no ground for an inferiority complex and some recent lamentations on the decline of British history – and especially of economic history – have gone much too far.

Anyhow, I have been much influenced by the British school of economic history, while disregarding Parisian gurus. And I welcome this opportunity to pay tribute to scholars who combine the resort to archival sources, according to well-established principles of scholarship, with a strong grounding in economics, including economic theory, and with proficiency in quantitative methods. They achieve a happy compromise between the theoretical and mathematical approach of American cliometricians, and the empiricism, associated with childlike conceptualisation, which remains too frequent on the Continent and especially in France. Above all, there is a climate of free, untrammelled discussion (which is, in some respects, still more lively in the United States), and the most senior historians are never sure that their views will be unchallenged. I have done my best, in some chapters of this book, to give a fair account of such debates. Some readers may find that I have analysed the pros and cons at excessive length; but the idea was to supply readers with basic data and to leave them to make up their minds. History is stifled by dogmatism, ideology and parochialism; it only thrives under liberty.

1 ❧ England and France in the eighteenth century: a comparative analysis of two economic growths*

The economic historian interested in the key problem of growth is bound to find the comparative approach particularly fruitful. A systematic comparison of the eighteenth-century English economy with that of another country – and France as the leading Continental power at that time seems the obvious choice – should bring out more clearly what factors were peculiar to England and might therefore have determined what is a unique phenomenon, the English Industrial Revolution of the eighteenth century.

The first point to be made is that the forwardness of England and the backwardness of France, clearly noticeable on the eve of the French Revolution, were not of sudden or recent appearance; this disparity between the two countries had already been evident early in the century, say at the death of Louis XIV. Moreover, to find an explanation for the contrasts between the social and economic structures of France and England we should have to look at the problem over a long period (going well back into the Middle Ages; one would stress, for example, the importance of wool in English history: wool production, the wool trade and woollen manufacture early made England part of the international economy and stimulated the rise of capitalism). That task cannot be attempted here, but it must at least be stressed that developments during the seventeenth century had a different effect on the two economies, which partly accounts for the time-lag between them at the beginning of the eighteenth century.

As is well known, a similar point was made some fifty years ago by J. U. Nef, who pressed it very hard with his assertion that the reason

* This article was edited for publication in R. M. Hartwell (ed.), *The Causes of the Industrial Revolution in England* (London, 1967). It had been first published in French in *Annales ESC*, XXI, 2, March–April 1966, pp. 254–91.

why England was the first country to undergo the eighteenth-century Industrial Revolution was simply that, unlike other countries and particularly France, she had already undergone a first industrial revolution in the late sixteenth and early seventeenth centuries, which meant that her lead had been established some two centuries earlier than was generally thought.[1] But this thesis has been strongly criticised from the British side, and little of it remains intact today.[2] The 'first English industrial revolution' existed chiefly in Nef's imagination: he attached far too much importance to a few technical innovations, to the understandably fast growth of the handful of new industries (coal excepted, their role was a very minor one – yet he ignored the slow growth in the major woollen industry), and lastly to a few non-representative cases of entrepreneurial giantism.[3]

Nevertheless, Nef deserves our thanks for having stressed the importance of the fast rise in English coal production and consumption during the century after 1540, and its influence on technological progress through stimulating the development and adoption of some completely new techniques, such as furnaces fired by coal or coke, which were quite unknown on the Continent. This early adoption of mineral fuels gave English inventiveness an impetus which proved to be lasting and which in France was lacking.[4] Again, it is possible that Nef was right in maintaining that between 1540 and 1640 England had an absolute lead over France in mining and metal production and also

1 J. U. Nef, 'A Comparison of Industrial Growth in France and England from 1540 to 1640', *Journal of Political Economy*, XLIV, 3, 4, 5, June, August, Oct. 1936, pp. 289–317, 505–33, 643–66; see also by the same author: 'The Progress of Technology and the Growth of Large-Scale Industry in Great Britain, 1540–1640', *The Economic History Review*, V, 1, Oct. 1934, pp. 3–24; 'Prices and Industrial Capitalism in France and England, 1540–1640', *ibid.*, VII, 2, May 1937, pp. 155–85; 'L'Industrie et l'État en France et en Angleterre (1540–1640)', *Revue Historique*, CXCI, 1941, nos 1 and 2, pp. 21–53, 193–231.

2 See particularly D. C. Coleman, 'Industrial Growth and Industrial Revolutions', *Economica*, n.s., XXIII, 89, Feb. 1956, reprinted in E. M. Carus-Wilson (ed.), *Essays in Economic History*, III (London, 1962), pp. 345–7; D. C. Coleman, 'Technology and Economic History, 1500–1750', *The Economic History Review*, 2nd series, XI, 3, April 1959, pp. 506–7, 509–10, 512; B. E. Supple, *Commercial Crisis and Change in England, 1600–1642* (Cambridge, 1959), pp. 2–8; F. J. Fisher (ed.), *Essays in the Economic and Social History of Tudor and Stuart England in Honour of R. H. Tawney* (Cambridge, 1961), pp. 6–7; Y. S. Brenner, 'The Inflation of Prices in England, 1551–1650', *The Economic History Review*, 2nd series, XV, 2, Dec. 1962, pp. 271–3.

3 On the other hand, Nef overstated the stagnation of French industry during the same period. He also went much too far when he spoke of a 'phenomenal acceleration' in English industrial output between 1540 and 1640.

4 W. H. Chaloner and A. E. Musson, *Industry and Technology* (London, 1963), pp. 20–1, 24–5, 29; 'The Origins of the Industrial Revolution', *Past and Present*, XVII, April 1960, p. 76; below, pp. 95–9.

had a higher output per head for products such as woollen goods and glass, and possibly for industrial output as a whole.[5]

However, it was after 1640 rather than before that significant disparities between the economic evolution of the two countries appeared. As is well known, recent research has produced a black picture of French economic history in the 'tragic seventeenth century' (admittedly, an overstated expression). This work has shown that after a relatively prosperous start to the century, the 1630s saw the beginning of a long period of stagnation and decline – turning in mid-century during the Fronde into collapse – which lasted up to the 1720s. Prices – and especially food prices – over the century show a downward trend, and more significantly, extreme instability; there were frequent and violent economic and demographic crises, attended by terrible mortalities; there was monetary famine and 'tightness of money', which crippled business activity and brought down rents and industrial and commercial profits; there was unemployment and pauperism. In view of all this, it is no wonder that industrial production stagnated and even declined.[6] Colbert's policy of industrialisation was really nothing but a desperate effort to counteract this declining trend; it was undertaken in the highly unfavourable conditions of deflation, falling prices, incomes, and consumption, and ended in semi-failure. Although some of his new industrial undertakings survived and developed later, many others declined and quickly disappeared; and on the whole, if there was any increase in total industrial output under Colbert's government, which is not certain, it was not very pronounced. It is true that recent research has shown that despite two great wars, several famines and protestant emigration, there were signs of recovery in the French economy during the latter part of the reign of Louis XIV, long thought to have been catastrophic. This may well reveal a rising underlying trend, a sign heralding the post-1715 growth, but any such recovery was largely counteracted by the bad effects of wars and

[5] Nef, 'A Comparison', p. 663.

[6] See P. Goubert, *Beauvais et le Beauvaisis de 1600 à 1730. Contribution à l'histoire sociale de la France du XVIIe siècle* (Paris, 1960), pp. 585–91, 595–6; graphs, 126–30, pp. 116–19 of the supplement; P. Deyon, 'Variations de la production textile aux XVIe et XVIIe siècles: Sources et premiers résultats', *Annales ESC*, XVIII, 5, Sept.–Oct. 1963, pp. 947, 950–3. See also P. Goubert, in F. Braudel and E. Labrousse (eds.), *Histoire économique et sociale de la France*, vol. II: *Des derniers temps de l'âge seigneurial aux préludes de l'âge industriel (1660–1789)* (Paris, 1970), pp. 329–48 (later abbreviated *HESF*, II); and vol. 2 of P. Léon, *Histoire économique et sociale du monde*, P. Deyon and J. Jacquart (eds.), *Les Hésitations de la croissance, 1580–1740* (Paris, 1978).

famines.[7] Therefore, even if there are a few positive items to enter on the French balance sheet for the seventeenth century, the general picture remains most unfavourable, and the population of France in 1715 or 1720 was hardly higher than it had been in 1600.

On the English side of the Channel the picture is certainly different, and English historians are on the whole optimistic in their estimation of England's economic performance during the seventeenth century. England was not, of course, totally unaffected by the adverse economic climate of the seventeenth century; there were periods of difficulty and stagnation, for example in the 1620s, during the Civil War and at moments in the wars against Louis XIV; England's main industry, woollen manufacture, went through a series of crises and its growth over the century as a whole was relatively modest; chronic poverty and underemployment were serious problems. But there is nothing to compare with the recurrent violent crises or the deep and lasting depression to be seen in France after 1630. The reversal in the trend of price movements and of the economy in general reached England later than France, about 1650, and in England the subsequent fall in prices was smaller, while short-term price fluctuations seem to have been – at least after 1661 – less violent, less irregular, and hence less injurious to economic activity.[8] F. J. Fisher was able to conclude that the global output of agriculture and industry increased slowly but appreciably during the century, and that despite the rise in population, average income per head probably rose.[9]

There are also other signs of economic progress, especially after 1660, for which there is no parallel in France: for example, the expansion of the English home market, due principally to the growth of London, which far exceeded that of Paris; the 'frontier-like' development of the northern and western counties;[10] and the fast and prolonged growth during the seventeenth century of English foreign

[7] P. Léon, 'La Crise de l'économie française à la fin du règne de Louis XIV (1685–1715)', *Information historique*, XVIIII, 4, Sept.–Oct. 1956, pp. 132–7; Deyon, pp. 953–5; P. Goubert, *Louis XIV et vingt millions de Français* (Paris, 1966).

[8] J. Meuvret, *Etudes d'histoire économique. Recueil d'articles* (Paris, 1971), pp. 103–4, 117–19, 123; A. B. Appleby, 'Grain Prices and Subsistence Crises in England and France, 1590–1740', *Journal of Economic History*, XXXIX, 4, Dec. 1979, pp. 865–87; also Brenner, pp. 276, 281–2; G. N. Clark, *The Wealth of England from 1496 to 1760* (London, 1946), pp. 108–10; E. H. Phelps Brown and S. V. Hopkins, 'Seven Centuries of the Prices of Consumables, Compared with Builders' Wage-Rates', *Economica*, n.s., XXIII, 92, Nov. 1956, pp. 299–301, 305, 312–13.

[9] Fisher, *Essays*, p. 3; F. J. Fisher, 'The Sixteenth and Seventeenth Centuries. The Dark Ages in English Economic History?', *Economica*, n.s., XXIV, 93, Feb. 1957, pp. 6–9, 12, 15, 16.

[10] Fisher, in *Economica*, pp. 10–11.

trade, largely thanks to early colonial expansion, which meant that from the 1660s England had an important trade in the re-export of exotic products, a trade which continued to rise and was the chief factor in the growth of English trade as a whole, at a time when French colonies and colonial trade were still relatively insignificant.[11]

Thanks to this slow but quite steady growth, at the beginning of the eighteenth century England already had a definite lead over France in several important fields. First, in agriculture: various technical improvements were now in use over a large part of the country, productivity was higher and more regular than in France, a fact which, together with England's geographical advantages, helps to explain why bad years were less disastrous in their effects. Secondly, in industrial technology: the earlier innovations which resulted from the use of coal as a fuel had been supplemented by the great burst of inventive activity of the late seventeenth and early eighteenth centuries, which threw up among others the major inventions of Savery, Newcomen, and Darby. Thirdly, England was also leading in the commercial field, with a higher volume of trade, both in relation to the population and in absolute terms,[12] with a much larger merchant navy, and with a faster accumulation of merchant capital. And she had won the first battles in the struggle for command of the seas and dominion over America. Lastly, England's superiority was also very evident in the financial field, where the establishment of the National Debt and the Bank of England were signs of a political and economic structure well in advance of France: attempts by Louis XIV to set up a National Bank foundered on the objections of the bankers who thought it incompatible with a 'pure monarchy', and John Law's attempt a few years later to transplant English financial institutions to France ended in disaster.[13]

In 1688 Gregory King asserted that England had reached a higher level of wealth than any other country, Holland alone excepted, and

[11] R. Davis, 'English Foreign Trade, 1660–1700', *The Economic History Review*, 2nd series, VII, 2, Dec. 1954, pp. 150–4, 159–63, and 'English Foreign Trade 1700–1774', *ibid.*, XV, 2, Dec. 1962, p. 285; D. A. Farnie, 'The Commercial Empire of the Atlantic, 1607–1783', *ibid.*, XV, 2, Dec. 1962, p. 206.

[12] E. Levasseur, *Histoire du commerce de la France, Première partie: avant 1789* (Paris, 1911), p. 405.

[13] H. Lüthy, *La Banque protestante en France, de la révocation de l'édit de Nantes à la Révolution* (Paris, 1959 and 1961, 2 vols.), vol. I, pp. 94–7, 290–1, 414; R. Mousnier, *Les XVIe et XVIIe siècles* (Paris, 1954), p. 299; C. P. Kindleberger, 'Financial Institutions and Economic Development: A Comparison of Great Britain and France in the Eighteenth and Nineteenth Centuries', *Explorations in Economic History*, XXI, 2, April 1984, pp. 117–19.

estimated the French average income per head at 20 per cent lower than the English; a generation later, just after the Treaty of Utrecht, Daniel Defoe was writing of England as 'the most flourishing and opulent country in the world'.[14] These opinions were certainly not unjustified, in view of England's modest but growing prosperity in the seventeenth century, when France was stagnant and even declining. Whatever the causes of this disparity – different socio-economic structures, political circumstances – once the unfavourable economic climate of the seventeenth and early eighteenth century had lifted and the French economy started to grow, it was already behind the English and began with a serious handicap. If it is accepted that the Industrial Revolution was merely the crown stage of a long process of growth and change, it is important to our understanding of the British 'take-off' in the last third of the eighteenth century that it came after about two centuries of growth – admittedly broken at times, but never for very long – whereas the growth of the French economy at the same period dated back less than half a century and followed a century of stagnation. It was in fact during this 'tragic' post-1630 seventeenth century that France was clearly outdistanced by England, and despite her relatively fast growth during the eighteenth century she was never able to catch up.

We have seen that the economic developments of France and England during the seventeenth century are in clear contrast; but for the three-quarters of a century between the end of the War of the Spanish Succession and the French Revolution the picture is quite different. In both countries this was a period of growth, and the available statistical data point to the somewhat surprising conclusion that the rates of growth were not at all dissimilar.[15]

Let us start with what is best known, foreign trade, which is also the sector where French growth was fastest – faster in fact than the British. The total foreign trade of England and Wales (imports + exports + re-exports) had an average yearly official value of £13 million for the five years 1716–20 and £31 million for the five years 1784–8, which

[14] Quoted by P. Deane and W. A. Cole, *British Economic Growth, 1688–1959. Trends and Structure* (Cambridge, 1962), p. 38, and M. Ashley, *England in the Seventeenth Century (1603–1714)* (London, 1952), p. 230.

[15] Naturally, statistics from the eighteenth century can give only rough orders of magnitude or very approximate indexes of growth, and they should be used with caution. A stronger warning applies to the calculations of national aggregates; the work of J. Marczewski and J. Toutain on France, P. Deane and W. A. Cole on Britain was received with reservations by many scholars. However, it would be a kind of intellectual Luddism to refuse to use their results.

means it multiplied by 2·4.[16] On the other hand, the average yearly value of France's foreign trade was 215 million livres tournois for 1716–20 and 1 billion 62 million for 1784–8, which means a fivefold increase.[17] However, the English official values were calculated at more or less constant prices, so that in fact they give a rough index of the volume of trade, while the French figures are at current prices. Since prices rose about 60 per cent between the 1730s and the 1780s, the comparison is only valid if we deflate the figures for 1784–8 to constant prices. But this would still leave an increase in the *volume* of French trade which at lowest is of the order of 1 to 3, and even so is higher than the English. True enough, it has been argued that available statistics overestimate the growth of French commerce,[18] but there is no doubt that in any case, the value of French foreign trade was by 1715 markedly lower than that of the English, and by the eve of the Revolution had reached about the same level (though the value per head of the population was naturally still much lower).

We must, of course, take into account the very low level to which French trade had fallen at the end of the War of the Spanish Succession, but it nevertheless grew faster than the English up to the time of the French Revolution. Moreover, there were several branches of international trade in which the French secured or maintained a dominant position; they continued to be the main suppliers of manufactured goods to Spain, and through Cadiz to Spain's American Empire, while the British had the monopoly of the smaller Portuguese and Brazilian markets; they dominated the markets of Italy and the Levant. Thanks to spectacular progress in sugar and coffee cultivation in San Domingo and to the low prices of these products, which competed successfully with those of the British West Indies where soils were becoming exhausted and production costs were higher, the French snatched most of the entrepôt trade in colonial produce from the English merchants and developed a large and fast-growing re-

[16] E. B. Schumpeter, *English Overseas Trade Statistics, 1697–1808* (Oxford, 1960), pp. 15–16, Tables I–IV.

[17] A. M. Arnould, *De la balance du commerce et des relations commerciales extérieures de la France dans toutes les parties du globe particulièrement à la fin du règne de Louis XIV et au moment de la Révolution* (Paris, 2nd edn, year III, 3 vols.), vol. III, Table 10; Levasseur, p. 512, n. 2.

[18] D. S. Landes, 'Statistics as a Source for the History of Economic Development in Western Europe: The Protostatistical Era', in V. R. Lorwin and J. M. Price (eds.), *The Dimensions of the Past. Materials, Problems and Opportunities for Quantitative Work in History* (New Haven and London, 1972), pp. 63–4. See, however, Riley (n. 62 below), p. 109 n. 1, who confirms my view.

export trade to Northern Europe. The British on the whole did not do well in European markets, where they came up against protective tariffs and French competition. In absolute terms, the increase in English exports to Europe was slow; they did not double between the beginning of the century and the 1780s; Europe's share in English total exports also diminished, falling from about four-fifths to under a half. English commercial expansion was due almost entirely to the fast growth of her colonial trade and especially of trade with the American possessions, which up to the revolt of the Thirteen colonies provided English industry with an almost fully protected market.[19] This 'Americanisation' of foreign trade is also noticeable, though less marked, in France; French colonial trade, despite losses of territory due to the Seven Years War, grew tenfold between 1716–20 and 1784–8, when trade with countries outside Europe made 38 per cent of total trade. French trade, then, was still more oriented on Europe than the English, and this European trade was growing almost as fast as total trade, certainly faster than that of England with the Continent.[20]

This optimistic picture of French foreign trade needs, however, to be qualified on several points. In particular, its relative position seems to have been more favourable during the first half of the period under review, that is before the Seven Years War. Up to the end of the forties, in fact, the development of English trade was 'painfully slow', because of the stagnation in the export of woollen goods and in re-exports; fast growth came only after 1748, with an annual rate of growth of 3·9 per cent between 1745 and 1760. At first, French trade, despite the whiplash of the '*Systeme*', grew at a rate similar to the English, but after about 1735 it accelerated sooner and faster, doubling in value in under twenty years (between 1736–9 and 1749–55). But this spurt was cut short by the Seven Years War, during which French trade was driven off the seas by the Royal Navy and fell 50 per cent, while English trade continued to grow. Between 1763 and 1771 there was a sharp recovery, whose chief effect, however, was to recover lost ground, and this was followed by distinct stagnation in the 1770s and then an outright recession during the American war. It was only on the very eve of the Revolution that French trade again became buoyant and reached a

19 Davis, 'English Foreign Trade, 1700–1774', pp. 294, 298; Farnie, p. 214; Deane and Cole, pp. 34, 86, 88; Schumpeter, pp. 10–11; also pp. 216–18, 234–5.

20 It is true that the main growth in French trade with Europe was made by re-exports (of colonial produce) which increased eightfold, while exports of French products barely trebled. Cf. Levasseur, pp. 487, 512, n. 2; Arnould, vol. I, pp. 326–7; II, Table 2; III, Table 12.

record level, before collapsing in 1793. English trade on the other hand prospered during the Seven Years War, suffered some slowing down during the 1770s and a fall during the American war; after the peace of 1783 it picked up very sharply, to make a rapid and sustained growth until the end of the century. There are also signs that the competitive position of French products deteriorated after 1770 and that they were losing ground in the Levant, in Spain (where the protectionist policy of Charles III was a further obstacle) and in Spanish America.[21] In addition, the course of British trade was much less irregular, because it did not suffer as much from the wars.[22]

Symptoms of an incoming crisis have been observed under the apparent prosperity of French colonial trade on the eve of the Revolution;[23] though the danger must not be overstated, an undoubted weakness of French trade was its great dependence on San Domingo, which in the 1780s was responsible for three-quarters of the trade with the French colonies and also supplied most of the re-exports, which themselves made about one-third of total exports. The proportion of re-exports was almost as great in English trade, but the British colonial empire was larger and more various than the French so that British colonial trade was more diversified; moreover, until 1776 it included as one of its chief markets the Thirteen colonies, with their fast-rising European population, their relatively high standard of living and expanding demand for manufactured goods of all sorts. Further, the percentage of manufactured goods to total exports was higher in British than in French trade – about two-thirds as against two-fifths in the 1780s; the leading French exports were coffee, sugar, and wines, linen and silk goods taking second place.[24]

However, in France, as in England, commercial expansion was a strategic factor in the growth of industry. This is a more difficult

[21] Davis, 'English Foreign Trade, 1700–1774', pp. 285–8, 294–3; Schumpeter, pp. 13–14; Deane and Cole, pp. 29–30, 42–9, 310–11; Levasseur, pp. 511, 521, 523; E. Labrousse, *La Crise de l'économie française à la fin de l'Ancien Régime et au début de la Révolution* (Paris, 1943), pp. xxxvi–xxxix.

[22] But there are also some striking parallels in its development, with alternating phases of fast growth (between the War of the Austrian Succession and the Seven Years War) and of slow growth or stagnation (after 1713, during the 1770s).

[23] F. Crouzet, in F. G. Pariset (ed.), *Bordeaux au XVIIIe siècle* (Bordeaux, 1968), pp. 316–23; Paul Butel, *Les Négociants bordelais, l'Europe et les iles au XVIIIe siècle* (Paris, 1974), pp. 382, 385; R. Stein, 'The State of French Colonial Commerce on the Eve of the Revolution', *Journal of European Economic History*, 12, 1, Spring 1983, pp. 105–17.

[24] E. Levasseur, *Histoire des classes ouvrières et de l'industrie en France avant 1789* (Paris, 2nd edn 1900, 2 vols.), vol. II, pp. 556–7; Levasseur, *Histoire du commerce*, pp. 515, 518 n., 521, n. 2.

question to discuss, because of the shortage of really satisfactory quantitative materials and the highly conjectural character of the structures which have been erected on the shaky foundations of those we possess. For England, W. Hoffmann's index shows that industrial production just trebled between 1700 and 1799; the later index of real output in commerce and industry established by Phyllis Deane and W. A. Cole goes up from 100 in 1700 to 285 in 1790, which means an average rate of growth of 1·17 per cent per year; more recent research suggests lower figures, at least for the pre-1760 period.[25] For French industry, Jean Marczewski published only some provisional results; according to these, the gross physical product of French industry and handicraft at current prices rose from a yearly average of 385 million livres for the decade 1701–10 to 1,573 million for 1781–90, which means its volume increased fourfold, in fact at a mean average rate of growth of 1·91 per cent per year.[26] But it seems that fuller and more precise calculations would modify these conclusions, reducing the rate of growth to little more than 1 per cent per year, which would be very close to the figure Deane and Cole obtained for English production. The idea that English and French industrial production increased at much the same pace between the early eighteenth century and the French Revolution may appear surprising, but comparison of the evolution of the main industries in each country appears to bear it out.

As regards the woollen industry, Deane considers that in England its output rose about 150 per cent in the eighteenth century taken as a whole. For France, Pierre Léon puts the increase between the early eighteenth century and 1789 at a mere 60 per cent, i.e. a mean rate of growth of 0·9 per cent per year. Later, T. J. Markovitch calculated that the volume of French wool textiles production rose by 144 per cent from 1702/4 to 1784/6, i.e. at a mean yearly rate of 1·1 per cent – roughly in his view at the same pace as the English wool industry. In France the linen industry was very important, in terms of labour force and value of output perhaps bigger than the woollen industry;

[25] W. G. Hoffmann, *British Industry, 1700–1950* (Oxford, 1955), Table 54, Part A; Deane and Cole, p. 78, Table 19. The index given by these authors refers to ten-year averages centred on the year quoted. See also N. F. R. Crafts, 'British Economic Growth, 1700–1831: A Review of the Evidence', *The Economic History Review*, XXXVI, 2, May 1983, pp. 182–4; C. K. Harley, 'British Industrialization before 1841: Evidence of Slower Growth during the Industrial Revolution', *Journal of Economic History*, XLII, 2, June 1982, pp. 267–89 (especially 272, 276, Table 5, 284, Table 8, 285).

[26] J. Marczewski, 'Some Aspects of the Economic Growth of France, 1660–1958', *Economic Development and Social Change*, IX, 3, April 1961, Tables 1 and 3; P. Léon, in *HESF*, II, p. 521.

according to Pierre Léon, its growth during the eighteenth century was faster than that of wool. In Britain, linen manufacture was of little importance at the beginning of the eighteenth century and though it later grew fast in Scotland, particularly at mid-century, by national standards it remained a relatively minor activity, and its growth, though sharp, can have had little consequence for industrial output as a whole. As for the silk industry, imports of raw silk into England slightly more than doubled between the beginning of the century and the 1780s, but the English silk industry remained small in comparison with the French, which was growing altogether faster: according to Léon, the number of looms at work in Lyons increased 185 per cent between 1720 and 1788.[27]

For cotton, the picture is of course different – but not as different as one would think. There is no need to dwell on its phenomenal growth in Britain. Net imports of raw cotton rose from just over 1 million pounds weight in the early eighteenth century to a yearly figure of over 15 million in 1780–9 (and in this last year to 30 million). However, in France the cotton industry was also growing very fast; J. Marczewski has calculated that its rate of growth between the first and the ninth decades averaged 3·8 per cent per annum; this was similar to the English growth rate but starting initially at a lower level. Thus in 1786 English net imports of cotton were 18 million pounds weight, French only 11 million. This shows the English cotton industry with a definite superiority, but the margin is not so great as it became later, and France had then the advantage in the production of printed cottons. It must also be remembered that until the very last years of the century cotton's contribution to British national income remained relatively small.[28]

For the mining and metal industries the quantitative data are very unsatisfactory. French coal production was of course much lower than

[27] Deane and Cole, pp. 52–3, 205, 207; P. Léon, 'L'Industrialisation en France en tant que facteur de croissance économique du début du XVIIe siècle à nos jours', *Première conférence internationale d'histoire économique, Stockholm, 1960* (Paris and The Hague, 1960), pp. 175–6, 178–9; *id.*, in *HESF*, II, p. 519; T. J. Markovitch, *Histoire des industries françaises. Les industries lainières de Colbert à la Révolution* (Genève, 1976), especially pp. 458, 460, 484–6; this last work is based upon archival sources, very thorough and rather reliable.

[28] Deane and Cole, pp. 50–2, 163; Léon, 'L'Industrialisation', p. 178; Levasseur, *Histoire des classes ouvrières*, p. 524–6, 545, 690; Marczewski, Table 7; P. Bairoch, *Révolution industrielle et sous-développement* (Paris, 1963), pp. 235–6, 305–7; C. Ballot, *L'Introduction du machinisme dans l'industrie française* (Paris, 1923), p. 120; Lüthy, vol. II, pp. 663–5; S. D. Chapman and S. Chassagne, *European Textile Printers in the Eighteenth Century. A Study of Peel and Oberkampf* (London, 1981), p. 8, Table 1.

British, but in the eighteenth century it started to grow very fast and by the time of the Revolution had some national importance. As for the iron industry, although there is still much that is obscure and controversial about its evolution in England during the first part of the century, its growth up to about 1760, in fact up to the time of Henry Cort's inventions, was certainly slow; it was only as a result of Cort's inventions that iron production showed dramatic increase, doubling in ten years. Some figures suggest that until the 1780s output in France grew faster. At all events, on the eve of the Revolution, France probably had an output of from 130,000 to 140,000 tons of pig-iron, as against only 60,000 in England.[29]

This brief survey thus does not contradict the impression left by estimates of global industrial output, and as regards *volume of output*, French industrial performance up to the Revolution compares not unfavourably with the English. France was producing less coal, non-ferrous metals, ships and cotton goods than Britain, but more woollens, linens, and silks, as well as more iron. French total industrial production was appreciably higher than the English, but production per head remained smaller, as it had already been in the seventeenth century.

It is true that in industry, as in foreign trade, French performance seems to have been relatively better in the first half of the period under review than in the second. Recovery in output after the depression of the later years of Louis XIV occurred before 1720 in some sectors (Dauphiné, Amiens), after this date in others (Beauvais for example). The recovery was sharp: output of woollens seems to have doubled at Amiens between 1715 and 1750 and trebled at Beauvais between 1724 and 1735. In any case, after 1730 growth was

[29] Léon, 'L'Industrialisation', pp. 177, 179; P. Léon, 'Techniques et civilisations du fer dans l'Europe du XVIIIe siècle', *Le Fer à travers les âges. Hommes et Techniques* (Nancy, 1956), p. 233; B. Gille, 'La Métallurgie française d'Ancien Régime', *Revue d'histoire de la sidérurgie*, V, 2, April–June 1964, p. 156; H. d'Herouville, 'Réflexions sur la croissance', *Etudes et conjoncture*, XIII, 11, Nov. 1958, p. 997; E. F. Heckscher, 'Un grand chapitre de l'histoire du fer: le monopole suédois', *Annales d'Histoire économique et sociale*, IV, 14, March 1932, p. 132; Levasseur, *Histoire des classes ouvrières*, vol. II, p. 675; Marczewski, Table 8; Bairoch, pp. 238, 247–8, 313–14; Deane and Cole, pp. 55, 221; T. S. Ashton, *An Economic History of England. The 18th Century* (London, 1955), p. 124; B. R. Mitchell, with the collaboration of P. Deane, *Abstract of British Historical Statistics* (Cambridge, 1962), p. 221; M. W. Flinn, 'The Growth of the English Iron Industry, 1660–1760', *The Economic History Review*, 2nd series, XI, 1, August 1958, pp. 151–2; Léon, in *HESF*, II, pp. 321, 527; C. K. Hyde, 'The Adoption of Coke-Smelting by the British Iron Industry, 1709–1790', *Explorations in Economic History*, X, 4, Summer 1973, p. 408.

general and quite fast.[30] English industrial growth at this period was somewhat sluggish: Deane and Cole observed a faster pace only in the 1740s and 1750s, and even this movement slackened after 1760. Not everyone will agree with this interpretation, but there is broad agreement about an acceleration during the 1780s in all manufacturing output, which signifies that England had truly entered the Industrial Revolution.[31] In France, according to Ernest Labrousse, there was a slackening in industrial growth from mid-century and after 1770 prolonged stagnation. The old textile industries stopped growing and in some districts – for example Amiens, Normandy, Brittany, and Languedoc – even declined. The agricultural depression around 1780, the worsening lot of the poorer classes, made the difficulties of industry more acute and were a preface to its collapse in 1788–9. These difficulties should not, however, be overestimated, since the stagnation of the old industries (also noticeable in England, where competition from cotton damaged wool and linen) was in part compensated by the fast rise of new industries – cotton in particular, but also coal, iron, glass, and chemical products. However this may be, during the eighteenth century, French industry certainly displayed considerable vitality and buoyancy.[32]

There remains agriculture, a thorny question which will be considered in the next chapter. According to J. Toutain, France had a 60 per cent increase of the deflated agricultural product between 1701–10 and 1781–90; this figure is undoubtedly too high. On the other hand, Deane and Cole have estimated the growth in real output of British agriculture between 1700 and 1790 at 35 per cent. As in the preceding cases, some roughly parallel growth is not to be excluded. Admittedly,

[30] Goubert, *Beauvais*, pp. 586, 589; P. Deyon, 'Le Mouvement de la production textile à Amiens au XVIIIe siècle', *Revue du Nord*, XLIV, 174, April–June 1962, pp. 204, 207; P. Léon, *La Naissance de la grande industrie en Dauphiné (fin du XVIIe siècle–1869)* (Paris, 1954, 2 vols), vol. I, pp. 118 ff.

[31] Deane and Cole, p. 78, Table 19; Ashton, *The 18th Century*, p. 125; A. H. John, 'Aspects of English Economic Growth in the First Half of the Eighteenth Century', *Economica*, n.s., XXVIII, 110, May 1961, pp. 176–90. According to Crafts and Harley (see n. 25), the acceleration of the 1780s has been overestimated by most writers; still they do not deny it existed.

[32] C. E. Labrousse, *Esquisse du mouvement des prix et des revenus en France au XVIIIe siècle* (Paris, 1933, 2 vols), pp. 506–8, 548, 557; *La crise*, pp. viii, x, xxii–xxiii, xxxii–xxxvii, 177; Deyon, 'Le Mouvement de la production', pp. 207–8; Levasseur, *Histoire des classes ouvrières*, pp. 527, 682, notes 6 and 7; Lüthy, vol. II, p. 594; Léon, 'L'Industrialisation', p. 179; 'Structure du commerce extérieur et évolution industrielle de la France à la fin du XVIIIe siècle', in *Conjoncture économique, structures sociales. Hommage à Ernest Labrousse* (Paris – The Hague, 1974), pp. 415–21; Markovitch, p. 486.

English agricultural techniques underwent great improvements during the eighteenth century, for which there is no equivalent in France, but French agriculture was not as conservative as is often thought and eighteenth-century France did not suffer the famines and mass mortalities which had been so frequent in the seventeenth.[33]

As regards the global growth of the two economies, for Britain the Deane and Cole index of total output rises from 100 in 1700 to 190 in 1790 (and Crafts has a doubling from 1700 to 1780), for France an index of the gross physical product at constant prices, as computed by Marczewski, rises from 100 to 260 between the first and ninth decades of the century; the last figure is undoubtedly too high.[34] But between 1700 and 1781 the population of France apparently increased 28 per cent (from 21·5 to 26 millions), that of England and Wales 39 per cent (from 5·1 to 7·0 millions).[35] The growth in average real output and income per head might therefore have been roughly of the same order of magnitude in both countries – and possibly faster in France.[36]

As we have seen, however, at the beginning of the eighteenth century France was behind England, especially as regards the level of average industrial output, foreign trade, and incomes; as both economies grew at about the same rate in the next three-quarters of a century, France could not overtake her rival (although some ground was no doubt made up during the second third of the century), and the close similarity in the rates of growth, which in this paper is deliberately stressed because it has often not been recognised, ought not to disguise the differences between them. In the 1770s, though the economic power of France was, like in the seventeenth century,

[33] J. C. Toutain, *Le Produit de l'agriculture française de 1700 à 1958* (Paris, 1961, 2 vols, *Histoire quantitative de l'économie française*, vols I and II), vol. I, pp. 213, 215; vol. II, pp. 128 (diagram 110), 133, 136, 139, 204, 276; Deane and Cole, p. 78, Table 19; Chapter 2, pp. 52–4.

[34] Deane and Cole, pp. 78–9; Marczewski, 'Some Aspects', Table 4; his figures are tainted because of Toutain's mistakes. The last estimates – by Crafts and Harley – of British national product give a somewhat slower growth than Deane and Cole.

[35] E. A. Wrigley and R. S. Schofield, *The Population History of England, 1541–1871. A Reconstruction* (Cambridge, 1981), pp. 528–9, Table A3. 1; J. Dupâquier, *La Population française aux XVIIe et XVIIIe siècles* (Paris, 1979), pp. 34, 37, 81–2, 87; 'La Non-Révolution agricole du XVIIIe siècle', *Annales ESC*, XVII, 1, Jan.–Feb. 1972, p. 83; E. Le Roy Ladurie, in *Seventh International Economic History Congress. Edinburgh 1978. Four 'A' Themes* (Tonbridge, 1978), p. 122.

[36] A rise of the French income per capita is undoubted, but no figure can be presently given. For England, there was an increase of 20–30 per cent from 1700 to 1760 and then stagnation; Deane and Cole, p. 78, Table 19; Crafts, p. 183, Table 5.

clearly superior in mercantilist terms,[37] England was still the more 'developed', the richer country, with certainly a higher average income per head. England was more urbanised, more industrialised,[38] more involved in international trade; industry employed a higher percentage of the active population and contributed more to national income, roughly over one-quarter, as against one-fifth in France.[39] Moreover, the subsistence sector had virtually disappeared from England as early as the seventeenth century, ousted everywhere by the mercantile and monetary economy; in France the quasi-autarchic subsistence sector was still important and prevailed in extensive areas, acting as a brake on the growth of the economy as a whole (mostly because of obvious geographical reasons).

The fundamental difference between the two economies, however, is in the technological field. The relatively fast (but extensive) expansion of French industry during the eighteenth century took place within a framework which was still, as regards organisation and methods, largely the traditional one. Some changes can be observed, for example the tendency towards concentration and growth of commercial capitalism, the migration of industry from the towns to the countryside, the appearance of new products or even of new industries such as cotton, but in general the traditional structures held. On the eve of the Revolution, the French economy was not basically different from what it had been under Louis XIV: it was merely producing much more. In England, on the other hand, where growth during the first half of the century was of the 'French' type, that is, within the traditional framework, after 1760 some revolutionary changes appeared and economic structures were modified in depth by a series of technical inventions which heralded a general revolution.

This is the heart of the matter: Britain was the place where all the basic inventions which created modern industry – the spinning machine, the flying shuttle, the power-loom, the printing drum, the coke furnace, puddling, and most revolutionary of all, the steam engine – were made, perfected and introduced into industry. In France inventions were far fewer and restricted to improvements for the silk

[37] P. O'Brien and C. Keyder, *Economic Growth in Britain and France, 1780–1914. Two Paths to the Twentieth Century* (London, 1978), pp. 57, 60.

[38] Possibly the difference in this respect between the two countries was not large; cf. O'Brien and Keyder, pp. 92–3; P. Bairoch, 'International Industrialization Levels from 1750 to 1980', *Journal of European Economic History*, XI, 2, Autumn 1982, p. 281, Table 4.

[39] These estimates are possibly wrong, but nothing better can be suggested.

industry (Vaucanson and later Jacquard) and the chemical industry (Berthollet and Leblanc). Eighteenth-century France had some excellent technicians in fields like shipbuilding, ordnance (Gribeauval), and public works, not to mention many marvellous craftsmen, but their talent was not applied to the improvement of industrial techniques. French industry only developed on the technical side through taking up foreign machines and techniques, and to assimilate them usually required the help of foreign technicians, most of them British, though some were Swiss or German.[40]

England experienced a real outburst of inventiveness, which in France was almost completely lacking, and this decisive British superiority in ingenuity and willingness to innovate is the basic fact which accentuated the structural discrepancy between the two economies during the second part of the eighteenth century, and which we must now try to explain.

This is a difficult task, all the more so because the foregoing analysis has removed one convenient explanation: if, as was long believed, British output had increased much faster than the French, British inventiveness could then very easily be explained as a function, a by-product, of growth. But as things are, the parallel growth in output in the two countries makes the British superiority harder to understand, since there seems nothing specific or unique about the development of the English economy, or at least of a large part of it. And in so far as individual genius remains something of a mystery, it will never be fully explained why England had so many great inventors in the eighteenth century. All the historian can hope for is to understand the environment which favoured the making of inventions and which made manufacturers eager to take them up.

The earliest economic historians, when they considered this question, attached great importance to the English institutional framework. Efforts by the State to control and regulate industry had been abandoned as early as the seventeenth century, and though the relevant laws were still theoretically in force, they were never applied; at the same time, the guild system had fallen into decay.[41] Eighteenth-century England was thus a country of *laissez-faire*, in which the field was left free for individual initiative. In France, on the other hand, the

[40] See particularly P. Léon, 'Tradition et machinisme dans la France du XVIIIe siècle', *Information Historique*, XVII, 1, Jan.–Feb. 1955, pp. 5–14.

[41] T. S. Ashton, *The Industrial Revolution, 1760–1830* (London, 1948), pp. 11–12.

guilds survived and their members resisted the development of large-scale enterprises and the introduction of new techniques. Moreover, Colbertist regulations, by prescribing detailed standards of workmanship, discouraged innovations. And in England, such vestiges of corporate regulation and public control as did survive, as for example in the woollen industry, had precisely the effect of encouraging routinism.

Historians like Levasseur, however, went too far in envisaging eighteenth-century French industry as imprisoned in the double strait-jacket of guilds and regulations, which they saw as an insuperable barrier to progress and the reason why French inventions were so few.[42] Nowadays, it is accepted that the guild system was never general in France and in fact did not apply to the greater part of industry; it was unknown in the economic life of many towns, for example Lyons, in royal manufactures, in rural domestic industries, and in new industries such as cotton.[43] Moreover, the system went into rapid decline in the second half of the century, as did Colbertist regulations, which had always been evaded and which from mid-century were less and less strictly enforced, as governmental circles were converted to *laissez-faire* policies. The contrast betweeen French 'dirigism' and English liberalism should thus not be overestimated and it seems that the influence of the institutional framework, though real, was limited.

Some recent historians have stressed the importance of socio-psychological factors, involving a distinct contrast between the English and French social structures and 'scales of value' to explain the British superiority in inventiveness and the entrepreneurial spirit.[44] These writers have shown, with justice, that there was greater vertical social mobility in eighteenth-century England than in France, but it is odd that they should emphasise an aspect of the problem which seems both disputable and of secondary importance. They maintain that in England the social barrier separating the landed classes from industry and commerce, the barrier, that is, between the aristocracy and the business world, was relatively low. But this can have very little bearing

[42] Levasseur, *Histoire des classes ouvrières*, vol. II, p. 305. A. Toynbee and W. Cunningham also overestimated the influence of *laissez-faire* on the English side.

[43] The rise of this industry was possibly delayed by the prohibitions against printed cottons which remained in force until 1759, though Chapman and Chassagne, p. 190, doubt it.

[44] See D. S. Landes, *The Unbound Prometheus* (Cambridge, 1969), pp. 49–52, 66–74; H. Perkin, *The Origins of Modern English Society, 1780–1880* (London, 1969), pp. 63 ff.; A. Milward and S. B. Saul, *The Economic Development of Continental Europe, 1780–1870* (London, 1973), pp. 34–5.

on the problem, since the Industrial Revolution was certainly not the work of the British aristocracy nor even of the gentry. As we know, England had the Duke of Bridgewater and his canal and some great landowners who took an interest in business, but on the whole active participation and investment in industry by the nobility and gentry seems to have actually declined during the eighteenth century, notably in metallurgy (it has been maintained, however, that it gave legitimacy to the pursuit of profit). Moreover, despite the contrary assertions of some English-speaking sociologists, the French nobility was not a close caste, nor was it totally uninterested in business. It controlled a good part of the metallurgical and glass industries and the coal-mines; it invested in foreign trading ventures and West Indian plantations, and on the eve of the Revolution a number of *grands seigneurs* like the Duke of Orleans and the Count of Artois were active in enterprises concerned to introduce English technology into France.[45]

No one, however, will deny that the social prestige of business was lower in France than in England, that the ideal of *vivre noblement* (that is of doing nothing) was stronger there, contempt for work more widespread. But here, too, caution is necessary. For example, writers have often stressed that the French bourgeois who got rich in business retired from it as soon as possible to buy land or public office. And the sale of offices has been rightly criticised as an important factor in diverting capital and talents away from productive activities (tax-farming and financial deals with a government perpetually hard-up played the same role). But this factor was much less important in the eighteenth than in the seventeenth century, as the State was no longer resorting to mass creations and sales of offices. As for the diversion of capital to land, this was also a marked feature in England, where it was the dream of every merchant who got rich to become a country gentleman: and though he himself fairly often retained an interest in the business which had made his fortune, it very rarely survived into the next generation.

As regards our present problem, vertical mobility and scales of values may well be less important than differences between the two countries in the mentality of the men actually engaged in business. In English society there was a more 'capitalist', a more commercial, a more acquisitive spirit; and according to contemporary accounts there was in England a harshness, a ruthlessness, a concentration on the

[45] There has been a good deal of discussion about the French nobility; see particularly G. Chaussinand-Nogaret, *La Noblesse au XVIIIe siècle: de la féodalité aux Lumières* (Paris, 1976).

pursuit of gain, which was absent in the more easy-going France of the *Ancien Régime*.[46] Yet the French social and psychological environment was not basically hostile to innovation, and many manufacturers were quite ready to take up foreign inventions (although they often had difficulty in making them work). French merchants too displayed plenty of initiative and daring in overseas ventures. In any case, such observations are primarily descriptive and quite superficial, leaving the differences in the two mentalities unaccounted for.

Basically, the problem is still obscure and new research is needed into the relationship between the English and French social structures on the one hand and the entrepreneurial mentalities and attitudes on the other. What is most needed is a close analysis at the local or regional level, since to speak of English society and French society as a whole only leaves one with dubious generalities. After all, the Industrial Revolution was not made in England but in a few small districts of England – south Lancashire, some sectors of the East Midlands and Yorkshire, Birmingham, and the Black Country.[47] The inventors and innovators were recruited from the middle class of these industrial districts, from the merchant-manufacturers and the skilled, well-to-do artisans, and England's wealth in qualified cadres of this type was certainly an important factor. A detailed comparison between these English nurseries of the Industrial Revolution and some French industrial centres would be very instructive. Another pointer is the fact that most of the English discoveries were the product of joint effort, as for example with the notable collaboration of Black, Watt, Boulton and Wilkinson over the steam engine; in France, a larger and more rural country, where manufacturing was more dispersed, an element of isolation may have hampered this type of co-operation and cross-stimulus.

Another difficult question is the influence of the Enlightenment. The relationship between the Industrial Revolution and the English philosophical and scientific movement of the late seventeenth century and the eighteenth century is well known. Recent research has stressed the importance of the belief, which goes back to Newton, that industrial progress was possible through observation and experiment; it has shown that most of the inventions (although largely the work of

[46] See Landes, pp. 71–2.

[47] The idea of the Industrial Revolution as a 'regional phenomenon' has been developed by S. Pollard, *Peaceful Conquest: The Industrialization of Europe, 1760–1970* (Oxford, 1981), especially pp. 3, 14, 20, 40–1.

practical men with little education) were backed by systematic thinking, that British scientists and manufacturers were often in close contact, for example in bodies such as the Birmingham Lunar Society, and that scientific knowledge had penetrated industrial society down to a very modest level. But the philosophical and scientific movement was at least as powerful in France, which had plenty of scientists, some of whom, like Buffon and Réaumur, tried their hand at industrial research; scientific societies and academies existed there in profusion and numbered business men among their members; belief in progress and the wish to improve man's material condition were at least as widespread as in England, and Diderot's *Encyclopédie* is striking proof of the interest cultivated people took in technology. But unlike what happened in England, all this intellectual activity had very little practical result; discussions in learned societies remained theoretical in character and those who took part lacked a sense of the concrete.[48] A study of this question which also took education into account would again be very useful. In Britain, dissenters and Scotsmen played a major role in the Industrial Revolution because, thanks to the dissenting academies and the much more advanced Scottish educational system, they were the best-educated section of the middle class. French businessmen had either a very elementary or a purely classical education. This difference may have had some consequences.[49]

To sum up, although neither the differences in social structure and mentality between the two countries in the eighteenth century, nor the features of the English social environment which favoured the entrepreneurial spirit should be minimised, the contrast does not appear to be as sharp as is often said. Moreover, the real influence of such concrete differences as did exist is still obscure, and though they may in some respects account for British technical superiority, they can only

[48] There is a large literature on this problem; see particularly Ashton, *The Industrial Revolution*, pp. 14, 16; A. E. Musson and E. Robinson, 'Science and Industry in the Late Eighteenth Century', *The Economic History Review*, XIII, 2, December 1960, pp. 222–44; Musson and Robinson, *Science and Technology in the Industrial Revolution* (Manchester, 1969); Musson, *Science, Technology and Economic Growth in the Eighteenth Century* (London, 1972); P. Mathias, 'Who Unbound Prometheus? Science and Technical Change, 1600–1800', article of 1972, reprinted in *The Transformation of England* (London, 1979), pp. 54–5; also 'Science and Technology During the Industrial Revolution: Some General Problems', *ibid.*, pp. 72–87; J. R. Harris, *Industry and Technology in the Eighteenth Century: Britain and France. An Inaugural Lecture delivered in the University of Birmingham on 27th May 1971* (Birmingham, 1972), pp. 15–16; 'Skills, Coal and British Industry in the Eighteenth Century', *History*, LXI, no. 202, June 1976, pp. 167–9.

[49] On the whole the level of literacy was higher in the eighteenth century in Britain than in France.

be a secondary factor in comparison with strictly economic forces. After all, technical progress is closely bound up with economic phenomena, and the explanation we are looking for must be first and foremost an economic one. The contention is that the French did not innovate because, unlike the British, they were not made to do so by the strong pressure of economic forces.

Did this pressure arise from demand? Several writers have maintained that a fast growth in the demand for manufactured goods, from both the home and the export markets, presented British industry with a challenge it could meet only by a technical revolution. This is an attractive hypothesis, but its major premise, that there was an abnormally fast growth in demand in eighteenth-century England is still unproved, and in any case there seems no reason why effective global demand should have grown much faster in England than in France.

There was population growth in the two countries, but at a faster pace in England than in France: this increase in population from 1700 to 1781 was respectively 39 per cent and 28 per cent, as already mentioned (but in absolute numbers, France gained three times more people than England). There has been much debate about the relationship between the industrial and demographic revolutions, but some of the contributors are surely right in stressing that while population growth was doubtless a necessary condition for the Industrial Revolution, it was by no means a sufficient or decisive one, since it was general throughout Western Europe, in particular the upsurge which occurred around mid-century.[50]

Turning to average real incomes per head, they certainly rose in England during the first half of the eighteenth century, when the population was almost stationary, food prices falling, and money wages rising; the internal market therefore expanded, consumption of many articles increased, there was a broadening in range and improvement in quality; A. H. John has pointed out that this permanently affected the level of consumption in most classes and even aroused an appetite for mass consumption. This progress, however, did not last, for from mid-century the expansion of the economy was absorbed by the upsurge in population, and average output per head hardly

[50] This problem would need much fuller treatment in the light of recent research.

increased afterwards.[51] Development in France seems to have been roughly parallel, with a rise in average incomes during the first half of the century followed by a degree of stagnation. Labrousse has shown that, from the 1760s, food prices and rents were rising faster than money wages, which means a fall in real wages, affecting not only the urban wage-earner and the landless rural proletariat, but also many poor peasants with some land of their own, who derived part of their income from wages; a large section of the population therefore became poorer, and this must have meant a fall in its average consumption of manufactured goods. However, the rise in rents and agricultural profits was at the same time enriching a not insignificant part of the population, not only the 'feudal' landlords but also the well-to-do peasants. This was a stimulus to trade, and in particular trade in colonial products, and to industry and urban development, and produced a rise in non-agricultural incomes. There is therefore no reason why average effective demand for manufactured goods should have decreased, except possibly during the late 1770s and the 1780s when, according to Labrousse, the fall in food prices brought about a general stagnation.[52] But, and this is the important point, the slowing down in French demand would have come only after the English had made their main innovations, which were achieved during a period of prosperity on both sides of the Channel.

There is also the demand from foreign markets to consider. In both countries it was more buoyant and increased much faster than internal consumption (although it absorbed a much smaller proportion of output); but as we have already seen, British exports of manufactures increased no faster than French, with the important exception of cotton goods.[53] In addition it must be said, against a currently held opinion, that French losses of colonial territories as a result of the Seven Years War had little effect on exports, since few French goods were taken up by the Canadian and Indian markets, which were only

[51] Ashton, *The 18th Century*, p. 232; John, pp. 180–3, 190; Deane and Cole, pp. 18–19, 21, 41, 80–1; also note 36 above and p. 89 below. There is presently a broad consensus that real wages stagnated or even fell during the second half of the eighteenth century.

[52] Labrousse, *Esquisse*, vol. II, pp. 379, 382–3, 444, 497, 598–9, 610–11, 617; *La Crise*, pp. xxv–xxviii, xxxi.

[53] Schumpeter, p. 12; Deane and Cole, p. 59; see also *Past and Present*, XVII, April 1960, p. 74, and K. Berrill, 'International Trade and the Rate of Economic Growth', *The Economic History Review*, 2nd series, XII, 3, April 1960, p. 358, which stresses the importance of England's capture of the expanding market for this article of mass consumption.

of potential value; nor did England derive much immediate advantage from her conquests.[54]

In fact, the important differences between the English and French markets for manufactured goods are to be observed in their structure rather than their evolution.

In the first place, the British home market – unlike the French – was a truly national market, since the country was an economic unit and there were no internal customs or tolls. This factor should not be overstressed, since the principal French customs unit – the 'Five big Farms' – covered a population about as large as Britain. Nevertheless, as K. Berrill rightly stressed, during the eighteenth century Britain and her colonies formed the largest 'free trade area' in the world. Furthermore, the small size of the country, its configuration, and the early improvement to its transports, contributed to making this national market a reality and internal circulation much more active than in France.[55]

Again, demand within this market was more intense, because as we have already seen, from the beginning of the eighteenth century Britain had a higher average income per head and a higher standard of living. There is no doubt that the British masses were better fed, better clothed, better shod than their French counterparts; the percentage of really poor in the total population may have been smaller and that of well-to-do middle-class people greater. In consequence, if average demand for manufactured goods did not grow faster than in France, it still kept to a higher level for the whole of the period under review.[56]

Lastly, the pattern of consumption was also different, though not in the sense often claimed. Some English-speaking writers maintain that France had only luxury industries such as silk, crystals, porcelain, cabinet-making, which were unsuited to machine production, while England specialised early in making cheap goods for a mass market, which could be mass-produced by machinery in factories.[57] France certainly had luxury or semi-luxury industries which catered for the upper classes; their relative importance was greater than in England and they were little suited to mechanisation. But, in addition, France had large industries which catered for popular consumption, turning out coarse woollens and linens for the peasantry, for West Indian

[54] Deane and Cole, p. 85, n. 2. [55] Berrill, p. 358; John, pp. 185–8.

[56] The 'high' standard of living of the bulk of the British people must not be overestimated.

[57] *Past and Present*, XVII, April 1960, pp. 79–80; Clark, pp. 169–70.

slaves and for the Spanish colonies. Now this production for the masses was not large-scale mass production, since the market was fragmented and the places of manufacture dispersed; moreover, it catered for an unfastidious clientèle and used very cheap rural labour, so there was no pressing need to make technical improvements. On the other hand, it appears that British superiority in the eighteenth century was in the manufacture of good quality products suitable for middle-class consumption; and when Frenchmen complained (at any rate before the 1780s) about British competition, they stressed the superior quality, finish and appearance of the goods manufactured in Britain. In part the contrast was a reflection of the differing social structures of the two countries and their colonies: England, relatively speaking, had a larger middle class and the fast-growing population of the Thirteen colonies had a standard of living close to that of the middle classes in Europe. English industry was therefore not catering for a true 'mass market' – this appeared only in the nineteenth century – but was in a position to make longer production runs than the French.[58] In the result, output had to be both somewhat standardised and of good quality, which undoubtedly encouraged increased division of labour and technical improvements in order to keep prices low, and also the concentration of work in factories, to maintain quality by better supervision.

We may also wonder whether the growth in demand for manufactured goods was not more regular in England than in France, where recurrent crises and wars were more serious interruptions. T. S. Ashton has pointed out that in England the number of patents rose during periods of expansion and optimism and decreased during depressions or wars. Therefore if economic fluctuations were much more violent in France, this could have had a discouraging effect on innovation. Since it is generally agreed that short-term fluctuations in eighteenth-century industrial output were due mainly to variation in harvest yields, a comparison of grain prices on both sides of the Channel is of interest. In this respect, J. Meuvret observed that the amplitude of fluctuations in wheat prices markedly decreased in both countries after 1741; none the less, fluctuations remained sharper,

[58] One wonders whether writers who have maintained that mass consumption was encouraged in Britain by a relatively equalitarian distribution of income have ever visited a large country house... Chapman and Chassagne, pp. 214–15.

more violent in France (she, however, did not suffer any more from country-wide famines after 1709/10).[59]

As for fluctuations in output, it is known that in some centres in France production fell about 50 per cent in the course of a business cycle, but such cases are exceptional. In England two reasonably well-founded manufacturing series, one for printed goods and the other for West Riding cloth, show that in several cases output fell 20 per cent or even 25 per cent in the course of a given cycle.[60] As a hypothesis, we might conclude that fluctuations were less violent than in France, probably because a larger proportion of output was intended for export, so that in a year of bad harvest the foreign, and especially the non-European, demand was more likely to compensate for the fall on the home market.

The impact of the wars of the eighteenth century has stimulated some interesting debates among British historians: for them the problem centres on whether their favourable effects – such as encouraging output and technical innovation in the metal industries – were outweighed by their depressive effects on other branches of the economy.[61] For France the question hardly arises, since there is no doubt that the balance was unfavourable in view of the very serious interruption to seaborne trade during hostilities. Admittedly, out of the three wars the only really disastrous one for France was the Seven Years War. But whatever the outcome of particular battles and the conditions of peace, in time of war the Royal Navy was always in command of the seas, leaving France, despite the use of neutral ships, to a large extent cut off from overseas countries and particularly her colonies. The British sea lanes, on the other hand, were kept open and British commerce, despite French privateering, had real protection. French trade thus fell sharply during each of the wars, though the worst collapse was naturally during the Seven Years War, when its annual average was barely half that of the preceding years; even so, the situation was little better during the American war; only the War of the

[59] Meuvret, p. 119; Appleby, pp. 866, 870, 882.

[60] Labrousse, *Esquisse*, vol. II, p. 549; *La Crise*, p. xl; Deyon, 'Le Mouvement de la production', p. 211; Ashton, *The 18th Century*, pp. 248–9.

[61] A. H. John, 'Wars and the English Economy, 1700–1763', *The Economic History Review*, 2nd series, VII, 3, April 1955, pp. 329–44; Ashton, *The Industrial Revolution*, pp. 90–1; *The 18th Century*, pp. 126–7; *Economic Fluctuations in England, 1700–1800* (Oxford, 1959), pp. 69–83; L. D. Neal, 'Interpreting Power and Profit in Economic History: A Case Study of the Seven Years War', *Journal of Economic History*, XXXVII, 1, March 1977, pp. 20–35; W. W. Rostow, *How It All Began. Origins of the Modern Economy* (New York, 1975), pp. 42–4, 235.

Austrian Succession was without really adverse effects. The fall in French exports caused a decline in industrial activity but from Labrousse's figures, the recession was not so great as in foreign trade, which is normal since the greater part of industrial output was distributed on the home market. The adverse influence of the wars should therefore not be overstressed, and indeed H. Lüthy and A. Rémond have maintained that on the whole France was fairly prosperous during the Seven Years War.[62] On the other hand, while English foreign trade rose significantly during the Seven Years War, it fell during the War of the Austrian Succession and fell badly (although less than the French) during the American war. A relationship might be seen between the innovations of the 1760s and the optimism, the confidence in expansion, aroused by England's crushing victories; yet the disaster of American independence was immediately followed by acceleration in the rate of economic growth. On the whole, British maritime and colonial victories do not appear to have been important factors in British technical superiority; it was only during the Revolutionary and Napoleonic wars that complete command of the seas gave Britain the monopoly of overseas markets and thus a stimulus to growth.[63]

There are, then, a number of interesting divergences to be noted between the character and evolution of demand for manufactures in France and England; but these appear less important than those to be observed on the supply side of industry, in the analysis of productive factors.[64]

The Industrial Revolution was not something gratuitous, a triumph of technical progress for its own sake, but a determined effort to solve some concrete problems facing British industry; the character of the

62 Labrousse, *Esquisse*, vol. II, p. 548; Levasseur, *Histoire des classes ouvrières*, vol. II, p. 551, n. 2; Lüthy, vol. II, pp. 12, 42–4, 357–8; A. Rémond, 'Trois bilans de l'économie française au temps des théories physiocratiques', *Revue d'histoire économique et sociale*, XXXV, 4, 1957, pp. 420–1. These views are confirmed by recent research: J. C. Riley, *The Seven Years War and the Old Regime in France. The Economic and Financial Toll* (Princeton, 1986).

63 H. J. Habakkuk, *American and British Technology in the Nineteenth Century. The Search for Labour-Saving Inventions* (Cambridge, 1962), pp. 185–6. Also O'Brien and Keyder, pp. 75–6, 98–9, 197. The dominating position in the international economy which Britain eventually achieved was largely the product of two centuries of aggressive and successful mercantilism, but the connection of this policy (the dividends of which came only gradually) with the Industrial Revolution is tenuous.

64 Some neo-classical writers have denied that demand played a major part in the coming of the Industrial Revolution.

most significant inventions reveals what those problems were. The inventions were designed to make possible the replacement of relatively scarce and expensive resources, such as wood, water power and labour, by others which were relatively plentiful and cheap, such as coal, steam power, and capital, the last in the form of labour-saving machines and processes.[65] This underlying character reflects the fact that English industry in the eighteenth century suffered from relative shortages, particularly of fuel in the iron industry and of labour in textile manufactures, and that such bottlenecks were hampering expansion in output. In other words, unless a technical breakthrough was achieved, the available productive factors were inadequate (except through an excessive rise in prices) to meet the relatively fast increase in demand which started in mid-century when the population growth made itself felt. The contention is that these shortages and bottlenecks, which in England exerted strong pressure in favour of innovation, did not exist in France.[66]

In the primary iron industry the contrast is quite evident. Admittedly, we must not overestimate the wood 'famine' which some writers say existed in England from the early seventeenth century; there was no exhaustion of resources nationally, but at worst local shortages. Michael Flinn has shown that between 1550 and 1750 charcoal prices rose little higher than prices in general, and that ironmasters could secure a fuel supply either by systematic copse 'cultivation' or by moving their works to remote and wooded districts. Even so, in any region, every attempt to increase output meant a fast rise in marginal costs, so that prospects for expansion were limited, and fuel costs were markedly higher in England than in Sweden. On the other hand, from the sixteenth century coal had been cheaper than charcoal in terms of heat output per unit. The ironmasters were aware of the economic advantages of coal, and they also knew that vast reserves of it lay hidden underground. There was therefore a strong incentive to look for methods allowing the substitution of coal for charcoal in blast furnaces, a search which began in the sixteenth century. When it had been successful, by the early eighteenth century, and especially when, from *c.*1750 onwards, coke pig-iron had become less expensive than charcoal pig-iron, ironmasters who wished to take advantage of the growing demand for iron, were induced increasingly

[65] Ashton, *The 18th Century*, pp. 108–9; *The Industrial Revolution*, p. 91; Rostow, p. 130.
[66] This interpretation will be discussed in more detail in Chapter 2.

to replace charcoal, which was expensive and limited in supply, by coke, which was a cheaper and much more elastic source; eventually, in the last quarter of the century, ironmasters found they either had to go over to coke smelting or close down. Technical progress therefore resulted from the pressure of growing demand on inadequate wood resources, and this explains why coke smelting was discovered and taken up in England rather than in countries where supplies of wood were cheaper and more elastic.[67] In France, where large forests were still extant, the situation was quite different, and though there was some pressure on wood resources during the eighteenth century and prices rose sharply, such shortages as developed remained purely local and French ironmasters were never faced with the choice between innovation or extinction; and in France coal was scarce and expensive.[68]

Moreover, in England the growing demand for coal for both industrial and domestic purposes during the eighteenth century led to deeper working of the mines, which created the need for more efficient pumping devices; and this of course was a powerful incentive in the development of the steam engines, which was in fact a by-product of the rise of the British coal industry. The same incentive was lacking in France, because of the different balance between wood and coal resources.

A contrast between France and England is also evident in the textile industry, but here it is in the supply of labour. The putting out system (domestic labour allied with commercial capitalism) which prevailed in the industry had many advantages, but also the disadvantage that expansion of output was hampered by rising marginal costs. Once the development of an industrial centre had passed a certain limit, to increase production work had to be put out over an ever-widening

67 M. W. Flinn, 'Timber and the Advance of Technology: a Reconsideration', *Annals of Science*, XV, 12, June 1959, pp. 109–20; Habakkuk, pp. 157–8; G. Hammersley, 'The Charcoal Iron Industry and its Fuel, 1540–1750', *The Economic History Review*, XXVI, 4, November 1973, pp. 593–613; C. K. Hyde, 'The Adoption' (note 9), pp. 397–418, and *Technological Change and the British Iron Industry 1700–1870* (Princeton, 1977); Brinley Thomas, 'Was There an Energy Crisis in Great Britain in the 17th Century?', *Explorations in Economic History*, XIII, 2, April 1986, pp. 124–52.

68 See Labrousse, *Esquisse*, vol. II, pp. 346–7; Andrée Corvol, *L'Homme et l'arbre sous l'Ancien Régime* (Paris, 1984), pp. vi, 631; Institut d'histoire moderne et contemporaine, *Aspects de la recherche sur l'histoire des forêts françaises. Table-Ronde, Paris. 2 février 1980* (Paris, 1980); Groupe d'histoire des forêts françaises, *Histoire des forêts françaises, Guide de recherche* (Paris, 1982), pp. 60, 76, 95, 132; D. B. Young, 'A Wood Famine? The Question of Deforestation in Old Régime France', *Forestry*, XLIX, 1, 1976.

area, and at a period when communications were slow this meant increased distribution costs, which were soon exceeding profits; the worker spent too much time going to and fro; supervision of the work was becoming impossible and the risks of bad workmanship and of embezzlement of the raw materials were growing. Putting out could, of course, be concentrated on a restricted area where the workers could be made to work longer and faster, but such attempts were thwarted by a regressive labour supply, since the bait of increased earnings was not enough to lure the worker away from his traditional way of life, with its leisure hours and convivial drinking sessions.

There is plentiful evidence of the appearance of this kind of situation during the first half of the eighteenth century in a number of English industrial districts where the putting-out system had developed early and was widespread, with the result that all available labour within reasonable reach of each centre was used up. Nor was there an unlimited supply of mobile labour: the innovations in agriculture, far from creating unemployment, were stimulating demand for labour, which contradicts the older view that England was at this period suffering from large-scale rural underemployment and that there was a mass exodus from the countryside to the industrial centres. We must also remember that up to mid-century the population grew only very slowly. Although it then started growing fast, a number of years had to pass before a large supply of new hands was available for the labour market, and by this time demand was again increasing. There was therefore a relative shortage of labour in industrial districts, as is proved by the quite sharp rise in money wages there (not found in the south of England) during the first half of the eighteenth century.

Manufacturers were therefore faced with high and rising labour costs, which was particularly embarrassing in a young industry like cotton, which in practice had to build up its labour force at the expense of the older industries. There must therefore have been great difficulty during the 1750s in meeting the fast-growing demand for cottons, particularly for export to the colonies. But in the 1760s and 1770s, when there was some slackening in foreign demand, the rise in manufacturing costs was really dangerous. It was now imperative to reduce labour costs and therefore to invent and take up labour-saving machinery. The relative shortage of labour which affected English industry seems therefore to have been one of the most powerful incentives to innovation, not only in the cotton industry but in several others as well.[69]

In France the situation is again obviously different. The countryside was relatively less industrialised, the relaxation of the regulations against rural manufactures (especially after the decree of 1762) freed vast reserves of labour, and this meant it was possible to put work out in a wider area around the industrial centres without unduly increasing labour costs. Moreover, since the rise in the French population was due solely to a fall in deaths (whereas in England there was also an increase in births), in France the number of people of working age may have grown faster. Lastly, and most important, there was in the French countryside a large pool of semi-employed proletarians which putters-out could use without bringing pressure on wages. Labrousse has shown that this proletariat increased fast during the eighteenth century, outpacing the agricultural demand for labour and glutting the labour market.[70]

In sum, during the first half of the eighteenth century, industrial growth in England had reached limits not to be crossed without a technological breakthrough, which the increase in population and in demand from the 1740s made imperative. In France, on the other hand, there was no shortage of labour, output could be increased to meet demand without looking for drastic innovations. This may rank as the most important of the differences to be observed between England and France, but it was in part due to England's earlier and more intense industrialisation, and hence to the situation in the seventeenth century.

There remains the question of capital resources. In eighteenth-century England capital was relatively abundant, as is shown by the fall in interest rates over a long period; Ashton saw this as the deciding factor in the Industrial Revolution, but most British historians have not followed him.[71] In any case, there was the same fall in interest rates in France. From what little we know about the financing of French industry in the eighteenth century there is nothing to suggest that its

[69] Habakkuk, pp. 132–6, 144–7, 161–3; Landes, pp. 57–60; Ashton, *The Industrial Revolution*, pp. 109 sqq., 125; *The 18th Century*, p. 47; Deane and Cole, pp. 59, 96–7; John, 'Aspects', pp. 178, 189; Schumpeter, p. 12.

[70] Labrousse, *Esquisse*, vol. II, pp. 491–2, 598–9; *La Crise*, pp. xxix–xxxi.

[71] Ashton, *The Industrial Revolution*, pp. 11, 58, 94.

development was hampered by a shortage of capital resources[72] – especially at a time when industrial investment had a very low threshold and the earliest spinning jennies, for example, could be got for a few pounds sterling. We know, of course, that the English banking system was much more advanced than the French, but banks played only a minor and indirect part in financing the Industrial Revolution: industries for the most part financed themselves, through ploughing back profits. However, in England capital accumulation was at a faster rate than the growth of other factors of production, especially labour supplies, and this was a powerful incentive to innovation.[73] Things may have been different in France, but this could only be proved by research into the problem, which has not yet been done.

This analysis may appear inconclusive because in many cases it has tried to play down the 'sharp contrasts' between the French and English economies dear to the textbooks, contrasts which have been given too readily as the explanation for Britain's superior inventiveness and economic lead. There is no wish to deny that differences existed between the two countries, though many seem to have been less pronounced than is generally thought, and a matter of degree rather than kind. What is important is that these differences nearly all point in the same direction: in all the various fields investigated, in England the conditions for innovation seem to have been more favourable than in France.[74] The accumulation of these relative differences, many of them small but important as regards factors such as fuel and labour supplies, seems to have been sufficient to set in motion a cumulative and self-sustaining process of technical advance; in France there was no such movement, because there was no need for it. In a paper read in Paris in 1961, David Landes used an illuminating metaphor borrowed from nuclear physics: he spoke of a 'critical mass', a piling up of various factors favouring England's growth which triggered off a chain reaction – the Industrial Revolution.[75] In France, on the other hand,

[72] For a different view see Lüthy, vol. II, p. 41, and C. Fohlen in his Introduction to the French edition of T. S. Ashton, *The Industrial Revolution* (Paris, 1955), pp. xvi–xviii.

[73] Habakkuk, pp. 1–3, 132; and Chap. 5 below.

[74] Of course, many of these differences had deep historical roots, and for example, the contrast between the English and French colonial markets has its origin in the settlement of the English in Virginia and Massachusetts and of the French in Canada and San Domingo.

[75] D. S. Landes, 'Encore le problème de la Révolution industrielle en Angleterre', *Bulletin de la société d'histoire moderne*, 12th series, XVIII, p. 6. This expression was also used in 1962 by P. Lebrun; see P. Lebrun *et al.*, *Essai sur la Révolution industrielle en Belgique, 1770–1847* (Brussels, 2nd edn, 1981), pp. 33–41; particularly p. 36, note 1.

there was no such critical mass, which is why France did not start spontaneously an Industrial Revolution. The external stimulus of serious competition from cheaper English goods, first in foreign markets and after the treaty of 1786 in France itself, was needed to set in train a number of French efforts, intensified during the 1780s, which aimed at introducing the new English technology into France. At this date English industry had a clear superiority, but was only just entering the stage of fast growth and widespread revolutionary changes; France was not disastrously behind, and the Industrial Revolution might have taken off there with only a few years' delay in relation to England. But the 'national catastrophe' which the French Revolution and the twenty years war meant to the French economy[76] would intensify the discrepancy and make it irremediable. In 1815 it would be more pronounced than in 1789, because during this quarter of a century, despite a delaying effect due to the wars, the British economy had continued to change and to make rapid growth.[77]

[76] M. Lévy-Leboyer, *Les Banques européennes et l'industrialisation internationale dans la première moitié du XIXe siècle* (Paris, 1964), p. 29.

[77] See F. Crouzet, *L'Economie britannique et le Blocus continental (1806–1813)* (Paris, 1958, 2 vols., 2nd edn., 1987), vol. II, pp. 863–72, and the introduction to the 2nd edition (Paris, 1987); 'Les conséquences économiques de la Révolution. A propos d'un inédit de Sir Francis d'Ivernois', *Annales historiques de la Révolution française*, 34th year, nos. 168 and 169, pp. 182–217, 336–62; reprinted as Chapter 10 of the French edition of the present book.

2 Criticisms and self-criticisms of a comparison*

The previous chapter derives from two lectures delivered at the London School of Economics in January 1964; the text was revised and published in *Annales ESC* in 1966. This was a period when French historians tended to exaggerate England's 'modernity' and the lead it enjoyed with respect to France, whereas English-speaking historians were inclined to gloat over the stagnation and archaism of France. When I began to draft these lectures, I believed that growth in the eighteenth century must have been much more vigorous in Britain than in France, but I soon realised that a number of preconceptions needed correcting. This article therefore belongs to the revisionist school as far as the economic history of France is concerned, a school which a number of French, British and American historians have joined in the course of the last twenty years and which has been mainly concerned with the nineteenth and twentieth centuries.[1] In order to combat the clichés which were then current, I had at times opted for somewhat extreme formulations but I had tried to avoid being provocative. I had not wanted to shock or offend my English audience, a large part of which was very taken aback by my hypotheses, nor had I wished to lay myself open to the charge of chauvinism. It is a little ironical, therefore, to find myself accused by an

* The 1966 article – which is reprinted in Chapter 1 – has provoked a certain amount of debate, and it has therefore seemed useful to review the question some twenty years later. I have not attempted, however, to survey all of the studies published in the last two decades on eighteenth-century France and England, and I have referred mainly to those which mention my original article or which are directly concerned with a comparison between the two countries. I have no wish to accord this article more importance than it merits or to deck myself with laurels.

[1] This effort culminated in François Caron's remarkable synthesis, *An Economic History of Modern France* (New York, 1979); French edition: *Histoire économique de la France* (Paris, 1981); an extreme version of it may be found in an article by R. Cameron and C. E. Freedeman, 'French Economic Growth: A Radical Revision', *Social Science History*, VII, 1, Winter 1983, pp. 3–30.

English author of having unfairly denigrated the eighteenth-century French economy![2]

An eminent historian described my original article as 'stimulating', which, in academic circles, means that it is of some interest to read but does not stand up.[3] Others have criticised the article more directly (but without a detailed discussion of it), on the absurd pretext that it implies a deliberate attack upon the French Revolution, as if I had charged it with having shattered the impetus of French growth.[4] In general, however, my conclusions have been accepted in France. Thus, Pierre Léon, in his authoritative contribution to the second volume of the *Histoire économique et sociale de la France*, suggested a growth rate for French industrial production, from the beginning of the eighteenth century to 1789, of between 1·5 per cent and 1·9 per cent per year, which, he observed, comes very close to that suggested by me, on the basis of Jean Marczewski's findings. Pierre Léon also accepted my conclusions regarding the growth rates of national product in Britain and in France, and as regards a similar increase in the *per capita* product of the two countries.[5] In 1974, he added:

> In the light of the very detailed studies conducted by Jean Marczewski and François Crouzet, it really does seem as though, from around 1700 to around 1780, France and England advanced at the same pace towards modern industrialisation, with a relatively high annual growth rate of over 1 per cent. The two dominant powers in Europe thus achieved a complete break with the slow, almost imperceptible evolution which industry had known in the past.[6]

In a more sober vein, François Caron wrote: 'During a good part of the eighteenth century, France underwent a demographic, agricultural

[2] N. F. R. Crafts, 'Industrial Revolution in England and France: Some Thoughts on the Question, "Why was England First?"', *The Economic History Review*, XXX, 3, August 1977, pp. 438–41. Some authors have taken the rehabilitation of the French economy still further, as the reader will discover below.

[3] E. Le Roy Ladurie, 'The Chief Defects of Gregory King', in *The Territory of the Historian*, translated by Ben and Sian Reynolds (Hassocks, 1979), p. 185. This remark was made in the context of criticisms of the work of J. Toutain (see below, p. 52), but actually I had only referred to his conclusions in passing and had presented them as hypothetical.

[4] See below, Chapter 3, pp. 105–6.

[5] In F. Braudel and E. Labrousse (eds.), *Histoire économique et sociale de la France*, vol. 2, *Des derniers temps de l'âge seigneurial aux préludes de l'âge industriel (1660–1789)* (Paris, 1970; referred to from here on as *HESF*), pp. 521, 527. In the conclusion to this work (pp. 699, 708), Ernest Labrousse himself expressed his agreement with Léon's perspective on the rapid growth of several French industries during the eighteenth century. My article was heavily indebted to earlier studies by Pierre Léon.

[6] In *Conjoncture économique, structures sociales. Hommage à Ernest Labrousse* (Paris–The Hague, 1974), p. 407.

and industrial growth parallel to that of England',[7] but, this being so, the discrepancy between the two countries which existed at the beginning of the eighteenth century was maintained.

This point of view has even been endorsed by the late Albert Soboul, the advocate of the most traditional, jacobino-leninist interpretation of the French Revolution. In his *La Civilisation et la Révolution Française*, Soboul did draw quite heavily on my article, although he was not overgenerous with quotation marks. He wrote as follows:

> Statistical data, although their value is obviously only approximate for the eighteenth century, surprise us somewhat by revealing that the rhythms of growth [of industry] in England and France were remarkably close to each other ... Taking population increase into account, François Crouzet, whose study I follow here, reckons that the growth in average real production and *per capita* income was approximately the same for both countries. It is only fitting that the parallelism in rhythms of development, at any rate up until the 1780s, be emphasised...[8]

More recently, Jean-Charles Asselain, an economist, has also expressed his agreement with most of my suggestions. Even if, Asselain observes, one allows that Marczewski has exaggerated French growth somewhat and that Deane and Cole have by the same token underestimated English growth, 'one must accept that, in quantitative terms, at any rate, France's industrial growth was not inferior to that of England during the greater part of the eighteenth century'. Asselain continues: 'At first sight, a comparison of growth rates also belies the thesis of Great Britain's superiority, since the growth of foreign trade and of industrial production ran roughly parallel in both countries throughout the eighteenth century.' However, since England was more developed at the beginning of the century, this parallelism implies that the gap was not closed but simply stabilised. It is true that Asselain placed greater emphasis than I had done upon 'the different nature' of the two economies, which 'the similarity in rhythms of growth' should not be allowed to obscure. French growth remained typically 'extensive' in character, whereas the English economy displayed a 'tendency to give rise to an increasing flood of inventions, especially in a group of industrial branches which were engines of growth, as they opened up outlets for each other and drew each other on', to such an extent that the gap between the two countries was becoming wider by around

[7] Caron, pp. 12, 17, rightly observes that 'France was ... a great industrial country rather than a great industrialised country.'

[8] A. Soboul, *La Civilisation et la Révolution Française. 1: La Crise de l'Ancien Régime* (Paris, 1970), pp. 342–7 and 351–2, particularly 343 and 346.

1770. Asselain also regards the timelag between the beginning of the growth in agricultural production and the demographic spurt as highly significant, a timelag which was one generation in England but which did not exist in France. This occasioned a rise in nominal and real wages in England, which affected both supply and demand, by widening available markets and by making labour more costly. Finally, Asselain recalls the 'vulnerability of the French economy', and of agriculture in particular; the growth of French industry was therefore precarious and the catastrophe which followed the Treaty of 1786 demonstrated its fragility, along with England's superiority.[9]

The *Annales* article, which was soon translated and published in a widely available collection,[10] aroused more interest in Britain and the United States than in France;[11] it was the object of serious debate on the part of several economic historians and the starting-point for a new analysis of the problems which it had tackled.

Most commentators were prepared to accept the conclusion which I had advanced, namely, that the growth rates of the British and French economies had been very similar, from the beginning of the eighteenth century up until the 1780s, although the unreliability of the quantitative data upon which it was based had led me to present it as conjectural. Thus, David Landes, who mistrusts 'guessestimates' of France's national income in the eighteenth century and who often adopted a pessimistic approach to the French economy, has nevertheless written: '... it seems reasonable to suppose that income per head was moderately lower than in Britain at the beginning and that it kept pace fairly well until the last quarter of the century'.[12] Emmanuel Le Roy Ladurie's later criticisms of Toutain has, admittedly, caused Landes to declare that my work ought in fact to be reassessed, given Toutain and Marczewski's overestimation of French growth, and also Michel Morineau's writings.[13] Milward and Saul, on the other hand,

[9] J.-C. Asselain, *Histoire économique de la France du XVIIIe siècle à nos jours*. 1. *De l'Ancien Régime à la Première Guerre Mondiale* (Paris, 1984), pp. 88, 93, 97–8, 102–8.

[10] F. Crouzet, 'England and France in the Eighteenth Century: A Comparative Analysis of Two Economic Growths', in R. M. Hartwell (ed.), *The Causes of the Industrial Revolution in England* (London, 1967), pp. 139–74. This translation was slightly abridged.

[11] See A. Milward and S. B. Saul, *The Economic Development of Continental Europe, 1780–1870* (London, 1973), p. 117.

[12] D. S. Landes, *The Unbound Prometheus* (Cambridge, 1969), p. 13.

[13] D. S. Landes, 'Statistics as a Source for the History of Economic Development in Western Europe: The Protostatistical Era', in V. R. Lorwin and J. M. Price (eds.), *The Dimensions of the Past. Materials, Problems and Opportunities for Quantitative Work in History* (New Haven and London, 1972), pp. 73–4. In fact, if one takes Toutain and Marczewski's figures (together with

claim that '...on the whole it does not seem unreasonable to accept that the overall rate of growth of the French economy in the eighteenth century was about, or slightly above, 1 per cent per annum. It was, therefore, growing at about the same rate as, or perhaps slightly faster than, the British economy';[14] likewise the industrial product *per capita*. Ralph Davis, in spite of his doubts about several points in my article (see below), nevertheless asserted that the national incomes of France and England had more than doubled during the first three-quarters of the eighteenth century, with France probably enjoying a slight advantage between 1730 and 1770.[15] As for W. W. Rostow, after having carefully examined the quantitative data, he recognised that aggregate indices should be used with caution and admitted that Toutain had exaggerated the growth of French agriculture, he none the less concluded that 'from the 1720s, French production and trade moved up more rapidly than that of Britain'; thus, 'from the 1720s until 1783, France, from a depressed base, gained relatively on Britain. Both moved forward thereafter, Britain with greater momentum, but the period of revolution and war set back France severely'.[16]

Peter Mathias and Patrick O'Brien, and the latter in collaboration with Caglar Keyder, have started out again from scratch, producing new calculations of France's and England's production in the eighteenth century, although again relying, it must be admitted, on the same substratum (the figures of Marczewski and his team, on the one hand, and those of Deane and Cole on the other), but with significant developments, including backward extrapolations in particular. They have thus constructed two 'hypothetical growth curves' of total *physical* product, at constant prices, whose aspect is fairly striking: on a basis of 100 for 1715, the index for 1785 is 199 for France and 145 for Great Britain.[17] These authors are mindful of the criticisms levelled at the work of Toutain and at the *Histoire quantitative de l'économie française* in

those of Deane and Cole), one arrives at a faster growth for France than for England (up until the Revolution, of course); this is the conclusion that D. R. Leet and J. A. Shaw, for example, come to, in 'French Economic Stagnation, 1700–1960: Old Economic History Revisited', in *Journal of Interdisciplinary History*, VIII, 3, Winter 1978, p. 538. It was in assuming that these figures were too high that I proposed roughly similar rates of growth.

[14] Milward and Saul, pp. 29, 31, 38; they identify a 'very small' and shrinking development gap between the two countries.

[15] R. Davis, *The Rise of the Atlantic Economies* (London, 1973), pp. 288, 301.

[16] W. W. Rostow, *How It All Began. Origins of the Modern Economy* (New York, 1975), pp. 94, 170–9. C. Trebilcock has arrived at the same conclusion, in *The Industrialization of the Continental Powers, 1780–1914* (London, 1981), pp. 112–13.

[17] For 1790–1, the indices are 210 and 157.

general, but they maintain that their curves fit, 'by and large', with the 'qualitative' conclusions of French historians (and with the periodisation advanced in the *Histoire économique et sociale de la France* in particular). They have also calculated the per capita commodity output at constant prices, which, between 1715 and 1785, rose by 41 per cent in France[18] and by only 5 per cent in Great Britain; they admit that these latter figures underestimate the growth of the British economy, since services played a more important role there than in France, but the gap remains a considerable one, even if one takes this tertiary sector into account.[19]

O'Brien and Keyder have calculated, on the basis of the above series of production at constant prices, that the average annual growth rates for the period 1701–10 to 1781–90 were:[20]

	Agricultural production (%)	Industrial production (%)	Total Commodity production (%)
Great Britain	0·4	1·1	0·7
France	0·6	1·9	1·0

These authors have also calculated that, in 1701–10, the commodity production of France could have been two and a half times that of Britain, which is compatible (the French population being three times the size of the British one) with G. King's idea that the income per capita of the English in 1700 was 10 to 30 per cent higher than that of the French. Since total physical production later increased more rapidly in France than in Britain, the relative gap between the two aggregate products, on the eve of the Revolution, had increased. As far as per capita product was concerned, France had very probably caught

18 This means an average rate of growth of 0·5 per cent per year. J. C. Riley and J. J. McCusker, 'Money Supply, Economic Growth and the Quantity Theory of Money: France, 1650–1788', *Explorations in Economic History*, XX, 3, July 1983, pp. 280, Table 2, 282, have calculated a rate of 0·3 per cent per year for the growth of output per capita and consider that a higher figure, like 0·5 per cent, is possible; see below, note 27.

19 P. Mathias and P. O'Brien, 'Taxation in Britain and France, 1715–1810. A Comparison of the Social and Economic Incidence of Taxes Collected for the Central Governments', *Journal of European Economic History*, V, 3, Winter 1976, pp. 607–9, 611, 613, Tables 3, 4, 5, 6.

20 P. O'Brien and C. Keyder, *Economic Growth in Britain and France, 1780–1914. Two Paths to the Twentieth Century* (London, 1978), p. 57, Table 3.1; *id.*, 'Les Voies de passage vers la société industrielle en Grande-Bretagne et en France (1780–1914)', *Annales ESC*, XXXIV, 6, November–December 1979, p. 1301.

up and, in the 1780s, its per capita product 'seems to have been' above the British level: O'Brien and Keyder's calculations present it as being, for 1781–90, 14 or 37 per cent (depending upon the exchange rates adopted) higher than that of Britain. The latter enjoyed, however, thanks to the sale of services abroad and to income accruing from foreign investments, an imports surplus amounting to 10 per cent of domestic product (while this surplus was very small in the case of France), which increased the quantity of goods which were available in England. Therefore, the per capita incomes of the two countries 'could not have been very far apart', but it is possible that France had a slight advantage.[21] It is worth noting that O'Brien and Keyder are very prudent and make no attempt to conceal their doubts when they formulate their conclusions. This is because they have used Toutain's figures in their calculations, and they mention that they are 'controversial' and regarded with scepticism by numerous French specialists (which is something of an understatement), so that the results obtained for France are probably too high.[22]

These authors are just as cautious in their presentation of another of their discoveries; in the years 1781 to 1790, the productivity of the workforce employed in commodity production was higher in France than in Britain (two or three times higher in industry, which more than compensated for the much lower productivity of French agriculture). They acknowledge that this is a somewhat difficult view to admit.[23] This is not the place to embark upon a technical discussion of this point and I will simply quote some sensible remarks made on this subject by J.-C. Asselain:

> Quantitative history has recently produced one of the 'shocking' results we have come to expect of it ... a figure [for the productivity of French industry] which is genuinely hard to believe, and whose exaggerated size can be explained by a whole series of statistical biasses ... This undoubtedly suspect assessment has nevertheless the real virtue of reminding us just how little we really know and also, more precisely, of acting as a counterbalance to the opposite error, which is traditionally committed, of judging industry as a whole, in a far too exclusive manner, in terms of the nucleus of 'modern' industry.[24]

[21] Although real wages were higher in Britain, by a full third, if not more; O'Brien and Keyder, pp. 62, 70, Table 3.7.

[22] O'Brien and Keyder, *Economic Growth*, pp. 51, notes 9 and 10, 57, 60, 61, Table 3.3, 77, note 4, 194; 'Les Voies de passage', p. 1287; P. O'Brien, in D. Johnson, F. Bédarida, F. Crouzet, (eds.), *Britain and France. Ten Centuries*, (Folkestone, 1980), pp. 176–7.

[23] O'Brien and Keyder, pp. 87, 91, Table 4.3, 103, 146.

[24] Asselain, p. 96.

Rondo Cameron and C. E. Freedeman have written as follows of the work of O'Brien and Keyder: 'Neither their methods nor their sources are immune from criticism, but, as far as that is concerned, the same thing could well be said of virtually every quantitative assertion in history.'[25]

Is it therefore possible to conclude that I had been quite cautious in suggesting that '... the growth in average real output and income per head might therefore have been roughly of the same order of magnitude in both countries'?[26]

It is worth adding that the most recent quantitative studies on the growth of the British economy in the eighteenth century arrive at growth rates which are lower than those posited by Deane and Cole, which had been used in my 1966 article (and also by O'Brien). N. F. R. Crafts, for example, gives the following figures:[27]

Rates of average growth per year of real product (%).

	Agriculture	Industry	Total product	Per capita product
1700–1760	0·60	0·71	0·69	0·31
1760–1780	0·13	1·51	0·70	0·01
1780–1801	0·75	2·11	1·32	0·35

The main novelty here is that growth (particularly that of industry and of trade) was clearly less rapid between 1780 and 1800 than Deane and

[25] Cameron and Freedeman, p. 8.

[26] Crouzet, 'England and France in the Eighteenth Century', p. 154; see p. 25.

[27] N. F. R. Crafts, 'British Economic Growth, 1700–1831: A Review of the Evidence', *The Economic History Review*, XXXVI, 2, May 1983, pp. 183, Table 3, 187, Table 5, also 182–4, 186, 194. Crafts had presented somewhat different rates earlier, in R. Floud and D. McCloskey (eds.), *The Economic History of Britain since 1700, Volume 1: 1700–1860* (Cambridge, 1981); see p. 2, Tables 1.1 and 1.2, also p. 5, where he wrote: 'The growth of the [English] economy prior to 1780 ... was similar to that of other areas of Europe – France, for example' (he cites Rostow, O'Brien and Roehl as his authorities). In the same work (p. 64, Table 3.2), W. A. Cole gave new estimates for the English national product at constant prices, according to which rates of growth would be calculated as follows: 0·77 per cent per year for 1700–80, 0·82 per cent for 1700–90. C. K. Harley, however, in 'British Industrialization Before 1841: Evidence of Slower Growth During the Industrial Revolution', *Journal of Economic History*, XLII, 2, June 1982, p. 286, Table 9, argues for a slower total growth than does Crafts, but the difference is very slight as regards per capita income:

	Rate of growth per year (%)	
	National income	Per capita income
1700–1770	0·56	0·27
1770–1815	1·31	0·33

Cole had supposed. On the other hand, these writers would have underestimated the growth of agriculture prior to 1760 and overestimated it after that date. As for the growth of per capita product, it was markedly slower than Deane and Cole had assumed.

It is not in a spirit of self-congratulation that I have reviewed the conclusions several authors have reached; I merely wished to show that broad agreement had been reached as to the correctness of the hypothesis which I had originally advanced in 1964. I am only too ready to allow that my demonstration is far from being a conclusive one. In all studies, the same materials (Deane and Cole's statistical series, on the one hand, those of the ISEA on the other) were, by and large, used, and subjected to more or less refined or barbarous handling, so as to be completed or corrected. No amount of sophistication in the use of statistics would enable one to compensate for their shortcomings.[28]

The real bone of contention is France's agricultural production (one cannot be certain that English agricultural production is better known, but it has not aroused such fierce passions). In my 1966 article, I had quoted, not without some reservations, a recently published work by J. Toutain. However, in 1968, this study was subjected to a devastating critique by Emmanuel Le Roy Ladurie, in an article whose title, 'The Fantastic Accounts of Gregory King', showed more charity and courtesy towards the living than the dead, for really it was Toutain whose shortcomings were under fire, whereas honest Gregory King had done the best he could with the means at his disposal at the time. Toutain's study is described as a colossus with feet of clay, resting upon 'extremely fragile foundations', which are 'sawn off' by a critical examination and turn out to be evanescent; more particularly, he accepts figures for the production of 1701–10 which are far too low, so that the growth during the rest of the eighteenth century is overestimated. Le Roy Ladurie's critique is a wholly convincing one.[29] Nevertheless, British and American experts have gone on using

[28] Note also S. Pollard's critique, in *Peaceful Conquest: The Industrialization of Europe, 1760–1970* (Oxford, 1981), p. 39, namely, that in a period when industrialisation is regional, it is misleading to use national statistics.

[29] E. Le Roy Ladurie, *The Territory of the Historian*, p. 190. See also, M. Morineau, 'Y a-t-il eu une révolution agricole en France au XVIIIe siècle?', *Revue historique*, CCXXXIX, 486, April–June 1968, pp. 303–5; M. Garden, in P. Léon, *Histoire économique et sociale du monde*, vol. 3, L. Bergeron (ed.), *Inerties et Révolutions, 1730–1840* (Paris, 1978), pp. 173, 190, 192–3.

Toutain's study, as we have seen, merely emphasising that his estimates were on the high side.[30]

It is true that researches into the yield of tithes, conducted under the supervision of Le Roy Ladurie, have provided a more solid foundation, namely, archival sources, than have the phantasies of earlier authors. The first overall conclusions to be drawn were that the real agricultural product of France rose between 1700–9 and 1780–9, by at least 25 per cent and at the most 40 per cent, thus clearly less than Toutain had maintained. Subsequently, Le Roy Ladurie has gone further: 'The undeniable growth of French agricultural product must have come close to 40 per cent between 1715 and 1789, but it can hardly have been higher than that.'[31] It has, admittedly, been emphasised that the production levels at the end of Louis XIV's reign were abnormally low, lower, indeed, than those achieved in Mazarin and Colbert's days; therefore a part of the post-1715 growth – up until 1750, and possibly even beyond – was just 'recovery'. This is a plausible line of argument, but I am not concerned here with the very long term, only with the eighteenth century. Sources on tithes, their use and their interpretation have also given rise to controversies which it would be pointless to linger over.[32] In any case, the increase in French agricultural production implied by the study of tithes would seem to be of the order of that proposed for Great Britain by Deane and Cole (35 per cent from 1700 to 1790). However, more recently, Eric Jones suggested that the increase in *English* agricultural production was 61 per cent from 1700 to *1800*.[33]

Michel Morineau's theses would seem, however, to undermine this

30 O'Brien and Keyder, p. 27, remark, with regard to the estimates of the *Histoire quantitative* and of Deane and Cole, that, for all their faults, 'the estimates have been properly constructed and are the best available for the time being'.

31 E. Le Roy Ladurie, 'Tithes and Net Agricultural Output (Fifteenth to Eighteenth Century)', in *The Territory of the Historian*, p. 202; Le Roy Ladurie, in G. Duby and A. Wallon (eds.), *Histoire de la France rurale*, vol. 2, *L'Age classique des paysans, 1340–1789* (Paris, 1975), pp. 394–6, 417, 580; E. Le Roy Ladurie and J. Goy, *Les Fluctuations du produit de la dîme. Conjoncture décimale et domaniale de la fin du Moyen Age au XVIIIe siècle* (Paris–The Hague, 1972), pp. 23–4, 369 ff.; see also Garden, in Léon, vol. 3, p. 193; Labrousse, in *HESF*, II, pp. 460–2, 696. H. Neveux has suggested that, as a consequence of increasing specialisation, total production had grown more than that of cereals.

32 See J. L. Goldsmith, 'The Agrarian History of Preindustrial France. Where do we go from here?', *Journal of European Economic History*, XIII, 1, Spring 1984, pp. 175–99, who has some harsh criticisms of French works on rural history and the 'ideological blockages' from which their authors suffer.

33 In Floud and McCloskey, pp. 67–9; Jones adds that this estimate is 'purely illustrative'. According to recent growth rates calculated by Crafts (p. 55), one would arrive at an increase slightly under 50 per cent between 1700 and 1780.

apparent parallelism. He has repeatedly denied that there was an agricultural revolution in France in the eighteenth century (I would have no hesitation in granting this point), or even prior to 1840; but he did not maintain that there was a complete standstill in French agriculture. His basic idea is that, between the fifteenth and the middle of the nineteenth century, the average yields of corn underwent fluctuations, in the course of which they attained the same maximum on several different occasions, without ever passing beyond it. One of these occurred after 1750 but, since yields had fallen to a low level at the beginning of the century, the subsequent recovery appeared all the more vigorous, at any rate in the two villages of Hainaut, which Morineau studied with great care, and which he considered typical of the whole of North-West France. A 'recovery' was undoubtedly involved, but this again is not relevant to the present case (it would merely illustrate the notion that, at the beginning of the eighteenth century, the French economy was in a trough, while the English economy was expanding).[34] Altogether, there has been a consensus among most specialists of eighteenth-century French agriculture that both a technical revolution and immobilism can be ruled out, in favour of an increase in production, through a large number of 'small steps', of local and scattered efforts, with strong regional variations. Harvests and prices no longer oscillated as wildly as in the seventeenth century and ceased to have such catastrophic consequences; 'scarcity eased off', in spite of a population increase of six or seven million.[35] Le Roy Ladurie has even written of the end of the 'cold economy', which prevailed since the fourteenth century, and of a 'genuine' but 'hesitant' growth, with a slight increase of corn yields in the zone of open fields.[36] From my point of view, this is rather reassuring!

I want now to pass from quantitative questions to problems of

[34] Morineau, 'Y a-t-il eu une révolution agricole', p. 326; Morineau, *Les Faux-semblants d'un démarrage économique: agriculture et démographie en France au XVIIIe siècle* (Paris, 1971), pp. 31, 35, 93–5, 104–6 and the graphs between pp. 160 and 161; Morineau, 'Cambrésis et Hainaut: des frères ennemis?', *Revue historique*, CCLVII, 522, April–June 1977, pp. 332, note 2, 341. Between 1701–10 and 1781–9, the increase in tithes was 48 per cent in one village and 61 per cent in the other.

[35] Garden, in Léon, vol. 3, pp. 174–5, 183, 193–5; Asselain, pp. 36, 40, 47, 49. Morineau also accepts the view that harvests were more regular in the eighteenth century. He writes: 'There was therefore some progress, as I would take some care in emphasising', but he deems it peripheral, fragmentary, minor, ambiguous, costly and impoverishing.

[36] Le Roy Ladurie, in Duby and Wallon, vol. 2, pp. 395–6; this contribution earned him savage criticisms from M. Morineau, 'History and Tithes', *Journal of European Economic History*, X, 2, Autumn 1981, p. 446.

interpretation. One of the aims of my 1966 article had been to consider the origins of the Industrial Revolution in a new light. However, my approach left me vulnerable to criticism. Peter Mathias, for example, judged that the search for an operative variable which would allow one to differentiate between the English experience and that of all the other countries, for a factor present in England but absent elsewhere, was a methodological error, linked to the vain quest for a monocausal explanation of the Industrial Revolution; he believed that there were too many factors which could have had an influence and that their mutual interactions were too complex. Comparative history is not genuinely scientific, although it can supply, if not proofs, at any rate indications as to the relative importance of the various forces which were involved. Furthermore, in the case which concerns us here, 'many aspects of Britain's economic development in the eighteenth century were certainly not unique to herself' and, in a comparison with France, 'common features ... stand out as prominently as so-called unique ones'. Mathias concludes, therefore: 'If England's growth was not unique in most, if not all, particulars its uniqueness ... lay in the combination of relationships that focused within England during the eighteenth century but in no other European power.'[37]

Milward and Saul, however, have criticised such a position for being tautological; they have also expressed some regret that historians have been too much preoccupied with why it was in Britain that the Industrial Revolution arose first. This is to measure other societies too much in terms of the British yardstick, and to regard them as aberrations with respect to the British norm (this is a valid criticism of my original article, which revolved around this question). Be this as it may, Milward and Saul also reckoned that it was very hard to isolate *one* single economic factor which was operative in eighteenth-century Britain, but not in a number of other European countries, whose economies were in fact very diverse (England, they noted in passing, more closely resembled France than France did Romania). It is even difficult to give a precise definition of the *economic* differences between England and the other countries; all one can say is that it was more 'developed', and that it had attained to a greater 'maturity'. But this situation can only be understood if one takes account of the global

[37] P. Mathias, 'British Industrialisation: Unique or not?', in P. Léon, F. Crouzet, R. Gascon (eds.), *L'Industrialisation en Europe au XIXe siècle* (Paris, 1972), pp. 497–9, 502–3; 'La Révolution industrielle en Angleterre: un cas unique?', *Annales ESC*, XXVII, 1, January–February 1972, pp. 35–7; *The Transformation of England* (London, 1979), pp. 12–16.

historical experience during the centuries prior to the Industrial Revolution; if the latter did not take place in the most productive, the richest and the most powerful country, i.e. France, it was because of the nature of this long-term process of development. Milward and Saul reckon that the problem was fundamentally a social one; but it was not so much a question of 'social attitudes', which they feel have been too much discussed, as of social structures, which are themselves the outcome of a long-term process in economic history.[38]

N. F. R. Crafts advanced a more radical and more detailed methodological criticism of my article in 1977. In his view, the question 'Why was England first?', raised by several authors, myself among them, was a badly formulated one, which cannot be properly answered and ought therefore to be discarded (it may even have distorted our understanding of the economic history of the eighteenth century).[39] Crafts believes that economic development in general, and technological progress in particular, are stochastic processes, highly uncertain in their nature and as regards the dates at which they produce results, and involving, furthermore, a random variable (which is not to say that they are lotteries or that no causal relationships are involved); specialists in technological innovation tend to agree on this point. England was, admittedly, the first to realise the truly decisive innovations, but that does not mean that it had *ex ante* greater chances than France of doing so.

One ought not to perpetuate the common mistake of *post hoc ergo propter hoc*, especially if one only has a single set of observations to hand.[40] Just because England was the first country to carry through an Industrial Revolution, one cannot therefore claim that conditions there were especially propitious (although this may have been the case), that the probability of it making the decisive inventions was higher than elsewhere, and that its economy was superior to that of the other countries. Even where there is little probability *ex ante* of an

[38] Milward and Saul, pp. 30–4, 38–40, 114.

[39] Crafts, 'Industrial Revolution in England and France', pp. 429–31, and, for what follows, 433–4, 436–41. Crafts has also rebuked me for having stated at the beginning of my article that a comparison between England and France can help to understand economic growth in general, a notion which he described as 'otiose'. No doubt I deserved this rebuke, for I had clearly fallen for the fashion which prevailed at the time that every empirical study needed to have theoretical implications.

[40] Crafts sums up (p. 441) by noting that one ought not to expect too much from comparative economic history, for 'some of the uncontrolled experiments that history performed were unique, non-repeatable events'.

economy making decisive progress, it may nevertheless, if it has a good opportunity early on, so position itself as to enable it, eventually, to win the race against another country, a race which is only contested once. Thus, the fact that in 1790 Britain was more 'advanced' and had every chance of making further progress in the industries that were then the leading ones, does not necessarily mean that, around 1740, there was a greater probability of its achieving the Industrial Revolution; its situation in 1790 does not oblige us to find reasons, extending far into its history, for its inevitable supremacy. Britain's ultimate ascendancy does not justify the postulate that it possessed the elements of that superiority long before. To the question as to whether the English economy was visibly superior to that of France in the middle of the eighteenth century, one must answer, Crafts maintains, with a 'resounding no'; considered as a whole, the French economy of this period has been unjustly and prematurely set aside as inferior to the English. Crafts borrows from Rostow various figures, which refer to the respective situations of the two countries in 1700 and in 1780, and which demonstrate that France enjoyed a superiority in absolute terms and a faster growth in almost all domains. He quotes Peter Mathias on the impressive French achievement in science and innovation, and he recalls that, according to S. T. McCloy,[41] the French twice came close to inventing the spinning jenny, before Hargreaves had managed to do so. Crafts also rejects the point of view of those such as David Landes, who have come to the conclusion, on the basis of the situation at the end of the eighteenth century and the beginning of the nineteenth, that the French were less open to innovation than were the British. The French were, after all, at war in this period, the English had taken the lead, but this situation tells us nothing in particular about the ex ante potential of France. The 'unjust treatment' which France has suffered at the hands of economic historians derives in part from the incorrect formulation of the question 'Why was England first?', for France's inferiority is here simply a corollary of England's chronological priority. However, Crafts does, it must be admitted, insist that he never claimed that the Industrial Revolution was a wholly fortuitous event and that the likelihood of its arising in France was greater than that of its occurring in England.

In response, W. W. Rostow chided Crafts for having neglected the acceleration in the rhythm of invention which took place in Britain, by

[41] S. T. McCloy, *French Inventions of the Eighteenth Century* (Lexington, Kentucky, 1952).

contrast with France, from the 1760s onwards; French observers of the period were the first to realise that they were losing ground. Furthermore, one ought also to distinguish between invention and innovation; the stochastic hypothesis cannot be applied to the latter, on account of the 'innovatory zeal' which was widespread in England after 1760 – to a far greater degree than in France – and which covered much more ground than a small number of 'decisive' inventions. Rostow admits that it was not inevitable that the Industrial Revolution should have taken place in England, but he maintains that various factors made it more probable that it should have occurred there rather than in France. There was not one unique match, that might have been won by a weaker team, but rather a whole series of challenges. Rostow thus concludes that the Industrial Revolution was not 'a random walk'.[42] Crafts answered that Rostow had accepted his main thesis, namely, that the Industrial Revolution should be considered in terms of probabilities and that, as a consequence, it had still to be demonstrated that the English economy was 'superior' to the French. Crafts reproached Rostow with having overestimated the inventiveness and innovatory zeal at work in this period in England and he noted that their impact upon growth, such as is shown by a calculation of total factor productivity, had anyway been insignificant before 1780. Crafts maintained that it was impossible to formulate an answer to the question 'Why was England first?', and likewise to discover the causes of the Industrial Revolution by means of the comparative method.[43]

I find Crafts' theoretical or philosophical arguments perfectly valid. There is good reason to react against the frequent indulgence in explanations of the *post hoc ergo propter hoc* kind, and some of Crafts' ideas are very appealing, namely, the notion that one should think of the Industrial Revolution in terms of probabilities, that there is a random element to the date at which particular inventions occur and that the response to economic incentives is an uncertain one. Conversely, flattering to French *amour propre* though Crafts' perspectives on France's economy in the eighteenth century may be, it is nevertheless the case that everything that we know of France and England during the Enlightenment suggests that France was qualitatively inferior to

[42] W. W. Rostow, 'No Random Walk: A Comment on "Why was England First?"', *The Economic History Review*, XXXI, 4, November 1978, pp. 610–12.

[43] N. F. R. Crafts, 'Entrepreneurship and a Probabilistic View of the British Industrial Revolution', *The Economic History Review*, XXXI, 4, November 1978, pp. 613–14; its author acknowledged that his article of 1977 had been deliberately provocative.

England. My 1966 article was meant to show that the gap was not so yawning a one as the 'Vulgate' had traditionally argued, but I cannot subscribe to Crafts' claim that such a gap did not exist at all. Furthermore, the comparative method may not be a panacea but it is still, to my mind, a fruitful approach to problems.

As far as the basic issues are concerned, two economic historians have discussed my proposals in some detail, agreeing with some and rejecting a number of others. Thus, the late Ralph Davis favoured a more traditional conception of the comparison between France and England;[44] he held that real and important contrasts existed between the social structures of the two countries (which I would be the last to deny), so that English society provided a climate that was more congenial to innovation than French society. The former was more 'open', it included the dissenters (for which there was no equivalent in France) and it was less subject to state regulation. Thus, industrial innovation was pursued with more vigour and accepted with greater eagerness in England than in France. Davis has also emphasised the differences between the agrarian structures of the two countries, the brake to economic expansion constituted by the French peasantry, and he wrote: 'The agricultural base of the French economy once more revealed in the 1770s and 1780s, its inability to sustain prolonged growth', whereas, by the second half of the seventeenth century, England had to all intents and purposes solved the problem of its food supplies. It was in fact the attempts to modernise agriculture which triggered off the French Revolution: 'Perhaps it was now impossible for France to undergo its industrial before its political revolution.' Davis went on to observe that the demographic spurt of the eighteenth century in England had occurred on the basis of a historical maximum, since the population had not fallen during the second half of the seventeenth century, whereas in France there had first been a recovery from the losses of the late seventeenth and early eighteenth century; in addition, after 1770, a Malthusian trap began to make itself felt (although symptoms of this were also evident in England[45]). Finally, Davis reckoned that France suffered from the lack of a large colonial

[44] The final two chapters of *The Rise of the Atlantic Economies* are concerned with this comparison.

[45] It is not wholly accurate to claim that English population had not diminished after the middle of the seventeenth century. See below, pp. 70 and 71. I will return to the question of the different agricultures of the two countries. Milward and Saul, p. 41, also reckon that the Revolution had its roots in the *Ancien Régime*'s incapacity to resolve the problem of agricultural production.

market for its industry, of the kind furnished by the Thirteen Colonies.[46]

Admittedly, Davis also believed that many of these factors had nothing to do with the triggering of the Industrial Revolution, which in his view amounted to a particular innovation, namely, the transformation of the technology of cotton spinning, which set in motion some remarkable changes.[47] But why were spinning machines invented? Davis reckoned that it was because England needed to economise on labour (although he rejected the notion that there was a relative shortage there by comparison with France), and because the atmosphere conducive to innovation, which was mentioned above, 'brought forth the inventors'.[48] For all the respect one owes to the memory of an excellent historian, whose early death is a cause for deep regret, his contribution to the debate strikes as a limited one.

W. W. Rostow, on the basis of the statistics concerning the issuing of patents (whose number rose much more sharply in England than in France, in the course of the eighteenth century), has concluded that the operational demand for inventions was lower in France than on the other side of the Channel, and therefore that the French entrepreneurs had not displayed the same innovatory zeal as their British rivals.[49] Rostow has accepted, for a number of sectors,[50] my hypothesis that the English ran up against difficulties which necessitated, far more urgently than elsewhere, the introduction of new technologies: 'the economic pressure to innovate was less in France than in Britain'. This passage continues, however, as follows:

> it is the responsiveness of British society to the economic challenges and opportunities that emerged in the eighteenth century that, I believe, made the difference ... What distinguished Britain from France, as the eighteenth century wore on, was the greater scale of the inventive effort that went into the breaking of crucial technological bottle-necks, and the greater scale of the entrepreneurial corps that introduced them as the century moved towards its close.

46 Davis, pp. 289, 293, 296, 298, 305–10, 313.

47 This view of the problem has been accepted by Crafts, 'Industrial Revolution in England and France', pp. 431–2.

48 Davis, pp. 311–13; see below, p. 92.

49 Rostow, *How It All Began*, pp. 175–8. It is true that statistics for Great Britain are for the number of patents granted, whereas those for France refer to the number approved by the Academy of Sciences (according to McCloy); they are therefore not exactly comparable and probably involve a bias against France (although it is the broad trend which is important). R. Roehl, 'French Industrialization: A Reconsideration', *Explorations in Economic History*, XIII, 3, July 1976, p. 250, had drawn almost the opposite conclusions.

50 In particular, the industrial use of coal, the development of 'coal fuel technology', with its fall-out, but not the cotton industry (see below, p. 92, note 143).

This difference was too great, in Rostow's mind, to be explained in terms of discrepancies in per capita income, percentages of the population that were living in cities, and so forth: 'Crouzet is inclined to explain the difference in terms of the sharper challenges confronted by the British, challenges which more urgently required technical innovation than in France. I am inclined to seek the answer in another direction'.[51]

The other direction to which Rostow refers is that of English Nonconformists and Scottish Presbyterians. Drawing his inspiration from T. S. Ashton and from E. Hagen's attempt at quantification,[52] Rostow has emphasised that there is 'a formidable disproportion' between the presence of dissenters among inventors and innovators and their numbers as regards the population as a whole. At the end of the seventeenth century, Rostow adds, the puritans' ardour shifted from theological debates to 'the market place', although it was the dissenters' minority position, a minority excluded from public life, which directed them towards 'modernising activities'. It was the dissenters who showed the necessary patience, determination and, indeed, obstinacy for the long, slow and painful task which would turn an intuition into an invention that could actually be put to use. However, under these circumstances, there was a direct relationship between the religious problem of the seventeenth century and the locus of the Industrial Revolution. After a series of bitter conflicts, England had managed to resolve this problem (at home and in Scotland) by means of toleration, after the Revolution of 1688. This was for non-economic reasons but it occurred in such a way as to strengthen England's economy, which, in spite of having a much smaller population than France, was fortunate enough to be able to call upon 'big battalions' of potential innovators among the dissenters.

On the other hand, the Revocation of the Edict of Nantes was doubly damaging to France, for it both deprived it of entrepreneurs and further reinforced the creative capacities of its rivals, and of England in particular. Admittedly, French eighteenth-century society, Rostow observes, was also on the move, with considerable opportunities for

[51] Rostow, *How It All Began*, pp. 177–80, 183–4, 253, no. 48.

[52] E. E. Hagen, *On the Theory of Social Change. How Economic Growth Begins* (London, 1964), pp. 296–7; using a sample of some 92 'innovators' for the period of the Industrial Revolution, Hagen discovered that 41 per cent of those English and Welsh innovators whose religious denominations were known, were Nonconformist, although the latter category represented only 7 per cent of the population of England.

vertical-mobility and with some businessmen who were vigorous entrepreneurs; but the reserves of entrepreneurial talent had been reduced and so much so that, to take one example, the French were quite unable to profit from the potential mass market in cotton fabrics which was very much within their grasp. Rostow therefore concludes that: '... the British Nonconformists contributed a scale and a thrust to the generation and application of new technology that larger France could not match. They were, in my view, the critical margin France denied herself in 1685.' One could admittedly, Rostow adds, invoke the examples of Holland and of the Thirteen Colonies, which had not had the same 'political and social inhibitions' as France but did not achieve an industrial breakthrough either; however, the profitability of industrial enterprise in these places was insufficient.[53]

Rostow's account implies that development be considered in the very long term and that a broad framework be used. If England's economic superiority is to be understood, the whole of the country's history in the modern period (together with that of France), and its political and religious history in particular, must be taken into account. Furthermore, David Landes' recent book on watch-making is grist to Rostow's mill; the persecution of the Huguenots and the Revocation of the Edict of Nantes, 'devastated' the French watch industry and helped to transfer to England and to Geneva predominance in this branch.[54] However, on the one hand the haemorrhage of talent occasioned by the emigration of the Huguenots had begun long before the Revocation and, on the other hand, contrary to what the casual reader of Rostow's book might suppose, not all the protestants did leave France. Besides, though Peter Mathias has written ironically of the notion that Nonconformists were the 'secret weapon' of economic growth, he places much emphasis, in his *First Industrial Nation*, upon the role that dissenters played in the English economy of the eighteenth century, upon the effects of their value system, of their minority status and of the solidarity networks binding them one to the other.[55] However, if the 'historical compromise' of

[53] Rostow, *How It All Began*, p. 175, 184–9.

[54] D. S. Landes, *Revolution in Time. Clocks and the Making of the Modern World* (Cambridge, Mass., and London, 1983), pp. 92–3, 412–13, notes 19 and 21. Landes rejects the thesis of W. Scoville, in *The Persecution of Huguenots and French Economic Development, 1680–1720* (Berkeley, 1960), who had denied that the Revocation had damaging effects upon the French economy.

[55] P. Mathias, *The First Industrial Nation. An Economic History of Britain 1700–1914. Second Edition* (London, 1983), pp. 7, 142–5.

1688–9 really played the crucial role that Rostow claims, one cannot help but wonder why three-quarters of a century had to pass before English inventiveness manifested itself on a large scale. Conversely, the 'prosperity' enjoyed by England at the end of the seventeenth century had begun under the Restoration, and the Glorious Revolution did not increase it overmuch. Everything suggests that the presence of Nonconformists in England constituted *a* difference with respect to France; I do not believe that it constituted *the* difference.[56]

After this reminder of the criticisms and observations to which my 1966 article gave rise, it seems appropriate to return to a number of problems touched upon there which have been further illuminated by research in the last twenty years.

At the beginning of the article I had emphasised the initial advantage enjoyed by England at the beginning of the eighteenth century,[57] as a consequence of the more favourable conjuncture from which it had benefited, by contrast with France, in the course of the seventeenth century ('conjuncture' being understood here in a purely descriptive sense, namely, the more or less prosperous or depressed situation of an economy, and not, *à la Braudel*, as a *deus ex machina*).

Several historians have confirmed the hypothesis that there was a perceptible difference in the economic development of the two countries in the seventeenth century and in their position at the beginning of the eighteenth. Pierre Goubert, for example, has produced a strong statement of this point of view, observing that, during the second half of the seventeenth century, 'recession, depression, or at any rate stagnation, were glaringly apparent' in France, whereas Holland and England had more or less escaped this great depression.[58] However, one should not push the contrast between France and England to the point of caricature, as Robert Mandrou, both because of his complete ignorance of conditions across the Channel and because of his ideological bias, has done.[59] It is going too far to claim that, after a 'total'

[56] Recent research has not confirmed the notion that there was a clear contrast between Anglican and dissenting schools, although some authors had represented the latter as being like business schools!

[57] A line of argument which Caron, *Histoire économique*, p. 17, accepts. See also O'Brien and Keyder, *Economic Growth*, pp. 57, 194; P. Chaunu, *La Civilisation de l'Europe des Lumières* (Paris, 1971), p. 351.

[58] Goubert, in *HESF*, vol. II, pp. 329–30, 347. A. Corvisier, *La France de Louis XIV, 1643–1715. Ordre intérieur et place en Europe* (Paris, 1979), pp. 139, 146, 153, criticises this excessively sombre balance sheet.

[59] R. Mandrou, *Louis XIV en son temps* (Paris, 1973), especially pp. 21–9, 309–11, 376–81, 386, 403 and Chapter V, pp. 404 ff. According to Mandrou, around 1660, the whole of the French

triumph in 1713, England found herself 'at the head of Europe if not of the world'[60] and that she was 'ready for the great industrial adventure',[61] which in fact only began half a century later.

Nevertheless, when I wrote my original article, I was still too much influenced – like most French historians of my generation – by F. Simiand and Ernest Labrousse, especially as far as the meaning of price movements and their relationship with production were concerned, and by the concept of the 'general crisis' of the seventeenth century. That century had, admittedly, seen several grave crises, but most scholars would now question the notion that it had ever known *one* generalised and continuous depression.[62]

Indeed one ought to add a little light and shade to the sombre picture that had been drawn, up until around twenty years ago, of the seventeenth-century French economy, and in particular of the state of things at the end of Louis XIV's reign. Admittedly, new research into agriculture, and into tithes in particular, has confirmed that there was indeed long-term stagnation – up until 1720 – in cereal production, and that the latter suffered several collapses, in the short term, during wartime.[63] However, alongside this rural stagnation, there was some progress in trade, industry (in rural manufactures in particular) and capitalist organisation. As far as manufactures are concerned, Pierre Deyon, who had emphasised their archaic condition when writing in 1966, took a much less sombre view in a subsequent book; he even noted that those of France and England had undergone virtually

economic machine was jammed, industry and trade were blocked and so doomed to relatively low levels of development, the country was hit by a 'monetary malediction'(?); as for the second part of Louis XIV's reign, it was a time of protracted crisis, whereas England's economic advance is presented in glowing colours, although not without many errors.

60 *Ibid.*, p. 376. Corvisier, p. 340, writes that the treaties of 1713–14 were not disastrous for France, and that it is premature to speak of England as being already dominant; this term is also deemed anachronistic by P. Deyon and J. Jacquart, in the volume they edit of P. Léon, *Histoire économique et sociale du monde*, vol. 2, *Les Hésitations de la croissance, 1580–1740* (Paris, 1978), p. 505; they, like Chaunu (p. 20), prefer to speak of a shared ascendancy, between France and England, although they recognise that the latter held some trump cards, both economic and socio-political, which account for her successes in the War of Spanish Succession.

61 Deyon, in the work mentioned in note 60, pp. 204–8.

62 See Morineau, in Léon, *Histoire économique et sociale*, vol. 2, pp. 86–9, 98–101, 104–5, 193–4; Deyon, in the same work (p. 578), emphasises that the concept of a 'general crisis' has been dealt some hard blows.

63 E. Le Roy Ladurie, in *Seventh International Economic History Congress. Edinburgh 1978. Four 'A' Themes* (Tonbridge, 1978), p. 11; Jacquart, in Léon, vol. 2, pp. 350–3; H. Neveux, 'Les Mouvements longs de la production céréalière en France du XIVe au XVIIIe siècle', *Bulletin du département d'histoire économique, Faculté SES. Université de Genève*, no. 8, 1977–8, pp. 20–4. The latter argues for a depression of around fifty years at the end of the seventeenth century and the beginning of the eighteenth.

simultaneous ups-and-downs in the course of the seventeenth century. It is admittedly true that England enjoyed better results after 1688, but the overall picture of French industry at the end of Louis XIV's reign contains both positive and negative components. As for foreign trade, Jean Delumeau has described its development after 1660, which, though slow and irregular, was evident and characterised by the crucial fact of the emergence of French colonial trade. It would therefore be an error to suppose that in 1715 France was ruined.[64]

It is, nevertheless, the case that the English economy was ahead of the French at the beginning of the eighteenth century, as recent studies have clearly confirmed. England, together with the United Provinces, was in a category apart; one could describe it as 'an advanced pre-industrial economy'.[65]

There can be no doubt that England in the seventeenth century, especially in its latter half, displayed many signs of economic progress, on a broad front and in almost all sectors (whereas in France, innovation, where it existed, was localised). There would be little point in reviewing the increasing prosperity and the innovations of the period; to be brief, agriculture was changing, industry and foreign trade were expanding and diversifying, a new system of public finance and an embryonic banking system were established. D. C. Coleman has therefore emphasised what he calls 'the divergence of England', from the middle of the seventeenth century on, which consisted in the main in a rise in the standard of living, in the gradual accumulation of a reserve of disposable income that was larger and more widely distributed than in any other part of Europe; all of which served to guarantee a particular extension and depth to the domestic market. Coleman has identified the causes of these developments as being the rise in agricultural productivity after 1650, the advance of the 'frontier' in the North of England and the increase in the percentage of the population that was living in towns and engaged in non-agricultural

64 See in particular, D. Richet, 'Croissance et blocages en France du XVe au XVIIIe siècle', *Annales ESC*, XXIII, 4, July–August 1968, pp. 781–2, 785–6; J. Delumeau, 'Le Commerce extérieur français au XVIIe siècle', *XVIIe siècle*, no. 70–1, 1966, pp. 90, 94 ff., 104–5; P. Deyon, 'La Production manufacturière en France au XVIIe siècle et ses problèmes', *ibid.*, pp. 47–63; Deyon, in Léon, vol. 2, pp. 287–8; Corvisier, pp. 12, 151, 346.

65 For A. Maddison, *Les Phases du développement capitaliste* (Paris, 1981), pp. 35, 39–40, the United Provinces having a more advanced economic structure and England having borrowed large sums from them, the latter was a follower country rather than a leader. As for Morineau (in Léon, vol. 2, pp. 189–91), he observes that England had not had to bear the burden of the Thirty Years' War, so that revolution broke out in the country which was the most exempt from the misfortunes of the early seventeenth century and which was the least hurt by taxation.

activities. In France, Coleman added, domestic demand continued for a longer time to be depressed, the standard of living of the masses was lower, because of an inadequate agricultural base, and of other causes, like the absence of an integrated national market such as England was fortunate enough to possess.[66]

The same notion of 'divergence' features in the work of Eric Jones, who maintains that England, during the seventeenth and the beginning of the eighteenth century, had an exceptionally vigorous performance, by comparison with that of the Continent (including, when all is said and done, Holland), through the improvement of the volume, methods and organisation of production. Jones is careful not to attribute everything to agriculture, but he reckons that the main divergence arose in that sector, a judgement that accords with Denis Richet's views on France. Richet has in fact highlighted the French contrast between progress in trade and industry and stagnation of the rural areas, the distortion, after 1680–90, between the depressed cereal economy and the expanding capitalist sector.[67] Jones believes that the depression in Continental Europe was caused by the fall in cereal prices, which was itself triggered by decline in population.[68] England did not escape this fall in cereal prices either, but it was late in coming, less severe and less protracted. However, what made England so distinctive was her atypical response, through innovation, to the difficulties occasioned by the fall in prices. The innovation that was pioneered in these years was mixed farming, based upon the introduction of fodder crops, which created a 'virtuous circle' and guaranteed increases in production (J. Jacquart observes that, thanks to the new methods, farming remained profitable, well-to-do cultivators did not suffer from the same difficulties as in France). However, we still need to know how it was that the English had managed to develop this system, when the Continentals had failed to do so. Jones lays particular emphasis upon the system of land ownership and of cultivation which prevailed in England: the predominance of large estates, the peculiarly British relationship between landlord and tenant, which favoured investment in agriculture. On the Continent, on the other

[66] D. C. Coleman, *The Economy of England, 1450–1750* (Oxford, 1977), pp. 197–200 (note that his analysis extends as far as 1750). J. Jacquart, in vol. 2 of Léon, p. 462 and elsewhere, emphasises the pauperisation of rural France.

[67] Richet, 'Croissance et blocages'; see note 64.

[68] This view of a depression resulting from a fall in agricultural prices has been challenged by Morineau, in Léon, vol. 2, pp. 86–9, 98.

hand, social structures tended to deprive agriculture of capital (the French upper nobility was an absentee class, which lived off its seigneurial dues and, Jones has observed, made no improvements in its estates, whereas English magnates were beginning to take an interest in agronomy).[69] The 'Agricultural Revolution' was not, as the reader will discover below, a crucial factor in the Industrial Revolution, but what concerns us here is the importance of agriculture in 'the divergence of England' from mainland Europe.

England enjoyed the immense advantage of having overcome famine or at least of having reduced the deleterious effects of bad harvests, so that they no longer resulted in demographic disasters.[70] It is worth recalling that the last famine to affect England *on a national scale*, though, admittedly, a truly murderous one, was that of 1596–7; at the regional level, subsistence crises continued to occur for longer, in poor and isolated zones, such as present-day Cumbria, but the last real famine there dates from 1623. After 1650, the classic subsistence crisis had disappeared from England, and A. A. Appleby was thus prepared to assert that the latter had solved the problem of feeding its population sixty years before France (where famines had come to a definite end, according to Emmanuel Le Roy Ladurie, by 1715–20), although R. B. Outhwaite has qualified this view, observing that demographic immunity to bad harvests was by no means complete.[71]

B. A. Holderness has considered this question of crises in a long-term perspective, and, in a very evocative passage, recalls the resemblances between southern England and northern France which together 'formed perhaps the most productive, and naturally most

[69] E. Jones, 'English and European Agricultural Development. 1650–1750', in R. M. Hartwell (ed.), *The Industrial Revolution* (Oxford, 1970), pp. 42–3, 52–3, 58, 62, 65–9, 71. J. Jacquart, in Léon, pp. 412, 468, reckons that the ruling classes' offensive against the peasantry was more successful in England than on the Continent; hence the progress of agriculture in that country.

[70] J.-P. Poussou, in Léon, vol. 2, p. 49.

[71] A. B. Appleby, *Famine in Tudor and Stuart England* (Stanford, 1978); 'Grain Prices and Subsistence Crises in England and France, 1590–1740', *Journal of Economic History*, XXXIX, 4, December 1979, pp. 865–7, 883; R. B. Outhwaite, 'Dearth and Government Intervention in English Grain Markets, 1590–1700', *The Economic History Review*, XXXIV, 3, August 1981, pp. 393, 397, 401–2; Le Roy Ladurie, in Duby and Wallon, vol. 2, p. 386. According to Appleby, from the sixteenth century on, subsistence crises were less grave in England than in France. Subsequently, according to E. A. Wrigley and R. S. Schofield, *The Population History of England, 1541–1871. A Reconstruction* (Cambridge, 1981), pp. 325, 328, 354, 372, in England, bad harvests affected nuptiality and fertility much more than mortality (although they could result in epidemics). V. H. T. Skipp, *Crisis and Development: An Ecological Case Study of the Forest of Arden, 1570–1674* (Cambridge, 1978), has studied a small region in the Midlands in which the link between bad harvests and mortality was probably broken as early as 1538. In Scotland, admittedly, the connection persisted up until the 1690s.

fertile, cereal-growing region in agrarian Europe, and the different experience of the two countries is therefore doubly significant'. The 'most obvious contrast' between these two large regions, 'at the simplest, most fundamental and most poignant level' lies in 'the infrequency and comparative mildness of hunger crises in England after 1350' compared with the frequency and gravity of such episodes in France. So it was that England had a 'secure basis' upon which to diversify its economy, in both the industrial and the commercial domains (which depended largely on the capacity of the agricultural sector to produce surpluses of foodstuffs and raw materials), without running up against the blockages and setbacks suffered by France. Holderness reckoned that medieval England, although it was technically backward in many respects, 'was still one of the best favoured and least precarious economies in Europe'. In subsequent centuries, England maintained and even increased its initial advantage and, from 1350 onwards, the contrast between English and French society grew sharper (although their main demographic fluctuations ran parallel to each other and, as Holderness observed, there was an element of chance in the outcome, for England had not undergone a series of devastating wars at home and had a better endowment of natural resources). Holderness also made the interesting observation that the contrast between the two countries would seem to be reflected in their respective historiographies, with French historians having paid most attention to cycles, fluctuations and the circular flow of economic change (which ends up in zero growth in the long term), to what Emmanuel Le Roy Ladurie has called 'immobile history', whereas British historians have been concerned above all with '(the) long period of hard training in the exercise yard' of economic development, which their country had undergone during three or four centuries, and which had given it an invaluable advantage even before the start of the eighteenth century.[72] One must add, however, that few British historians share the miserabilist obsession of the majority of their French colleagues!

Indeed, several authors have emphasised the 'very long term growth' (R. M. Hartwell) from which England benefited during the two centuries prior to the Industrial Revolution and which the other countries of Europe did not experience. S. Kuznets has arrived at the

[72] B. A. Holderness, *Pre-Industrial England. Economy and Society from 1500 to 1750* (London, 1976), pp. 232–4. The passage from which I am quoting constitutes the conclusion to his book.

figure of 0·4 to 0·5 per cent per year for the total product and 0·2 per cent for the per capita product, between 1500 and 1750. These are quite modest rates (growth was, furthermore, fairly irregular), but by no means negligible.[73] It is of course tempting to emphasise this long-term growth and the deep roots of the Industrial Revolution (such as the 'commercialisation' of the economy, its market orientation, features which developed early and were quite pronounced). If one subscribes to this line of argument, one would see the Industrial Revolution as having emerged quite naturally out of the most advanced of the *Ancien Régime* economies, which had attained to such a degree of maturity that it effected the transition to a higher stage without any particular force, whether exogenous or endogenous, impelling it.[74] However, to invoke an argument of this kind is merely to sidestep the difficulty.

If we return now to the seventeenth century, which is a kind of statistical desert as far as aggregates are concerned, the only acid test of economic performance has probably to be a demographic one. As far as France is concerned, the very bleak hypotheses, which were at one time current, have now been abandoned. According to Emmanuel Le Roy Ladurie, between 1570 and 1730 the French population curve was a sinusoid between a ceiling of twenty millions and a floor of eighteen millions, with linear adjustment producing a horizontal straight line for a hundred and sixty years. J. Dupâquier has arrived at a more cheerful assessment, arguing that population was more or less stationary during Louis XIV's reign, and that upward movements in the birth-rate compensated rapidly for peaks in mortality; the total that he produces for France within its present borders at the beginning of the eighteenth century is a little higher than the figure for the beginning of the seventeenth century. J.-P. Poussou holds an intermediate position, but he emphasises the demographic disasters at the close of the Sun King's reign. From my own perspective, the important point is that, even if one opts for the most optimistic estimate, France's population only increased by a modest amount (perhaps 10 per cent at

[73] R. M. Hartwell, *The Industrial Revolution and Economic Growth* (London, 1971), p. 31; S. Kuznets, 'Capital Formation in Modern Economic Growth (and Some Implications for the Past)', *Troisième Conférence internationale d'Histoire économique. Munich, 1965* (Paris–The Hague, 1968), vol. I, pp. 30–1, 33–4.

[74] All the more so given the difficulty (see below, p. 102) of identifying any direct, immediate causes of the 'explosion' of innovation at the end of the eighteenth century. Conversely, it is possible to see no necessary connection between the Industrial Revolution and the various changes occurring during the two centuries prior to it.

the utmost) in the course of a century, with sharp fluctuations in the meantime.[75]

England's demographic history, now well known, thanks to E. A. Wrigley and R. S. Schofield's book',[76] was undoubtedly less turbulent and tragic than that of France. Admittedly, after a steep rise during the sixteenth century and the first half of the seventeenth,[77] the population of England levelled out and even fell, from a maximum of 5,281,000 inhabitants in 1656 to a minimum of 4,865,000 in 1686, but the main reason for this fall (accounting for 58 per cent of it) was large-scale emigration, which probably involved the loss of some 500,000 persons between 1630 and 1680; furthermore, demographic indicators can hardly be said to be favourable during the seventeenth century, particularly between the 1640s and the 1680s.[78] After 1686, population began to rise again, but only very slowly, and it was a full eighty years before the figure that had been reached at the mid seventeenth century was definitively exceeded. However, whereas the figure for 1701 was lower than that for 1641, it was nevertheless 23 per cent higher than that for 1601, which implies that the best part of the growth of the first half of the century (28 per cent between 1601 and 1656) had been preserved. Furthermore, seventeenth-century England did not experience the violent fluctuations suffered by the population of France; it was, as we have seen, virtually immune to the disastrous effects of poor harvests; high mortality peaks were rarer and less steep.[79]

Wrigley and Schofield account for these contrasts by invoking the original demographic system that was operative in England. This was a 'low pressure' system, whose regulator consisted of variations in

[75] Le Roy Ladurie, in Duby and Wallon, vol. 2, pp. 359–61, 363, 576; he points out, however (p. 386), that the last third of the seventeenth century saw a diminution in the kind of large-scale disasters which cause spectacularly high mortality rates, and, more especially, the end of plagues (the one in Marseilles in 1720 being merely an episode, tragic, but short-lived and localised); J. Dupâquier, *La Population française aux XVIIe et XVIIIe siècles* (Paris, 1979), pp. 11, 43, 45, 67–8, 87; J.-P. Poussou, in Léon, vol. 2, pp. 42, 47–8, 50. According to Poussou, there was a population peak in 1705, higher than that of the beginning of the seventeenth century; Dupâquier has underestimated the effects of the crisis of 1709–10, and the 1715 figure was lower than that for 1705.

[76] For what follows, see Wrigley and Schofield, pp. 208–11, 228, 441, 533.

[77] D. M. Palliser, 'Tawney's Century: Brave New World or Malthusian Trap?', *The Economic History Review*, XXXV, 3, August 1982, pp. 339–53; the strong demographic growth between 1540 and 1640 did not create any Malthusian trap, but it stimulated the economy; Wrigley and Schofield, p. 440: the drop in fertility at the beginning of the seventeenth century meant that England avoided the dangers of the 'positive check'.

[78] A fall in nuptiality and in life expectancy, a rise in mortality: Wrigley and Schofield, pp. 161–2, 236, 413–14, 417.

[79] *Ibid.*, pp. 325, 328, 335, 341, 354, 372, 414.

fertility (or, rather, in the last resort, in nuptiality and age at first marriage), which guaranteed an equilibrium between population and resources (an equilibrium which actually improved between 1650 and 1750). On the other hand, France and the other European countries had 'high pressure' systems, in which mortality (or, to be more precise, high mortality peaks) was the regulator. Thus, the positive checks had disappeared from England by the seventeenth century, and perhaps even earlier (although England experienced several years of high mortality resulting from epidemics, in the second quarter of the eighteenth century), whereas it was still a crucial fact in France at the beginning of the eighteenth century. Since its standard of living was low, French population was vulnerable to short-term shocks and both the death-rate and the birth-rate were higher than in England.[80]

Wrigley and Schofield have also calculated an index of real wages which falls sharply from 1571 to 1606 and then rises almost uninterruptedly from 1626 to 1741.[81] From the 1690s, and even earlier, this index also becomes more stable, which suggests that there was an improvement in the production and distribution of foodstuffs. England therefore enjoyed an exceptionally long 'benign' period; for a whole century she benefited from the advantages which derive from a rising level of real incomes and she underwent as a consequence certain structural changes (in the pattern of demand, in particular, which operated to the advantage of goods other than basic necessities),[82] without this rise having provoked an increase in population such as to prevent further progress. Wrigley and Schofield regard this as the explanation for 'the divergence of England' mentioned by Coleman, a divergence which raised the country to levels of prosperity unknown in

80 *Ibid.*, pp. 1, 9, 162, 268–9, 328, 451–3, 467, 469, 471–3, 478–9. However, J. Dupâquier, pp. 67–9, denies that mortality was the main regulator of French population under Louis XIV; more crucial determinants, according to him, would be variations in the birthrate in response to variations in mortality: young unmarried people only had to increase their nuptiality in order to compensate for the devastating effects of high mortality rates. D. R. Weir, 'Life Under Pressure: France and England, 1670–1870', *Journal of Economic History*, XLIV, 1, March 1984, pp. 40, 42–4, admits that between 1670 and 1739, the demographic history of France was more 'turbulent' than that of England (French mortality rates were more sensitive to variations in the price of grain); but he denies that France, in relation to England, had a 'high pressure' system; nuptiality was sensitive to economic jolts in the two countries.

81 I am quoting here their moving average of twenty five years.

82 The ages pyramid of the period 1626–96 had the same favourable effect, with the dependency ratio (percentage of children and old people) being at its minimum (it was higher in the early eighteenth century, and clearly much higher at its end); Wrigley and Schofield, pp. 443–4, 448–9.

the pre-industrial world. This 'good fortune', namely, the unusual length of this benign period, was partly the 'gift', as it were, of the economic and demographic régime of early modern England. On the one hand, age at marriage and fertility tended to adjust themselves *slowly* to economic changes; this is why there was a long period of late marriages and therefore of somewhat low fertility and reproduction rates, which brought significant economic advantages, thanks in particular to a relatively low rate of dependence. On the other hand, the English economy was capable either of supporting a population growth at a rate of 0·5 per cent per year without inducing a fall in real wages, or of guaranteeing a rise in real wages of 0·5 per cent per year if there was nil demographic growth.[83] Admittedly, Wrigley and Schofield's index of real wages has been criticised by Michael Flinn, who felt that it rested upon a narrow and 'terribly frail foundation'.[84] It is worth noting, anyhow, that as early as 1971 Pierre Chaunu had observed that the Malthusian blockage experienced by England after 1640, through the rise in the age at first marriage and the fall in the birth-rate, had prepared the way for the explosive 'growth' of the eighteenth century.[85]

Pierre Chaunu had also observed that it was during the seventeenth century that England and Scotland had acquired a strong lead in literacy, so that, by 1700, the percentage of persons able to sign their names on documents was roughly twice as high in England as in France (although some regions of France were as literate as the most advanced areas of Britain). Since literacy advanced at the same pace on both sides of the Channel during the eighteenth century, the British held on to their lead. This is a fact of considerable importance, even if one does not wholeheartedly endorse Pierre Chaunu's conclusion: 'It was in the seventeenth century that England gained the trump cards which ensured its take-off at the end of the eighteenth century. Seventeenth-century England had invested in brains.'[86] It had also invested in colonies. Thus, in 1700, New France, with its 15,000 European inhabitants, was twenty times less populated than were the

[83] Wrigley and Schofield, pp. 319, 408–9, 439–40, 481–2. These authors reckon that the peculiar features of the English marriage system helped to prepare for the Industrial Revolution but were not themselves capable of triggering it.

[84] M. W. Flinn, 'The Population History of England, 1541–1871', *The Economic History Review*, XXXV, 3, August 1982, pp. 455–6. This index was calculated on the basis of that of Phelps Brown and Hopkins, completed, for the period after 1712, with that of E. Gilboy.

[85] Chaunu, pp. 136–7. [86] *Ibid.*, pp. 145–8.

English colonies of North America, whose natural resources and economic possibilities were moreover far superior.[87]

I shall end this retrospective account with one question: were the causes for England being ahead of France at the beginning of the eighteenth century mainly structural or, conversely, were circumstances partly responsible?

The former position is held by historians who are violently opposed to the *Ancien Régime*,[88] and by American neo-institutionalists. Thus, according to North and Thomas, economic competition at the end of the seventeenth century had produced some winners (England and the United Provinces), some 'also rans' (such as France) and clear losers (Spain, Italy and Germany). 'For the first time in history, some regions and nations had been able to escape the iron teeth of the Malthusian trap'; in England, real wages and real per capita income had progressed, in spite of the increase in population; in France, on the other hand, they had stagnated, even though the population had not risen.[89] For North and Thomas, the lack of sustained growth in France was to be attributed to the fact that the State had not managed to develop 'an efficient set of property rights'; conversely, England had imitated the property rights and institutions of Holland, indeed so successfully that after 1700 she overtook the latter from the point of view both of efficiency and of rapidity of growth. England had established an institutional framework which 'provided a hospitable environment for growth' and 'the stage was now set for the industrial revolution' which, nevertheless, as I ought yet again to remind the reader, only finally arrived half a century later.[90]

D. R. Leet and J. A. Shaw have countered this interpretation with a very simple but nevertheless pertinent objection, namely, that France's 'institutions', reckoned by North and Thomas to be 'medieval', remained largely the same in the eighteenth century as they had been in the seventeenth, and yet the French economy underwent a relatively rapid growth (more rapid, in the view of these authors, than that of England). This implies that France's economic misfortunes in the seventeenth century should be attributed to non-institutional causes, above all the handicap of virtually continuous

[87] Deyon, in Léon, vol. 2, pp. 237, 241, 243. [88] For example, Mandrou, p. 21.

[89] According to Morineau, in Léon, vol. 2, p. 101, France also experienced a rise in real wages.

[90] D. C. North and R. P. Thomas, *The Rise of the Western World. A New Economic History* (Cambridge, 1973), pp. 103, 105, 117–18, 127, 146, 155–6.

warfare.[91] The perspective of these two American historians thus converges with that of several French specialists. Emmanuel Le Roy Ladurie has emphasised the part played by war in France's demographic misfortunes: 'The tremendous wars of the classical age . . . had, on three separate occasions between 1560 and 1715, checked French demographic growth.'[92] J. Jacquart has emphasised the important role played by wars in causing agricultural depression and reducing the peasantry to poverty, both by their direct effects and by the voracious fiscalism to which they gave rise in France, while England was more or less spared such depradations.[93]

The case for the institutionalist hypothesis is strengthened, however, by the testimony of John Harris, whose researches in French archives have uncovered many cases of

> avoidance of commercial and industrial innovation by businessmen pleading the excellence of existing local or national regulations, of low social mobility in the industrial context, the workmen not looking to rise to an entrepreneurial role, the noble requiring a royal privilege to preserve his status before he would enter on anything so demeaning as industrial enterprise. The magnificent illogicality of the French tax, tariff and toll structure created a world of economic Kafkaism, with the entrepreneur as anti-hero.[94]

These observations refer to the eighteenth century, but they are valid *a fortiori* for the seventeenth also.

What I have written in the above pages makes it plain that there is a wide consensus among historians as to the very pronounced differences between the English and French economies at the end of the seventeenth and the beginning of the eighteenth century. One voice, however, has been raised in opposition to this consensus in recent years, that of Immanuel Wallerstein. This curious book is neo-marxist and in sympathy with the Third World, but it is also stuffed full of

91 Leet and Shaw, pp. 532–5, 538–44. These authors maintain that, prior to the nineteenth century, political events determined economic progress; they attribute to these events a crucial role in the chronology of French growth, with wars (especially those waged on French soil) proving damaging for the latter. Had it not been for 'the Napoleonic holocaust', France could, they claim, have overtaken England. Rostow, *How It All Began*, p. 253, note 46, has also rejected North and Thomas's views on 'property rights' in France.

92 Le Roy Ladurie, in Duby and Wallon, vol. 2, p. 389.

93 Jacquart, in Léon, vol. 2, pp. 380–1, 385, 406; also, Dupâquier, pp. 18, 20–1; Corvisier, pp. 146, 151–2, 343, who notes that the French economy did nevertheless stand up to the ordeal of two long periods of war.

94 J. R. Harris, *Industry and Technology in the Eighteenth Century: Britain and France. An Inaugural Lecture delivered in the University of Birmingham on 27th May 1971* (Birmingham, 1972), p. 9. In the seventeenth century England became by and large a *laissez-faire* country, as far as industry was concerned.

sophistries, half-truths and contradictions;[95] nevertheless, it contains a number of ideas which deserve to be taken seriously, particularly as regards the problem with which we are concerned here.

Wallerstein argues that the 'core' of the European world-economy in the period 1600–1750 was in north-west Europe; in Holland and Zeeland, in London, the Home Counties, and East Anglia, and in northern and western France (on the other hand, a good part of the French kingdom did not belong to this centre); 'economically these zones were more alike than different'. Wallerstein goes on to add: 'My strong suspicion is that there was far less of a difference between the real agro-industrial efficiencies of England and France in this period than we tend to assume. The small differences that emerged as of 1763 were magnified *politically* into the significant differences of a century later.'[96]

Wallerstein has argued that, even in agriculture, there were only 'relatively minor' differences between the two sides of the Channel prior to 1750, even as regards productivity. He doubts that French agriculture was as backward as is commonly supposed and maintains rather that there were parallelisms between, for example, the rise of stockbreeding in England and that of viticulture in France. England did, admittedly, become a large exporter of cereals, thanks to the bounties instituted by the Corn Law of 1688 (*sic*),[97] but northern France used also to 'export' to other less fertile French provinces, and the south of France exported to Mediterranean countries. In both countries, the development of industry was encouraged by a high degree of protection and there was a shift towards rural areas.[98] Wallerstein's views may at first seem surprising but, upon second thoughts, it is not at all absurd to maintain that England's economic evolution up until the start of the Industrial Revolution was not fundamentally different from that of the rest of Western Europe, if one

[95] I. Wallerstein, *The Modern World System: II: Mercantilism and the Consolidation of the European World-Economy, 1600–1750* (New York, 1980).

[96] *Ibid.*, pp. 37, 81; also 120, 288.

[97] Curiously enough, Wallerstein (pp. 260–2, 267–8) is here reviving eighteenth-century views (p. 138), and those of W. Cunningham (1882), regarding the significance of this Corn Law, which is held to have stimulated exports and therefore agricultural production, and, indirectly, merchant shipping; it is therefore supposed to have led the English to concentrate on foreign trade, therefore on the navy, etc. This, in Wallerstein's view, accounts for their subsequent victories over France. In a review of this book, Eric Jones has written of a 'surprising explanation of Britain's eventual success in terms of state support for farm exports', *The Economic History Review*, XXXIV, 2, May 1981, p. 343.

[98] Wallerstein, pp. 83–91.

excepts a higher degree of regularity which may be largely explained in terms of the country being an island and thus immune to invasion and devastation.

Wallerstein allows, however, that there were serious differences between France and England as regards colonies, trade and finance. Yet if important settler colonies were founded by the English in the course of the seventeenth century, it was because the development of their industries needed external outlets, whereas France, which had a huge (albeit poorly integrated) domestic market, had scarcely any need to increase its foreign trade. In this case, as in a number of others, Wallerstein (and also Fernand Braudel, as we shall see below) has attributed a determinant role to the difference in size between England which, being small, had no choice but to turn its attention towards the outside world, and France, a huge country.[99] This explanation is of course vulnerable to the usual criticisms levelled at a crude geographical determinism.

As far as public finance and banking were concerned, England was far more successful than France, because, appearances notwithstanding, the English state was just as 'strong' by 1689 as the French monarchy (which was absolute in theory but not in practice) and, from the beginning of the eighteenth century, it became manifestly the stronger of the two. Wallerstein's thought revolves around this crucial point; in a capitalist system, a state is strong if it enables the owners of the means of production to extract the highest possible surplus, by helping them in particular in their struggle against their competitors on the world market, by armed force if necessary, which presupposes a capacity to mobilise the country's resources for military purposes. But the key factor is the existence of a stable 'hegemonic bloc' (to use Gramsci's term), which balances out the interests of the owners of means of production.[100] The seventeenth century saw serious attempts on both sides of the Channel to strengthen the state, but they enjoyed more lasting success in England, where the two Revolutions resulted in a stable compromise, with the reconstitution of a unified ruling class, and with the adoption of a political strategy by means of which the

[99] *Ibid.*, pp. 101–4, 267. See also pp. 112 and 99–101, for other bizarre views, for instance about the replacement of wood with coal in England, which Wallerstein rightly attributes to a different 'ecology' from that of France, but he goes on to commit the shocking error of confusing 'timber', which was used for shipbuilding and was imported from the Baltic, and 'wood' for making charcoal, which never entered international trade.

[100] *Ibid.*, pp. 11–14, also 94, 102.

state devoted itself to stimulate economic development at the expense of other countries. France, because of its peculiar geography – its large size and its heterogeneity, did not achieve a compromise of this nature but merely an 'imposed truce' under Colbert; the reconciliation of the upper classes, which, after their divisions in the seventeenth century, accounted for England's stability in the eighteenth, was never achieved in France, where, in the end, the state's weakness was to bring about the Revolution of 1789.[101]

It is undoubtedly true that the making in England of a genuine ruling class (such as France has never had), together with its takeover of the state, were phenomena of the greatest importance, as Pierre Chaunu had already observed.[102] Furthermore, Wallerstein is quite right to point out that the strongest state is not the one which has the most developed apparatus or whose decisions are the most arbitrary; he is also justified in rejecting the old clichés about a constitutional and liberal England, which tended to favour private enterprise and mass production, by contrast with an absolutist and bureaucratic France, which was supposed to stifle such developments.[103] However, the curious thing about Wallerstein's position is that it leads him to put the emphasis upon political factors (he holds that the strength or weakness of a state depends upon politics rather than upon economics) and upon political decisions respecting the economy (he attaches great importance to the Navigation Acts and, quite unjustifiably, to the Corn Law of 1689).[104] Finally, Wallerstein has rehabilitated the military factor: 'Military strength is one key to efficacity in this regard' (the struggle against economic rivals); the 'crucial Battle of Barfleur' (which was in 1692, and not in 1694) gave the English at a single stroke mastery of the seas.[105] There is some justification for such positions but what is surprising is that they have been formulated by an author who, in the

[101] *Ibid.*, pp. 116–25, 246, 285–7. However, some other passages appear to minimise the differences between the compromises realised in the two countries, at the end of the seventeenth century, between the old aristocracy and the 'new capitalists', and between the monarchy and the nobility (pp. 142, 284–5). Differences between the social structures of the two countries are also described as 'minor'.

[102] Chaunu, pp. 202, 362; he sees also in the 1680s a significant divergence between France and England, when the 'reformations' of the nobility in France served to reinforce social rigidity. See also his suggestion, pp. 198–200, that one should not exaggerate the contrast between the English and French political systems of the eighteenth century.

[103] Wallerstein, pp. 94, 102, 113–14.

[104] *Ibid.*, pp. 102, 113, 179, 236; he also remarks, on p. 264, that the state's intervention (through the prohibition of imports) was the crucial factor in the growth of textiles production.

[105] *Ibid.*, pp. 113–14, 248.

United States, has been the high priest of the cult of Fernand Braudel, who had been fiercely opposed not only to old-fashioned military and political history, but also to any consideration of the military and the political dimension.

Be this as it may, Wallerstein has argued that the 'ultimate triumph' of England in the course of the second One Hundred Years War (which he sees as coming to an end, curiously enough, in 1763) was a victory not of liberalism, but of the strongest, least democratic and most mercantilist state in Europe.[106] However, this was also a state which enjoyed some strong support from abroad – from the United Provinces. Wallerstein is very insistent on this point. The reconciliation between England and Holland at the end of the seventeenth century enabled the English to borrow from Amsterdam and the international Huguenot community, to set up the Bank of England, to contain France militarily and to establish Walpole's stable, one-party (*sic*) state, whereas France's finances descended into chaos.[107] Wallerstein concluded his account as follows: 'It was this steady increase in the relative strength of the English state – rather than significant differences in how French and English production was organized in the period from 1600 to 1750 or in their value systems – that accounted for the ability of England to outdistance France decisively in the period from 1750 to 1815.'[108] Wallerstein's study on the Industrial Revolution itself will be eagerly expected.

At the end of my 1966 article, I had expressed some regret at not having examined the problem of the relations between the political revolutions which England underwent in the course of the seventeenth century and the Industrial Revolution of the following century.

It is worth going into this problem, for marxist or *marxisant* historians hold that, if England was the first country to carry out the Industrial Revolution (regarded as the blossoming of industrial capitalism), it was because, a century before, it had been the first country to make a bourgeois revolution, which had liquidated

[106] *Ibid.*, pp. 115, 258, 268, 286.

[107] *Ibid.*, pp. 115, 277–9, 281, 283, 285, 288. Wallerstein acknowledges, on pp. 249 and 277, that neither France nor England could hope to be strong on both land and sea at the same time, that it was natural for France to lean towards expansion on the Continent, and that in fact she had no choice. This is once again, with some justification, to favour the geographical factor.

[108] *Ibid.*, p. 288. He had noted, on p. 120, that the *small* differences existing prior to 1763 enabled the English subsequently to pull ahead in terms of productivity and economic dominance, an advance for which the rise of their foreign trade and their colonies had also prepared them (p. 104).

feudalism and eliminated all obstacles to the free advance of capitalism. Conversely, France, which had to wait until 1789 for its bourgeois revolution, was unable to rival England on the economic plane.

Christopher Hill has enlarged upon this theme in his book, *Reformation to Industrial Revolution*, which is now widely regarded as a classic. Hill argues that the English Revolution of the seventeenth century transformed the economic and social life of the country and gave rise, as early as the seventeenth century, to 'revolutions in trade and industry which had far-reaching effects on the whole of society'. Because of these changes, and because it had founded 'a political system within which commercial and industrial capital had freedom to develop', the Revolution 'created the conditions for that uniquely favourable balance between population and resources in England from which the Industrial Revolution was to result'.[109]

On the French side, Albert Soboul has likewise stressed that the path from feudalism to capitalism had as revolutionary a character in seventeenth-century England as in France at the end of the eighteenth. In both countries, feudal relations of production were abolished 'as categories or structurally'. The English Revolution 'played an equivalent role in the history of England to that of the French Revolution in the history of France'. To a very great extent it 'cleared a path for the development of capitalism', by sweeping away the last vestiges of the feudal order, by abolishing monopolies, by lessening the influence of the guilds etc.[110] G. Lemarchand has written that, during the sixty or eighty years following 1640, the last vestiges of the feudal mode of production (FMP) were liquidated, by revolutions that were bourgeois in the sense that they shattered the institutional barriers which impeded the free advance of capitalism and they enabled the merchant upper bourgeoisie to have a share in political power.[111]

The main objection that one can raise to the crucial role that these historians appear to be attributing to the revolutions of the seventeenth century is that by 1640 there was not much feudalism left to abolish. Actually Lemarchand admits that it had been steadily declining in England since the fourteenth century; the manor had disintegrated

109 C. Hill, *Reformation to Industrial Revolution* (Harmondsworth, 1969), pp. 14–16, 22, and Chapters 3 to 5 of the third part of the book.

110 Soboul, *La Civilisation*, vol. II, pp. 66, 68–9.

111 G. Lemarchand, 'Un cas de transition du féodalisme au capitalisme: l'Angleterre', *Revue d'histoire moderne et contemporaine*, XXV, April–June 1978, p. 297. It is worth noting the somewhat embarrassed formula employed with respect to 'bourgeois' revolutions.

and had assumed the form of the large estate, which was rented out to tenant farmers and worked by wage-earning labourers. The FMP had ceased to be dominant as early as the sixteenth century; it had at first continued in symbiosis with the new capitalist mode of production (CMP), but this latter prevailed fairly quickly, without being 'coopted' by the feudal mode (as was to be the case in France in the modern period), so relentless was its advance and so weakened had feudalism been as early as the fifteenth century. Soboul himself has written that in England 'there had been a free and rapid development of capitalism, linked with the utter dissolution of rural communities through the mediation of rent in money'; in France, things proceeded at a slower pace, in spite of a more radical revolution, because the dissolution of peasant communities had never been completed and because rents in kind survived.[112]

Whatever the validity of this scheme, the major point is the idea that the transition from feudalism to capitalism in England was a process which took a very long time and that it was already very advanced well before the Revolution of 1640 to which, when all is said and done, Soboul and Lemarchand (whose marxist–leninist credentials can not be suspected) did not attribute a crucial importance.[113] Thus, English agriculture was in the main commercial and capitalist. The Long Parliament did, admittedly, abolish a number of 'feudal' survivals (such as the Court of Wards) in the field of property rights, together with a number of restrictions upon free enterprise, but it is hard to believe that these details were anything more than finishing touches. Christopher Hill has certainly exaggerated the influence of the political revolution upon the 'Agricultural Revolution' of the seventeenth century (a revolution that was still modest both in its nature and in its spread). His account becomes more convincing when it deals with the impact of the Navigation Act and of the Commonwealth's foreign policy upon the 'Commercial Revolution' and upon the emancipation of England from Dutch tutelage. Finally, is it really necessary to point out yet again that there was no social revolution in England in the seventeenth century and no significant transfer of power to the advantage of the 'bourgeois' and the 'capitalists'? Furthermore, the peculiarities of the evolution of agrarian society in England, of its

112 Soboul, vol. II, p. 66; Lemarchand, pp. 277–82, 286–7, 304.

113 Lemarchand is very eclectic and draws into his argument multiple factors in order to explain the transition from the FMP to the CMP. Of course, it is quite another matter to decide whether this transition is or is not a pseudo-problem.

passage from the FMP to the CMP (if this jargon has to be used), are beyond dispute, and proved to be a major factor in the Agricultural Revolution, but the causal relation linking this latter and the Industrial Revolution, as we shall see below, was rather weak.

A second objection to Christopher Hill's thesis concerns chronology. Lemarchand himself has observed that the development of capitalist industry, that is, the Industrial Revolution, occurred at least a century after the disappearance of the FMP, and he has shown some surprise (as have a number of other authors) at the fact that this revolution had not arisen during the 'period of rupture', between 1689 and 1715 (or 1720), when the FMP had all but disappeared and when there took place a 'genuine boom' (*sic*), together with a number of technical inventions.[114] We should recognise, nevertheless, that the 'divergence of England' did become apparent ... at the Restoration.

As for eighteenth-century France, Lemarchand has written that she 'experienced a significant economic expansion but [that] her basic structures did not greatly change, which gave rise to grave imbalances after 1770'. Yet feudalism does not feature among the three series of causes which, according to Lemarchand, account for the absence of an Industrial Revolution in France, namely, the relative abundance of wood, water and labour; the cast of mind of the businessmen which, formed by an education which was still humanist and religious, had not turned towards technical matters; and, finally, the attitude of certain merchants who, since they enjoyed a *de facto* monopoly within the framework of commercial capitalism, had no particular incentive to increase production.[115]

Curiously enough, it was an English marxist, Tom Kemp, who formulated the idea that the French economy had been blocked by a system that was still feudal, and that it was necessary to shatter that system if an Industrial Revolution were ever to be realised. Kemp accepts, albeit begrudgingly and with reservations, that growth may have pursued a parallel course in France and Britain: 'the curve of income per head and total output [of France] moved unmistakably upward; at a rate, it has been claimed, comparable with that in

114 Lemarchand, pp. 295, 297–8, 301–2: Soboul, while he makes the liquidation of the last vestiges of feudalism a necessary condition for the development of industrial capitalism, does not suggest that this condition is a sufficient one; vol. II, pp. 64–5.

115 Lemarchand, p. 298; also his earlier article, 'Bilan et perspectives de recherches: Le XVIIe et le XVIIIe siècles en France', *Annales historiques de la Révolution française*, 1969, no. 198, pp. 647–8.

England'; further on he admits that the French economy was not immobile and displayed 'a capacity for change and expansion which has enabled the claim to be made that the growth in production and in average income per head was about the same as that in England'. However, Kemp maintains that quantification is 'misleading', for profound changes were blocked by various factors which are not really susceptible to quantification: 'They depend upon an analysis ... of the totality of social relations.' Kemp's account continues:

> The fact that growth took place, in some spheres at an impressive rate, does not, therefore, seem to be the significant thing about French development in this period. Rather the emphasis must be upon the comparatively narrow scope for entrepreneurship of a modern kind in a society which remained overwhelmingly agricultural and traditional. What seems significant is not the fact that growth took place ... but rather the lack of conditions for carrying through a structural transformation. To explain this it is necessary to look outside the sphere of production ... at the character of the society. Stress has therefore been laid on the ways in which the general characteristics of the old régime limited the possibilities of economic transformation.

Given conditions of this sort, after 1780, the divergences between the French and English economies became more pronounced, with tensions and symptoms of crisis appearing in France and with industry making great strides in England. As far as Kemp is concerned, 'France appears basically as a feudal society in the eighteenth century'; even industrial and commercial undertakings had a 'feudal' character, with very little productive investment or entrepreneurial spirit. In such conditions, tendencies towards inertia continued to be 'overwhelmingly strong', especially in agriculture. Capitalist development could not intervene 'as long as the grip of the old social relations had not been broken or loosened'. Kemp heaps up all the most traditional clichés regarding the French economy of the *Ancien Régime*, and his refusal to resort to quantification is, it must be said, frankly obscurantist (an attitude which is to be found among a number of historians of the Left, when statistics do not agree with their ideology).[116]

The best response to Kemp must be the following perspicacious passage from Emmanuel Le Roy Ladurie:

> The contradictions between bourgeoisie and feudalism, and between capitalism and feudalism ... only play a fairly weak role, since in the countryside, it is actually the *seigneurie* (centred on the demesne) which is the matrix for the capitalism of the big

[116] T. Kemp, *Economic Forces in French History* (London, 1971), pp. 66, 69–72, 74–6. See also the whole of his first four chapters; note 1, on pp. 79–80, shows that my 1966 article was one of his targets.

farmers, when it exists. This capitalism, though not without some internal disagreements, is embedded in the *seigneurie*; it pits itself against the familial, plot-holding economy of the peasant masses (which was the real obstacle to change).[117]

This observation quite clearly breaks with the usual 'catechism' regarding the *Ancien Régime.*

I had indeed neglected in my 1966 article to survey the differences between the agrarian systems of England and France or to analyse their possible consequences for the industrialisation process.[118] I would have needed, admittedly, to extend the field of analysis, probably too much so. One would have, indeed, to take account of the geographical factor, which Patrick O'Brien and D. Heath reckon to be as important as the institutional one, for England has a higher percentage of fertile soils than France and natural conditions which are more suitable for stockbreeding, which is a fact of some significance. Furthermore, if one wished to understand differences in land ownership and in patterns of tenancy, one would have to go back a long way, to the medieval period itself, and to developments taking place, as Marc Bloch had long ago pointed out, between the eleventh and the thirteenth centuries; one would have to begin by comparing the French *seigneurie* and the English manor, and even the feudal systems of the two countries. At any rate, 'the disappearance of the peasantry' in England (by the end of the seventeenth century, less than a quarter of the land was still in the hands of owner-occupiers) and its survival in France, the concentration of both ownership and cultivation of land in the one country, and their fragmentation in the other,[119] were processes which took several centuries. One must likewise take a long-term view if one is to grasp why the density of rural population was, in the seventeenth

[117] Le Roy Ladurie, in Duby and Wallon, vol. 2, p. 591; see also pp. 431–2, where he shows that the nobility's fiscal privileges favoured the progress of large-scale farming: 'fiscal iniquity and modernisation went hand in hand'. R. Forster, 'Obstacles to Agricultural Growth in Eighteenth-Century France', *American Historical Review*, LXXXV, 6, October 1970, p. 1614, reckons that the retardative effects of the seigneurial régime have been much exaggerated.

[118] I did look at this problem in another article, 'Agriculture et Révolution industrielle. Quelques réflexions', *Cahiers d'Histoire*, XII, 1–2, 1967, pp. 67–86. S. Pollard, *Peaceful Conquest*, p. 40, gives a summary of the traditional view regarding England: 'No peasants, no feudal privileges, but a class of wage-earners accustomed to working for wages.'

[119] Forster, pp. 1601–3, provides a pertinent discussion of the consequences of this fragmentation. See also C. Heywood, 'The Role of the Peasantry in French Industrialization, 1815–1880', *The Economic History Review*, XXXIV, 3, August 1981, pp. 359–60, who condemns the thesis, which dates back to Arthur Young, that small family farms act as a brake upon industrialisation. It is worth noting that in England some of the cradles of the Industrial Revolution were areas of small farms and even division of landownership.

and eighteenth century, much lower in England than in France (according to Michel Morineau, the former had not been, at the beginning of the fourteenth century, a part of the *monde plein*). This was an important advantage, which may have helped to set the Agricultural Revolution in motion or at any rate to make it possible; whereas in France strip farming and concentration on cereal production still tended to prevail, in England the amount of cultivable land available per person employed in agriculture (and, consequently, the productivity of labour) and the capital/land and capital/labour ratios were higher and therefore more favourable. The animals, being both input (as supplying draught and manure) and output, are the key element in agricultural capital, so much so, indeed, that O'Brien, Heath and Keyder have placed the beast/land ratio at the very heart of their explanation of France's agricultural backwardness with respect to England; but they note that only a study concerned with the long term would explain how English cultivators had managed to accumulate a larger stock of productive assets, and of animals in particular, per unit of cultivated land; an advantage which had been won as early as the beginning of the eighteenth century and probably long before, and which increased as time went on, guaranteeing them increasing yields.[120] The specifically English landlord–tenant relationship was also something that had developed gradually over a period of time, and there is a general consensus (at any rate, among English-speaking historians) that it favoured a relatively high rate of reinvestment of rents and of profits. Conversely, French landowners, including the greatest of them, who were drawn to Paris and Versailles, took no interest in their land and in its improvement, did not invest in it, squeezed more heavily their tenant farmers than was the case in England (and the *gros fermiers* in particular, who were the equivalents

[120] For all of this, see M. Bloch, *Les Caractères originaux de l'histoire rurale française* (Paris, 1952, 2nd edn.), p. 132; P. O'Brien, 'Agriculture and the Industrial Revolution', *The Economic History Review*, XXX, 1, February 1977, pp. 167–9; in D. Johnson *et al.*, pp. 200, 202; P. O'Brien and D. Heath, with C. Keyder, 'Agricultural Efficiency in Britain and France, 1815–1914', *Journal of European Economic History*, VI, 2, Autumn 1977, pp. 349–53, 362, 374–77, 380–1, 390; O'Brien and Keyder, 'Les Voies de passage', p. 1294; O'Brien and Keyder, *Economic Growth*, pp. 129–30, 132, 138–9. See also M. Morineau, *Les Faux-semblants*, pp. 68–9, 76, 84, and 'History and Tithes', pp. 475–6; J. Mulliez, 'Du blé, "mal nécessaire". Réflexions sur le progrès de l'agriculture, de 1750 à 1850', *Revue d'histoire moderne et contemporaine*, XXVI, 1979, pp. 3–47; the animal/land ratio was higher in some French regions than in the openfields of the Paris Basin.

of the 'farmers' on the other side of the Channel, and the sole potential agents of agricultural progress).[121]

One cannot help but wonder, none the less, whether there has been a tendency, going back as far as the travellers and agronomists of the eighteenth century, Arthur Young in particular, to exaggerate the superiority of English agriculture. Michel Morineau has observed, half in jest, that 'it was the English farmers who gave French agronomists a feeling of guilt'; reviewing the various figures quoted by Arthur Young for agricultural yields, Morineau has found that the English traveller was heavily biassed against France and that, taken all in all, the French wheat yields *c.*1789 were not so bad by comparison as Young had asserted. After having made calculations which extrapolated backwards the English data for 1837, Morineau concludes that the average wheat yield in England in 1789 was from 40 to 50 per cent higher than that of France. However, if one restricts the comparison to north west France, where soil and climate resemble those of England, the latter's advantage in yield per hectare falls to 28 per cent. Morineau holds that this figure allows one to scale down the progress in efficiency which is habitually attributed to English agriculture during the eighteenth century, at the end of which the latter's output was not managing to keep up with the country's demographic growth, as England, which had been an exporter of cereals on a large scale at mid-century, was becoming a net importer.[122]

P. O'Brien has pursued a similar line of argument, expressing some doubt 'about the *uniquely* progressive state of British agriculture from 1660 to the mid eighteenth century'; 'there appears to be nothing extraordinary about the British achievement from 1700 to 1850'. The post-1750 period saw a rapid rise in agricultural prices and a very clear and continuous shift in the intersectorial terms of trade to the detriment of industry, which means that agricultural production did not increase enough to satisfy the rising demand of the industrial and urban economy. Therefore, the performance of agriculture, whose production increased at only a third of the speed of that of industry during the eighteenth century, does not deserve the extreme praises that have been heaped upon it.[123]

121 Forster, pp. 1605–15 (whose views are accepted by Rostow, *How It All Began*, pp. 82–5); also see above, p. 66–7.

122 Morineau, *Les Faux-semblants*, pp. 73, 76–9, 82, 84; 'History and Tithes', pp. 474–6.

123 O'Brien, 'Agriculture and the Industrial Revolution', pp. 173–5.

To return now to France, Michel Morineau, who can hardly be said to belong to the 'optimistic' school, has argued that in 1789 French population had not broken through the ceiling of food supplies, the asymptotic limit determined by cereal production (in other words, it had not fallen into a Malthusian trap); he does, admittedly, allow that a process of generalised immiserisation was in progress, that is, a 'contraction' of the people's standard of living, but he declares that the starving point had not been reached. Morineau speaks of 'rural French provinces that were by no means too backward in their technical development and their performance, but were overloaded by a middling peasantry which was not well-off, and by a swelling proletariat of journeymen'. A number of other passages in *Les Faux-semblants* and a subsequent article are, admittedly, more sombre, and suggest that, after an economically satisfactory first half of the century, the second half reverted to catastrophe; France, Morineau asserts, was a country which did not experience genuine growth (that is, a rise in per capita product), and where the increase in food production lagged behind the rise in population.[124]

Regardless of the precise discrepancy between the performances of British and French agriculture in the eighteenth century, a major problem is that of the effects of the indisputable differences between them upon the industrial development of the two countries, as it is often held that there exist close links between agrarian systems and 'the state of preparation for industrialisation'.[125]

Thus, Eric Jones has argued that the progress of agriculture in Southern England from the middle of the seventeenth century, and the resulting increase in cereal production, had affected farmers in regions less suited to grain cultivation, such as the West and North of the country, and even the Midlands; they responded by turning towards stockbreeding and above all by looking for non-agricultural sources of income, that is, by developing domestic industry. Jones admits that proof that such specialisation increased between 1650 and 1750 is hard to come by, but he claims that the advent of cereals surpluses stimulated rural industrialisation. The regions which benefited from these surpluses accumulated capital and business expertise, a semi-

[124] Morineau, *Les Faux-Semblants*, pp. 68–9, 321, 325, 329–31, 334; 'Cambrésis et Hainaut', pp. 331–2, note 4, 342.

[125] Pollard, p. 47.

proletariat formed, which gradually was 'divorced' from the land and became available for the purposes of factory industry.[126] More recently, Sidney Pollard has applied to England the 'protoindustrialisation' model, which had been meanwhile developed; he has identified a striking negative correlation between those regions which were favoured from the agricultural point of view and those in which industry developed, at first in the traditional form of rural domestic industries, organised according to the putting-out system, then in its modern form; the latter were almost all either areas of mediocre agricultural potential (the Pennines), or zones which had barely been touched by the Agricultural Revolution (the belt of clay soils in the Midlands). The Pennines and the Midlands were both regions in which cultivators obtained a poor return for their labour (the inhabitants had therefore to supplement their incomes with industrial work) and in which wages were low (which tended to attract the putters-out).[127] Another factor was the existence in neighbouring regions of a commercial agriculture, whose surpluses made it possible for protoindustrial workers to be fed. Subsequently, if one agrees with the model developed by Franklin Mendels and Charles Tilly, a dynamics internal to protoindustrialisation brought about the birth of the factory system and the gradual substitution of it for the domestic system, and therefore industrialisation *stricto sensu*.

However, Donald Coleman, who is sceptical of the value of the concept of protoindustrialisation, at least as far as Great Britain is concerned, has denied that the regions in which this phenomenon occurred were all poor, hilly, barren ones. This was certainly not true of East Anglia or of the Black Country; in the Pennines, moreover, industry was established in the valleys and not on the hills. It is possible that in certain areas the population turned towards industrial work because poor soils did not give them a sufficient income, but the rise of English rural industries began at the end of the Middle Ages, during a period when real wages were rising, and Coleman claims that

126 E. L. Jones, 'Agricultural Origins of Industry', in his *Agriculture and the Industrial Revolution* (Oxford, 1974), pp. 130–1, 137–9; the original version of this article had been published in *Studi Storici* in 1968, and therefore predated Franklin Mendels' famous article on 'protoindustrialisation'.

127 Pollard, p. 5. For a valuable discussion of the relationship, in the West Riding of Yorkshire, between the agrarian system and the development of industry, see Pat Hudson, *The Genesis of Industrial Capital* (Cambridge, 1986), Chapter 3 (pp. 57 ff.), 128.

the causes for the development of these industries were quite diverse and could not be reduced to the low wages factor only.[128]

Coleman's observations may just as readily be applied to France, where 'protoindustrialisation' occurred both in 'rich' provinces (Normandy, Picardy) and in very poor regions (inland Brittany, Cévennes). Furthermore, since France had a plentiful supply of agricultural journeymen and of plot-holding peasants, conditions there were at least as favourable for protoindustrialisation as in England, as far as the cost of labour was concerned. If it is true that an Industrial Revolution can spontaneously emerge from protoindustrialisation, why was it that this phenomenon did not arise in France?

There is another, older conception of the relationship between agriculture and the Industrial Revolution. To begin with, it is argued that the Agricultural Revolution was a necessary condition of the Industrial Revolution: if there had not been an increase in the productivity of agricultural labour, it would not have been possible for England to feed its industrial and urban population, whose rapid increase industrialisation was bringing about, both in absolute terms and, crucially, as a percentage of total population; indeed, without this increase in agricultural productivity, the Industrial Revolution would have aborted. Secondly, agriculture, owing to the progress it had made, is held to have made a positive contribution to the growth of industry, by providing it with labour, capital and markets. Paul Bairoch has produced the most elaborate formulation of this argument, especially with respect to markets; he has argued that it was the increased demand for textiles and for iron implements, on the part of an expanding agriculture, which had set the Industrial Revolution in motion. Since the Agricultural Revolution began in England much earlier than it did in France, it was only to be expected that the Industrial Revolution should have started up first in Great Britain.[129] Indeed, given that in the eighteenth century (and even for a part of the nineteenth century) it was not *materially* possible for a country the size of England to feed a significant part of its population with imported foodstuffs, it must be admitted that the Agricultural Revolution was a

[128] D. C. Coleman, 'Proto-Industrialization: A Concept Too Many', *The Economic History Review*, XXXVI, 3, August 1983, pp. 440–45. See also L. A. Clarkson, *Proto-Industrialization: The First Phase of Industrialization?* (Basingstoke and London, 1985).

[129] P. Bairoch, *Révolution industrielle et sous-développement* (Paris, 1963), pp. 77 ff.; Bairoch, in C. M. Cipolla, *The Fontana Economic History of Europe*, vol. 3, *The Industrial Revolution* (London, 1973), p. 470.

necessary or, rather, an enabling or 'permissive' condition for large-scale industrialisation. I would not go any further than that, however.[130]

Besides, it is reasonable to suppose that the increase in agricultural productivity helped to boost demand in eighteenth-century England (although I would not attribute so decisive a role to it as Bairoch does), whereas the low and stagnant productivity of French agriculture tended to depress the standard of living of the mainly peasant masses and, consequently, the demand for manufactured goods.[131] On the other hand, there have been lively discussions (although I will not enter into the details here) concerning the impact that the course of British agricultural prices may have had upon the demand for manufactured articles.[132] I will simply observe here, in agreement with Patrick O'Brien, that it is by no means proven that the redistribution of incomes which took place, to the detriment of wage-earners and to the benefit of tenant-farmers and landowners, as a result of the rise in agricultural prices during the second half of the eighteenth century, significantly enlarged the market for industrial products. According to O'Brien, it was in the expanding towns that industry found new outlets; moreover, conspicuous consumption by landowners was in part of imported goods. I have discussed in some detail the transfer of capital from the agricultural to the industrial sector in another chapter, where the reader will see that it was not really very substantial, at any rate directly. As for labour, there can be no doubt that agriculture made some available for the industrial and urban sector, but it should be borne in mind that the surplus rural population which left the land was by no means 'driven off' by enclosures but was mainly the product of natural increase; in industrial areas (where age at first marriage was lower than elsewhere), the latter increase was so large,

130 Morineau, 'History and Tithes', p. 447.

131 Crouzet, 'Agriculture', pp. 78–82; Coleman, *The Economy of England*, p. 200.

132 See Chapter 1, p. 32 (and Crouzet, *De La Supériorité*, p. 216), with respect to the thesis of A. H. John, according to which the fall in the prices of foodstuffs during the first half (and the second quarter, in particular) of the eighteenth century stimulated the consumption of manufactured articles and enlarged their market in an enduring way; there is basically the same view in Jones, 'Agricultural Origins', p. 138, where it is argued that, given the slow demographic growth between 1650 and 1750, demand from industrial regions kept agricultural prices up, and regions of progressive agriculture bought more manufactured articles. Conversely, J. V. Beckett, 'Regional Variations and the Agricultural Depression, 1730–50', *The Economic History Review*, XXXV, 1, February 1982, pp. 35–51, maintains that the depression hit cereal-growing regions not stockbreeding ones, and that there is no proof that it stimulated the demand for industrial products. It is hardly likely that industry would have benefited first from a fall and then from a rise in agricultural prices.

indeed, that industry to a great extent generated its own manpower. We should bear in mind, however, both the view of many English-speaking historians, who hold that in England agrarian 'institutions' did not favour as much as in France the retention of a population surplus in agriculture,[133] and the work of Jean-Pierre Poussou, who has shown how much migratory movement there was, and how mobile the work-force was, in eighteenth-century France.[134]

If it is correct to argue, as I would, that the causal relationship in England between the Agricultural Revolution and the Industrial Revolution was a weak one (for the impetus to industrial change did not come from the agricultural sector), the lack of the former in France cannot have been an important factor in the non-existence of the latter.[135]

When, in 1966, I had considered the problem from several different angles, I came to the conclusion that the most pronounced contrast between England and France consisted in the fact that the former suffered from relative shortages in vegetable fuels and labour, which did not exist in the latter country. Crafts later made the astute observation that these shortages boil down to an energy crisis: a labour shortage is tantamount to a shortage in animal power, and the steam engine was at first a way of making it easier to exploit mines, and therefore facilitated the substitution of mineral fuels for those of vegetable origin.[136]

This hypothesis had been inspired by a paper given by David Landes in 1961; in his *Unbound Prometheus*,[137] he returned to, and developed the argument that the search by the British, in the eighteenth century, for machines and other inventions, had its origins in the more and more pronounced inability of the traditional systems of production to keep pace with increasing demand: 'It was in large measure the pressure of demand on the mode of production that called

[133] O'Brien, 'Agriculture and the Industrial Revolution', pp. 175–80. See also E. L. Jones, 'Agriculture and Economic Growth in England, 1650–1815: Economic Change', in *Agriculture and the Industrial Revolution*, pp. 85–127; also the introduction to the same author's *Agriculture and Economic Growth in England, 1650–1815* (London, 1967).

[134] J.-P. Poussou, *Bordeaux et le Sud-Ouest au XVIIIe siècle, Croissance économique et attraction urbaine* (Paris, 1983).

[135] Morineau, *Les Faux-semblants*, p. 95, appears sceptical about such a connection, even in 'agronomically' progressive countries.

[136] Crafts, in Floud and McCloskey, vol. 1, pp. 11–12.

[137] The first version of which appeared in volume VI of the *Cambridge Economic History of Europe*, which was published in 1965, when my article was at the printers.

forth the new techniques in Britain.'[138] Crafts has observed that there are only two purely economic hypotheses that can account for the innovations of the eighteenth century, namely, the one which invokes relative shortages and the energy crisis (where it is argued that the rise in production and in the stock of capital tended to overtake that of the supply of labour and of natural resources; changes occurring as a consequence in relative prices would then have stimulated the search for innovations) and the one which invokes an increase in demand, across a broad front and very rapidly, which would also have put pressure upon the factors of production and provoked 'a vigorous innovative response'.[139] The mechanism involved would in part have been the same in either case, but I hope that I have demonstrated that demand did not rise much faster in England than in France. There is some broad consensus regarding the explanation of the technical lag between England and France, in terms of 'bottlenecks' and obstacles on the supply side. 'It is a commonplace', writes Peter Mathias, 'to remark that Britain had been fortunate in her scarcities since the sixteenth century' and, in John Harris's view, she had the right bottlenecks.[140]

This hypothesis seems to me to be still valid today, but it needs to be qualified, if it is to match the chronology of inventions and innovations, and also the fluctuations in demand (and we must begin by making sure that these 'bottlenecks' really did exist!).

If one takes the long-term view, it is beyond dispute that technical progress in the British iron industry arose out of inadequate wood resources, while demand was growing, and of the fact that the iron industry could not develop without resorting to coal. If, however, one adopts a short-term view, a number of difficulties arise. There is no reason whatsoever to think that Abraham Darby's invention was connected to any worsening in the wood 'shortage', which had existed for the best part of a century; in addition, there is something perplexing about the half-a-century (or thereabouts) timelag between the invention of the coke-smelting process and its diffusion. The latter phenomenon was, admittedly, conditioned by economic factors, by changes in the relative costs of using charcoal and coke in blastfurnaces, and

138 Landes, *The Unbound Prometheus*, pp. 65, 77, 112, also 43, 84–9, 166, 194.

139 Crafts, 'Industrial Revolution in England and France', p. 435; Crafts in Floud and McCloskey, vol. 1, p. 11.

140 Mathias, 'British Industrialisation', in Léon *et al.*, *L'Industrialisation*, p. 508; Harris, *Industry and Technology*, p. 3.

therefore in the 'availability' or 'shortage' of these two fuels. Nevertheless, the link between bottleneck and invention (or even innovation) only seems to be close in the case of a few large ironworks with coke-fired blastfurnaces, which were set up to supply the Army and Navy during the Seven Years War.[141]

Likewise, no one can dispute that there is some causal connection between the invention of the steam engine and mining of tin and copper in Devon and Cornwall, but of coal also. But no one has managed to demonstrate that Savery and Newcomen built their engines as a direct response to increasing difficulties encountered in pumping out seepage water from pits. As for Watt's machine, it was the work of a genius, and one can never give a strictly economic explanation for the timing of inventions of that order. It is worth noting, nevertheless, that, prior to his association with Boulton, James Watt was backed financially by Dr John Roebuck, who was involved in the development of coal-mines in the vicinity of Edinburgh.

These examples lend credence to Crafts' thesis that economic factors were more important for the spread of inventions than for the very fact of inventing, that it is difficult to establish a correlation between these factors and inventions, and that there was a random element in the dating of specific inventions.[142]

The notion that a relative shortage of labour in England was responsible for the invention of textile machinery has been rejected by several historians. Ralph Davis, for example, had argued that the main region where the cotton industry flourished in France was Normandy, where several industries were competing for labour, which had therefore become rare.[143] It is certainly true that one cannot speak of a shortage of labour at the national level in eighteenth-century England, where many were underemployed, even in years of prosperity. Moreover, Wrigley and Schofield's index of real wages, which had risen from the 1620s up until the early 1740s, displays a fairly flat

[141] See n. 29 and 67 of Chapter 1, for references to C. K. Hyde's works. As for puddling, it was only the last and most satisfactory of several processes for transforming pig-iron into iron.

[142] Crafts, in Floud and McCloskey, p. 12.

[143] Davis, *The Rise of the Atlantic Economies*, p. 312. See also Crafts, 'Industrial Revolution in England and France', p. 435; Rostow, *How It All Began*, pp. 181–3, is sceptical on this point, claiming that nothing suggests that the plentiful supply of labour in France rendered unprofitable the introduction of new textile machines; this is clearly correct, given the huge increases in productivity that these machines brought about, but my argument was concerned with the invention and not the diffusion of these machines. For the same reason, I would contest his argument that mechanisation resulted in a large increase in employment in the cotton industry and that the necessary manpower was none the less found.

tendency during the middle decades of the eighteenth century; then, after a brief rise and a peak in 1781, the index falls for a whole generation. These fluctuations do not lend credence to the idea of a shortage of labour, for such a shortage would have brought about a rise in wages. This index is, admittedly, a national one, heavily weighted in favour of wages in Southern England and therefore perhaps unduly pessimistic.[144]

Nevertheless, it is difficult to deny the existence of local labour shortages, of pockets of 'overemployment', in particular in the North of England, where money wages increased rapidly between 1750 and the late 1760s, and in an activity as labour intensive as cotton-spinning. In this respect, the boom in cotton exports from 1750 to 1763 may have fostered the quest for cotton-spinning machines. Moreover, these same years saw migrations of manpower towards areas which were poor from the agricultural point of view but where industrial activity was increasing, such as Lancashire, the West Riding and the hosiery districts in the East Midlands; still merchant-manufacturers had to put out spinning outside their own counties.[145] As far as cotton printing is concerned, S. D. Chapman and S. Chassagne have found that France and Germany were suffering from the same shortage of highly-skilled workers as Britain, but that the latter was hit by a sharp rise in labour costs, because these workers organised themselves in clandestine unions which imposed 'restrictive practices', and to such effect that their employers lost no time in adopting the newly invented cylinder printing.[146] Finally, it is worth quoting François Caron's observation that 'the whole of French growth in the eighteenth century gives the impression of being based upon an enormous accumulation of human labour, precisely to the extent that it was readily available everywhere. This is probably the main difference between France and England.'[147]

A new variant on the explanation in terms of labour costs has

[144] Wrigley and Schofield, pp. 432–3; these authors regard the end of the eighteenth century as a 'malign' period, when England was threatened by a Malthusian trap (pp. 408–12, 439–42). Their wages index has been criticised by Flinn (see above note 84).

[145] Pollard, *Peaceful Conquest*, p. 6. E. E. Hunt, 'Industrialization and Regional Inequality: Wages in Britain, 1760–1914', *Journal of Economic History*, XLVI, 4, Dec. 1986, pp. 937–8, 941, 947, stresses the wages rise in Northern England from 1760 to 1800, which changed the wages geography of Britain.

[146] S. D. Chapman and S. Chassagne, *European Textile Printers in the Eighteenth Century. A Study of Peel and Oberkampf* (London, 1981), pp. 192–3, 198–9.

[147] Caron, *Histoire économique*, p. 13.

recently been advanced, which reminds us of the crucial but often forgotten fact that the cotton industry originated in the East, that it developed in Europe as a way of providing substitutes for imports, by producing ersatz East India goods, and that, given the skill of Indian spinners and weavers and the much lower wages paid there than in Europe, this development could not have been a spontaneous one.

The traditional textile industries had been threatened at the end of the seventeenth century, both in England and in France, by the flooding of the market with East India goods, which were the height of fashion; the governments of both countries responded in largely the same way, by banning the importation of East Indian goods and also the manufacture of cotton textiles. However W. W. Rostow has observed that this policy was taken much further in France, where not only pure cotton textiles but also mixed ones, such as linen and cotton, were banned. In England, on the other hand, the manufacture and printing of fustians and other mixed articles were tolerated, so that a 'cotton industry' did in fact develop and was of some importance by the middle of the eighteenth century; English yarns were still, however, inferior to Indian ones, and this led to the invention of machines which could produce good quality yarn, especially for warp. In France, the prohibition of cotton goods was lifted in 1759, but it was too late to catch up with the English.[148] K. N. Chaudhuri has also emphasised that the Europeans could not compete with the Indians in both the quality and the price of handspun yarns, and he has suggested that the competition of authentic East Indian goods might have been 'a contributory factor' to the setting in motion of the Industrial Revolution, for, without machines to achieve a cut in costs, it would have been impossible to counter the comparative advantages enjoyed by India.[149]

This suggestion was welcomed and elaborated by Fernand Braudel.[150] Moreover, Chapman and Chassagne have observed that

[148] Rostow, *How It all Began*, pp. viii, 63–4, 66, 130–1. His observation on France is open to dispute; anyhow numerous cotton-printing works were established just outside the French borders and were able to set up in business within the kingdom itself after 1759. See note 43 of Chapter 1.

[149] K. N. Chaudhuri, *The Trading World of Asia and the English East India Company 1660–1760* (Cambridge, 1978), pp. 237–8, 273; 'Some Reflections on the World Trade of the XVIIth and XVIIIth Century: A Reply', *Journal of European Economic History*, VII, 1, Spring 1978, pp. 227–8.

[150] F. Braudel, *Civilisation matérielle, Economie et Capitalisme, XVe–XVIIIe siècle*, vol. 3, *Le Temps du Monde* (Paris, 1979), pp. 490, 495.

the Peels, by contrast with Continental cotton printers, such as Oberkampf, ventured into cotton-spinning quite early on, because they wanted to lower the prime cost of the grey cloth they were using, in order to compete with India. Since the English had the closest relations with India, they were by the same token most vulnerable to its competition, and they therefore had the strongest incentive to seek out alternatives to Indian artisanal techniques (not only in spinning but also in printing, in which field they perfected copper plate, and then cylinder processes).[151]

The merit of the above explanations is that they refuse too insular an approach and interpret the progress and mutation of the English cotton industry in terms of the international context. One must, however, bear in mind that cotton goods coming from India were banned on the English domestic market; some were of course smuggled in, but such luxury articles were not meant for the same market as fustians and other British 'cotton goods', which were in effect well protected. It is true that Indian competition was not held back by such obstacles on third markets, including those of the British colonies, where East India goods could be re-exported. Yet this rivalry had not prevented a rapid rise of exports of English 'cotton goods' during the two decades prior to the invention of spinning machines. Furthermore, textile imports to London by the East India Company were both large and steady, in spite of some cyclical fluctuations, from around 1725 up until the 1740s, then they tailed off as a result of the wars in India and in the West; as to their prices, they rose on trend. These data do not suggest fierce competition between East India and English cotton goods.[152]

There is some risk of historians' discussions going around in circles, always reprocessing the same information, until new research into primary sources brings out fresh raw materials. We therefore owe a great deal to John Harris's studies, based upon archive sources, on the problem of the transfer of technology between England and France in the eighteenth century; he has thus produced many precise data

151 Chapman and Chassagne, pp. 13, 18–19, 198, 214.

152 Chaudhuri, *The Trading World of Asia*, pp. 105–8, figs. 15–20, 272, 284, 286, 293, figs. 21–6, 297–302, 547–8, Table C.24; 'The Economic and Monetary Problems of European Trade with Asia during the Seventeenth and Eighteenth Centuries', *Journal of European Economic History*, IV, 2, Autumn 1975, pp. 352, 354–7.

From 1750 to 1763, there was an increase in the share of British-produced cotton goods which were exported; the growth of exports then slowed down, but production accelerated, thanks to the domestic market; see Chapter 6 below, p. 253.

documenting the former's technological lead over the latter, the modalities of its 'divergence' and, as a consequence, the origins of the Industrial Revolution.[153] John Harris has revived, but refined, elaborated and corrected J. U. Nef's hypothesis regarding the importance of the early development of the coal industry in Britain, and of the gradual spread, beginning in the sixteenth century, of the use of coal in an increasing number of industries.[154] This diffusion had significant, though subtle effects, for it demanded technical innovation: one cannot introduce coal into an industry without at the same time effecting some change or other in the equipment or methods that one is 'importing' from another branch. This is how what Harris calls coal–fuel technology was developed, a technology which comprised a tried-and-tested ensemble of know-how and a whole panoply of plant and tools; this ensemble would be gradually perfected, through a series of 'spin-offs' as some elements of technology were transferred from one industry to another. This was how the art of building furnaces was improved and reverberatory furnaces in particular, which were used in glassworks from 1612 on, adapted to the smelting of non-ferrous metals in the 1680s, and judged by foreign visitors in the eighteenth century to be one of the distinguishing marks of British technology; the same was true of the boiler-maker's art, of the techniques involved in the making of crucibles in refractory clay capable of standing up to high temperatures (a very important feature in a number of industries), and also, at

[153] J. R. Harris, *Industry and Technology*; 'Skills, Coal and British Industry in the Eighteenth Century', *History*, LXI, 202, June 1976, pp. 167–82; 'Saint-Gobain and Ravenhead', in B. M. Ratcliffe (ed.), *Great Britain and her World, 1750–1914. Essays in honour of W. O. Henderson* (Manchester, 1975); 'Attempts to transfer English Steel Techniques to France in the Eighteenth Century', in S. Marriner (ed.), *Business and Businessmen, Studies in Business, Economic and Accounting Policy* (Liverpool, 1978), pp. 199–233; 'Michael Alcock and the Transfer of Birmingham Technology to France before the Revolution', *Journal of European Economic History*, XV, 1, Spring 1976, pp. 7–57; 'The Diffusion of English Metallurgical Methods in Eighteenth-Century France', *French History*, II, 1, March 1988, pp. 22–44; 'The Transfer of Technology between Britain and France and the French Revolution', in C. Crossley and I. Small, eds., *The French Revolution and British Culture* (London, 1989), pp. 156–86. I would also emphasise the interest of Chapman and Chassagne's recent study, *European Textile Printers*; one of its virtues is to bring down comparison from the macro- to the microeconomic level; the authors thus make a clean sweep of some accepted ideas, and while they bring out many resemblances between the two undertakings, they also demonstrate that productivity was far higher at Peel's than at Oberkampf's (pp. 211–14).

[154] Nef had made the mistake of seeing coal as the agent of a so-called 'first industrial revolution' (see Chapter 1, p. 12–13), whereas it was used mainly for domestic consumption, and also of restricting himself to the period 1540–1640, while important innovations in the use of coal were achieved during the half-century after 1660.

a more humble level, the practices involved in the cutting of coal or in the stoking of furnaces.

In all of these different domains and, just as crucially, in metal-working, England made great progress in the course of the seventeenth century; indeed, by 1700–10, she was assured of a lead that could hardly be challenged. Yet the process was to go on and it was in the 1780s that the last significant lacunae in coal–fuel technology were filled, with puddling, rolling of iron and the rotative steam engine.[155]

Harris reckons that the introduction of coal–fuel technology played a key part in setting England on the path to the Industrial Revolution. In particular, it gave a powerful stimulus to the inventiveness of the English, inasmuch as it familiarised employers, managers, foremen and skilled workers with technological change, it showed them the advantages that accrued from observation and experimentation, and it gave them the aim of cutting costs; it also created a 'technological optimism' and brought innovation even to the attention of the ordinary worker. Indeed, the skills needed to operate this technological system were perfected in a purely empirical manner, by practical men rather than by scientists, and at shop floor level; it was a question of craft skills, which were the prerogative of skilled workers and could only be 'learned by doing', through a long apprenticeship on the job.[156]

This technology was of course peculiar to England, for the other countries of Europe, and France in particular, only used coal on a much smaller scale and continued to employ wood or charcoal as the main fuel in industry. For about two centuries, England pursued a lone path. Harris emphasises how long term the process of developing coal–fuel technology was, but he also makes it clear that these refinements were interconnected and achieved on a broad front, with a mutual cross-fertilisation of techniques in various industries and with the transfer from one to the other of a whole set of processes and equipment which were all bound up with the use of coal.

Harris has also shown just why it was that France had such difficulties, right up until the beginning of the nineteenth century, in adopting coal–fuel technology. His argument is that France was trying to compress into a short period of time the extended apprenticeship undergone by the British, that the technology involved formed an interconnected whole, which could not be imported bit by bit, and that

[155] See, in particular, Harris, *Industry and Technology*, pp. 3–9.

[156] Harris, 'Skills, Coal', p. 168.

only men who were used to it were capable of introducing it abroad (they only arrived in sufficient numbers after 1815).[157]

Given these conditions, it is tempting to suppose that the early emergence and development in England of technologies for the use of coal and/or metal-working, and their concentration in this country, at a time when they were ignored in France (for the simple reason that England had a large number of rich, easily workable coalfields, well served by waterways, whereas France was much poorer in such resources), may to a great extent account for England's 'divergence' and for its being 'first'. This would bring us back to a 'geological' explanation, of the kind so scorned by social scientists.[158]

Admittedly, Peter Mathias has levelled an objection at Harris's hypothesis. He is prepared to admit that the 'divergence' established by the progress of coal–fuel technology had its roots in the seventeenth century and that a 'strategic' sector was involved, of great importance for the future; Mathias emphasises, however, that this sector continued to be a small one for a long time, and that it was in no position to have an effect upon growth rates and industrial performance at the national level at any point prior to 1780; after that date, however, this technology made possible a whole range of advances, which gathered momentum as it progressed. Harris responded that a technological gap ought not to be measured in terms of growth rates, and that 75 per cent of the gap separating France from England in 1790 had already been hollowed out by 1750.[159] One can also observe that Harris has neglected the textile industries, and cotton in particular; but he has suggested that the coal and metal-working technologies, which had been set up before the invention of textile machinery, had made it possible for the latter to be developed and perfected. Harris also states that he had not meant to advance a monocausal explanation, that he

[157] Harris, *Industry and Technology*, pp. 9–17; 'Attempts to transfer', p. 277, and also 199, 218, 228. This latter article gives a detailed account of the failures of the numerous attempts made in France in the course of the eighteenth century to produce genuine steel, in spite of support by government and of the employment of first class scientists; one humble, but in fact crucial cause of this failure was an incapacity to master the technology of refractory clays. Harris's article on Saint-Gobain and Ravenhead also shows the difficulties a 'high tech' French firm encountered when it tried to use coal (pp. 384 ff.).

[158] According to Pollard, *Peaceful Conquest*, pp. 4, 21, there has been too much underestimation of the part played by natural resources, and by coal in particular.

[159] Mathias, 'La Révolution industrielle', pp. 37, 43; see also his intervention, and that of J. R. Harris, in Léon and others, *L'Industrialisation*, pp. 505, 511.

was concerned with just *one* factor and that this did not rule out those mentioned by other historians.[160]

Be this as it may, Mathias agrees with Harris that, from the beginning of the eighteenth century, the English enjoyed a clear superiority in several technological domains: mining, the use of coal as a fuel and metal-working in particular. Those who specialised in these craft techniques were relatively few in number – especially for the more sophisticated among them – but groups of them were to be found in large towns and in the various industrial mining districts. Since these specifically British techniques were attuned to England's endowment in natural resources (coal and metallic ores in particular), there were kinds of technological 'pyramids', combining raw materials, equipment, processes and know-how.[161] Thus, one must stress not only geology but also human capital – the workmen and craftsmen skilled in coal and metal-working techniques – and also the pool of entrepreneurs which England could call upon in the middle of the eighteenth century, in relatively greater numbers, it would seem, than was the case in France. There were both big and small businessmen, who were alert to any opportunity for making money, skilled in organising production in response to market signals, and also endowed with confidence, energy, and, indeed, with aggressiveness. The combination of this human capital and of the new technologies was bound to be an explosive one, but these technologies were themselves the creation of the workers' skill and the businessmen's astuteness.

One can argue that the Industrial Revolution arose out of the confluence of two different currents of technical progress. The first current was that of coal–fuel technology, which involved the use of coal by a widening range of different industries, together with associated technical improvements; this current was an old one, continuous but slow, and it did not involve many opportunities for rapid increases in productivity. The second current was that of textile machinery, which emerged quite suddenly in the form of the spinning jenny and the water-frame (although they had been anticipated by the knitting machine, the Dutch loom for ribbon-making, the silk-throwing mills,

160 Harris, 'Skills, Coal', p. 181; *Industry and Technology*, p. 9.

161 Mathias, in Léon and others, pp. 504–6; 'La Révolution industrielle', pp. 41–4; 'Skills and the Diffusion of Innovations from Britain in the Eighteenth Century', an article first published in 1975, and republished in *The Transformation of England*, pp. 33–6; Hartwell, *The Industrial Revolution and Economic Growth*, p. 295, observes that the important thing was not science, where France was ahead of England, but skills, where the latter was superior.

the flying shuttle and the Lewis and Paul machine); these machines brought about huge increases in productivity and that of Arkwright imposed a new form of organisation of work – the factory system. This breakthrough had revolutionary consequences, bringing about the rapid creation of a new and substantial industry, namely, the machine-spinning of cotton, which also served as a model for the other textile industries. The Industrial Revolution was truly on its way when these two currents converged, in the 1780s and 1790s, when, for instance, Watt's engine was used to power textile machines, which were themselves constructed of cast and wrought iron, and not anymore of wood (as they had been before), and when the engineering industry was born.

A full two decades after I had drafted my original article, research into the origins of the Industrial Revolution still seems somehow akin to the quest for the Holy Grail, to borrow a phrase from Peter Mathias. Perhaps Crafts was right to have argued that a comparison of the British and French economies in the eighteenth century gave no chance of arriving at a valid conclusion on this problem of origins. Furthermore, historians are still divided as regards the performances of the two countries, whether they are considered separately or compared one with the other.

There is more dispute over these matters in the case of France, for, where England is concerned, the debate tends only to be between the 'insularists', who insist upon the uniqueness of English economy and society, and those who admit that, in many respects, there was nothing particularly exceptional about them. At the beginning of this chapter we saw that Ralph Davis had judged my views on the economic position of eighteenth-century France to have been too optimistic; Tom Kemp's sombre perspective on these matters was also delineated. As for Michel Morineau, he holds an extremely pessimistic view, reckoning that France at the end of the *Ancien Régime* was moving backward, unlike the rest of Europe, that agricultural production was declining, as were the traditional industries, so severely hit by the treaty of 1786; as population kept on rising, France was caught in a trap which led inexorably to her impoverishment, to a 'generalised immiserisation'. In Morineau's view, France's technical backwardness placed her in a situation of inferiority; she was 'powerless, in the short term, to come to terms with the new needs of new inhabitants ... unprepared for the changes that the future would bring'.[162]

Conversely, some writers have gone much further than I had done in

[162] Morineau, *Les Faux-semblants*, pp. 331, 334; and see above p. 86.

'rehabilitating' the French economy of the eighteenth century. This is the case, as I have already observed, with Crafts, and the same is true of Richard Roehl. The latter has used the criteria of backwardness formulated by Alexander Gerschenkron, and he has claimed that in no sense can they be said to apply to eighteenth-century France. Indeed, it is quite the reverse and Roehl reckons that France set out very early on the path to modern industrialisation, around the middle of the eighteenth century, that is a little before England; at any rate, he believes that the industrialisation processes of the two countries had many aspects in common.[163] This may seem to be an extreme position, and yet J. Marczewski had suggested as early as 1960 that if there had been a take-off in France, it could be placed around 1750, that is, before the British one. T. J. Markovitch has, more recently, written in a similar vein: 'France was, alongside England, the main pioneer of the modern Industrial Revolution.'[164] And Pierre Léon considered that France at the end of the eighteenth century was an 'industrial nation ... in the grip of powerful forces for renewal, undergoing a complete transformation internally'.[165]

Other historians hold a median position. This is the case with Denis Richet who has, on the one hand, identified a Malthusian trap, with population continuing to expand right up until the French Revolution, while agricultural production had no elasticity; but, on the other hand, he has judged that industrial and commercial activities were making a much more substantial contribution than in previous periods (one of the enduring achievements of the Enlightenment).[166] Clive Trebilcock wonders first of all if 'the promising French developments of the eighteenth century' might not have been merely 'surgical improvements to an arthritic frame', which in the end rejected them, and he reminds us that the *Ancien Régime*'s attempts at economic modernisation helped to unleash the Revolution, which was itself catastrophic for the economy; but he concludes that 'clearly, the late French edition of the ancien régime was not in itself incompatible with economic progress'.[167] These testimonies may be rounded off with a quotation

[163] Roehl, pp. 238, 255, 268; Asselain describes Roehl's ideas as paradoxical, in *Histoire économique de la France*, p. 15.

[164] J. Marczewski, in W. W. Rostow (ed.), *The Economics of Take-Off into Sustained Growth* (London and New York, 1963), p. 129; T. J. Markovitch, 'La croissance industrielle sous l'Ancien Régime', *Annales ESC*, XXXI, 3, May–June 1976, p. 647; 'La Révolution industrielle: le cas de la France', *Revue d'histoire économique et sociale*, LII, 1974, no. 1, p. 123.

[165] Léon, in *HESF*, vol. II, p. 422.

[166] Richet, pp. 786–7.

[167] Trebilcock, pp. 115–18, 125.

from a young scholar: 'to believe that traditional capitalism was lethargic, one would need to be a Jacobin or a Colbertist'.[168]

It would clearly be prudent not to push revisionism too far, for it is itself liable to be revised in turn. Charles Kindleberger has reminded us that eye-witness accounts of contemporaries, together with a number of simple tests, do not bear out the notion that the per capita income of the French was higher than that of the British, on the eve of the Revolution. Kindleberger stresses, moreover, that France's financial institutions were a century behind those of Great Britain: the hundred and six years gap between the founding of the Bank of England and that of the Bank of France is not just a symbolic one.[169] If we adopt a different point of view, and consider demography, this too is not in France's favour at the end of the *Ancien Régime*: mortality was stable, while it had been falling in England since 1731 (and life expectancy had been rising there), nuptiality and fertility of marriages were falling, and the age of first marriage rising, whereas it had been falling in England. Wrigley and Schofield record that, at the mid eighteenth century, population growth rates were the same on both sides of the Channel but, after 1770, the English rate increased 'powerfully' and overtook that of France, where demographic growth was clearly weakening when her rival was embarking upon an impressive expansion.[170] Nor should we forget that there was a 'crisis of the French economy at the end of the *Ancien Régime*'.[171]

In the last resort, one can readily understand why it was that the Industrial Revolution did not begin in France, for it is hard to discern any force there which was tending to effect a thoroughgoing transformation of economic structures. Yet it remains somewhat difficult to see what set it going in England; we lack, in particular, an adequate explanation of the timing of its first, tentative steps, that is the causes behind the constellation of inventions and innovations which cluster around 1770 and, more precisely, the causes behind the invention of cotton-spinning machinery, since it is there that, in the last analysis, the Gordian knot lies.

[168] F.-X. Caron, *Quarante négociants anoblis au XVIIIe siècle. Etat, Elites et Question Sociale au siècle des Lumières* (*3e cycle* thesis, University of Paris–Sorbonne, 1984), p. 618.

[169] C. P. Kindleberger, 'Financial Institutions and Economic Development: A Comparison of Great Britain and France in the Eighteenth and Nineteenth Centuries', *Explorations in Economic History*, XXI, 2, April 1984, pp. 104–6, 109–10, 120.

[170] Chaunu, *Lumières*, pp. 138–9, 155–6; Dupâquier, *La Population*, pp. 105, 107; Wrigley and Schofield, *Population History of England*, pp. 215, 236, 262. The mortality rate was lower in England than in France. Weir, pp. 33–5, takes a more optimistic view.

[171] This was the title of Ernest Labrousse's classical book.

It is admittedly true that, by the middle of the eighteenth century, England had an 'advanced' economy, which was making progress on a broad front, though slowly and without any Draconian change. It is likewise true that the social, political and intellectual environment favoured innovation and, besides, according to the hypothesis which I advanced in 1966 and which I would still, in all essentials, wish to defend, progress was checked by bottlenecks, in the cotton industry in particular. Now, Hargreaves and Arkwright's inventions were realised only a short time after a period of very rapid expansion in the export of cotton goods; in more general terms, an acceleration in the growth of England's total exports (which took place between 1744 and 1760) preceded the innovatory 'constellation' observable around 1770. One can perhaps follow Rostow in identifying 'some oblique linkage' of foreign trade and technical progress,[172] but one cannot be certain.[173] The explanation of the changes that took place around 1770 cannot help but be a tentative one; indeed, this is so much the case that it is tempting to subscribe to Crafts' view that innovation had for a part a random character. After all, Hargreaves' and Arkwright's inventions could have been fortuitous.

Conversely, once the first technological breakthrough was achieved, everything is as clear as day. The success of Richard Arkwright and his associates, who had been the pioneers of the factory system in the 1770s, demonstrated the remarkable opportunities for profit-making that the new technology offered,[174] and many followed in their tracks,[175] especially when the depression, political in origin, which had prevailed during the 1770s, had come to an end and when demand recovered dramatically at the end of the American War of Independence, which reopened large markets to British industry (France did not benefit from the peace of 1783 to the same degree and the treaty of 1786 was very shortly to shake a number of industries there). At this

[172] Rostow, *How It All Began*, p. 130. See also below, Chapter 6, pp. 253, 260–2.

[173] See the rather negative conclusions of C. P. Kindleberger, 'Commercial Expansion and the Industrial Revolution', *Journal of European Economic History*, IV, 3, Winter 1975, pp. 623–32. One can also observe that the diffusion of these innovations began during a period in which exports fell, at the end of the 1760s and in the 1770s: it would have been stimulated by such difficulties. But you cannot have your cake and eat it too (as is the case also with the argument regarding the effect of agricultural prices, see note 132, above).

[174] Chapman and Chassagne, p. 215, have also pointed out that the success of a few large calico-printing works was the occasion and the stimulus for the transition from the proto-factory to the factory proper.

[175] We should not forget the annulment, in 1785, of Arkwright's patents, though, admittedly, they had not stopped the pirates.

same moment, the growth in population was accelerating, and the convergence (as noted above) was effected between the new current of technical progress in textiles (which, beginning with cotton, soon had imitative effects in other textile industries) and the traditional current of coal, metal-working and machinery technologies. One therefore moved from a breakthrough in one relatively narrow sector to an advance on a much broader front and, consequently, to an acceleration of global growth;[176] the cumulative and self-sustaining process of innovations, which can be compared to a chain reaction, was unleashed. The Industrial Revolution was both or, rather, in succession, unbalanced and balanced growth. It has been compared to a two stages rocket, but the curious thing is that the first was the smaller one and its firing is hard to explain; on the other hand, the detonator of the 'explosion' of the 1780s was undoubtedly the peace of Versailles. France had not undergone the first stage of change; it was therefore only natural that she should have experienced some difficulty in her attempts to imitate England's second innovatory push, a difficulty that was exacerbated by the troubled condition of her economy in the 1780s.

[176] Even if this acceleration was less pronounced than one had thought, as Harley and Crafts' calculations suggest (see above, p. 51).

3 When the Mediterranean looked to England

The problem of the origins of the Industrial Revolution aroused the interest of a scholar who had been called 'the greatest living historian', Fernand Braudel, and, towards the close of his monumental study, *Civilisation matérielle, Economie et Capitalisme, XVe–XVIIIe siécle*, he was prompted to compare the economies of England and France in the early modern period. The fact that he makes no mention of the article, which is reprinted as Chapter 1 of this book, although it had been originally published in *Annales* (which he edited), makes his perspective of especial interest; he actually observes that no one has ever attempted a serious study of Anglo-French competition using statistical comparisons.[1]

Braudel also wrote, it is true, the following passage:

> Certain historians reckon that it was the Revolution and the Empire which caused France to fail in its industrial transformation and in its competition with England in the struggle for the first place in Europe and in the world; an opportunity had, in their view, been missed. It is certainly true that France, owing to adverse circumstances, surrendered the entire globe to exploitation by Britain's merchants; it is also the case that the combined effects of Trafalgar and Waterloo weighed very heavily upon France. Nevertheless, one ought not to disregard the opportunities that had been missed prior to 1789.[2]

In a note at the end of the volume in question, Braudel informs us who the historians referred to above are, namely, Maurice Lévy-Leboyer, François Crouzet and Pierre Chaunu, but nowhere does he specify where precisely it was that such judgements had been expressed.[3] The reader who has the patience to read through Chapters 2, 10 and 11 of

[1] F. Braudel, *Civilisation matérielle, Economie et Capitalisme, XV–XVIIIe siècle*, vol. 3, *Le Temps du Monde* (Paris, 1979), p. 328. See also, vol. 1, *Les Structures du quotidien: le Possible et l'Impossible*, and vol. 2, *Les Jeux de l'Echange*. Except in passages where I have specified otherwise, all references to Braudel in the present chapter are to this work.

[2] Braudel, vol. 3, p. 38. [3] *Ibid.*, p. 550, n. 76.

De la Supériorité de l'Angleterre sur la France will be able to decide for himself whether Braudel's summary is a fair assessment of my position and, at any rate, he will find that I never wrote that the Revolution and the Empire had resulted in a 'missed opportunity'. I had, admittedly, argued that France had fallen further behind England during the period 1793–1815,[4] but I had never denied that there was already, in 1789, a significant gap between the two countries. Furthermore, my 1966 article emphasised that England had already gained a clear lead by the start of the eighteenth century, and even earlier; it had also pointed out that one had to go fairly far back into the medieval period if one wanted to understand a number of differences in the social structures of the two countries, which had significant consequences for their economic history. Braudel also admits that the Revolution interrupted the experience of modernisation, under the impact of English competition, which had been started by the trade treaty of 1786, and that the wars of the Revolutionary and Empire period enabled England to win 'a monopoly over a limitless market, that of the whole world'. 'From this perspective', Braudel goes on, 'the arguments of those who hold the French Revolution and the Napoleonic wars responsible for the economic backwardness of France at the beginning of the nineteenth century have a certain weight.'[5] I was pleased to read this, though I myself had never held the Revolution and the subsequent wars solely 'responsible' for France's backwardness. And I am in agreement with Braudel when he observes that 'the industrial backwardness of France, evident from the nineteenth century on, cannot be explained without going back a fairly long way in time'.[6]

As for 'missed opportunities' prior to 1789, Braudel mentions the loss suffered by France in 1713 of free access to the silver of Spanish America (this would have been the sole occasion – when the merchants of Saint Malo were venturing into the South Seas – that France for a short period came close to taking the lead), the loss of Canada and in

[4] See P. O'Brien and C. Keyder, *Economic Growth in Britain and France, 1780–1914. Two Paths to the Twentieth Century* (London, 1978), pp. 60–1, 151: if one considers development across the whole period from 1780 to 1913, it was during the period 1793–1815 that the gap between Great Britain's per capita physical product and that of France was at its widest (to the detriment of France).

[5] Braudel, vol. 3, pp. 326–7; likewise (vol. 2, p. 188), he observes that the French economy had collapsed at the beginning of the Revolution, before the war had broken out.

[6] *Ibid.*, p. 38.

practice of India in 1762 (*sic*).[7] These observations cannot but strike one as surprising, coming as they do from an inveterate enemy of *histoire événementielle*; one is likewise startled by the importance ascribed, in a passage quoted above, to two battles which, though certainly quite spectacular affairs, were merely the end point of a long process. Braudel sees commercial relations and economic rivalries in mercantilist, that is, bellicose terms, as if competition for trade naturally ended in war for trade. Yet, given this perspective, it is startling to find that there is not a single line on the Royal Navy and on its patient conquest of the mastery of the seas.

Another 'missed opportunity for France', much further back in the past, was her loss of the advantage she had from the holding of the Champagne fairs on her soil; this was 'the first and last time' that she had 'the economic centre of the West on her own territory'.[8] The establishment of the maritime connection between Italy and the Low Countries, at the beginning of the fourteenth century, put France 'outside the crucial capitalist circuit of Europe'. Hence Braudel's staggeringly profound conclusion: 'The moral to be drawn from this is that one never loses on one occasion only. Nor does one win upon one occasion only.'[9] As for the observation that France was not, either in the sixteenth century or later, at the centre of the 'European world-economy' – the real centres having been Venice, Antwerp, Genoa, Amsterdam and London – this is a self-evident truth and explains nothing.[10] One is tempted to say: 'this is just too bad'.

At any rate, for Braudel, it was in 1783 that, in spite of its defeat in the American War of Independence, England had 'won control of the world economy', and that the failure of France's bid for this hegemony was sealed; in fact, the French monarchy had never made a bid of this kind – much as a supercilious nationalist might reproach it for this – and it was in many respects the *Ancien Régime*'s fault if the 'sharing out of the world' was at France's expense; the *Grande Nation*'s bid for hegemony was in fact made by the Directory and by Napoleon. Indeed, 'the real duel for world domination was not just between France and England but still more between the latter and Holland, which had literally been drained of its substance' in the course of the American War. This is an interesting and important observation, and

[7] *Ibid.*, also pp. 22, 276. The preliminaries to the peace of 1763 were signed in 1762; this probably accounts for the initially surprising date.

[8] Braudel, vol. 3, p. 38. [9] *Ibid.*, p. 94. [10] *Ibid.*, pp. 276, 301.

one that reminds us that we should not confine ourselves to a purely Anglo-French framework. Yet the duel between England and Holland was a seventeenth-century matter; an alliance against France, in which the United Provinces were merely a second, took its place from 1689 onwards. Admittedly, the United Provinces' participation in the War of American Independence was disastrous for them, but it had been a war quite unlike those of the previous century, and Britain's superiority, on the commercial, naval and colonial planes, had been established long before, together with Holland's reduction to the status of satellite, which, as Braudel emphasises, gave to England much financial support. Conversely, no matter what proofs may exist of the strength of the English economy immediately after 1783, which Braudel is quite right to remind us of and I would be the last to deny, at this date it was not yet the 'dominant' economy and it would take the 'Napoleonic' wars to assure it of this position, as W. W. Rostow has quite rightly pointed out.[11] It seems to me anyway excessive to assert that Louis XVI's France '[could] only breathe the air of the wider world through London' and that it '[had fallen] from Charybdis into Scylla', that is, from the clutches of Holland into those of England.[12]

In Braudel's explanation of England's victory over both Holland and France, he ascribes great importance to the formation of a national market, including first England and then the whole of the British Isles. Braudel observes that London took a long time to catch up with Amsterdam which was 'freer and more alert in its movements' (why? and what are these expressions supposed to mean?), but then 'the huge town' on the Thames overtook it, because it had access to a large domestic market, whereas Holland, which was tiny, did not have a real national market.[13]

As for France, it '[fell] victim to its giantism', to the vastness of its territory, which was the main cause of its inertia; it therefore had a fragmented, regionalised economy, which hindered the establishment of connections between different areas and the spread of technological progress. Furthermore, it had been 'prematurely overpopulated ... in terms of its capacities at that period ... [it was] loaded down with men, with vagabonds, with useless mouths to be fed, and with undesirable elements'.[14] England was clearly smaller (especially if one considers it

[11] W. W. Rostow, *The World Economy. History and Prospect* (London, 1978), p. 122.

[12] For the whole of this paragraph, see Braudel, vol. 3, pp. 276, 321, 325, 327.

[13] *Ibid.*, pp. 24, 252–3.

[14] *Ibid.*, pp. 269, 277–8, and vol. 1, pp. 36–7.

in the strict sense, and disregards Wales and Scotland), and, at a time when communications were difficult, had certainly benefited from its modest size and had been more easily unified from the economic point of view; it had also benefited from the lower density of its rural population. However, one should not exaggerate the contrast between the two countries, for France was not Russia or China; the Paris basin constitutes an ensemble comparable to that of London, although with the handicap (which is perhaps not an overwhelming one) that it is not surrounded by sea. John Harris observes that economic activity was not so dense in France as in England, since the former was a larger country, but he adds: 'This may itself be a less serious difference than it first seems, for industrial development in Britain was not evenly spread, but the product of hectic growth in a number of regions: comparable development could initially have taken place in France at similar regional growth points, leaving behind areas of lower industrial productivity and prosperity.'[15]

Moreover, Braudel, having asserted that a perfect national market did not exist in France in 1789 (no one had ever claimed that it did), goes on to observe that in the eighteenth century there took place 'a vigorous unpartitioning of the provinces', an increase in trade, an 'advance of the French national market', which 'began to play its part', and, finally he notes that, from the end of the seventeenth century, France tended to form a national market (although he adds further on that France's 'coherence' would only 'be fully established with the completion of its railway system').[16] The reader must orient himself as best he may in this confusing account. It is also hard to see just why the contrasts between 'rich' regions and 'areas of darkness', a dichotomy which is not specific to underdeveloped countries and which is also to be found to a degree in Britain also, should be regarded as so disadvantageous a factor,[17] or why the rivalry between Paris and Lyons was 'one of the unacknowledged weaknesses of the French system'.[18] Nor can one readily grasp how it was that the English economy could be held to be better balanced, 'less vulnerable to outside forces' (whereas in fact it was more open to the outside world),

[15] J. R. Harris, *Industry and Technology in the Eighteenth Century: Britain and France* (Birmingham, 1972), p. 2.

[16] Braudel, vol. 3, pp. 269, 273–4, 297, 468. However, Braudel rightly observes that internal customs, tolls etc. were not an insuperable obstacle to trade.

[17] *Ibid.*, pp. 287–9 ff. [18] *Ibid.*, pp. 278, 282–3, 285–6.

and with products more necessary to the Dutch than were those of France (what, then, of the wines of Bordeaux?).[19]

It is to be regretted, on the other hand, that Braudel did not go on to develop his interesting suggestion that a territorial state such as France, involved in a slow and costly process of political construction (a commitment often disregarded by foreign economists), had too much on its hands to involve itself in the conquest of world markets.[20] It is also a pity that Braudel did not enlarge upon the idea which he came across in a brilliant essay by Sir John Hicks (which he quotes), namely, that England was one – indeed, the last – of the maritime, mercantile City-States, belonging to the same lineage as Venice and Amsterdam, but having a larger territorial base and being more easily defended (since it was an island); such advantages enabled it to extend its domination ever further and to become, more fully than its predecessors, the warehouse of the world.[21]

To return now to the English national market, Braudel shows that, between 1453 and 1558, England 'became an island'; the loss of her possessions in France and the breach with Rome saved her from the dangers of giantism, and enabled her to differentiate herself from the Continent so that, from then on, she devoted herself to domestic tasks and to expansion in the new worlds.[22] This is a brilliant idea, but one which perhaps mingles politics too much with economics. Braudel then goes on to emphasise, quite correctly, the role of London, 'creating, and created by, the national market'.[23] 'By contrast with France', Braudel writes, 'which was too huge, divided against itself and torn between Paris and Lyons, England had only one head, albeit an enormous one',[24] whose superiority over Paris lay in its not being only 'a vast, parasitical machine, a thing of luxury and wastage', but also a very active port which came to dominate the whole of England and later of the British Isles. Yet Braudel's account seems to be again contradictory for, on the one hand, he asserts that London 'built and orientated the life of England from A to Z',[25] whereas, on the other, 'the Industrial Revolution in England arose, to a great extent, on the fringe of large-scale capitalism, independently from London'; it was the work of provincial towns such as Birmingham and Manchester.[26]

19 *Ibid.*, p. 220. 20 *Ibid.*, p. 252.
21 J. Hicks, *A Theory of Economic History* (Oxford, 1969).
22 Braudel, vol. 3, p. 302. 23 *Ibid.*, p. 303. 24 *Ibid.*, p. 313.
25 *Ibid.*, p. 316, also vol.2, pp. 25–7.
26 Braudel, vol. 3, pp. 255, 266.

Braudel continues his analysis by bringing out two factors, the first of which has often been neglected. It concerns the extraordinary stability of sterling from 1560–1 to 1931, which goes to show that 'nothing in England happens the same as anywhere else', and which was 'a crucial element in England's greatness' (although its economic effects are not described in detail). The second factor is the 'Financial Revolution', as P. G. M. Dickson terms it, and the creation by England of a consolidated public debt of a modern type, which played a key role in the wars against the Bourbons, who had never managed to 'nationalise' their finances. Braudel tries to account for these successes achieved by England, which derived from 'a series of good fortunes which set her, at times unaware, on the path to modern solutions', in terms of 'pragmatic responses' to successive crises, which turned out in the long term to be imbued 'with the highest wisdom'. Yet Braudel's explanation of the stability of the pound tails off into rhetoric; for him, this stability was 'the repeated result of the aggressive tension of a country tied to a particular destiny, because it was an island that had to be defended, because it had to make its way in the world, and because it had a clear notion of who its adversaries were, whether Antwerp, Amsterdam or Paris. The stability of the pound was thus an offensive weapon.' It is a pity that Braudel also falls into the elementary confusion between 'paper money' and bank notes.[27] It is anyway hard to grasp just why the fact of being an island should have encouraged aggression for it did, after all, guarantee England's security once the English navy had become powerful. On this reckoning, the French, whose capital was but a few days' march from the frontier, would have been still more 'tense'.

Where the more direct factors behind the English Industrial Revolution are concerned, it is startling to see Braudel reviving the myth, first propagated by J. U. Nef, of the 'first English Industrial Revolution'. Nef's 1934 article, Braudel observes, 'has lost nothing of its explanatory power'. Indeed, none of the authors who have criticised Nef's thesis are quoted by Braudel (also, although the increasing recourse to coal as an original feature of the English economy is rightly emphasised, recent studies of this question, such as those by J. R. Harris, are ignored). This is perhaps why he asserts that by 1642

[27] *Ibid.*, pp. 305–9, 312, 322, 324. See also, vol. 2, pp. 468–71, 479–82. Is one supposed to take the term 'remained' literally in the sentence: 'A fantastic share of the wealth of the country [France] remained in the hands of farmers[-general]'?, vol. 2, p. 482.

'England had become the first industrial country in Europe, and such she would remain', with 'a relatively enormous level of investment'. Braudel goes on to observe that, 'by dint of stretching Nef's thought somewhat, it can be said that the English revolution which was to assert itself in the eighteenth century had already begun in the sixteenth century, and had progressed in stages'.[28]

Fortunately, however, the so-called 'sudden take-off' at the end of the sixteenth century and the beginning of the seventeenth[29] does not blind Braudel to the maturation of the English economy around 1700. The slowness of its evolution does, admittedly, irritate him ('everything seems to drag ... the Industrial Revolution is forever being born'), but he rightly notes that England was not any more an underdeveloped country, that the different sectors of the economy were linked up, 'each of them being sufficiently developed so as not to risk becoming, at the first prompting', a dangerous bottleneck. It was thus ready to go forward.'[30]

However, 'an Industrial Revolution, considered as a global phenomenon, cannot be constructed solely from inside, through a balanced development of the various sectors of the economy; it has to rely also – and this is a *sine qua non* – upon a domination of foreign markets.'[31] Braudel therefore places a strong emphasis upon the 'Commercial Revolution' which England underwent in the eighteenth century; and, while allowing that the links with the Industrial Revolution were both close and reciprocal, so that the two revolutions helped each other along,[32] he seems in general to attribute the leading role to foreign trade, which '[was] far and away the frontrunner', and which helped 'to raise [the economy] above itself(?).' Braudel admittedly acknowledges that many writers have minimised the part played by foreign trade, and, while pointing out that this debate is related to the one 'between those who account for capitalist growth solely in terms of the virtues of an *internal* evolution and those who see it as having been built up from the outside, through a systematic

[28] Braudel, vol. 3, pp. 477–9. There is a confusion in this passage also. It is correct that the penetration of coal into an industry often entailed a degree of concentration, so that undertakings tended to grow in size, but, in the sixteenth and seventeenth centuries, these were 'furnace' industries – glassworks, breweries, copper smelters, etc . . . ; 'Manufacture . . . with its huge workshops and their maddening din . . . its masses of workers' only appeared with the textile factories of the end of the eighteenth century.

[29] Braudel, vol. 2, pp. 397–8.

[30] Braudel, vol. 3, pp. 508–9, 468; and vol. 2, pp. 113, 399.

[31] Braudel, vol. 3, p. 477.

[32] *Ibid.*, p. 502: the Commercial Revolution cannot by itself explain the Industrial Revolution.

exploitation of the world', he concludes, somewhat disarmingly, that 'this is a debate that can never be resolved, because both explanations are valid'. It is nevertheless clear, even if the reader has some difficulty in understanding it right away (owing to a highly confusing passage, to which I shall return, concerning English 'customs papers'), which conclusion Braudel favours.[33] He makes no reference to any of Paul Bairoch's works, one of which appeared in *Annales*, which suggest that before 1780 foreign trade was not an engine of growth for England's economy. As for the building of England's 'very large merchant empire', Braudel accounts for it largely in terms of force, quoting India and Canada as examples; as bad luck would have it, these conquests did not provide British industry with any important markets prior to the nineteenth century; he then goes on to emphasise once again that, from 1793 on, the wars of the Revolutionary and Napoleonic period 'obliged [England] to seize the world'. Yet the Industrial Revolution was already well on its way. This is of small import to Braudel, who concludes by quoting the 'startling' judgement of an Indian historian, who claims that the 'surpluses' extracted from India were equivalent to a considerable part of English savings; the Nabobs' money swelled the level of England's wealth. 'This was the level', observes Braudel, 'at which the English successes were pitched.'[34]

Likewise, Braudel's explanation of the mechanisation of the English cotton industry (as I noted above) rests upon the (somewhat strained) use to which he puts a few lines by the talented Indian historian, K. N. Chaudhuri. England had, Braudel maintains, to produce more cheaply than India, which would be only possible with machinery.[35] This explanation by differential labour costs is then generalised, on the basis of accounts by eighteenth-century observers, who had been struck by the high prices and high wages prevailing in England. By the late seventeenth century, Braudel observes, England was a country of high prices, which was a sign of the predominance '[it was] then beginning to establish'. Although Braudel admits that these could be 'hindrances' also, for the decadence suffered by Italian industry has been explained in terms of high wages, he nevertheless reckons that it was the high prices prevailing on the domestic market in England 'which encouraged it to modify its means of production (machinery

33 *Ibid.*, p. 302: the victory over Holland, in placing England at the very centre of the world economy, drew the Industrial Revolution into being.

34 *Ibid.*, pp. 497, 500, 502–3.

35 *Ibid.*, pp. 490, 495; see above pp. 93–5.

emerges because men cost too much)'. One wonders, however, whether Braudel is right to accept the account of Accarias de Sérionne, who maintained that English trade turned away from Europe in the course of the eighteenth century and gravitated towards more distant countries (America, in particular), because the excessively high price of labour made it impossible to compete with the French. Elsewhere, Braudel rightly stresses that the Industrial Revolution occurred in the main in northern England, which was a peripheral area, where prices and wages were lower than in the South ('In terms of theory, this is an exception, indeed, virtually a scandal'); and he observes that: 'Industrialisation invariably thrives if it can take root in poor countries, their poverty being to their advantage. Consider present-day South Korea, or Hong Kong, or Singapore or, in earlier times, Northern Europe by contrast with Italy.'[36]

It may be a mistake to seize upon a few passages which are, all in all, relatively brief, and which are scattered into the fabric of a meandering and discursive exposition, which altogether does not present any systematic or coherent interpretation of the Industrial Revolution. Braudel jeers at the many explanations of it that have been advanced, judging them to be 'spuriously illuminating'; 'How can one help but be disoriented', he adds, 'as one comes across the hundredth argument for or against?'[37] When, however, one reads that England 'did not advance towards a single goal, it was rather that, in the course of a rising tide of powerful life, she encountered the outcome of a multitude of cross-currents which carried the Industrial Revolution forward',[38] one can readily sympathise with the condescension that 'cliometricians' have expressed for 'literary' economic history.

In fact, in the last analysis, Braudel seems to believe that England's superiority over France consisted in its being 'more nervous', because it was smaller, and because it felt, if not besieged, at any rate threatened by hostile neighbours. England '[was] a wary, aggressive and tense country, which intended to lay down the law and to police things at home and abroad also'. Its 'artificial' wealth prevailed over the massive natural wealth of France. 'Let us once again praise what is *artificial*', Braudel exhorts (in another passage, he describes this as 'man's real masterpiece'). 'If I am not mistaken, it was England rather

[36] Braudel, vol. 2, pp. 145–6, 265; vol. 3, pp. 500, 521. It is worth recalling that wages rose rapidly in the north of England in the middle of the eighteenth century.

[37] *Ibid.*, p. 481. [38] *Ibid.*, p. 509.

than France which lived throughout the years in a state of tension. Yet it was this very tension which fuelled the genius of Albion.'[39] What can Braudel have meant by describing England as 'nervous'? He presumably did not mean that millions of Englishmen lived on their nerves for two or three centuries. Was he thinking just of the ruling classes, in spite of Voltaire's Lord *Qu'importe*? or of Fielding's Squire Western? Or did he have the governments of the day in mind? The epithet fits men such as William of Orange or the two Pitts, the Elder and the Younger, seized with a devouring passion for the struggle against France, but it is hardly appropriate to Walpole or Lord North. Was it meant to apply to businessmen? Yet extreme tension only afflicted a small minority, those fiercely intent upon maximising their profits. This use of the epithet 'nervous' is in fact an excellent example of Braudel's frequent habit of personalising entities. Consider, for instance, those passages in his book on the Mediterranean in which he refers to the peninsulas as 'these leading characters of the sea'. Such anthropomorphisms explain nothing and may well lead the ill-informed reader astray.

Braudel's analysis was plainly organised around the theme of England's primacy, which was regarded as being not only qualitative but quantitative also (it was described, as we have seen, as the first industrial country in Europe, deserving this description as early as 1642, and having '[a] huge production'). This analysis was undermined, however, by Peter Mathias and Patrick O'Brien's contribution to the Prato Conference in 1976, which was devoted to taxation in Britain and France in the eighteenth century.[40] This accounts for the addition of a bizarrely titled section, 'Statistics illuminates but does not resolve the problem.' Braudel frankly admits his embarrassment, his dismay even, when confronted with evidence which had been marshalled long before (for example, by Jean Marczewski and T. Markovitch) but which he himself had neglected. Because on this occasion this material was presented by two eminent English historians, in the context of a series of meetings which were one of his main sources of information about current research, Braudel had no

39 Braudel, vol. 3, pp. 269, 303–4, 325, 330.

40 This contribution has been published as P. Mathias and P. O'Brien, 'Taxation in Britain and France, 1715–1810. A Comparison of the Social and Economic Incidence of Taxes Collected for the Central Governments', *Journal of European Economic History*, V, 3, Winter 1976, pp. 601–50.

choice but to take account of it, although he described Mathias and O'Brien's 'truth test' as 'still incomplete'.[41]

Braudel has therefore expressed some dismay at the fact that 'it has become plain that France enjoyed a degree of superiority', indeed, so much was it the case that it was she, and not Britain, that should have had the Industrial Revolution; France's GNP in the eighteenth century was 'twice as big as that of England'.[42] In fact, it could hardly be otherwise, given the overwhelming superiority of France in population, unless one were to posit a per capita income four or five times lower in France than in England, which is improbable in the extreme. Finally, Braudel allowed that, around 1783, per capita incomes for the English and the French were in a ratio of 7·31 to 6.[43] Braudel was also somewhat disconcerted by Mathias and O'Brien's demonstration that the growth of the French economy had been faster than that of England in the eighteenth century and by their observation that the burden of tax had been higher on the English than on the French side of the Channel: 'This runs quite counter to the habitual assertions of most historians, who have an image of France as a country crippled by taxes imposed by an absolute monarch.' However, disregarding Mathias and O'Brien's observations on the socially regressive character of English taxation, which was predominantly indirect, Braudel goes on to remark that 'by contrast with English taxpayers, the French were subject to an onerous "social" levy, which benefited the feudal lords and the Church. It was this social tax which limited in advance the appetite of the Royal Treasury.'[44] Yet were the rents collected by English landowners not a 'social' levy? And did the Anglican Church not receive tithes, just as the Gallican Church did?[45] Be this as it may, Braudel has resigned himself to the fact that, in terms of the value of aggregate production, France was the giant and that 'perhaps ... we have underestimated France's growth in the eighteenth century'. Why then did the giant not win? Because, it would seem, of the English

[41] Braudel, vol. 3, pp. 328–30; see also p. 312. [42] *Ibid.*, p. 329.

[43] He observes that this gap is a 'noteworthy' one, but lower than the English cartoonists of the time believed; he reproduces, on p. 328, an engraving of 1792 which contrasts a well-fleshed Englishman with an emaciated Frenchman, while failing to note that it is a counter-revolutionary caricature (though one, it is true, which harps on a traditional theme).

[44] Braudel, vol. 3, p. 329.

[45] According to Mathias and O'Brien, it is possible that rents and tithes were lower, relatively speaking, in England than in France, but the crucial fact was the 'broader economic base' for indirect taxation that Britain possessed, because a larger part of her production and consumption passed through the market (and also because her per capita income was higher).

nervousness and tension mentioned above, and because one should not forget 'the part played by circumstances' (is this perhaps a euphemism for *événementiel*?)

> If conservative and reactionary Europe had not become the mercenary of England and laboured on her behalf, one would perhaps have had to wait longer for victory over revolutionary and imperial France. If the Napoleonic wars had not excluded France from world trade, England would have found it less easy to impose its harsh rule upon the world.[46]

But had not views of this kind, from 'certain historians', already been condemned by Braudel, as we saw above? The Industrial Revolution was, moreover, well on its way by 1793 and we know that, in Braudel's view, England had 'won the empire of the world economy' as early as 1783.[47]

Braudel uses an impressive quantity of documentation, but its nature accounts for some weaknesses of his work. It includes a scattered sample of archival documents, whose interpretation at times required a somewhat more critical method. Thus, a 'compilation of English statistics' in the archives of the *Quai d'Orsay* was the basis of a map of 'Britain's world trade in 1792'; it shows whether England's balance of trade with its various partners was favourable or unfavourable, and the caption concludes that, all in all, there was 'a positive balance of over five million' (pounds sterling); the drawback is that in 1792 the only statistics for England's foreign trade available are 'official values', which are values in name only and do not enable any serious calculation of the balance of trade.[48]

One of Braudel's favourite sources is travel accounts, and although such testimonies should in no way be despised, certain precautions ought to be observed. General Pillet, author of *L'Angleterre vue à Londres et dans ses provinces* (1815), is taken to be 'a reliable witness, in no way blinded by hate, and one who would seem to have a natural tendency to be impartial',[49] whereas in actual fact he was an out-and-out Anglophobe; anyway, his brief testimony regarding the workers' wretchedness at the time of the cyclical crisis of 1811 teaches us nothing about long-term change in the condition of the working class during the Industrial Revolution.

[46] Braudel, vol. 3, p. 330. [47] *Ibid.*, p. 321.

[48] *Ibid.*, pp. 522–3, Map 55; likewise, vol. 2, pp. 177, 179–80; the need to subject early trade statistics to rigorous criticism is not mentioned.

[49] Braudel, vol. 3, p. 533; on this book see note 60 to Chapter 14.

It is also startling to see what frequent recourse Braudel has to old and wholly obsolete works, such as John Francis's *The London Stock Exchange*, which he quotes several times.[50] There is something fairly random about Braudel's selection of more recent studies, although he does use the main textbooks; one cannot but wonder, for instance, why, from Eric Jones's many publications on agriculture, he should only have mentioned (several times) an article published in *Studi Storici*.[51] Altogether, Braudel's information regarding England is often incomplete or obsolete. This is especially true in matters of historical demography, an astonishing shortcoming, given the close links between the Cambridge Group and the *Annales* school. Wrigley and Schofield's book was, admittedly, only published in 1981, but it was the culmination of a series of earlier researches, which Braudel does not take into account at all. He reproduces a graph of mortality and natality rates in England between 1700 and 1840, which he borrows from G. M. Trevelyan's *English Social History* (1942; the graph is on p. 342 and not on p. 361, as the caption mentions); Trevelyan had himself borrowed it from a work by G. T. Griffith, first published in 1926.[52] It is true that, all in all, Braudel pays little heed to demography, a common enough failing in a man of his generation, and he writes: 'No error of judgement is therefore possible: industrialisation played a key part in setting the English population growing'; the debates which have developed around this problem are merely hinted at in a few lines,[53] and the specific character of England's demographic history is not remarked.

No historian, after all, can claim to have read everything on every problem. Yet one comes away from Braudel's book with a feeling of uneasiness, especially because of ambiguity and vagueness in the use of economic concepts or even simply of economic terms. One cannot help but wonder, for instance, what meaning the distinction between 'nominal prices' and 'real prices'[54] is supposed to have, since the term 'real' is normally applied to a series from which the impact of price changes has been eliminated. One is also bound to wonder how the graph of the real wages of bricklayers built up by Phelps Brown and Hopkins can 'express the attempts made by economic historians to

[50] Braudel, vol. 2, p. 544, note 427, p. 545, note 446, p. 571, note 306.

[51] For example, Braudel, vol. 3, p. 483.

[52] Braudel, vol. 3, p. 489, fig. 51. Griffith's figures are nowadays regarded as useless.

[53] *Ibid.*, pp. 488–9.

[54] *Ibid.*, p. 534.

isolate, from a prices-wages dialectic, something resembling a *pro capite* income'.[55] At the risk of seeming pedantic, I must observe that Braudel invariably uses these two words, instead of the usual per capita, or 'per head', the latter being a perfectly satisfactory formulation. But, more seriously, one can regret the confusion, repeated in another passage, between the wages of a category of workers and the income per head of the population of a country as a whole.[56]

This confusion has some serious consequences for, noting that Phelps Brown and Hopkins's real wages graph is falling on trend from 1750 to 1800, nay up to 1817, and confusing this graph with that of national income per head (increase of which is the sign of 'modern' economic growth), Braudel writes as follows: 'I would claim, contrary to the repeated assertions of others, that the beginnings of the English Industrial Revolution were sustained by a growth *which was still Ancien Régime in character.* There was no miracle, no *continuous growth* before 1815, even before 1850, and some would claim not even before 1870.' Braudel in fact maintains that between 1817 and 1850 the rise in real wages was in part offset by the dramas of an excessively rapid urbanisation and by the decline in the quality of life.[57] But he confuses quantitative and qualitative factors, which are two different aspects of the condition of the people. It is curious that Braudel had not learned from economists, whether marxists or non-marxists, that there could be at the same time a rise in national income per head and a fall in real wages for certain categories of workers, through the redistribution of national income to the detriment of wage-earners and to the benefit, for example, of military expenditure in time of war, or else of investment, as S. Pollard has argued.[58] Though Braudel was a friend of Eric Hobsbawm, the latter's studies on the standard of living are, admittedly, not quoted. It is true that Wrigley and Schofield's new index (like the one produced by Phelps Brown and Hopkins) bears out Braudel's contention regarding the decline in working-class standards of living at the beginning of the Industrial Revolution, but this index recovers after the early years of the nineteenth century. As for income per head, its sustained rise is beyond dispute, well before 1850, let alone 1870!

[55] *Ibid.*, p. 533, fig. 58, and p. 535.

[56] This confusion derives, admittedly, from an article by P. Bairoch (quoted in Braudel, vol. 3, p. 257), according to which one obtains the per capita national income by multiplying the daily wage of the labourer by a coefficient which remains fixed over a long period. This is nevertheless no excuse for mixing up the two concepts.

[57] Braudel, vol. 3, pp. 511–12, 532–4.

[58] See below, pp. 168–9.

Braudel also claims that 'the customs papers' (which is a bizarre turn of phrase, given that English customs statistics were kept in huge ledgers) do not allow one to calculate England's trade balance: 'The customs figures ... refer only to commodities leaving or entering English ports. They record neither movements of capital nor the slave trade which, being "triangular", was beyond their control,[59] nor the freight earned by the merchant navy, nor the money sent home by Jamaican planters or by Indian nabobs;[60] nor the profits from the country trade in the Far East...'[61] This curious passage betrays a confusion between balance of trade and balance of payments, which would be severely penalised in an undergraduate's essay. Be this as it may, the studies by A. H. Imlah and some others would have presented Braudel with more precise information regarding these two balances, from 1796 and 1816 respectively.[62] One hopes that recourse to them would have helped save him from falling into the trap of 'official values', and from believing that England's trade balance had been consistently and strongly in its favour from 1700 to 1771, a fact which is meant to demonstrate that the two countries (France being in the same position) 'lived comfortably off the rest of the world',[63] whereas in fact it is a negative trade balance which shows that a country is sponging off others, either because it is borrowing from them or because, as in the case of England much later on, it is earning income from its overseas investments.

A long section entitled 'What role should one attribute to the conjuncture?' makes interesting reading also. It has the virtue of offering a very clear definition of the difference in perspective of English and 'French historians' (or, at any rate, a number of the latter). For the former, the conjuncture would be the product of events and processes intrinsic to each country; for the latter, it would be in part an exogenous force, even as regards England, and one which enveloped both England and Europe (this is not inaccurate, though the British, because they live on an island, tend to forget it); in

59 In fact, two of the sides of the 'triangle' – exports to Africa and returns from America – were registered by the customs.

60 These returns were not in cash but in commodities or bills of exchange.

61 Braudel, vol. 3, pp. 502–3.

62 A. H. Imlah, *Economic Elements in the Pax Britannica* (Cambridge, Mass., 1958), pp. 37–8, 70–1, Tables 2 and 4.

63 Braudel, vol. 2, p. 175, fig. 16. This sentence shows up Braudel's mercantilism (see also, vol. 3, p. 502); he rejects the notion that international trade can be advantageous to the various parties concerned.

addition, it is 'a reality in itself', 'the world's weather'. Braudel sees the proof of this in a comparison of England's and France's prices graphs between 1770 and 1817; he acknowledges there is a problem about the 1780s: the falling trend, which Labrousse believed he had detected in France, only found expression in England as stable prices, but Braudel is quick to define them as stagnation. Since he is faithful to the time-honoured fallacies of Simiand, which posit an indissoluble link between price rises and growth ('rising prices determine a spurt in production and population'), Braudel concludes that England, much like the unhappy France of Louis XVI, was 'also troubled by a cheerless conjuncture', since 'for a dozen years the [price] rise which had up until then favoured the English economy was checked'. From 1791, on the other hand, the economic weather became favourable once again. Hence Braudel's conclusion that the Industrial Revolution, between 1781 and 1815, had 'two breaths, the first of which was difficult, whereas the second was easy'.[64] Quite the opposite was in fact the case: from 1783 to 1792, there was 'rapid' growth, almost uninterrupted prosperity, culminating in the boom of 1789 to 1792; during the Napoleonic wars, there were grave difficulties, which slowed down but did not check the impetus of the Industrial Revolution.

It is worth mentioning that, if the graph of English prices fluctuated less sharply than the French one, it was because 'at the centre of the world, the water does not boil as much as elsewhere'; this is just one of many metaphors (cotton 'leads the dance'; 'the European economy calls the tune') which are scattered through Braudel's study but which do not explain very much.[65]

It is not so surprising to find that Braudel hardly mentions the institutional and political framework of the English economy in the eighteenth century. I would simply point out that the division of political power between Crown and Parliament is presented as proof that the division of labour is 'ubiquitous' in England;[66] that the latter is said to have passed 'fairly rapidly under mercantile domination, after the Revolution of 1688'; that merchants '[were] everywhere ... soon they [were] ruling England, which had been made amenable to their interests and passions'.[67] Readers should need no reminding that Parliament and government remained firmly in the hands of landowners until well after the Reform Act of 1832. There were at most a

[64] Braudel, vol. 3, pp. 528–32. [65] *Ibid.*, pp. 531, 511, 301. [66] *Ibid.*, p. 518.
[67] *Ibid.*, pp. 39, 516.

few dozen merchants in the House of Commons (although the ruling class did, it is true, show concern for commercial interests). More well-founded is Braudel's notion that, appearances notwithstanding, the eighteenth-century English state was stronger than the so-called absolutist monarchies of the Continent, and that it was, in particular, more able to impose a substantial tax load. Yet 'it too was bureaucratised ... running to fat', and it was 'more or less dependent upon a precocious capitalism, whose teeth were already sharp';[68] it was aggressive and quite prepared to resort to violence.

What is surprising is the paucity of Braudel's references to social structures and to their impact upon the economy. Given the kind of remarks that Braudel does make, this may be just as well. Under the Tudors, we are told, the English aristocracy consolidated its advantages and its privileges; henceforth, the furthering of its fortunes ceased to depend upon the good graces of the Crown. When, therefore, in 1640, the King attempted to reassert his unchallenged authority, it was too late. The aristocracy and the big bourgeoisie – which was very soon to overtake the former – went on to weather the difficult years of the Civil War and blossomed with the Restoration.[69] How would an ill-informed reader judge this example, which Braudel deems a 'magnifying' and 'clear' one? Would he not draw the conclusion that it was the aristocracy that made the Revolution, which had begun in 1640 with the meeting of the Long Parliament, that is, with Charles I's renunciation of the 'unchallenged authority' which he had been wielding for the previous ten years? How is it that Braudel has wholly disregarded everything that English marxists have written regarding the part played by the English revolution in the elimination of feudal survivals and in the clearing of a path for the free advance of capitalism? Indeed, he quotes only one text from Marx himself – which is particularly inaccurate: 'After the restoration of the Stuarts, the landed proprietors ... abolished the feudal tenure of land, i.e. they got rid of all encumbrances which it bore and indemnified the State by taxes on the peasantry and the rest of the people ...'[70] 'This must', Braudel observes, 'have swept away traditional life.'[71] 'In Queen Anne's reign', Braudel goes on to note, 'the English whigs, who were all very rich, were referred to as the "wallet-men" or as the "moneyed"

[68] *Ibid.*, pp. 39, 519; his perspective here resembles that of I. Wallerstein (see above, pp. 76–8), to whose dactylogram (then unpublished) Braudel refers.

[69] Braudel, vol. 2, p. 422.

[70] K. Marx, *Capital*, vol. I, ch. xxvii, p. 676.

[71] Braudel, vol. 3, p. 244.

men',[72] whereas the leaders of the Whig faction were the biggest landowners in the country.

There is of course a good dose of miserabilism in Braudel's study. We learn that London contained a number of quite terrible quarters, on the fringe of the city which were 'often shanty towns'; we are told that its population consist[ed] 'of a handful of the elect, numerous servants and wretches', whereas in fact London was characterised by the importance of its middle classes, as was English society as a whole.[73] Braudel even lapses into a kind of historical Luddism ('the power loom ... was a real calamity in social terms'[74]), forgetting that mechanisation was a preliminary condition for the improvement of the standard of living for the people. Taken all in all, Braudel's *Weltanschauung* is disillusioned and gloomy.

Finally, I must draw attention to the surprising number of minor inaccuracies that Braudel's pages on Britain contain.

Thus, we are told 'that sowing-machines were only rarely used (for instance at Town and Coke) in the progressive county of Norfolk'.[75] If this strikes one as a little strange and one refers to the source quoted in the note, that is, J. D. Chambers and G. E. Mingay's *The Agricultural Revolution*, one reads that the drill 'was not generally used for sowing corn before well into the nineteenth century, and on the farms of East Norfolk, the homeland of Townshend and Coke',[76] that is, the famous improving landowners, Turnip Townshend and Coke of Holkham. La Fontaine's monkey had thought Piraeus to be a man...

One is equally startled to read that English agriculture's demand for iron in 1780 could be calculated at '200,000 or 300,000 tons per year',[77] since at this date England was only producing 50,000 to 60,000 tons of pig-iron. In fact, Paul Bairoch, quoted as the source for these figures, had written that, in the sixty years prior to 1780, the total consumption of iron for agricultural implements was between 180,000 and 360,000 tons.[78] Braudel rightly observes that what is original in the evolution of English agriculture could only have occurred within the framework of large estates, from which the seigneurial régime had been more or less eliminated, '200 acres, then, or 80

[72] *Ibid.*, p. 204. [73] Braudel, vol. 1, pp. 488, 490.
[74] Braudel, vol. 3, p. 514, also 513, 515.
[75] *Ibid.*, p. 483.
[76] J. D. Chambers and G. E. Mingay, *The Agricultural Revolution 1750–1880* (London, 1966), p. 2.
[77] Braudel, vol. 3, p. 487.
[78] P. Bairoch, *Révolution industrielle et sous-développement* (Paris, 1963), p. 87.

hectares',[79] but he confuses estate and farm, that is landownership and land cultivation. It is lucky that the acre is measured correctly here, and not as 'equivalent to 150 square metres', as the key to one of Braudel's maps has it.[80] It is also a little difficult to understand how 'English peasants' could be settled in the Scottish Highlands.[81]

Yet these slips are not only concerned with agriculture. Thus, we hear of 'Ambrose Crowley's giant blast-furnace, in 1729',[82] when in fact this ironmaster died in 1713 and a significant aspect of his concerns, which were indeed gigantic for the period, was that they did not produce pig-iron but were restricted to the making and working of bar-iron, and therefore did not have blastfurnaces. The author whom Braudel uses as his source is in fact responsible for the mistaken date but not for the reference to the blastfurnace...[83] Braudel's hasty reading of this same book accounts for another surprising assertion, namely, that 'the firm of Whitbread ... around the 1740s, supplied 750,000 Londoners' [with beer],[84] whereas Samuel Whitbread started business in 1742 and even as late as his death in 1796, in no sense had a monopoly of the London market. As far as finance is concerned, Peter Laslett is severely chided because 'he would have us believe' that the East India Company and the Bank of England had prior to the beginning of the eighteenth century only a very slight influence upon commercial and industrial activity as a whole; one wonders how the Bank, founded in 1694 as an expedient in war finance, could ever, in a matter of years, have given 'an additional impetus to business'.[85] As for the landbanks, which first appeared in 1695 (and 1696), they did not so much 'multiply' as have a short and disastrous lifespan.[86] We also hear from Braudel of 'the creation of the office of Lord Treasurer in 1714, which prepared the establishing of the Board of Treasury',[87] when in fact this ancient office was suppressed with the advent of the Hanoverians and put into commission, that is, replaced by a Board.

After the invention of spinning machines, Braudel informs us,

[79] Braudel, vol. 3, p. 485. [80] *Ibid.*, vol. 2, p. 28, Map 2. [81] *Ibid.*, p. 268.

[82] *Ibid.*, p. 286.

[83] L. A. Clarkson, *The Pre-Industrial Economy in England 1500–1750* (London, 1971), p. 98, mentions the value of Ambrose Crowley's 'buildings and equipment' in 1728, but with regard to metal-working not iron-making; he goes on to speak of 'industrial giants like Crowley', hence no doubt the idea of a giant blast furnace. It is worth mentioning that R. Mandrou, in *Louis XIV en son temps* (Paris, 1973), p. 411, had put the first coke-fired blast furnaces in Sussex.

[84] Braudel, vol. 2, p. 297; the misinterpreted source is again L. A. Clarkson, p. 99.

[85] Braudel, vol. 2, pp. 401 and 399.

[86] Braudel, vol. 3, p. 316. [87] Braudel, vol. 2, p. 469.

'imports of raw cotton increased from the West Indies, the East Indies and, after a short while, from the Southern English colonies in America';[88] whereas in fact cotton only began to be grown in the United States after their independence, and after E. Whitney's invention. 'Canal madness' ('mania' is the English way of putting it) did not begin 'in 1755', with the few miles of the Sankey Navigation; this phrase ought properly to be applied to the boom in the promotion of canals around 1790, and the 'huge investments' devoted, according to Braudel, to the improvement of rivers in the first quarter of the eighteenth century are, even 'relatively speaking', a figment of his imagination.[89] Furthermore, reference to 'the Westminster practical schools', where 'battalions of lawyers were trained', can hardly be said to evoke the reality of the Inns of Court.[90]

At one point in his study, Braudel writes:

> If the Industrial Revolution had not been, for Hanoverian England, a New Deal, the world would have toppled either towards a Russia whose fortunes were dramatically in the ascendant or, more probably, towards the United States, which were constituted not too easily as a kind of republic of United Provinces, with proletarian ships, analogous, all other things being equal, to those of the sea-beggars of the sixteenth century . . .[91]

What does the New Deal have to do with all this? Let us conclude this catalogue of bizarre items concerning England with the observation that great territorial States have the same means of domination as the City-State: 'The navy, the army, violence and, if necessary, cunning, treachery even – think of the Council of Ten or, much later, the Intelligence Service';[92] I am surprised that the C.I.A. was not mentioned, for good measure (and of course, strictly speaking, one should say Secret Intelligence Service – or MI6).

Will specialists on other countries reap as rich a harvest as I have done? I would note merely that, if this book were to come into the hands of 'boat people' (after all, in the United States, Braudel is sold in drug-stores and airports), they would likely be shocked by the reference to 'the liberation of Vietnam in 1976'.[93] Likewise, many French academics will hardly believe their eyes when they read the following passage: 'When Jean-Paul Sartre (April 1974) writes that what one must do is to break up the hierarchy, and prevent any one man from

[88] Braudel, vol. 3, p. 490; conversely, see p. 576, note 125 of the same volume.
[89] *Ibid.*, pp. 505 and 316.
[90] *Ibid.*, p. 519. [91] Braudel, vol. 2, p. 509. [92] Braudel, vol. 3, p. 251.
[93] *Ibid.*, p. 543.

depending upon any other, he has to my mind got to the heart of the matter.'[94] This was a curious profession of faith on the part of a master who, for over thirty years, had been building up an empire, such that even the most ingenuous observer would suppose that he was not averse to wielding power over others.

94 Braudel, vol. 2, p. 458. D. Landes, in *The New Republic*, 3 September 1977, pp. 29–30, was the first to put forward some of the remarks made here.

4 The sources of England's wealth: some French views in the eighteenth century*

I

'England is not worth a quarter of France, either by the number of her people ... or by the fertility of her soil ... However, for three or four years, England has paid to the Prince of Orange nearly 80 million per year, and this without reducing the people to beggary or obliging them to give up cultivating their land.'[1] This remark by Boisguillebert, in 1697, was echoed by François Chaumont in 1760:

> The territory of Great Britain is only about a third of France and her lands do not compare with ours in goodness; so her population ought not to be more than one third of ours. Her trade, her riches ... ought to follow the same ratios. However, England has a population ... nearly equal to one half of ours. She has a very rich agriculture, more than twice our trade, an immense shipping; as for credit, she bears the burden of a debt larger than ours ... What can be the reasons for this conjunction of advantages?[2]

Such remarks, which occur in several other writings, show that the wealth and prosperity of eighteenth-century England were to Frenchmen something of a riddle. The purpose of this paper is to examine how they tried to answer the riddle and to find the reasons for the economic

* The following abbreviations are used throughout the notes to this chapter:

AE MDA	Archives du Ministère des Affaires Etrangères, Mémoires et documents, Angleterre
AE CPA	Archives du Ministère des Affaires Etrangères, Correspondance politique, Angleterre
AN	Archives Nationales
AN AMB	Archives Nationales, Archives de la Marine, B
BN MF	Bibliothèque Nationale, Paris, Manuscrits français

References have been simplified; readers who want more detail can go back to the original publication.

[1] Boisguillebert, *Le Détail de la France sous Louis XIV*, reprinted in *Économistes financiers du XVIIIe siècle* (Paris, 1843), I, p. 216. The 80 million are, of course, French *livres*. Boisguillebert (1646–1714) was an economist who criticised Louis XIV's policies.

[2] BN MF 10716.

superiority of their neighbour. It is based not only on the printed contemporary literature, but also on unpublished materials, mainly from the archives of the French Foreign Office and the Ministry of Marine; indeed, these records contain a large number of memoranda, which put forward explanations for 'the wealth of England'. Of course, this study tells more about French public opinion in the eighteenth century than about the 'real' British economy, which was imperfectly known and understood in France – as will appear from some fanciful notions.[3] However, there were some astute comments by French observers and the kind of 'official view' of England which emerges from some of the *mémoires* might well have had some influence upon French policy.[4]

All the Frenchmen who visited England in the eighteenth century agreed that she was an affluent country, with a much higher standard of living, especially for the lower orders, than in France.[5] From Voltaire (*Lettres philosophiques*, 1734) onwards, it was a well-established *leitmotiv* that the English *paysan*[6] lived in comfort: he ate white bread, plus meat and fish, he drank tea, he wore shoes (not clogs) and good clothes (and his womenfolk were quite elegant), he had a well-furnished and clean house in a pleasant and well-built village. Free from fiscal exactions, many cultivators could acquire a competence and although, as some writers admitted, most people were not in fact as well off, they were well-fed and cleanly dressed, there was no serious poverty and there were no ragged and hungry-looking wretches, and no beggars.[7]

Owing to their admiration for the British constitution, many travellers can be suspected of having worn rose-coloured spectacles,

[3] A. Bourde, *Agronomie et agronomes en France au XVIIIe siècle*, 3 vols. (Paris, 1967), 1, p. 277, n. 4.

[4] However, caution is necessary: some memoranda were written by officials, diplomats or secret agents, but some others by unsolicited private persons, while a number are anonymous.

[5] F. Acomb, *Anglophobia in France, 1763–1789* (Durham, NC, 1950), p. 41. This consensus is rather impressive and might be taken into account in discussions about the English standard of living.

[6] It is obvious from the contexts that this word applied to well-to-do farmers or yeomen; but French readers could believe that it concerned the bulk of the population, as in France.

[7] Voltaire, *Lettres philosophiques* (Paris, edition Garnier-Flammarion, 1964), p. 64; J. B. Le Blanc, *Lettres d'un Français sur les Anglais*, 3 vols. (The Hague, 1745), II, pp. 64–5; *Lettres de Madame du Bocage contenant ses voyages en France, en Angleterre, en Hollande et en Italie, faits pendant les années 1750, 1757 et 1758* (Dresden, 1771), pp. 5, 53; Abbé Coyer, *Nouvelles observations sur l'Angleterre par un voyageur* (Paris, 1779), p. 164; F. de la Rochefoucauld, *La Vie en Angleterre au XVIIIe siècle ou Mélanges sur l'Angleterre (1784)* (Paris, 1945), p. 33; J. Cambry, *Promenades d'automne en Angleterre* (Paris, 1791), pp. 13, 21.

Similar views had been put forward before Voltaire; see *Lettres sur les Anglais et les Français et sur les voyages, par le Sr. Muralt, gentilhomme suisse* (1725), pp. 2, 19.

but similar views appear in the French Foreign Office records; two memoranda of 1733 and 1736 stress the flourishing condition of England, where 'abundance and even opulence prevail in almost all orders of society'. In 1781, it was pointed out in connection with plans for invading England, that the countryside 'is abounding in every kind of victuals, the roads are superb, the people are rich', so that, after its landing, the French army would have no problem in getting food supplies.[8]

However, such remarks were often mixed with anxiety before the rise of England's wealth and power, inasmuch as many Frenchmen were convinced that England aimed at monopolising world trade and, to begin with, at destroying the trade of France. In 1714 a document written for the French Foreign Secretary, the Marquis de Torcy, expressed the fear that 'France would become dependent on England, like Spain on her neighbours, to get from abroad what is not produced in the Kingdom; in this case, our manufactures and our navigation will die out and England will become formidable through an increase in population, employment and riches.' In 1733, 'the financial and maritime power of the English, which gets every day larger and more dangerous', was said to be soon 'able to destroy or at least disturb the trades in which France has hitherto held her own ... The English will always want to encroach upon France ... and keep her subordinate.' In 1747, Silhouette, who was later *contrôleur général des finances* (in 1757, for eight months), wrote that 'the English are planning to exclude any rival from America and ... to monopolize that Continent's trade', by conquering in particular the French possessions in North America. In 1760, England was accused of intending to restrict the French to 'the internal trade' of their country.[9]

There was even an inferiority complex among French officials before English dynamism. In 1711, when peace negotiations started, the chief clerk of the French Foreign Office urged that British demands for bases in the Pacific Ocean should be rejected. If England took possession, for instance, of one of the Juan Fernandez islands (off the Chilean coast),

> we must be sure that, however desert it may be to-day ... within a few years, one would see there a large number of inhabitants, some well-built harbours and the largest *entrepôt* in the world for the manufactures of Europe and Asia, which the English would supply to the Kingdoms of Peru and Mexico ... 60 million in gold and silver which the

[8] AE CPA, Supplement 8; AE MDA, 6 and 53; BN MF, Nouvelles acquisitions 20089.

[9] AE CPA, 261 and Supplement 8; AN AMB[7], 414.

mines produce each year would be the purpose and the fruit of their industry. What efforts that nation, skilful in trade and powerful at sea, would make to appropriate this enormous income... ! What resources would she find among individuals to supply the capital for the ventures in that new colony!

France would lose her former markets for her silks, linen and gildings, and she would grow weaker, while the English would become richer and 'the most formidable nation in Europe'.[10] Eighty years later, in 1792, a former French diplomat in London, D'Aragon, wrote about Lord Macartney's embassy to China, saying that it was 'apparently absurd', but actually a deep and shrewd manoeuvre, with the likely result that 'not only all European nations would be expelled from Kanton [*sic*] and Macao, but the trade of the whole of Asia would fall into English hands'.[11]

Still, some French observers were more guarded in their views of England's economy. They were aware of its fluctuations, of the financial burden resulting from heavy war expenditures, also of the sluggishness in woollen goods exports; they pointed out in the 1730s that France was overtaking England on the markets of the Levant and in the carrying trade of West Indian sugar; they also maintained that the quality of some lines of French manufactures was superior to that of English goods.[12] And there were also more general and far-reaching criticisms of the English economy. In 1733, a writer stressed that the growth of English industry had gone too far and might become dangerous; if some of its markets were lost, the 'countless multitude' of workmen who were employed in industry would be threatened with unemployment.[13] In 1760, F. Chaumont forecast that, in the future, England's prosperity would be disturbed, so that she would be wise not to try to extend it anew, as 'seapower has bounds which cannot be overstepped'.[14] Rather curiously, such critical remarks become more frequent in the 1770s and 1780s: England had reached the zenith of her power, she could not progress any more and her decline was inevitable, as the proper balance between agriculture, industry and trade had not been maintained, while the prices of foodstuffs and labour had become too high. On the other hand, France had much bigger potentialities;

[10] AE CPA, 233, 'Raisonnement de Pegnet, premier commis du Mis de Torcy'.

[11] AN AMB[1], 762.

[12] AN AMB[7], 3, 4, 6, 7, 8, 9, 12, 370, 434; AE MDA, 6, 63, 68; AE CPA, 425, Supplement 8; Muralt, p. 17; Fougeret de Montbron, *Préservatif contre l'Anglomanie* (Minorca, 1757), pp. 11–12; *Supplément à l'espion anglais* (1781), pp. 150 ff.

[13] AE CPA, Supplement 8. [14] BN MF 10716.

her power was more consistent with the 'natural order of things'; she was capable of a much larger population and output; her future prospects were therefore far brighter.[15]

II

However, most French commentators were convinced that England was more prosperous than France and they tried to explain her superiority. Several of them produced 'lists of factors', which compare honourably with those of modern textbooks, but there is one factor which appears in all those lists and which, moreover, many writers singled out as the key to Britain's wealth and power: her foreign trade, which is always said to be 'immense', 'enormous' and 'prodigious'.

According to Voltaire,

> trade, which has made richer the citizens of England, has helped to make them free, and this freedom has, in its turn, enlarged trade ... It is trade which has gradually created the Navy, thanks to which the English are masters of the seas ... Posterity might be surprised that a small island, which has from her own only some lead, tin, fuller's earth and coarse wool, has become, thanks to its trade, powerful enough to dispatch in 1733 three squadrons ... to three uttermost ends of the earth.[16]

The same views appear under the pen of Dutot, in 1738,[17] and in several memoranda in the French Foreign Office archives, written during the 1730s and 1740s: as one of them puts it in 1736, 'trade makes the wealth of England which owes to it her navy and the multiplication of her manufactures.'[18]

After the mid eighteenth century, this monocausal explanation was challenged. In 1760, F. Chaumont stressed that England's trade was based upon the products of the country: wheat, horses, salt meat, cloth, minerals; without such natural resources, a country cannot enjoy 'a genuine trade'; moreover England had preserved the primacy of agriculture.[19] The physiocrats rejected, of course, the 'treasure by forraign trade' explanation. Quesnay admitted that the Royal Navy had become formidable thanks to sea-borne trade, from which the

15 Acomb, pp. 9, 59–61, 63, 65–6, 120; Bourde, pp. 379–81; AE CPA, 499, 500; AE MDA, 56.

16 Voltaire, p. 66.

17 Dutot, *Réflexions politiques sur les finances et le commerce* (1738), reprinted in *Économistes financiers du XVIIIe siècle* (Paris, 1843), I, p. 1002; Dutot had been cashier of the French East India Company.

18 AE MDA, 6 and 68; also AE CPA, 368 and Supplement 8; BN MF 12162.

19 BN MF 10716.

British government had been able to borrow on a large scale. But trade, though the nation's creditor, was not the nation; one had 'to make a distinction between the territorial patrimony of the English nation and that of its trading republic'; land, which was 'the only source of all wealth and all expenditure', was the basis on which England had built up her credit.[20]

Despite those criticisms, an undiluted mercantilism survived until the French Revolution in many French Foreign Office documents; a memorandum of 1770 proclaimed: 'The wealth and power of States is founded only upon sea-borne trade'; in 1775, one M. de Roussille stated that 'Neptune's trident has become the sceptre of the world', which England had conquered thanks to her trade and navigation; in June 1789, the French 'consul' in London, Herman, wrote: 'The wealth of England is nothing but the fruit of her large trade', and in July 1792, D'Aragon echoed him: 'This nation [England] supports itself and is able to support itself through its trade only.'[21]

Such assumptions led to overestimations of the part which trade and industry played in the British economy and to some strange views. 'Less than half the soil of England is cultivated', asserted a writer in 1765; 'as all its inhabitants are inclined through self-interest and political principle towards trade and the sea, there is a shortage of men to clear the land which remains in waste.' 'All Englishmen are born seamen, the highest lords in the land pride themselves to be so'; this was the peremptory view of the French ambassador in London, the Comte de Guines, in 1773; likewise, the Comte de Custine wrote in 1786: 'The few villages which exist inland are almost deserted ... The population is on the coasts and in the manifold manufactures, everybody is seaman or mechanic.'[22]

As for explaining the growth and prosperity of British trade, there was also a large consensus, which was markedly mercantilist. Indeed, geographical factors are sometimes mentioned, for example, the

[20] Fr. Quesnay, *Physiocratie ou constitution naturelle du gouvernement le plus avantageux au genre humain*, 2 vols. (Paris, 1767–8), II, pp. 277–82; also A. Oncken (ed.), *Oeuvres économiques et philosophiques de F. Quesnay* (Paris, 1888), p. 524.

[21] AE MDA, 56 and 73; AN AMB[1], 762.

[22] AE MDA, 61 and 52, 'Mémoire sur l'Angleterre', by Guines, 1773; AE CPA, Supplement 28, 'Lettre de M. de Custine sur l'état de l'Angleterre', 3 April 1786. Adam-Philippe, comte de Custine (1740–1793) had fought during the American war of independence; *maréchal de camp* in 1783, he was a deputy at the States-general in 1789. A nobleman of radical views, he commanded the army of the Rhine in 1792 and conquered the Rhineland; but, having suffered some setbacks, he was guillotined. His grandson was the famous traveller in Russia.

insular situation of England, which made her 'naturally a trading and maritime nation', her need to import many foreign goods (such as wines, salt, linen, silks) and the abundance of raw materials which she and her colonies supplied.[23] But the decisive factor was thought to be the wise and skilful policy of a government which was constantly anxious to promote foreign trade and merchant shipping, which knew the right 'maxims' and 'principles' for this purpose, and which embodied them in perfectly devised laws.[24]

It was widely accepted in France that the English government was 'more convinced than we are that the main asset of state is trade', and that its policy was supported by the country unanimously; a memorandum as early as 1699 states that 'Parliament (which is the whole nation) protects trade; the King encourages it on all occasions. Many noblemen ... are openly interested in trade ... The whole nation, generally speaking, is in trade.' The same views (especially about the solicitude of Parliament for trade) appear frequently,[25] and we cannot but quote Voltaire in *Essai sur les moeurs*:

> What made the power of England is that all the parties have ... combined since the time of Elizabeth to promote trade. The same Parliament which had the head of its King cut off, busied itself with maritime projects, like in the most untroubled times. The blood of Charles I was still warm, when that Parliament, though almost entirely made up of fanatics,[26] passed in 1650 [*sic*] the famous Navigation Act.[27]

However, this attention to commercial matters was often thought to be pushed too far by the English, who were said to be 'jealous in trade'; this meant not only that they were suspected of aiming at a monopoly of sea-borne trade and of resenting any gain made by other countries, but also that they were accused of sharp practice, of seeking after unilateral advantages and of denying to other countries – and especially to France – any kind of reciprocity. In 1698, Louis XIV's instructions to his ambassador in London stated: 'There is no place in the world where the laws of equality, which are so just and so necessary

[23] BN MF 10716; AN AMB⁷, 381, no. 29; Plumard de Dangeul, *Remarques sur les avantages et les désavantages de la France et de la Grande-Bretagne ... traduites de l'anglais du Chevalier John Nickolls* (actually, the author was French) (Amsterdam, 1754), pp. 77 ff.; Butel-Dumont, *Essai sur l'état du commerce de l'Angleterre*, 2 vols. (Paris, 1755), I, p. 114.

[24] See, for instance, BN MF 12162; AE MDA, 6; AN AMB¹, 762.

[25] AE CPA, 361 (also 362, 368); AN AMB⁷, 499 and 500; AE MDA, 56.

[26] Obviously, Voltaire had no inkling that capitalism might be the offspring of puritanism!

[27] Voltaire, *Essai sur les moeurs et l'esprit des nations* (Paris, Garnier edn, 1963), II, pp. 695–7. However, Quesnay deplored that in England the landed interest and the State were subordinated to mercantile views: Acomb, p. 46.

to trade, are more considerably offended than in England.'[28] In 1712, C. de Fenellon wrote that the English were 'very jealous and diligent as regards their trade', which was almost entirely on their own account and in their own ships; customs duties and trade regulations aimed at 'this only point to obtain and to retain for [their] nation all possible advantages without sharing them with the subjects of other powers'.[29] Montesquieu thought on similar lines when he stressed that England, 'jealous in the highest degree of the trade which is made with her', refused to be bound by treaties of commerce with other countries and maintained a complete independence in the matter of customs duties.[30] Many other writers did denounce the selfish, unjust, proud and grasping policies of 'the modern Carthage', whose lack of fair-play went as far as repressing the smuggling of French goods![31]

Despite those strictures, most French observers could not but admire the regulations which England enforced to promote her trade. They praised her protectionist policy, the 'principles' of which Silhouette defined rather accurately in 1747: prohibition or heavy duties upon foreign manufactures; duty-free export of English manufactures, but prohibition of the export of raw materials (such as wool) which could be used by foreign manufacturers; and duty-free import of most raw materials. These arrangements were generally seen as securing a favourable trade balance and as discouraging the consumption of foreign luxuries, while stimulating exports of British goods.[32] However, towards the end of the *Ancien Régime*, some French writers, such as the physiocrats, who had become converted to free-trade views, criticised the excesses of English protectionism. In 1783, the Abbé Morellet lamented that Englishmen 'failed to recognize the true principles of the liberty of trade' and that 'the jealousy of trade' was 'a

[28] AE CPA, 208, 'Mémoire concernant le commerce, la navigation et les colonies pour servir d'instructions au Sr. Comte de Tallard', 14 March 1698; this document seems to be based on two memoranda by merchants in AN AMB^7, 499. This view had been put forward earlier in Jacques Savary's famous *Le Parfait Négociant*, published in 1675 and reprinted several times later on; his chapter on trade with England is simply a list of maltreatments inflicted on French merchants in England (1759 edn, I, pp. 120–5). However, a memorandum of 1711 to the Conseil de Commerce pointed out that England had imposed excessive duties upon French goods only after France had set the example, and asserted that Englishmen did business 'more nobly' than any other nation (AN F^{12}, 55 and AMB^7, 499).

[29] BN MF, Nouvelles acquisitions 20542, 'Réflexions sommaires sur le commerce d'Angleterre', 28 September 1712 (this is actually a draft of instructions for French negotiators).

[30] Montesquieu, *De l'Esprit des loix* (Paris, Seuil edn, 1964), pp. 652–3.

[31] See, for instance, AE MDA, 6; AE CPA, 360; AN AMB^1, 760 and 761, B^7, 18 and 22; Acomb, p. 9.

[32] BN MF 12162; AE MDA, 63; *Encyclopédie*, XVII, 'Vingtième', p. 870.

mistake truly national, popular, universal', which no government could defy.[33]

As for the Navigation Acts, they made a deep impression upon French opinion. According to J. F. Melon, writing in 1734, 'the English owe the great progress of their shipping and their trade to the famous Navigation Act . . . The result for England was the necessity to export everything which was in surplus and to import what was necessary, while the merchant's profits, the costs of transport and of building ships were also to the advantage of the nation.' In 1753, a memorandum sent by the French minister in Hamburg asserted that, thanks to those Acts, the English 'have enabled themselves to make single-handed almost all the commercial operations which their products and their needs give them the opportunity to do. Such is the system which has made England so flourishing and has raised her to the degree of power at which we see her'.[34] However, some French observers realised that the Navigation Acts were not the only factor responsible for the growth of English shipping; they mentioned the part played by the coastal traffic – especially for carrying coal to London, the low cost of ship-building thanks to cheap timber from Northern Europe and America and the fact that English ships 'put to sea . . . with so few seamen that they are able to navigate more cheaply than other nations. The result is that English ships are often given preference to get cargoes in foreign countries.'[35]

Among the various trades in which England was engaged, three were deemed in France to be particularly 'advantageous': the Portuguese trade, the trade with the 'Spanish Indies' and the trade with England's own colonies.

Special attention was paid to the Portuguese trade. According to the French ambassador in Madrid, writing in 1756, the English 'have attracted the whole trade of Brazil and India; they have destroyed the manufactures . . . of Portugal and have bought all its produce in order

33 AE MDA, 6, 'Tableau de l'administration de Mylord Shelburne et exposition de ses principales vues sur l'économie intérieure et la politique extérieure'. Morellet was reporting on his private talks with Lord Shelburne, who, he wrote, was in favour of free trade, but had to proceed very gradually; see also Acomb, pp. 8–9, 49–50, 71, 73.

However, in 1787, D'Aragon was praising the system of bounties on export of English goods as one of the main factors for the growth of British trade: AN AMB[7], 62.

34 J. F. Melon (ex-secretary to John Law), *Essai politique sur le commerce* (1734), reprinted in *Economistes financiers du XVIIIe siècle* (Paris, 1843), I, pp. 750–1; AN AMB[3], 81, no. 29; also BN MF 10716, and AE MDA, 56.

35 BN MF 10716; AE CPA, 361; AN AMB[7], 392; Coyer, letter XXII, pp. 172 ff.

to introduce their own goods. They have encouraged the laziness and indolence which prevail easily among people of the South; finally, thanks to their activity, they have appropriated immense riches.'[36] Many other documents stress the large markets in Portugal for British manufactures (and also for dried cod from Newfoundland) and the 'prodigious quantities' of English goods which were re-exported to Brazil; still more valuable was the very large favourable balance of trade which England enjoyed and which was settled with gold from Brazil. A memorandum of 1783 estimated that 'over 300 million [of French *livres*] have passed . . . into the hands of the English in return for their supplies to the luxury and to the needs of the Portuguese. This was the first spring from which England's prosperity was derived'; having appropriated 'the raw material of all exchange, the gold from Brazil', her merchants used it to buy everywhere in Europe the raw materials and manufactured articles which their country did not produce; 'in this way, they established their large carrying trade'. According to another document of 1770, gold from Brazil was 'the main artery of English power', inasmuch as it was completed by bullion from Spanish America: the consumption of English goods was made easier, public credit was supported, interest rates were kept low.[37]

The Spanish colonies received far less attention than Brazil, and this mainly during the quarter of a century which followed the peace of 1713, when the French were worried by both the excessive advantage which England was taking from the privileges she had gained at Utrecht, and the smuggling trade which was developing between the British West Indies and the Spanish possessions. That traffic was said to bring 'immense' and 'prodigious' profits to English merchants and to be injurious to the legal trade which France was conducting through Cadiz. The British were suspected of wanting to monopolise the trade with the Spanish Indies and therefore their output of precious metals, so that the manufactures of the rest of Europe would be annihilated.[38]

[36] AN AMB^7, 400, 'Mémoire sur le Portugal', by the Duc de Duras, 1756.

[37] AN AMB^7, 12, 267, 268 and 412; AE MDA, 6, 56 and 63; BN MF 12162. From H. E. S. Fisher, *The Portugal Trade. A Study of Anglo-Portuguese Commerce 1700–1770* (London, 1971), it appears that the French did not overestimate too much the importance for England of her relations with Portugal and Brazil; even the figures they give for exports of gold to England seem rather accurate. However, since 1760, British exports to Portugal were declining, owing to the fall in the output of Brazilian gold; see Fisher, pp. 7–8, 13–17, 19–24, 30–3, 41–6, 125–30, 133, 135–6, 138.

[38] AE CPA, 361, 362, Supplements 7, 8; AN F^{12}, 647–8; AN AMB^7, 344.

On the other hand, Britain's trade with her own colonies, which was ignored in documents of the early eighteenth century, later attracted increasing attention. Even as early as 1736, a memorandum asserted that 'England owes the best part of her trade to her colonies', which were well-populated and where output was increasing fast; they sent to her five-sixths of their produce and gave large outlets to her manufactures as well as employment to 4000 merchant ships. In 1747, Silhouette wrote: 'The riches which the English extract from America, from their own colonies and also from Brazil, are the foundations of their power'; and he stressed the importance of the tobacco trade from Virginia and Maryland and of the rice exports from South Carolina. Documents of the 1770s repeat the view that trade with the colonies in the New World is the main factor of England's prosperity.[39] The 'americanisation' of British trade during the eighteenth century had not gone unobserved in France.

III

The emphasis upon foreign trade and its mercantilist framework did not blind French commentators to the 'real economy' of England. André Bourde has shown that the improvements which English agriculture had achieved, and especially the Norfolk system, were revealed to the French reading public first by the *Lettres* of the Abbé Le Blanc in 1745, and later, with more technical details, by a number of works published in the mid-1750s.[40] Earlier, however, in 1729 and 1732, two memoranda in the French Foreign Office archives had observed that, in England, land was better cultivated than elsewhere, livestock more numerous, farm buildings better maintained; agriculture had reached 'a high degree of perfection', as Englishmen had taken great care to ascertain the quality of their soils and the kind of continuous rotation each field could bear, so that land was constantly under cultivation, either for grain or for vegetables.[41]

As early as the 1730s, the French Foreign Office had also been

39 AE MDA, 6, 32 and 56; BN MF 12162.

40 Bourde, pp. 277–96, 302–8; among the books alluded to are those by Plumard de Dangeul and Butel-Dumont; *Encyclopédie*, III, 'Culture', written by Véron de Forbonnais; *Les intérêts de la France mal entendus dans les branches de l'Agriculture*, 3 vols. (Amsterdam, 1756), by A. Goudar and French translations of several English works on agronomy. Henceforth there was a constant flow of panegyrics of English agriculture. Owing to the full study of this literature by Bourde, the problem of agriculture will be dealt with briefly here.

41 AE CPA, 368 and Supplement 8.

informed that England had become an exporter of grain on a large scale to many European countries.[42] Later on, those grain exports and the bounty on them were to be seen by many writers as the decisive factor for the prosperity of English agriculture. Voltaire wrote in 1756 that 'agriculture, which had long been neglected, took eventually for them [the English] the place of the Potosi mines ... cultivation was particularly encouraged when, in 1689, the granting of awards for exporting grain was started'. Two years earlier, Plumard de Dangeul had built up a sort of model of economic growth triggered off by the 1689 Corn Law, which had brought benefits to all branches of the economy.[43] Such views, were, of course, eagerly taken up by the physiocrats, who with a few other writers, considered the progress of her agriculture as the decisive cause of England's wealth and of her military power.[44]

The technical aspects of English agriculture were not ignored, however, even by writers who were not agronomists; it was understood that continuous rotations ('land never rests') had broken the vicious circle of traditional agriculture; thanks to them, livestock was more numerous and better; in its turn it produced more manure, which ensured 'abundant harvests'.[45] It is worth pointing out that French travellers were impressed by the large areas devoted to grass or pasture and by the 'prodigious' numbers of cattle, sheep and horses, as well as by the large size of those animals;[46] in a word, they had guessed that

[42] AE MDA, 6 and 8: within 3 or 4 years, those grain exports have brought in 60 million of French *livres*, 'which have diffused money among the cultivators and the lower orders ... If this relief had been absent, distress would have become acute owing to a surabundance, as nothing, after famine, is to be feared more than the fall in food prices' (1739).

[43] Voltaire, *Essai sur les moeurs*, II, pp. 695–7; Plumard de Dangeul, pp. 93, 96–7; Bourde, pp. 303 ff.; BN MF 10716; F. Chaumont writes in 1760 that England 'by this bold stroke (the Corn Law) drove away for ever famine from her territory'.

[44] G. Weulersse, *Le mouvement physiocratique en France de 1756 à 1770*, 2 vols. (Paris, 1910), I, pp. 544, 565, 577; II, 523, 706; Bourde, pp. 285, 289, 303; Le Blanc, II, p. 65; Coyer, Letter XXI, pp. 164–71.

[45] See especially AE MDA, 61 and 74, 'Mémoire sur l'Angleterre par M. le Marquis de Biencourt' [Charles, Marquis de Biencourt (1747–1824) was then colonel of an infantry regiment; *maréchal de camp* in 1788, he was a deputy at the States-general, where he stood out for his radical views (which he held already in 1784; cf. below); he spent the rest of the Revolutionary period quietly, in his country house]; La Rochefoucauld, *La vie en Angleterre*, II, pp. 198–200, 209–11, 215, 225; *Voyage philosophique d'Angleterre fait en 1783 et 1784*, 2 vols. (Paris, 1787), II, pp. 178 ff.; also Bourde, pp. 294, 304, 307.

[46] The fact that there were no wolves in England was sometimes seen as a reason for this huge number of animals and for the fact that they stayed in the fields day and night. But some other writers explained it by the scarcity and high price of labour: 'English agriculture aims mostly to exploit its land without the help of a large population' (1765). Cf. AE MDA, 61; AE CPA, 499 and Supplement 28, 'Lettre de M. de Custine'; *Lettres de Madame du Bocage*, pp. 5, 53; La Rochefoucauld, pp. 192, 200; Cambry, p. 13.

agriculture was more 'animal-intensive' in England than in France, as O'Brien and Keyder have demonstrated.[47]

Some underlying causes of agricultural progress were also mentioned: the security and liberty which landed property enjoyed,[48] the habit of landowners, including the highest 'milords', to reside on their country estates, their interest in agriculture, their readiness to make experiments, to invest and to grant long leases to their farmers, who in their turn made 'large advances' to the land; the beneficial influence of agricultural societies and the prizes they awarded; the role of Parliament, which had encouraged the reclamation of marshes and wastes, as well as the enclosure of common and other lands.[49] It was also said that 'the Englishman is never satisfied with what he has obtained; his mind gets bored when in rest ... The desire to increase always his property by continuous speculations destroys in him the love of tranquillity which inclines all well-to-do men towards idleness.' Another writer offered a pre-Toynbeean 'challenge and response' explanation: the English farmer had to resort to a 'rational and learned' husbandry, in order to extract good harvests from a soil 'lacking in vegetative salts and which sunbeams reach only after having fought with losses the winds and the fogs'.[50]

Until the last decades of the eighteenth century, technological progress was more conspicuous, especially to foreigners, in agriculture than in industry.[51] Of course, it was well-known in France that England had a large wool industry, 'which is the basis of her trade', and that it produced a wide range of woollens and worsteds, which were often superior in quality to, and cheaper in price than, French goods. The superiority of England was also generally recognised for various other articles, such as those in metals and especially steel goods.[52] As for the explanations of this superiority, they were quite

[47] P. O'Brien and C. Keyder, *Economic Growth in Britain and France, 1780–1914. Two Paths to the Twentieth Century* (London, 1978), pp. 113 ff.

[48] AE MDA, 61; La Rochefoucauld, p. 211, adds equality: nothing but their difference in wealth separates the *grand seigneur* and the farmer.

[49] Butel-Dumont, I, pp. 53–4; AE MDA, 61 and 74; also Bourde, pp. 285, 289–91, 303. Le Blanc had explained the preference of landowners for living in the country by 'the smoke of coal' which made London unattractive; and according to Butel-Dumont, landowners devoted themselves to 'the study of the most advanced sciences', to the benefit of agriculture. Enclosures are mentioned not infrequently, but without comment in most cases.

[50] AE MDA, 61; *Voyage philosophique*, II.

[51] Acomb, p. 9; A. Rémond, *John Holker, manufacturier et grand fonctionnaire en France au XVIIIe siècle, 1719–1786* (Paris, 1946), pp. 29, 55–6.

[52] In particular, articles in polished steel; *Lettres de Madame du Bocage*, p. 50; AE CPA, 499; AE MDA, 32 and 56. On the misfortunes of steel-making in eighteenth-century France, see J. R.

simple; for the wool industry, the quality of the English raw material was considered as a most important factor; it resulted from the improved breeds of sheep, from the excellent grass and roots which were their food, from the mild and wet climate, and from the *éducation sauvage* – the fact that they lived outside, day and night, all the year round. England had also some fuller's earth, which scoured wool so well that it could be dyed beautifully.[53] Some writers mentioned the activity and ingenuity of English manufacturers, who 'often invent new and lovely fabrics', and who supervised most carefully their making, as well as the skilfulness of English workers who carried out their duties to perfection and with 'extreme celerity'.[54] In this respect, John Holker, who knew both countries well, thought that English workmen, who were well-fed, lived in comfort and enjoyed economic freedom, were therefore able to work much harder than the French, who were miserable and crushed by taxes.[55]

However, some French observers were puzzled by the competitive edge which British goods enjoyed, even while the 'dearness' and 'excessive price' of labour were obvious in England. The answer was, of course, better technology, but this factor was discovered rather late. Still, as early as 1745 the Abbé Le Blanc wrote: 'England is the country where one finds the largest number of these machines ... which truly multiply men by saving their labour, and thanks to which one man is made to produce the work which, without such help, would employ thirty people.'[56] In 1753, a report sent from Hamburg pointed out that the English sold much more jewellery there than the French, owing to lower prices, as they employed machinery to make those articles.[57] But, as J. R. Harris has stressed, it was only during the 1780s that Frenchmen fully realised 'that British technology was advancing on a broad front ... and would take a long time to match with a front of

Harris, 'Attempts to Transfer English Steel Techniques to France in the Eighteenth Century', in S. Marriner (ed.), *Business and Businessmen* (Liverpool, 1978), pp. 199–233.

[53] AN AMB[7], 388; AE CPA, 368, and Supplement 8; Bourde, pp. 795 ff., 810 ff., analyses the long discussions about sheep-farming and how to improve it in France. It is correct that French wools were of inferior quality and this was a drawback as, during the eighteenth century, demand turned towards fine cloths.

[54] AN AMB[7], 388; AE CPA, 361; Rémond, pp. 139–40.

[55] Rémond, pp. 91 and 148, memoranda by Holker of 1756 and 1762. However, the quality of English workmen was questioned by a few writers.

[56] Le Blanc, I, p. 63; he gave as examples a steel-polishing machine, which one child could operate, and a pumping engine (obviously a Newcomen engine) in a coal mine.

[57] AN AMB[7], 388. It is likely that jewellery included things like Birmingham 'toys'.

equal strength'.[58] This was obvious not only to experts and businessmen,[59] but also to intelligent laymen.

In 1784, the Marquis de Biencourt drew up a long list of English manufactured goods, which were either new or made more cheaply and of better quality thanks to new methods; he wrote also about 'water mills' to card and spin cotton, wool and silk: each of them produced as much as 3,600 persons; in most of them water was raised by the fire-engines 'which M. Watt has perfected'. The English were constantly making new discoveries: 'The whole of nature is unceasingly studied, requested, worked upon, fecundated, husbanded.'[60] Two years later, Custine was also impressed by 'the fire-engine, used everywhere to drive machinery which simplifies labour'; it was 'put in motion by burning coal which is dirt cheap in all the provinces. It serves as substitute for a great deal of waterpower and drives mills to spin and card cotton, which, thanks to it, can be attended by children.'[61] Biencourt had observed that 'an English workman does more work than six Frenchmen and does it better, so that the country can withstand foreign competition despite the dearness of labour'; the author of *Voyage philosophique* made similar observations after visiting a large distillery near London, and then wondered about the origins of the inventive spirit which Englishmen were displaying and of the large undertakings they created. Just as in the case of agriculture, he put forward a 'challenge and response' model. England, being a small country, did not abound in essential foodstuffs and raw materials; labour was expensive, because the population was not large and because a super-abundant money supply pushed up the cost of living; moreover the burden of taxation was 'enormous'. An Englishman was thus threatened by want and poverty; he had therefore to be constantly active and he was 'irresistibly led to spring forward beyond the limits of his station in life. So everything is speculation, enterprise or manufacture'. In industry, particularly, there was little difference in the degree of finish which workmen gave to the goods they made; therefore, 'a master manufacturer can only raise

58 J. R. Harris, *Industry and Technology in the Eighteenth Century: Britain and France* (Birmingham, 1972), p. 16.

59 Cf., for instance, memoranda on the 1786 treaty (AN F^{12}, 658^{A}) and by Thouret, from Rouen (quoted by Rémond, p. 45, n. 128); they stress the use of labour-saving machinery in the textile industries, thanks to which England makes up for a population smaller than France's and also manufactures inexpensively. They also point out the advantage gained from the cheapness of coal, which is used either for driving machinery, or in finishing and dyeing operations.

60 AE MDA, 74. 61 AE CPA, Supplement 8, 'Lettre de M. de Custine'.

himself above the general either by giving new shapes to the articles he makes, or by reducing the number of workmen's days through simplified processes; or by substituting new machinery for human hands'.[62] This substitution, according to a petition by the merchants of Nantes (1792), had allowed English masters to pay higher wages to their workers, so that consumption had increased and therefore the demand for agricultural products. 'Thus, through a system which seems paradoxical, the English have grown richer by consuming', but thanks to an enormous trade surplus and therefore to the detriment of other nations.[63] For his part, Biencourt had observed that 'Englishmen are sensible enough to manufacture for the people much more than for the rich', so that they were able 'to sell a great deal and regularly'.[64]

IV

It was mentioned earlier that several writers had drawn up lists of factors which explained England's economic superiority.[65] Such lists include in particular institutional and social factors; and they imply, more or less openly, a criticism of the *Ancien Régime*, which emerges quite early in the eighteenth century, and which comes not only from *philosophes*, but also from diplomats, officials or persons sending memoranda to the Foreign Office, who might have been expected to be more respectful to established institutions.

Curiously enough, geographical factors are rarely mentioned, except, as it has been seen earlier, the small size of England and her lack of natural resources;[66] but not much was made of her insular situation and the security which it brought. There are also fewer references to the English 'national character' than one might expect.[67]

On the other hand, 'the nature of government' in England is frequently seen as a cause of the country's wealth. 'The English constitution is wonderfully suited to trade', F. Chaumont wrote in

[62] *Voyage philosophique*, II, pp. 149, 156, 162, 164.

[63] J. Meyer, *L'Armement nantais dans la deuxième moitié du XVIIIe siècle* (Paris, 1968), p. 252.

[64] AE MDA, 74. Other writers had stressed as a favourable factor the fact that Englishmen had become used to luxury goods; but Biencourt congratulated them to refuse the 'asiatic luxury which France is spreading everywhere' and which was bound to ruin Europe.

[65] Each writer has, of course, his own list; we can present only a sort of synthesis, while trying to point out whether a given point of view is frequent or rare.

[66] But there was no complete consensus on this point.

[67] Generally, Englishmen were considered as hard-working, active to the point of restlessness, and ingenious.

1760, but much earlier it had been stressed that, under this constitution, which was 'at one and the same time popular, aristocratic and monarchic', liberty and property were secure, the powers of the king were limited and he did not interfere with business, Parliament was always ready to pass new laws to encourage trade and was anxious to safeguard public credit. Moreover, government was not burdensome and expensive: the king's court did not try to impress the populace through showy ostentation; the provinces were not handed over, 'like elsewhere', to the arbitrary rule of 'commissioners' (the *intendants*); the number of law-courts and judges was not excessive; as for religion, clergymen did not live in luxury, churches did not keep 'sterile treasures, which have made Rome a huge hospital and her territory a desert' (Biencourt). In peace time, the army was kept small, so that more men were available for agriculture and manufactures. Thanks to the freedom of the press, the nation was enlightened about its economic interest.[68] As a free country, England had also, to her advantage, welcomed foreign craftsmen, driven from their homes by religious persecutions; with obvious gratification, Voltaire enumerated all the new manufactures which the Huguenots, those 'useful citizens', had introduced in England, making her independent from France for the supply of many goods.[69] England also enjoyed economic freedom, which, indeed, some commentators tended to overestimate, being impressed by the free exportation of most goods – including grain – the duty-free import of raw materials and the absence of internal customs: they thought that trade was 'absolutely free', forgetting the protectionist system and the survival of many traditional regulations of industry.[70]

The English system of taxation was praised too from an early date. Taxes were established by law, 'according to the rules of justice', and raised with little expense; since the land tax was calculated according to the taxpayer's property, and paid by the landowner and not by the farmer, this was a factor in agriculture's prosperity.[71] The other taxes were excise and customs duties upon foreign goods, and none was

[68] BN MF 10716; AE CPA, 368 and Supplement 8; AE MDA, 74; *Encyclopédie*, XVII, 'Vingtième', p. 870; Coyer, letter XXI, pp. 164 ff.

[69] Voltaire, *Essai sur les moeurs*, pp. 695–7; Le Blanc, II, p. 233; AE CPA, Supplement 8.

[70] AE CPA, 368; AE MDA, 6 and 74; BN MF 10716; Acomb, pp. 8, 12, 13, 47, 49; Bourde, p. 830.

[71] Its immutability (so that improvements of land did not make it liable to heavier tax) and the fact that it did not affect the circulating capital of farmers were also praised: Weulersse, I, pp. 466, 544 n. 3.

levied upon manufactures or manufacturers. However, the physiocrats did not approve of this system and maintained that the predominance of customs and excise was a vicious sort of taxation, which raised prices and wages to the prejudice of landowners and cultivators.[72]

As for social factors, and especially 'social values', they were often stressed by French observers. As early as 1699, it was noticed that 'merchants are considered with much honour in the whole Kingdom' [England]; in 1729, a memorandum asserted that 'the condition of trade is in that country upon a more honourable footing than in any other': some merchants were knighted and became mayors or members of Parliament.[73] This theme was picked up by Voltaire, who wrote about the 'legitimate pride' of the English merchant, who 'dares to compare himself, not without some reasons, to a citizen of Rome'; he dedicated his tragedy *Zaïre* (1733) to *M. Falkener, marchand anglais*, expressing his 'pleasure to be able to tell my nation how merchants are considered in your country, how much esteem is entertained in England for a profession which ensures the greatness of the State, and the superiority with which some of you represent their country in Parliament'.[74]

Frenchmen were also impressed by the absence of *dérogeance* in England: 'Many noblemen of the highest rank and standing are openly interested in trade, and several of their children are actually merchants; the richest and most distinguished gentlemen trade openly without losing their rank in any way.' To this view of 1699, Le Dran, a clerk in the French Foreign Office, added in 1718 that, England being a small country, 'people who have money are obliged to put it into trade, as they cannot invest it in land or in public offices, which are not purchasable. The highest noblemen are not reluctant to take a share in trading companies; one can even see peers of the realm and gentlemen who have no property apprenticing their younger sons to shops' – a theme which is echoed by several other writers, though a book

72 AE CPA, 368 and Supplement 8; AE MDA, 6; Voltaire, *Lettres philosophiques*, p. 64; *Mémoires et observations faites par un voyageur en Angleterre* (The Hague, 1698), p. 257; Acomb, p. 49.

73 AN AMB[7], 499, 'Observations sur l'inégalité'; AE CPA, 368, 'Remarques sur le commerce d'Angleterre'.

74 Voltaire, *Lettres philosophiques*, p. 67; *Zaïre* (Bibliothèque de la Faculté des Lettres de Lyon edn, Paris, 1889), pp. 3–4. The dedication was to Sir Everard Fawkener (1684–1758), who had been Voltaire's host during part of his exile in London. He was a merchant-mercer, but shortly afterwards, he was knighted and appointed ambassador to Turkey (1735); later on, he was secretary to the Duke of Cumberland and Joint-Postmaster General (1745). His story illustrates the upward mobility in English society, but also the gentrification process among merchants.

published in 1698 had pointed out: 'It is very rare for peers of the realm to apprentice their younger sons to any trade, as it is said to have been done in the past; I even believe it is not done at all any more. For Knights' sons, nothing is more usual.'[75] Still, Voltaire stressed that 'the younger son of a peer of the realm does not scorn trade' and that, just at the time 'Milord' Oxford and 'Milord' Townshend were ministers, their brothers were merchants.[76] The Swiss traveller Muralt seems to have been the only one to notice that many English merchants retired, once they had made a fortune, to live as country gentlemen; other writers maintained that the sons of merchants or manufacturers always carried on their fathers' business, so that firms could grow powerful.[77]

There are thus some symptoms of a propensity to idealise English society, especially its commitment to business. 'There are few lords, gentlemen, burgesses, merchants, widows, orphans, artisans who do not have some share in a ship', asserted the Irish refugee Barry in 1728. In 1740, F. Chaumont maintained that society in London was egalitarian, 'despite the existence of titles, of a nobility, and of distinctions', and so propitious to trade, which was 'the profession of equality'. As for Biencourt, he considered as a major asset for England that the nation was not 'like elsewhere overburdened by a multitude of idle, lazy families to which the State has granted privileges'.[78]

Finally, Frenchmen paid a good deal of attention to the problem of credit in England, and firstly, of course, to the government's ability to borrow large sums and to the strength of its credit. A memorandum of 1733 stressed that the wealth and the power of England were multiplied by 'the immense credit which England has known how to establish and to preserve'; the enormous debts she had accumulated during the War of Spanish succession 'have not impaired confidence and have even helped to increase the circulation of specie'. How could this paradox be solved? 'The stability of the value of coins, which are never changed' was a factor, as 'this safety established credit, which is the soul of trade'; but, according to a document of 1748, 'the attention by the English government to ear-mark funds in order to be able to pay the interests on its debts and the creation of the sinking fund are the

75 AN AMB[7], 499; AE MDA, 68, 'Sur le commerce d'Angleterre', 1718; *Mémoires et observations*, p. 294.

76 *Lettres Philosophiques*, p. 67.

77 Muralt, p. 16; AE CPA, 368; BN MF, Nouvelles acquisitions 20089.

78 AE CPA, 364; BN MF 10716; AE MDA, 74.

two main causes of the ease with which the nation borrows at home and abroad'.[79] Such views appear not infrequently later on, but another theme emerges, which was destined to be widely accepted in France: the fragility of an economic system based upon credit. F. Chaumont wrote in 1760: 'This credit on which everything hangs in England, hangs itself on very little, despite the false glamour from which it benefits.'[80]

The importance of commercial credit and *the fall of interest rates* were also noticed rather early as factors which stimulated trade as well as land improvements – with borrowed money. The Bank of England is mentioned at a later date, at least in the documents which have been examined; however, its operations were said to be among the causes of England's power, as the circulation of 'paper money' had, by 1783, increased threefold her means of payment and her resources for trade, and had given her a powerful navy.[81]

V

Rien de nouveau sous le soleil ... There are, indeed, few factors, which modern historians have called forth in order to explain England's economic growth during the eighteenth century, of which French observers and writers of that period had not caught a glimpse at least. They thus mentioned the role of foreign trade, supported by seapower, as an engine of growth; the precocious improvement of agriculture; political and economic freedom; the absence of legal barriers within a mobile society; a system of 'social values' which was congenial to economic progress; the making of consumption goods for the many rather than of luxury articles; the rapid accumulation of capital, low interest rates, an elaborate credit system.[82] On the other hand, French officials, and also the French reading public, were reasonably well-informed about England's economy and the reasons for its superiority.

[79] AE CPA, 368, 425 and Supplement 8. [80] BN MF 10716.

[81] AE MDA, 6 and 56; also Bourde, p. 304; Weulersse, I, p. 398. Chaumont explained the development of credit in England by the fact that 'finance [i.e. operations with the government] did not show those scandalous fortunes which give a distaste for any other activity and attract all capital'.

[82] Though many travellers comment upon the condition of the roads, which were generally thought to be good, the role of transport as a factor of economic progress is not much mentioned. However, in December 1789, the French 'consul' in London, Herman, announced the recent opening of the Thames and Severn canal and wrote: 'Englishmen do not lose sight of the advantages which much ease in internal circulation can procure ... This immense work has not cost a *sol* to the government' (AN AMB^{1}, 762).

However, they were also presented with many strange and even fantastic 'observations' and explanations. Such distortions or aberrations resulted from prejudices – in the literal meaning of this word. Some of them were voiced by diehard mercantilists, obsessed with foreign trade and its strict regulation; some others by *philosophes* or their followers, who looked across the Channel for the reverse of *Ancien Régime* France, in order to present it to Frenchmen as a model – and found it, of course. Under its extreme form, this current of thought built up a mythical image of English economy and society, which had little relation with English realities. The creation of myths was a basic aspect of the Enlightenment – an expression of the alienation which the French intelligentsia felt towards the *Ancien Régime* and a weapon to fight it.[83] Anyhow, Englishmen were seen as philosophers, steeped in a 'republican' spirit and prompted by a 'zeal for the common cause', which was 'the source of the power' of their country; they were like members of a large family and considered themselves as co-owners of Britain, so that they all worked for the commonweal; this was the reason for their unceasing activity, and their search for all projects and inventions which could be useful to the country. This 'philosophical spirit' was at the root of English economic progress.[84] One may well wonder if Richard Arkwright or John Wilkinson would have found this portrait of the eighteenth-century entrepreneur a good likeness.

Post scriptum

At first sight, there is some contradiction between this chapter and those which precede. The theme here, however, is the views of eighteenth-century Frenchmen, and it has been stressed that they were sometimes whimsical. Strangely enough, many common ideas about differences between the British and French economies in the eighteenth century were first expressed by eighteenth-century travellers and polemicists, and were later repeated by many serious historians. My article of 1966 (Chapter 1) was an attempt to challenge this conventional wisdom, and deliberately went too far in some respects. However, I never denied that the two economies were

[83] A recent and interesting contribution to the study of anglomania is C. Bruneteau and B. Cottret (eds.), *Un inédit de Louis-Sébastien Mercier. Parallèle de Paris et de Londres* (Paris, 1982), with a good introduction.

[84] Butel-Dumont, I, pp. 398–400; also Goudar and Roland de la Platière, quoted by Bourde, pp. 289 and 308.

different, that a serious gap divided them. Of course, Voltaire and many others overestimated the gap between the standard of living of the English and the French people; none the less, there was a gap. Moreover many writings which are quoted in this chapter confirm my view that England was ahead of France in the late seventeenth and early eighteenth century. As for the interest which eighteenth-century Frenchmen took in the Navigation Acts, it has been vindicated recently by O'Brien and Keyder, who have stressed the role of seapower, of colonial conquests – and, in a word, of British mercantilism.[85]

[85] This study was first published in P. L. Cottrell and D. H. Aldcroft (eds.), *Shipping, Trade and Commerce. Essays in Memory of Ralph Davis* (Leicester, 1981), pp. 61–79. The late Annik Pardailhé-Galabrun, *ingénieur* CNRS, had done most of the archive work.

5 ❧ Capital formation in Great Britain during the Industrial Revolution*

I

Capital played a central part in the classical economists' theory of development. To Adam Smith, Ricardo and their followers (and, as a consequence, to Karl Marx), the accumulation of capital was the fundamental determinant of economic growth and progress. However, the early historians of the Industrial Revolution, at the end of the nineteenth and the beginning of the twentieth century, did not pay much attention to the question of capital formation; they were far more interested in the institutional and technical aspects of the Industrial Revolution, or, indeed, in its social consequences, in the rise of the factory system and of industrial capitalism (with 'capital' and 'capitalism' often being confused). They did, nevertheless, formulate a number of ideas regarding capital formation, emphasising for example that the mechanisation of industry involved a considerable expenditure of capital; most of them claimed that the plentiful supply of capital in eighteenth-century England, and the speed with which it was accumulating, had been a decisive factor of the Industrial Revolution. Other historians, however, pointed out that innovators had often been hampered by difficulties in raising the capital they needed, which implied some shortage of capital. So began a controversy which has continued up until our own days.

* The first part of this chapter is a summary of the introduction to my book, *Capital Formation in the Industrial Revolution* (London, 1972), which is a collection of seven articles on this question. The original text is sixty-nine pages long, and has copious notes, to which the interested reader should refer.

The second part of this chapter is a revised version of a paper given at the International Economic History conference of Aix-en-Provence in 1962; it was reprinted in English translation as Chapter 6 of the above-mentioned book (pp. 589–642). Capital formation can be defined as 'additions made during a particular period of time to the stock of goods which are for use in future production' (J. Hibbert).

The inter-war period saw the publication of a number of monographs which brought to light many useful data about the sources from which the pioneers of the Industrial Revolution had drawn their capital, and, more particularly, about the process of accumulation, within industrial concerns through the regular ploughing back of profits. One particularly important study was that by T. S. Ashton on the eighteenth-century iron industry, the basic conclusions of which were generalised in his later books.[1] Ashton showed that Nonconformist and Quaker ironmasters developed their firms rapidly, 'by dint of ... unremitting thrift': they tended to live very frugally and to reinvest at once most of their profits. Another important study was that of J. Lord on the firm of Boulton and Watt, which emphasised how much difficulty the inventor of the steam engine and his partner had experienced in finding the necessary capital for developing their machine.[2] Lord's conclusion, namely, that in the eighteenth century 'the capitalisation of a large industrial firm ... was a difficult business',[3] exercised a strong influence upon the conceptions of British economic historians, many of whom tended to believe, in the inter-war period, that the innovators and entrepreneurs of the Industrial Revolution had been hampered by scarcity of capital (all the more so given that Lord stressed the 'tremendous increase' in fixed capital during this period).

This idea did of course clash with the other widespread notion of an abundance of capital in England as one of the main forces behind the Industrial Revolution. But this Gordian knot was elegantly untied by Michael M. Postan, in a 1935 article, which was the first serious discussion of capital formation which both had a historical perspective and was conducted in economic terms.[4] On the one hand, eighteenth-century England did not suffer from a shortage of capital on a nationwide or aggregate basis; but, on the other, the imperfections of the capital market were such that new firms, depending solely on the

[1] T. S. Ashton, *Iron and Steel in the Industrial Revolution* (Manchester, 1924).

[2] J. Lord, *Capital and Steam-Power, 1750–1800* (London, 1923, Second Edition 1966, with an introduction by W. H. Chaloner). In fact, Lord had overestimated the difficulties encountered by Boulton and Watt.

[3] Lord, p. 104.

[4] M. M. Postan, 'Recent Trends in the Accumulation of Capital', *The Economic History Review*, VI, 1 October 1935, pp. 1–12; this article was reproduced in Crouzet, *Capital Formation*, pp. 70–83. Of course, whenever one speaks of a shortage or an abundance of capital, these notions should always be understood in a relative sense; it is a matter of shortage or abundance in relation to other factors of production or in relation to other countries.

personal savings of their founders, with the additional backing of those of their relatives and friends, hardly benefited from the fact that England was the richest country in Europe. There was no 'general reservoir of national savings' but 'a multiplicity of small, disjointed pools', and the conduits connecting them to industry were 'few and meagre'; furthermore, psychological and institutional obstacles prevented the use for investment in industry of most of the considerable capital which had accumulated in the country, and of landed wealth in particular.

Thus, 'the insufficiency of capital was local rather than general and social rather than material';[5] it could nevertheless be sorely felt by the pioneers of the new industry. Shortly afterwards, in another innovatory article, Herbert Heaton pointed out that the initial capital requirements of eighteenth-century industrialists were really very modest and that they could have recourse to a variety of sources in order to supply them.[6]

On the other hand, some bold, attractive but ill-founded views were advanced. Consider, for example, Earl J. Hamilton's hypothesis, formulated in 1942, that the Industrial Revolution had been financed by a 'profit inflation', resulting from wages lagging behind prices (which were rising rapidly) and producing a bout of forced saving.[7] However, Hamilton was using indexes of the prices of foodstuffs and of the wages of London building artisans, which were in no way representative of the movement of prices and costs in industry; during the second half of the eighteenth century, prices of manufactured articles rose less than money wages and, from 1799–1803 onwards, they underwent a long-term fall. It was increased productivity which accounted for the expanded profits, the ploughing back of which swelled industrial capital accumulation.[8] As for Eric Williams (who was subsequently, and for a long time, Prime Minister of Trinidad), he claimed, in 1944, but with little in the way of proof, that the profits

5 Postan, 1935, pp. 2–5, 1972, pp. 71–5.

6 H. Heaton, 'Financing the Industrial Revolution', *Bulletin of the Business Historical Society*, XI, 1, February 1937, pp. 1–10; also reprinted, in Crouzet, *Capital Formation*, pp. 84–93.

7 E. J. Hamilton, 'Profit Inflation and the Industrial Revolution, 1751–1800', *Quarterly Journal of Economics*, LVI, 2, February 1942, pp. 256–73. Hamilton had published a tentative version of this argument as early as 1929 and he advanced it once more in 1952, in 'Prices and Progress', *Journal of Economic History*, XII, 4, Autumn 1952, pp. 325–49.

8 See the conclusive criticism of D. Felix, 'Profit Inflation and Industrial Growth: The Historic Record and Contemporary Analogies', *Quarterly Journal of Economics*, LXX, 3, August 1956, pp. 441–63; writers such as T. S. Ashton, P. Deane, R. M. Hartwell and D. S. Landes have seconded these objections.

from the slave trade had been the source of the capital which was invested in British industry.[9]

Conversely, after the Second World War, study of capital formation was undertaken more systematically, in large part under the influence of economists. Indeed, the latter shifted their attention from short-term fluctuations, with which they had been preoccupied during the crises of the inter-war period, and devoted themselves to the problems of long-term growth. Reviving the theory of classical political economy, they once more attributed a crucial role in the process of growth to capital accumulation. With these influences at work, economic historians in the post-1945 period paid more attention to capital formation; there was also consensus respecting a very simple model, inspired by that of Harrod and Domar, which presupposed that increasing formation of capital in England had led quite naturally to the Industrial Revolution; the plentiful supply of capital was thus seen as the crucial advantage which accounted for Britain's early start. T. S. Ashton, in his synoptic account of 1948, stressed the importance, which to him was crucial for the unleashing of the Industrial Revolution, of the substantial fall in interest rates which occurred during the early decades of the eighteenth century and which had made it very much easier to invest.[10]

Yet some economists, who were attempting an analysis, in historical perspective, of relations between capital formation and economic development, gave a wholly new twist to discussions regarding the first of these concepts. So much was this the case that the debate tended to concentrate upon the question of the quantitative relation which investment bore to national income during the epoch of the Industrial Revolution, i.e. the investment proportion.

In 1954 and 1955, W. A. Lewis argued that an Industrial Revolution could be defined as 'a sudden acceleration of the rate of capital formation', such that it moved from 4 to 5 per cent of national income,

[9] E. Williams, *Capitalism and Slavery* (Chapel Hill, North Carolina, 1944). This argument was not borrowed from Marx, as some have supposed. See on this question S. L. Engerman, 'The Slave Trade and British Capital Formation in the 18th Century: A Comment on the Williams Thesis', *Business History Review*, XLVI, 4, Winter 1972, pp. 430–43; Engerman shows that the slave trade's contribution to the financing of investment in Great Britain in the 18th century could at best have represented only a minimal fraction of total investment.

[10] T. S. Ashton, *The Industrial Revolution, 1760–1830* (London, 1948), pp. 7–11. Actually, interest rates, after having fallen to a very low level between 1736 and 1759, rose again slightly, during the period which saw the start of the Industrial Revolution. Most historians would now hesitate before endorsing Ashton's argument.

that is, the rate usual in traditional economies or in underdeveloped countries, to 12 or 15 per cent, which is the minimal rate in advanced industrial countries.[11] This hypothesis of a doubling of the investment proportion during the Industrial Revolution was revived, refined and spread far and wide by W. W. Rostow in his 1956 article on 'the take-off' and in his famous *The Stages of Economic Growth* (1960).[12] Rostow defined take-off as 'the interval during which the rate of investment increases in such a way that real output per capita rises';[13] a necessary condition for this would be that the proportion of net investment to national income rose from 5 per cent to over 10 per cent. Rostow also maintained that this phenomenon had occurred in Great Britain between 1783 and 1802, but this assertion was not supported by any precise quantitative data regarding eighteenth-century England, but merely by argument and by references to the example of several other countries during their industrialisation in the nineteenth and twentieth centuries.

Rostow's hypothesis made such a sensation that the International Economic Association held a special conference at Konstanz, in September 1960, in order to discuss it. A paper on 'The Take-Off in Britain' was delivered jointly by Phyllis Deane (who had been working for several years upon a study of Britain's economic growth from the seventeenth to the twentieth century) and H. J. Habakkuk.[14] These authors accepted Rostow's – and Lewis's – basic idea, namely, that the investment proportion had roughly doubled during the Industrial Revolution, for this view agreed with the quantitative data available to them, but they rejected outright Rostow's claim that this change had been compressed within the short period of the last two decades of the eighteenth century. They presented data respecting the increase of investment in the sectors most deeply affected by the Industrial

[11] W. A. Lewis, 'Economic Development with Unlimited Supplies of Labour', *The Manchester School*, XXII, 2, May 1954, p. 155, and *Theory of Economic Growth* (London, 1955), pp. 201–2, 207–8, 225–6, 235. This hypothesis derived from the study of underdeveloped countries in the twentieth century, India in particular. S. Kuznets had made this same suggestion, but in more tentative form, in 1953.

[12] W. W. Rostow, 'The Take-Off into Self-Sustained Growth', *Economic Journal*, LXVI, 261, March 1956, pp. 25–48, and *The Stages of Economic Growth. A Non-Communist Manifesto* (Cambridge, 1960).

[13] Rostow, 'The Take-Off into Self-Sustained Growth', p. 25.

[14] P. Deane and H. J. Habakkuk, 'The Take-Off in Britain', in W. W. Rostow (ed.), *The Economics of Take-Off into Sustained Growth* (London and New York, 1963), pp. 63–82. At Konstanz, A. K. Cairncross and S. Kuznets supported these criticisms of Rostow's 'excessively dramatic' conception.

Revolution – canals, iron, cotton – and these showed that this increase could not have had so momentous an effect upon the national rate of capital formation. It was therefore only during 'the railway age', and in the 1840s in particular, that this rate could have reached, and then exceeded 10 or 12 per cent. During the previous period, on the other hand, its increase was gradual and fairly slow.

These lines of argument were developed and refined by Phyllis Deane in a number of subsequent studies[15] and one can fairly claim that they were by and large accepted in the 1960s and 1970s. A summary of her position might run as follows:

- Towards the end of the seventeenth century, the annual rate of capital formation in England may have reached 6 per cent of national income in a very prosperous year, such as 1688, but on average it did not exceed 3 per cent.
- This rate did not perceptibly increase during the first half of the eighteenth century; then it rose, perhaps reaching 5 or 6 per cent on the eve of the War of American Independence.
- There was an indisputable increase in the rate of investment during the last two decades of the eighteenth century, but it is very unlikely that it exceeded 1 or 1.5 per cent of national income, so that around 1800 this rate was not higher than 6 or 7 per cent.
- This rate probably fell during the Napoleonic Wars, and during the post-war depression.
- It was only from the mid-1830s that any clear change took place in the level and structure of investment, as a result of the building of railways and of the generalisation of machine technology; the investment proportion rose rapidly, to reach a permanent 10 per cent in the 1850s.

All in all, the change had been a gradual one and the Industrial Revolution had been achieved with an average net rate of investment a good deal lower than 10 per cent of national income.

[15] P. Deane, 'Capital Formation in Britain before the Railway Age', *Economic Development and Cultural Change*, IX, 3, April 1961, pp. 352–68; this article is reprinted in Crouzet, *Capital Formation*, pp. 94–118; P. Deane and W. A. Cole, *British Economic Growth, 1688–1959: Trends and Structure* (Cambridge, 1962; Second edition, 1967); P. Deane, *The First Industrial Revolution* (Cambridge, 1965); see also, 'New Estimates of Gross National Product for the United Kingdom 1830–1914', *The Review of Income and Wealth*, series 14, no. 2, June 1968, pp. 99–100; 'The Role of Capital in the Industrial Revolution', *Explorations in Economic History*, X, 4, Summer 1973, pp. 349–64. Miss Deane has added different nuances to her conclusions in each of these studies.

The success enjoyed by Phyllis Deane's theses derived in part from their being in harmony with the results of other empirical studies on several advanced countries in the nineteenth century; these studies had also revealed a very gradual increase in the rates of capital formation; no direct, simple or uniform relationship emerged between the level of capital formation and the rate of growth of production or of incomes, and no proof of a cause and effect relation between these two variables. In addition, econometric analyses showed that the increase in physical capital inputs had been responsible for only a limited fraction of the recent growth of output in advanced economies. Finally, theorists questioned the central role which had formerly been attributed to capital formation in economic growth; investment appeared as only one of the sources of the latter (emphasis was placed upon the 'residual', that is, scientific and technical progress, the development of education), and the accumulation of capital was therefore reckoned to be of less importance than its utilisation, than improvements in its quality and efficiency. Reversing the causal relation between savings and growth, some economists even maintained that it was this latter which drew investment along behind it.[16]

Under these circumstances, Rostow's hypothesis regarding a sudden and dramatic acceleration in capital formation at the end of the eighteenth century was abandoned, although actually he had been quite correct to posit a doubling in the proportion of investment – with the proviso that it be regarded as happening during the Industrial Revolution in the extended sense of the term, between the middle of the eighteenth century and the middle of the nineteenth.[17] Nevertheless, the Industrial Revolution is no longer seen as the outcome of a significant acceleration in the accumulation of capital, nor is a high proportion of investment seen as a necessary condition for 'modern' economic growth.

However, Phyllis Deane's views have never been universally accepted. Her starting point – a rate of investment of 5 per cent in good years, at the end of the seventeenth century and at the beginning of the eighteenth century – is an important element in her argument; yet it rests upon her interpretation of data furnished by Gregory King, which are quite plausible but not wholly reliable. Furthermore, during

[16] See Crouzet, *Capital Formation*, pp. 16–19, for detailed references to studies by S. Kuznets, R. M. Solow, E. F. Denison, etc.

[17] J. R. T. Hughes stressed that Rostow had only made a mistake as regards timing; 'Measuring British Economic Growth', *Journal of Economic History*, XXIV, 1, March 1964, p. 71.

the International Conference of Economic History at Munich, in 1965, Simon Kuznets disputed this figure; employing arguments which are arithmetical and logical, but none the less striking, he suggested that the net rate of investment in pre-industrial England should be somewhere between 1 and 2.8 per cent of national product.[18] If this was indeed the case, the second half of the eighteenth century would have seen an increase in this rate which was greater than that posited by Phyllis Deane, even if the rate did not exceed 5 or 6 per cent around 1800.

At this same conference, Sidney Pollard criticised Phyllis Deane's sources and methods (especially her use of doubtful estimates taken from eighteenth- and nineteenth-century authors), and then went on to present his own estimates of the gross formation of capital in Britain, sector by sector, and for a number of periods. Pollard arrived at rates of capital formation which are clearly higher than those of Deane and, in his view, closer to those posited by Lewis and Rostow: 6.5 per cent around 1770, 9 per cent in 1790–3 (boom years, admittedly), 11 per cent in 1830–5. He therefore maintained that the investment effort of the British economy during the Industrial Revolution (especially at its beginning) and the burden that the people had therefore to bear, had been underestimated.[19] Actually, Pollard's calculations, although more detailed and systematic than those of Deane, are often overgenerous and tend to overestimate. Furthermore, he has calculated gross investment and its proportion to gross national income, so that his conclusions do not completely 'rehabilitate' Lewis and Rostow's views, for they had always discussed the net rate of capital formation. Nevertheless, Pollard's labours give some reason to suppose that Phyllis Deane's estimates may well have been somewhat too low. One should add that Pollard had started an ambitious team research project on capital formation in Britain from 1750 to 1850, employing a quantitative approach and exploiting primary sources, with the target of calculating rates of investment on more solid foundations than had been the case before. A conference was held at Sheffield in 1969, and its

[18] S. Kuznets, 'Capital Formation in Modern Economic Growth (and Some Implications for the Past)', *Troisième conférence internationale d'histoire économique. Munich, 1965* (Paris–The Hague, 1968), vol. I, pp. 15–53; see in particular, pp. 30–5. On the other hand, Kuznets has maintained that the *gross* rate of capital formation was high in traditional economies, because of the short lifespan of physical capital, whose rapid deterioration required frequent repairs and replacements.

[19] S. Pollard, 'The Growth and Distribution of Capital in Great Britain, *c.* 1770–1870', *Troisième Conférence*, vol. I, pp. 335–65; see below pp. 160, n. 28, and 168–9, about other works by Pollard.

proceedings constitute a very useful volume,[20] which stresses, *inter alia*, the serious methodological difficulties which were encountered. Sources would seem to be absent for some branches of the economy, while for others they are over plentiful but scattered (for example, the archives of canal companies, of turnpike trusts, and of enclosure commissions); furthermore, they are awkward to use, because of the often archaic methods of book-keeping employed, which, for instance, do not allow one to distinguish between maintenance and new works. A study of this nature has to proceed on the basis of samples, and large numbers of extrapolations are necessary in order to construct aggregate series. Admittedly, a new method, microeconomic in nature, has been perfected by S. D. Chapman, for a study of fixed capital formation in the cotton industry; it relies upon the use of numerous fire insurance policies covering textile factories, which provide valuations of buildings and machinery. Sources of this nature, together with the method used in exploiting them, have been considered by some historians with reservations, but the results obtained by Chapman, along with those of David Jenkins (for the West Riding wool industry), are of great interest. However, they have not yet been integrated into general studies on capital formation and, besides, only a few branches of industry lend themselves to researches of this nature.[21]

As regards the overall problem of capital formation, the debate remained at a standstill for a number of years; then, in 1978, with the publication of volume VII of the *Cambridge Economic History of Europe*, a far more thorough treatment of the problem, by Charles Feinstein, appeared.[22] This study is extremely detailed, painstaking and systematic; it calculates, sector by sector, both the stock of capital in Great

[20] J. J. P. Higgins and S. Pollard (eds.), *Aspects of Capital Investment in Great Britain, 1750–1850. A Preliminary Survey* (London, 1974). See also note 172.

[21] S. D. Chapman, 'Fixed Capital Formation in the British Cotton Manufacturing Industry. 1770–1815', *The Economic History Review*, XXIII, 2, August 1970, pp. 235–66 (reprinted, with additions and a synopsis of a discussion, in Higgins and Pollard, *Aspects of Capital Investment*, pp. 57–119; Chapman has made use of insurance policies in several later works); D. T. Jenkins, *The West Riding Wool Textile Industry, 1770–1835: A Study of Fixed Capital Formation* (Edington, 1975); D. T. Jenkins and K. G. Ponting, *The British Wool Textile Industry, 1770–1914* (London, 1982), pp. 32–9.

[22] C. H. Feinstein, 'Capital Formation in Great Britain', in P. Mathias and M. M. Postan (eds.), *The Cambridge Economic History of Europe*, vol. VII, *The Industrial Economies: Capital, Labour and Enterprise*, Part I (Cambridge, 1978), pp. 28–96 (see in particular Table 28, p. 91); see also his chapter 'Capital accumulation and the industrial revolution', in R. Floud and D. McCloskey (eds.), *The Economic History of Britain since 1700, Volume I: 1700–1860* (Cambridge, 1981), pp. 128–42. Feinstein's calculations, unlike those of Phyllis Deane, are based upon series at constant prices (of 1851–1860).

Britain for four different dates, between 1760 and 1860, and the ten-yearly averages for investment flows during this period. Feinstein's conclusion is that, from the 1760s to the 1850s, the increase in the volume of investment was very large (roughly speaking, it increased by ten times), but most of the time it simply followed the growth of national income, so that the investment proportion (calculated in relation to GNP) only changed appreciably between the 1760s and the 1790s, when it climbed from 8 per cent (1761–70) to 10 per cent (1771–80), then to 14 per cent (1791–1800); it fell back to 10 per cent during the Napoleonic wars (1801–10), but from 1811–20 to 1851–60, it remained stable at 13–14 per cent; it was not affected by the building of the railways, for this was carried through by diverting savings from house-building. As Feinstein has stressed, his analysis by and large confirms the earlier hypotheses of Lewis and Rostow, for it shows that there was indeed a rise in the investment proportion at the beginning of the Industrial Revolution (all the more so, given that in his opinion this rate had been less than 8 per cent prior to 1760 and had increased in the 1740s and 1750s).

Feinstein's study was of such high quality that it seemed to close the debate which had been initiated a quarter of a century before; indeed, Phyllis Deane acknowledged that his estimates for capital formation were the best that had been produced.[23] Nevertheless, an article by N. F. R. Crafts has reopened the debate. Crafts does not dispute Feinstein's calculations of the volume of investment in Britain, but he charges him with having compared these figures to a series for national income at constant prices, taken from Deane and Cole, which, according to Crafts, underestimates British national income. Crafts has produced new calculations of the investment proportion, based upon Feinstein's data on capital formation on the one hand, and upon his own, new calculations of national product on the other. The relation between gross domestic investment and gross domestic product would have developed as follows: 1700: 4 per cent; 1760: 5.7 per cent; 1780: 7 per cent; 1801: 7.9 per cent; 1811: 8.5 per cent; 1831: 11.7 per cent. The sharp rise in the investment proportion which, according to Feinstein, had occurred between the 1760s and the 1790s, is thus very much reduced, so that sixty rather than thirty years would

[23] Phyllis Deane, in the 1981 edition of *The First Industrial Revolution*, p. 167, note 1. However, Larry Neal, in *Journal of Economic History*, XXXIX, 3, September 1979, p. 757, observed that Feinstein's calculations for the eighteenth century could have been on the high side, on account of a bias occasioned by his use of a Paasche index for the prices of capital goods.

be needed for this ratio to increase by five points; this, as Crafts emphasises, is a return, by and large, to the positions of Deane and Cole.[24]

These 'variations' may make the reader feel somewhat sceptical; all the more so, perhaps, given Feinstein's admirably honest and modest admission that his estimates are conjectural. It is probable, indeed, that, for sheer want of the necessary sources and data, calculation of the exact investment proportion in the eighteenth century and in the early nineteenth will also remain akin to the quest for the Holy Grail. Be this as it may, the important point is that the Industrial Revolution did not demand of Britain, at the national level, massive and prolonged exertions of saving, for the proportion of national income which was invested was relatively low, even if one opts for the upper estimate, that is to say, Feinstein's figures.[25]

This state of affairs had been something of a surprise to Deane and Cole themselves, but upon reflection it seems quite normal: for a long time, the technological and structural changes which were associated with the Industrial Revolution and which rendered industry more capital intensive were concentrated in a small number of branches, such as cotton spinning and the primary iron industry; these latter, in spite of their rapid growth, only made a minor contribution to national product and they were not in a position to make a serious impact upon the aggregate rate of saving. It is true that there was a very rapid increase of investment in these branches, at rates of 5 or 6 per cent per year, and perhaps more.[26] This is important, for economists have stressed the role played by the increase in the stock of capital, which, because it embodies innovations, could well be more significant than the aggregate investment proportion, with which the controversy whose history we are sketching here has perhaps been too much concerned. Besides, a more efficient and more productive use of savings can have more influence upon growth than a greater propensity to save; now, the largest part of investment in industry was

[24] N. F. R. Crafts, 'British Economic Growth, 1700–1831: A Review of the Evidence', *The Economic History Review*, XXXVI, 2, May 1983, pp. 194–5. On the other hand, Crafts accepts Feinstein's notion that there was a rise in the investment proportion in the first half of the eighteenth century.

[25] According to Feinstein, there was a sharp increase in the investment proportion during a fairly short period at the end of the eighteenth century. I will reconsider below the question of short-term fluctuations in investment.

[26] See Chapman, 'Fixed Capital Formation', pp. 247, 252.

concentrated in branches whose productivity was rapidly increasing and whose profitability was high.

Of course, one should also bear in mind that the greater part of investment was made in non-industrial sectors of the economy, namely, agriculture, transportation, housing and other social overheads. According to Charles Feinstein, the share of industry and commerce in fixed capital formation rose from 20 per cent in 1761–70, to 29 per cent in 1811–20 and 36 per cent in 1851–60.[27]

Furthermore, within industry itself, investment in fixed capital represented only a relatively small share of capital formation; recent studies of the structure of capital in firms, and of the relation between fixed and circulating capital, have shown that the second continued, in spite of the rise of the factory system, to be predominant. Admittedly, the appearance, for the first time in the history of industry, of large concentrations of fixed capital was a crucial aspect of the Industrial Revolution, but one ought not to exaggerate either its precocity or its rapidity. The proportion of fixed capital to total assets remained for a long time very low, even in the most mechanised undertakings.[28]

It is easy enough to account for this situation. Given the nature of technology at the beginning of the Industrial Revolution, fixed plant was relatively simple and cheap. Thus, around 1795, a spinning jenny could be bought for six pounds, a mule for thirty pounds; one could buy a small steam engine for one hundred and fifty to two hundred pounds, a large one for five hundred to eight hundred pounds. The water-powered spinning-mills, according to Arkwright's system, were worth from three thousand to five thousand pounds in the 1780s (and a small, horse-driven spinning-mill less than a thousand pounds); only the large steam-driven spinning-mills, which first appeared in the 1790s, were worth as much as ten or fifteen thousand pounds. Even in the iron industry, the building of average size works, with one or two blast furnaces and a forge, did not require a substantial quantity of capital. Moreover, recent studies have stressed that industrialists going into business could have recourse to a number of expedients in

[27] Feinstein, 'Capital Formation in Great Britain', Table 29, p. 93. In 1961, Deane had suggested that, at the end of the eighteenth century, the annual flow of new capital in the main industries did not exceed two million pounds sterling, or around 1 per cent of national income.

[28] See S. Pollard's two pioneering articles, 'Capital Accounting in the Industrial Revolution' (1963) and 'Fixed Capital in the Industrial Revolution in Britain' (1964), both of which were reprinted in Crouzet, *Capital Formation*, pp. 119–61; also M. M. Edwards, *The Growth of the British Cotton Trade, 1780–1815* (Manchester, 1967), pp. 213–14, 257–9, Appendix E, Tables 1–7.

order to limit their expenditure on fixed capital. Thus, instead of building a brand new factory, they could convert an existing building, such as a corn-mill, a barn, a warehouse or some dwellings (this was a common practice at the end of the eighteenth century in the cotton industry); they could also rent a factory, or part of one, instead of buying it outright; they could likewise rent – or buy second-hand – the machinery they required.[29] Many firms therefore had quite modest beginnings, and then gradually increased the scale of their operations, enlarging their buildings and buying new machinery. It was actually rare for very large 'lumps' of investment to be indispensable. All in all, during the first stages of the Industrial Revolution, the need for investment in fixed capital was modest, the threshold for entry in industry – factory industry included – was low, especially in textiles (although the emergence of a number of giant firms, with assets running into tens or even hundreds of thousands of pounds, should not be forgotten). The total sums of money which provided 'the material envelope' for the new technology were thus relatively small.

These observations regarding the British economy's capital requirements have of course influenced discussions as to whether there was a shortage or an abundance of capital during the Industrial Revolution. The shortage thesis, which had been in favour during the inter-war period, has now been abandoned, and scholars tend rather to emphasise that England, even prior to its industrialisation, was a 'rich' country. From the time of the Restoration on, per capita income was higher than that of many present-day Third World countries, and its economy generated a surplus which was available for investment. The ease with which London was rebuilt after the Great Fire of 1666, the ease, likewise, with which numerous joint-stock companies were floated at the end of the century, shows that there was not an actual shortage of capital; that is, rather, that there was a lack of opportunities for profitable investment, a situation which may have persisted into the early eighteenth century. As far as the latter is concerned, we have overwhelming proof of England's wealth in this period, which is especially clearly reflected in the huge loans which were successfully launched by government in order to finance its wars, and which amounted to seven hundred and seventy million pounds between 1688

[29] Feinstein, 'Capital Accumulation', p. 133, shows that investment in machinery, although increasing very fast, was less than the expenses involved in the construction of the buildings in which the machines were set up.

and 1815. This figure may be compared with the highest estimate we have of the total cost of setting up a system of inland navigation in Great Britain between 1750 and 1830, namely, twenty million pounds. After 1815, Great Britain's plentiful supply of capital is again proven by exports of capital abroad, which occurred on a considerable scale from the 1820s on.

Given these circumstances, recent years have seen a consensus among economic historians to the effect that Great Britain did not suffer, either before or during the Industrial Revolution, a shortage, whether absolute or relative, of capital, such as might have checked its economic growth. We have gone back to the view, held by 'very old economic historians', that there was in fact an 'abundance' of capital. It is true, however, that this is no longer regarded as the decisive cause of the Industrial Revolution, but only as a permissive factor, for capital was, relatively, even more abundant, and rates of interest lower, in eighteenth-century Holland, which did not undergo an economic revolution.

However, the notion that, Britain being a rich country, aggregate savings were more than sufficient to finance the Industrial Revolution, is, in some respects, an ahistorical one. Indeed, institutional and social obstacles could well have blocked or slowed down the mobilisation of savings for productive ends. Actually, in eighteenth-century England, a very large flow of income went into the hands of the upper class, which had a high propensity to consume, to spend in pursuit of a life of luxury and pleasure; a large share of its personal savings was used to acquire durable consumer goods, to build country houses, to travel and to subscribe to government loans; such behaviour did not lead to capital formation and did not create savings in the sense of modern national accounting. On the other hand, though, large landowners carried out productive investments involving substantial sums of money, mainly in agriculture and transportation.

At any rate, economic historians have in recent years accorded a great deal of importance to the problem of capital supply and capital mobility, which involves the conduits or channels, the financial intermediaries, the procedures and mechanisms through which the gaps between savers and investors were closed.

The question of the 'sources of capital' is studied in detail in the second part of this chapter; it stresses the predominance of 'internal' financing of industry. During the Industrial Revolution, the majority of firms involved were initially launched with a quite modest capital, which had been accumulated in traditional industry or in the trading of the raw materials or finished products of such industry; their development was made possible by the regular reinvestment of profits. All in all retained profits were the main source of long-term capital, and 'external' capital, provided by landowners, overseas merchants, banks etc., only played a supporting role.[30] Here I shall only stress the role of commercial credit and pose the problem of the relations between banks and industry.

Since long-term investment in buildings and machinery was relatively small, the industrialists' main need, in quantitative terms, was short-term credit to finance inventories. They were able, however, to take advantage of the elaborate machinery of credit which had been in existence prior to the Industrial Revolution; by inserting themselves in it, they were able to acquire circulating capital, which allowed them to invest their own resources in fixed capital. Industrialists could buy their raw materials on credit from merchants and, although they themselves had to grant credit to their clients, they could either have their drafts on the latter discounted, or get advances from commission agents to whom they consigned their goods. It was also fairly common for young firms to benefit as well from accommodation made available by established merchants who were patronising them. They were thus able to start in business with a very small capital of their own, which was inferior to that they actually employed. Some writers, such as S. Pollard, therefore reckon that the 'web of credit' was at the centre of the process of capital accumulation and that merchants, who supplied industry with a large part of its circulating capital, thus played a crucial part in the process.[31] However, one should not exaggerate the importance of commercial credit, for it was very unstable; some authors hint that a firm could actually prosper without having capital resources of its own, but actually this led straight to bankruptcy.

30 These conclusions, which I had formulated in 1962, in the main hold good today; however, Edwards, p. 214, maintains that the ploughing back of profits was not as important a factor in the growth of firms as I had supposed, and that those which wished to develop had other ways of gaining access to funds. Likewise, M. W. Flinn, in *The Origins of the Industrial Revolution* (London, 1966), pp. 44–5, has pointed out that most of the new investment made in industry at the end of the eighteenth century occurred in new industries, such as cotton, which therefore could not have been financed by a ploughing back of profits. To which one can reply that much of the capital involved came from neighbouring branches of industry, organised on the domestic system.

31 Pollard, 'Fixed Capital', in Crouzet, *Capital Formation*, pp. 154–61; 'The Growth and Distribution of Capital', pp. 356, 358–61, 365.

As for the problem of relations between the British banking system of the eighteenth century and industry, I myself, taking my cue in the main from L. S. Pressnell's study[32] had stressed in 1962 that these relations had in fact been closer than was generally believed. Since then, Rondo Cameron has taken the argument much further[33] and scholars have tended to stress the by no means negligible role played by banks in capital formation. Admittedly, the traditional view that English banks did not finance long-term investment remains by and large valid, but with some serious qualifications. As Peter Mathias has observed, 'as more case histories reveal the number of instances in which this generalization about the banks not financing industrial investment was broken, the generalization may itself come under suspicion.'[34] Indeed, we now have knowledge of numerous direct loans from banks to industrialists, loans which – though occasional – were crucial for the survival or expansion of the firms which received them; moreover, the renewal or prolongation of short-term advances agreed to by the banks turned them fairly often into long-term loans. None the less, English banks mainly dealt in short-term credit, but the emphasis which has recently been placed upon circulating capital and trade credit gives an added importance to this type of financing, which was the banks' main contribution to capital formation. On the one hand, the banks, by means of discounts, overdrafts and short-term advances, released the industrialists' own capital so that it might be used for long-term investment, and this made it easier for them to expand. On the other, by the credit they gave to merchants, who were themselves both suppliers and customers of industry, the banks underpinned the whole system of trade credit and the circulation of bills of exchange. Finally, it was through the mediation of banks that the savings of large landowners, and of the social groups close to them (lawyers, clergymen, well-to-do widows), were activated, injected into the circulation of credit and used in part for capital formation. However, it should not be forgotten that the integration of the country's financial system and even the setting up of the network of country banks happened

[32] L. S. Pressnell, *Country Banking in the Industrial Revolution* (Oxford, 1956).

[33] R. Cameron, and others, *Banking in the Early Stages of Industrialization. A Study in Comparative Economic History* (London, 1967), especially, pp. 18, 41, note 45, where he criticises me for being over-cautious in my conclusions.

[34] P. Mathias, *The First Industrial Nation. An Economic History of Britain 1700–1914. Second edition* (London, 1983), p. 158; this work contains a number of excellent pages on the problems treated here (pp. 130–6, 156–9).

relatively late, at the end of the eighteenth century; indeed, the banking system was 'a response to industrialization rather than a causal factor, the banks were capital-servicing rather than capital-forming institutions' (B.L. Anderson).[35]

In spite of the importance of circulating capital and short-term credit, long-term financing could still be a problem for industrialists. This accounts for historians' attention to the eighteenth century capital market, which, although 'imperfect', was nevertheless very active. The London market has been studied by P. G. M. Dickson, in his important work, *The Financial Revolution in England*.[36] It existed only in embryonic form at the end of the seventeenth century, but it greatly extended, and it became less imperfect, more efficient in the course of the eighteenth century; however, its principal function was the financing of the National debt, both consolidated and short-term. Dickson has shown that government funds constituted the basis of the pyramid of commercial credit; yet the London capital market did not make any significant, direct contribution to capital formation, perhaps in part because of the Bubble Act.[37] A more important phenomenon, as far as the present study is concerned, though one that is still not well known, is the rise of provincial financial markets, which were largely independent, were fuelled by local savings and served the local economies. Most of the capital for turnpike trusts, canals, docks and bridges companies was raised locally, through the flotation of shares, bonds and annuities. There were also local markets for mortgage loans, which have been studied, as far as Lancashire is concerned, by B. L. Anderson. He has shown that the practice of lending and borrowing against mortgage was very widespread in that county from the beginning of the eighteenth century, and in all classes of society; the intermediaries in such transactions were often local attorneys, who forged the mortgage market into something approaching a rudimentary capital market, which was both active and flexible, and which undoubtedly did much to develop the region, by mobilising dormant savings and by making it easier to borrow. Anderson therefore reckoned that the Financial Revolution of the beginning of the eighteenth century was not restricted to London and to the 'public'

35 B. L. Anderson, 'The Attorney and the Early Capital Market in Lancashire' (1969), reprinted in Crouzet, *Capital Formation*, pp. 223–55, see p. 253.

36 P. G. M. Dickson, *The Financial Revolution in England. A Study in the Development of Public Credit, 1688–1756* (London, 1967).

37 See below, p. 187.

sector of government loans, but also occurred in the provinces of England.[38] These markets of course continued for a long time to be imperfect; personal relations and family connections played a crucial part in them. Savings were specific, capital heterogeneous and investment was highly localised; capital did not move freely from one market to another, and there were several rates rather than *one* rate of interest.

Altogether, recent studies confirm that the supply of capital was not a serious problem in eighteenth- and early nineteenth-century England, for it was endowed with a sophisticated and innovating financial system.[39] More generally, such studies have tended to bridge the gap, whose existence had been assumed for the period of the Industrial Revolution, between industry and the other sectors of the economy. This is one aspect of the broader tendency to see the Industrial Revolution as a phenomenon of 'balanced growth' and of gradual advance on a broad front, rather than as a sudden breakthrough in a limited sector. The formation of industrial capital is thus linked to a previous accumulation within the economy as a whole, so that the small, disjointed pools of capital of which Postan had written in 1935, were not so few, meagre or isolated as he had implied; indeed, they were united by a network of conduits, which made it possible for the great landowners' wealth to be invested in the improvement of agriculture and transportation, and that of merchants to irrigate industry. It is true, however, that there is still much debate over the problem of intersectorial flows of capital, especially towards and away from the land.

Peter Mathias has written that it is impossible to judge whether the net flow of capital was towards or away from the land. On the one hand, new recruits, drawn from trade, industry and the professions, were continually swelling the ranks of the landed classes; they were investing in the purchase of land the fortunes they had won in business. On the other hand, a part of the landlords' and tenant-farmers' savings were invested in transport, or else were integrated, through the banks'

[38] See B. L. Anderson, 'The Attorney and the Early Capital Market in Lancashire', and his other publications (drawn from an unpublished thesis), namely, 'Provincial Aspects of the Financial Revolution of the Eighteenth Century', *Business History*, XI, 1, January 1969, pp. 11–22; 'Money and the Structure of Credit in the Eighteenth Century', *Ibid.*, XII, 2, July 1970, pp. 85–101. These studies show that small investors played a far more important role than has often been supposed.

[39] This does not of course mean that numerous firms did not experience difficulties in getting hold of the capital they needed.

intermediation, in the circulation of credit.[40] Sir John Habakkuk, however, has stressed that landowners were pre-eminently consumers and borrowers, who, moreover, only rarely borrowed for the purpose of productive investment; their economic activities should therefore not be overestimated. Nevertheless, Habakkuk allows that there were a fair number of exceptions and that the relatively small sums which landlords invested productively may in fact have played a crucial role, especially in the construction of a transport system which was a prerequisite of industrial progress.[41] Yet, as far as industry is concerned, one is tempted to keep to Postan's view that a very small part of the wealth of rural England 'found its way into the new industrial enterprises.'[42]

This problem of the flow of capital between agriculture and the rest of the economy leads on naturally to a discussion of the marxist views on 'primitive accumulation', as they assign to changes in agriculture a leading part in the rise of industrial capitalism in eighteenth-century England, that is, in the Industrial Revolution. But Marx's 'primitive accumulation' (which is termed 'primitive' because it precedes capitalist accumulation and is not the outcome of the capitalist mode of production) is wholly different from the accumulation or formation of capital as it is understood by non-marxist economists (nevertheless, a number of authors, considering themselves as marxist without ever having read Marx, are unaware of the difference and employ the term 'primitive accumulation' without knowing what it means and sometimes distorting it seriously). It refers to the historical process by which the polarisation is achieved between the owners of the means of production on the one hand, and the 'free' workers ('free' in the sense of being deprived of any rights over these means of production) on the other; the basis for this process was the expropriation of the peasant through the enclosures of the sixteenth and eighteenth centuries, which led to the triumph of capitalist agriculture and created a landless proletariat, available for employment in factories. Marx did admittedly mention other aspects of primitive accumulation also, namely, the looting and exploitation of colonies, the slave trade, the 'trade

40 Mathias, *The First Industrial Nation*, pp. 52–3, 60, 131.

41 See, in particular, H. J. Habakkuk, 'Economic Functions of English Landowners in the Seventeenth and Eighteenth Centuries', in H. G. J. Aitken (ed.), *Explorations in Enterprise* (Cambridge, Mass., 1965), pp. 330–40; 'La Disparition du paysan anglais', *Annales ESC*, XX, 4, July–August 1965, pp. 661–3.

42 Postan, 'Recent Trends', in Crouzet, *Capital Formation*, p. 72.

wars' between European states, and the creation of the national debt – all factors which were operative in late seventeenth-century England and which increased and concentrated capital, merchant capital in particular. But Marx stresses that this latter is incapable by itself of achieving the transition from the feudal mode of production to capitalism, the necessary condition for the latter being the expropriation of the peasantry.[43] 'Primitive accumulation' being very different in nature from capital formation, which is the topic of the present chapter, there is no need to discuss it at length; let me simply point out that the transformations undergone by English agriculture did indeed concentrate great wealth in the hands of the landed oligarchy, but that a small part of it only was 'converted' into industrial capital, contrary to what certain marxists have, without providing any proofs, asserted;[44] as to the relation of cause and effect between the formation of a rural proletariat and the Industrial Revolution, this has yet to be proved.

Another controversy, which is not without its ideological undertones either, concerns the relations between capital formation and the standard of living of the British people, and of the labouring classes in particular. For a long time, it had been supposed that the Industrial Revolution had required considerable investment (and, if one follows Lewis and Rostow's account, a sharp increase in the percentage of national income that was invested); since it had often at the same time been presumed that there was a relative shortage of capital, the conclusion was that this investment effort could not have been carried through without a heavy pressure upon the level of consumption by the working class. Authors on the left and on the right had been agreed on this point, with the former condemning the greed and harshness of the employers, and the latter stressing that this system of forced saving had been an indispensable requirement for the success of the Industrial Revolution, which subsequently had made possible a rise in the standard of living. The most elaborate exposition of these views was published by S. Pollard, in 1958; he maintained that the British

[43] K. Marx, *Capital. A Critical Analysis of Capitalist Production* (London, 1974 edition), Book 1, Part VIII, chs. xxvi–xxxii, especially pp. 667–71 and 686–716.

[44] For example, J. Saville, 'Primitive Accumulation and Early Industrialization in Britain', *The Socialist Register* (London, 1969), pp. 250–67. There is a more sophisticated marxist analysis in M. Dobb, *Papers on Capitalism, Development, Planning* (London, 1967), pp. 26–30, where he attempts to identify the link – which is missing in Marx – between primitive accumulation and capital formation during the Industrial Revolution.

economy had had to support an 'exceptional burden' and a 'formidable stress', in order to accumulate the real resources that were necessary for investment; this accumulation could only have been achieved at the expense of consumption, and capital formation had absorbed all increases in production, from which the workers had not benefited. Pollard regarded this as providing an explanation as to why the standard of living of the working class had risen so slowly in the course of the Industrial Revolution, for the first two generations which had lived through it had to be sacrificed to the imperatives of growth.[45] Other authors, such as W. A. Lewis, W. W. Rostow and, from a different point of view, Eric Hobsbawm, did revive the classical economists' model, according to which growth demands a redistribution of incomes at the expense of wage-earners, who are merely consumers, and to the advantage of those classes which reap the profits, thanks to which the latter accumulate savings and therefore invest; the benefits arising from the increase in production went to these classes and, as a consequence, the workers' standard of living remained stagnant or even declined.[46]

These interpretations depended upon the postulate that there had been a large and rapid increase in the investment proportion. They became less credible after Phyllis Deane's calculations, which suggested that this increase had in fact been slow and gradual, so that it could no longer be an a priori reason for a decline or a stagnation in the standard of living of the people. That such a decline had ever occurred was also firmly denied by the proponents of the 'optimistic' school in the controversy over the standard of living; they likewise rejected the idea that there had been a redistribution of the national income to the detriment of wage-earners (one should perhaps add that the rates of profit in industry, although often high, would not have left much of a margin for a substantial rise in wages at the expense of ploughing back). However, Charles Feinstein has made an original contribution in this field also; he has produced figures for per capita consumption, after the appropriate deductions for government expenditure and

[45] S. Pollard, 'Investment, Consumption and the Industrial Revolution', *The Economic History Review*, XI, 2, December 1958, pp. 215–26; also S. Pollard and D. W. Crossley, *The Wealth of Britain 1085–1966* (London, 1968), pp. 181–2, 187.

[46] Lewis, 'Economic Development', pp. 156–7; *Theory of Economic Growth*, pp. 226, 231–6; Rostow, 'The Take-Off into Self-Sustained Growth', pp. 38–40; *Stages of Economic Growth*, pp. 46–50; E. J. Hobsbawm, *Industry and Empire. An Economic History of Britain since 1750* (London, 1968), pp. 51, 56–7, 72.

investment, during the Industrial Revolution. It turns out that this average consumption remained stable (or stagnant, if one prefers), without any appreciable improvement, but without any deterioration either, for some sixty or so years, between the decades 1761–70 and 1811–20; it was only after 1820 that a substantial rise occurred. The working classes therefore had to wait a long time before reaping some benefits of industrialisation (all the more so given that average consumption is not a reliable index of their standard of living, and that Feinstein reckons that there was a redistribution of income to their disadvantage during the Napoleonic Wars). Feinstein has, however, calculated that the rise in the investment proportion was only a minor factor as regards the stagnation of consumption; and the same was true of government expenditure during the wars, for the main factor exerting pressure on the standard of living was the rapid growth of population, 'the unlimited supply of labour' at a subsistence wage, as W. A. Lewis had suggested (which accords with some other studies published in recent years regarding the fall in real wages and the reality of a Malthusian trap at the end of the eighteenth century). We saw above that Crafts had disputed Feinstein's calculations regarding the investment proportion, but, as far as per capita consumption is concerned, his estimates give the same result, namely, stability or stagnation between 1760 and 1820; the only difference is that the subsequent rise is slower in Crafts' reckoning than according to Feinstein.[47] The poverty of the people during the Industrial Revolution cannot be explained in terms of the pressure from investment.

All in all, economic historians have in recent years shown a degree of scepticism regarding the crucial role that had been previously attributed to capital in the beginnings of 'modern' economic growth; they have abandoned the simple neo-classical models, in which increased accumulation of capital led quite naturally to the Industrial Revolution; nor do they believe any more that there was a shortage of capital in the eighteenth century, or a sharp increase in the investment proportion at the end of this same century. The Industrial Revolution was achieved with a rate of investment that can be regarded as quite modest if one considers the level of capital formation in the economy as a whole, and which is really quite low if one only takes industrial capital into account. The relative abundance of capital in eighteenth-

47 Feinstein, 'Capital Accumulation', pp. 135–8; Crafts, 'British Economic Growth', p. 198.

century England, and the increasing facilities for obtaining it (thanks to the progress made by the financial system), are still considered to be important, but simply as a 'permissive' factor and not as a determining cause of the Industrial Revolution. Some authors are indeed tempted to assert an inverse causal relationship between the two phenomena, so that accumulation would be a result rather than a precondition of industrialisation, and capital formation would be a response to the growth of income. Others, in their quest for the origins of the Industrial Revolution, have put the emphasis upon demand rather than upon supply, upon the pressure exerted by demand (in particular, that emanating from the home market) upon the traditional modes of production.[48]

Be this as it may, a crucial aspect of the Industrial Revolution was undoubtedly the increasing efficiency in the use of capital goods (for, in its essence, the substitution of the factory system for the domestic system is a better utilisation of capital), together with the continuous improvement throughout the eighteenth century in the quality of the capital stock; at any moment, this latter had a higher productivity than it had before, as new capital and an increasing proportion of replacement capital embodied new techniques.[49] The unending flow of innovations in the technology, organisation and management of firms, as well as in the financial system itself (which made possible a better allocation of savings vis-à-vis investment requirements) lay at the heart of the Industrial Revolution, which was first and foremost a technical revolution. Recent thinking may have placed too much emphasis upon 'balanced growth', and thereby neglected the decisive role played by a small number of technological breakthroughs occurring at critical points, together with the rapid increase of investment in fixed capital, that is, embodying technical progress, in a few branches of the economy. At any rate, the debate regarding the functional relations between capital formation, economic growth and technological progress is far from being closed.[50]

[48] But these perspectives on demand have been criticised; see p. 261, n. 150.

[49] J. Mokyr, 'Growing-up and the Industrial Revolution in Europe', *Explorations in Economic History*, XIII, 4, October 1976, p. 372, stresses, with good reason, that a large number of elements of the new technology were embodied into new investments, which made capital and technical progress complementary and practically inseparable; and he concludes: 'Nobody, after all, has argued that capital accumulation was dispensable.'

[50] A valuable recent contribution is: Pat Hudson, *The Genesis of Industrial Capital. A Study of the West Riding Wool Textile Industry, c. 1750–1850* (Cambridge, 1986).

II

The sources of capital which were tapped for investing in British industry during the Industrial Revolution will now be investigated. Where did the money come from for the setting up and the development of the undertakings in which technological innovations were applied and 'embodied' – mills where cotton, wool or flax was spun by machinery, coke-using ironworks, engineering shops, etc.? Admittedly, some historians have suggested that this problem is an artificial, or at any rate an insoluble one. They contend that the available data being too contradictory, all that emerges is that the capital which financed the Industrial Revolution came from very varied sources, nay, from all sectors of the economy.[51] However, these different sources are by no means of equal importance and it is not impossible to establish a hierarchy between them; moreover the study of capital formation must include research into the sources of capital. True enough, aggregate quantitative data are not available, and one has to rely mainly on individual cases of business firms, but these do not exist in large numbers and the value of the available sample is uncertain. Only a provisional survey, which attempts to synthesise existing works is possible. It will deal solely with capital formation in industry, basically during the period from 1760 to 1830, with occasional forays on either side of these dates.[52]

A distinction must, at the start, be made between two significantly different aspects of the problem: on the one hand, the origin of the 'initial outlay' which allowed new firms to build up their factories out of nothing, or existing ones (which had started in a small way) to enter large-scale manufacturing; and, on the other hand, the financing of the later expansion of these enterprises.

In both cases we shall distinguish between 'internal' and 'external' sources of capital; on the one hand, capital which came from within industry itself, which was already present there as the Industrial Revolution got under way (it will appear to have played a preponderant part) and on the other hand, capital which had accumulated in other sectors of the economy. Among the former are the capitals which

[51] Ashton, *The Industrial Revolution*, pp. 94–5; C. Wilson, 'The Entrepreneur in the Industrial Revolution in Britain', *History*, XLII, 1957, p. 112.

[52] The choice of 1830 as *terminus ad quem* has the disadvantage of concealing some changes that were becoming apparent at about this time, such as a different part played by banks in financing industry, and the growing number of joint stock companies.

were supplied by craftsmen (*artisans*, in French) or small manufacturers.

Their contribution seems to have been substantial, allowing for the fact that, at the beginning of the Industrial Revolution, the threshold of entry in 'factory' production was relatively low, especially in the textile industry, where even the largest production units were small, the plant rudimentary and inexpensive; consequently the initial outlay involved in setting up a factory was modest – at the end of the eighteenth century a few thousand pounds would finance a substantial cotton mill.[53] In circumstances such as these a large number of industrial enterprises of the second half of the eighteenth century were founded by 'self-made men' of modest origin, on a small initial capital, provided by profits from production on a small scale; and thanks to the rapidity of accumulation – a topic we shall consider later – many of them subsequently experienced a phenomenal expansion.[54] Examples abound, especially in the textile industry. James McConnel came to Lancashire from Scotland in 1781 to be apprenticed to a manufacturer of textile machinery; after working as a journeyman-spinner and having built machines himself, he entered into partnership in 1791 with John Kennedy – whose background and beginnings were the same as his – and two Manchester fustian warehousemen; it was their activities on what was in fact an 'artisan' level that enabled McConnel and Kennedy to save a capital of £1,770 with which they set up on their own account in 1795 – the starting point of their meteoric rise that, twenty years later, made them the largest cotton-spinning firm in Britain. Several other young Scotsmen who came to Lancashire at the same time and also became prominent fine cotton-spinners – James Kennedy, Adam and George Murray – and the Welshman, Robert Owen – had parallel careers; working as artisan machine-makers and mule-spinners, they amassed within a few years the capital to set up proper factories. Thanks to the profits resulting from the strong demand for cotton yarn, many Lancashire artisans, who had installed some of the new spinning machines in their workshops, were able to follow suit during the last twenty years of the

[53] See above, pp. 160–1, and Crouzet, *Capital Formation*, pp. 37–9, 85–8; also D. C. Coleman, *The British Paper Industry, 1495–1860. A Study in Industrial Growth* (Oxford, 1958), pp. 232–3.

[54] On the problem of the 'self-made' man, see P. Mathias, *The First Industrial Nation*, pp. 156–7, and F. Crouzet, *The First Industrialists. The Problem of Origins* (Cambridge, 1985), pp. 126ff. It was not at all easy, however, for a workman or even a small master, to acquire a modest amount of capital – a few pounds or a few dozen pounds.

eighteenth century.[55] In the Peak District, some 'small men', who had started with jennies workshops, were eventually able to have mills with steam-driven mules.[56]

The same pattern can be seen, but at a later date, in the West Riding woollen industry, which retained its essentially artisan structure until the beginning of the nineteenth century. A fair number of woollen mills were established by master-clothiers, who started with scribbling mills to card their own wool and do jobwork for their neighbours, then added some spinning jennies and a few looms. Later on, in the mid nineteenth century, wealthy clothiers set up the first large factories for power-loom weaving. In two or three generations, according to Crump, more than one enterprising family transformed its clothier's warehouse into a huge mill.[57]

Although the iron industry needed much more capital than the textile industry, some large enterprises were also established with funds accumulated in artisan activities. The most striking example is that of the three Walker brothers who set up a small foundry near Sheffield in 1741 and rose gradually from 'workshop' (in 1746 their capital was only £600) to large-scale manufacturing. One could also cite Abraham Darby I who started as an artisan making equipment for malt mills, became a partner in an iron and brass foundry in Bristol and, by selling his share in this business (already a large one), was able to set himself up at Coalbrookdale in 1709; Isaac Wilkinson, who saved enough money as a foundry worker and foreman to set up as an ironmaster in 1740. T. S. Ashton estimates that many of the eighteenth-century ironmasters were former artisans of the secondary metal trades, who had made good. And one stage higher, it was some small ironmasters who supplied the capital for the establishment of several large ironworks – e.g. those of Clyde and Muirkirk in Scotland.[58]

[55] *A Century of Fine Cotton Spinning, 1790–1906. McConnel and Co. Ltd. Ancoats, Manchester* (Manchester, 1906), pp. 8–9; G. W. Daniels, 'The Early Records of a Great Manchester Cotton-Spinning Firm', *Economic Journal*, XXV, 1915, pp. 175–7; also his *The Early English Cotton Industry* (Manchester, 1920), pp. 122, 126–8, 141–2; P. Mantoux, *The Industrial Revolution in the Eighteenth Century*, rev. ed. (London, 1928; trans. from the French), p. 383.

[56] S. D. Chapman, *The Early Factory Masters. The Transition to the Factory System in the Midlands Textile Industry* (Newton Abbot, 1967), pp. 56, 59–60, 92, 216.

[57] W. B. Crump, *The Leeds Woollen Industry, 1780–1820* (Leeds, 1931), p. 26; W. B. Crump and G. Ghorbal, *History of the Huddersfield Woollen Industry* (Huddersfield, 1935), pp. 69, 71, 74, 82, 84, 89, 90.

[58] T. S. Ashton, *Iron and Steel in the Industrial Revolution*, 2nd edn (Manchester, 1951), pp. 25–7, 46–8, 209–10; A. Raistrick, *Dynasty of Iron Founders, The Darbys and Coalbrookdale* (London,

There is also the case of Josiah Wedgwood, who began with no capital at all, worked as a journeyman, then, after two short-lived partnerships, set up on his own in 1759; he amassed a small capital and expanded his business, which enabled him to build the Etruria factory in 1769.[59] In the paper industry one can also find some large enterprises – e.g. the Crompton firm – growing out of small family concerns.[60]

The role of 'artisan' capital was thus quite important,[61] but possibly its importance tended to decrease as technical progress and concentration inevitably raised the threshold of entry into 'factory' industry. However, this happened with significant time-lags between the various branches of industry; in a highly capitalistic industry, like the brewing of porter in London,[62] the threshold may have been beyond the reach of the small entrepreneur by the beginning of the eighteenth century, and, by the end of the century, tens of thousands of pounds were needed to set up an ironworks;[63] nevertheless, this still left a wide field of action open to 'artisan' capital, e.g. such industries as the secondary metal trades. Also, small entrepreneurs could often obtain outside help in order to found large factories. Some of this capital was supplied by wealthier people – the merchant-manufacturers – who were also considerable investors of their own.

As early as the middle of the eighteenth century several branches of British industry were organised on a commercial capitalism basis – the putting-out system – and dominated by powerful merchant-manufacturers. Naturally, these men, who were used to organising and financing production and who provided 'the historical transition', as

1953), pp. 17, 19–20, 23, 26, 50; W. H. Chaloner, 'Isaac Wilkinson, Potfounder', in L. S. Pressnell (ed.), *Studies in the Industrial Revolution. Essays presented to T. S. Ashton* (London, 1960), p. 25; H. Hamilton, *The Industrial Revolution in Scotland* (Oxford, 1932), pp. 165–6; A Birch, *The Economic History of the British Iron and Steel Industry, 1784–1879* (London, 1967), pp. 196–7.

59 R. M. Hower, 'The Wedgwoods: Ten Generations of Potters', *Journal of Economic and Business History*, IV, 1932, pp. 285–8, 291; N. McKendrick, 'Josiah Wedgwood: An Eighteenth Century Entrepreneur in Salesmanship and Marketing Techniques', *The Economic History Review*, 2nd series, XII, 3, April 1960, p. 408.

60 Coleman, pp. 161, 238, 245.

61 With artisan capital, one can connect that of the 'managers', the top employees of large industrialists, who often retired when they had saved enough money to set up on their own. G. Unwin, *Samuel Oldknow and the Arkwrights. The Industrial Revolution at Stockport and Marple* (Manchester, 1924), p. 51, stresses their importance in the cotton industry; T. C. Barker and J. R. Harris, *A Merseyside Town in the Industrial Revolution: St Helens 1750–1900* (Liverpool, 1954), p. 68, in the coal industry.

62 P. Mathias, *The Brewing Industry in England, 1700–1830* (Cambridge, 1959), p. 23.

63 Ashton, *Iron and Steel*, pp. 100, 163; A. H. John, *The Industrial Development of South Wales, 1750–1850. An Essay* (Cardiff, 1950), pp. 35–6.

P. Mantoux wrote, 'between the master-craftsman of the Middle Ages and the modern industrialist',[64] did not hesitate to encourage the rise of the factory system by investing in it the abundant capital at their disposal.[65] The main stimuli for these investments came from the high profitability of mechanised production, and from the desire to ensure a regular supply of semi-finished goods (e.g. cotton yarn) or to control the quality of the products. It is typical that Richard Arkwright should have been given financial backing by two rich merchant-hosiers, Jedediah Strutt of Derby and Samuel Need of Nottingham, who went into partnership with him; they probably provided the greater part of the £13,000 he invested before 1774 to perfect his invention and build his first two mills. A few years later J. Strutt built the spinning mills of Belper and Midford. His cash-book for the years 1780–9 shows the transfer of large sums from his hosiery business to his expanding cotton mills, which his sons made into one of the biggest cotton firms in the country.[66]

A number of merchant-manufacturers of Manchester and the surrounding area followed this example after 1780 by investing in the building of mechanised spinning mills the capital they had acquired as middlemen. Peter Drinkwater was one such, a wealthy manufacturer and exporter of fustians, who built two spinning mills at Northwich and Manchester. Samuel Oldknow was another example; around 1790 he was the first manufacturer of muslins in England – but he operated on the putting-out system. In 1786 he decided to embark on mechanised spinning and he was able to put his idea into practice from 1790 thanks to the huge profits he had made; he built a steam-mill in Stockport and a large water-mill in Mellor. At the same time most of his fellow calico manufacturers in Stockport turned over to spinning.[67]

64 Mantoux, p. 487.

65 The rates of profits and capital accumulation seem to have been high for the merchant-manufacturers during the last quarter of the eighteenth century. S. Oldknow made a fortune in a few years by manufacturing muslins (Unwin, pp. 16, 42, 45). Moreover, before the Industrial Revolution proper, some prototypes of 'factories' – the silk-spinning mills of the first half of the eighteenth century – had been largely financed by merchant-manufacturers of silks and by silk merchants. See W. H. Chaloner, 'Charles Roe of Macclesfield (1715–81): An Eighteenth-Century Industrialist', *Transactions of the Lancashire and Cheshire Antiquarian Society*, LXII (1950–1), pp. 134–5; A. P. Wadsworth and J. de Lacy Mann, *The Cotton Trade and Industrial Lancashire, 1600–1780* (Manchester, 1931), p. 305; Unwin, pp. 23–5, 27.

66 R. S. Fitton and A. P. Wadsworth, *The Strutts and the Arkwrights, 1758–1830. A Study of the Early Factory System* (Manchester, 1958), pp. 1, 47, 50, 60, 63–4, 77–8, 81.

67 W. H. Chaloner, 'Manchester in the Latter Half of the Eighteenth Century', *Bulletin of the John Rylands Library*, vol. 42 (1959), p. 48; also, 'Robert Owen, Peter Drinkwater and the Early

A careful quantitative study has led S. D. Chapman to conclude that investment in cotton spinning mills on Arkwright's techniques before 1800 in the Midlands was characterised by a preponderance of capital supplied by merchants-hosiers and other merchant-manufacturers; things were not different in Lancashire; in the Blackburn area, nearly all manufacturers were former middlemen, chapmen or dealers in linen and cotton cloth.[68]

Capital supplied by merchant-manufacturers played also a crucial part in the creation of the first Scottish cotton-spinning mills; they were the work of such men as David Dale, founder of New Lanark (1786) and two other mills, James Monteith and the Buchanan brothers, who had started as weavers of fine linen in Glasgow or Paisley and then become importers of linen yarn which they put out to domestic weavers.[69]

In the woollen industry the first large mills were nearly all established by wealthy merchant-manufacturers, such as Benjamin Gott, who built the great Bean Ing mill in 1792, again financed by profits he had made as a woollen cloth merchant and as a putter-out. In the next few years several merchants from Leeds, Halifax and Huddersfield followed his example in setting up mills.[70] In the worsted industry the trend was much the same; it was highly capitalistic and had been dominated by rich merchant-manufacturers since the early eighteenth century. An excellent monograph has described the typical case of John Foster: he set up as a putter-out in Queensberry in 1819; his business rapidly prospered and in 1834 he had a capital of £11,185; he began spinning and weaving for himself, at first in a small rented mill, then at Black Dyke Mills which he started to build in 1835.[71]

In the light metal industries, where commercial capitalism was likewise well developed, merchant-manufacturers set up also their

Factory System in Manchester, 1788–1800', *ibid.*, vol. 37 (1954), pp. 85–7; Unwin, pp. 39, 72, 85, 103, 123–5.

68 Chapman, *The Early Factory Masters*, especially pp. 17, 19–20, 23–6, 77, 216; also his 'Fixed Capital Formation in the British Cotton Industry', pp. 248–9; and 'The Peels in the Early English Cotton Industry', *Business History*, XI, 2, July 1969, p. 62.

69 Hamilton, *Industrial Revolution in Scotland*, pp. 124, 126–9, 136–7; M. L. Robertson, 'Scottish Commerce and the American War of Independence', *The Economic History Review*, 2nd series, IX, 1, August 1956, p. 130.

70 Crump, pp. vii, 2, 13, 255; H. Heaton, 'Benjamin Gott and the Industrial Revolution in Yorkshire', *The Economic History Review*, III, 1931, pp. 45–8, 51.

71 E. M. Sigsworth, *Black Dyke Mills. A History of John Foster and Son* (Liverpool, 1958), pp. 137–41, 155, 159, 165, 172–4, 176–7, 218.

own factories, like the one Peter Stubbs established in Warrington in 1802.[72]

The capital provided by merchant-manufacturers thus appears as a very important factor in the birth of the factory textile industries; moreover, they were able to invest on a much larger scale than the artisans, and their intervention partially explains the upsurge of investment (which we shall discuss later) that resulted in the founding of numerous cotton mills in the years following 1783.

Up to now we have been analysing the financial contributions from traditional forms of industry – the artisans and commercial capitalism – at the outset of the Industrial Revolution, but as it gathered momentum, factory industry, not content with financing its own expansion, was soon providing capital for the creation of new enterprises and this transfusion helped the Industrial Revolution to go from strength to strength.[73] Thus Richard Arkwright lent considerable sums to Samuel Oldknow,[74] and the great ironmasters – such as the Darbys, Reynolds and Crawshays – built new ironworks or lent money to their less wealthy colleagues.[75] They also played an important part in financing the first tinplate factories.[76] In other cases, a shift of capital from one industry to another took place: thus the development of coal-mining at the end of the eighteenth century was largely financed by the coal-using industries – the ironmasters, but also in South Wales the copper-smelting industry and, around St Helens, the owners of the Cheshire salt-works.[77]

But in some cases there was no direct link between the industry providing the capital and the one in which it was invested. Thus a large part of the money which Samuel Garbett and John Roebuck invested in the Carron Company came from the profits made by the sulphuric

[72] T. S. Ashton, *An Eighteenth Century Industrialist. Peter Stubbs of Warrington. 1756–1806* (Manchester, 1939), pp. 1, 9, 20, 26–7.

[73] See J. R. Harris' interesting remarks in 'Michael Hughes of Sutton. The Influence of Welsh Copper on Lancashire Business, 1780–1815', *Transactions of the Historic Society of Lancashire and Cheshire*, vol. 101 (1949), p. 162.

[74] Unwin, pp. 85, 140, 156.

[75] John, *Industrial Development of S. Wales*, pp. 31–2; Ashton, *Iron and Steel*, p. 53; Raistrick, pp. 13, 70; J. P. Addis, *The Crawshay Dynasty. A Study in Industrial Organization and Development, 1765–1867* (Cardiff, 1957), p. 158. Between 1753 and 1757, the Coalbrookdale Company founded ironworks at Horsehay and Ketley; later it received large loans from R. Reynolds.

[76] W. E. Minchinton, *The British Tinplate Industry* (London, 1959), pp. 17, 95.

[77] T. S. Ashton and J. Sykes, *The Coal Industry of the Eighteenth Century* (Manchester, 1929), pp. 5–6; E. D. Lewis, *The Rhondda Valley. A Study in Industrial Development from 1800 to the Present Day* (London, 1959), p. 37; John, *Industrial Development of South Wales*, pp. 36, 38; Barker and Harris, pp. 58–61.

acid factory they had founded at Prestonpans in 1749.[78] As for the St Helens Crown Glass Company, founded in 1826 (now Pilkington Brothers), it was mainly financed by Peter Greenall, a member of a rich brewing family, in conjunction with the Pilkington brothers; the latter invested (for £13,000 in three years) the profits of their family distilling business.[79]

The capital, which made possible the creation of large-scale 'factory' industries, came, then, mainly from industry itself. Besides, as T. S. Ashton noted, the technical innovations of the eighteenth century tended – by accelerating production and transport – to free funds which were formerly used as circulating capital (its circulation was, however, very slow) and which could be thus transformed into fixed capital.[80]

The Industrial Revolution was not, however, entirely self-financed, and capital from external sources also made an important contribution in the initial stages. The most important – indeed perhaps the only important – supply of such capital came from commerce, especially from merchants who invested large sums in the industries producing the goods they sold. The most spectacular example is that of the iron merchants and wholesale ironmongers in Bristol and London who played a decisive part in establishing the South Wales iron industry. This region had no industrial tradition and its expansion was due solely to the arrival of entrepreneurs and capital from England; the capital was principally of mercantile origin. Thus, the Cyfarthfa works was built in 1765 by Anthony Bacon who had made his fortune in a variety of enterprises, including iron trading. After his death the works was taken over in 1786–7 by Richard Crawshay, a self-made man who had become a prosperous iron merchant in London, and he was to make it the largest ironworks in Britain. Other works were built by partnerships of ironmasters and merchants, but it was the latter who supplied the greater part of the capital, and often went on to take an active part in the management; the Ebbw Vale and Nantyglo iron-works are examples, as they were financed by the Harford brothers,

[78] R. H. Campbell, *Carron Company* (London and Edinburgh, 1961), pp. 7–10; also 'The Financing of Carron Company', *Business History*, I, 1958, pp. 21–3. On the other hand, cf. A. H. John (ed.), *The Walker Family. Iron Founders and Lead Manufacturers. 1741–1893* (London, 1951), p. iv.

[79] T. C. Barker, *Pilkington Brothers and the Glass Industry* (London, 1960), pp. 30–2, 58–62, 78.

[80] Ashton, *An Economic History of England. The Eighteenth Century* (London, 1955), pp. 90, 100, 110–12.

who were wealthy Bristol Quakers, and likewise the works of Penydarren, Tredegar and Abernant. Iron merchants and ironmasters were also joint financers of the tinplate industry.[81]

In other industries 'merchant' capital, usually from an associated trade, played a much less important, although by no means negligible part. It seems that London coal merchants invested in the Northumberland and Durham coalfields, London and Bristol merchants in the South Wales coal mines; in 1750 the coal magnate in the St Helens area was Sarah Clayton, the daughter of a wealthy Liverpool merchant.[82]

In the textile industries, purely commercial capital was of secondary importance compared with that supplied by merchant-manufacturers. However, the foundation of the largest mechanised flax-spinning firm in Britain was largely financed by merchant capital. It was set up by John Marshall, who financed in part the building of his first mill in 1791 by disposing of the modest linen-draper's business left to him by his father. He subsequently expanded his spinning mill in 1793 by forming a partnership with Thomas and Benjamin Benyon, two rich woollen merchants from Shrewsbury, who subsequently financed the construction of a second mill there by selling their draper's business.[83]

D. C. Coleman points out that in the paper industry a number of businesses were created or taken over and developed with the help of capital provided by stationers – wholesale paper merchants. He mentions particularly the two London stationers, H. and S. Fourdrinier, who used capital from their trading business to finance the development of the 'Fourdrinier' machine (derived from an invention by the Frenchman Robert) which was the starting point of mechanisation within the paper industry (but the Fourdriniers were bankrupted).[84]

In the brewing trade, there was a different pattern of capital movement from commerce to industry; a fair number of enterprises were established or taken over by merchants who dealt in the raw materials of brewing, especially malt merchants.[85]

[81] Addis, pp. 1–12; John, *Industrial Development of S. Wales*, pp. 24–5, 32–5, 116. In 1788 nine out of twenty-five people occupying an 'entrepreneurial position' in the South Wales iron industry were merchants.

[82] E. Hughes, *North Country Life in the Eighteenth Century. The North-East, 1700–1750* (London, 1952), p. 163; John, *Industrial Development of S. Wales*, pp. 26–7; Barker and Harris, pp. 25–7, 46, 50, 53.

[83] W. G. Rimmer, *Marshalls of Leeds, Flax-spinners, 1788–1886* (Cambridge, 1960), pp. 10–14, 22–3, 26–7, 36–41, 44, 55; also Chapman, *Early Factory Masters*, pp. 17, 77, on investment by drapers and mercers in the Midlands cotton industry.

[84] Coleman, pp. 163–9, 179–83, 187, 235–6.

[85] Mathias, *The Brewing Industry*, pp. 255–6.

There were also cases – but one gains the impression that they were relatively scarce – where merchants invested their capital in industries unconnected with their former businesses. The Pleasley cotton-spinning mill in Derbyshire was founded in 1785 by five partners, of whom one was a Nottingham brass merchant and three were drapers. In 1803 three Bristol linen-drapers went into partnership with J. Homfray, a professional ironmaster, to operate the Hirwaun iron-works.[86]

It may seem surprising that there has so far been, in this discussion of 'merchant' capital, no mention of capital accumulated in the colonial trade. Some writers (e.g. Eric Williams) did maintain that the huge profits made in colonial trade were used to finance the Industrial Revolution, which was thus based on colonial exploitation and the slave trade. A. P. Wadsworth asserted also that Liverpool 'fertilised' Lancashire, where 'new branches of capitalist enterprise' were created with the profits of the trade in slaves and colonial produce. H. Hamilton, for his part, claimed that the Glasgow tobacco lords financed the beginnings of the Scottish Industrial Revolution, after the American War of Independence had destroyed the tobacco trade, and diverted their capital into the cotton industry.[87] These are attractive theses, but their authors were unable to provide supporting evidence, and they have been abandoned. In particular, recent research has shown that there was no substantial transfer of capital from the tobacco trade (which, anyway, was not ruined by the independence of the United States) to the Scottish cotton industry ('colonial' capital, on the other hand, played some role in the rise of the iron industry around Glasgow).[88]

As a matter of fact, the fortunes amassed by West India planters and merchants, or by East India nabobs, were used to buy landed estates in Britain or Government stocks, and to make mortgage loans to planters, but not for investment in industry. As. R. Pares neatly remarked, the West India merchants built 'more Fonthills than factories'.[89]

In fact one can find only a very few cases – and these seem

[86] S. Pigott, *Hollins. A Study of Industry. 1784–1949* (Nottingham, 1949), pp. 21–4; John, *Industrial Development of S. Wales*, pp. 31–2, 34.

[87] Wadsworth and Mann, pp. 212, 224; H. Hamilton, pp. 3–5, 120; above, pp. 151–2.

[88] T. M. Devine, *The Tobacco Lords: A Study of the Tobacco Merchants of Glasgow and their Trading Activities, c. 1740–90* (Edinburgh, 1975), pp. 34–48; see also Cameron *et al.*, *Banking in the Early Stages of Industrialization*, p. 65.

[89] K. G. Davies, 'Empire and Capital', *The Economic History Review*, 2nd series, XIII, 1, August 1960, p. 110.

exceptional – of direct investment of 'colonial' capital in the new 'factory' industries. Anthony Bacon admittedly had important colonial interests; it is also worth noting that some Bristol West India merchants set up a copper-smelting works near Swansea in 1737 and that in 1778 the Sirhowy ironworks was established by a group of London tea and spices merchants. There were also important 'East India investors' among the sponsors of the British Cast Plate Glass Manufacturers (1773); and R. Dunmore who, with the Buchanans, set up the Ballindalloch spinning mill, was a former West India merchant, but his is a special case.[90]

All this does not amount to much, but, on the other hand, there is no doubt that the rise of colonial trade influenced indirectly British industry and stimulated its growth by widening its markets and enriching the country. However, as Ashton points out, the Industrial Revolution gathered momentum after 1783, by which time England had lost the thirteen colonies and the sugar islands were on the decline.[91]

As for 'landed' capital, i.e. that of the great landowners, it seems to have played an altogether minor part in financing the Industrial Revolution, with the exception of coal-mining; its contribution was much less important in the eighteenth than in the late sixteenth and early seventeenth century, when the landowners had supplied large funds to industry, and it tended to decline.[92] This withdrawal of landed capital can be explained mainly by competition from other outlets for investment which seemed both safer and equally profitable: agriculture (enclosure and technological progress absorbed vast sums, attracted by the increase in grain prices during the second half of the eighteenth century), turnpike trusts and canal shares, Government stocks. Moreover, technological progress raised the costs of investing in mining or in the metal industries and placed them beyond the reach of the mere gentry, inasmuch as at the same time its consumption expenditures were increasing. It is also possible that there was a psychological block, in that direct involvement in industry was felt to be beneath a gentleman. Eventually the net flow of capital may have been from industry into land-owning, as the newly rich industrialists,

[90] John, *Industrial Development of S. Wales*, pp. 8, 25; Barker and Harris, p. 113; Robertson, p. 130; Devine, p. 180.

[91] Ashton, *An Economic History*, p. 125.

[92] See L. Stone, 'The Nobility in Business, 1540–1640', in *The Entrepreneur. Papers presented at the Annual Conference of the Economic History Society at Cambridge, England, April 1957*, p. 14.

such as Richard Arkwright, Samuel Whitbread I or T. Williams, hastened to buy large landed estates.

Until the eighteenth century large landowners had supplied the iron industry with a large slice of its capital, but during the first half of the century they took an increasingly less active part in production,[93] while continuing to supply part of the fixed capital by leasing blast furnaces, forges and water-mills to the ironmasters. But they subsequently retreated even further and, with one or two exceptions, they seem to have taken no part in the financing of the large ironworks which are typical of the Industrial Revolution.[94] As for the textile industries, investment by landowners seems to have been almost nil, although some instances are recorded in Scotland and in the West Riding. There is also, of course, the strange story of Major John Cartwright and Revolution Mill.[95]

The situation was, however, different in the coal industry, where, throughout the eighteenth century, a large part of the capital was supplied by landowners who themselves exploited the mines, and who included even members of the aristocracy, like the Duke of Bridgewater. Even when some of them preferred to lease the rights of working their deposits to capitalist entrepreneurs, the latter were often of the same social class; the Northumberland–Durham coalfields thus had their colliery gentry. However, even in this industry, a withdrawal of landed capital is noticeable; in the St Helens area it began before 1750; it happened after this date in South Wales, where the landowners who had hitherto dominated the coal industry began to give up working their collieries and leased them to English industrialists or merchants.[96]

It could be possible, however, that industrial entrepreneurs drew from 'landed' sources part of their capital. Some writers have suggested this, pointing out that many eighteenth-century industrialists came from rural families. However, many of them – like Abraham

[93] E.g. R. L. Downes, 'The Stour Partnership, 1726–36. A Note on Landed Capital in the Iron Industry', *The Economic History Review*, 2nd series, III, 1, August 1950, pp. 90–6.

[94] Ashton, *Iron and Steel*, p. 209; John, *Industrial Development of S. Wales*, p. 8; Birch, pp. 86–90.

[95] See W. H. Chaloner, 'The Cartwright Brothers. Their Contribution to the Wool Industry', *Wool Knowledge*, II (1953), p. 18.

[96] Ashton and Sykes, pp. 1–3; Barker and Harris, pp. 24–5, 27, 45; John, *Industrial Development of S. Wales*, pp. 9–10, 36–7; also, his 'Iron and Coal on a Glamorgan Estate, 1700–1740', *The Economic History Review*, XIII, 1943, pp. 93–4, 103. According to D. Spring, 'The English Landed Estate in the Age of Coal and Iron: 1830–1880', *Journal of Economic History*, XI, 1, Winter 1951, pp. 3–24, especially pp. 4–6, 11, 14, 20–1, after 1830 landowners' interest and participation in industrial enterprises revived.

Darby I, R. Crawshay, D. Dale, J. McConnel – left the land early on and obtained no capital from it for their later enterprises. On the other hand, Samuel Whitbread I, son of a rich Bedfordshire yeoman, used the £2,600 inherited from his parents for his initial outlay when he set up as a brewer in 1742; and some yeomen farmers, like Joshua Fielden, combined farming with industry and developed the latter up to the 'factory' level.[97] But it is difficult to believe that income from the land made more than a marginal contribution to their success. My view is that, in the eighteenth century, the ownership or exploitation of a small rural property facilitated the entry of some entrepreneurs into industry and supplied them with some capital (and gave them a means of obtaining more by mortgage); but this entry was only on a small scale – as an artisan or small merchant-manufacturer – so that if these yeomen-industrialists went on to found large enterprises, they did it with capital accumulated through industrial production.[98]

It was accepted for a long time that the English banking system, despite its precocious development, played no direct part in the financing of the Industrial Revolution; recent research has modified this opinion by showing that the banks did often underwrite the expansion of existing concerns, as we shall see later. But as far as helping to found or start off new firms is concerned, L. S. Pressnell supports the traditional negative theory: 'The evidence', he writes, 'is all against it.'[99] The story that Richard Arkwright, on his arrival in Nottingham, managed at first to interest Wright's Bank in his invention and that they some time later withdrew, remains typical.[100] Indeed, the Carron Company received some advances from several Scottish banks in its early years, supposedly on a short-term basis, but it used these partly for building purposes. In the same way, John Marshall, in 1792–3, was allowed an overdraft (in April 1793, £3,783) by Beckett and Co.'s bank.[101] These seem to be isolated instances, however, to be explained perhaps by the personal credit of the beneficiaries who had already a strong local position. But, towards the end of our period,

97 Mantoux, pp. 379–82; Mathias, *The Brewing Industry*, pp. 257, 261; Daniels, *Early English Cotton Industry*, pp. 141–2; also Chapman, 'The Peels', p. 61.

98 Marriages with landowning wives were also advantageous to both M. Boulton and J. Wilkinson. See E. Roll, *An Early Experiment in Industrial Organization, being a History of the Firm of Boulton and Watt, 1775–1805* (London, 1930), pp. 10, 100; Chaloner, 'Isaac Wilkinson', p. 35.

99 Pressnell, *Country Banking*, p. 337.

100 Mantoux, p. 228; Fitton and Wadsworth, p. 63 (but both authors point out that the authenticity of the anecdote is unproven).

101 Campbell, 'Financing of Carron Company', pp. 23–5, 29–30, 33; Rimmer, pp. 37, 55.

when the banking system had developed and consolidated, it was possibly more ready to back new enterprises; thus, in their early years, the Greenall-Pilkington glassworks on the one hand, and the firm of John Foster on the other, were allowed permanent and considerable overdrafts by their local banks.[102]

One last source of capital remains to be considered, which, for want of a better word, we shall call 'Miscellaneous'. I refer to capital provided by members of the professions, by tradesmen, by road hauliers, by builders, by fund-holders, not to mention the very rare instances of foreign capital (i.e. Dutch). Such capital can be glimpsed in copper and coal mining, in the paper industry, and it was also attracted by the boom in cotton-spinning after 1783.[103] It played no important part directly, but entrepreneurs found in it a useful source of supplementary capital and borrowed from relatives, friends and members of their own Nonconformist sects. Such was the case with John Marshall in 1792–3, and W. G. Rimmer comments humorously that old ladies – rich widows or spinsters – were a very convenient source of capital for him. Probably this remark is widely applicable...[104]

It is thus obvious that the founders of 'factory' industries obtained capital from diverse sources, but that these sources were of unequal importance; industry itself supplied most of the capital for its own transformation; commerce provided an important supplementary reservoir, but the part played by landed capital, bank capital and 'miscellaneous' sources seems very small. Within industry the analysis made above confirms the thesis that capital moved from the 'secondary' to the 'primary' or 'basic' industries; commercial capital showed a similar backward motion. Thus we see a flow of capital into the primary iron industry coming from the light metal trades or from iron merchants; then from the primary iron industry into coal-mining. Cotton-spinning mills were similarly financed with funds amassed in the making or merchanting of textile goods.[105] The reasons for this are

102 Barker, pp. 63, 77, 95; Sigsworth, pp. 175–6, 178.

103 Ashton, *An Economic History*, p. 127; also his *The Industrial Revolution*, p. 107; Roll, p. 103; Lord, p. 133; John, *Industrial Development of S. Wales*, p. 27; Barker and Harris, pp. 34–5; Coleman, pp. 160–3; Wadsworth and Mann, p. 495; Mantoux, pp. 376–7; Chapman, *Early Factory Masters*, pp. 21–2, 77, 81, 92–6, 99.

104 Rimmer, pp. 36–7. Admittedly such capital came, in fact, from land or from trade. See also A. J. Robertson, 'Robert Owen and the Campbell Debt, 1810–1822', *Business History*, XI, 1, January 1969, pp. 17–18, on the help given to Robert Owen by his four sisters-in-law, David Dale's daughters, who were unmarried, but very rich.

105 In the same way, industries making copper goods in London, Bristol and Birmingham financed to a great extent copper-smelting works (and even copper mines). See John,

evident: the deficiencies of basic industries at the onset of the Industrial Revolution compared with consumer goods industries; bottlenecks in the production of semi-finished goods such as cotton yarn or bar-iron; high profitability from such productions once technical innovations had cut down costs; the desire of the users of these products to ensure a constant supply and to take a share in the high profits obtained in the primary industries.

Naturally, when examined in detail, capital flows are complex, and each industry, each industrial district has its own pattern of finance; the importance of 'merchant' capital in the South Wales iron industry is not found in other siderurgical areas; massive investment by merchant-manufacturers seems to belong only to cotton-spinning; coal-mining is an exception because of the preponderance of landed capital.

On the other hand, capital from diverse sources was used not only in each industry, but often in many individual enterprises. Of course we can find some which were founded solely on 'artisan' or 'commercial' capital, but generally speaking an entrepreneur had to rely on various sources to collect enough capital to found a sizeable new undertaking. We need only mention John Marshall supplementing his original 'commercial' capital by borrowing from family and friends, by a bank overdraft and by the support of two successive groups of partners. The formation of a partnership was an entrepreneur's natural expedient when in need of capital; this pattern of business organisation, which was predominant during the Industrial Revolution, provided, particularly for men of modest origin, an opportunity of supplementing the limited capital they had acquired as artisans or petty industrialists, through the support of richer individuals; it was mainly in this way that much commercial capital came to be invested in industry. Thus in 1702 Abraham Darby I went into partnership with some Bristol merchants to establish his foundry; then with J. Peters and G. Prankard in 1709 to set up at Coalbrookdale; then with R. Champion in 1711 and T. Goldney in 1716 – the latter being both Bristol iron merchants. In South Wales many ironworks were founded by partnerships which united ironmasters, like the Homfrays, and merchants from Bristol or London.[106]

Industrial Development of S. Wales, pp. 28–9; H. Hamilton, *The English Brass and Copper Industry to 1800* (London, 1926), pp. 219, 234, 236.

106 Raistrick, p. 6; John, *Industrial Development of S. Wales*, pp. 33–5.

Borrowing was another resort, loans being frequently obtained from relatives and friends; we need only to cite once again the cases of John Marshall, Samuel Whitbread I and M. Boulton, all of whom are illustrations of Peter Mathias' excellent observations on the importance of kinship in the financial structure of eighteenth-century business.[107]

Loans obtained from outside the family were often secured by a mortgage; Abraham Darby mortgaged half of Coalbrookdale to T. Goldney to get a loan of £1,600, probably for the construction of a blast furnace. M. Boulton mortgaged his own and his wife's lands, then the 'premiums' paid by some of the users of Watt's steam engines; Oldknow mortgaged his lands at Mellor to Richard Arkwright for a loan of £12,000 in order to build Mellor Mill.[108]

One can wonder, still, whether this system of finance was adequate to the needs of a fast-growing large-scale industry. This problem has been discussed earlier,[109] and one will only add that it is debatable whether the main obstacles to the mobilisation of savings were of a legal or psychological nature. A. H. John is inclined to favour the former theory, stating that many people would have been ready to invest in industry, had it not been for the risk of losing their entire fortune thereby, because unlimited liability was then the general rule. On the other hand, Ashton thinks that the Bubble Act did nothing to impede the rise of large-scale industry, because the latter did not need joint stock incorporation. Pressnell adds that the limited-liability company would probably not have spread widely, even if there had been no legal difficulties, as is proved by the slowness with which English industrialists adopted it once the legal obstacles had been removed.[110]

Anyway, there is no doubt that in the eighteenth century capital had

107 Mathias, *The Brewing Industry*, pp. 261, 271; also Roll, pp. 10–11, 100.

108 Raistrick, pp. 6, 50; Roll, pp. 10, 100, 102–3; Unwin, pp. 16–17, 85, 140, 147, 156; also Coleman, pp. 162, 247–50.

109 See above, pp. 161–6.

110 John, *Industrial Development of S. Wales*, p. 53; Ashton, *An Economic History*, p. 119; Pressnell, *Country Banking*, p. 285; also Dickson, *The Financial Revolution*, p. 489; S. G. Checkland, *The Rise of Industrial Society in England, 1815–1885* (London, 1964), pp. 13–14, 203–4. Of course, it was possible to create a joint stock company by private Act of Parliament; and 'illegal' companies, created without authorisation, were almost never prosecuted. In the mining industry they were fairly numerous. In manufacturing, they are exceptional. An example is the British Cast Plate Glass Company studied by Barker, pp. 47–50, and Barker and Harris, pp. 113 ff. It was founded in 1773 by Act of Parliament and built a big plate-glass factory near St Helens. It had, among its stockholders, members of the aristocracy, West and East India merchants (see p. 182), copper and coal magnates and, later, London bankers.

a highly personal and specific character; it was far from being the abstract and mobile factor of production it was to become in the nineteenth century; personal relationships were still at the bottom of most investments. On the other hand, Boulton and Watt had serious financial difficulties, but they managed to overcome them; as for the Carron Company, its initial vicissitudes seem to be the result of special circumstances: over-ambitious plans at the outset, under-estimation of building costs, and the founders being ruined in other ventures.[111] Reading records or histories of firms, one does not have the impression that the pioneers of the Industrial Revolution came up against insurmountable problems in raising the long-term capital they needed; what harassed them much more was the 'scarcity of money', of short-term credit, about which they complained incessantly.[112]

On the whole, the eighteenth-century capital market seems, to twentieth-century eyes, badly organised, but the creators of modern industry do not seem to have suffered too much from its imperfection.[113] We shall reach the same conclusion when we consider, after the problem of the initial outlay for the founding of enterprises, that of financing their expansion.

The simple answer to this question is the overwhelming predominance of self-finance. Enterprises increased their capital by ploughing back immediately, regularly and almost automatically the greater part, or even the whole of their profits. As we shall see, this increase was very rapid so that machinery and production were expanded at an accelerating rate. Thus most of the additional capital required for expansion was provided from industry's own resources, from the savings of the industrialists. This fact is so obvious as to be almost a cliché and the point is not worth labouring.

The widespread practice of systematically ploughing back profits is, of course, related to specific psychological attitudes and to a certain pattern of mentality: it is largely due to the 'frugality' of the pioneers of the Industrial Revolution. Their origins were often humble, and they were as hard on themselves as they were on others; business was their consuming interest and they continued to lead the simple lives to

[111] Campbell, 'Financing of Carron Company', pp. 23–4, 27–8, 30–1.

[112] Cf. Wilson, 'The Entrepreneur', p. 115, and H. J. Habakkuk, *American and British Technology in the Nineteenth Century. The Search of Labour-Saving Inventions* (Cambridge, 1962), pp. 70–3, 174–6.

[113] In any case, English industry, compared with that of the Continent, seems to have overflowed with capital. On the capital market, see above, pp. 165–6.

which they had been early accustomed, practising a stringent personal economy and a rigid austerity. They withdrew from their business each year only a small part of its profits for their personal needs, or else they paid themselves a small salary, hardly any higher than a skilled workman's wage. The case of the Walker brothers has become famous; at the beginning they paid themselves a wage of 10*s*. a week, and not until 1756, fifteen years after the founding of their firm, did they allow themselves a dividend of £140, about 2·5 per cent of their firm's capital value. This annual dividend was later increased, but at a slower rate than their capital grew: in 1768 it was £700, or 1·8 per cent of their capital. There is an abundance of similar cases: in the partnership deed signed by McConnel and Kennedy with the Sandfords in 1791, there was a proviso that the profits should be left to accumulate, and that if one of the partners wanted to withdraw his share, he would have to pay interest on it until he had replaced it in the firm; McConnel and Kennedy, as managers, received a salary of £40 a year.[114]

The fact that many, nay the majority of eighteenth-century industrialists belonged to Noncomformist sects definitely reinforced their tendency to abstinence, hard work and thrift, and helped to keep them faithful to their simple and frugal way of life, even when they had made a fortune (as with the Darbys), and to discourage them from conspicuous expenditure or aping the upper classes; thus religion was a factor in the rapid accumulation of capital.[115]

We must not, however, over-emphasise the frugality of these early industrialists. Once they had built up their businesses and secured their fortunes, they nearly always relaxed somewhat, withdrawing more money and adopting a more comfortable way of life. Some of them bought landed estates and built themselves large mansions. Mathias describes how the great brewers withdrew considerable sums from their firms and did not at all restrict themselves to a spartan way of life.[116] At Marshalls, from the early years, between 1793 and 1804,

[114] Ashton, *Iron and Steel*, pp. 48, 158, 160, 224; also his *The Industrial Revolution*, pp. 95–7; John (ed.), *The Walker Family*, pp. v, 2–9 ff.; R. Butler, *The History of Kirkstall Forge through Seven Centuries, A.D. 1200–1924* (2nd edn, York, 1954), p. 28; S. Pollard, *Three Centuries of Sheffield Steel. The Story of a Family Business* (Sheffield, 1954), pp. 10, 12, 18; Daniels, 'The Early Records', p. 177. At Kirkstall Forge the partners only took a salary of £30 per annum; at Newton Chambers the 'wages' of the partners were 'absurdly low' – £80 per annum from 1799 to 1811 for G. Newton; and there were no dividends. At Marsh in Sheffield the partners received 29*s*. a week from 1816 to 1819, then £100 per annum and after 1825, £200.

[115] Ashton, *Iron and Steel*, pp. 211, 218, 220, 223, 225.

[116] Mathias, *The Brewing Industry*, pp. 261, 264–5, 553.

the partners drew out a third of the gross profits each year, as an average, and let the other two-thirds accumulate; J. Marshall used to draw £1,800 a year, a large sum then, and, after 1804, £3,000 (between 1793 and 1804, however, his fortune had increased twenty times over!); between 1815 and 1828 his household expenses amounted to £6,000 a year. Rimmer estimates that from 1815 to his death in 1845 he devoted only a limited part of his resources to his flax-spinning mills and spent nearly £1 million in improving his social position.[117]

In spite of all this, there is no doubt that entrepreneurs, at the outset of the Industrial Revolution, reinvested immediately most of their profits (and even the interest on capital), in order to finance expansion; and even after these requirements were met, they left the greater part of their earnings with the firm, which then paid them interest, usually at the rate of 5 per cent. Most of the firms we have mentioned adopted this policy, e.g. the Walker brothers, Newton Chambers, J. Marshall and Co., McConnel and Kennedy. At Cyfarthfa also, in the 1790s, R. Crawshay systematically reinvested his profits each year, a custom kept up by his successors; in 1821 William Crawshay I wrote characteristically to his son that the profit was to be 'left on the spot . . . to support that which created it'. At Pleasley Mill, profits made in the early years were never distributed, but either kept in reserve or reinvested. The first dividend was paid in 1796, after ten years of production, and then it was only £439 for a total annual profit of £1,439.[118]

This state of affairs enabled a number of enterprises – possibly most of them – to finance expansion entirely from their own resources. John points out that self-finance was the rule in the South Wales iron industry. Mathias makes the same observation about the brewing industry. To which we can add that the Crawshays never borrowed, so that Cyfarthfa was completely self-financed. John Marshall, who had borrowed a lot to start his flax-spinning mill, was able to finance his considerable expansion after 1794 from his profits; the Marsh firm in Sheffield was able to do likewise on a lesser scale.[119]

Many firms, however, had to look outside for the capital they needed to expand. They could choose one of several methods. The first was to

[117] Rimmer, pp. 47, 70, 91, 97–102.

[118] Ashton, *Iron and Steel*, pp. 48, 158; John (ed.), *The Walker Family*, p. v; Pollard, *Three Centuries*, p. 12; Daniels, 'The Early Records', pp. 177–8; Addis, pp. 155–6; Pigott, pp. 37–40.

[119] John, *Industrial Development of S. Wales*, pp. 41–2; Mathias, *The Brewing Industry*, p. 252; Addis, p. 159; Rimmer, p. 47; Pollard, *Three Centuries*, p. 18.

take new partners into the firm; it was the simplest way but it had serious disadvantages, especially for individualists whose dispositions were autocratic, like most entrepreneurs of the Industrial Revolution, as it could lead soon to disputes about the management of the firm and the distribution of profits. There are actually very few examples among the larger concerns, whose owners usually wanted as few partners as possible, so that one more often sees them manœuvring to oust irritating associates. There is, however, one important exception: at the beginning of the nineteenth century, the great London breweries had embarked on a campaign destined to secure their outlets through control of the retail sales of beer (tying the trade). This necessitated an enormous capital outlay that could not be met by accumulated profits and they were forced to take in new partners, usually wealthy merchants and bankers.[120]

Firms more usually borrowed – on mortgage, bond or note of hand – from family and friends, solicitors and attorneys (or through their agency), or from other manufacturers or merchants with whom they had connections. Such loans were normally made on a temporary basis, but they sometimes became quasi-permanent, or else a second loan was sought in order to pay the first. John considers that semi-permanent loan capital played a secondary but not unimportant role (compared with self-finance) in the expansion of the South Wales metal industry. In some firms, like the Llanelly Copper Company, the proportion of loan capital to paid-up capital was very high.[121]

The third method was for firms to obtain help from banks, whose contribution, as Pressnell's work and other studies (Mathias) have shown, was more important than had hitherto been realised. Firstly, many industrialists also became bankers, either by creating their own banks, or by going into partnership with bankers; John Wilkinson, Robert Peel, the Feredays, Walkers, Homfrays and Guests are all examples. This extension of interests, clearly observable after 1793 and more so after 1797, was often necessitated by the scarcity of specie, which was indispensable for paying wages. In any case it allowed the 'industrial bankers' to receive deposits, issue bank-notes and tokens (these proliferated after John Wilkinson had set the example in 1787) and start a circulation of bills of exchange. Such procedures provided

120 Mathias, *The Brewing Industry*, pp. 300–4, 324.

121 John, *Industrial Development of S. Wales*, pp. 40, 42–6, 167. Birch, *The Economic History*, pp. 208–9, stresses the vital role of loans on security in the iron industry.

them not only with means of payment, but also with capital, as repeated short-term loans eventually increased their long-term borrowing. Moreover, they frequently borrowed from the banks in which they were partners, for the needs of their own enterprises, and this practice of taking clients' deposits for their own use resulted in evading the laws on partnership and mobilising capital from varied sources.[122]

On the other hand, country banks (and sometimes London banks too) granted substantial credits to industrialists. True, they were theoretically on a short-term basis only; long-term loans were ruled out by liquidity requirements, by the inadequacy of the banks' own resources, by the problems resulting from unlimited liability and bankruptcy laws, and finally by the legal limitation of interest rates which diverted banks' reserves into Government stocks. Banks considered factories a 'bad risk', and some made it a strict principle never to lend them money on mortgage. Consequently, financing of industry by the banks mainly took the form of discount of bills of exchange and temporary advances by means of overdrafts for fixed amounts. But the banks thereby supplied circulating capital which allowed industry to tie up in fixed capital a larger part of its own resources.[123]

Besides, what happened was that such short-term advances were converted to long-term loans after a time, either by being repeatedly renewed over the years, or by an overdraft being consolidated into a loan. As Mathias explains, this was the common fate of banking capital once it fell into the hands of manufacturers. Lastly, the banks did make direct loans on mortgage, personal bond or promissory note. Pressnell thinks that such loans may have been frequent, but it was unusual for banks to grant a first loan on a new mortgage, or new loans on an existing mortgage; generally, they were more ready to accept a mortgage as collateral or security for an earlier advance.[124] Examples of long-term loans by banks to industry, however, are few: there were some in South Wales, notably those made by the Brecon Bank to the Clydach and Plymouth (1813, £54,000, on mortgage)

[122] Pressnell, *Country Banking*, pp. 13–29, 291–2, 322; Ashton, *An Economic History*, pp. 174, 182–3.
[123] Pressnell, *Country Banking*, pp. 18, 285–6, 326; Ashton, *An Economic History*, pp. 183–4.
[124] Pressnell, *Country Banking*, pp. 294, 296–7, 299, 305, 308–9; Mathias, *The Brewing Industry*, p. 304. See also Campbell, 'Financing of Carron Company', p. 33, and R. Butler, *The History of Kirkstall Forge through Seven Centuries* (Kirkstall, 1945), pp. 69–71.

ironworks; from 1822 to 1876, the Llanelly Copper Company received bank credits equivalent to £25,000 in supplementary capital.[125] Pressnell thinks that the Cornish mines were also financed on a considerable scale by local banks such as Praed of Truro.[126] By contrast, the part played by banks in the textile industry seems to have been limited to short-term credit by discount.[127] As for the great London breweries, they were closely linked with banks, who sometimes financed their expansion, as for example, for the Anchor Brewery, but these were special cases, mainly because of the close family ties between brewers and Quaker bankers.[128]

In conclusion we can generalise John's observations on the Welsh iron industry; having noted that long-term bank loans to industry were exceptional, he goes on to say: 'But the total effect of tapping the banking system at so many points . . . is to reverse the accepted view of a rigid division between the growing industrialism and early banking system and to substitute one in which the latter, though not perhaps consciously, played a not unimportant part in the industrial development of this period.'[129]

Moreover, the development of credit as a whole and of the banking system, which was one of the concomitants of the Industrial Revolution, indirectly helped capital formation. The mere fact that industrialists could, firstly, buy their raw materials on credit and, secondly, obtain advances from the commissioners and merchants through or to whom they sold their goods, meant that they could procure thus part of their circulating capital and invest a larger part of their own resources in fixed capital.[130] This complex credit chain was, of course, held together by capital supplied to trade by banks, brokers and 'capitalists'. Also, the rise of the London discount market at the beginning of the nineteenth century enabled banks from industrial areas, which were short of capital, to have bills discounted in London, through the agency of bill-brokers, thanks to the surplus capital provided by banks from agricultural districts. This beginning of a

[125] John, *Industrial Development of S. Wales*, pp. 44, 48; Pressnell, *Country Banking*, pp. 308, 328–9.

[126] Pressnell, *Country Banking*, pp. 322–5, 330–2. [127] *Ibid.*, pp. 334–6; also pp. 340–2.

[128] Mathias, *The Brewing Industry*, pp. 283–4, 294–5, 297, 300–5.

[129] John, *Industrial Development of S. Wales*, p. 49; also Ashton, *An Economic History*, p. 184.

[130] See, for example, L. J. Williams, 'The Welsh Tinplate Trade in the Mid-Eighteenth Century', *The Economic History Review*, XIII, 3, April 1961, pp. 441, 447; also Sigsworth, pp. 221–2.

centralised money market meant that more short-term, and indirectly more long-term, capital was available for industry.[131]

However useful these transfusions of 'external' capital may have been, the 'internal' resources of industry seem to have been even more predominant in financing expansion than for initial outlays to set up industrial concerns. Naturally, what permitted the Industrial Revolution to proceed at a relatively swift pace was that profits, the ploughing back of which made expansion possible, were at a high level. A study of profits during the Industrial Revolution is outside the scope of this chapter. We may therefore only mention that all the firms we have discussed achieved high net profits: in good years, they were often in excess of a 15 or even 20 per cent return on capital employed (at Cyfarthfa, in 1796–7, they reached 52 per cent!);[132] losses are correspondingly rare, except in the lean years after 1815, and even in a poor year profits were respectable, especially when one remembers that the partners of a firm first assured themselves of a fixed interest (generally 5 per cent) of their capital, and only the earnings over and above this were considered as 'profits'; they were, in fact, *net* profits, and statistics dealing only with such figures tend to minimise the return on capital. In the years 1792–1807 Benjamin Gott had an average return on the capital he had invested of 19 per cent, and John Marshall seems to have fared no worse; he was expecting his capital to bring in 15 to 20 per cent per annum.[133]

It is true that these findings apply to 'progressive' firms in particularly profitable industries, and no doubt many other firms had a less brilliant record. After 1815, moreover, profit margins became narrower as a result of the secular fall of the prices of manufactured goods. But although profits per unit of output dropped, there is no evidence that gross profits or return on capital were noticeably affected

[131] Pressnell, *Country Banking*, pp. 97–9, 102–8, 225, 401, 434–7; Ashton, *An Economic History*, p. 184; F. Crouzet, *L'Economie Britannique et le Blocus Continental, 1806–1813* (Paris, 1958, 2 vols., 2nd edn., 1987), pp. 123–4. Also Dickson, p. 485 on the circular process of long- and short-term lending, which had emerged embryonically by the 1750s between the agricultural districts, London and the industrial districts.

[132] John, *Industrial Development of S. Wales*, p. 41, n. 2. Other examples: Ashton, *Iron and Steel*, p. 160; Pigott, pp. 37–8; Mathias, *The Brewing Industry*, pp. 264, 553; R. P. Beckingsale (ed.), *The Trowbridge Woollen Industry as Illustrated by the Stock Books of John and Thomas Clark, 1804–1824* (Devizes, 1951), p. xxxi.

[133] Rimmer, pp. 47, 56, 69–71, 160; also A. J. Robertson, p. 30.

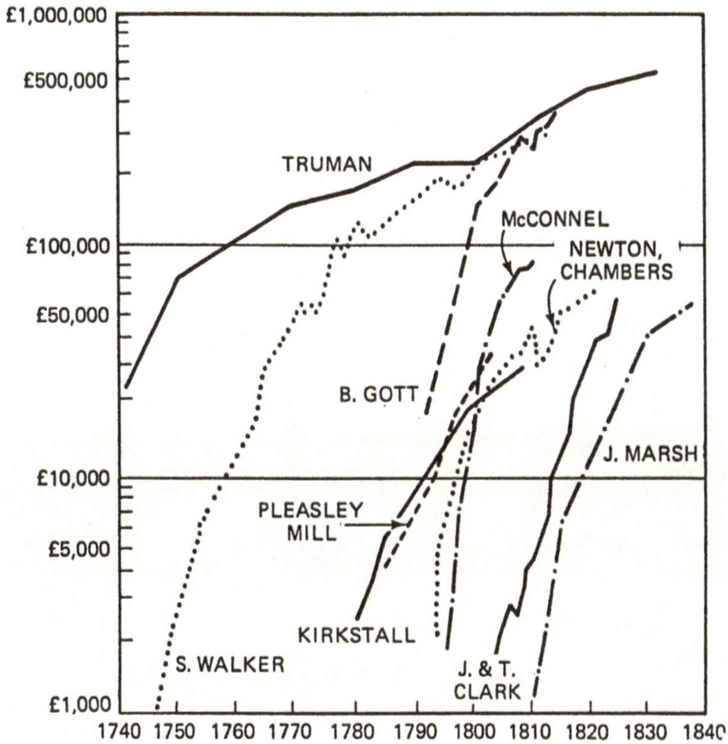

Graph 5.1. The growth of capital of various industrial firms (semi-logarithmic scale with three modules).

– except during some bad years of the Napoleonic wars and during the severe postwar depression.[134] In fact high returns on capital were the result of technological innovations which brought considerable economies in real production costs, while demand was buoyant and possession both of capital and entrepreneurship so scarce as to have monopolistic elements.[135]

Anyhow, the regular reinvestment of the largest part of these high profits ensured a rapid accumulation of capital within industrial

134 A. D. Gayer, W. W. Rostow and A. J. Schwartz, *The Growth and Fluctuations of the British Economy, 1790–1850. An Historical, Statistical and Theoretical Study of Britain's Economic Development* (Oxford, 1953, 2 vols.), pp. 653–4; also *Parliamentary Papers 1834*, XIX, p. 185; Rimmer, p. 309, graph 8. According to Edwards, *The Growth of the British Cotton Trade*, pp. 23, 190, in the cotton industry, profits reached a peak during the peace of Amiens, after which they fluctuated violently at a lower level.

135 S. Pollard, *The Genesis of Modern Management* (London, 1965), pp. 285–6.

Table 5.1. *Rate of growth of capital of various industrial firms.*

	Year	Capital £	Average rate of growth per year %	
1 *Metal industries*				
Coalbrookdale Co.	1709	2,800	4·17	3·49
	1809	166,000		
	1851	366,000		
S. Walker and Co.	1746	600	16·92	9·86
(Rotherham)	1780	122,000		
	1812	299,000		
R. Crawshay and Co.	1790	14,000	11·17	6.50
(Cyfarthfa)	1813	160,000		
	1835	238,000		
Kirkstall Forge	1779	1,800		10·18
	1808	29,578		
Newton Chambers and Co.	1793	2,270		12·62
(Sheffield)	1821	63,306		
J. Marsh and Co. (Shefffield)	1813	1,013		17·63
	1838	58,000		
Cheadle Brass Co.	1734	3,600		4·95
	1804	106,000		
2 *Textile industries*				
McConnel and Kennedy (Manchester)	1795	1,770		29·80
	1810	88,375		
Pleasley Mill	1790	5,000		15·30
	1804	36,000		
Gott and Wormald (Leeds)	1792	20,000		13·73
	1815	397,000		
J. and T. Clark (Trowbridge)	1804	1,634		18.65
	1825	59,258		
J. Foster and Co. (Black Dyke Mills)	1834	11,185		16·10
	1867	1,463,155		
J. Marshall and Co. (Water Lane, near Leeds)	1794	14,000	15·70	
	1803	52,000		9·15
	1828	272,000		
3 *Breweries*				
Truman, Hanbury and Buxton (London)	1741	23,000		3·68
	1830	575,000		
Barclay Perkins (London)	1784	95,000		
	1830	759,000		4·68

N.B. I have abbreviated the names of firms, particularly because they often changed them.

Sources for Graph 5.1 and Table 5.1

Coalbrookdale: [a] Raistrick, pp. 6, 244, 297.
Walker: [b] John (ed.), *The Walker Family*, pp. 2–25.
Crawshay: [c] John, *Industrial Development of S. Wales*, p. 41; Addis, pp. 83, 173.
Kirkstall: Butler, pp. 27, 29, 110.

concerns. We have tried to estimate it by using a number of statistical series drawn from firms' accounts, which show the evolution of their capital. They have been used in the preparation of Graph 5.1 and Table 5.1 on pages 195–6, in which we have calculated the average annual rate of growth of capital for these firms (and some others). Unavoidably these calculations are somewhat vitiated by arbitrary choices; fortunately in the majority of cases the amount of initial capital was known (in the case of Gott and Wormald we have started in 1792 when they went over to the factory system) and it served as a *terminus a quo*; for the *terminus ad quem* we simply took, in some cases, the last available figure (e.g. for McConnel and Kennedy); in others, in order to eliminate the perturbations of the post-1815 crisis, we took the highest figure before that date. Such choices leave one open to criticism; moreover some series cover a very short period so that findings are sometimes influenced by business cycles and by the specific problems of each firm (such as the withdrawal of one partner which explains the irregularity in the Newton Chambers graph). Lastly, we cannot be sure that these series are really comparable, given the variations in accounting methods from one firm to another;[136] the sample is in any case ridiculously small.

Table 5.1 (*cont.*)

Newton Chambers: Ashton, *Iron and Steel*, p. 160.
Marsh: Pollard, *Three Centuries*, pp. 8, 10, 11, 18.
Cheadle Brass Co: Hamilton, *English Brass and Copper Industry*, pp. 246, 248.
McConnel and Kennedy: Daniels, 'The Early Records', p. 178.
Pleasley Mill;[d] Pigott, pp. 37–8.
Gott: *Accounts of Co-partnership*, Gott MSS (Brotherton Library, Leeds). See also Crump, p. 255; Heaton, 'Financing the Industrial Revolution', pp. 9–10.
Clark: *The Trowbridge Woollen Industry*, p. xxxi.
Foster: Sigsworth, p. 218.
Marshall:[e] Rimmer, pp. 310–11.
Breweries: Mathias, *The Brewing Industry*, pp. 554–8.

Additional notes

(*a*) These figures must be completed and corrected by Birch, *The Economic History*, pp. 61–2, 65–6. Value of the concern: 1708: £2,804; 1740: £21,323; total capital value: 1798: £95,000; 1805: £111,000 (for Coalbrookdale only); net total value of the three concerns: 1809: £166,000; this means the value of the investments and undistributed profits which had been sunk into the firm, and not the capital strictly speaking.
(*b*) After 1812, this firm declined and went into liquidation.
(*c*) Capital of the Cyfarthfa firm, the London house not included.
(*d*) In this case the figures are for paid-up capital.
(*e*) The rate of growth was slowed down when the Benyons withdrew in 1804, and other partners in 1824.

136 For a discussion which shows the pitfalls concealed by apparently simple account books and the possibility that they may have been falsified, see A. Birch, 'Carron Company, 1784–1822:

We must, therefore, treat these graphs and calculations with caution; interesting conclusions seem to emerge nevertheless. The clearest is the extremely high rate of growth of capital in the concerns considered; most of the graphs describe part of a parabola; and although the highest average annual rate of growth – that of McConnel and Kennedy at nearly 30 per cent – is obviously exceptional, rates ranging from 15 to 20 per cent are fairly common, especially among textile firms, over periods from 15 to 30 years. These almost vertical 'take-offs' are an essential feature in the process of the Industrial Revolution.

Secondly, growth rates are higher for the series which cover a short period than for those covering a long period (e.g. Coalbrookdale or the breweries); moreover the curves are almost vertical during the early years of a firm, but later on slope towards the right. In short, there is a more rapid growth in the early stages of a firm's history than in its later years. This is clearly marked in the cases of Walker, Newton Chambers, Marsh (in their first ten years the rate borders on 30 per cent per annum), Marshall, Gott, even McConnel and Kennedy. This slowing down of expansion is quite normal: it is more difficult to maintain rapid growth when a firm has reached a large size than during its 'take-off'; moreover, at the beginning, the owners of a business reinvest virtually all the gross profits, but after a while they want to live more comfortably, so draw out more. It also happens that the firm cannot absorb for its expansion all the capital it is accumulating, and then withdrawals must be increased to avoid heavy capital charges and new outlets must be found for the surplus resources. This seems to have happened quite often after 1815, when one finds big industrialists, like J. Marshall, William Crawshay II or the Fosters, investing their surplus capital in British or foreign Government stocks, later in railway shares or on the money market.[137] It also seems that after the early years of the nineteenth century the difficulties caused firstly by the Continental Blockade, then by the depression following the Napoleonic wars, combined with the secular fall in profit margins, resulted in a slower accumulation of capital for some firms;[138] others, however, like Marsh or Foster, maintained a high rate of growth.

The Profits of Industry during the Industrial Revolution', *Explorations in Entrepreneurial History*, VII, 2, 1955, pp. 66–79; A. R. Hall, 'Note on Carron Company 1784–1822 ... by A. Birch', *ibid.*, IX, 1, 1956, pp. 44–6; A. Birch, 'Carron Company 1784–1822: A Reply', *ibid.*, IX, 1, 1956, pp. 46–9; Campbell, *Carron Company*, pp. 137, 163–9.

137 Rimmer, pp. 47, 94–6; Addis, pp. 156–7; Sigsworth, p. 224; also Heaton, 'Financing the Industrial Revolution', p. 9.

138 See Rimmer, p. 310, graph 11.

We have little information about the pre-1780 period, but it seems possible that the accumulation of capital was slower before than after that date; Coalbrookdale and the breweries would seem to bear this out; on the other hand, the rate of growth of capital of S. Walker and Co. during their first decades is very rapid. Nor must we forget the large fortunes made in the eighteenth century by men like Josiah Wedgwood, R. Arkwright or Samuel Whitbread I who, starting with nothing, left £500,000 or so at their deaths.[139]

Thus only more detailed research would show if the growth rates of industrial concerns' capital were subject to significant variation during the Industrial Revolution (and notably if they reached a peak during the last twenty years of the eighteenth century) and also whether the rate was higher in the textile than in the metal industries, as our figures would seem to indicate. But it seems certain that in many cases this rate was bordering on 15 per cent per year over fairly long periods, which is really very high.[140] True, we have taken examples among particularly successful firms, whereas many others grew more slowly, stood still, or even disappeared. We must not forget that the death rate for firms was very high during the Industrial Revolution and that, as Mathias points out, referring to breweries, even the most lucrative business soon degenerated if it fell into incompetent hands, and a vast capital could be eaten away within a few years.[141] Moreover, although some innovators quickly made huge profits, for example, Richard Arkwright, there were others, like Boulton and Watt, whose capital increased only slowly. It would therefore be unwise to generalise from these examples in order to estimate, even roughly, the long-term trend in capital formation in British industry as a whole, or even in its different sectors. Moreover, if the capital resources of firms accumulated steadily and swiftly, investment in fixed capital was realised much more irregularly, by successive stages, as is shown if one considers the fluctuations of investment.

The study of investment in industry at the end of the eighteenth century and the beginning of the nineteenth comes up against serious

139 McKendrick, p. 408; Fitton and Wadsworth, pp. 94–5, 97, 178; Mathias, *The Brewing Industry*, p. 308. For the later period, Jedediah Strutt's three sons are supposed to have had a fortune of £1 million in 1813; R. Crawshay is said to have left £1·5 million on his death in 1811, and J. Marshall between £1·5 million and £2·5 million in 1845 (Addis, p. 19; Rimmer, pp. 97, 321).

140 This guess-estimate is considered as valid by Cameron *et al.*, p. 39.

141 Mathias, *The Brewing Industry*, pp. 265–8, 272.

difficulties, because of the shortage of sources, and particularly of quantitative data. We are therefore restricted to qualitative data, in particular to information about the construction or enlargement of factories, the installation of new machinery, etc. In default of a precise chronology of investment, one can still sketch a graph of their short- and medium-term fluctuations.

Starting with an analysis of this sort, covering the years 1790–1850, Gayer, Rostow and Schwartz formulated a most interesting interpretation. According to them the process of investment is discontinuous by nature, and shows sharper fluctuations than current production; the large-scale increase in productive capacity is in fact concentrated on a small number of short periods, which occur in the late phases of expansion of a number of business cycles. Gayer and his team labelled the latter 'major cycles' to distinguish them from the 'minor cycles' which usually separate them and during which investment is restricted; thus these bursts of intensive investment recur approximately every nine years.[142] This attractive thesis seems on the whole to be borne out by fact.

Discontinuity of investment first appears at the level of the firm; mainly because a concern lacks the necessary financial resources to undertake heavy construction at short intervals, especially in the course of each business cycle. The only history of a firm to study this question in any detail, Rimmer's study of John Marshall's flax-spinning mills, shows that plant was increased or replaced during a small number of short periods – five between 1791 and 1840 – separated by fairly long intervals when the fixed capital hardly changed. J. Marshall built his first factory, *Mill A*, at Water Lane, in 1791–2; growth was rapid from 1793 to 1800; *Mill B* was built in 1794–5 at Leeds, and another at Shrewsbury in 1796–7. But from 1800 to 1814, capacity did not increase. In 1815, with his factories working at full capacity, and demand high, Marshall decided to build *Mill C* which increased his capacity by 55 per cent. In 1818 the fall in the prices of heavy yarn led him to change to the production of fine yarn, for which he installed new machinery, the gill frames, whence a reorganisation of his mills, achieved in 1820–2. In 1825, in the middle

[142] Gayer *et al.*, pp. 534–5, 540, 533–62; W. W. Rostow, *British Economy in the Nineteenth Century* (Oxford, 1948), pp. 54–5. This thesis has been criticised – but not convincingly – by R. C. O. Matthews, 'The Trade Cycle in Britain, 1790–1850', *Oxford Economic Papers*, N.S., VI, 1, February 1954, pp. 4–10, 13.

of the boom, he decided to build a fourth mill, *D* (1826–7), but the 1826 crisis brought about the decision in September 1827 to change over to wet spinning, based on Philippe de Girard's invention, which involved a complete reorganisation and re-equipment lasting from 1828 to 1835 and the construction of *Mill E*. Eventually, in 1838, Marshall decided to construct a huge new factory, in Egyptian style, Temple Mill.[143]

In the history of other firms that we know less well, the same discontinuity seems apparent; thus, from 1750 to 1755 or 1757, Coalbrookdale underwent considerable reorganisation and expansion, marked by the construction of the Ketley and Horsehay blast furnaces; then investment seemingly came to a halt, to start again about 1783 with the installation of rolling mills and new steam engines; this was followed by a long pause. At Kirkstall Forge there seem to have been three phases of investment, 1785–96, 1818, 1835–9, separated by long interruptions.[144]

We must not, however, exaggerate the irregularity of investment by industrial concerns. Rostow has in fact noted that there were exceptions: for instance, after the invention of the hot-blast in 1828, the Scottish iron industry regularly increased its capacity, apparently unaffected by cyclical fluctuations, because expectations of high profits had been engendered by this innovation.[145] On a different level, Samuel Walker's diary shows that his firm realised an amazing variety of small investments from 1741 to 1782, many of which were increasing its capacity. At Pleasley Mill new machinery was bought almost every year of the two decades following 1790. Likewise, the Strutts invested almost continuously during the Napoleonic Wars, repeatedly enlarging and rebuilding the Belper and Midford spinning mills.[146]

Moreover, according to Gayer, the concentration towards the end of major cycles applies mostly to the 'decisions to invest'; the existing capacity is by then fully employed and a mood of optimism is prevalent; but the projects are often realised after the peak, during a depression, and tend sometimes to mitigate its effects. Many of the examples quoted support this thesis, particularly Marshall's decisions

[143] Rimmer, pp. 33–4, 54–5, 85–6, 135–9, 142, 153–5, 165–80, 186–90, 196, 198, 200–3, 207–8, 212, 311, graph 12.

[144] Raistrick, pp. 68–70, 96, 225–6; Butler, *History of Kirkstall Forge*, p. 139.

[145] Rostow, *British Economy*, p. 54; R. H. Campbell, 'Investment in the Scottish Pig-Iron Trade, 1830–1843', *Scottish Journal of Political Economy*, I, 3, October 1954, pp. 245–8.

[146] John (ed.), *The Walker Family*, pp. 2–24, *et passim*; Pigott, p. 39; Fitton and Wadsworth, pp. 219, 221.

of 1791, 1796, 1818 and 1825; also S. Oldknow building Mellor Mill and B. Gott, Bean Ing in 1792; the Crawshays building three blast furnaces in 1824; Greenall and the Pilkingtons tripling the capacity of their glassworks in 1834–5. Investment decisions do, however, occur also contra-cyclically, in periods of depression – as Gayer and his team have admitted.[147] This tends to happen when firms (like Marshall in 1827) adopt some technological innovation to enable them to combat depression more effectively by reducing costs.

The discontinuity of investment that can be observed on a micro-economic scale recurs at a macro-economic level,[148] and much of Britain's fixed industrial capital was installed during a few relatively short 'bursts' or 'waves' of investment. There is no point in looking for such movements in the first three-quarters of the eighteenth century, because industrial machinery was too primitive. The iron industry might be an exception, and some writers have noted bursts of growth, and especially the creation of new ironworks, during the War of the Austrian Succession, and still more the Seven Years War.[149] The first unmistakable wave of investment, however, occurs in the years 1783–92, though it had started before 1780 in the cotton and metal industries where it was to reach its height. Arkwright and his associates, the manufacturers whom he authorised to use his patents, and those who pirated his machinery, set up about twenty mechanised spinning mills, investing a capital estimated in 1782 at £200,000.[150] The American War of Independence may have checked such developments, but it encouraged investment in the iron industry, above all in South Wales, by hindering imports of Swedish and Russian iron and creating a demand for armaments. In any case the peace of 1783, and the suspension, followed by the cancellation, of Arkwright's patents were quickly followed by a boom in the cotton industry; numerous spinning mills, powered at first by water, and later by steam, were set up (in 1788 they were said to be 145), to say nothing of the many small carding or spinning workshops, the 'jenny factories'. In Scotland there

[147] Above, pp. 176–7; Addis, p. 68; Barker, p. 77; Gayer *et al.*, p. 649.

[148] Investment by firms is discontinuous but not erratic; it may be partly determined by circumstances specific to each enterprise, it may sometimes be contra-cyclical, but all things considered, the majority of investments are commanded by general factors and they happen simultaneously.

[149] John, 'War' (see below n.164), p. 332.

[150] Fitton and Wadsworth, pp. 71, 77–8; Daniels, *Early English Cotton Industry*, p. 100; Chapman, *Early Factory Masters*, pp. 67–8, 72, 75.

was a strong burst of activity, starting with the building of the Deanston (1785) and the New Lanark (1786) mills; by 1787 Scotland had nineteen spinning mills. Imports of raw cotton in 1785–8 were three times what they had been in 1776–81. This boom was interrupted by the 1788 crisis, but after that it went on with renewed vigour until early 1793, and many mills were set up towards its end, in 1791–2.[151] The Welsh iron industry was also developing rapidly. Penydarren ironworks was set up in 1784, Blaenavon in 1789 and Ebbw Vale in 1791; elsewhere ironworks were being converted to the Cort puddling and rolling process – Coalbrookdale, for example, installed rolling mills – and in Scotland the Clyde and Muirkirk works were founded in 1786 and 1789 respectively.[152] It was thus a decisive decade, which saw the creation of large-scale industry, and the spread of mechanisation. The cycle culminating in 1792 was definitely a 'major' one, although the total value of industrial investment cannot have been very high.[153]

By contrast, the 1793 crisis and the difficulties attendant on war with France slowed down new industrial investment, until about 1798 – though the iron industry was probably less badly affected. However, the major cycle 1797–1803 stands out by a second wave of investment which reached its peak in the years 1799–1802. We know that in July 1799 eight new spinning mills were under construction in Manchester, the existing ones were being enlarged, machine-makers were working full-time; and at the beginning of 1802, twenty new mills were under construction. Even more spectacular progress was to be seen in the iron industry, and in a sense this wave of investment belonged to iron, as the first one had to cotton. A sharp increase in the prices of pig- and bar-iron in 1796 (caused by the raising of protective customs duties, by the difficulties of importing from the Baltic, and by a growing demand, while technological progress was improving productivity) ensured huge profits for the ironmasters, stimulated and made possible considerable investment: new ironworks were set up, and the capacity of existing ones increased. Thus, nineteen blast furnaces were built in

151 Fitton and Wadsworth, pp. 82–6, 198, 200–5; Unwin, pp. 85, 103, 115, 119, 123; Mantoux, pp. 251–2, 376–7; Hamilton, *Industrial Revolution in Scotland*, pp. 124, 126–7; M. L. Robertson, p. 129; Chapman, *Early Factory Masters*, pp. 77, 143.

152 John, *Industrial Development of S. Wales*, pp. 25–6; Raistrick, pp. 95–6, 225–6; Hamilton, *Industrial Revolution in Scotland*, p. 163; Addis, p. 11.

153 Ashton, *Economic Fluctuations in England, 1700–1800* (Oxford, 1959), pp. 131–2, 165; Gayer *et al.*, pp. 7, 16–17, 535.

Shropshire from 1796 to 1806, and eighteen in Staffordshire between 1796 and 1800. In South Wales, five new ironworks were established between 1799 and 1802, and nine blast furnaces built between 1796 and 1800 in Glamorgan alone. Altogether at least sixty-seven blast furnaces were built between 1796 and 1802 in Britain, and in 1802, twenty-two others were under construction. Investment in copper mining and smelting and in pottery works was also active.[154]

On the other hand, when war with France broke out again with its attendant crisis in 1803, it was the start of a long period – the Napoleonic Wars – when new industrial investment seems to have been limited, even in good years like 1806 and 1809. Gayer's team in fact states that investment was almost nil and that no new 'factories' were built between 1808 and 1811; this is going too far, however, because in the cotton industry the first mills for power-weaving were being built at that time, while various firms were expanding or modernising their equipment – but it was still nothing like the 1802 boom. Things were much the same in other industries: we know that several worsted mills were built in Bradford and Keighley, that steam power was introduced in many factories in the light metal trades at Birmingham, that two copper-smelting works were set up near Swansea; all this does not add up to much, and the capacity of the major industries does not seem to have increased significantly. During the last years of the Napoleonic wars the situation remained unchanged, except for some expansion in the Staffordshire and South Wales iron industries.[155]

Napoleon's defeat was not followed by a significant wave of investment, even in 1818, a year of prosperity; quite the reverse: the post-war depression was characterised by a net disinvestment in the worst-hit sectors, such as the iron industry, and many ironworks either closed down or were pulled down. Not until the major cycle culminating in 1825 do we see a 'tremendous expansion of plant', in the years 1824–5. Thanks to a strong demand for exports and to a burst of intense speculation, factories were working at full capacity and heavy investment was undertaken in several industries. Cotton is a case in point; the number of mills in Manchester increased from 49 in 1823 to 63 in

[154] Gayer *et al.*, pp. 8, 35, 41–3, 72; Crouzet, *L'Economie britannique*, pp. 81, 86; Edwards, pp. 13–14, 184; R. Meade, *The Coal and Iron Industries of the United Kingdom* (London, 1882), p. 609. The growth of the iron industry entailed a shortage of coal and the opening of new pits.

[155] Crouzet, *L'Economie britannique*, pp. 865–9; Gayer *et al.*, pp. 58, 60, 69–72, 94; Edwards, pp. 15, 185; Chapman, 'The Peels', p. 79.

1826; tens of thousands of power-looms were installed. The iron industry benefited too, partly thanks to the demand from railways, and the coal industry was also stimulated; in 1824, 1825 and 1826, sixty blast furnaces were built.[156]

The 1825–6 crisis, however, put paid to the boom, and there followed, until 1832, a period of instability and chronic unemployment, for both men and machinery. Prices and profits dropped, bringing with them a marked falling-off of investment. Though technological progress went on and industrialists were encouraged to improve productivity to offset the reduction of profit margins, Gayer thinks that in the cotton industry there was no substantial addition to plant, while in other industries fixed capital increased only sporadically.[157]

After 1832 came a new major cycle culminating in 1836, again characterised by considerable investment in the cotton and iron industries – sparked off for the latter by the first railway boom. But this is outside our period, and anyhow we have said enough to show that a great deal of the investment which created large-scale industry in Britain was made, before 1840, during four relatively short periods. This conclusion agrees with that of Gayer, Rostow and Schwartz, except on one point: bursts of *industrial* investment are fewer and more spaced out than their 'major cycles', because some of the latter, for example 1808–11 and 1816–19, are mainly distinguished by investment in non-industrial sectors.[158]

It remains to identify the factors that caused these bursts of investment and their location over time. They seem to have been connected with technological innovations, and the attraction for capital of a possible reduction of costs. The two first bursts obviously coincided with the diffusion of Arkwright's, Crompton's, Cort's and Watt's inventions; it seems also that the bursts culminating in 1825 and 1836 were largely connected with the power-loom, the self-acting mule, the hot-blast process and railways. Innovation could play a direct part – as when an industry adopts a new technique on a massive scale – or an indirect one, when it creates either a new demand for industrial products (e.g. railways) or simply conditions favourable to industrial expansion (e.g. the building of canals in a region like South Wales).[159]

156 Gayer *et al.*, pp. 111–12, 127, 171–2, 185, 194 n. 6, 195–6, 198, 212, 230.
157 *Ibid.*, pp. 171, 173, 212, 221–2, 224, 556 n. 1.
158 *Ibid.*, pp. 242–3, 259, 264; Checkland, pp. 17–19.
159 Gayer *et al.*, p. 38.

Secondly, investment waves come at a time when demand is high and industry's productive capacity is fully- or even over-employed. The investment, massive for its time, undertaken by the cotton industry in the decade 1783–92 is a direct result of the bottleneck which prevailed in the production of yarn while people were crying out for cotton fabrics. As for explaining such high levels of demand, one must bear in mind, of course, the secular increase in internal consumption caused by the growth of population and by higher average incomes, but this does not account satisfactorily for the suddenness of these bursts of investment, which, according to Gayer, is rather linked to export demand. Throughout the Industrial Revolution 'the controlling element in the growth and fluctuations of the British economy . . . was its foreign trade', or, to be precise, exports of manufactured goods. Thus major business cycles begin with a gradual increase in exports, which is followed by an upsurge of investment; the two phenomena are moreover connected: increased exports cause a rise in both direct and derived demand and supply also entrepreneurs with the resources needed for investment; one sees very clearly a multiplier effect.

The buoyant state of British exports in the years following the 1783 peace, their recovery during the wars against the French Revolution after the 1793 crisis, and likewise the increased demand from abroad in 1822–5 and 1832–6, were thus decisive in unleashing waves of investment and supplying both the stimulus and the capital they needed.[160]

Monetary conditions seem to have played a much less important or direct part. On the whole, however, bursts of investment coincided with periods of easy credit, for example, after 1783 and after the suspension of cash payments in 1797. Good harvests and low corn prices in 1797–8, 1820–3 and 1832–5 may have helped stimulate expansion during the subsequent major cycles by increasing consumers' real incomes.[161]

That these bursts of investment were often suddenly halted is obviously due to the crises of 1793, 1803, 1825 and 1836, which caused a sharp drop in demand, curtailed credit, and showed businessmen that their hopes of unbroken expansion were too optimistic. In addition, an investment boom brings with it unstable conditions, in which the least upset can provoke a crisis, since prices, wages and costs are rising and the money market becomes overstrained; a time comes

160 *Ibid.*, pp. 16 n. 1, 532–4, 647. See also Matthews, pp. 17, 31–2; Checkland, p. 15.

161 Gayer *et al.*, pp. 559–60, 563–4; Ashton, *An Economic History*, pp. 60–1.

when the prospect of new investment being profitable seems less likely and so investment tends to fall off, thus helping to create crisis conditions.[162]

One difficult question remains: that of the long period from 1803 to 1822 when investment, while far from negligible, never took on a boom-like character. It is surely no coincidence that this period was the time of the Napoleonic wars and the depression that followed them. Gayer and his team did, in fact, claim that the French wars caused British economic growth to slow down, particularly where it concerned industrial plant, which was increased more slowly than in the years preceding the French wars, or in the period after 1820 – the time of greatest expansion in industrial capacity. Gayer maintains that if these wars had not happened, economic growth and technical progress would have been swifter – and differently orientated. The slowing down was not due solely to the disruption of foreign trade caused by military and political developments (notably the Continental Blockade) but also – and mainly – to the diversion of capital away from industry towards other sectors. On the one hand, the enormous sums absorbed in massive loans to the Government and forced exports of capital for military expenditures abroad, made productive investment at home relatively less important than before 1793 and after 1820; on the other hand, the influence of wartime conditions caused a shift of investment towards agriculture (owing to the high prices of corn which lasted throughout the wars), the building of merchant ships, harbours and docks and short-term financing of foreign trade. Typical of this period were short- and medium-term investment in foreign currency, and long-term investment in agriculture and Government stocks.[163] We should, no doubt, qualify this interpretation for the period of the war against the French Revolution, given the burst of investment from 1799 to 1802, but it was entirely borne out by research on the period of the Continental Blockade, the climax of the French wars, when the slowing down of growth is the most pronounced. It has been mentioned above that capital of industrial concerns seemed to accumulate more slowly during the Napoleonic wars; moreover, it was then necessary to keep relatively more circulating capital because of the difficult conditions in foreign trade and this

162 Gayer *et al.*, pp. 560–2. However, Matthews, pp. 4–10, emphasises the mania element in boom years, which eventually kills off investment.

163 Gayer *et al.*, pp. 648–9, 651–2; Cameron *et al.*, p. 27.

affected investment in fixed capital, just when inflation had made its costs rise.[164] Moreover T. S. Ashton had pointed out that, during the eighteenth century, medium-term fluctuations in interest rates (determined by variations in the volume of Government borrowing) influenced the decisions to invest, not only in the building trade or in public works, where the cost of capital is an important element of costs, but also in most industries; obviously such fluctuations do not affect much the profitability of industrial investment, but in wartime industry suffers from a shortage of capital because the legal maximum rate of interest, imposed by the Usury Laws, diverts all the available savings into Government stocks.[165]

This thesis was criticised, because of the fragmentation of the capital market – or rather markets, as people who bought government securities were not the same as those who invested in industry – which sheltered the provinces from the tension which prevailed in London during the wars; because also much investment, being financed 'internally' from firms' own resources, was thus hardly sensitive to variations in the market interest rate (it seems, however, that provincial businessmen did watch the level of interest rates in London). On the other hand, Pressnell pointed out that, during the French wars, there were long periods when it was impossible to borrow on mortgage. Conversely there is a correlation between the lowering of interest rates from 1783 to 1792 and the burst of investment that characterises this period; similarly, after 1815, interest rates dropped rapidly to reach a lowest point in 1824, which coincides with a new burst of investment.[166]

After a lull in the debate, a new and powerful shot was fired in 1984 by J. G. Williamson. Many of his predecessors had been Keynesians, to

[164] Crouzet, *L'Economie britannique*, pp. 868–71. On the other hand, some scholars feel that the wars speeded up Britain's economic growth; but John, a leading advocate of this view, was the first to admit that his analysis did apply to the War of the Austrian Succession and to the Seven Years' War, but neither to the War of American Independence nor to the revolutionary and Napoleonic wars; A. H. John, 'War and the English Economy, 1700–63', *The Economic History Review*, 2nd series, VII, 3, April 1955, pp. 329–44.

[165] Ashton, *The Industrial Revolution*, pp. 9–11, 58; *An Economic History*, pp. 27–9; *Economic Fluctuations*, pp. 84–6, 104–5.

[166] See, for instance, John, 'War', pp. 341–3; L. S. Pressnell, 'The Rate of Interest in the Eighteenth Century', in Pressnell (ed.), *Studies in the Industrial Revolution*, pp. 183–4, 195, 198–9; Gayer *et al.*, p. 652. H. J. Habakkuk, 'The Eighteenth Century', *The Economic History Review*, 2nd series, VIII, 3, April 1956, pp. 434–6, accepts the validity of Ashton's thesis about the most severe periods of war, but thinks that for the rest of the time, interest rates had little influence upon investment.

whom investment demand was the critical variable, while he has used the neo-classical view of savings as an active constraint; he has also used some recent quantitative work which stresses the slow rate of growth of the British economy in the late eighteenth and the early nineteenth centuries. Instead of marvelling at England industrialising despite a modest investment proportion, he exposes the slowness of growth, as a result of insufficient capital formation. In his view, the responsibility lies with the wars, which raged for 36 of the 60 years from 1760 to 1820, and with the enormous loans which government floated to finance them. Britain was not a low saver, but a country which devoted to its war effort a substantial part of its savings, so that the private sector was deprived of capital. Actually, the gross rate of savings (private capital formation plus government borrowing) was close to 25 per cent of national income during the decade 1791–1801 and was on average 18 per cent for the period 1761–1820; but the French wars kept capital formation below the level it would have reached if peace had been maintained; productive investment was 'crowded out', economic growth and industrialisation were markedly slowed down.[167]

However, according to the best available calculations, the average ratio of productive investment remained fairly stable during the French wars; there was no inverse correlation between government borrowing and private investment – which both had a peak during the late 1790s. For some part at least, government loans were subscribed thanks to an increase in total savings and not at the expense of investment, as the richer classes, owing both to patriotism and to self-interest, displayed a greater propensity to save and to lend to government. As for the latter's fiscal and monetary policy, it was not damaging to the ability of industry to finance investment through ploughing back of profits. These remarks do not, however, destroy the 'crowding out' hypothesis. A basic fact remains: for over two decades, very large sums (of the same order of magnitude as total private investment) were borrowed every year by government. It is unlikely that such heavy and repeated drains had no effect upon private investment, that some of the moneys which went into the funds were

[167] J. G. Williamson, 'Why was British Growth so Slow during the Industrial Revolution?', *Journal of Economic History*, XLIV, 3, September 1984, pp. 687–712. Criticism by J. Mokyr, 'Has the Industrial Revolution Been Crowded Out? Some Reflections on Crafts and Williamson', *Explorations in Economic History*, XXIV, 3, July 1987, pp. 293–319.

not diverted from use in industry, whatever the fragmentation and imperfection of the capital market. Still, it must be recognised that there were no signs of serious tension on the market, of brutal diversion in financial flows, of shortage of funds for investing. Interest rates were, on an average for the war period, 20 per cent higher than in peace time, despite inflation; for a short time only, did government have to borrow at a rate over 6 per cent. So one can only say that the investment proportion would have been higher but for the Napoleonic wars.[168]

Unfortunately many other important problems remain – and will no doubt remain – unsolved for lack of statistical data. It is, for example, impossible to determine the ratio between net and gross capital formation; we have no information about the longevity of fixed capital in our period, and we can only assume that machinery was quickly replaced, given the swiftness of technological progress, and this naturally restricted *net* capital formation.[169]

Another problem – important because of its connections with technological progress and economic growth – is that of capital intensity in industry. The Industrial Revolution certainly made British industry more capital intensive, when compared with other factors, especially labour; it was labour-saving. We do not know, however, the exact extent of this change, and some innovations, moreover, were also capital-saving; this needs to be precisely estimated, bearing in mind variations according to periods and industries. We also need to know the effect of the capital and labour factors on entrepreneurs' decisions to invest. In a study of the cotton industry in the mid nineteenth century, Blaug states that technological innovation increased the real capital invested per workers' *capita*, but not per net unit of output. This, he thinks, was caused by progress in the machine-making industry, which reduced the cost of machinery; he thus challenges the idea that the Industrial Revolution was dominated by capital-using innovations.[170]

[168] P. K. O'Brien, 'The Impact of the Revolutionary and Napoleonic Wars, 1793–1815, on the Long Run Growth of the British Economy', *Review Fernand Braudel Center*, XII, 3, Summer 1989, pp. 345–56; F. Crouzet, 'The Impact of the French Wars on the British Economy', in H. T. Dickinson, ed., *Britain and the French Revolution, 1789–1815* (Basingstoke and London, 1989), pp. 202–5.

[169] J. Marshall, in 1798, had only 13 out of 126 frames dating from before 1793; in 1811 all those that were pre-1801 were replaced (Rimmer, pp. 46, 84 n.1).

[170] M. Blaug, 'The Productivity of Capital in the Lancashire Cotton Industry during the Nineteenth Century', *The Economic History Review*, 2nd series, XIII, 3, April 1961, pp. 358–60, 363–7, 369–70; see also, however, Mathias, *First Industrial Nation*, p. 143.

The problem has been tackled on a more general level in a well-known study by H. J. Habakkuk. He suggests that until about 1800 the rate of capital accumulation was faster than the growth of the available labour force. The result was a relative shortage and an increasing cost of labour, in other words a bottleneck which led manufacturers to develop and adopt innovations that were labour-saving and more capital intensive. By this means they hoped to avoid slowing down the accumulation of capital owing to narrowing profit margins. Thus, an increased demand for British manufactured goods was met, not by an extension of the domestic system, but by the creation of the factory system. The abundance of capital in relation to labour would explain, combined as it was with the improvement of internal transport and the fast rise of foreign trade, the growth 'over a broad front' that took place in the last twenty years of the eighteenth century.

After 1800, however, and even more after 1815, the supply of labour was more elastic, the shortage of labour vanished and there was even a great deal of underemployment. Capital could be accumulated without any pressure from wages, and capacity went up noticeably; this was favourable to technological progress, by offering many opportunities for trying out and applying new techniques. But the trend was more towards diffusing and improving existing techniques than discovering and adopting more advanced methods, especially those which were labour-saving, because the incentive for the latter had lost strength. This resulted in a slowing down of technological progress during the years after 1815. In order to offset the effects of a superabundant labour force, more substantial investments should have been made than was the case, but various obstacles prevented this, in particular an insufficient demand for manufactured goods because of the low purchasing power of British and foreign consumers after 1815.

Habakkuk maintains that, as a general rule, abundance of capital compared with other factors – particularly labour – creates the most favourable conditions for technological progress, because the bottlenecks which occur force the development and adoption of innovations that increase capital intensity and save on manpower. Such innovations, moreover, offer the best prospects of sustained progress and conform more closely to long-term economic trends – while this is not the case with inventions which save capital or natural resources.[171]

[171] Habakkuk, *American and British Technology*, pp. 132–3, 135–6, 138–42, 162–5, 168, 177–8, 180, 185–6, 188. See below, pp. 364–7, for a similar approach to a comparison between Britain and the Continent.

This study has tried only to survey the state of research about capital formation in Britain during the Industrial Revolution. It has perhaps also thrown light on some aspects of the latter. Thus, industry would seem to have financed from its own resources most of its mutation, and this emphasises the spontaneity of the Industrial Revolution, its characteristically organic growth within the already dynamic and complex economic structure existing in England around 1760. Its autonomy was not, however, complete, and the influence of foreign trade – as much in supplying supplementary 'merchant' capital as in giving exports-led impetus to bursts of investment – is not to be neglected. The Industrial Revolution also seems to have been a swift and continuous process as far as the speeding up of capital accumulation is concerned, but discontinuous and relatively slow when it comes to investment operations. The picture is rather one of energetic 'take-offs', but by stages, with some slipping back, than of a smooth ascent. The most pronounced irregularities, however, were caused by outside circumstances – in particular the French wars.[172]

[172] C. H. Feinstein and S. Pollard, *Studies in Capital Formation in the United Kingdom 1750–1820* (Oxford, 1988), is a most important contribution to several of the problems which are discussed in this chapter. J. Mokyr, *The Economics of the Industrial Revolution* (Totowa, 1985), pp. 38, 50 n. 60, has some excellent critical remarks on my views. P. Richardson, 'The Structure of Capital during the Industrial Revolution Revisited: Two Case Studies from the Cotton Textile Industry', *The Economic History Review*, XLII, 4, November 1989, pp. 484–503, presents some 'revisionist' ideas.

6 Towards an export economy: British exports during the Industrial Revolution*

The term 'the export economy' has been applied by S. B. Saul to Britain during the period 1870–1914, which saw the peak of influence of foreign trade in the economy, at least in a purely statistical sense, the ratio of foreign trade to national income having been at its maximum in the 1870s and 1880s and falling only moderately thereafter.[1] The origins of this peculiar position of the British economy have never been investigated in depth, while work by A. H. John, D. E. C. Eversley, and P. Bairoch, seems to have established that during most of the eighteenth century (up to *c.* 1780) exports played only a marginal role in the growth of the British economy, which received its main impetus from the home market.[2] This implies that important changes took place at some time after 1780 in the relationship between the progress of exports and national economic growth.

This is the problem with which the present chapter is concerned; it will cover the period from the 1780s to 1873, when Britain had definitely become an 'export economy' – though some incursions in the early and mid eighteenth century have been deemed necessary – and it will investigate four main points: (a) the periodisation of the growth of British exports, in order to ascertain the stages by which Britain

* Reprinted from *Explorations in Economic History*, XVII 1, January 1980, pp. 48–93.

1 S. B. Saul, 'The Export Economy, 1870–1914', *Yorkshire Bulletin of Economic and Social Research*, XVII, 1, May 1965, p. 5; also P. Deane and W. A. Cole, *British Economic Growth 1688–1959* (Cambridge, 1967, 2nd edn), pp. 28, 311.

2 A. H. John, 'Aspects of English Economic Growth in the First Half of the Eighteenth Century', *Economica*, NS, XXVIII, 110, May 1961, pp. 176–90; D. E. C. Eversley, 'The Home Market and Economic Growth in England, 1750–1780', in E. L. Jones and G. E. Mingay (eds.), *Land, Labour and Population in the Industrial Revolution* (London, 1967), pp. 206–59; P. Bairoch, 'Commerce international et genèse de la révolution industrielle anglaise', *Annales ESC*, XXVIII, 2, March–April 1973, pp. 541–71. For a different view, see: W. E. Minchinton, *The Growth of English Overseas Trade in the Seventeenth and Eighteenth Centuries* (London, 1969), pp. 36–52; K. Berrill, 'International Trade and the Rate of Economic Growth', *The Economic History Review*, 2nd series, XII, 3, April 1960, pp. 351–9.

became an 'export economy'; (b) the changing commodity structure of exports, in order to find out what kind of products were mainly responsible for the increase in exports; (c) the changing geographical distribution in exports, in order to specify the leading markets on which those goods were sold; (d) finally, the growth of exports will be confronted with the available data on national income and industrial production.

This study will be primarily descriptive, rather than analytical and will be concerned only with *domestic* exports, the re-exports of 'colonial and foreign goods' being left out. It faces familiar problems in its quantitative sources. The only statistics of English (and later British) exports, which are available up to the last years of the eighteenth century were computed by the Customs according to the system of 'official values' (OV), i.e., at constant prices; historians generally agree, though, that they provide rough, but reliable indices of the volume of exports.[3] Moreover, during most of the eighteenth century, when average prices were stable, there was probably not much difference between the official values of exports and their market values.[4] On the other hand, the sharp advance in the general price level and the upheaval in the price structure, which started in the 1780s, created a serious gap between official and market values and made the former a source of inaccuracies, especially for analysing the commodity structure of exports. Fortunately, from 1796 onward, annual totals of the 'declared' or 'real', i.e., current values of exports (CV), based on the declarations of exporters, became available, and, after 1814, they are complemented by detailed figures by commodities and countries of destination, which have been extensively utilised. Moreover, the late Ralph Davis revalued exports at current prices for a group of three years in each decade, from 1784/6 to 1854/6, with a breakdown among the main areas of destination and the major commodities.[5] We have

[3] G. N. Clark, *Guide to English Commercial Statistics, 1696–1782* (London, 1938), pp. 37–9; A. H. Imlah, *Economic Elements in the Pax Britannica* (Cambridge, Mass., 1958), pp. 20–3; B. R. Mitchell and P. Deane, *Abstracts of British Historical Statistics* (Cambridge, 1962) (cited below: *Abstract*), p. 275; T. S. Ashton, Introduction to E. B. Schumpeter, *English Overseas Trade Statistics, 1697–1808* (Oxford, 1960), pp. 4–6; P. Deane, *The First Industrial Revolution* (Cambridge, 1965), p. 62; Deane and Cole, pp. 42–5. Appendix I, pp. 315–17.

[4] J. F. Shepherd and G. M. Walton, *Shipping, Maritime Trade and the Economic Development of Colonial North America* (London, 1972), pp. 177–84, Appendix II; also R. Davis, 'English Foreign Trade, 1700–1774', *The Economic History Review*, N.S., XV, 2, December 1962, p. 285, note 2; Minchinton, p. 15, note 3.

[5] R. Davis, *The Industrial Revolution and British Overseas Trade* (Leicester, 1979), pp. 94–101, Tables 41 to 48. He had kindly allowed us to use his tables before they were published.

Table 6.1. *Mean rates of growth per year of exports from England and Wales.*

Years	%
1697 to 1714	2·8
1714 to 1744	0·9
1744 to 1760	3·0
1760 to 1781	−1·5
1781 to 1800	5·1

also used A. H. Imlah's volume series for exports from the United Kingdom from 1796 onward, and some other volume series which have been computed with his index of the price of exports as deflator.[6]

These time series have been processed by computer to calculate their mean rates of growth per year for various periods or subperiods. These calculations have been made between bench-mark years by exponential adjustment, so that all the values between those years are taken into account.[7] Absolute and relative deviations from the long-term trend of each series have also been systematically calculated and they have been used to pinpoint accurately the turning points between the periods of acceleration and deceleration.

The stages of growth

The eighteenth century, taken as a whole, did not see a remarkably fast growth of English exports: from 1697 to 1800, their mean rate of growth per year is only 1·5 per cent. But, a most interesting feature is the existence of five fairly distinct periods (about 20 years long) of alternating growth and stagnation or decline. This alternation, which had been pointed out by Deane and Cole,[8] is confirmed by the analysis of the deviations from trend and by the calculation of exponential rates of growth between the turning points which they reveal (see Table 6.1). It was only during the last of those phases, starting in the 1780s, that British exports underwent a really fast and sustained growth, a well-known fact that this paper can only confirm.

[6] A list of the various time-series, which have been used, and of their sources is given in appendix; so detailed references to them are not supplied.

[7] All rates of growth quoted in this chapter have been computed by this method. So the position in the business cycle of the first and last years of the periods for which they are calculated has no serious influence on the growth rate.

[8] Deane and Cole, p. 47, also Table 14, p. 48.

(a) From 1697 to 1714, despite (or because of) the war of Spanish succession, the rate of growth is markedly higher than for the whole century; deviations from trend are mostly positive and increasing to a peak in 1714.[9]

(b) Then comes a 30-year period of much slower growth and even stagnation of exports, which fluctuated around £5 million. From +26·7 per cent in 1714, deviations fall, irregularly but clearly, to −20.3 per cent in 1744 and are negative for a majority of years. If the declining trend which had developed from 1714 to 1727 was interrupted by a rather strong recovery from 1728 to 1738, this upsurge was cut short by the outbreak of war with Spain in 1739 and, in the early 1740s, up to 1744, exports were depressed.[10]

(c) In 1745, exports started to recover and they rose very fast up to 1750, when official values were 75 per cent above their 1744 level, and the deviation from trend was +27·9 per cent. Though exports declined afterward to 1755, they rose later to new record figures in 1759/61 and in 1764, when for the first time their official value exceeded £10 million. Deviations from trend are constantly positive from 1748 to 1768 (except in 1755), but they reach their peak in 1760 (+28·2 per cent) and then start to decline.[11] The period from 1745 to 1760 was thus one of relatively marked progress for exports.

Deane and Cole have attributed much importance to the turning point of the mid-1740s and to the 'dramatic increase' in exports which followed; they have maintained that the period 1745–60 witnessed an advance almost as spectacular, if not nearly as regular, as after 1780.[12] There was indeed a significant change in the pace of British exports, but, if the jump from 1744 to 1750 was very sharp (at a rate of growth per year of 9·8 per cent), it was short-lived and the growth from 1750 to 1760 was much slower (1·4 per cent per year); this jump was more an end-of-war and postwar recovery and boom, resulting from the release of foreign pent-up demand and also from exceptional sales of grain

[9] Deane and Cole, p. 48; P. Mathias, *The First Industrial Nation. An Economic History of Britain 1700–1914. Second edition* (London, 1983), p. 89; A. H. John, 'Agricultural Productivity and Economic Growth in England, 1700–1760', in E. L. Jones (ed.), *Agriculture and Economic Growth in England, 1650–1815* (London, 1967), p. 180.

[10] Deane and Cole, p. 48; Ashton, in Schumpeter, p. 13; Ashton, *Economic Fluctuations in England, 1700–1800* (Oxford, 1959), pp. 58–60; Minchinton, pp. 14–16; John, in Jones, pp. 180, 190.

[11] This is why we have chosen 1760 as the turning-point.

[12] Deane and Cole, p. 48; also Davis, 'English Foreign Trade', p. 295. But these views have been mitigated in W. A. Cole, 'Eighteenth-Century Economic Growth Revisited', *Explorations in Economic History*, X, 4, Summer 1973, pp. 328, 331, 333.

Table 6.2. *Mean rates of growth per year of exports*

	Years	%
From England and Wales (OV)	1781–1792	7·0
	1792–1800	5·0
From Great Britain (OV)	1781–1792	6·9
	1792–1802	5·9
	1802–1814	3·1
From the United Kingdom		
(OV)	1802–1814	3·2
Imlah's volume series	1796–1814	1·9
	1802–1814	2·0
Current values	1796–1814	1·7
	1802–1814	0·7

abroad,[13] than the beginning of a sustained growth of exports, while the high level of overseas sales in 1759/61 is related to the special circumstances of the Seven Years' War.[14] Anyway, the rate of growth of exports from 1744 to 1760 is markedly lower than from 1781 to 1800 and most of the progress which had then been achieved was cancelled by the depression which followed.[15]

(d) After the end of the Seven Years' War, English exports reached, in 1764, a record figure of £11·5 million, which was not exceeded before 1788, but they declined in the following years up to 1769 and, if they recovered somewhat in 1770 and 1771, they suffered in the 1770s an almost uninterrupted fall which brought them in 1781 to £7 million, i.e., lower than in any year since 1745. Deviations from trend decreased sharply after 1760, to reach eventually the low level of −39·4 per cent in 1781. From 1760 to 1781, the rate of growth per year of exports is negative, at −1·5 per cent. These 20 years not only of stagnation, but of actual decline in the volume of exports, are quite unique in the history of British trade in the eighteenth and nineteenth centuries; but their importance has been often overlooked, though they are a strong argument for those scholars who stress the role played by the home market in British economic growth at the beginning of the

13 Ashton, *Fluctuations*, pp. 46, 183, Table 3; Ashton, in Schumpeter, p. 12; Minchinton, pp. 25, 27, 43, 63, Table 7; John, in Jones, p. 179; John, review of Ashton, *Fluctuations*, in *Kyklos*, XVII, 2 (1964), pp. 278–9; Cole, p. 338.

14 Ashton, *Fluctuations*, pp. 60–1; Davis, 'English Foreign Trade', pp. 295–6; Minchinton, pp. 14–16; Cole, pp. 329ff., 339.

15 See also Deane and Cole, p. 48, Table 14; P. Deane and H. J. Habakkuk, 'The Take-Off in Britain', in W. W. Rostow (ed.), *The Economics of Take-Off into Sustained Growth* (London, 1963), p. 81, Table 3.

Industrial Revolution.[16] Though difficulties in European markets played a part at first,[17] the main cause of this depression was the conflict with the 13 colonies, starting with their boycott of British goods and culminating in an unsuccessful war against America, France, Spain, and Holland.

(e) After the trough of 1781, exports rose very fast and unceasingly until 1792, with only a slight setback in 1785 and some slowing down from 1784 to 1787; exports from Great Britain (OV) increased by 141 per cent from £7·6 million in 1781 to £18·3 million in 1792 (see Table 6.2).[18]

However, several writers have pointed out rightly that part of this upsurge of exports was a rebound from the artificially low level to which they had been forced by the War of American Independence, a result of the cessation of hostilities and of the backlog of export orders accumulating in markets which had been cut off from Britain during the war; the low starting point of 1781 (or even 1783) exaggerates the steepness of the growth curve.[19] These views can be supported mathematically; first, despite the fast growth from 1781 to 1800, the rate of growth of English exports for the century 1697–1800 (1·5 per cent) is slightly lower than for 1697–1760 (1·6 per cent), so that the post-1781 gains did not quite cancel the losses suffered during the depression of the 1760s and 1770s; second, the deviations from trend, though recovering from their 1781 low point, remain negative until 1789; it was only from 1790 onward that the 'recovery' gave way to a new growth.

Moreover, the fact that the American war had not been victorious helped to make this post-war rebound more pronounced and sustained than after earlier successful wars. Instead of having to hand back enemy territories which she had occupied, Britain recovered some colonies which she had lost; there was no cessation of subsidies to allies (which had stimulated exports during the Seven Years' War), as she had fought alone; the enemy markets which reopened were much

16 Eversley, pp. 209, 236, 247–9; Bairoch, p. 558.

17 Ashton, *Fluctuations*, pp. 46, 61; Ashton, in Schumpeter, p. 14; Minchinton, p. 17; M. W. Flinn, *The Origins of the Industrial Revolution* (London, 1966), p. 58.

18 With Davis' current values, the rise would be faster (except at the end of the period), because of the increase in prices: from 1784/6 to 1794/6: +76% (OV: +54%); from 1794/6 to 1804/6: +72% (OV: +46%); from 1804/6 to 1814/16: +16% (OV: +53%); *The Industrial Revolution*, pp. 94–7.

19 Deane and Habbakkuk, p. 78; Deane, *First Industrial*, p. 66; Flinn, p. 60.

Table 6.3. *Percentage increases between the quinquennial average official values of exports from Great Britain*

Years	%
1783/87 to 1788/92	+35
1788/92 to 1793/97	+ 9
1793/97 to 1798/1802	+45
1798/1802 to 1803/07	+ 2
1803/07 to 1808/12	+23

larger than formerly: not only Spain and France, but also Holland and the United States.

Even so, the truly spectacular and unprecedented character of the upsurge of exports in the 1780s must not be underestimated; it was 'both more rapid and sustained than in any previous period' and there was undoubtedly during those years a decisive change of momentum in the course of British exports, which entered an entirely new stage.[20] Moreover, their fast growth was sustained for another decade.

The uninterrupted upsurge of British exports came to an end in 1793, when the outbreak of war with France brought about a serious slump. The peak figure of 1792 was not exceeded before 1796 and the average official value for the 5 years 1793–7 was only 9 per cent higher than for the preceding quinquennium (see Table 6.3). But there was a new and very sharp upsurge of exports from 1798 to 1802, so that the rate of growth of British exports from 1792 to 1802 (5·9 per cent) is only one percentage point lower than from 1781 to 1792, a difference which cannot be interpreted as a sign of deceleration; the continuous increase, without any cyclical fluctuation, which had taken place after 1781, was obviously exceptional and, war or no war, a more normal pattern, involving some years of recession, was bound to reappear. It would be absurd to project the 1781–92 trend to find out the export figures which would have been reached if the war had not broken out. The 1790s and early 1800s are clearly a prolongation of the 1780s and, taken together, these 20 years are one of the major leaps forward in the history of British exports.[21]

However, the growth rates in Table 6.2, the figures in Table 6.3, and the deviations from trend show that there was a definite slowing

20 Deane and Cole, p. 47; Deane and Habakkuk, pp. 77–8; also Ashton, in Schumpeter, p. 14; Mathias, p. 98.

21 This is stressed by Deane and Habakkuk, pp. 78–9.

down in the progress of exports after 1802, a year which was a new turning point in the fluctuations of British exports growth rates.[22]

The deviations from trend of the various time-series reach peak positive figures between 1799 and 1802, but they tend to decline from 1803 onward, a movement which was to go on after the end of the wars. The volume of exports drifted downward from 1802 to 1808 and, despite the new peak figures which it reached in 1809, 1810, and 1814, its recovery during the later years of the Napoleonic war was far less pronounced than the upsurge it had known around 1800.[23] As for the current values, their growth rate from 1802 to 1814 is extremely low. After the fast growth of exports from 1782 to 1802, came therefore a phase of much slower growth, which actually extends astride the Napoleonic war and the post-war years.

It is obvious that the short-run fluctuations of British exports during the French wars were largely influenced by military and political developments abroad, but the impact of the wars on the long-run growth of exports and on the movements which have just been delineated is far less clear.

Two factors are often quoted as having strongly stimulated British exports during the wars: hostilities crippled Britain's major competitors on the Continent and gave to the British Navy effective control of oceanic routes, so that Britain alone could take full advantage of markets enhanced by growing population and incomes in Europe and America. However, the impact of those factors must not be overestimated.

There is no doubt that the Revolution and the war seriously harmed French industry during the 1790s, that its output and its exports more or less collapsed. Moreover, they interrupted for some time the attempts which had been made in France in the 1780s to introduce British innovations and, as technology was progressing rapidly in Britain, the gap between the two countries widened.[24] But, as the rise of British exports in the 1790s and 1800s resulted mainly from the spectacular upsurge of cottons exports, the French competition which was crippled by Revolution and war was a *potential* much more than an actual competition, as the pre-1789 French cotton industry was not

[22] M. M. Edwards, *The Growth of the British Cotton Trade, 1780–1815* (Manchester, 1967), p. 74.

[23] With Imlah's volume figures, there is a decrease of 2 per cent from 1798/1802 to 1803/7 and an increase of only 14 per cent from 1803/7 to 1808/12.

[24] M. Lévy-Leboyer, *Les banques européennes et l'industrialisation internationale dans la première moitié du XIXe siècle* (Paris, 1964), pp. 23, 27–32.

competitive with the British and did not export much.[25] The other industrial areas of the Continent suffered far less than France from internal disturbances and wars, and the difficulties of the cotton industries of Saxony and Switzerland came mostly from British competition enhanced by British technological superiority (from which they were actually saved by the Continental Blockade after 1806). It is thus difficult to see which of Britain's competitors in cotton were really crippled by the wars.[26] Other British manufactured goods, however, possibly did displace French articles which either were no longer competitive or could no longer reach their former markets. A test-case might be linens and silks, two French specialities which, before the Revolution, were very competitive with similar British goods. Actually, exports of British linens did increase very slowly during the 1790s and 1800s, while exports of silks rose somewhat up to 1796, but declined markedly afterward.[27] In both cases, the substitution of British for French products does not seem to have been significant. However, linens and silks everywhere then were suffering from the competition of cottons and such French products might have been replaced, not by similar British goods, but by British cottons – and there is evidence, though at the end of the wars period, that this actually happened.[28]

As for Britain's ascendancy at sea, it was not before the later years of the Napoleonic war that it was both absolute and fully used, through the enforcement of the Orders in Council of November 1807, to favour British trade by cutting off competitors from overseas, i.e., American markets, and giving Britain a monopoly there. Previously, the Continentals were not prevented from exporting to the United States or to the French or Spanish colonies. It is true that they did not make much inroad into the United States market, but this had nothing to do with the war: the French had discovered to their disappointment during the peace years after 1783, that they could not compete there with the cheaper goods and better trading organisation of the British. However, the greatest gain to British trade from 1808 onward came from the

25 And the 'crippling factor' ought to have had its strongest impact during the early years of the Revolutionary war, when the French economy was collapsing; actually, from 1792 to 1797, British exports to Europe fell sharply and total exports did not increase much.

26 Though, after 1807, the Continental cotton industries suffered from the shortage and high price of cotton wool, which resulted from the British Orders in Council and the American Embargo.

27 See Table 6.5.

28 Edwards, pp. 56, 60.

opening of Brazil and of the Spanish colonies, which was a consequence of the political and military events in the Peninsula in 1807 and 1808, much more than a benefit accruing directly from sea power.[29]

British sea power did, however, make easy the conquest of a number of enemy colonies, which henceforth were supplied by Britain rather than by the Continentals. This gave to the British, during the later years of both wars, new markets, which were not insignificant: during the 4 years 1798–1801, the 'Conquered West Indies' received 5·3 per cent of total British exports (OV).[30]

Another factor, which has been mentioned as a stimulus to British exports, is the unrequited capital export by the government in wartime both for the maintenance of British troops abroad and as loans or subsidies to allies. However, such expenditures did not become really heavy before 1808.[31]

To sum up, the wars brought about some trade diversion to the benefit of Britain and to the detriment of the Continentals, but this diversion does not seem to have been very large, except for the opening of the Latin American market, from 1808 onwards, but a large part of the additional exports thus engendered only offset the loss of the markets in Europe and the United States at the same time. On the other hand, such redirection does not seem to have played the dominant part in the export boom of 1798 to 1802, when there was more trade creation than trade diversion, thanks to the fall in the prices of cotton goods. Moreover, the boom in exports to the United States, which was responsible for a large share of the increase in total exports during the 1790s, was only stimulated marginally by the war: in so far as American national income and foreign purchasing power were pushed upward by the profits of the neutral and indirect carrying trades. The main factor was the increase in demand from the American home market.

On the other hand, the wars also had some serious negative impact

[29] Part of the trade which was thus carried directly with those territories was only a substitute for a former circuitous or illegal trade.

[30] In 1808, their share was 4·8 per cent; we do not have separate figures for those territories after 1808; see also Table 6.9. The slaves' revolt in San Domingo – an indirect effect of the French Revolution – also favoured British trade.

[31] A. D. Gayer, W. W. Rostow, and A. J. Schwartz, *The Growth and Fluctuations of the British Economy, 1790–1850* (Oxford, 1953), II, p. 647; J. L. Anderson, 'A Measure of the Effect of British Public Finance, 1793–1815', *The Economic History Review*, XXVII, 4, November 1974, p. 618, Table I.

Table 6.4. *Mean rates of growth per year of exports from the United Kingdom*

		Imlah's volume series (%)	Current values (%)
A.	1814–1846	4·3	1·1
	1846–1873	4·7	5·7
	1814–1873	4·5	3·4
B.	1802–1826	2·5	−0·5
	1826–1848		2·7
	1848–1873		5·6
	1826–1856	5·6	
	1856–1873	3·8	

upon exports, through the sudden closures of markets, when European countries joined France against England or were occupied by the French armies. In particular, the Continental Blockade, which, despite extensive smuggling and the ingenuity of British merchants in finding new trade routes and new outlets, was pretty effective at times in closing most European markets to British goods, and the dispute with the United States from 1807 onward, culminating in the war of 1812, were undoubtedly instrumental in the slowing down of the growth of British exports during the Napoleonic war.[32] It is also possible that the impoverishment of European countries by protracted warfare and the stagnation in Britain of consumption per capita, which affected imports and therefore the purchasing power of foreign countries, had deleterious effects upon British exports. On the whole, and in the long run, the French wars seem to have been either slightly unfavourable or simply neutral towards British exports and the ubiquitous military and political factors might conceal the influence of some purely economic forces.[33]

The progress of British exports after the French wars is shown in Table 6.4. The periodisation in part B of the table has been suggested by the deviations from trend. Their decline, which had started during

[32] See F. Crouzet, *L'Economie britannique et le Blocus Continental, 1806–1813* (Paris, 1958, 2 vols., 2nd edn, 1987).

[33] As the deceleration which started after 1802 went on after the war, it might be part of a long-term fluctuation, independent from the influence of political and military developments. According to J. G. Williamson, 'Why Was British Growth so Slow During the Industrial Revolution?', *Journal of Economic History*, XLIV, 3, September 1984, pp. 709–10, the rate of growth per year of British exports of manufactures, from 1793 to 1815, would have been 16 per cent higher, if peace had been maintained.

the Napoleonic war, after 1802, goes on after the peace, to a nadir in 1826, both for volumes and values. But, after 1826, deviations in the volume and the value series behave differently. Deviations in volume rise progressively to reach a peak (+25·6 per cent, against −28·2 per cent in 1826) in 1856, after which they tend to fall again. After the fast growth of export volume from 1782 to 1802, there was thus a phase of markedly slower growth up to 1826, followed by a period of acceleration and fast growth from 1826 to 1856 and a deceleration thereafter – despite the boom of the late 1860s and early 1870s. On the other hand, if the periods considered are those delimited by 'political' changes (the end of the wars, the triumph of Free Trade), the rates of growth of volume are quite close and seem to have been just a little higher for 1814–46 than for 1781–1814.[34]

As for the current values, their deviations from trend fall sharply from 1802 to 1826, but their curve is U-shaped, with its bottom from 1826 to 1848, where they fluctuate around a low level, and it is only from 1849 onward that they rise very sharply to a peak of +74·5 per cent in 1872. Moreover, unlike the volume figures (which do not cease to rise on trend, despite the postwar slumps), the current value of British exports, after a very slow growth from 1802 to 1814, tends to fall from 1815 to the late 1820s and only starts to rise again clearly in the late 1830s.[35] There is therefore during the first half of the nineteenth century, not only a different periodisation in the course of volumes and values, but also a contrast between the fast growth of the volume of exports and the much slower growth of their values.[36]

This contrast resulted from a marked fall in the prices of exports during this period; cotton yarn and cloth had the sharpest fall and its impact was aggravated by the growing proportion of cotton textiles in total export volume. Those falling prices resulted mainly from increasing mechanisation and higher productivity, so that they must not be

[34] It is difficult to be definite, because Imlah's volume series starts in 1796, and the rate of growth for 1781–1814 must be calculated on the different official values series.

[35] Imlah, pp. 37–8, Table 2.

[36] This differential manifested itself from the turn of the century (see Table 6.2); the index of the average price of exports, which has been computed by Imlah (p. 94, Table 8) has its peak in 1802; an index of British industrial prices reaches its peak in 1814; G. Hueckel, 'War and the British Economy, 1783–1815: A General Equilibrium Analysis', *Explorations in Economic History*, X, 4, Summer 1973, p. 388, Table 3. According to C. K. Harley, 'British Industrialization Before 1841: Evidence of Slower Growth During the Industrial Revolution', *Journal of Economic History*, XLII, 2, June 1982, pp. 271, 286–9, prices of cotton fabrics were steady from 1770 to 1815, but those of other manufactures rose by 50 per cent; from 1815 to 1841, cottons fell by 45 per cent.

interpreted as a sign of 'economic adversity', inasmuch as the volume of exports grew rapidly.[37] But L. G. S. Sandberg has also shown that there was a substantial and (after 1830) continuous decline in the average quality of British cottons exported, as an increased share of them was shipped to low-income countries (especially India), which bought only low-quality goods.[38]

However, from 1852 onward, the average prices of exports rose, so that the contrast between the rates of growth of volume and of value disappears for the period 1846–73, when actually export values grew faster than volumes.

On the other hand, the rate of growth of export volume from 1846 to 1873 is only slightly higher than from 1814 to 1846 and this raises doubts about Imlah's views on 'the failure of the British protectionist system', i.e., its alleged retardative impact upon industrial output and exports, and the 'success of British Free Trade policy', which he makes largely responsible for a phenomenal and unprecedented growth of exports after 1842.[39] Imlah argued that the Corn Laws restricted the expansion of the British home market and the purchasing power of foreign countries, especially in Northern Europe, while the import of grain was a spasmodic, emergency trade, paid for in part by gold, so that the additional purchasing power which it brought to foreign countries did not result in an immediate or equivalent response in their buying of British goods; otherwise there was a high degree of export–import dependence in British trade with many areas, with exports being the dependent variable.[40] However, there is much good sense in J. H. Clapham's older views that, up to the 1840s, Britain did not need large regular imports of grain and that freer importation of the other articles which were kept out by protection (foreign timber, sugar, and coffee, French wines, German linens) would not have had much influence upon exports; and that 'no amount of tariff manipulation or reciprocity could have opened very much wider the European markets', given the decidedly protectionist policy of France, Austria–Hungary, and Russia (a fact which Imlah overlooks) and the existing

[37] Imlah, pp. 93, 100, 102–9.

[38] L. G. Sandberg, 'Movements in the Quality of British Cotton Textile Exports, 1815–1913', *Journal of Economic History*, XXVIII, 1, March 1968, pp. 1, 7–9, 13, 19–20.

[39] Imlah, pp. 115, 117, 123, 125–8, 132, 156–7, 163–7. Actually, Imlah has made a serious mistake in using as benchmark the years 1842 (depression) and 1873 (boom); the rate of growth is heavily overestimated for the Free Trade period.

[40] This is confirmed by R. C. O. Matthews, *A Study in Trade-Cycle History: Economic Fluctuations in Great Britain, 1833–1842* (Cambridge, 1954), pp. 43 sqq.

Table 6.5. *Mean rates of growth per year (%), principal British exports (official values)*[a]

Product	1697–1760	1760–1783	1783–1792	1792–1802	1802–1814	1783–1814
Woollen and worsted manufactures	0·9	−2·2	4·9	4·9	−1·4	1·8[b]
Cotton yarn and manufactures	2·8	2·9	10·7	17·3	8·4	12·3
Linens	6·6	−1·6	6·4	0·5	2·6[c]	2·2[c]
Silks	1·2	−2·2	0·8	−0·7	−0·7	−1·1
Iron and steel, unwrought and wrought	3·5	0·3	9·6	3·1	1·4	2·3
Nonferrous metals and manufactures	1·5	0·8	6·9	1·9	−4·9	−0·5
Total exports	1·6	−1·4	6·0	5·9	3·1	4·1

[a] Exports are from England and Wales up to 1791, from Great Britain later. Calculated by exponential adjustment, and expressed in percentage.
[b] The data used stop in 1808; woollen hats are included, except for 1802–14.
[c] The data used stop in 1812.

reasonably open channels for British goods through the Low Countries and various German states.[41] If British protectionism slowed down the growth of British exports, it cannot have done so by much; that the growth of export *volumes* accelerated from 1826 to 1856, to slow down later, seems independent of tariff policy.

This survey of the course of British exports during the eighteenth century and the first three-quarters of the nineteenth shows that the alternation of periods of growth and stagnation or decline in the *volume* of exports, which Deane and Cole observed in the eighteenth century, seems to have existed also in the nineteenth, with the difference that there was no period of actual decline (like the 1770s), but only an alternation of phases of faster (1782–1802, 1827–56) and of slower (1803–26, 1857–73) growth. In the long run, the growth of British exports would display a 'cyclical' pattern, with long fluctuations in its rate of 40 to 50 years.[42] The growth of export values was

[41] J. H. Clapham, *An Economic History of Modern Britain*, vol. I (Cambridge, 1939 edition), pp. 479–81; R. G. Wilson, *Gentlemen Merchants. The Merchant Community in Leeds (1700–1830)* (Manchester, 1971), pp. 113, 116, on the impact of *foreign* protection on British woollens exports.

[42] We put cyclical between inverted commas, because we do not want to imply that there was a self-generating movement like in the short-term business cycle.

a function of both volume and prices. From the time *c.* 1790 when the price stability of the eighteenth century came to an end, the fluctuations in the rate of growth of export values are quite pronounced, with two periods of fast growth (when both volume and prices of manufactured exports rose together), from 1782 to 1802 and from 1849 to 1873, and in-between periods of slower growth or even decline. This will have an important impact upon the relationship between exports and national product.

The sectors of growth

During most of the eighteenth century – up to the 1760s – exports of woollens and worsteds grew at a slow pace (0.9 per cent per year between 1697 and 1760 or 1772, against 1·6 per cent for total English exports; see Table 6.5),[43] while shipments of certain other goods, such as linens, cottons, metals, metal manufactures, and coal, progressed more and, in some cases, much more rapidly. The result was a steady and pronounced decline of the share of woollens in total exports (from 70 per cent in 1700/9 to 44 per cent in 1760/9) – though they remained by far their largest single component – and an increase in the share of the 'other' goods, reflecting the broadening of the British economy and the widening range of its competitive manufactures.[44] The percentage contributions of these various commodities to the increase of total English exports between 1699/1701 and 1772/4 can be calculated:[45]

Woollens and worsteds	21·1
Linens, silks, cottons, hats	20·6
Metals and metal manufactures	21·3
All other goods	37·0

From the 1780s, this 'balanced growth' on a broad front was to give way to a different pattern. The method used to analyse this development will be to ascertain the contribution of each major group of exported commodities to the growth of British exports, by calculating

43 Deane, *First Industrial*, p. 53. N.B. the terms woollens (which include worsteds), cottons, cotton goods (or fabrics, or manufactures), linens, silks, apply only to cloth woven of those materials; we write of wool, cotton, or linen *products* when twist and yarn are added.

44 Tables and comments in: Schumpeter, p. 12; Mathias, p. 432, Table 15; Minchinton, pp. 24–5; Eversley, p. 223, Table 1; Deane and Cole p. 30.

45 From figures in Davis, 'English Foreign Trade', p. 302. The share of cottons was only 3·7 per cent.

Table 6.6. *Contributions of the principal products to the increase of total British exports (current values)*[a]

Product	From 1784/6 to 1794/96 (%)	From 1794/96 to 1804/06 (%)	From 1804/06 to 1814/16 (%)	From 1784/86 to 1814/16 (%)	From 1814/16 to 1844/46[b] (%)
Woollen and worsted yarn and manufactures	18·1	6·0	22·8	14·0	10·8
Cotton yarn and manufactures	28·8	72·8	31·5	52·8	45·9
Other textiles[c]	10·4	3·3	8·6	6·9	9·8
Iron and ironwares	9·6	3·6	—	—	16·9
Nonferrous metals and manufactures	10·0	3·8	12·3	7·9	16·6
All other goods	23·1	10·5	24·9	18·3	—

[a] The symbol — indicates that an actual decrease took place in the category between the years indicated.

[b] Pertains to exports from the United Kingdom (excluding exports to Ireland). Other columns pertain to Great Britain and include exports to Ireland.

[c] Linens (including linen yarn), silks, hats, haberdashery, garments.

Source. Percentages calculated from R. Davis, *The Industrial Revolution and British Overseas Trade* (Leicester, 1979), pp. 94–7, 100.

the marginal changes in exports of these groups, i.e., the proportion of the net change in exports of each of them to the net change in total British exports.[46] The results of these calculations are given in Table 6.6, which is based on R. Davis' current values; as his first figures are for 1784/6, we have used *official values* for calculating the percentage contributions of the major groups to the growth of total exports from 1780/2 to 1790/2:[47]

Woollens and worsteds	35·7
Cotton goods	16·3
Linens	4·8
Silks	1·1
Iron and ironwares	8·9
Nonferrous metals and manufactures	5·5
All other goods	27·8

46 If X are total exports and X_c the exports of cottons, the contribution of cottons to the growth of total exports between the years t_0 and t_1 is: $C_c = (X_c t_1 - X_c t_0)/(Xt_1 - Xt_0) \times 100$. However, there is a difficulty for several periods, when some items are increasing and some others decreasing; in such cases, the percentages which have been calculated are those between the *net* increase in the exports of each growing item and the '*gross*' increase of total exports, i.e., the sum of those increasing items.

47 As the changes in the price structure were not too serious during this period, this calculation is valid.

During the 1780s, the exports of all the major commodities (except silks) increased at a fast pace (see Table 6.5), including those of woollens, which had been so sluggish earlier in the century. Of course, exports of cottons grew much more (10·7 per cent per year in volume between 1783 and 1792) than those of other goods (except ironwares), but they started from low levels (£336,000 OV, in 1780/2); thus, though their volume increased nearly fivefold in 10 years, their contribution to the growth of total exports (OV) from 1780/2 to 1790/2 was relatively modest (16 per cent) and much inferior to that of woollens. For the slightly later period from 1784/6 to 1794/6 and in current values, their contribution is substantially larger (29 per cent), but those of woollens, of the other textiles, and of 'all other goods' remain very large, while that of ironwares is again under 10 per cent.

It seems therefore that the leap forward of exports in the 1780s (and even the early 1790s) was not based mainly on the technological and organisational innovations in the cotton and iron industries and that the significance of those industries for the export trade at that time must not be overestimated.[48] Though the spectacular rise in cotton exports was a novel and crucial development, there was still a general advance on a broad front like that earlier in the century.

It was only during the 1790s and 1800s that the position changed rather drastically. The growth of the volume of cotton products exports accelerated and, from 1792 to 1802, reached the amazing and record rate of 17·3 per cent per year;[49] it was to go on during the next decade at a slower, but still impressive pace. As for woollens exports, they maintained from 1792 to 1802 the same relatively high rate of growth (4·9 per cent) as from 1783 to 1792, but their volume (and its deviation from trend) reached a peak in 1801 and then fell markedly.[50] For the other types of goods, the rates of growth were much more modest after 1792 than from 1783 to 1792, and for silks and nonferrous metals, there was an actual fall in the volume of exports after 1796 and 1802, respectively.[51]

As a consequence of those differentials in the rates of growth after 1792, cotton goods (and yarns, which had started to be exported in growing quantities from 1794) were responsible for 72·8 per cent of the

[48] Ashton, in Schumpeter, p. 14; Ashton, *Fluctuations*, pp. 62–3; Davis, 'English Foreign Trade', p. 298; Mathias, p. 98; Deane and Habakkuk, p. 78.

[49] There was an especially sharp rise in 1798 and 1799; Edwards, p. 73.

[50] Ashton, *Fluctuations*, p. 76; Wilson, p. 111: in the West Riding, the strong upward trend in activity since 1783 was broken down by a crisis in 1801 and lean years followed.

[51] Between 1803 and 1815, the OV of iron goods exports never reached their peak of 1802.

great (72 per cent) increase in British exports (CV) between 1794/6 and 1804/6, while the contribution of woollens was only 6 per cent, and that of metals and metal manufactures 7·4 per cent.[52] These figures are consistent with the conclusions of M. M. Edwards who puts in the 1790s and 1800s (later than his predecessors) the period of decisive progress for the cotton industry, and with Deane and Cole's view that the rise of the cotton industry at the end of the eighteenth century was partly compensated by a slowing down in the growth of the other textile industries.[53]

However, between 1804/6 and 1814/16, the contribution of cotton goods and yarn to the increase of total exports (which was itself modest: 16 per cent) was much smaller than for the preceding decade, falling to 31·5 per cent, the same as woollens and other textiles together, with a compensating larger share for nonferrous metals and manufactures and 'other goods'. These changes resulted both from a recovery of non-cotton exports in 1814/16 and from the fall in the prices of cottons.[54] None the less, from the resumption of war, up to 1812, cotton products were entirely responsible for the increase in total British exports, which, without them, would have actually declined.[55] And finally, if we compare the current values of exports in 1784/6 and 1814/16, we find that exports of cotton products had increased by 2283 per cent, while those of woollens, other textiles, nonferrous metals, and 'other goods' had increased three- or fourfold only and iron goods exports had actually fallen, and that cottonwares were responsible for over half (52·8 per cent) of the increase in total exports, against 14 per cent for woollens, 7 per cent for the other textiles, 8 per cent for nonferrous metals, and 18 per cent for 'other goods'. Though the ascendancy of the cotton industry is not overwhelming, the low level of its exports in the 1780s must be remembered and, on the whole, the growth of British exports during those crucial 30 years was very much 'unbalanced'.

The enormous increase in the overseas sales of cotton goods was due mostly to their relative cheapness compared with other fabrics and to

[52] From 1794/6 to 1804/6, the CV of cotton products exports increased 330 per cent; that of the other groups between 18 per cent (woollens) and 31 per cent (nonferrous metals).

[53] Edwards, pp. 8, 10, 12–14, 49–50, 73; Deane and Cole, pp. 54, 212–13.

[54] While the prices of non-cotton exports fell far less or not at all; Imlah, p. 106.

[55] If we compare the OV of exports in 1800/2 and 1810/12, exports of woollens, other textiles, metal goods, and 'other goods' show a marked fall, while cotton goods and yarn progress by 236 per cent.

the fact that they enjoyed an elastic demand; thanks to the opening of new cotton lands in the United States and to technical innovations in Britain, prices of cotton yarn and cloth fell, possibly as soon as the 1780s and certainly from the 1790s, generating a disproportionate expansion in demand. There was a substitution of British cottons for other fabrics – linens, silks, mixtures of cotton and linen, possibly woollens – and for non-British cotton goods, which previously had been either produced locally or imported from Britain and other countries (for instance, East India cotton goods); there was also the creation of a broader market, through the overall expansion (in volume) of the demand for textiles, thanks to the falling prices of British cottons.[56]

The fast growth of cottonwares exports brought about a spectacular change in the commodity structure of British exports, with the ratio of cotton products to total exports rising dramatically; concomitantly the shares of woollens and of linens, silks, and ironwares came down sharply.[57] There was thus, for a time, a reversal of the trend toward a broadening of the base of the British export trade which had prevailed in the eighteenth century, and the dramatic expansion from the 1780s to the 1810s was very narrowly based, becoming even more so. On the contrary, the decades after the end of the wars were marked by a renewed, though rather slow, diversification of British exports.

Between 1814 and the 1840s, the export of cotton products increased so rapidly in volume[58] that, despite the fall in their prices, their values advanced at a higher rate than those of total exports (1·4 per cent per year against 1·1 per cent). Exports of wool products grew quite slowly in volume and hardly at all in value,[59] while exports of linens, metals, and metal goods displayed higher rates of growth than during the wars. This period was thus still dominated by cotton: cotton yarn and goods were responsible for 46 per cent of the increase in value of total British exports between 1814/16 and 1844/6.[60] The contribution of

56 Edwards, pp. 8, 31–3, 35, 239–41; Deane, *First Industrial*, pp. 63–4; Berrill, p. 358; Imlah, p. 104. The fast increase in cotton yarn exports from 1794 corresponded also in part to a substitution by Continental weavers of British machine-spun yarn to locally hand-spun yarn.

57 Deane and Cole, p. 30; Imlah, p. 104, Table 9.

58 Though more slowly than before 1814.

59 Though Davis' figures show a larger increase than the declared values – and also for linens exports (whence the differences in Table 6.8); *The Industrial Revolution*, pp. 97–100.

60 Imlah, p. 127, gives a higher figure (72 per cent) for the contribution of cotton products to the increase of total exports from 1816/20 to 1838/42 because of his different method of calculation.

Table 6.7. *Mean rates of growth, principal exports (percentage per annum)*[a]

Product	1814–1846	1846–1873	1814–1873
A. Declared values			
Cotton yarn and manufactures	1·4	4·8	2·8
Woollen and worsted yarn and manufactures	0·1	6·3	2·9
Linens	2·8	4·3	3·3
Metals and metal manufactures	3·2	5·7	5·1
Coal	8·3	8·7	9·2
Total exports	1·1	5·7	3·4
B. Volumes at 1880 prices			
Cotton manufactures	5·5	4·0	5·1
Woollens and worsteds	1·5	4·6	3·4
All other goods	3·4	5·7	5·1
Total exports	4·3	4·7	4·8

[a] Calculated by exponential adjustment.

Source. (A) B. R. Mitchell and P. Deane, *Abstract of British Historical Statistics* (Cambridge, 1962), pp. 302–4. (B) A. H. Imlah, *Economic Elements in the Pax Britannica* (Cambridge, Mass., 1958), pp. 94–7, 208–15, Tables 8, II, III, and IV.

wool products was modest, that of other textiles – mostly linen products – far from negligible;[61] but, the novel and significant development was the important contribution made by metals and metal manufactures, which were responsible for about a third of the increase in total exports.[62]

However, Imlah has rightly pointed out that most of the increase in the value of textiles exports resulted from the progress of yarn and twist exports.[63] From 1814/16 to 1844/6, cotton yarn exports increased in volume over twice as much as cotton cloth; in value the former increased over threefold, while cloth rose only 13 per cent; twist and yarn were thus responsible for 69 per cent of the increase in cotton products exports. Woollen yarn exports were negligible in the 1810s, but exceeded £2 million in 1844/6,[64] even though woollens and worsteds exports had fallen since 1814/16. Likewise, exports of linen yarn were trifling before 1832, but they rose rapidly in the 1830s and were responsible for nearly one half of the increase in linen products exports between 1816/20 and 1838/42.[65] In addition, exports of

[61] The increased importance of linens exports results partly from the inclusion of exports by the Irish linen industry, which were excluded from previous figures of exports from Britain.

[62] The trend toward an increasing contribution by this group started in the late 1820s.

[63] Imlah, p. 127.

[64] Davis' figures (*The Industrial Revolution*, p. 100).

[65] Imlah, p. 127; Clapham, I, p. 249; *Abstract*, pp. 195, 202.

nonmanufactured iron rose also much faster than those of ironwares and accounted for 62 per cent of the increase in iron products exports between 1814/16 and 1844/6. M. Lévy-Leboyer has stressed that these developments resulted from continental protectionism and from the progress in the production of finished goods in European countries: they were an example of international division of labour, with Britain expanding her sales to Europe of semifinished, capital-intensive goods, in which she had large comparative advantages, rather than those of labour-intensive goods.[66]

From 1846 to 1873, the position was quite different, but quite simple: exports of all the main categories of goods grew rapidly, both in volume and – still more – in value (see Table 6.7). But, this time, cotton products were rather the laggards, mostly because of the cotton famine during the American Civil War: their rates of growth per year were lower than those of total exports.[67] On the contrary, exports of woollen products, of metals and metal manufactures, of coal, and of 'other goods' grew at a faster pace than total exports. Still, because cotton products accounted for a large share of total exports, their contribution to the increase of the latter's values, between 1844/6 and 1871/3, remained considerable (27·4 per cent), though far less than during the preceding 30 years. The relative contribution of metal goods also fell markedly, while that of woollen products increased, but the largest contribution to the advance of total exports came from 'other goods' (33·3 per cent). This was a period of diversification of exports and of general – and rapid – advance on a broad front.

As the absolute increase in the value of British exports from 1844/6 to 1871/3 was enormous (£186 million) and far superior to that of 1814/16 to 1844/6 (£12·5 million), the percentage contributions of the main products to the total growth of exports, from the end of the Napoleonic wars to the Great Depression (Table 6.8, column 3), are close to those of the later period and display therefore a pattern of 'balanced growth'.

During the combined period, 1814–73, the changes in the commodity structure of British exports are now clear.[68] The share of cotton products in the value of total exports continued to increase, but much more slowly than during the French wars, to reach a peak (about 50

[66] Lévy-Leboyer, pp. 177–8, 180–1.

[67] From 1849 to 1861, the growth of exports of cotton products had remained rapid.

[68] Imlah, pp. 104, 107, Tables 9 and 10; Deane and Cole, p. 31, Table 9; Mathias, p. 434, Table 17.

Table 6.8. *Contributions of the principal products to the increase of total United Kingdom exports*[a]

Product	From 1814/16 to 1844/6 (%)	From 1844/6 to 1871/3 (%)	From 1814/16 to 1871/3 (%)
A. Current values (Davis)			
Woollen and worsted yarn and manufactures	10·8		
Cotton yarn and manufactures	45·9		
Other textiles	9·8		
Iron and ironwares	16·9		
Nonferrous metals and manufactures	16·6		
All other goods	—		
B. Declared values			
Woollen and worsted yarn and manufactures	3·9	13·7	13·3
Cotton yarn and manufactures	46·4	27·4	29·3
Linen yarn and manufactures	13·7	3·1	4·0
Metals and metal manufactures	35·9	22·4	23·8
All other goods	—	33·3	29·7
C. Volumes at 1880 prices			
Woollen and worsted yarn and manufactures	9·9	13·3	12·6
Cotton yarn and manufactures	54·6	26·1	31·8
All other goods (including metals)	35·5	60·7	55·6

[a] The symbol — indicates that exports in the category decreased between the years indicated.
Source. (A) R. Davis, *The Industrial Revolution and British Overseas Trade*, pp. 97, 100; (B) (see (A) in Table 6.7; (C) See (B) in Table 6.7.

per cent) in the 1830s, then to fall back gradually to 31 per cent in 1871/3. Woollen products continued their relative decline. The metal group, by contrast, experienced a steady rise (at least up to the 1850s), reaching just over 20 per cent of total exports values. The marked rise of the share of 'other goods' completes this trend toward diversification, which was none the less limited by the supremacy of textiles (which remained over 50 per cent of total exports in the 1870s). Even so, while the first upsurge in the value of British exports – from 1782 to 1802 – had been the result, above all, of the dramatic rise of cotton goods exports, the second, in the 1850s and 1860s, was much more broadly based.

The markets for growth

During the eighteenth century, up to the dispute with the colonies, there had been three major trends of change in the geographical pattern of English exports.[69] First, the share of total exports which went to Continental Europe had fallen markedly, from 82 per cent in 1700/1 to 40 per cent in 1772/3.[70] Second, exports to the British colonies in America – and especially to those of North America – had increased at a fast pace, so that the share of America in total exports had risen from 10 per cent in 1700/1 to 37 per cent in 1772/3.[71] Third, a less important, but still significant development had been the progress of exports to other 'captive markets', in Ireland, Africa, and the East Indies. If one compares exports from England and Wales (OV) in 1700/1 and 1772/3, the respective percentage contributions of the main areas to their increase appear as:

Europe	4·2
North America	41·8
West Indies	18·2
British Islands	14·6
East Indies	13·5
Africa	7·8

The period from the 1780s to the end of the Napoleonic wars presents an intricate and shifting pattern of changes in the geographical distribution of British exports, largely as a consequence of the French wars, with their sudden closings or openings of markets, which forced British exporters to display a great deal of adaptability and ingenuity in switching their shipments from one market to another. These short-run kaleidoscopic changes cannot be considered in detail here,[71] but the most significant shifts in the destination of exports appear in Table 6.9, in which the contributions of the main geographical areas to the increase in Britain's total exports have been

69 *Abstract*, p. 312 (the percentages given in the text are calculated from the figures in this table: they refer to official values and to exports from England); Davis, 'English Foreign Trade', pp. 286–91, 302–3; Davis, *A Commercial Revolution* (The Historical Association, 1967), pp. 20–1; Davis, *The Rise of the Atlantic Economies* (London, 1973), pp. 306–7; Ashton, in Schumpeter, pp. 10–11; Minchinton, pp. 26–31; Flinn, pp. 58–9; Deane and Cole, p. 34; Deane, *First Industrial*, pp. 55–6; D. A. Fairnie, 'The Commercial Empire of the Atlantic, 1607–1783', *The Economic History Review*, XV, 2, December 1962, p. 214.

70 Actually, exports to Europe had risen up to *c.* 1760, but had fallen sharply afterward and were in 1772/3 hardly higher than in 1700/1.

71 The growth of exports to North America was proportional to the increase of the latter in population; Harley, p. 280.

71 They have been studied for the period of the Continental Blockade in Crouzet, *L'Economie britannique*.

Table 6.9. *Percentage contributions of the major geographical areas to the increase in total British exports (official values)*[a]

Area	From 1783/87 to 1788/92 (%)	From 1788/92 to 1793/97 (%)	From 1793/97 to 1798/1802 (%)	From 1798/1802 to 1803/07 (%)	From 1803/07 to 1808/12 (%)
Northern Europe[b]	16·5	—	30·5	24·2	—
Southern Europe[c]	6·5	—	8·4	7·7	46,8
Europe	22·5	—	38·9	31·9	(45·4)[f]
British North America	2·8	3·3	5·5	—	5·4
United States	25·7	48·9	22·6	27·1	—
British West Indies	16·8	16·3	12·6	—	}
Conquered West Indies		15·8	7·5	—	} 44·3
Foreign territories in America[d]	0·4	0·2	0·5	19·6	}
America	45·6	84·4	48·7	—	(48·4)[f]
British Islands[e]	10·1	2·1	7·2	21·4	3·5
East Indies	18·9	13·7	—	—	—
Africa	2·9	—	5·1	—	—

[a] The symbol — indicates that exports to the area decreased between the quinquenniums considered.
[b] France and all countries to the north.
[c] Countries south of France, including Turkey.
[d] Foreign West Indies and Latin America.
[e] Ireland, Isle of Man, and Channel Islands.
[f] Calculated as percentages of subtotals to the sum of increases in subtotals.
Source. Calculated for the years 1783–1802 from Public Record Office, Customs 17/8 to 24; for the years 1802–12 from F. Crouzet, *L'Economie britannique et le Blocus Continental, 1806–1813* (Paris, 1958), vol. II, p. 885, Table 3 (mainly based on Customs ledgers at the Public Record Office).

calculated from each quinquennial average of their official values[72] to the next, between 1783 and 1812. It shows that the advance of exports was achieved by a succession of shifts between the main trading areas in Europe and America,[73] one or two of them absorbing most of the additional exports for a few years, and also making good for the set-backs in other quarters, but giving way to different markets afterward.

In the mid-1780s, the recovery of exports from the depression of the American war was mainly due to rising European demand; but 67 per cent of the increase in exports to Europe between 1783 and 1788 resulted from the sharp rise in exports to France, following the Eden

[72] Current values would be more satisfactory, but Davis' figures do not give the same complete coverage.
[73] The East Indies were important in the early years, but later on exports to them decreased.

Treaty of 1786. After 1788, the advance of exports to Europe slowed down markedly and it gave way to a sharp fall with the beginning of war against France in 1793. On the other hand, exports to the United States more than doubled within the 4 years after 1788 and they went on rising almost continuously up to 1801. They played a decisive part in the last phase of the leap forward of exports in the late 1780s and early 1790s; the export boom which culminated in 1792 was America-based and not Europe-based.[74] As, moreover, new markets were opened in the West Indies during the war, the New World was responsible for nearly the whole of the additional exports which were achieved between 1788 and 1798.[75] Then, for a few years up to 1802, there was a 'return to Europe' and a partial reversal of the previous switch toward America, owing to a rapid recovery and increase of exports to Northern Europe, which played a vital part in the progress of exports during those years; the export boom of 1802, unlike that of 1792, was Europe-based. However, this movement was reversed as soon as war broke out again in 1803: exports to Europe declined, shipments to the United States rose rapidly again, and it was thanks to increased exports to the New World that total exports were maintained at an average high level between 1803 and 1807.[76] During the late years of the French wars, the Continental Blockade as well as Jefferson's and Madison's policies brought about sharp falls in average exports to Northern Europe and to the United States, while the invasion of Portugal and Spain by the French and the Peninsular war opened widely to British exporters the markets of those countries and their American possessions; exports to Southern Europe[77] and to Latin America expanded enormously and more than made good the losses suffered in more northerly regions; these two areas were the outlets for the new exports of the years 1808/12. Finally, the collapse of

[74] There is no reason to speak of an 'invasion of Europe' by British manufactures during the 1780s, thanks to their price advantage resulting from the recent technological breakthroughs. If one is to find such an 'invasion' of the Continent, it is during the few years from 1798 to 1802; but it was an invasion by cotton goods and cotton yarn: exports of cottons to Europe rose from £701,000 in 1797 (OV) to £4,773,000 in 1802 (see Edwards, pp. 14, 54, 63, 67, 243–4, Tables B/1 and 2).

[75] The 'Americanisation' of British trade, which had been set back by the conflict with the 13 colonies, had been resumed and intensified: in 1798, the share of America in total exports reached 61 per cent (OV); it was 34 per cent in 1783/7 and 49 per cent in 1808/12.

[76] This shift was not as pronounced as the earlier ones and, because of the small increase in total exports between 1798/1802 and 1803/7, the figures for the contributions of the various areas in column 4 of Table 6.9 are not very significant.

[77] Which were bolstered also by heavy smuggling from Malta to Mediterranean countries.

Napoleon's Empire brought about an ultimate shift to Northern Europe in 1813 and 1814.

However, if this 30-year period is considered as a whole, it is clear that the New World – and especially the United States, despite the vicissitudes in the last years of the wars – played a decisive part in the growth of British exports, though the contributions from Europe, the East Indies, and Ireland were not unimportant, as is shown in the following calculation of the percentage shares of the cumulated *additional* exports to the main trading areas in the grand total of cumulated *additional* exports (OV) which were achieved between 1783 and 1812:[78]

Northern Europe	10·8	
Southern Europe	11·9	
Europe		22·7
British North America	2·6	
United States	32·3	
West Indies and Latin America	24·9	
America		59·8
British Islands	7·6	
East Indies	10·0	
Africa	nil.	

From the end of the Napoleonic wars to the 1840s, the growth of the value of British exports to Europe was quite slow, but only a shade slower than that of total exports (see Table 6.10). Indeed, the value of exports to Europe shows a falling trend up to the early 1830s, while their volume stagnates up to the late 1820s. This recession was more pronounced than that in total exports and contemporaries had some grounds to think that the protectionist policies of most European countries were building up against British manufactures a 'Second Continental Blockade', which may have stimulated exporters to divert their shipments to non-European markets. Still, exports to Europe revived in the 1830s and their contribution to the increase of total exports values between 1814/18 and 1842/6 is not negligible (see Table 6.11), while their share of total exports, after a dip in the 1820s,

[78] Additional exports are those over the 1783 level. Rather different results emerge from the comparison of Davis' current values for 1784/6 and 1814/16 (*The Industrial Revolution*, pp. 94, 97), as exports to Northern Europe had strongly recovered in the immediate postwar period.

Table 6.10. *Mean rates of growth, exports from the United Kingdom to the major geographical areas (percentage per annum)*[a]

Area	Current values 1814–1846	Current values 1846–1873	Volumes at 1880 prices 1814–1846	Volumes at 1880 prices 1846–1873
Northern Europe[b]	0·9	6·7	4·1	5·7
Southern Europe[c]	1·0	5·8	4·2	4·8
United States	−0·6	3·9	2·6	2·9
America except USA	0·2	4·4	3·4	3·4
Asia, Australasia, Africa	4·4	6·6	7·7	5·6
Total exports	1·1	5·7	4·3	4·7

[a] Rates of growth by exponential adjustment.
[b] France and countries to the north, but includes Austria–Hungary for 1846–73.
[c] Includes Turkey, the Middle East, and North Africa, as well as Austria–Hungary for 1814–46.
Source. B. R. Mitchell and P. Deane, *Abstracts of British Historical Statistics* (Cambridge, 1962), pp. 313–15, 318, 321, and 324 for the declared (current) values; volumes have been calculated by deflating the current values series by an index of export prices taken from A. H. Imlah, *Economic Elements in the Pax Britannica* (Cambridge, Mass., 1958), pp. 94–6.

Table 6.11. *Percentage contributions of the major geographical areas to the increase in current values of total United Kingdom exports*[a]

Area	From 1814/18 to 1842/46 (%)	From 1846/50 to 1869/73 (%)
Northern Europe	15·2	35·7
Southern Europe	13·9	12·5
Europe	29·1	48·2
United States	—	13·1
West Indies and Canada	—	4·6
Latin America	17·9	9·1
Africa	8·6	2·5
Asia and Australasia	44·4	22·3

[a] The sign — means that an actual decrease occurred in exports to an area. For sources and definitions see Table 6.10.

returned to its previous level; but they made only a modest contribution to the cumulated additional total exports which were achieved from 1814 to 1846 (see Table 6.12).[79]

The course of exports to the United States in the same years was

[79] Gayer, II, pp. 543–4 and Matthews, p. 70; Europe is not the dynamic factor of the export trade and has a minor influence only on the fluctuations of the British economy.

Table 6.12. *Cumulated additional exports to the major geographical areas as percentages of total cumulated additional exports from United Kingdom (current values)*[a]

Area	From 1814 to 1846[b] (%)	From 1847 to 1873[c] (%)
Northern Europe	8·2	26·3
Southern Europe	5·4	13·7
Europe	13·6	40·0
United States	4·5	17·2
West Indies and Canada	—	2·6
Latin America	28·8	9·5
America	9·9	29·3
Africa	8·7	2·7
Asia } Australasia }	44·3	17·5
Australasia		10·5

[a] For sources and definitions see Table 6.10.
[b] For 1814–46 additional exports are calculated on the base of the average of the 3 years 1814/16, because the 1814 figures for some areas are abnormal.
[c] Additional exports are calculated from the base level of 1846.

extremely peculiar.[80] Not only did they fluctuate wildly, but, after a fall in the postwar years, they rose to a peak in the boom of 1836, only to fall back in the 1840s to low levels (in 1842/6, 23 per cent under 1814/18, CV), so that the rate of growth of their values from 1814 to 1846 is negative and their share of total exports fell from 17·4 per cent in 1814/18 to 11·1 per cent in 1842/6.[81] Nonetheless, as R. C. O. Matthews has demonstrated, the proportional fluctuations of exports to the United States being of much greater amplitude than in exports generally, the state of the American market was – at least in the 1830s – the most important single factor in bringing prosperity or depression to British export industries.[82]

Most of the increase in the value of British exports resulted therefore from demand in markets outside Europe and the United States,[83] which were largely 'new' markets for British manufacturers: Asia (i.e., mostly India),[84] Africa and Latin America. Indeed, exports to Asia

[80] The coefficient of correlation between exports to the USA and total exports (CV), for the period 1814–46, is only +0·33, while it is much higher for the other regional series.
[81] And their rate of growth in volume (2·6 per cent per year) is quite modest.
[82] Matthews, pp. 43–5.
[83] And also outside the traditional markets in Britain's American colonies: exports to the West Indies and to Canada declined almost continuously.
[84] At the end of the period, exports to Australia, which are included in the series 'Asia', had become important.

and Africa grew almost continuously and at a fast and accelerating pace (4·4 per cent per year in values, 7·7 per cent in volumes), and they were responsible for 44·4 per cent of the increase in the value of total exports from 1814/18 to 1842/6 and for 53 per cent of the total cumulated additional exports of this period; their share of total exports rose meanwhile from 7·9 to 21 per cent. Exports to Latin America increased less significantly and more irregularly, with growth slowing down greatly after the boom of 1824/5. Though an uncertain, expensive, and disappointing market,[85] Latin America still made a notable contribution to the growth of British exports, absorbing 29 per cent of total cumulated additional exports down to 1846.

This shift of British exports toward some of the less developed countries in the trading world is remarkable.[86] The traditional explanation is that the hot climates and low standards of living prevailing in those areas – whose markets were moreover unprotected – made cheap cotton goods (which formed the bulk of their imports from Britain) especially acceptable and in growing demand there.[87] A more sophisticated interpretation is that exports to those areas were the dependent variable of imports from them by Great Britain and that they accelerated from 1820 onward owing to the growing demand for tropical produce in Britain and other advanced countries, which resulted itself from their rapid growth in population and incomes.[88]

However, in volume, the contribution of Asia, Africa, and Latin America to the increase of total exports is markedly less than in value (46 per cent, against 71 per cent), while that of Europe is higher. The fall in export prices being most marked just after 1815 and slowing down later tends to minimise the growth of values to Europe, to which export volumes stagnated during the sharp fall in prices, while enhancing that to Asia and Africa, with their continuous progress in export volumes.

The period from 1846 to 1873 witnessed a growth of export values to all the main areas much more rapid than that between 1814 and 1846; the rate of growth of volume, though, did not increase markedly,

[85] D. C. M. Platt, *Latin America and British Trade, 1806–1914* (London, 1972), pp. 3–4, 6–7, 9–11, 22, 29–31, 33–4, 36–7, 57–8, 65.

[86] The share of 'advanced countries' (Northern Europe + USA) fell from 44 per cent of total exports (CV) in 1814/18 to 27 per cent in 1842/6.

[87] Clapham, I, p. 481; Imlah, p. 128.

[88] Mathews, pp. 72, 77–8; Gayer, II, p. 544; J. R. Hanson II, 'The Nineteenth-Century Exports of the Less Developed Countries', *Journal of Economic History*, XXXIII, 1, March 1973, pp. 305–6.

except to Northern Europe (see Table 6.10). Indeed, exports to Northern Europe showed the highest rate of growth (6·7 per cent per year for values) and made the largest contribution to the increase of total exports between 1846/50 and 1869/73 (36 per cent), though accounting for only 26 per cent of cumulated additional total exports achieved from 1847 to 1873. Exports to Asia, Australia, and Africa grew slightly more slowly, but their contribution to the increase of total exports (25 per cent) and their share of cumulated additional exports (31 per cent) were smaller than during the period 1814–46. This area and Northern Europe were responsible for 61 per cent of the increase in total exports between 1846/50 and 1869/73, an interesting concentration upon the most advanced and the least developed trading partners of Britain.[89] On the other hand, exports to Southern Europe grew at the same rate as total exports, while those to America – especially to the United States[90] – increased much more slowly; none the less, those areas made a contribution to total growth which was not negligible. In geographical distribution, as in commodity structure, the fast growth of British exports in the 1850s and 1860s was broadly based, though Northern Europe, Asia, and Australia were particularly strategic.

In every period from the 1780s to the 1860s, a small number of markets was responsible for most of the growth of British exports; the Americas, though playing a vital role from the 1780s to the end of the French wars, were thereafter far less important.

Exports and national income

'The growth in the importance of foreign trade can be illustrated by measuring its value against national income.'[91] Unfortunately, for the eighteenth century, we have neither export values at current prices nor reliable national income estimates. None the less, down to the 1770s official values of exports were unlikely to have been much different from their market values, while a few national income estimates, however tentative and uncertain, can give some rough orders of magnitude. The available data are presented in Table 6.13 and, despite their conjectural character, might support some conclusions.

[89] In Northern Europe, the Western countries (France, Belgium, Holland) had the fastest growth and contributed 17 per cent to the increase in total exports.

[90] Clapham, II, pp. 229–30, on the relative decline of the US market for Britain, following the Civil War.

[91] Deane and Cole, p. 28.

Table 6.13. *Exports and national income in the eighteenth century*[a]

	National income (£ million) (A)	Exports (£ million) (B)	Ratio of exports to national income (%) (C)
1. *c.* 1688	48	4	8·3
2. 1700	58·5 or 52	4·4	7·5 or 8·5
3. 1759	85	9·9	11·6
4. 1770	130	9·9	7·6
5. 1783	160	12·4	7·8
6. 1801	232	41·4	17·8

[a] N.B. Most figures in this table are highly tentative.

Notes. Figures are for England and Wales up to 1770, for Great Britain in 1783 and 1801. Export figures are triennial averages centred on the year specified, of official values, except in 1801, when declared values have been used; the OV of 1783 has been raised by 20 per cent to take into account the price rise.

Sources. **1.** Column A: Deane and Cole, p. 156. Column B: R. Davis, 'English Foreign Trade, 1660–1770', in Minchinton, pp. 79, Table 1, 85, note 4, 93; Davis, *English Overseas Trade, 1500–1700* (London, 1973), p. 56; Deane and Cole, pp. 310, note 2, 319. We have assumed that the volume of exports in 1686/8 was the same as in 1699/1701, i.e. £4·4 million, that this figure corresponded more or less to current values in 1699/1701 and we have adjusted it to take into account the rise in prices from 1688 to 1701 (about 10 per cent, according to *Abstract*, p. 468). The ratio in column C is higher than in Deane and Cole, pp. 228, 309 (5 to 6 per cent), who have relied on King's trade figures which, according to Davis, underestimate the exports of 1688. **2.** Column A: Bairoch, in *Annales*, XXVIII, pp. 556–7 (gross national product). Column B: Original official values for 1699/1701. **3.** Column A: Estimations of Joseph Massie, adjusted by Deane and Cole, p. 279. **4.** Column A: Deane and Cole, p. 156. **5.** Column A: Deane and Cole, p. 262, Deane and Habakkuk, p. 75. **6.** Column A: Deane and Cole, pp. 158–60, 161, Table 36. Column B: *Abstract*, p. 282; exports from the United Kingdom, somewhat inferior to those from Great Britain.

First, during most of the century up to the 1780s, the ratio of domestic exports to English national income (which we shall call the exports proportion) was quite modest[92] and remained generally under 10 per cent. However, this ratio did not rise regularly and it underwent a fluctuation which fits rather well with the changes in the rate of growth of exports which have been analysed earlier. It rose substantially between 1700 and 1759 (though the ratio given for the latter year must not be taken at its face value), as exports grew undoubtedly faster than national output.[93] But most of this increase took place during the stage of relatively fast growth of exports from 1745 to 1760, while there had been only a small advance during the quasi-stagnation from 1714 to 1744. Indeed, A. H. John had suggested that the rise in

[92] Though we find for the early period a ratio of exports to income higher than other writers; see notes to Table 6.13, 1.

[93] Deane and Cole, pp. 310–11; Harley, p. 286; N. F. R. Crafts, *British Economic Growth during the Industrial Revolution* (Oxford, 1985), p. 45, Table 2.11.

Table 6.14. *Exports as a percentage of national product, 1801–1871*

Year	At current prices (A)	At constant prices (B)
1801	17·8	8·0
1811	13·6	6·8
1821	12·6	7·6
1831	11·0	8·0
1841	11·1	10·4
1851	14·3	15·2
1861	19·2	20·2
1871	24·7	23·6

Source. National product is taken from P. Deane and W. A. Cole, *British Economic Growth 1688–1959* (2nd edn, Cambridge, 1967), p. 166, Table 37 (current prices), p. 282, Table 72 (constant prices). Exports (triennial averages centred on the quoted year) are from B. R. Mitchell and P. Deane, *Abstract of British Historical Statistics* (Cambridge, 1962), pp. 282–3 (declared values); and A. H. Imlah, *Economic Elements in the Pax Britannica* (Cambridge, 1958), pp. 94–7, Table 8 (volumes at 1880 prices). As Deane and Cole have calculated national product at constant prices with the Rousseaux index as deflator and as this index stands at 102 in 1880, the comparison with Imlah's volume series is valid.

exports after 1748 was so fast that it had to be met partially by a transfer of output from the domestic to the foreign market.[94] On the other hand, the sharp fall in the exports proportion in Table 6.13 from 1759 to 1770 and 1783, which would have brought it back, at the end of the American war, to its level of the turn of the century, tallies perfectly with the negative growth of exports from 1760 to 1781.[95] Of course, this fall of the ratio supports Eversley's view of a widening gap between export and home demand from 1750 (we would rather say 1760) to 1780, and his thesis that during this crucial period for the Industrial Revolution, foreign demand was not a major factor of expansion.[96]

Only in the last 20 years of the century did the exports proportion rise suddenly and rapidly, owing to the marked difference between the rate of growth of exports – 4·6 per cent per year from 1783 to 1800 in volume and even more in value – and that of total output which, according to Deane and Cole, was only 1·5 per cent in real terms (or 1·8 per cent, with different base and weights).[97] From our calculations, the

[94] Review of Deane and Cole, in *Kyklos*, XVII, 2, 1964, p. 278; and in Jones, p. 186.

[95] Deane and Cole, p. 262, note 1, point out that their figure for national income in 1783 might be too high (but our majoration of the exports OV by 20 per cent might also be excessive). See below, p. 260.

[96] Eversley, pp. 221, 229, 236, 247–9; also Flinn, p. 58. However, foreign demand may have been an important factor in the case of the cotton industry from 1750 to 1763; see pp. 105, 253.

[97] Deane and Cole, pp. 80, Table 20, 280, 311. Crafts, p. 45, Table 2.11, gives 63 per cent for 1780–1801.

ratio of the current value of exports to national income reached about 18 per cent *c.* 1801, having more than doubled since 1783.[98] Though Britain, around 1800, showed signs of becoming an 'export economy', this development was not to proceed further for several decades.

This retrogression appears in Table 6.14, which is more valid than our guess-estimates for the eighteenth century, as it is based on Deane and Cole' series of national income figures at 10-year intervals (which, though still tentative in the early nineteenth century, are not to be mistrusted too much) and on the current values of exports.[99] The exports proportion at current prices fell steadily and markedly from its peak in 1801 to 11 per cent in 1831, and did not rise again before mid century.[100]

Deane and Cole have explained the fall of the ratio from 1801 to 1811 by two factors.[101] First, the war slowed down the growth of exports: in 1810/12, their current values were not higher than in 1800/2, while national product at current prices had increased about 30 per cent. Second, industrial prices, i.e., export prices, had fallen absolutely (5 per cent according to Imlah's index) and still more relatively to agricultural prices, which had risen.

In the post-1811 period, export values fell after the war, then stagnated on trend up to the early 1830s and for the whole period from 1814 to 1846 grew at the very slow rate of 1·1 per cent per year; on the other hand, national income at current prices increased 13 per cent from 1811 to 1831. The explanation of this contrast lies largely in the movement of prices; export values bore the brunt of the rapid fall in the prices of manufactures and especially of cotton products (which, moreover, were enlarging their share of Britain's exports), while the prices of many other goods and services did not come down as sharply; Imlah's index of export prices falls 58 per cent from 1810/12 to 1830/2, while Gayer's index of domestic commodities falls 36 per cent only between the same dates.[102]

98 This is a higher ratio than that (14 or 15 per cent) given by Deane and Cole, pp. 28, 309, and Deane and Habakkuk, p. 68, note 2. See also W. A. Cole, 'Factors in Demand, 1700–80', in R. Floud and D. McCloskey (eds.), *The Economic History of Britain since 1700, Volume 1: 1700–1860* (Cambridge, 1981), p. 38.

99 Exports are from the UK, national income figures for Great Britain. But this results only in a slight underestimation of the exports/product ratio in the first three decades of the nineteenth century.

100 Deane and Cole, pp. 29, 310; also P. Bairoch, *Révolution Industrielle et sous-développement* (Paris, 1963), pp. 259–60.

101 Deane and Cole, pp. 161–2.

102 Imlah, pp. 94–5, Table 8; *Abstract*, p. 470.

However, as the volume of exports progressed much faster (4·3 per cent per year from 1814 to 1846) than their value and as it has been found in other cases, such as the United States from the 1860s to 1913, that the removal of price changes can markedly alter the relationship between trade and output over time,[103] we have calculated the ratios between exports and national income at constant prices (Table 6.14, column B). They still show a decline in the exports proportion from 1801 to 1811, but there is a slight rise from 1811 to 1831, when the ratio is back to its 1801 level, and a marked advance from 1831 to 1841.

In real terms, therefore, we need not think that from the early 1800s to the 1830s demand from the home market was expanding faster than demand from abroad[104] or that there was a serious diversion of resources from exports toward domestic investment and consumption.[105] None the less, it is important that, during a period which saw the highest rate of growth of British industrial production during the nineteenth century,[106] and when Britain's industrial and commercial supremacy was almost unchallenged, there was little relative aggrandisement of the export sector in real terms and a definite setback at current prices.

However, after 1848, the growth of export values accelerated sharply with a yearly rate of 5·7 per cent from 1846 to 1873, while there was also some acceleration in the growth of volume. On the other hand, there was some slowing down in the progress of industrial production and, possibly, of total national real product.[107] The exports proportion, both at current and at constant prices, increased sharply after 1841; it more than doubled in 30 years, to reach a peak at 24–25 per cent on the eve of the Great Depression. The figures of Table 6·14 are corroborated by those which can be calculated from Miss Deane's subsequent yearly figures from 1830 onward for the gross national product of the United Kingdom at factor cost:[108]

[103] Saul, p. 5; J. D. Gould, *Economic Growth in History. Survey and Analysis* (London, 1972), pp. 225–6.

[104] Deane and Cole's view, pp. 29, 310–11.

[105] Except during the Napoleonic war, when some diversion toward domestic investment in agriculture and toward defence is likely. See also below, about the switch of some industries towards the home market.

[106] Deane and Cole, p. 170, Table 38.

[107] Deane and Cole, pp. 170, Table 38, 297, Table 77, 311, Table 83.

[108] P. Deane, 'New Estimates of Gross National Product for the United Kingdom 1830–1914', *The Review of Income and Wealth*, series 14, no. 2, June 1968, pp. 104–5, Table A. With triennial averages centred on the year specified, like in Table 6.14, the ratios are as follows: 1831, 8·6%; 1841, 10·4%; 1851, 13·5%; 1861, 15·9%; 1871, 19·8%.

Ratios of the value of exports to GNP yearly averages (%).

1830/9	9·4
1840/9	10·6
1850/9	15·1
1860/9	17·2
1870/3	19·9

Results are similar with Charles Feinstein's more recent series of Britain's Gross Domestic Product (decade averages) at constant (1851–60) prices:[109] ratios of exports at constant prices to those GDP figures are of the same order of magnitude as those in column B of Table 6.14:

	(%)		(%)
1801–10	7·8	1831–40	9·8
1811–20	8·2	1841–50	13·0
1821–30	8·2	1851–60	18·9

It is clear that it was only after 1850 that Britain really became 'an export economy'. Before this, there had not been any regular increase in the ratio of exports to national product, but rather some long swings, with peaks at current prices *c.* 1760 and 1801, and troughs *c.* 1781 and 1831.

As for the statistical relationship between exports and the growth of British national income, P. Bairoch has estimated that, between 1700/10 and 1780/90, foreign demand was responsible for 5 to 9 per cent (his favourite percentage being 6·5 per cent) of the *increase* in England's total product, and the home market for 91 to 95 per cent of this increment. He has also calculated that the home market absorbed 92 to 95 per cent of the *total* output realised during this period and exports 5 to 8 per cent only.[110] These calculations, which allow to exports a marginal role only in British economic growth for most of the eighteenth century, are open to some criticisms on points of detail, but they appear roughly valid; indeed, if one calculates, from the figures in Table 6.13, the ratio of the additional exports to the increase in

[109] C. H. Feinstein, 'Capital Formation in Great Britain', in P. Mathias and M. M. Postan (eds.), *The Cambridge Economic History of Europe*, vol. VII, *The Industrial Economies: Capital, Labour and Enterprise*, Part I (Cambridge, 1978), p. 91, Table 28. Imlah's exports series has been recalculated at 1851 – 60 prices by using Rousseaux prices index.

[110] Bairoch, in *Annales*, pp. 557–8, 568.

Table 6.15. *Additional exports as percentages of increases in national product*[a]

Period	At current prices (%) (A)	At constant prices (%) (B)
From 1783 to 1801	40·3	
1801 to 1811	−0·6	1·7
1811 to 1821	[b]	10·2
1821 to 1831	1·2	8·9
1831 to 1841	11·4	19·5
1841 to 1851	34·5	34·2
1851 to 1861	37·1	54·5
1861 to 1871	39·4	33·5
1801 to 1841	3·9	11·7
1841 to 1871	37·9	37·0
1783 to 1871	28·3	
1801 to 1871	27·0	27·0

[a] The additional exports have been calculated between 3-year averages centred on the year specified.

[b] Both exports and national income were lower in 1821 than in 1811; the decrease in exports amounted to 44 per cent of that of national income.

Source. See Tables 6.13 (for 1783) and 6.14.

national income, between 1700 and 1783, it is 6·5 to 6·9 per cent and so falls in the same range as Bairoch's.[111]

However, Bairoch has admitted that the situation was quite different after 1780 and he has suggested that from the 1780s to the 1860s foreign demand absorbed about 30 per cent of the United Kingdom additional output and powerfully contributed to industrial expansion.[112] Borrowing his method, we have calculated in Table 6.15 the incremental ratios between the additional exports and the increase of national product for successive periods of the late eighteenth and nineteenth centuries.

It appears that the contribution from foreign demand to the increase

[111] If the national income figure for 1759 is not too far off the mark, this ratio would have been much higher for the period 1700–59: 17 to 21 per cent; for 1759 to 1783, it would be only 3 per cent.

[112] Bairoch, p. 570.

of national product between 1783 and 1871 (28 per cent) was of the order of magnitude proposed by Bairoch, but with significant fluctuations over time. During the decisive stage of the Industrial Revolution, in the 20 years which followed the peace of 1783, the incremental ratio of exports to national product seems to have been as high as 40 per cent; but, from the early 1800s up to the 1830s and even *c.* 1841, it was quite low, not only at current, but also at constant prices; it rose sharply in the 1840s and from 1841 to 1871 it was about 37 per cent. This movement fits fairly well with several of our preceding conclusions.[113]

A rough calculation, which is still more tentative, as long as yearly series of the current values of exports and of national product are not available,[114] seems to show that the aggregate additional exports were equivalent to one-half of the cumulated additional national output from 1783 to 1801; but, from 1802 to 1841, owing to the recession of exports values in the postwar period, the ratio would have been minute, while it rose to 33 per cent for the period from 1842 to 1871. As for the percentage of total cumulated exports to total cumulated national product, it would have been about 13 per cent for the periods 1783 to 1801 and 1802 to 1841, but over 18 per cent for 1842 to 1871.

For the later period, thanks to Miss Deane's yearly series for national product, one is on firmer ground; the ratios (in %) between aggregate additional exports and the cumulated additions to national product are as follows:

1830 to 1849	11·6
1850 to 1873	28·8
1830 to 1873	21·7

Over the same years, 1830–73, total exports amounted to 14·8 per cent of the sum of yearly GNP.

Without forgetting that exports are not income, there is a strong case for suggesting that they were a powerful engine of growth for the British economy from the end of the war of American Independence up to the first years of the nineteenth century, and again after the late 1840s; but in between their influence on long-term growth was very

[113] With the series of GNP figures of Miss Deane, the results are somewhat different for the period 1841 to 1871.

[114] Yearly national income figures have been calculated by extrapolation between the years for which they are available in Deane and Cole; also exports values from 1783 to 1795.

modest, though, of course, foreign demand was a crucial factor in short-term fluctuations.[115]

Exports and industrial production

As British exports were mostly – and increasingly – made of manufactured goods, the rise of overseas sales had a relatively greater impact on the demand for manufactures than on the growth of national income; moreover, the problem with which economic historians have been mainly concerned is the relationship between foreign trade and the *Industrial Revolution*. It would be most useful therefore to compare the evolutions of exports and of industrial production. For the eighteenth century, W. A. Cole has built up estimates of the gross value of industry's final output and calculated the share which was exported: it increases from 21 per cent *c.* 1700 to 31 per cent *c.* 1760–5; it falls back to 27·6 per cent *c.* 1780 and 1785, but increases again to 34·5 per cent *c.* 1800. The exports proportion would have risen from one-fifth to a full third – a figure which had often been suggested for the late eighteenth century.[116] After 1800, unfortunately, the figures which are available for industrial production are for its 'added value' or contribution to national income, which is net of the cost of raw materials, while exports values are 'final values' FOB, incorporating some transport and marketing costs. The ratios between exports and industrial production values are thus extremely high and can in no way be indicators of the actual share of industrial output which was exported. Still, the changes in this ratio over time can be interesting.

It seems that this ratio increased significantly from *c.* 1700 to *c.* 1760 and then fell back between 1760 and 1780, but without a complete loss of its previous gains.[117] There was, of course, a rise of the ratio in the

[115] Gayer, II, pp. 533, 545.

[116] Cole, in Floud and McCloskey, p. 40, Table 3.1. Harley, p. 282, Table 7, suggests much lower percentages. See also R. Davis, *English Overseas Trade 1500–1700* (London, 1973), p. 8, who estimated this share at over one quarter *c.* 1700. The present writer (*L'Economie britannique*, p. 63) had estimated previously that, *circa* 1804, exports amounted to 35 or 40 per cent of final industrial output; this was likely too much.

[117] This is corroborated by a comparison of the growth of exports volumes and of the index of industrial production (excluding building) of W. G. Hoffmann, *British Industry, 1700–1950* (Oxford, 1955), Table 54, part A. Though this index is not reliable, it is interesting that it grows very slowly up to 1760 and then accelerates – a movement quite different from that of exports. Some figures of industrial output at current prices, which Dr P. O'Brien has calculated and kindly allowed us to use, show a ratio of exports to output higher in 1780 than in 1701.

Table 6.16. *Exports and production in three industries (ratios of the value of exports to the value of the industry's final product)*[a]

	Wool (%)	Cotton (%)	Iron (%)
c. 1695	*c.* 40		
c. 1760		*c.* 33	
c. 1772	*c.* 45	*c.* 22	
1781/83		16	
1787/89		23	
1795/97		37	
1799	*c.* 55		
c. 1805	31 or 37		18
1805/07		66	
1815/17		58	
c. 1818			26
1819/21		54	
1820/24	23		18
1829/31		56	
1830/34	19		21
1839/41		52	
1840/44	19		30
1849/51		62	
1850/54	25		40
1859/61		64	
1860/64	30		40
1869/71		67	
1871/74	43		38

[a] N.B. Figures in this table for the eighteenth and the early nineteenth centuries are highly tentative.

Notes. The proportions in the table have been calculated from the following sources:

Wool. Estimates of the value of production and exports for 1695, 1772, 1799: Deane, 'The Output', pp. 209–10, 215, 220, Table 3, except the current value of exports for 1799, which is the figure of Davis for 1794/6, adjusted according to the increase in volume and the likely price rise. For 1805, Deane, 'The Output', p. 220, and Deane and Cole, p. 196, Table 47, have two different figures for the final value of output; we give therefore two alternative percentages, calculated from Davis' current values of exports for 1804/6 (*The Industrial Revolution*, p. 96). After 1805, the percentages are those of Deane and Cole, p. 196, Table 47, of the value of exports of woollen manufactures (yarn not included) to final product.

Cotton. Estimates of 'gross value cottons' (Great Britain) up to 1815/17 and afterward 'value final product' (UK) from Deane and Cole, pp. 185 and 187, Tables 42 and 43; exports at current prices up to 1815/17 from *ibid.*, Table 42, but they have been corrected for 1760 and 1772, as a majoration of the official values by a third, which Deane and Cole have applied, does not seem justified. For 1781/3, we have used Davis' current values for 1784/6 (*The Industrial Revolution*, p. 94), with an adjustment. From 1819/21, we have recalculated Deane and Cole's percentages of exports to product, from the exports figures in *Abstract*, pp. 302–4 (they include yarn), and the results are slightly different.

Iron. Estimated values of gross product, from Deane and Cole, p. 225, Table 56. The percentages are different, having been recalculated from the exports figures for iron, hardware, and machinery, in *Abstract*, pp. 302–4.

last 20 years of the eighteenth century, but it was not as large relatively as for the exports/national income proportion, as industrial production grew faster during those years than total output.

In the nineteenth century, the ratio of exports current values to industrial production's added values fluctuates with the exports/national income ratio: from a peak *c.* 1801, it falls to 1831. This fall is so sharp that it cannot be entirely explained by the much bigger share of cotton products, with their precipitous price fall, in exports than in total industrial output, and it might correspond to an actual decline in the proportion of output which was exported[118] – at least at current prices, for in volume exports rose faster than industrial production. The explanation might lie in the shift in exports toward lower quality goods, especially cheap cottons, and semifinished goods, not paralleled to the same degree in the structure of output for the home market. On the other hand, from 1841, there is a sharp upsurge of the exports/industrial production ratio, owing to both an increase in the rate of growth of exports and a decrease in that of industrial production, at least in volume.[119]

These hypotheses can be completed by looking at the exports/production ratio in some of the main industrial sectors, where data are somewhat more satisfactory. Such an analysis confirms the view that this ratio fluctuated over time and that there was a succession of shifts between the foreign and the home markets (see Table 6.16).

This will appear from the comparison of the respective growth rates of net imports of cotton wool in Britain (which give a rough index of production) and of the volume of cotton goods exports:[120]

[118] P. O'Brien's yearly series of the value of industrial output at current prices has a growth rate of 2·6 per cent per year from 1814 to 1846, while exports current values grow at 1·1 per cent only.

[119] Rates of growth per year:

	Hoffmann's index (excluding building) (%)	Volume of exports (%)
1814–1846	3·7	4·3
1846–1873	2·9	4·7

[120] Net imports of cotton wool into Great Britain up to 1814; consumption of cotton wool in the UK afterward; *Abstract*, pp. 177–9. Volumes of exports are the official values up to 1814; Imlah's series of volumes at 1880 prices (pp. 208–10, Table II) has been used afterward, but it concerns only cotton *manufactures*; if yarn was included, the rate would be slightly higher for 1814–46. See also Deane and Cole, pp. 51, 59, Tables 15 and 16.

	Net imports	Volume of exports
	(%/year)	(%/year)
1697–1749	2.6	0.1
1749–1772	2.3	10.9
1760–1783	5.3	2.9
1783–1792	14.1	10.7
1792–1802	10.1	17.3
1802–1814	1.4	8.4
1814–1846	6.6	5.5
1846–1873	2.3	4.0

During the first half of the eighteenth century, the 'cotton' industry was quite small, its exports were minute and the rather slow growth which it enjoyed resulted almost entirely from increased home demand. But, from 1750 exactly, and up to the early 1760s, there was a 'meteoric ascent' of exports, which far outstripped the increase in inputs of cotton;[121] the proportion of exports to total output reached between a third and a half *c.* 1760. Then, after 1763, the growth of exports slowed down markedly, while that of production accelerated; exports' share of production declined and seems to have been only about 16 per cent in the early 1780s; all this during the celebrated technological transformation of cotton spinning.[122] In the 1780s, both imports of cotton wool and exports of manufactures grew very rapidly, but inputs more so than export volumes, and it was only in the 1790s that exports rose so decisively that the ratio of their value to that of total output increased spectacularly to a peak of two-thirds *c.* 1805.[123] This was also the period when cottons exports first played a decisive part in the growth of total exports.[124] However, during the postwar years, the share of exports (current values) in the final product of the cotton industry declined to somewhat over 50 per cent during the 1820s and 1830s; the home market seems thus to have increased its share – in value, but likely also in volume – during this period of fast growth of the cotton industry.[125] The postwar stagnation of cotton products exports, the decline in their quality and the increasing proportion of yarn and twist in their total contributed to this relative

121 Deane and Cole, p. 59; John, in *Economica*, pp. 184–5; John, in Jones, p. 176.

122 Eversley, pp. 224–5; Bairoch, in *Annales*, p. 565.

123 From Deane and Cole, p. 185, Table 42. Also Edwards, pp. 25–6; Davis, *The Industrial Revolution*, p. 96.

124 See above. For the period 1783–1814, the rates of growth per year are 5·5 per cent for imports of cotton, 12·3 per cent for exports of cotton products.

125 Deane and Cole, pp. 187–8; also Matthews, p. 151, Table 25.

decline. After 1846, the growth of both production and exports volumes slowed down,[126] but the former much more than the latter, while export values increased sharply; thus, exports' share of the value of the industry's production rose again and reached 67 per cent in 1869/71.

For the woollen industry, the position in the eighteenth century is far from clear, the available data and the glosses upon them being hypothetical and often contradictory.[127] Still, it seems that the exports/production ratio was already quite high (possibly 40 per cent) at the end of the seventeenth century,[128] and that, despite slow growth during most of the century (0·9 per cent per year from 1697 to 1772), exports volume advanced somewhat faster than production and slightly enlarged its share of total output: Hoffmann's index of the output of woollen and worsted cloth in the West Riding – which was the region with the fastest growth – progressed at only 0·8 per cent per year from 1739 to 1772.[129] Though the ratio must have fallen during the depression of exports in the 1770s, it certainly rose a good deal in the 1780s and 1790s; the rate of growth of export volume is 4·9 per cent per year from 1783 to 1802, much higher than that of the Hoffmann's West Riding index (1·7 per cent from 1783 to 1792, 0·6 per cent from 1792 to 1802); according to P. Deane, at the close of the century over two-thirds of the industry's output were exported[130] – a figure which seems too high and ought to be reduced to between 50 and 60 per cent. But, as the volume of woollen exports fell markedly after 1801, and as their values declined and stagnated for a long time after the end of the wars, the ratio of exports to output fell sharply during the early nineteenth century to a level around 20 per cent, where it remained up to the late 1840s. On the other hand, the fast rise of the value of woollen and worsted cloths and yarn exported after 1848 (6·3 per cent per year from 1846 to 1873) brought about a sharp increase in the exports/output ratio, which exceeded 40 per cent in the early 1870s.

An overwhelming share of the output of the iron industry in the

[126] The rates for 1846–73 are influenced by the Cotton Famine and growth remained fast up to 1860, but there is a deceleration in the consumption of cotton wool from 1845.

[127] P. Deane, 'The Output of the British Woollen Industry in the Eighteenth Century', *Journal of Economic History*, XVII, 2, June 1957, pp. 220, 222, and Deane and Cole, p. 52; criticised by Wilson, pp. 50–1.

[128] Deane, 'The Output', pp. 209–10; Wilson, p. 42; Davis, *English Overseas Trade*, p. 8; see also Ashton, *Fluctuations*, p. 75.

[129] Hoffmann, Table 54, part A.

[130] Deane, 'The Output', p. 221.

eighteenth century went to the home market.[131] Exports of iron goods nevertheless grew quite fast up to 1771 (with a yearly rate of 3·6 per cent from 1697 to 1771), and W. E. Minchinton has rightly noticed that their weight grew faster than total English bar-iron consumption, so that the ratio of export weights to supplies increased from 8 per cent in 1715 to about 20 per cent in 1770 and possibly more.[132] But exports fell sharply from 1771 to 1779/81 and, though they grew rapidly in the 1780s (at a yearly rate of 9·6 per cent from 1783 to 1792), this advance was not maintained, the growth rate falling to 3·1 per cent from 1792 to 1802 and to 1·4 per cent from 1802 to 1814. On the other hand, British production of pig-iron seems to have more than doubled from *c.* 1760 to 1788, and to have increased fourfold between 1788 and 1806 (while the official value of exports of iron and steel goods increased only 65 per cent between the last two dates); of course, the total supplies of raw materials to the secondary iron industry did not rise as much, as imports of bar-iron grew quite slowly and eventually decreased from the late 1790s; moreover, a large part of the output of pig-iron was used directly as castings.[133] We have attempted some rough calculations of the ratio between the pig-iron equivalents of iron goods exported and the total consumption of pig-iron in Britain (home production + equivalent of the bar-iron imports); this would give ratios of 20 per cent *c.* 1788, 22 per cent *c.* 1796, and 20 per cent *c.* 1805.[134] On the other hand, the current value of iron goods exported *c.* 1805 is 17·5 per cent of the estimated value of the iron industry's gross product.[135] It seems therefore that the fast expansion and technological mutation of the iron industry – especially in its primary branch – in the late eighteenth and early nineteenth century were not accompanied by a rise of the exports/output ratio for iron goods, and

[131] John, in *Economica*, pp. 183–4. There were practically no exports of unwrought iron (pig-iron, bar-iron) and all exports of iron goods were supplied by the secondary iron industry.

[132] Minchinton, p. 42; confirmed by Deane and Cole, pp. 51, 55, 58–9; Bairoch, p. 561.

[133] Deane and Cole, pp. 51, Table 15, 221; Eversley, p. 236.

[134] From data in *Abstract*, pp. 131, 140, 145; Deane and Cole, pp. 55, note 3, 221–2. Wrought iron has been converted to a pig-iron equivalent on the assumption that 1 ton of bar or wrought iron contained 33 CWT of pig. One can also calculate the ratio of the weight of iron and steel goods exported to the total supplies of bar iron (home produced and imported), as the chief raw material of the secondary iron industry. On the assumption that one half of the pig-iron produced in Britain was cast (Deane and Cole, p. 223, note 1), this would give ratios of 27 per cent *c.* 1788, 30 per cent *c.* 1796, 31 per cent *c.* 1805; these figures are comparable to the ratios given by Minchinton for the earlier period.

[135] Current values according to Davis, *The Industrial Revolution*, p. 96; product from Deane and Cole, p. 225, Table 56.

that the additional production was for the most part absorbed by the home market.[136]

Iron's exports proportion seems to have risen during the immediate postwar years, when the industry suffered a severe depression, but it fell to 15 per cent in the late 1820s; exports thereafter picked up, with traditional sales of hardware increasingly complemented by growing shipments of semifinished products and machinery; though production also advanced substantially, the export ratio increased and approached 30 per cent in the early 1840s; after 1850, it rose suddenly to around 40 per cent.[137]

All the main British industries contributed to the rise in the ratio of exports to national income and industrial production in the 1780s; but, after 1792, the cotton industry and, to a lesser degree, the woollen industry were responsible for the whole of the further increase in the ratio which took place and created for a time an 'export economy'. After the early years of the nineteenth century, there was a setback and a shift of all industries – at least as far as values of exports and production are concerned – toward the home market. A new strong rise in the ratio of exports to industrial production did not take place before the mid nineteenth century, but this time it was very broadly based, on an increased exports proportion in all major industries.

Last, some conjectural examples of the incremental ratios between the additional value of exports by the main industries and the additional output they achieved can be suggested.

For the cotton industry, the ratios (in %) would be:[138]

From 1760 to 1784/86	13
From 1784/86 to 1805/07	87
From 1805/07 to 1839/41	42
From 1839/41 to 1869/71	79

As it could be expected, the contribution of exports to the growth of the cotton industry was small from 1760 to the mid-1780s, but it was

[136] And also by the substitution of home produced bar-iron to imports. However, there is a good deal of qualitative evidence about the strong dependence upon exports in the secondary iron trades of Birmingham and Sheffield, but it was given during the Parliamentary enquiry about the Orders in Council in 1812 and tended to stress the importance of exports, which were said to absorb in good years about half the output of these towns; Crouzet, p. 71, note 89.

[137] Deane and Cole, p. 224.

[138] Calculated from the sources quoted in the notes to Table 6.16 and especially from Deane and Cole, pp. 185, 187, Tables 42 and 43.

overwhelming during the 20 years or so which followed;[139] it fell back during the four next decades to become again very large from *c.* 1840 to *c.* 1870. In the woollen industry, the ratio of additional exports to additional output might have been very high (83 per cent) between 1772 and 1799, but it would be nil during the first four decades of the nineteenth century, before rising again to a high figure (about 40 per cent) between 1850/4 and 1870/4. As for the iron industry, if we use the same system of pig iron equivalents as earlier, the contribution of export demand to the increase in output (both in weight) would have been about one-fifth between *c.* 1788 and *c.* 1805. If the additional value of exports is compared with the additional value of the industry's gross product, the ratio would be 32 per cent from *c.* 1805 to 1835/9 and 43 per cent from 1835/9 to 1870/4.[140] For British industry as a whole, it is likely that the incremental ratio of exports to output was modest before 1780, but high from 1781 to 1802, after which it fell back to a low level from the 1800s to *c.* 1840 but was high again in the 1850s and 1860s.

With much that is conjectural and tentative, this paper has not been able to consider the whole gamut of problems relevant to its theme. The multiplier effects and the backward linkages of exports expansion, which Deane and Habakkuk have mentioned as important in the late eighteenth century,[141] have been neglected, with the question of the gains from trade and the influence of an enlarged market, thanks to growing foreign demand, upon the division of labour, technological innovation, and transfer of resources to high productivity sectors. Moreover, domestic exports have been considered per se and arbitrarily isolated from imports and from the related variable of the terms of trade. Indeed, there has deliberately been no attempt to tackle the problem of the sources of export expansion. Was foreign demand for British goods an exogenous, independently determined and random variable?[142] Or should the explanation of its accelerations be sought 'at home rather than abroad', i.e., in the increase of British demand for foreign products, resulting itself from rising population and incomes in Britain, as Deane and Cole have maintained for the eighteenth

139 Bairoch, in *Annales*, pp. 565–6, gives estimates quite close to ours.

140 Sources for these estimates in notes to Table 6.16; Deane and Cole, p. 255, Table 56; above, note 134.

141 Deane and Habakkuk, p. 80.

142 This was the view, for the mid eighteenth century, of John, in Jones, pp. 179–80.

century?[143] Or did internal economic growth of itself lead to higher productivity in the export sector and thus to increased exports?[144] This paper does not pretend to answer these questions and, if the impact of conditions on foreign markets has been stressed in several cases, this was as an explanation of relatively short-term movements of exports, especially during the French wars.

It seems that the pattern which emerges from this study is more intricate than is generally supposed, with a succession of shifts in the balance between foreign and home demand, in the role of the main industries in export expansion, and in their various export markets. Finally, the most interesting finding might be the contrast between several periods and their specificities. Particularly, in accordance with W. W. Rostow's intuitions, the 20 years from 1782 to 1802 have a marked originality, owing to their very high rate of growth of exports,[145] to the 'leading sector' part which cottons played in export expansion, to the predominant role of American markets, and to the undoubtedly strong impact of foreign demand on Britain's economic growth (and though export expansion came after the technological breakthroughs, it certainly accelerated their diffusion). On the other hand, the later years of the French wars, after 1802, and the postwar period display slower growth of exports, diversion to underdeveloped countries, and a limited contribution to economic growth. Only in the mid nineteenth century did Britain become a fully-fledged export economy.

Appendix

Statistics and their sources

1. Exports from England and Wales, 1697–1800, official values (OV): Mitchell and Deane, *Abstract*, pp. 279–81; Schumpeter, Table II (for 1792–1800). For 1697–1708, this series uses the adjusted figures with

[143] Deane and Cole, pp. 83–9, 312; Cole, pp. 329–42. A recent econometric study rejects Deane and Cole's view that variations in retained imports (and therefore in home demand) preceded and influenced variations in exports; it maintains that the evidence points in the opposite direction, i.e. exports as causal variable; see T. J. Hatton, 'Quantitative Economic History at the University of Essex', *Journal of European Economic History*, XI, 3, Winter 1982, pp. 747–8; T. J. Hatton, J. S. Lyons, S. E. Satchell, 'Eighteenth-Century British Trade: Homespun or Empire Made', *Explorations in Economic History*, XX, 2, April 1983, pp. 163, 175, 178–9.

In some periods of the first half of the nineteenth century, foreign markets might have been a dumping ground for an over-production which the home market would not absorb, with manufacturers expanding their overseas sales in order to keep their factories going.

[144] Saul, p. 11.

[145] Flinn, p. 61, maintains that this was induced by fortuitous and ephemeral circumstances.

revised estimates of the values of woollens of Deane and Cole, pp. 319, 322.

2. Exports from Great Britain, 1772–1814, OV: *Abstract*, p. 281; Crouzet, *L'Economie britannique*, p. 885, Table 3 (for 1805–12).

3. Exports from the United Kingdom, 1801–53, OV: *Abstract*, pp. 282–3.

4. Exports from the United Kingdom, 1796–1873, current (declared) values (CV): *Abstract*, pp. 282–3.

5. Exports of UK products, 1796–1873, volume at 1880 prices: Imlah, pp. 94–7, Table 8.

6. Exports from England and Wales, 1697–1791, and from Great Britain, 1792–1814, OV, of cotton yarn and manufactures, linen yarn and manufactures (up to 1812), silk yarn and manufactures, iron and steel goods, nonferrous metals and manufactures: *Abstract*, pp. 293–5.

7. Exports from England and Wales of woollen and worsted yarn and manufactures (hats included), 1697–1808, Mrs Schumpeter's values; from Great Britain, 1792–1814, hats not included, OV: *Abstract*, pp. 293–5.

8. Exports from the United Kingdom, 1814–73 (in fact, from Great Britain excluding exports to Ireland, 1814–29, but there is no difference with UK exports, except for linens, for which an adjustment has been made), CV, of cotton, wool, linen yarn and manufactures, metals and metal manufactures, coal: *Abstract*, pp. 302–4.

9. Exports from the United Kingdom, volume at 1880 prices, of cotton manufactures, woollen manufactures, goods other than cottons and woollens: Imlah, Appendix, Tables II, III, IV, pp. 210–15.

10. Exports from the United Kingdom to the main geographical areas, 1814–73, CV: *Abstract*, pp. 313–15, 318, 321, 324.

11. Exports from the United Kingdom to the main geographical areas, 1814–73, volume at 1880 prices: series 10 deflated by the exports prices index of Imlah, pp. 94–7.

Postscriptum

Some suggestions made in this study have been criticised by N. F. R. Crafts, who has calculated new estimates of national income in the eighteenth century.[146] He considers as unacceptable the figure of

[146] N. F. R. Crafts, 'British Economic Growth, 1700–1831: A Review of the Evidence', *The Economic History Review*, XXXVI, 2, May 1983, pp. 197–9.

£160 millions for the national income of 1783 (which had been borrowed from Deane and Cole) and he proposes a much lower one – 105 millions (in 1780). As a consequence, the ratios between the increment of exports and that of national income are:[147]

	(%)
1700–1760	21·2
1760–1780	3·5
1700–1780	13·0
1780–1801	19·3

The present study underestimates the share of national product which was exported during the period 1700–80, but greatly overestimates it for the last two decades of the century. As Crafts' estimates of national income are an improvement upon Deane and Cole's, it is quite possible that his percentages must be preferred to mine.

As far as industrial production is concerned, the new series of its values, which W. A. Cole has built up (and which has been mentioned above), would show that exports were responsible for 40 per cent of the increase in output from 1700 to 1800 and therefore made a 'substantial contribution' to industry's growth.[148] Crafts gives roughly the same ratio (43 per cent) for the eighteenth century as a whole, but he found that industrial production grew more slowly than Cole's figures imply, during the two sub-periods 1700–60 and 1780–1800, for which, consequently, the incremental ratio of exports to industrial production would be, in both cases, 58 per cent. The contribution of exports to industrial growth would be larger before 1760 and after 1780 than Cole and the present writer have suggested; on the other hand, Crafts accepts that this contribution fell back between 1760 and 1780.[149]

Altogether, Crafts comes to a conclusion which is not greatly different from those of Bairoch and this study: during the eighteenth century, the ratio of exports to Britain's national income was never

[147] On the other hand, his ratios Exports/National income (p. 197, Table 8) are not too far from those suggested here:

	%
1700	8·3
1760	12·4
1780	10·5
1801	15·3

[148] Cole, in Floud and McCloskey, p. 40; also, pp. 64–5.

[149] Crafts, 'British Economic Growth', pp. 197–8.

very large; but during the last twenty years of the century, exports made a strong contribution to the growth of industrial output.[150]

150 *Ibid.*, p. 199.
Some writers deny to exports any role in economic growth; see i.e. R. P. Thomas and D. N. McCloskey – and also Von Tunzelmann – in Floud and McCloskey, pp. 99–102, 144–6.
J. Mokyr (ed.), *The Economics of the Industrial Revolution* (Totowa, NJ, 1985), pp. 21–3, has two excellent pages on 'Foreign Trade and Empire', with references to some recent work.

7 Great Britain's response to the French Revolution and to Napoleon*

Why did a revolution not break out in late eighteenth-century England, making a pair with the one in France? Although this question is frequently posed, it is probably as misleading as the one which asks why France did not then undergo an industrial revolution. There is in either case the same mixture of insularity and universalism, the same assumption that the experience of a given country, taken as a model, would have to be shared by all civilised nations. In fact, neither a revolutionary situation nor a revolutionary spirit existed in George III's England. Which is not to imply that the English *Ancien Régime* was lacking those 'abuses' which old textbooks declared to be rife in Louis XVI's France, for its political system in particular, which was basically oligarchical, was also riddled with corruption. Nor was the English *Ancien Régime* without conflicts; it was simply that the forces favouring equilibrium were powerful and England lacked in the main the multiple dysfunction which makes a revolution possible and even probable, the explosive mixture of a large number of dangerous ingredients which had been building up on the other side of the Channel.

There was no need to raise one's sword against absolutism and centralising bureaucracy for, since the Glorious Revolution of 1688, the English monarchy had been a limited one, there was no 'big government' to complain about, extensive liberties were guaranteed His Majesty's subjects and political practice was evolving towards a parliamentary régime, although the sovereign had the last word in the choice of ministers. There was no danger of an 'aristocratic revolution' for, although George III and his juvenile Prime Minister, Pitt the Younger, had excluded the great Whig families from power, Charles

* An earlier version of this chapter was published in F. Crouzet (ed.), *Les Hommes d'Etat célèbres*, vol. V, *De la Révolution française à la Première guerre mondiale* (Paris, 1975), pp. 52–9.

James Fox and his circle were, for all their bitterness, prepared to wait patiently for the time when the death or terminal madness of the king would allow their friend, the Prince of Wales, to call them back to office (notwithstanding the good relations they enjoyed with certain French 'liberal nobles', they did not play the same role of sorcerer's apprentices). Nor was there any conflict between nobility and bourgeoisie over the question of privileges. Indeed, the English nobility, who were anyway few in number, hardly possessed any at all and the gentry – landowners who were commoners but led a gentlemanly life – was an open group, into which affluent merchants or lawyers could readily be integrated. In a society which had no 'orders', social mobility was real. Moreover, there was no class of arrogant but impoverished *minor nobilitas*, and there were few *déclassé* intellectuals with dreams of overturning the social order. Among the 'middle classes', the pursuit of wealth, in an expanding economy, was sufficient to absorb the energies of businessmen who, save for a few exceptions, at this stage were hardly concerned that landowners had a monopoly over political power, in as much as the landed oligarchy was adept at promoting commercial and industrial interests. There was no agrarian crisis either, such as might have exploded in a 'Great Fear', with the burning of muniments and country houses. England no longer had many genuine peasants, smallholders scratching a meagre living; it was a land of solid and prosperous tenant-farmers and, if their labourers were often wretched, they were at least immune from serfdom, 'feudal' dues, the *taille* and the *vingtième*. As for workers in industry, the sheer diversity of their conditions of employment and status, the predominance of domestic work, scattered throughout rural areas, delayed the formation of class consciousness and political awakening. Besides, the standard of living of the masses was superior to that enjoyed on the Continent, at least prior to the costly wars waged against France. If Élie Halévy has exaggerated the influence of Methodism, as if it had been an opium distracting English workers from the path of revolution, it was nevertheless real enough. Finally, the factor that actually detonated the French Revolution – the financial crisis which toppled the *Ancien Régime* and brought about the calling of the States-General – was lacking in England. The English fiscal system was more rational and more productive than the French one and, though the American War of Independence had destabilised the country's finances, Pitt had managed to re-establish fairly rapidly a sound situation. His government enjoyed remarkable authority and prestige and was not discredited as the ministers of the dying French *Ancien Régime*.

England thus had social and political structures which were both open and stable, quite different actually from those of France and as yet not significantly forced off balance by the revolution in technology that was just then beginning. England's élites – the well-to-do strata from which the political class was recruited – were in the great majority satisfied by the prosperity and liberties which they enjoyed, and were full of self-confidence; the common people, rightly or wrongly, were fairly content with their lot, even though they were excluded from participation in politics. There were, however, minorities which suffered from a degree of frustration and desired reforms. The faults of the political system had for long been met with indifference; yet, from around 1770 on, a 'radical' movement had appeared,[1] which sought to purify political life and, in particular, to reform a Parliament which they regarded as corrupt and unrepresentative. This movement had been encouraged by George III's blunders and by the defeats suffered in America; it was particularly influential among members of the dissenting sects, who, owing to the Test Act, laboured under a juridically inferior status, and its avant-garde were the 'rational dissenters', rationalist intellectuals whose positions were often close to the ideology of the French Revolution; won over to the cult of natural rights, liberty and progress, they dreamed of radical reforms, sometimes even of manhood suffrage. Milieux such as these could not help but be sensitive to the inspirational example on the other side of the Channel, which was therefore grafted on to a congenial native stock. Yet the groups involved were few in number and, though capable of wielding some influence over the middle classes, were cut off from the masses by their relative affluence, their culture, their intransigent laissez-faire views and by the fact that some industrialists known for their harsh treatment of their workers came from the entrepreneurial nursery of the dissenting sects. Likewise, the oligarchs of the Whig opposition, owners of or members for pocket boroughs, were not the kind of men who would consider electoral reform an urgent matter, still less would they lead a popular uprising. Moreover, in 1780, the Gordon riots, which had sent areas of London up in a blaze and cost

[1] One should perhaps say 'reappeared', for there had been oppositional tendencies before, and one cannot rule out the possibiliy that there was some linkage with the Republicans of the seventeenth century.

many lives, had demonstrated to the well-to-do how dangerous demagogic appeals to the populace were. Men of property in other countries were not slow to draw the appropriate lesson from the revolution which had broken out in France, all the more so given that it was egalitarian, popular and bloody, and the chances of seeing the sequence of events which had unfolded in France (whose success derived in part from its being unexpected and, aside from the forgotten age of Charles I and Cromwell, unprecedented) being reproduced elsewhere were very much diminished. Indeed, it can be argued that England had externalised her revolution, which had been carried out in America in 1776.

Nevertheless, the first episodes of the French Revolution were greeted by British public opinion (which disapproved of the *Ancien Régime*) with quasi-unanimous satisfaction and even sympathy. These attitudes were, it is true, not unmixed with condescension, for the French were only then setting out on paths of liberty that England had blazed a full century earlier. Some of the English, moreover, expressed satisfaction at the humiliation of their hereditary enemy, the house of Bourbon, and at the weakening of France; this was the attitude of, for instance, the Prime Minister. The English attitude was also that of disinterested spectators, for no one in the summer of 1789 imagined that the events in France would constitute a political lesson for the English. It was only from the end of 1789 that things began to change. Events in France helped to revive and spur on the radical movement, which had been involved since 1787 in a campaign for the granting of equal rights to dissenters; the Revolution even aroused quasi-millennarian hopes among some Radicals. But a number of Anglicans became anxious and responded, during the winter of 1789–90, with a campaign for the maintenance of the Test; they charged the dissenters with wishing to imitate the French revolutionaries and destroy the established Church. It was this 'alarmist' position on the part of Anglicans which prompted the ideological battle over the French Revolution and prepared for the general polarisation of public opinion in regard to it.

The full implications of this debate only became apparent with Edmund Burke's contribution. Burke had been hostile to the French Revolution from the summer of 1789; he had condemned it publicly in February 1790, and in November 1790 he published his *Reflections on the Revolution in France and on the Proceedings in certain Societies in London relative to that Event*; the preposition 'in', together with the second section of the title, are significant, for they suggested that the French Revolution had a universal relevance and that ill-intentioned Englishmen were proposing to imitate it, which, indeed, was Burke's view. This book was a masterly and resounding gospel of the Counter-Revolution and, as such, it has been the basis of all subsequent conservative and traditionalist philosophies. Yet at first it was not well received, and it is not accurate to say that Burke with one blow had transformed English public opinion's sympathy for the French Revolution into hostility. The truth is that he provoked a host of responses from impassioned defenders of the Revolution and its works, notably Thomas Paine, an intransigent rationalist, democrat and republican, whose *Rights of Man* (March 1791 and February 1792), truly was a 'revolutionary catechism', which argued for a thoroughgoing reorganisation of society and enjoyed great success. 1791 therefore saw a major debate on the principles of 1789, during which British public opinion split into opposing camps with regard to the French Revolution, which became, albeit rather slowly, a political problem in England too.

Already existing reform societies took on a new lease of life, new clubs were founded, as were radical newspapers, both in London, the provinces and Scotland. The London Corresponding Society has proved of especial interest, on account of its structure, which consisted of sections capped by a central committee, its programme (manhood suffrage and annual parliaments) and its membership, which was recruited from socially modest, 'sans-culottes' like milieux, such as craftsmen and shopkeepers. Yet London was not alone in this, for Sheffield had a Constitutional Society, founded at the end of 1791, organised into 'divisions', which enjoyed great success among the small masters and workmen of the cutlery industry; Norwich, another industrial town, also had many popular societies.

In 1792, the reform societies therefore both proliferated and grew more radical; they were active in distributing Paine's works; they began to take an interest in social questions and their propaganda stirred up political activity among the 'lower' strata of society, which had not usually been involved in it. Some of these societies were in contact, through the sending either of motions or of delegations, with the French assemblies and the Jacobins' club, but their intentions were, so to speak, wholly innocent, for at this stage France had made no attempts at 'subversion' (contrary to what the English government believed).

The fall of the French monarchy on 10 August 1792 and the Republican victory over the Prussians at the battle of Valmy, together with some economic difficulties, lent further encouragement to agitation in England, which was to reach its height at the end of 1792, with the projects for a joint meeting of delegates from the various clubs, in the form of a people's Convention, and for the holding of a Scottish Convention at Edinburgh.

It should be clear from this account that England did not emerge unscathed from the contagion of revolution. Yet, one must avoid both underestimating the importance of the English 'Jacobins', as traditional historiography has tended to do (regarding their movement as an aberration by contrast with the main stream in the development of the country's politics), and the contrary danger of exaggerating it, as the members of the French Convention tended to do, believing that revolution was about to break out in England, or as some recent historians, intent upon reinventing a British revolutionary tradition, have done. Although this movement did become more radical in 1792, its militants, in spite of their foolishly incendiary and provocative language, never dreamed of taking arms and founding a republic (as their opponents and the government believed), for their real aim was parliamentary reform. Furthermore, although this movement had won a popular base, it mainly recruited from the middle class, drawing its membership from businessmen, professional men, dissenting ministers, and it was very much in a minority. An active minority can of course make a revolution; yet it has no chance of success, if it is running up against a government which is determined to defend itself and against a majority which is openly hostile to it, which was precisely the case in England.

A counter-revolutionary movement developed in parallel to the radical movement. Alarmed by the campaign for the repeal of the Test Acts and by the nationalisation of ecclesiastical property in France, Anglican elements had launched 'King and Church mobs' against their adversaries, especially in Birmingham, where the imprudent announcement of the holding of a banquet to celebrate the second anniversary of the Fall of the Bastille had led to violent riots on 14 July 1791, in the course of which dissenters' chapels and the residences of rich reformers were sacked, very probably with the connivance of the local authorities. The counter-revolutionary movement, which came into its own in 1792, won real popular support; it was given every encouragement by the government, which warned against seditious plots, and it was further strengthened by events in France during the summer, which spread anxiety among property-owners. As Macaulay has observed, after the 10th of August and the September Massacres, nineteen out of every twenty Englishmen who had a roof over their heads and a good shirt on their backs had become hostile to the French Revolution and to its British admirers. Loyalist, gallophobic and war-mongering organisations were founded, such as the Association for Preserving Liberty and Property against Republicans and Levellers, whose title is self-explanatory. The loyalists embarked upon a campaign of counter-propaganda that used a range of different methods, from sermons to caricature, a campaign also of threats, delation, prosecution and the hunting down of 'Jacobins'; it was so effective that many of the latter were forced to lie low or even to emigrate (to the United States or to France). These activities did much to stifle any movement that looked with favour upon the French Revolution. Moreover, the panic of 1792, plus Burke's and Pitt's manoeuvres, brought about a split in the Whig party, with the majority of them rallying to the government. The nominal leader of the party, the Duke of Portland, together with a number of his friends, finally entered the government in 1794; only a minority remained faithful to Charles James Fox, who wanted to go on 'listening to the French Revolution'.[2] Finally, when war had broken out with France,

[2] The rash statements and tactical blunders, which greatly harmed Charles James Fox's career, were very much to the fore in his attitude with regard to the French Revolution. Reliving in memory the struggles against Stuart absolutism, and always the champion of human rights, Fox greeted the Revolution with enthusiasm, as if through it France was at last setting out on the path of liberty; he hailed the capture of the Bastille as 'the greatest event yet to have happened in the world and by far the best', and the Revolution as 'the most glorious work ever realised by human integrity'. He persisted in his admiration even when the Revolution had radicalised and turned bloody. He declared that he wished to go on 'listening to' the French Revolution, that it was still a hugely beneficent force, whose virtues the British should make their own and whose crimes were merely the product of the hostility of foreign powers. He condemned the war policies adopted by Pitt, which were committing England to a crusade against liberty, on the side of continental despots, who might well one day turn against her; he rejoiced in France's successes against the coalition; he called for negotiations with the Republic, but he never recommended peace at any price. Fox's case is therefore an interesting one, for one can see in him a forerunner of those liberal *belles âmes* who applaud régimes that reign by terror. However, if there was blindness on his part, there was also confidence in the stability of English institutions and a conviction that panic at revolutionary contagion, of the kind entertained by the government and its supporters, was not justified. The Foxites condemned the counter-revolutionary repression, but they did not ally themselves with the English Jacobins, from

patriotism served to reinforce counter-revolutionary feelings; the opprobrium of treason was levelled at all those who admired the Revolution or called for reforms, all the more so given that many radicals condemned the war against France and demanded peace talks with her. Pitt's government was therefore able to deal severely with disaffected elements, since it enjoyed the support of the bulk of public opinion, including the working classes, which were little politicised and hated the hereditary foe of England.

In Scotland, where a 'Convention' of English and Scottish delegates met at the end of 1793, but was dissolved by the authorities, the sentencing of the 'five Scottish martyrs' to deportation to Australia terrified the radicals and quickly damped down agitation. It is true that the proceedings brought against the chief London 'Jacobins' in 1794 ended in a fiasco, in which the accused were acquitted; yet the suspension of Habeas Corpus in 1794 and, above all, the Two Acts of 1795, which effectively made all subversive propaganda tantamount to treason and severely restricted the freedom to hold meetings, brought the radicals' activities to a standstill. Finally, fears of a French invasion resulted in the passing of still more repressive measures, in 1798 and 1799, and these dealt the last blow to the radical movement.

Nevertheless, agitation for reform, and even sympathies for the French Revolution, were far more tenacious than one is often led to believe; they were not completely crushed, from the beginning of 1793, by the spectacle of the 'horrors' of the French Revolution, by the patriotic reaction against the traditional enemy of Britain and by government repression. The latter, be it noted, only gradually gained in intensity, and it is quite exaggerated to see it as a 'white terror'.

While some radical clubs disappeared, others remained active and continued their propaganda; this was especially true, for instance, of the London Corresponding Society, but it holds good for the Norwich and Sheffield societies also. They were assisted by the widespread discontent occasioned by the military defeats which England and its

whom their aristocratic connections separated them; and they kept themselves aloof from the hurly-burly, refusing to assume the leadership of popular and violent movements. Fox's vitality, his good-heartedness, his eloquence, his generosity, and even his impulsive behaviour and his love of gambling, make him an enduringly attractive figure. Furthermore, he was the spiritual father of the Whig-liberal tradition, which was to blossom in the nineteenth century. He had taught the young aristocrats with liberal sympathies in his circle that one had to accept reforms at their due time if one was to avoid revolution, and it is no accident that several of them were to form part of the government of 1830, around his friend and disciple, Lord Grey of the Reform Bill.

allies suffered and by economic difficulties – for which the war was held responsible. In 1795, the high cost of provisions led to many food riots and the Corresponding Society organised two large-scale, open air meetings in London, bringing together some 100,000 persons, at which calls for peace and the reform of Parliament were made; on 29 October, the king was barracked and threatened by the mob as he was making his way to Parliament; this presented the panic-stricken government with a pretext for passing the Two Acts, in spite of fierce protests and huge public meetings, the last of their kind for a long time.

These measures forced those radical societies which still survived to operate in a more and more clandestine way; they also delivered them into the hands of the most extremist elements, for moderates were discouraged by the ineffectiveness of the campaigns which they had run and by fear of the many informers and *agents provocateurs*. The radical societies were also infiltrated and manipulated by Irish revolutionaries, who were themselves liaising with the Irish emissaries based in Paris and with the Directory (which, in reprisal for the English government's support for Royalist rebels in Western France, sought to encourage subversion in England and in Ireland).[3] In imitation of the United Irishmen, associations of 'United Englishmen' and 'United Scotsmen' were founded, and the last radical societies, the corresponding societies in particular, became, after 1797, secret organisations, clearly republican in tendency, which dreamed of violent action – of instigating mutiny in the army, of making preparations to lend support to insurrection in Ireland and to a French invasion. A Jacobin conspiracy, of the kind that the government and its supporters had been fearing since 1792, was at last taking shape. These plots did not, however, constitute a real danger, except in Ireland, where there was both a revolutionary situation and a revolutionary movement, and where in 1798 there was a serious, though quickly crushed rebellion; they were the work of tiny groups, composed of fanatics who were recruited mainly in the Irish ghettos of London and of Lancashire. The government was naturally kept informed by its spies of the progress of these plots, they had no difficulty in extinguish-

[3] This policy, the brainchild of Carnot and Hoche, was based upon the dream of creating a *Chouannerie* in England and in Ireland; it was not put into action prior to 1795–6; conflicts and rivalries between the various French ministerial departments helped to bring about its failure. Previously, France had simply sent intelligence-gathering missions, such as that of the Reverend William Jackson, who was arrested and then poisoned himself in open court in Dublin (April 1795).

ing them in 1798 and 1799, by outlawing the 'united' societies and the Corresponding Society; a number of militants were imprisoned, but only one man, a catholic priest, James Coigley, upon whose person was discovered an appeal addressed to the Directory by a 'secret committee', was hung. Admittedly, some historians, E. P. Thompson foremost among them, have maintained that there existed a clandestine, revolutionary workers' movement, far more wide-reaching and insurrectionary than had been previously supposed, which showed itself during the strikes and bread riots, a huge number of which occurred between 1799 and 1801 (which accounts for the passing of the acts of 1799 and 1800 against workers' combinations, which had not only social but also political aims, any organisation of the 'lower classes' being considered suspect). We have little evidence as to how real this 'huge' movement was, but it is possible that Yorkshire was the scene of various clandestine activities which prefigured the Luddism of 1811–12. Be this as it may, this last 'revolutionary' (but in fact, truly marginal) phase of English Jacobinism was to have a final avatar in 1802, with the conspiracy of Colonel Despard, an ex-officer of Irish origin, who planned a kind of paramilitary putsch, in order to seize London, in combination with Ireland (where a final coup was in fact attempted by Robert Emmet in 1803).

By this date, English and Irish Jacobinism were dead. One should add that many of its supporters, who drew almost all their inspiration from the French Revolution, had been bitterly disappointed by the direction that this latter had taken and, in particular, by the aggressive, expansionist foreign policy of the *Grande Nation*. Wordsworth and Coleridge's road to Damascus was the invasion of the Swiss cantons by the French; many young intellectuals would, like them, foreswear their dreams of revolution, their belief in the philosophy of the Enlightenment, their interest in political action, and take refuge in the contemplation of nature, in the succour of religion and in the Burkean cult of tradition. After the Eighteenth of Brumaire, Bonaparte's despotism turned the last of France's admirers, with a few rare exceptions, away from her. When war recommenced, in 1803, the patriotic fervour which swept England was shared by the very same men who had condemned the war against the Revolution, and Wordsworth sung the praises of 'the men of Kent', who were in the front line against the enemy.

However, radicalism was not slow to raise its head again, albeit in a different form, drawing no direct inspiration from a France which had ceased to be revolutionary and, a fortiori, having no links with it. Nevertheless, there was continuity, as regards both ideas and tactics, between the democratic movement of the 1790s and the radicalism which emerged in the metropolis from 1806 onwards and which revived the campaign for parliamentary reform in 1809 (with serious disturbances in London in the following year, the Burdett riots). More significantly, a number of 'Jacobin' militants (such as Francis Place) resurfaced after several years and played an important role in the agitation of the postwar years. The writings of Thomas Spence, who proposed to abolish private property and preached a form of agrarian communism, and one of whose major books was published in 1801, show that the current of 'revolutionary' thought had never been obliterated. Moreover, the economic depressions of 1808 and 1811–12 prompted a political awakening both among the workers and among the middle classes of the provinces, especially among industrialists. The campaigns against the Orders in Council – measures directed against the Continental Blockade, but which had given rise to a conflict with the United States – brought about a division between an 'old', agricultural and mercantile, mercantilist and imperialist England and a 'new' industrial England, which was preoccupied with its liberty to do business and to trade, but was also aware that political reforms were necessary to guarantee such liberty. These campaigns also realised for the first time the union of the middle and working classes, which was to triumph in 1832.

Mention of this date should bring home to the reader just how long the reforms had to wait, and how long they had been delayed by the French Revolution. As revolutionary ideology failed, so conservatism triumphed, and it can even be claimed that English conservatism, as a self-conscious political force, was the product of the French Revolution. Before 1789, the established order had been so little challenged that people scarcely thought it needed defending, but the revolutionary threat had aroused dormant conservative forces and impressed upon all frightened property-owners the need to defend 'liberty and property'. It was this kind of conservatism, rather than repression, which had made it certain that the 'Jacobins' would be defeated. The Revolution and the war also exploded Whiggism – which had always been a politically ambiguous credo; its supporters had to opt for either its 'liberal' or its 'conservative' aspect; the majority of them leaned towards the established order. Fox and his friends, who were of the opinion that the power of the Crown and the alliance with the despots of continental Europe were more dangerous than the French threat, found themselves isolated and powerless; the motions for reform which they proposed periodically were rejected in Parliament by overwhelming majorities, and they were so discouraged that for a time they stopped taking their seats in the Commons. On the other hand, in the long term, the French Revolution may have taught the Tories (the revival by Canning of this forgotten nickname, in the early years of the nineteenth century, is itself significant), and the liberal aristocrats also, that it was wise to carry through reforms in good time if one wished to forestall violent explosions; but in the short and medium term it merely led to almost forty years of stasis and of a narrow, inflexible, coercive conservatism, which was not merely 'anti-Jacobin' but also anti-catholic, and which rejected even the most harmless innovations. This conservatism was, admittedly, strengthened by the imperatives of war and by the victory which brought it to a close.

Lasting, with two short interruptions, for twenty-two years, the war against revolutionary and Imperial France in fact dominated the history of England from 1793 to 1815. Yet Pitt had only decided fairly late in the day to make war against France, for he had at first reckoned that a country considered by him to be irremediably weakened by Revolution could not pose any threat, either on the ideological or the military plane, and he had therefore opted for neutrality (which, it is true, resembled a quarantine), when hostilities broke out on the Continent in the Spring of 1792. However, in November, he suddenly decided in favour of war (although admittedly he then very deftly waited for the French Convention to declare war on England, on 1 February 1793), when the opening of the mouths of the Scheldt to shipping had made it plain to him that France meant to establish a permanent presence in Belgium and when the Convention had formally opted for propagating by arms the revolutionary ideology. Pitt's programme was 'to halt the progress of French arms and principles', and to re-establish the European balance of power, by forcing France to hand back the territories it had conquered, to overthrow the Jacobins and to set up a constitutional monarchy, which would serve as a guarantee that France would no longer be a threat to the international order. The war was also meant to check the penetration of democratic ideas and to facilitate the struggle against the enemy within, but Pitt further counted upon seizing France's colonies and wrecking her naval and commercial power.

England was in the long run to attain her objectives, but only in 1814 and 1815, whereas Pitt had been convinced that a war against a country in a state of anarchy, whose finances were in ruins, would be quickly and easily won. In the meantime, the interminable 'French wars' were for the English a succession of successes with no tomorrow, of disappointed hopes, of wounding setbacks and of dangerous crises. In brief, these wars were for long a source of grave disappointment, but England finally was victorious.

The rebuffs suffered by England admittedly derived from factors that were by and large out of its control. One can, of course, emphasise the revolutionary government's success in mobilising the resources of the most populous country in Europe, the talent of the new French generals, the bravery of their troops and the emergence at their head of a military genius. Yet English specialists often feel no admiration, let alone respect, for the military qualities of the French armies, of their generals and of Napoleon himself. On the other hand, there is general agreement as to the disastrous consequences of the obsolete tactics and strategy of Britain's continental allies, and of their quarrels also. But the mistakes made by British statesmen were also partly responsible (during the early years, in particular) for the series of defeats suffered by the coalitions ranged against France (in spite of the opportunities offered by the sheer folly of France's own leaders, as at the time of the expedition to Egypt).

These coalitions were not generally the outcome of machinations by the British Cabinet, as people tended to believe in France, and they rather took shape spontaneously – as a response to French encroachments or through a desire for revenge; but the British government was their banker and their only conceivable leader. Actually English statesmen did manage, prior to 1813, neither to organise the coalitions in any real sense (indeed, they were often clumsy in their relations with their allies), nor to impose a coordinated strategy and clear war aims upon them. At the time of the first coalition, Pitt was not able to opt either for the ideological crusade against the Revolution (rather than against France) preached by Burke, or for a 'political' war aimed at re-establishing the European balance of power, or for a war of conquest. These objectives were in fact mutually contradictory and, moreover the English government, once it had disclosed its own expansionist ambitions, was no longer in a position to oppose those of its allies. Difficulties of this order were to blow the coalition apart, with Prussia being so preoccupied with the compensation that its allies had been forced to promise her in Poland, that it soon lost any enthusiasm for operations against France. Similarly, at the time of the second coalition, which had got off to a promising start, the Anglo-Russian landing in Holland prompted Austria to send an army in the direction of Belgium, in order to safeguard its own interests there, leaving the Russians to fend for themselves in Switzerland, where they were routed by Masséna.

It is true that the numerical weakness of the British army, which was for a long time incapable of lending any effective support to its partners, placed limits on any influence Britain might have on the strategy of the coalitions. England had begun the war with a regular army of 45,000 men, two-thirds of whom were immobilised in colonial garrisons, and it was only gradually that she succeeded in increasing the number of troops (through recourse to a whole gamut of expedients), in improving organisation and in producing competent generals; the expeditionary corps that she kept on dispatching to the Continent were therefore absurdly small for a long time. In addition, Pitt, his ministers and his successors turned out to be very poor strategists, ignorant of the basic principle that one's forces should be concentrated. In 1793, when the revolutionary government had not yet eliminated its enemies at home and set up large armies, the coalition could very likely have gained some signal successes, but Pitt had failed to grasp that, if the Revolution was to be crushed, Paris would have to be captured and therefore an energetic and concentrated offensive waged on the crucial front of the Low Countries. Pitt was convinced that victory was easily within grasp, and only sent there a few thousand men; leaving his allies to fight on the Continent, he made haste to seize sureties, in the West Indies in particular; then he attempted, but in a rather inept manner, to profit from the opportunities offered by the royalist insurrections in the Midi and in the West of France.

The British were therefore scattered far and wide, and squandered their meagre military resources (between 1793 and 1796, 35,000 soldiers and sailors died in the West Indies, not in battle but from disease); they embarked upon improvised and badly led expeditions, launched as and when the opportunity offered, belatedly and with some lack of seriousness, only to abandon them quickly without having pursued them with conviction. For years on end, in fact, the British adopted this same 'peripheral' strategy, involving soft but pointless diversionary activities, which at best brought them temporary successes and at worst landed them in costly fiascos and in hurried re-embarkations. This was the case at Toulon (1793), Quiberon (1795), the Helder (1799), in Southern Italy (1806), also at Corunna and at Walcheren in 1809. The English government also had recourse, admittedly, to subversion, for which purpose they set up professional intelligence services (such as the network known as The Correspondence, which operated from Jersey), but, in spite of its support for the royalist insurrections in the West of France, the latter were crushed in the end. As for the 'underground war', waged in the period of the Directory, with the purpose of bringing about counter-revolution at the top, it also ended in failure.

The war was therefore for a long time a disappointment for the British, with the hopes aroused by the formation of coalitions, and by their early successes (in 1793, 1799, 1805 and 1809), being dispelled in turn by the revolutionary *carmagnoles* and by Napoleon's *grognards*. Each time that her allies were crushed or defected, England found herself isolated once again and in a critical situation. The problem was compounded by the fact that military and political setbacks were often accompanied by economic difficulties. In spite of its wealth and the lead it enjoyed over other countries, the British economy was in fact vulnerable and sensitive to changes in the military and political conjuncture abroad, since it depended upon foreign countries for its supplies of a number of 'essential' products and, above all, for selling a large share of its industrial production. Moreover, the burden of heavy military expenditure (a part of which was carried out abroad), the shortcomings of the banking system, and the precariousness of the balance of payments created a risk of inflation and of depreciation in the value of bank notes. France was not slow to exploit this vulnerability, and Napoleon, in particular, from 1806 onwards, imposed a Continental blockade which was meant to asphyxiate England by shutting the Continental markets to its exports. The history of England from 1793 to 1815 was thus marked by a succession of crises which seemed to bring it to the brink of ruin and which, at any rate, were severe shocks.

So it was that, in 1797, the defection of Prussia and of Spain, together with the defeat of Austria, left England isolated; revolt was brewing in Ireland, and only a combination of unlucky circumstances – a hurricane, in particular – had prevented a powerful expedition led by Hoche from landing there, in December 1796. Because of the financial imprudence of Pitt, who had borrowed on a massive scale, and because of the panic aroused by fear of a French incursion (which in fact amounted to nothing more than the landing in South Wales of a 'black legion' of convicts and deserters), the bullion reserves of the Bank of England were almost exhausted, and it was found necessary in February to suspend the convertibility into gold of bank notes, which from then until the end of the war and beyond (1821) were de facto legal tender. In the months of May and June, the sailors of the squadrons at Spithead and the Nore, who were badly paid, badly fed, harshly disciplined and perhaps influenced by some 'Jacobin' agitators, mutinied, leaving the coast of England undefended, although the Directory failed to take advantage of this extraordinary opportunity. Likewise, in the following year, the improvised expeditions which it sent to Ireland were quite inadequate for the purpose and arrived too late, after the rebels had been defeated.

There was a further crisis in 1800–1, after the defeat and dislocation of the second coalition, when Tsar Paul I moved closer to France and urged the 'League of Armed Neutrality' to close the Baltic to the English, at a time when poor harvests were forcing them to import massive quantities of grain. Prices soared and there were riots; meanwhile Napoleon was organising his flotilla at Boulogne. In 1807, England was once again isolated, confronted with an almost wholly hostile Continent, after Napoleon had conquered the fourth coalition and had formed an alliance at Tilsit with Alexander I; he managed for several months to close off Europe to English goods, provoking serious economic difficulties and workers' riots in England. The same situation occurred again, but in a worsened form, when the Great Empire reached its apogee, after the defeat of Austria in 1809; a violent economic crisis broke out in England during the summer of 1810 and it was followed by a long and painful depression lasting almost two whole years; bank notes depreciated, industrial production sharply declined, unemployment and poverty were widespread. Roaming bands of Luddites, believing that machinery was depriving them of work, attacked workshops or factories and smashed their machines; revolution seemed to threaten, but there was no revolutionary party, or general conspiracy and the Luddites were mainly 'primitive rebels', lacking in real political objectives.

England did, however, survive these ordeals; defeats (suffered, mainly, by her allies) and crises shook her but never brought her to her knees. After each crisis, she managed to recover and waited for more favourable circumstances. This stubborn resistance to adversity was made possible by the resolution of the country's statesmen. Many people have been astonished that Napoleon's genius was finally laid low by adversaries who were far inferior. Pitt had been a great administrator and a very skilled politician in peacetime, but he turned out to be a mediocre *Kriegsführer.* His successors, with the exception of Canning, who was brilliant but given to intrigues, and Castlereagh, who was a great diplomat, were fairly lacklustre; this was especially true of Prime Ministers such as Spencer Perceval and Lord Liverpool. Yet these politicians were all tenacious, cool and confident of England's ultimate victory. England's traditions and basic interests made it impossible for her to admit that any great power – least of all France, her hereditary enemy – could subordinate the whole of the Continent to her hegemony. Only wholly critical circumstances and the general feeling of lassitude which reigned in 1801 brought the Cabinet in London to resign itself, reluctantly, to a recognition of France's natural frontiers and its influence over the 'Sister Republics', although it was hoping that French expansion would not proceed any further. Once this hope had turned out to be in vain, the peace of Amiens was broken and from that moment on (save in 1806, when Fox was in charge of England's diplomacy), no English Cabinet ever seriously envisaged a peace on an *uti possidetis* base, which would have ratified French hegemony in Europe. Indeed, the more victories Napoleon won and the larger his empire became, the less the British were ipso facto disposed to treat with him. 'Perpetual war', which at least guaranteed them naval and commercial advantages, seemed to them preferable to a peace which would recognise the power of France, which, as it grew unceasingly, became more and more unacceptable. Convinced that the domination of Europe by a Jacobin usurper of lowly birth was so monstrous a thing that it could not possibly last, ever prepared to attribute the defeats of the various coalitions to their allies' mistakes, aware that their naval power preserved them from direct attack, imbued with a sense of their own superiority and fired by a deep contempt for their enemies (Napoleon included), the British leaders would never admit to being defeated, in spite of the disheartening triumphs of the French armies.

Moreover, the British government enjoyed the support of the vast majority of the population. After the failure of the peace negotiations of 1796 and 1797 – because of the foolish intransigence of the French, after the crisis of 1797, there was a nationalisation of the war, a national awakening, and the growing conviction that England was struggling 'for its existence' (although it was really a matter of maintaining its rank as a great power). These developments were encouraged by the disappearance of the admirers of the French Revolution, by the imperialist character of French policies and by propaganda, which was intense by the standards of the period. Loyalism, patriotic fervour and a determination to resist were unambiguous, fiercely held feelings, especially widespread during the most difficult moments, when invasion seemed to threaten, as in 1798, and then again between 1803 and 1805, when remarkably extensive plans were made for the defence of the country, and 380,000 men enrolled in the Volunteers. Admittedly, there were always 'defeatists', who saw no possibility of victory and who, without openly calling for a compromise peace, tended to condemn continental adventures which, in their view, were doomed to fail; but the whigs, who were prone to such isolationist tendencies, were excluded from power, except for a few months in 1806–7. It is also true that economic difficulties led, upon several occasions, to the launching of 'peace petitions' signed by many industrialists and workers. Yet the great majority of the people was not affected by this pessimism, and tended rather to support the policy of all-out war advocated by the governments of the day, in spite of the successive economic crises (which were, admittedly, separated by years of prosperity), in spite of inflation, in spite of the crushing burden of taxation (including the income tax introduced by Pitt in 1799), which absorbed over twenty per cent of national income. During its struggle against Napoleon, England, however, suffered from political instability; although Pitt's position had at first been strengthened by the war, it was weakened as time went on, and the Catholic question led to his departure from office in 1801. After this date, and still more after the death of Pitt, in 1806, parties fragmented and divided into a number of factions, which demonstrates clearly that the political system was still that of the eighteenth century. The position of government was especially weak during the years of worst danger, from 1807 to 1812. Yet public opinion was not overmuch disturbed by the constant intrigues within the microcosm of politics, nor by the scandals which broke out (the mistress of the Duke of York, who was commander-in-chief of the army, was selling officers' commissions), nor by the final descent into madness of George III in 1810 and the accession of a Regent who was respected by few of his subjects.

It is true that the resolution of the English to pursue the war to the end would have carried little weight had it not been for the twenty miles of the Straits of Dover and for England's naval superiority which, being much more pronounced than during the wars against the Bourbons, guaranteed their security. The Royal Navy enjoyed a superiority which was, first of all, numerical. This had been clear from 1793 on and was further reinforced by the destruction or capture of dozens of French, Spanish, Dutch, Danish, Portuguese and other ships of the line, and notwithstanding the substantial shipbuilding programme embarked upon by Napoleon in the last years of his reign. England enjoyed a qualitative superiority also, not so much on the material as on the human plane, which became clear after a few initial waverings and which rendered the Royal Navy virtually invincible. Since it was always at sea, it had, notwithstanding some recruitment problems, sea-inured and battle-hardened crews, whereas the enemy's squadrons, which were blockaded in their ports, were reduced to inaction and lacked opportunities for training. As far as officers were concerned, the Revolution had destroyed the grand corps of the French Navy and replaced it by an incongruous and often mediocre mixture, whereas British officers formed a homogeneous and competent body, skilled in naval manoeuvres and combat, prone to take the offensive and convinced that victory would always be theirs. As for admirals, England had many excellent ones, and one genius, Horatio Nelson, who looked for every opportunity to destroy decisively the enemy; their French opposite numbers were often incapable or at any rate timid, suffering from an inferiority complex, committed to obsolete tactics and strategy.

However, in spite of their weakness at sea, the French and their allies several times drew up plans for landing in the British Isles, since this was the only way in which England could be vanquished. Yet each of these attempts ended in a fiasco or a disaster. Thus, the Spanish were defeated at Cape Saint-Vincent, and the Dutch crushed at Camperdown in 1797. Though Napoleon's grand design, in 1805, which involved bringing unexpectedly the combined Franco-Spanish fleet into the Channel, in order to protect the flotilla carrying the *Grande Armée* from Boulogne, was not quite as chimerical as has often been claimed, its ultimate success would have required commanders, crews and ships which he did not have. Actually the execution of the plan was so slow that the threat of the third coalition forced the Emperor to give up Channel-crossing, and the odyssey of Villeneuve ended, quite pointlessly, in the disaster of Trafalgar, which meant the indefinite adjournment of all invasion plans. Subsequent defeats (San Domingo, 1806; Aix Roads, 1809) obliged France to give up any battle-fleet strategy, but trade destroying tactics were no more successful. The Royal Navy was mistress of the seas; as Admiral Mahan saw quite clearly, English naval power was a crucial factor in the French wars, for it protected England's national territory and its trade from all attacks, enabled it to seize its enemies' colonies and to destroy their seaborne trade, and posed a constant threat to enemy coastlines. It is true that the 'peripheral' strategy, to which the British were tempted by the strength of their navy, was for a long time ineffective, but it did nevertheless bring some important successes. The battle of the Nile dashed Bonaparte's dreams of controlling the East and with one stroke reversed the strategic and diplomatic situation; victory at Copenhagen, in 1801, destroyed the League of Armed Neutrality; later, it was only the mastery of the seas which made it possible for the English to intervene in the Iberian peninsula. It would nevertheless be rash to claim that Trafalgar had sealed Napoleon's destiny, by condemning him to a *fuite en avant* which could only end in catastrophe.

England's mastery of the seas also helped it to stand up to the Continental Blockade and to counter it with a maritime blockade which embarrassed greatly the economies of the enemy countries; that of France in particular. While the economic war which Napoleon launched against England was not so unrealistic an enterprise as many historians have maintained and in fact dealt her some heavy blows, the Continental Blockade was only seriously enforced during periods which were too brief for these wounds to prove fatal. The English economy turned out to have more solidity and flexibility than Napoleon had imagined; British businessmen managed, by developing a vast and diverse system of contraband, which was aided and abetted by a huge network of accomplices on the Continent, to outwit the Emperor's interdicts; they also conquered substitution markets in the Americas.

Twice, moreover, Napoleon, by launching himself into the Spanish hornets' nest and into his Russian adventure, destroyed with his own hands the war machine that he had built, at the very moment at which it was beginning to give the results that were expected of it. If, therefore, England went through some difficult moments, she avoided disaster; if her economy was shaken, at least it was not ruined, and the crises which it suffered never forced its government to think of capitulating, and never unleashed a protest movement capable of obliging it to sue for peace or of overthrowing it. England's economic growth clearly slowed down but it did nevertheless continue, and her economic structures held steady.

England, Pitt declared shortly before his death, 'had saved herself by her own efforts and will go on to save the world by her example'. It is undoubtedly true that the unwavering resistance of the British, during the long years in which Napoleon reaped the laurels of glory, in itself held out some promise of victory, for it made the hegemony established by France over Europe precarious, and it weakened the Great Empire economically, by means of the maritime blockade, morally, because as long as England held firm she continued to be a hope and a rallying point for all of France's enemies, and militarily, thanks to its counterattack in the Iberian Peninsula. The Iberian Campaign had, however, only been decided upon on the spur of the moment, and it was conducted in the teeth of a whole series of criticisms, hesitations and disappointments, and at the price of great efforts, especially on the financial plane. Yet the army which fought in the Peninsula, though not very large, was solid, well trained, well armed and well provisioned; it had at its head a general, Wellington, who displayed great talent, genius even, who had a cold and tenacious will, was a meticulous organiser, managed to perfect a tactic capable of holding in check French attacks and was a skilled strategist, who took advantage of the mistakes made by Napoleon's marshals. Alternating defence with attack, Wellington managed to hold his position in Portugal, inflict defeats upon the French that were costly both in terms of men and of prestige, and then move into the offensive, liberating Spain and reaching Bordeaux and Toulouse in 1814. Had it not been for his support, the resistance of the Spanish armies and guerilla bands would have been rapidly quelled. The Peninsular War may well have worn out the *Grande Armée*, but it is as well to remember that for a long time it was little more than a diversion, an abscess that was a nuisance rather than a danger, and that Wellington's army did not play a major role until 1813, when it immobilised troops which would otherwise probably have guaranteed Napoleon a victory in Germany.

In fact, the English resistance and counter-attack were capable of undermining the Great Empire, but they could not by themselves overthrow it, in spite of a military effort which should not be underestimated (by the end of the Napoleonic Wars, the United Kingdom had more than 500,000 men in arms, which meant more than one out of every ten men who were of an age to serve). The war between England and France had, moreover, reached an impasse by the beginning of 1812, as it had done several times before. The deciding factors lay elsewhere, namely, the Russian winter and Russian open spaces, the continental coalitions at Leipzig which, by twice destroying the Grande Armée, dealt the fatal blows. England did not 'defeat' Napoleon, although in 1813 and 1814 Caslereagh's diplomacy and English subsidies cemented the coalition and prevented a compromise peace of the kind that would have left Napoleon his throne and France a part of her conquests; in this sense, England may be said to have been an indispensable catalyst. Circumstances then had it that the last victory over Napoleon was won by Wellington, a well-deserved honour no doubt for the army of his 'most constant' enemy, but in reality a secondary and peripheral affair. Nevertheless, Trafalgar and Waterloo still weigh heavily on the British national psyche, and a reader from abroad is always a little surprised by the one-sided and pent-up passion which continues to inform many English studies of the French wars, whereas British works on the world wars of the twentieth century are much more objective (even at times displaying a pro-German bias).

Whilst the exact weight of England's contribution to the failure of the imperial adventure is open to debate, there is little doubt that the role she played was a crucial one. Napoleon's defeat was first and foremost due to his failure to conquer his enemy on the other side of the Channel. And at any rate, England was the main victor in 1815. By the end of the second Hundred Years' War, she had definitively humbled her hereditary rival; she had chased her off the seas; she had destroyed her colonial empire and her trade; she had set up a system of 'barriers' on the Continent which would stand in the way of any attempts at expansion; she had deprived her of those areas (Belgium, the Rhineland) which would have given her a better economic balance; she had also, by favouring the restoration of the Bourbons, condemned her to political instability. England had also, it is true, installed Prussia on the Rhine, a mistake which was to prove fatal, both for Europe and for herself, but the harmful consequences of which were only to become apparent much later.

England could therefore settle down to enjoy the fruits of her naval, colonial and economic superiority. Her resources had in fact not been sufficient to prosecute both the war and a rapid process of industrialisation. Economic growth had thus been slowed down by the Napoleonic wars; taxes and government loans in particular had mopped up savings and 'crowded out' productive investment. The national debt, at constant prices, had risen from 244 million pounds sterling in 1791 to 704 million in 1821; its average increase had been equivalent each year to 8·5 per cent of national income (with the percentage being higher in the 1790s). Moreover, J. Williamson has calculated that, if there had been no wars between 1760 and 1820, English workers' standard of living would have risen by 65 per cent, whereas in actual fact it was stagnant at a low level, and after 1815 the burden of the public debt slowed down its improvement. Nevertheless, the wars had not brought the Industrial Revolution to a halt and, since they had done more damage to the economies of England's rivals than to her own, they had in fact increased the lead which she had enjoyed some twenty years earlier. As a result, England's commercial and industrial supremacy was assured for the greater part of the nineteenth century.

In other respects, the rigid conservatism which had arisen in reaction to the French Revolution had allowed unresolved problems to pile up, and had created tensions and imbalances in a society which was changing rapidly. Yet victory had also consolidated the institutions which had held firm against France's assault, so that, while England was prey after 1815 to some serious domestic turbulences, she again escaped revolution. Historians of an earlier generation used to speak of an 'English supremacy' in the eighteenth century; the expression is better applied, however, to the nineteenth century, which, since England was the only world power, the only superpower, was in many respects an English century.

An unexpiable conflict?[4]

In his letter of 14 July 1815 to the Prince Regent, Napoleon wrote to ask for the protection 'of the most powerful, the most constant and the

[4] This text was published in *Le Souvenir Napoléonien*, no. 264, June 1972, pp. 2–8.

most generous of [his] enemies'. Later, at Saint Helena, he declared that England had been 'the agent of victory, the linch-pin around which all the intrigues on the Continent had formed'. Subsequently many historians have maintained that England's hatred for Napoleon and its manoeuvrings to form coalitions against France were the key to the whole history of the Napoleonic period, while many English authors tend to assert that their country 'was struggling for its very existence' in this period, just as at the time of Philip II, Louis XIV and Hitler, against the Emperor's wish to obliterate the power of Albion. Hence the notion of a struggle to the death, of an unexpiable conflict. In the following pages, I hope to add some qualifications to this view, in particular by specifying the attitude of the antagonists to each other.

How Napoleon regarded England

Napoleon knew little of England; he never visited it, and it was only when he was on Saint Helena that he tried to learn English. He had had, all in all, very few contacts with the English prior to becoming their prisoner, if one excepts a number of interviews with diplomats and politicians during the peace of Amiens. It was only on his first and his last battlefields, at Toulon and at Waterloo, that he found himself face to face with English troops. He had, admittedly, some knowledge of English history and English institutions; when on Saint Helena, he drew an extensive and curious parallel between the English revolutions of the seventeenth century and the French Revolution, declaring that his own role in the latter had been both that of Cromwell and that of William of Orange! Yet Napoleon was also aware that his understanding of affairs on the other side of the Channel was defective, and his sense of irritation regarding the mystery of England comes across in the peremptory and at times contradictory nature of some of his judgements. The reasons for England's economic and naval power, in particular, quite eluded him and he was convinced, as were almost all Frenchmen of the day, that the English economy was an artificial and fragile edifice, resting upon the unhealthy foundation of credit, threatened by the 'gnawing worm' of its public debt, and therefore to be easily overthrown.

Although he had proclaimed in 1808 that 'England [was] the enemy of the world', Napoleon seems not to have nursed so fierce a hate for the English as is often ascribed to him. He is on record as describing

England as 'a nation which is fundamentally worthy of a great deal of respect', which was enlightened and an example to others; once again, on Saint Helena, he declared: 'In spite of the martyrdom imposed upon me by its ministers, the English people still has my respect.'

Indeed, Napoleon reserved his more violent judgements for Britain's leaders. Pitt, for him, was 'a real scourge, an evil genius', who 'set fire to the universe, and whose name will go down in history much as that of Erostratus has done, amid flames, lamentations and tears'; Napoleon was still more severe for 'the hideous followers' that Pitt left behind him, Castlereagh in particular, who 'raised all kinds of turpitudes and immoralities to their highest pitch'.

Napoleon accused the English ministers who had fought him of arrogance, impudence, ferocity, 'insolent Machiavellianism', 'profound immorality', 'cold egoism' and 'scorn for the destiny of men and the justice of things'. 'When all Europe', declared Napoleon, 'was engaged in mutual slaughter on account of their intrigues and their subsidies, they kept in the background and concerned themselves only with their own security, with the advantages to be gained for their own trade, with the sovereignty of the seas and with their monopoly over the whole world'. But these charges, which were often repeated by Anglophobes during the nineteenth century, were inspired either by the need to propagandise or by a natural resentment towards the men whom the Emperor held responsible for the failure of his plans, and he tended to distinguish between the English people and the 'English oligarchy', which, blinded 'by a handful of incorrigible émigrés', had made no attempt to understand him and had allied with the European aristocracy against France. 'I am dying before my time', he was to write in 1821, 'assassinated by the English oligarchy and its hired assassin [Hudson Lowe]. The English people will soon avenge me.' In Napoleon's view, Pitt had 'brought about the subjugation of the popular cause and the triumph of the patricians', who had corrupted the English constitution and 'turned the Cabinet of Saint-James into a corner shop'. Had Napoleon succeeded with his invasion plans, he would have given the English back their liberty: 'I would not have entered [London] as a conqueror but as a liberator; I would have been a second William of Orange, only with greater generosity and disinterestedness ... We would not have appeared before them as conquerors but as brothers, come to restore their liberty and their rights. I would have told them to gather together and to undertake their own regeneration.' Moreover, 'we were called by the wishes of a majority of the English ... the English people were groaning beneath the yoke of oligarchy; once their pride had been tactfully spared, they would straightway have come over to our side; we would then have seemed to them to be nothing else but allies come to deliver them'.

Upon several occasions, Napoleon also expressed some admiration for English institutions, whilst also drawing attention to 'the corruption of a bad administration ... the most defective in Europe', to the lack of foresight by a 'government preoccupied with domestic wranglings, and tending to direct its attention to any spot where there was some noise or other'. He regarded the English as 'our elders in matters of political legislation', and he recognised that 'in spite of its being composed of hateful, outdated and ignoble details, the English constitution nevertheless has, remarkably enough, led to happy and fine results' and that its 'foundations descend deep into the entrails of the earth'.

Hence Napoleon's regret that he had not been able to arrange a reconciliation between the two countries, which would, he believed, have been possible had it not been for the death of Fox, who was 'a model for statesmen' and whose passing 'has been one of the fatal blows suffered in the course of my career' (in actual fact, the Emperor had not shown too conciliatory a spirit at the time of the peace negotiations in 1806, when Fox was Foreign Secretary). 'England and France', said Napoleon, 'held the fate of the whole planet, and that of European civilisation in particular, in their hands. What harm we did each other! What good we could have done! With Fox's party, we could have reached an understanding ... We would have carried out, preserved the emancipation of peoples, the reign of principles: in Europe there would have been but a single navy, a single army, we would have ruled the world.' It is true, of course, that these projects dreamed up on Saint Helena of a union between England and France were fairly peculiar: 'England would naturally end up by being no more than an appendix [of France], for nature had decreed that it should be one of our islands, just as Oléron or Corsica are.'

Napoleon was therefore not possessed by a wild hatred towards England. Moreover, if the struggle against England, in order to challenge its maritime and commercial supremacy, had been his key objective, he would have concentrated upon this struggle, as Vergennes had done during the War of American Independence, and he would not have allowed himself to be dragged into continental adventures, which could not help but distract him from this objective and scatter his forces far and wide.

In fact, England had not been Napoleon's main enemy, in the sense that he had only devoted a relatively small part of his time and energy to combatting it. He had been appointed Commander-in-chief of 'the army of England' upon his return from Italy, in 1797, and a rapid inspection of the coastline convinced him that any invasion plans were ill-advised; he then threw himself into the Egypt expedition, which only posed a threat to English domination over India in the long term. After the Eighteenth Brumaire, Napoleon undertook preparations for an invasion, but they were not too serious and were mainly meant to force the government in London to enter into peace talks. Conversely, after the breach of the peace of Amiens, these preparations were revived on a grand scale and Napoleon was decided, if his fleet could win control of the Channel, to attempt an invasion of England. Yet it seems as if he felt little regret at abandoning this plan, when threatened by the third coalition, and setting out to win less dangerous laurels at Ulm and at Austerlitz. After Trafalgar, the invasion was indefinitely postponed, and, though Napoleon devoted a great deal of energy to the Continental Blockade and to the reconstitution of his navy, he several times neglected these tasks for new campaigns on the mainland, and he never took the decision to go in person and drive Wellington from the Iberian Peninsula. In his famous diatribe of 1811 to a delegation of Paris merchants, he declared that he was preparing to revive the war at sea and that, before ten years had passed, he would have conquered England. Yet this itself shows that it was a long-term objective.

On the other hand, Napoleon had not sought, or wished for, war with England. As soon as he had become First consul, he had proposed negotiations to her. The signing of the peace of Amiens was one of his greatest successes and did much to consolidate his power. The conditions of this treaty satisfied him and he hoped it would last. If it did not do so, Napoleon's responsibility for the breach of 1803 is restricted, from the juridical point of view. It was the English Cabinet which initiated the breach, by refusing to evacuate Malta, which it was formally committed to doing, by recalling its ambassador and by entering into hostilities. Napoleon was admittedly guilty of a number of imprudent gestures, which were seen by London to be provocations, and he refused to make some concessions which might have made it possible to postpone the war (which in fact came for him at a very inopportune time, since the reconstitution of the French navy had only just begun).

During the eleven years of war which followed, there were only once serious peace negotiations, in 1806, after Pitt's death, and the coming to power of the 'Ministry of all the talents', with Fox, the former admirer of the French Revolution, in charge of the Foreign Office. These negotiations very nearly succeeded, and this time it was Napoleon who was responsible for the breach, as he refused to grant the trivial concession demanded by the English, namely, that their protégés, the Bourbons of the Kingdom of Naples, be given Sicily or else be transferred to the Balearic Islands. Napoleon's intransigence convinced Fox, in spite of his own desire to come to terms, that an honourable peace was impossible; the Whig leader died soon afterwards. This was a missed opportunity and then, after Jena, Friedland and Tilsit, a negotiated peace between France and England had become an impossibility. Napoleon's new victories, in extending his domination up to the Vistula, had created a French hegemony over Europe that England could under no circumstances accept. Moreover, looking at it from the other side, how could one expect Napoleon to renounce, without having been defeated, his prodigious gains? By 1807 the die was cast, and the conflict could only be settled by the total defeat of one of the two antagonists.

Furthermore, from 1807 on, Napoleon never believed that a compromise peace with England was possible and he therefore wanted to force her to capitulate, either by stifling her through economic warfare or, in the longer term, by reconstructing his own navy. The problem remains whether these attempts to break an adversary that could not be attacked directly were in fact the engine of his policies as a whole and whether, more particularly, the need to integrate all Europe into his system, so as to make the Continental Blockade effective, did not draw Napoleon into a series of ever more dangerous adventures, into more and more unbounded schemes of conquest, which could only end in catastrophe. This is the *fuite en avant* theory, which holds that, after Trafalgar, Napoleon's destiny was mapped out in advance, as far ahead as Berezina and Waterloo. The Spanish affair and the attack on Russia, with their disastrous consequences for the Napoleonic edifice, lend credence to this line of argument. But Napoleon's desire to have Spain, and later Russia, respect the blockade, only played a secondary role in his decision to dethrone the Spanish Bourbons, and subsequently to march on Moscow. Such a mechanistic and mono-causal interpretation of Napoleon's policies is not at all satisfying. One would search in vain for a single explanation or objective of his policies. In this respect, the struggle against England is no more convincing a candidate than are the arguments about the defence of France's natural frontiers which were inherited from the Revolution, the oriental dream of a man from the Mediterranean, who had it in mind to march on Constantinople and on India, the reconstitution of Charlemagne's empire, or the politics of a Corsican clan chief, who wished to place each of his brothers and sisters on a throne. The only plausible explanation one can give of Napoleon's politics rests upon the dynamism, the will to power, the tireless activity of a man who only lived for action, and who used to say 'God's place is something I would not wish for myself, for it is a dead end', and 'I exploit opportunities and I push them to the limit'.

From Napoleon's point of view, there was not an inexpiable struggle against England, it is rather that she was the only one of his enemies that he was powerless to defeat, because the Straits of Dover are twenty miles wide and because the Royal Navy dominated the seas. It is this that accounts for the continuous war which lent a unity to the history of the Napoleonic Empire.

How the English saw Napoleon

By contrast, the British have displayed a remarkable unanimity in their hatred of Napoleon. Admittedly, even at the height of the war, he had a handful of admirers on the other side of the Channel, but these were isolated eccentrics or rebels, who had no influence. Their radicalism itself tended to make the radicals hostile towards Napoleon's 'despotism', which they charged with having smothered liberty in France; they were indignant about the aggression against Spain too. Admittedly, at the time of the troubles which broke out in a number of industrial regions of England in 1811–12, a few handbills were distributed, which had been allegedly issued by so-called secret committees, and which claimed that they were counting upon the French Emperor's help in unleashing the revolution, but these tracts were in reality the work of isolated energumens or of *agents provocateurs*. Of greater significance, in fact, was the defeatist or isolationist tendency, which was rife in Whig political circles, after they had been thrown back into opposition by the return to power of Mr Pitt's 'friends' in 1807. These people did not look favourably on Napoleon, nor did they relish the idea of a compromise peace with him, but, faced with his uninterrupted sequence of successes and with the failure of all attempts by England and its allies to contain French expansion, they were unable to discern any possibility of victory; moreover, the idea of England being involved in a 'perpetual war' caused them grave anxiety, for such a war would wreck its economy and its finances. The opposition therefore wished to husband England's resources, to avoid new continental adventures, which were doomed to failure; it condemned British involvement in the Iberian Peninsula and, had it returned to power, would probably have recalled Wellington's army.

But English public opinion as a whole, and the party in power in the years after 1807, never were affected by this grumbling pessimism, undoubtedly because their hatred for Napoleon was mingled with contempt. This attitude is obvious in the countless caricatures in which Napoleon features (this was the golden age of English caricature, featuring Gillray, Rowlandson, Cruikshank and many others). These caricatures, like the press and the pamphlets of the period, displayed an extreme violence in their attacks upon Buonaparte (as he was almost always called); he was presented as a tyrant, an assassin, a bandit chief, the enemy of mankind, the disturber of the peace of Europe; he was compared to the devil and accused of every conceivable crime. Some of the attacks were scurrilous: there was much jeering at the 'virtuous Josephine', it was claimed that Buonaparte's sisters had indulged in prostitution and that, at Jaffa, he had had those of his soldiers who were sick poisoned.

What is perhaps most interesting is the tendency to reduce and ridicule the person and the deeds of the enemy, so as to render him not merely hateful but despicable also, and thus to dispel the fears that he might have inspired in the English. In 1802, Gillray had represented Napoleon as a gigantic ogre, with huge teeth, about to devour everything before him. But, in 1803, he replaced this alarming spectacle with that of 'little Boney', a figure who reappeared time and time again in the years leading up to 1815. Little Boney was a Lilliputtian creature, with a hatchet face, with a chin that was pointed like a clog and with lank hair. He usually wore a huge plumed hat, which almost obliterated him; he was dressed in a long cloak, fitted with large boots and armed with a great sword, the whole of his tiny body being all but obscured by this outsized apparel. Napoleon was also always represented striking ridiculous attitudes, skipping, gambolling, and making uncontrolled gestures. This tendency systematically to denigrate Napoleon, to see him as nothing but a small man with trivial concerns, expresses, albeit with the exaggeration habitual in caricature, a deep-lying tendency in English culture. Indeed, English contemporaries, with only few exceptions, had never recognised any genius, any military or political talent, or even courage in Napoleon; for them, he was simply a coward, who had abandoned his troops in Egypt and who trembled desperately before the huge carcass of the big-bellied John Bull, to whom he was often opposed. This was clearly a residue of the current idea that the French were an inferior and grotesque race and an Englishman was worth at least two Frenchmen.

British statesmen tended to share many of these sentiments and therefore did not take Napoleon very seriously. An English minister made, in fact, a very revealing remark, in 1806, at a time when his government was considering whether to enter into negotiations with Dessalines, the leader of the black rebels of San Domingo; he declared himself to be in favour, observing that one could reasonably negotiate with '*un Empereur très noir*' since one had already done so with '*un Empereur très corse*'. It is easy to sense, in the attitudes of the English oligarchy towards Napoleon, a pride and an aristocratic arrogance with respect to a lowly born parvenu, who was also a former 'Jacobin'. This is a reason why English governments refused to recognise Napoleon as Emperor; in official documents and speeches, he was invariably Buonaparte or the Ruler of France and, in 1815, the man to be deported to Saint Helena was described as 'General Bonaparte'.[5] English statesmen did not admit that their enemy had military or political talents either. When the coalitions were defeated, this was always attributed to the errors of England's allies, to their disagreements, to their lack of effort or to their cowardice. Admittedly, Napoleon was no more of a good loser; on Saint Helena, he produced a long list of the 'grave mistakes' which Wellington had committed during the Waterloo campaign: 'His troops were admirable, but his disposition of them was pitiful ... His glory is wholly of the negative kind ... Fortune did more for him than he had done for her ...'.

[5] At the time of the 'return of the ashes', the latter, as they were taken from Saint Helena, were only granted, upon express instructions of the Admiralty, the number of cannon shots in the salute, delivered by HMS Dolphin, appropriate to the rank of general.

English statesmen therefore never lost their sang-froid when dealing with Napoleon, not even when his army was massed at Boulogne, not even in 1807, after Tilsit, when England was completely isolated, with the whole of continental Europe arrayed in coalition against her. They never despaired, for they felt able to count upon the superiority of their navy, which would halt any invasion, blockade France and smother it economically; they were convinced, moreover, that the domination of Europe by a Jacobin usurper was so monstrous and so contrary to the order of things that it could not endure; some also entertained the religious conviction that God was on the side of the English. Besides, the defeats of the coalitions were defeats for their allies rather than for England, which suffered almost no losses; except for short periods, her economy was not too hard hit by the Continental Blockade, and it remained prosperous; she went on reinforcing her maritime and colonial hegemony, by destroying or capturing the navies of the continental countries and by seizing their colonies. Hence the commonly held idea that the war was actually to England's advantage, since she had won much and lost nothing.

All of these factors help to explain why it was that the English had such unswerving confidence that they would be victorious at the last, and why they refused any compromise peace with the usurper or, more precisely, why they refused to recognise a 'greater France' that was capable of dominating Europe. This is actually the heart of the matter. Only when the second coalition had been defeated (a defeat which was all the more painful given that for a brief moment the allies had thought that they would prevail), and England, as a consequence, was isolated, only when the economic crisis of 1800–1 had struck, and only when public opinion had grown weary, did Addington's government resign itself to signing the peace of Amiens, which entailed the recognition of France's natural frontiers, including its possession of Belgium. But this step had been taken with a heavy heart and the English had let it be understood that French expansion should not be allowed to go any further. Once the First consul had overstepped this mark, England broke the truce, and she did not wish later to renew an experience which she judged to have been disastrous.

London was convinced that peace would allow France to consolidate her domination over the Continent and to extend it by means of further encroachments, and that she would also rebuild her navy and thereby threaten England again in the future, with altogether better prospects of success. The English therefore opted for war, on the grounds that, even if it did not offer any real hope of victory, it did at least enable them to inflict losses on the French navy, to disrupt her ship building programme by cutting off timber supplies from the Baltic, to ruin the foreign trade of France, to seize her colonies, and those of her allies, one by one. A 'perpetual war' thus seemed preferable to a Carthaginian peace. In one letter to Bernadotte, written in 1811, Napoleon shows that he understood the English position. England, he observed, 'does not want peace; she has rejected all my overtures; war swells her trade and her territory; she fears having to hand back [some of the colonies she had seized]; she does not want the new system confirmed by means of a treaty; she does not want France to be powerful.'

If there was an inexpiable conflict between Napoleon and England, it was only in the sense that English statesmen did not want to allow France to extend her domination of Europe beyond the limits that they had reluctantly accepted in 1802 (in fact, they would have preferred to enclose their neighbour within the frontiers of 1792, as they eventually managed to do in 1814), and because Napoleon had never accepted that his ambition should be thus contained. The Franco-English conflict represented a clash between two wills to power and to hegemony.

8 ❧ Wars, blockade, and economic change in Europe, 1792–1815*

The wars which raged almost continuously from 1792 to 1815 and which are generally, but not quite properly, called in English the Napoleonic wars, are the longest period of warfare which Europe has known since the early eighteenth century, and as they took place at a crucial stage of economic development, when the Industrial Revolution had just taken off in England and when its preliminary stirrings were showing in various places of the Continent, their impact upon the growth of industry in Continental Europe was quite serious. Unlike the twentieth-century world wars, the Napoleonic wars were not marked by large-scale physical destruction; though the productive potential of some towns or districts suffered from military operations or civil disturbances, such destruction was quite limited in space and time. On the other hand, most European countries suffered during the wars from bouts of paper-money inflation, which had undoubtedly serious consequences – especially in France during the Revolution, when the working capital of many merchants and manufacturers was destroyed through the combination of a sharp rise in their costs, of price control under the *maximum*, and of payment of government orders in depreciated *assignats*. Also, the diversion of resources to military purposes and the heavy burden of taxation and exactions must not be underestimated.

However, the impact of the wars upon the long-run development of industry, which this chapter will try to investigate, was felt mostly through the dislocations in international trade which were brought about by the twenty-year-long conflict between Britain and France and by the progressive involvement of all other European countries in this bitter struggle in which economic warfare played a prominent part. Those trade dislocations were at work during the whole war

* Reprinted from *The Journal of Economic History*, XXIV, 4, December 1964, pp. 567–88.

period and not only during the Continental Blockade – which was, of course, the most dramatic episode of the wars from the economic point of view, but which was also only their high-water mark; in fact most of the developments which are often thought of as characteristic of the blockade years (1806–13) had started much earlier, so that a longer view is needed to set the problem in its proper perspective.

Three main factors worked during the Napoleonic wars towards disturbing traditional trade relations: maritime blockade by the British, 'self-blockade' of the Continent imposed by the French, and lastly the large-scale redrafting of Europe's political map. Each of them had its own pattern of consequences for the Continent's industries.

I

First the British, thanks to their superior sea power, imposed upon the seaborne trade of Continental countries which were at war with them a number of restrictions which caused the decline and eventually the almost complete interruption of their seaborne trade; this led to serious difficulties and even to a complete and lasting collapse of the large sector of Continental industry which was dependent upon overseas trade.

The eighteenth century can be truly called the Atlantic stage of European economic development. Foreign trade, and especially trade with the Americas, was the most dynamic sector of the whole economy (for instance, French colonial trade increased tenfold between 1716 and 1787), and furthermore the demand from overseas markets was stimulating the growth of a wide range of industries as well as increased specialisation and division of labour. Owing to the superiority of sea transport over land transport, the eighteenth-century European economy was organised around a number of big seaports, the most prosperous being those with the largest share in the growing colonial trade, such as Bordeaux or Nantes; each of these had, not only its own industries, but also its industrial hinterland in the river basin of which it was the outlet. For instance, Bordeaux had shipbuilding yards, sugar refineries, distilleries, tobacco factories, and glassworks, while along the Garonne and its tributaries were to be found industries such as sail and rope making, foundries making guns for West Indiamen and boilers for sugar mills, manufactures of linens for slaves and woollens for planters, as well as cornmills producing fine flour for export to the West Indies. The seaboard provinces of France were undoubtedly the most industrialised in the eighteenth century, but the influence of the great seaports penetrated far into the interior; for instance, Pierre Léon has shown how much the industries of a landlocked province such as Dauphiné were also interested in the West India trade. And if this 'Americanisation' of trade and industry was the most pronounced for countries which owned a colonial empire (such as Britain, France, Holland, and Spain), its influence extended also farther to the east, to countries which had no colonies but were able to send goods to America as re-exports from the colonial powers, especially through Cadiz; so German linens, cutlery, and hardware reached the West Indian and Spanish-American markets. And the growing demand for colonial produce and for raw materials used for ship building stimulated seaborne trade and production for export along the whole European seaboard. So the eighteenth-century European economy was outward-looking, ocean oriented, and its most dynamic trading and industrial centres were geared to seaborne trade and American markets.

This 'Atlantic' sector was of course bound to suffer whenever relations with America were hampered. This had been experienced during the wars of the eighteenth century; but during the Napoleonic wars, the situation was much worse owing to the more complete mastery of the seas which was achieved by the Royal Navy and to the far longer duration of hostilities.

French colonial trade collapsed quite early in the war, owing mostly to the slave revolt in San Domingo which completely ruined 'the jewel of the Caribbean'; three-quarters of French colonial trade had been with San Domingo, and the sudden and complete destruction of such a valuable branch of trade dealt to several French ports and industries blows from which they did not recover. During the early years of the war, other maritime countries profited a good deal from the decline in French (and Dutch) trade and shipping, and ports such as Barcelona (up to 1796), Leghorn, Lisbon, Hamburg, Copenhagen, and later Trieste, enjoyed periods of great prosperity; but their trade booms all came to an abrupt end when these ports were occupied by the French or when their governments sided with France against England.[1] Still, up to 1807, most enemy ports were not put by the

[1] No significant industrial development resulted from such temporary trading booms; and if many merchants, in the Hanseatic towns or Trieste, for instance, made money through

British under rigorous blockade and they could go on trading under neutral flags; though direct relations between enemy ports and their colonies were forbidden by the British government, neutral ships (mostly American) were allowed to carry on an indirect trade by calling at some United States port on their way. So war with England did not cut at once all relations between Continental countries and the Americas or East Indies, but this trade did in fact decrease a good deal (especially exports of manufactured goods, because American ships often went to England for their return cargoes, and so Continental manufacturers lost ground in their own colonies).[2] Eventually such trade came to a complete stop when the British government decided to tighten its blockade.[3] In November 1807, Orders in Council prohibited in fact the indirect trade which neutral ships had been carrying between enemy countries and their colonies; an earlier order of January 1807 had forbidden neutrals to trade between enemy ports, thus destroying most of the active international coasting trade, especially between northern and southern Europe. Moreover, the last French and Dutch colonies were soon to be conquered by the British; and when, in 1808, the Spanish colonies sided with the Spanish insurgents against Napoleon, they fell into the economic orbit of England and their markets were lost to their traditional Continental suppliers of manufactured goods.

So in the later years of the Napoleonic wars, from 1807 onwards, Continental countries, nearly all of whom had by then sided willy-nilly against England, were subjected to a drastic sea blockade by the British; they were completely cut off from overseas markets and the most valuable part of their seaborne trade was destroyed. Some coasting trade was of course maintained, and the English permitted – even encouraged – relations with Britain herself; but though they were very active at some periods, they were no helpful substitute for Continental industries, because the Continent could export to England only foodstuffs and raw materials.[4]

smuggling activities or speculation, they used such capital after the wars for resuming their traditional trade and not for industrial investment.

[2] In Barcelona, indirect trade with the colonies through neutrals was in 1806 only a third of the direct trade in 1804. In Nantes, ships entering the port and clearing out had in 1806 a total tonnage of 54,000 as against 80,000 in the peace year of 1802. Moreover, trade through neutral ships did not prevent unemployment of national shipping and depression of shipbuilding.

[3] The reasons for this change of policy are mentioned in Chapter 9, pp. 330–3.

[4] The only exception was German linens, large quantities of which were imported into Britain (and re-exported) in 1809–10; American ships were also able to carry them from Tonningen or ports in the Baltic to Latin America.

It is well known that, as a consequence, the great seaports of the Continent, which had been the hubs of its economic life in the eighteenth century, were completely crippled from 1807 onwards. Harbours were deserted, grass was growing in the streets,[5] and in the large towns like Amsterdam, Bordeaux, and Marseilles, population did actually decrease. However, the collapse of industrial production in the ports and in their hinterland has not been as much noticed. It resulted from the loss of overseas markets and to a lesser degree from the difficulty in obtaining raw materials. In Marseilles, the value of industrial output fell from 50 million francs in 1789 to 12 in 1813.

Among the victims were, of course, shipbuilding and its ancillary industries, such as sail and rope making (Tonneins, east from Bordeaux, had 700 rope makers in 1783, 200 in 1801, none ten years later). Other industries to suffer were those processing imported colonial produce – especially sugar refining (Amsterdam had 80 refineries in 1796, 3 in 1813; Bordeaux 40 before the Revolution, 8 in 1809), also tobacco factories, and tanneries because of the shortage of hides which had been imported from South America. Also affected were industries which had been preparing foodstuffs for overseas markets or for provisioning ships, such as cornmills, distilleries, breweries (in Holland, and glassworks as a consequence), and those for salting, curing, drying, preserving of fish, vegetables, condiments (Marseilles had many such industries and their output fell very low). In Nantes and Hamburg, cotton printing was almost entirely wiped out. However, the most important casualty was the linen industry, which had been very widespread in several Continental countries in the eighteenth century, specially in western France, Flanders, Holland, and Germany. It was an export industry (in the 1780s, Bas-Maine had been exporting two-thirds of its output) with its main markets overseas, in the West Indies and in Spanish America, to which large quantities of French and German linens were re-exported through Cadiz. During the Revolution, French exports to those markets were almost completely stopped, and in Normandy, Brittany, and Maine, output collapsed, falling by as much as two-thirds in some districts; there was little recovery under the Empire, owing to the peninsular

[5] On 26 March 1808, the American consul at Bordeaux reported: 'From the Baltic to the Archipelago nothing but despair and misery is to be seen. Grass is growing in the streets of this city. Its beautiful port is deserted except by two Marblehead fishing schooners and three or four empty vessels which still swing to the tide' (quoted by F. E. Melvin, *Napoleon's Navigation System: A Study of Trade Control during the Continental Blockade* (New York, 1919), p. 48).

war; in 1810, Laval was making 18,000 pieces of linens, as against 36,000 in 1789. In Germany, the situation was not so bad, up to 1806–7, because exports to America went on and may have increased thanks to the fall in French competition; but after that date German linens also lost their overseas markets, and the linen-making districts of Westphalia, Saxony, and Silesia underwent a serious and lasting crisis; exports of linens from Landshut in the Riesengebirge fell from 174,000 *schock* in 1804 to 29,000 in 1811.

This decline of the linen industry (which can be observed also in Holland, Switzerland, and Italy) was of course in accordance with long-term trends in economic development: it was an archaic industry which was doomed anyway and which had already suffered in the eighteenth century from competition by the fast-rising cotton industry. Still there is no doubt that its decline and decay were greatly accelerated by the loss of overseas markets which it suffered during the Napoleonic wars, and the resulting crisis was so sharp that it made impossible for most centres of the industry any successful effort to adapt or to turn to other activities. In such a domestic manufacture, organised according to the putting-out system and with little fixed capital, the merchant-manufacturers were the key men; once they had lost their working capital, the industry was left in a hopeless condition.

The same remarks apply to the various industries which in the ports and in their hinterlands had been making consumption goods for overseas markets. They were of course small-scale industries, with generally an archaic technology, and at that stage they were not very susceptible to technical improvement and fast expansion. However their decline was unfortunate, as it did decrease opportunities for industrial employment and for accumulation of capital which could have been shifted later to higher productivity industries.

Moreover the 'Atlantic' sector of the European economy was not to recover when peace had been restored in 1815. There was of course a revival of traffic in the ports, but even where a fairly high level was attained, most of them had lost their position as international entrepôts and had become mere regional ports. As for their industries, they were relatively far less active. Such was the case, for instance, of Nantes, Bordeaux, Barcelona (P. Vilar writes that its career as a great colonial and international port was over), and Amsterdam, the 'general trade' of which did not revive. This was due to a number of reasons, including having lost touch with international trade during a period of rapid change and losing therefore the necessary skills, information, and capital; but including also the long-term decline in the importance of the West Indies in the world economy, the ruin of San Domingo, and the fact that the Latin American markets were henceforth, and for nearly a century, almost monopolised by the British, while the United States market had little demand for most of the Continent's traditional exports. These developments can also be considered as inevitable, owing to the technical advance and therefore lower prices of British industry and to superior British commercial organisation; in fact, before the war, British manufactures had been infiltrating the Spanish and even the French colonies, indicating that Continental industries had been dependent upon the maintenance of a high wall of protection under the old colonial system. Still, war conditions greatly helped the British to engross overseas markets and made it impossible for Continental industries to adapt fast enough to resist English competition and to regain a foothold in those markets after the peace.

Because of the permanent injury on many Continental industries by interruption of overseas trade, the war brought about a lasting deindustrialisation or pastoralisation of large areas (with, in some parts of France and Holland, a definite shift of capital from trade and industry towards agriculture). Seaboard districts failed generally to attract the new industries which developed during the wars, or when some new activities were attracted (like the wool industry in Denmark), they did not strike deep roots and declined after the peace – largely because those districts were outlying parts of a Continental empire at a time when land transportation was expensive. Such was the case of nearly the whole French seaboard, especially the western and southwestern provinces, and also Languedoc, on the Mediterranean, which had in the eighteenth century an important woollen industry working mostly for the Levant markets; in 1809, a German traveller commented that this industry was unable to modernise, owing to stagnating production, lost markets, and reduced profits. These provinces have been ever since, and still are, much less industrialised than northern and eastern France, and their relative underdevelopment has one of its major causes in the collapse of their traditional industries during the Napoleonic wars (of course, one has still to explain why they failed to industrialise again after 1815, but this is another story).

In France, this crisis was partly offset by the rise of new industries, but this did not happen in some other countries, such as Spain. There, industry had revived during the eighteenth century, especially in Catalonia, largely to answer the growing colonial demand; it was prosperous up to 1796, stagnated during the next twelve years, and collapsed in 1808; the loss of the colonial empire – and the devastation during the struggle against Napoleon – destroyed a vital part in the economic mechanism and worked towards a lasting pastoralisation of the country. In Portugal, there was some industrial progress up to 1806, mostly to supply the Brazilian market; but this was lost to the British in 1808, and in 1811, over one-third of industrial establishments were described as in a state of decay or closed. In Holland, the wars did not promote any significant industrial growth, while not only the 'port industries', but the manufacturing of woollens in Leyden, of silks and of earthenware in Delft was completely ruined. In Norway, war with England did bring about a sharp decline in its only industries – timber sawing and iron making – and the ruin of the business upper-middle class; and recovery after 1815 was hampered because England had turned to Canada for her timber supply, while Norway, annexed by Sweden, lost the Danish market for her iron.

The dislocation and eventual interruption of the Continent's seaborne trade, owing to maritime war and British blockade, brought about undoubtedly a collapse of the 'Atlantic sector' in the Continental economy, which had serious and lasting consequences.

II

There was, however, a second type of trade dislocation, the consequences of which were not so negative. This was the 'self-blockade' by Continental countries against British trade and especially their attempts at preventing imports of British manufactured goods. This was of course the purpose of the Berlin Decree and the Continental Blockade, but in France and her satellites, this policy was no innovation and had been enforced since the war had started. The self-blockade was never perfectly effective, and, except for short periods, many British goods were smuggled into the Continent; still, serious obstacles were erected against the import of such goods, which were made more expensive to consumers. Although the self-blockade was intended first and foremost as a means to force England into surrender, it acted practically, and from the point of view we are interested in, as a system of extreme protection, and its effect was to foster the growth of the industries which were the most seriously threatened by British competition.

The most important example in this respect is the cotton industry, and especially the spectacular rise of machine spinning upon a large scale. The cotton industry had grown quite fast during the eighteenth century in several parts of France, in Switzerland, and in Saxony and was well established there before the wars; but, though jennies had been introduced in France in the 1770s and in Germany in the 1780s and a handful of cotton mills had been established in France before 1793, hand spinning remained overwhelmingly predominant everywhere when the war started. From 1796 onward, however, machine spinning increased a great deal in France, and at the turn of the century cotton mills, using water frames or mules, and some of them driven by waterpower, were established in several other countries. Their simultaneous rise is very striking, as the first mills were built in Bohemia in 1797, in Switzerland (St Gall) in 1800, in Saxony (Chemnitz), Austria, Belgium (Ghent), and Holland in 1801, in Alsace in 1802. This was an answer to English competition, which during the 1790s had met with few obstructions except in France, and which was threatening with extinction the hand-spinning industries of countries like Saxony and Switzerland; but shortage of labour and difficulties in getting British yarns during the war of the second coalition may have had also some influence. However, during the first years of the nineteenth century, machine spinning spread relatively slowly (in each centre of the industry only a handful of mills was built), not only because of teething troubles in the use of the new machinery, but also because British competition was unabated and even stronger owing to a continuous fall in the price of English yarn.

In February 1806, imports of yarn were prohibited or surtaxed in France, and soon the Continental Blockade made such imports much more difficult and expensive for most countries than formerly – though they were never completely stopped, especially in Switzerland. Moreover, the simultaneous prohibition of British and of Indian cotton goods greatly increased the demand for locally produced yarns, and in Alsace, for instance, cotton printers were induced to start spinning mills and weaving sheds. There is a definite connection between these prohibitions and the boom in machine spinning which started in 1806 and developed up to 1810, with only one interruption in 1808.

Though in France, owing to an already high protection, progress had been rather fast during the preceding years, there was a sharp upward swing, and many new, relatively large mills were established.

The output of machine-spun yarn seems to have doubled from 1806 to 1808 and doubled again at least in the next two years. Lille, Roubaix, and Tourcoing had 32,000 spindles in 1806, 114,000 in 1808, and 177,000 in 1810; towns like Ghent and Mulhouse, where cotton spinning had been almost unknown before 1800, show a fast increase of the same order. However, the 1806 turning point was still more pronounced in Saxony, which before that date had been exposed to British competition and which enjoyed suddenly an unhoped-for prosperity; the number of mule spindles increased from 13,000 in 1806 to 256,000 in 1813. A fast growth took place also in lower Austria and in Switzerland, where the building of new mills went on during the unprosperous years after 1810, owing to increased difficulties in getting English yarn. And on the left bank of the Rhine, where machine spinning had been quite unknown before 1806, it made dramatic progress in the Gladbach-Rheydt district. At the end of the Empire, Continental Europe had built up, within a dozen years, a spinning industry which had, in very rough figures, over one million and a half spindles, of which one million were in France, over 250,000 in Saxony, and 150,000 in Switzerland (in 1811, however, Britain had 4,900,000 spindles). This fast growth was undoubtedly a direct consequence of the Continental Blockade, which of course did not create the industry but guaranteed its expansion. It brought about a concomitant decline in hand spinning, which by 1815 had almost entirely disappeared except in some isolated places. And it was accompanied by a good deal of technical progress, and especially by the substitution of the mule for the jenny and the water frame, which allowed the spinning of much finer counts of yarn. The mule was almost unknown in 1800 but became dominant after 1806, its triumph being helped by the crises of 1808 and 1811, which also increased concentration by wiping out the smaller firms and encouraging the creation of large, integrated concerns.

Technical progress took place also in other branches of the cotton industry: the flying shuttle was introduced in Switzerland in 1801, in Ghent shortly after, and in Mulhouse in 1805; cylinder printing started in Paris in 1797 and spread to Alsace and Switzerland around 1805, but was not taken up in Saxony. However, spinning was the only branch to undergo a complete technical revolution, and in others the innovations (including the Berthollet process for bleaching) did not come into general use. As a matter of fact, the sharp progress of machine spinning must not be taken as an index for the cotton industry as a whole.

In France, where the industry enjoyed a continuous protection against English competition, there was undoubtedly an important increase in cotton-goods output. The cotton industry was the only one which did not collapse during the Revolution and even managed to increase its output; though some centres were hurt, especially in printing, which had been working for overseas markets, some others developed fast during the Directory and the early 1800s, particularly Paris and Lille; around 1800, the French consumption of raw cotton was slightly larger than before 1789. Then the boom of the nineteenth century's first decade extended also to weaving and printing, especially in Ghent and around Lille and Mulhouse, and the raw-cotton consumption doubled at least within ten years; despite serious crises in 1808 and 1811, output remained generally at a high level at the end of the Empire.

In other countries, however, the story was rather different. In Saxony, English competition was increasingly dangerous between 1793 and 1806, hurting first the making of muslins, then the coarser goods. The industry was really saved by the Continental Blockade, but it seems that overall cotton-cloth production did not rise much during the next few years, an increase in calicoes for printing being offset by a fall in muslins. In Switzerland and Berg, the situation was more unfavourable, because the cotton industries of both countries were heavily dependent upon exports, which were made difficult by the protectionist policy of Napoleon which closed the French and Italian markets. Though the Swiss managed to switch their exports to Germany, the industries of both countries suffered, especially in Berg (which had boomed during the French Revolution) and in the cotton printing and muslin making of Switzerland. However, the situation would probably have been worse if these industries had been exposed to the full blast of English competition, and one may say that the Continental Blockade saved the Swiss as well as the Saxon cotton industry.

There is no doubt on the whole that the prohibition of British cotton yarns and goods which was instituted first in France and then in the countries which joined the Continental System gave to the Continental cotton industry a much needed protection, without which it would have been largely wiped out, as well as the opportunity of meeting the demand for cotton goods, which was expanding very fast owing to a shift in tastes and fashions (and to the fall of their prices).

On the other hand, one must stress that the balance sheet of the wars period was far from being entirely favourable to the cotton industry. First, the bitter and protracted struggle with England did certainly slow down the introduction of British machinery, production methods, and skilled workers (though it was in the thick of war that Lievin Bauwens smuggled out from England his first mules). Moreover, during the later part of the war period from 1808 onward, the cotton industry laboured under a serious difficulty – the shortage and high prices of its raw materials. This was due partly to the Continental Blockade but also to the American embargo and to a British Order in Council, of November 1807, which prohibited the carrying of raw cotton into enemy ports. However, except for a few months late in 1808, when many mills had to stand idle, there was never a real cotton famine and the shortage was alleviated by imports from the Levant overland and by cultivation in southern Italy, so that output could be increased again in 1810. Still, after 1807, manufacturers obtained their raw material at much higher prices than did their British competitors – at least twice and even four times higher; and the French were at a special disadvantage, because, owing to a more efficient customs system and to high duties upon raw cotton imposed in August 1810, prices were notably higher in France than in Germany, Austria, or Switzerland. This situation was one of the factors in the crisis which broke out in 1811 and hit the industry very hard, though output recovered the next year. There is no doubt that its expansion was hampered by these high prices of raw materials, and on the whole the cotton industry did not grow as fast on the Continent during the war period as in Britain. British consumption of raw cotton, which can be used as a rough index of output, did increase roughly fourfold between 1790 and 1810; we have no comparable figures for the Continent as a whole, but in France, which had the largest cotton industry, the consumption of raw cotton increased roughly threefold during the same period. Quantitatively, the Continent in fact lost ground to England, while in technology a twenty-year time lag persisted.

This fact has been stressed by various writers, such as Eli Heckscher, who have moreover pointed out that, when peace was restored in 1814 and 1815, the Continental cotton industries were hit very hard by British competition; in France, for instance, some of the largest manufacturers went bankrupt,[6] and prohibitions as severe as during the Continental Blockade had to be reimposed in order to save the industry. This has been seen as a proof of the Blockade's futility, since it did not succeed in making the industry competitive with England, and so the Continental cotton industry has been denounced as a typical 'hothouse' industry which developed under artificial conditions of wartime extreme protection and which constituted a serious misallocation of resources.

However this line of argument neglects two basic facts of the concrete economic situation in Europe during the late eighteenth and early nineteenth centuries. The first was that war was being waged and that England was using its mastery of the seas to dislocate the Continent's trade and to destroy some of its traditional industries. Though the Continental Blockade was intended as offensive economic warfare, it was also in fact a defensive reflex by the Continental economy, inasmuch as the war obliged it to labour under unfavourable conditions such as high prices of raw materials, a serious shortage of capital, and high rates of interest. It is most likely that if there had been no war, if relations with England had been maintained, if a moderate protection had been established, economic and technical progress on the Continent would have been faster. But after all, there was a war.

The second basic fact was the absolute ascendancy, the overwhelming superiority, which the British had achieved, so that no Continental industry, except silk, could be competitive with its English rivals – in fact, a full century was to elapse before foreigners were able to compete successfully with Lancashire mills, except for some special lines of goods such as fine printed cottons from Alsace. By 1800, Continental Europe was threatened by pastoralisation and the fate of India in the nineteenth century. In fact, countries like Spain, Portugal, and Sweden which fell into the economic orbit of England during the wars suffered

[6] In fact, the direct cause of this collapse was the sudden abolition in April 1814 of the high customs duties on cotton wool, which at a stroke depreciated manufacturers' stocks and brought sharply down yarn and cloth prices.

a crisis or a collapse of their traditional industries without any compensating rise of new ones; and countries where the cotton industry did not develop during the wars, like Italy or Spain, were to miss the first bus of nineteenth-century industrialisation. On the other hand, though the Continental Blockade did not reduce much the time lag in techniques between England and the Continent and though the development of the cotton industry (and of some others) under protection was a misallocation of resources, it was a necessary one and the only way to introduce the Industrial Revolution. As a matter of fact, the cotton industry was the strategic sector at that stage. It was the only one likely to expand fast, the best suited to machine production, and it required little capital; its development and technical improvement were the best way to introduce the new technology and to train workers and managers in the skills of machine production and the factory system; also they were the only possible basis for a machine-building industry. And truly its hothouse development during the Napoleonic wars did just that: it gave to the Continent its first experience of large-scale, integrated, mechanised industry; it created a new group of manufacturers with a progressive (and sometimes adventurous) outlook and a taste for technical advance and for expansion; moreover, jointly with technical change in the woollen industry, it gave birth to a machine-building industry in a few places, such as Paris, Liège, Verviers, Essen, Mulhouse, Zurich, and Chemnitz; it was of course much smaller than in England and not so advanced, but the quality of its mechanics and of its products improved and its rise was a necessary preliminary stage of industrialisation.

On the whole, the cotton industry and especially machine spinning had struck rather strong roots in Continental soil during the Napoleonic wars, and so the foundations for further industrialisation had been laid.[7] As a matter of fact, the beginnings of the Industrial Revolution on the Continent could be dated from the simultaneous establishment of machine spinning in various countries, around 1800, which has been pointed out earlier. As, moreover, it is not apparent to what other uses capital and labour resources could have been applied at this stage of

[7] During the postwar years, some centres of the cotton industry – especially in Germany and Austria – suffered serious difficulties under the impact of renewed British competition, but most of them managed to survive; in Bonn, however, by 1820, only one of the 12 mills which had been established under French rule, was still working.

economic development,[8] I can not think that the growth of the cotton industry was unfortunate from the point of view of economic growth. However, the 'bad thing' was that it created vested interests which during the postwar crisis clamoured for renewed protection and generally got it (especially in France), while in fact the industry could likely have developed more efficiently, with only a moderate amount of protection.

As for the Continent's wool industries, the 'self-blockade' had upon them an impact which was of the same kind as upon its cotton industry but not as powerful – because they were less in need of protection, because the Continent did not usually buy large quantities of English woollen goods, and because the possibilities of expansion were more limited. In France, the wool industry suffered badly during the Revolutionary period, as it was cut off by the war from its traditional markets in Germany, Spain, and the Levant; in 1795, production had fallen by two-thirds as compared with 1789. But a general revival followed, and during the Napoleonic period the prerevolution level of output was exceeded, though some old centres of manufacture went on decaying. However, the most interesting development took place in territories which had been annexed to France and which benefited both from strong protection against the British and from the opening of the large French market, which they could take advantage of, thanks to significant technical progress. This was especially true in Verviers, which at the turn of the century underwent within a few years (from 1799 to 1804) a true Industrial Revolution; the result was a sudden acceleration of growth, with output increasing at a mean average yearly rate of 6 per cent from 1800 to 1810, and a large increase in fixed capital and productivity. The woollen industry of Aachen also expanded a good deal, the value of its output increasing from 5 million and a half francs in 1786 to 11 million in 1811. But in many of the old French centres of the industry, technical change took place also upon a large scale; machine carding, spinning, and finishing became quite common. Protection through the self-blockade was, moreover, responsible for the taking off of a small woollen industry in Switzerland and in

[8] Improvement of agricultural techniques would have resulted in releasing labour which only industry could employ; moreover, home demand for foodstuffs was inelastic, export markets unstable, and the British market, which had a regular import demand, was largely closed right at the end of the wars by the new Corn Laws. Attempts at renovating archaic manufactures, especially the linen industry, would have led into a blind alley. Luxury industries, like silk, were not likely to expand fast and were unsuited to machine production.

the Dutch district of Tilburg and for expansion of the Moravian wool manufactures. Elsewhere, there was little change.

However, two important industries were not much affected by the closing of the Continent to British competition. The first was the silk industry: far from needing any protection against the British, this was much larger and more efficient.[9] The other was the iron industry: most centres of production stagnated during most of the war period, the Liège and Düren districts being exceptions, and the overall increase in output of pig-iron and iron seems to have been relatively small. As for technical progress, it was very limited – in France to the introduction of rolling mills. In various ironmaking districts (for instance in Berg during the blockade years), experiments were attempted to introduce the new English techniques of coke smelting, puddling, and crucible steelmaking, but nearly all of them failed and were given up. This stagnation may appear puzzling but can be easily explained: British exports of iron products to the Continent had been relatively small before the wars, and their interruption did not create a large vacuum to be filled up by local industries, while several centres of the iron industry (such as Berg) suffered from losing their overseas markets. As for the military demand for iron products, one must be careful not to overestimate it (naval guns were made of cast iron, but field guns of brass); it certainly helped to keep many ironworks active, but as it guaranteed to ironmasters a stable market for their output it acted, in fact, as a brake upon innovation.[10] On the other hand, prohibition of English goods seems to have stimulated steelmaking and the secondary metal industries, such as the making of hardware, cutlery, tools, buttons, harness pieces, and tinplate articles, but their expansion was not sharp enough to take the primary iron industry out of the doldrums

[9] However, different trade dislocations made their impact felt. During the Revolutionary period, the French silk industry underwent a serious crisis owing to a falling demand for luxury goods on the home market and to its being cut off from foreign markets; in 1801, its output was still about half that of 1789. At the same time, the silk manufacturers in Switzerland, Germany, and Austria were quite prosperous, owing to the elimination of French competition. However, the French silk industry recovered under the Empire and launched an export drive, which Napoleon tried to help as much as possible. This had unpleasant consequences in Switzerland and Germany, where the makers of ribbons in Basel and Barmen and of silks in Berlin were the main sufferers (but some centres of the industry remained prosperous). In Italy, there was little expansion of output.

[10] The recent book by D. Woronoff, *L'Industrie sidérurgique en France pendant la Révolution et l'Empire* (Paris, 1985), confirms that war, while protecting the French iron industry, was a factor of conservatism and not of innovation in technology; none the less, there were many minor improvements, which resulted in some overall progress. French output of iron fell during the 1790s, then recovered; after 1801, it was higher than in 1789, but less profitable.

which discouraged technical progress and investment – though the disappearance of many small firms was a forerunner of the post-1815 development.

A complete balance sheet of wartime dislocations would include also a study of the chemical industries, in which the shortage of traditional imported raw materials such as barilla and potashes resulted in drastic technical change and especially in the introduction of the Leblanc process for soda making. Though these new industries expanded fast, they were still relatively small at the end of the war period; but their rise was significant for future growth, just as was that of the machine-building industry. On the other hand, the making of ersatz for colonial produce had no importance in the long run; as an example, the beet-sugar industry was wiped out after 1814, not to revive in Europe before the 1830s.

III

To the trade dislocations wrought by the maritime and continental blockades must be added those which resulted from the large-scale redrafting of the political map of Europe during the wars, from the annexation to France of large areas, and from the drastic territorial changes which took place in Germany and Italy. These upheavals brought about frequent and important changes in the customs lines which crisscrossed the Continent and therefore, from the point of view of manufacturers, the closing of traditional markets and the opening of new ones.

The most important developments in this respect resulted from the annexation to France of Belgium and the left bank of the Rhine. Succeeding a period during which these districts had been battlefields and had suffered from French exactions, this had at first unfavourable consequences by interrupting traditional trade relations; but quite soon – roughly after 1800 – the industries of Belgium and the Roer department expanded very fast and enjoyed a remarkable prosperity under the Imperial régime. They shifted their sales from their former markets, mostly in Central Europe, toward the French market on which they concentrated. This integration with a huge protected and unified area of 30 million customers was the decisive influence which was responsible first and foremost for the fast expansion of the woollen industries of Verviers, Aachen, and Jülich, of the silk industry of

Crefeld, of the metal industries of Liège and Düren, and for the rise of the cotton industry in Ghent and Gladbach. Its impact was especially strong on the left bank of the Rhine, where, from 1806 onwards, the exclusion from France of Berg manufactured goods brought about a massive immigration of manufacturers and workers from Berg. Industry struck strong roots in this district, which had been overwhelmingly agricultural in the eighteenth century; by 1811, the Roer department had 2,500 industrial establishments with 65,000 workers, and, according to H. Kisch, 'French domination proved, in its long run effect, a true blessing.' The annexation of Mulhouse in 1798 and the integration of Alsace to the French customs area (outside of which it had remained under the Old Régime) had similar effects for this province, which benefited from an immigration of Swiss capital and labour. This expansion of Belgian and Rhineland industries was helped by comparative advantages they enjoyed over those of *l'ancienne France:* they had suffered less from the economic blizzard which struck French industry during the Revolution; their labour costs were cheaper owing to the existence of a destitute urban proletariat; and the woollen manufacturers had the luck that William Cockerill settled in Belgium and supplied them with excellent machinery, which allowed Verviers to achieve a precocious, fast, and perfect Industrial Revolution, without much trial and error.

However, territorial changes had for other industrial centres far less happy consequences, because they were cut off from their traditional markets without enjoying the compensation which Belgium and the left bank of the Rhine found in France. This was aggravated by Napoleon's protectionist policy which closed the markets of France and Italy, not only to the British but to his own vassals and allies, while trying to persuade them to admit French goods. The continuous annexations to France of new territories which were at once closed to their neighbours made things steadily worse. Moreover, many states, especially in Germany, raised their tariff walls, mostly for fiscal reasons. So Napoleonic Europe was far from being a 'common market' and was, in fact, bristling with obstacles to trade.[11]

The result was a general dislocation of trade relations and serious difficulties for countries which were exporting manufactured goods upon a large scale. The two main sufferers were Switzerland and Berg,

[11] New views on this problem in R. Dufraisse, 'L'Intégration "hégémoniale" de l'Europe sous Napoleon Ier', *Revue de l'Institut Napoléon*, CXLII, 1984, pp. 11–42.

which were both heavily dependent upon the French and Italian markets and which were badly hurt by the ultraprotectionist French tariff of 1806 and, a few months later, by their exclusion from the Kingdom of Italy. Berg exports fell one-third from 1807 to 1810. However, the difficulties which the two countries suffered during the Continental Blockade have been exaggerated; the growth of their industry was slowed down or stopped, they suffered from stagnation (especially the Swiss cotton, watchmaking, and jewelry industries and the ribbon making of Barmen), but no irreparable damage was done, there was no general deindustrialisation, except the disappearance of some Swiss centres of cotton printing. And one must not forget that Berg industries had grown fast up to 1806. As for Italy, which Napoleon made a *chasse gardée*, a preserve, an economic colony of France, surrounded by impassable custom walls except on the side of France, its industry survived nonetheless.[12]

On the other hand, recurrent and sudden changes in political frontiers and in customs regulations, as well as the violent and brutal methods which Napoleon used to enforce the blockade, did frighten and discourage businessmen, destroy security and confidence, and were baneful to entrepreneurship.

On the whole, there is no doubt that the manifold and serious dislocations which international trade suffered during the Napoleonic wars had an unfavourable and retardative effect upon the growth of Continental industry. In addition to causing the permanent decline of the 'maritime' and of the linen industries, they slowed down the progress of many industries as a result of serious and protracted crises, either during the French Revolution or in the later years of the Empire. During the 1790s, French industrial output collapsed and, though it recovered from 1796 onward, by 1800 it was at best 60 per cent of its pre-1789 level. The causes of this disaster were many, but the interruption of French foreign trade (not only through the British sea blockade, but also owing to the closing of Continental markets in enemy countries) was one of the most decisive. However, part of the damage was not irreparable; for instance, the wool and silk industries revived sharply under Napoleon, though some old wool centres had been mortally wounded. From 1802 to 1810, there was a powerful

[12] Grossly overdone are the lamentations and diatribes of B. de Cérenville against Napoleon (whom he charges with having deliberately tried to destroy Swiss industry). See Cérenville, *Le Système continental et la Suisse, 1803–1813* (Lausanne, 1906), pp. 17, 51, 117, 132, 141, 148 ff., 170, 173 ff., 180, 210–20, 279–81, 321.

outburst of industrialisation, but its first effect was only to make good earlier losses, and around 1810, the aggregate volume of industrial production was not much higher than in the 1780s (an increase of 50 per cent is the most optimistic hypothesis).[13] As for other Continental countries, they had benefited from the French collapse during the 1790s, but (except for cotton spinning and for the industries of Belgium and the left bank of the Rhine) there is little evidence of fast growth at the time of the Continental Blockade, and some important industries did certainly stagnate. Moreover, in 1810–11, a sharp crisis, aggravated by various dislocations connected with the Continental Blockade (overspeculation on colonial produce, enforcement of the Trianon decree), broke the momentum of the Napoleonic industrialisation. The last years of the Empire were of stagnation, and many business firms disappeared in the final collapse of 1813–14.

The balance sheet of the Napoleonic wars for the Continent as a whole might therefore be something like this: collapse of the 'maritime' industries, decay of the linen industry, stagnation of the primary iron industry, modest growth of the wool, silk, and secondary metal industries, relatively fast progress of the cotton industry, and a modest increase in overall industrial output. This was certainly smaller than the rise which had taken place meanwhile in Britain – though recent research has come to the conclusion that the Napoleonic wars had a retardative effect upon British industrial growth and investment in industry. So on the whole the impact of the wars was more unfavourable to the Continent than to England and made more serious its time lag. However, the rise of the cotton-spinning, machine-building, and chemical industries had laid foundations for future development, which was also to be fostered by the reforms which French dominion had introduced into many parts of the Continent, such as freedom of enterprise and abolition of the manorial system and the guilds.

Moreover, some other important developments had taken place within the Continental economy. One was the shift, which was to be permanent, in the location of Continental industries. Many industries located in seaboard districts had declined or collapsed, and moreover

[13] This is a very rough guess. The *Statistique de la France publiée par le ministère de l'agriculture et du commerce. Industrie,* I (Paris, 1847), xv–xvii, gives the value of industrial production for 1812 (and for *l'ancienne France*) as double the 1788 figure; but this seems over optimistic. On the other hand, according to W. Hoffmann's index (and to more recent computations as well), the volume of British industrial production did less than double between 1792 and 1815; W. G. Hoffmann, *British Industry, 1700–1950* (Oxford, 1955), Table 54.

such districts, with a few exceptions (mostly between the Seine and the Scheldt), did not benefit from the rise of new industries; even in Holland, industries developed inland, in Tilburg and Enschede. On the other hand, industrial centres which expanded or maintained their levels of output were as a rule inland, within a large area which extended between the Seine and the Elbe rivers; and some of the most important developments (as well as much accumulation of capital, largely through smuggling activities) took place in the ex-*Lotharingia*, with the fast growth of industries in the *Nord* department of France, in Ghent, Verviers, Liège, around Aachen, and in Alsace. This shows how unfortunate it was for France to be deprived of her 'natural frontiers' in 1814. The axis of the Continental economy had now moved from the Atlantic toward the Rhine,[14] and this was of course a forerunner of the growing concentration of European industry in northern and eastern France, Belgium, and northwestern Germany, which was to be so characteristic of the nineteenth and of the early twentieth centuries. There were also some interesting developments along an axis situated farther to the east, in Saxony, Bohemia, Austria, and even Hungary.[15]

This shift of industry from the seaboard to the heartland of western Europe was moreover the sign of another significant change. In the eighteenth century, the European economy had been outward looking and geared to overseas markets; all important industries had been heavily dependent upon the export trade.[16] However, during the Napoleonic wars, and especially at the time of the Continental Blockade, export industries had suffered the most and one could well say that the prosperity of each industrial centre had been inversely proportional to its dependence upon international trade – as is well shown by the story of the linen-making areas, of Lyons, of Switzerland, and of Berg. Moreover, the British had engrossed overseas markets. So the Napoleonic wars made most European industries inward looking and geared first and foremost to national markets (a typical case was Catalonia which, after the collapse of her colonial trade, turned

[14] This was helped by the accumulation of capital, through smuggling, in the hands of merchants in Basel, Strasbourg, Frankfurt, and Essen, and its subsequent use for investment in industrial ventures.

[15] Industrial growth in these countries was stimulated by the shift toward the east of trade routes across Europe at the time of the Blockade and by lower prices of raw materials.

[16] Because of obstacles to internal trade, high costs of land transport, and low incomes per capita, production upon a large scale could not be based on national or regional demand and had to rely upon export markets.

entirely toward the Spanish home market). This had been encouraged by the formation of larger economic units through the abolition of internal customs barriers. This development had run its full course in France, where the Revolution had created a national market which was relatively quite large, so that manufacturers to whom war and postwar conditions had made access to foreign markets difficult were encouraged to limit their ambitions within their own borders. In Central Europe, the situation was different because *Kleinstaaterei* maintained many customs barriers; still, larger economic units had been created and there was a clear tendency of Berg and Saxony industrialists to increase their sales on the German markets, especially in the eastern parts of Germany. Later on, the creation of large national markets through the Zollverein and Italian unity was of course to strengthen this trend. With a few exceptions (like Switzerland or Alsace) and up to the worldwide economic expansion of Germany in the late nineteenth century, Continental industries were to work mostly for their own national markets and for those of the neighbouring countries. This was in sharp contrast with England and her worldwide trading interests – but after all the inward-looking character of the Continental economy was a consequence of the decisive defeat which it had suffered in its struggle against British ascendancy. So the trade dislocations of the Napoleonic wars were responsible for some of the specific characters of Continental industry and for some of its differences with British industry – differences which they aggravated and which have persisted up to our own day.

Post scriptum

This essay is old, but it has not aged too badly. Its main suggestions have been found reasonable and have been taken up in most writings about the subject. I may, however, have somewhat overestimated the role of seaborne trade (and especially colonial trade) in the eighteenth century European economy, and so the impact of its decline during – and after – the wars.[17] The fact that in the 1780s French colonial trade had problems, which could have been harbingers of a serious crisis, might also have been mentioned. On the other hand, I think I have

[17] See R. Roehl, 'French Industrialisation: A Reconsideration', *Explorations in Economic History*, XIII, 3, July 1976, p. 244.

done justice to the 'positive' aspects of the Napoleonic era and specially to the industrialisation which took place.

It is not possible to mention new works which have been published since 1964. For France, the most important contribution has come from Louis Bergeron.[18] In English the work of Geoffrey Ellis, J. M. Diefendorf and the late Herbert Kisch must be mentioned.[19]

[18] Especially his *Banquiers, négociants et manufacturiers parisiens du Directoire à l'Empire* (Paris, 1978), but also several articles.

[19] G. Ellis, *Napoleon's Continental Blockade; The Case of Alsace* (Oxford, 1981); J. M. Diefendorf, *Businessmen and Politics in the Rhineland, 1789–1834* (Princeton, 1980); Herbert Kisch, *From Domestic Manufacture to Industrial Revolution. The Case of the Rhineland Textile Districts* (Oxford, 1989). Mention must also be made of articles by Martin Kutz on the foreign trade of 'Germany' and of 'Europe', which are valuable, particularly because of their attempts at quantification; see his 'Aussenhandel und Krieg 1789–1817', in W. Fischer, R. M. McInnis and J. Schneider (eds.), *The Emergence of a World Economy 1500–1914* (Wiesbaden, 1986), I, pp. 199–277. Kutz concludes that, despite erratic swings at the regional level, the volume of intra-European trade did not decrease because of the wars; their overall result, however, was to the detriment of French foreign trade and to the advantage of Britain.

9 ❧ Variations on the North Atlantic Triangle from Yorktown to Waterloo*

I

The role played by the United States in the economic history of the 'Napoleonic wars' period is easily underestimated. Of course, they stood apart from the two main contenders, Britain and France, and not only in the geographical sense. They were a 'small country', with under four million people in 1790, over seven in 1810, as against twenty seven and thirty respectively at the same dates for France,[1] and over fifteen for the United Kingdom in 1801. They were also a 'new country', of recent settlement, with economic structures less complex and sophisticated than in Western Europe. Thirdly, they kept out of the European wars up to June 1812, and Mr Madison's war lasted just thirty months; though they had been previously involved in the (not too serious) quasi-war with France of 1798–1800, and though their diplomatic relations with France and still more with Britain were under severe strain from 1807 onwards (with serious consequences for American trade), their experience was entirely different from that of France and Britain, which were in a state of war for over twenty years, with only the fourteen months long break of the Peace of Amiens (not to mention the civil strife in France during the 1790s). However, this very neutrality, which was something new for Americans who, either as 'colonials' or as 'rebels', had been belligerents in previous Anglo-French wars, and which was preserved longer than for any European neutral (such as Denmark), gave to the United States a unique

* This chapter was first published as: 'Variations on the North American Triangle from Yorktown to Waterloo: Substitution, Complementarity, Parallelism', in *Economics in the Long View. Essays in Honour of W. W. Rostow*, edited by Charles P. Kindleberger and Guido di Tella, volume 2, *Applications and Cases, Part I* (London, 1982), pp. 44–66.

[1] The 1810 figure does not include the population of the territories which were then annexed to France.

position; combined with their resources endowment, their geographical position, the enterprise of their merchants and shipowners, it made them play a crucial part in international trading between 1793 and 1812.

This chapter will explore some aspects of the triangular relationship between the United States, Britain and France[2] – a connection which might have turned into a three-cornered fight, if some American politicians, who wanted to declare war against *both* Britain and France, for having violated American rights, had had their way.

The first point is a substitution phenomenon. As a consequence of the European war, the United States found themselves suddenly having to substitute for France (and other countries) as a sea-trading power; they also infiltrated some trades which had been hitherto British preserves.

On the eve of the French Revolution, France had a large and prosperous (with, however, some concealed weaknesses) foreign trade, the value of which equalled that of Britain. She had also a large merchant navy: over 5,000 ocean-going ships of 729,000 tons burden (1785), second only to the British merchant fleet, with its 12,000 ships of 1,300,000 tons (1789).

However, the grand design, which had existed, of taking advantage of American independence for snatching from the British the valuable United States market, had failed utterly.[3] French exporters were unable to compete with the British in supplying textiles and iron goods for current consumption, while American importers and consumers reverted quickly to British manufactures to which they had been accustomed before the Revolution. French merchants were also unable to grant long-term credit on the same scale as the British. Moreover, many French firms which had been involved in trade with America during the war, had badly burnt their fingers, and first class houses kept to their traditional West Indian or East Indian connections. Anyway new trading and credit networks take some time to be woven,

[2] With some stress on the Franco-American side.

[3] Recent contributions to this question include: E. C. Papenfuse, 'An Uncertain Connection: Maryland's Trade with France during the American Revolution, 1778–1783', in *La Révolution américaine et l'Europe* (Paris, 1979), pp. 243–64; J. Meyer, 'Les Difficultés du commerce franco-américain vues de Nantes (1776–1790)', *French Historical Studies*, XI, 2, Autumn 1979, pp. 159–83; C. Fohlen, 'The Commercial Failure of France in America', in N. L. Roelker and C. K. Warner (eds.), *Two Hundred Years of Franco-American Relations. Papers of the Bicentennial Colloquium of the Society for French Historical Studies in Newport, Rhode Island, September 7–10, 1978*, s.l.n.d. (1984), pp. 93–119.

while it proved easy for British merchants to resume contacts with their former correspondents in the 'colonies'. The depression and instability which were rampant in the Confederation must also be taken into account. Frenchmen had hoped, Britons had feared that British trade with the thirteen colonies would be ruined by their independence; it was not and indeed it revived quickly, while Franco-American trade languished.

In any event, once war with England had started in 1793, French shipping and trade were left completely unprotected. During the eighteenth century, the French Navy had been inferior to the Royal Navy, both in numbers (of ships and – this was probably more serious – of able seamen) and in fighting capacity: crews, officers and admirals, training, tactics and strategy, were not up to English standards. Even under the favourable circumstances of the American War of Independence, the much-vaunted navy of Louis XVI just managed to hold its own. During the French Revolution, the navy was soon completely disorganised, owing to a breakdown in discipline and the emigration or dismissal of many officers. While the revolutionary government built up a new army which became a formidable force, they never managed to restore the navy to a satisfactory condition. A number of encounters with the British ended up in serious losses which further weakened the French and it was a much depleted fleet which Napoleon inherited – to send it to be uselessly butchered at Trafalgar. Later on, however, he made a serious effort to restore his navy and had a large number of new ships built, but he kept them safely in the ports, waiting for the moment when superiority in number over the British would have been achieved; this moment never came before his fall...

The French Navy was not able thus to organise and escort, as in earlier eighteenth-century wars, convoys of merchant ships, in order to maintain long-distance trade relations, especially with the French colonies. Such convoys were used only once, in 1794, in special circumstances, to save France from famine, by importing large quantities of grain from the United States.[4] The risks of capture for merchant ships flying the French flag were therefore very high, insurance premiums prohibitive. The French flag was wiped out from the high seas and the French merchant navy almost destroyed: around 1800, it

[4] This was the occasion for the battle of 'The Glorious First of June' in British parlance (*13 prairial an II* to the French). However, convoys of small coasters, creeping along the shore, were regularly organised.

had only 1,500 ocean-going ships left and in 1814 a few hundred – while the United Kingdom had over 21,000 ships of 2,400,000 tons burden.

What happened to the rest of French shipping is not quite clear. A good number were, of course, captured by the British, but they were mostly ships which were at sea at the beginning of the hostilities. For instance, in 1803, the shipowners of Bordeaux lost 63 of the 155 ships which they had at sea when war was resumed. But once it was known that war was on, few shipowners were foolish enough to send out ships under the French flag: indeed, the British did not have much to capture and this was one reason why they eventually turned against the neutrals. On the other hand, some French ships were sold to neutral owners, including American merchants; such sales could be either genuine or fictitious, in the latter case the ship remained French property under ostensibly neutral papers. This system of 'neutralisation' was widely used by the Dutch, once they were at war with England, and they transferred many of their ships under 'convenience flags' of tiny North German states, such as Kniphausen and Papenburg. Some fast ships were converted into privateers – privateering being a normal substitute for regular trade (Americans also resorted to it during the War of 1812);[5] and it is likely that many others just rotted away in port.

The picture is not as black for French foreign trade: its history, during the Napoleonic wars, appears as complex, with a number of sharp fluctuations, rather than some sudden collapse or continuous decline; there were depressions and revivals, attempts also at finding new orientations. None the less, even in its best years, the sea-borne trade of France was markedly smaller than before the war, and after 1807 – when Britain brutally tightened her sea blockade – it fell to a very low level, though it was not completely destroyed. However, it is now generally accepted that the 'maritime' or 'Atlantic' sector of the French economy, including industries which had backward or forward linkages with sea-borne trade, suffered during the Napoleonic wars serious and, in some respects, irretrievable losses.[6]

In sharp contrast with this decline stands the meteoric rise of American foreign trade and shipping, from 1793 onwards and up to

[5] But French privateering was less active under Napoleon than in the 1790s, because of increasing British command of the seas.

[6] This aspect is treated at greater length in chapter 8, pp. 297ff.

1807, when they were faced with serious problems. There is no need to quote more than a few figures; the value of total American exports had been $21 million in 1792; its record level of the period, in 1807, was $108 million, a five-fold increase within fifteen years, that is an average exponential rate of growth of 9·4 per cent per year (but, at constant prices, the advance would be less dramatic, by a factor of three).[7] As for American shipping, the tonnage of vessels engaged in foreign trade, which had already risen markedly from 1789 onwards, increased from 411,000 tons in 1792 to nearly one million (981,000) in 1809.[8] Within a few years, it had replaced the French as the second largest merchant fleet in the world. And the approximate share of the United States in world trade reached six per cent in 1800, while it had been two per cent twenty years earlier.[9]

A very large part of this spectacular progress was a direct consequence of the war between Britain and France, and of the destruction or inactivity of the ocean-going shipping of France and her allies. However some of this advance had nothing or very little to do with the war: especially the enormous increase in raw cotton exports. Its causes were Whitney's gin, the spread of cotton cultivation in the southern states, the fantastic growth of the cotton industry in Britain (plus a slower growth on the Continent). The value of cotton exports was next to nothing before 1793; it reached $14 million in 1807,[10] so that those exports were responsible for nearly one half the increase in *domestic* exports by the United States, which rose by $30 million between 1793 and 1807.

However, most of the expansion in other fields of American trade resulted from the wars and the new opportunities which they opened and which American merchants and shipowners were quick to grasp.[11]

[7] Imports rose more slowly, from $32 million to $139 million. All figures for US trade and shipping are from *Historical Statistics of the United States* (Washington, 1960).

[8] The percentage of US imports and exports, by value, which was carried on American ships, increased from 24 per cent in 1789 to 89 per cent in 1800; W. Woodruff, *America's Impact on the World. A Study of the United States in the World Economy, 1750–1970* (London, 1975), p. 262, Table XII.

[9] W. W. Rostow, *How It All Began. Origins of the Modern Economy* (New York, 1975), p. 117, Table 5.

[10] As cotton prices fell after 1799, the increase in volume is the most striking: 138,000 lbs in 1792, 66 million in 1807, 94 million in 1810.

[11] J. F. Shepherd and G. M. Walton, 'Economic Change after the American Revolution: Pre- and Post-War Comparisons of Maritime Shipping and Trade', *Explorations in Economic History*, XIII, 4, October 1976, p. 420, stress the 'drastic change' which took place in 1793, inasmuch as in previous years 'the relative importance of foreign trade was declining' for the American

In some years of the war period, European countries which had suffered bad harvests resorted on a large scale to the United States to obtain the grain and flour they needed; normally, they would have bought from the Baltic countries, the traditional granary of Europe; but during the wars trade relations with Baltic ports were at times entirely cut off, at some others, freight and insurance on trade with them were so high that it made American grain competitive, despite the longer haul over the Atlantic. This happened, for instance, to France in 1794, to Britain in 1801, to Spain and Portugal in 1811 and 1812.

Less spasmodic was the export from the United States to the Caribbean islands of foodstuffs and lumber. This trade was, of course, far from new, but it increased a good deal after 1793. The French colonies had been officially opened to American ships since 1784, but once the war had started, what remained of them became completely dependent on imports from the United States for their food supplies (in 1805, these imports exceeded $7 million). As for the British, after 1783 they had tried hard to restrict trade between their ex-continental colonies and their West Indian islands (and to reserve it to British ships), and to have the latter supplied as much as possible from British North America. This system had not been too successful and it became unworkable in war time. To prevent food shortages – which were thought especially dangerous in an era of slave revolts – the British Government had, though reluctantly, to authorise the islands' governors to suspend the Navigation Acts and to open their ports to American foodstuffs and lumber imported in American ships. The latter had the advantage of lower freights and insurance premiums than British ships,[12] which were driven out from the trade in the 1790s; while, of course, imports from British North America had the additional and decisive disadvantage of distance. It was estimated that in 1803–5 the British West Indies received from the United States two-thirds of their food imports and almost all their lumber, with 85 per cent of these imports on board American ships.

However, the most spectacular and important development in American foreign trade, owing to the war, was the capture of a large slice of the 'carrying trade' between European countries and their

economy, but also that the existing 'commercial base' was crucial for the ability of the US to take advantage of the new opportunities (for a different view, see below, pp. 326–7).

[12] Which were liable to capture by French privateers.

colonies. As mentioned earlier, owing to British ascendancy at sea, it was impossible for French ships to trade with the French colonies. The same fate overtook the two other colonial powers which willy-nilly joined France in the struggle against England: Holland in 1794, Spain in 1796, and both again after 1803. The French, Dutch and Spanish colonies would have choked if they had not been able to use neutral ships to keep up relations with Europe. At first, a British Order in Council of 6 November 1793 had prohibited neutral ships trading with the French colonies, but London retreated soon before American anger at the capture of many vessels; a fresh Order of 8 January 1794 (which was extended in 1798, confirmed by the King's Advocate in 1801, and renewed on 24 June 1803, when hostilities were resumed) only forbade neutral ships to trade directly between an enemy country and its colonies, implying that trade between enemy colonies and neutral ports would not be disturbed.

This allowed the development, from 1794 to 1807, of a peculiar commerce which grew fast and became very large. Neutral ships, mostly American (but including some European neutrals, such as Danes and Hamburgers), carried on trade actually between France, Holland and Spain, on the one hand, and their colonies (in the Caribbean, but also in the Indian Ocean and in South America),[13] on the other. They supplied the latter with foodstuffs, manufactured goods, wines and spirits, even slaves, and they brought back sugar, coffee, indigo, cotton, etc. But, on their way, they called at a neutral – generally American – port, in order to 'break' or 'interrupt' the voyage and to make it lawful in the eyes of the British. In many cases, this was just a 'formal' or even fictitious call: taking advantage of convenient American customs regulations, the cargo was landed and a bond given to pay import duties if the goods were not re-exported within a given period; actually the cargo was soon re-exported, the bond cancelled and a certificate of drawback granted, which could be used in case of British capture as evidence that this was not a 'continuous voyage' between two enemy ports, though, quite often, the same ship was used on both legs of the journey. Thanks to this system of fictitious 'bonded warehousing' and to the trade routes which were generally followed across the Atlantic, the detour to call at an American port on the way

[13] After Spain had entered the war against England in 1796, US trade with Spanish America increased very fast; exports to that area reached $13 million in the year 1806/7; 175 American ships entered the port of Havana within four months of 1805 alone.

from the Carribean to the Continent was not a cause of serious additional expense or delay. It was estimated in 1807 that the trade in Caribbean colonial produce was shared between Britain and the United States in the proportion of 60 per cent–40 per cent.[14]

The growth of this carrying trade brought about a large increase in imports into the United States (though most of them did not stay long on American soil) and a still larger one of re-exports of foreign goods. American re-exports had been quite small before the war: $1·8 million in 1792; as soon as 1796, they had jumped to $26 million; in 1801, they reached $47 million; they fell back during the peace of Amiens, when direct relations between European countries and their colonies were resumed, but they flourished again when the war broke out anew, to reach their peak in 1806 and 1807, at $60 million, thirty-three times more than in 1792, having risen much faster than American *domestic* exports. Indeed, in every year but two between 1797 and 1808, the value of re-exports exceeded that of domestic exports; they were the most powerful factor in the rise of total American exports, being responsible for 68 per cent of their increase between 1792 and 1807.

American ships were also employed in other new trades and in tramping activities with intricate patterns;[15] like the seventeenth-century Dutch in Colbert's words, they had become the *rouliers des mers*. They entered the coasting trade in Europe, between ports of countries which were at war with Britain: for instance, they carried wine from Bordeaux to northern Europe. As for the trade with India (the Jay treaty had opened British ports there to American ships) and China, it was also helped by the war, as Americans re-exported or even carried directly to Europe and to non-British colonies in America, large quantities of Indian printed cottons, tea and spices. Exports from British India in American vessels increased from 2,700,000 to 5,100,000 rupees (yearly average) between 1796–1800 and 1801–5.[16]

All this growing and eventually enormous carrying trade was bringing in a large invisible income: American net freight earnings are estimated to have risen from $7 million in 1792 to $31 million in 1801 and $42 million in 1807, making good a large part of the United States merchandise-trade deficit. Of course, thousands of American ships

[14] In 1806, the US re-exported 146 million lb of sugar and 47 million lb of coffee.

[15] Examples in F. Crouzet, 'Opportunity and Risk in Atlantic Trade during the French Revolution', in C.-L. Holtfrerich (ed.), *Interactions in the World Economy* (New York-London, 1989), pp. 90–150, specially 114–16.

[16] 1 rupee = 2*s*. 6*d*. = 1/8 £1.

were captured or seized by the British and the French (though capture did not mean inevitably condemnation and confiscation), but this was a business risk that could be reduced to a cost by insurance and up to 1807, it was a supportable cost.[17]

This upsurge of American foreign trade and shipping has been the theme of discussions which shall be only briefly mentioned. D. C. North and G. R. Taylor considered that it was a major factor in the fast economic growth which, according to them, took place in the United States during the very prosperous years from 1793 to 1807. The fluctuations in the American economy were directly correlated to those in foreign trade and to the military-political situation in Europe. The carrying trade enriched the main port-cities and stimulated a number of ancillary industries and services; moreover, it had a multiplier effect through the whole economy. This view of an export-led growth has been criticised by P. David; he does not see much evidence of a boom in the economy or of a large increase in per capita income; moreover, the economy was not open enough for a rise in exports to have a serious impact on the whole of it; the increase in foreign trade and shipping can therefore have made a small contribution only to the growth of national product. It can be added that the re-export of unmanufactured produce, however massive, has little stimulative effect upon an economy as a whole, and especially upon technological progress.[18]

According to a later article by C. D. Goldin and F. D. Lewis, American maritime expansion has been 'romanticised', but loses much of its legendary importance when confronted with statistical analysis, which leads them to conclude that 'had there been no change in the foreign sector from 1793 to 1807, per capita income would have been reduced by approximately three per cent', that is less than two dollars in 1800. On the other hand, they stress that 'though the rate of growth was modest', the buoyant foreign sector 'contributed significantly to the growth that did occur', increasing it 'by about one-quarter of a percentage point or slightly more than 25 per cent' (and 40 per cent if

[17] According to U. Bonnel, *La France, les Etats Unis et la guerre de course (1797–1815)* (Paris, 1961), pp. 317 ff., 407, from 1797 to 1812, the French captured at sea 1,434 American ships, of which 693 at least were eventually condemned.

[18] D. C. North, *The Economic Growth of the United States, 1790–1860* (New York, 1961); G. R. Taylor, 'American Economic Growth before 1840: An Explanatory Essay', *Journal of Economic History*, XXIV, 4, December 1964, pp. 439–42; P. David, 'The Growth of Real Product in the United States before 1840: New Evidence, Controlled Conjectures', *ibid.*, XXVII, 2, June 1967, pp. 186 *et seq.*; also W. W. Rostow, *The World Economy. History and Prospect* (London, 1978), p. 391.

other assumptions are made). However, 'even though the increase in trade ... did not dramatically increase incomes', it had longer range effects, such as urbanisation and other structural changes, so that the period of neutrality 'may have led to the emergence of a nascent national economy'.[19]

As for D. R. Adams Jr, his views are much more revisionist. He denies that the United States enjoyed an unparalleled prosperity from 1793 to 1807. The volume of domestic exports per capita never exceeded its level of 1792 and was actually much lower in some years. The fast rise of re-exports was achieved to the detriment of domestic exports; they suffered from the rise in freight rates, which was a kind of tax upon all American farmers and consumers. Socially and geographically, the benefits of neutrality were concentrated – to the benefit of a small number of shipowners, shipbuilders, bankers and big merchants, in North-eastern ports. The performance of the economy as a whole did not diverge from the long-run trend which prevailed before 1793. Adams, however, underestimates the spin-off from the growth of foreign trade and shipping; he also neglects the international context; as neutrals, the United States were in a better position than belligerent countries.[20]

A similar controversy has taken place in France, though at a far less sophisticated level: it has been maintained that the growth and prosperity of French sea-borne trade from the early eighteenth century up to 1789 was something superficial – epidermic, as E. Labrousse was fond of saying – without much impact upon *la France profonde*, so that the decline and collapse of the maritime sector during the Revolutionary and Napoleonic periods did not have far-reaching consequences (except at the local level, in the ports and in coastal districts) and did not prevent France from being rather prosperous during most of Napoleon's rule.

II

The rise of the American carrying trade and of the American merchant navy, which transported it, was basically a substitution for the direct

[19] C. D. Goldin and F. D. Lewis, 'The Role of Exports in American Economic Growth during the Napoleonic Wars, 1793 to 1807', *Explorations in Economic History*, XVII, 1, January 1980, pp. 6–25, and especially 15–16, 18–23 (and 24, Table A2, which shows that at constant – 1790 – prices, earnings from domestic exports and the carrying trade roughly doubled from 1793 to 1807).

[20] D. R. Adams, Jr, 'American Neutrality and Prosperity, 1793–1808: A Reconsideration', *Journal of Economic History*, XL, 4, December 1980, pp. 734–6.

relations, in their own ships, among France, Holland, Spain and their colonies, which the war had made impossible. On the other hand, there was no inverse correlation (except as far as shipping was concerned) between American and French (and Dutch and Spanish) maritime prosperity, but rather a good deal of complementarity, a sort of symbiotic relationship across the Atlantic. It was mainly thanks to the mediation of American ships that France and her satellites were able to retain some long-distance, transoceanic trade and especially some relations with their colonies. A counter-proof is the quasi-war of 1798–1800, during which French ports suffered a sharp fall of traffic (eight American ships entered Bordeaux in 1800, as against sixty-four in 1796), many bankruptcies and a serious depression. On the contrary, during the years 1803–7, which saw American trade at its zenith, French ports such as Bordeaux, Nantes and Marseilles, enjoyed a phase of 'semi prosperity' (P. Butel), which was actually the best (or the least unfavourable) of the whole war-time period. In 1805, 201 American ships entered Bordeaux, which was a large number, and in 1807 Marseilles received 97 of them.[21] Ostensibly, their cargoes were American property, in order to escape British capture, but part of this trade was actually on French account. A network of relationships, which had not existed in the 1780s, had been built up, especially as a number of French merchants had settled in the United States (especially in Baltimore and Philadelphia), often as refugees from the French colony of San Domingo (Haiti), after the slave revolt. It was during those same years that the irregular and volatile Franco-American trade made up a significant share of each country's total trade,[22] though much of it was not really between France and the United States, but between France and her colonies through American ships and ports (it is typical that sugar was then the largest 'American' export to France). Still, American shipping helped France to preserve some remains of her former trading position, and the Continent to be supplied with non-British colonial produce and without Britain's mediation.

However, in November 1807, the British cabinet issued its famous Orders in Council, which prevented *de facto* neutral countries from

[21] Many American ships laden with colonial produce went also to Antwerp and Amsterdam: the latter received 211 of them in 1806. Actually, in 1805, re-exports from the USA to Holland – \$15 million – were markedly higher than to France – \$9·9 million.

[22] From 1804 to 1807 exports to France averaged 12 per cent of total US exports; higher percentages were reached for abnormal years – 1795 and 1813.

trading with enemy ports; in conjunction with Napoleon's Berlin and Milan decrees, as well as with Jefferson's embargo, this was a deadly blow to the American carrying trade. It revived somewhat (but not with France) after the raising of the embargo and the British Order in Council of 26 April 1809, which put France, Holland and northern Italy – and them only – under strict and rigorous blockade and therefore allowed neutrals to trade with the outer fringes of Napoleonic Europe, in northern Europe and the Mediterranean. But the highest figure for American re-exports from 1808 onwards, $24 million in 1810, was a far cry from their 1807 peak.[23] Anyway, if the Orders in Council had struck this trade suddenly, it was doomed in the longer run, owing to the conquest by British forces of the last colonies which remained under French rule (in 1809 and 1810, and the Dutch East Indies in 1811), while the Spanish colonies had sided in 1808 with the Spanish patriots and therefore with Britain against Napoleon.[24] Eventually, Britain monopolised the carrying trade in the produce of both East and West Indies and 'became the grocer of Europe'.[25]

None the less, though the sea-borne trade of France fell to a very low level after 1807, it somewhat revived at times, for instance when both the British Government and Napoleon found that their interest was to relax the rigour of their respective blockades and to grant licences for a direct trade – in grain, wines or sugar – between the two countries. And there were the blockade-runners, ships which tried to break through the British sea-blockade. From July 1810 onwards, Napoleon granted special permits to American ships to trade directly between the United States and France. This was a highly risky venture, but it was attempted by a number of fast American ships, sailing mostly from Baltimore and during the winter, to take advantage of the long nights. Over thirty of those blockade-runners arrived each year in Bordeaux, which was their main destination, in 1811–13.[26] When leaving France,

23 A number of American ships went to Holland during a brief period after the aborted Erskine agreement of April 1809, and others to Tonningen in Denmark. Later on in 1810 and 1811 the US had a relatively large trade with Russia, as one of the few markets left open; see A. W. Crosby, *America, Russia, Hemp, and Napoleon: American Trade with Russia and the Baltic, 1783–1812* (Columbus, 1965), e.g. pp. 191, 224.

24 As the Spanish colonies – and Brazil – were opened to the British in 1808, when American trade was interrupted by the embargo, they managed to keep the lion's share in their trade, despite an active traffic by the Americans.

25 R. B. Sheridan, 'The Wealth of Jamaica in the Eighteenth Century: a Rejoinder', *The Economic History Review*, XXI, 1, April 1968, p. 60.

26 P. Butel, 'Guerre et commerce: L'activité du port de Bordeaux sous le régime des licences, 1808–1815', *Revue d'histoire moderne et contemporaine*, XIX, Jan.–March 1972, pp. 136, 142–3.

they were obliged to export French goods for a value equal to that of the imports they had brought in, with a given proportion of some articles such as silks (eventually 50 per cent of the total cargo), wines and brandies. It is possible that these exports, though actually forced upon the American market, did help to create there a taste for French goods which had not existed before, but which developed after 1815, when the United States became the largest foreign market of the silk industry of Lyons.

There is no need to dwell on the obvious complementarity between the American and British economies (J. Potter has written of a neo-colonial economic relationship),[27] in which the former almost specialised in primary production, the latter having a large manufacturing sector, which was exporting a significant part of its output, while its most dynamic industry was increasingly dependent on the United States for its raw material supplies. Moreover, from 1783 to 1802, exports were for Britain a major engine of growth, and the United States market played a crucial part in the fast growth of British domestic exports; at current prices, it took 21 per cent of them in 1784–6, 27 per cent in 1794–6 and 25 per cent in 1804–6; it was responsible for 26 per cent of the increase in total domestic exports from Britain between 1784–6 and 1804–6 (but 34 per cent for the period 1784–6 to 1794–6).[28] The United States were Britain's first customer and up to 1807, more than made good the losses of markets in continental Europe. As for American domestic exports, Britain bought over a third of them in the early nineteenth century (1802–7).

However, in the case of Britain – or rather the British Empire as a whole – there was also a good deal of competition with the United States. Shipping was, in this respect, a basic factor. For obvious geographical reasons, shipbuilding costs were much lower in timber-rich America than in deforested Britain, which had to import from northern Europe much of the materials. American ships were generally better built than the British, and their running costs were not higher. Their owners could offer cheaper freight rates while, as neutrals, they paid lower insurance premiums. Therefore, they drove out British ships from the sea routes which were open to competition and, to begin

[27] J. Potter, 'The Effects of the American Revolution on the Economic Relations between the former Colonies and the Mother Country', in *La Révolution américaine et l'Europe*, pp. 267–74.

[28] See above, Chapter 6, pp. 237–8. The percentages quoted have been computed from R. Davis' current values. The role of the US market was especially important from 1788 to 1798 and from 1803 to 1807.

with, from the direct trade between Britain and the United States. Before 1793 British ships were at least on a par with Americans on this route, but in 1802–4 American ships accounted for 82 per cent of the total tonnage of shipping which entered British ports from the United States and left them for the latter destination; in 1805–7, their share had risen to 92 per cent. They had also practically monopolised the traffic between their country and the British West Indies. As a result, shipbuilding declined in Britain and her colonies after 1803, while it boomed in the United States, which in 1805 built 129,000 tons as against 71,000 in Britain and 90,000 in the whole Empire.

Moreover, the rise of the American carrying trade in colonial produce had eventually baneful consequences for the British colonies. This did not happen in the 1790s, because of the 'destruction' of San Domingo, the world's first producer of sugar, which created a shortage of this commodity; but most sugar-growing territories increased their output in answer to higher prices, so that sugar prices peaked in 1798 and declined on trend afterwards, the seller's market having turned into a buyer's market.[29]

In the cut-throat competition that followed, the British were at a disadvantage: most of their Caribbean possessions were high-cost producers and, thanks moreover to lower transportation costs in American ships, foreign – mostly 'enemy' – sugar could undercut British-grown sugar on European markets.[30] From 1802 to 1806, re-exports of sugar from Britain fell by half, while imports increased (owing to British conquest of some enemy colonies), and while re-exports from the United States advanced sharply. In 1806 and 1807 the British West Indies suffered an acute depression and many planters were ruined or at least threatened with ruin.[31]

British North America was also depressed; owing to the war, it had lost to the United States, as mentioned earlier, the Caribbean market for its grain, lumber and fish.[32] As for the exports of cod from

[29] Though prices somewhat recovered from 1802 to 1805; but coffee prices fell also from 1805 onward.

[30] J. R. Ward, 'The Profitability of Sugar Planting in the British West Indies, 1650–1834', *The Economic History Review*, XXXI, 2, May 1978, pp. 199–200, Tables 1 and 2, on the rise in freight rates and insurance premiums on sugar from the British colonies to London.

[31] Ward, *ibid.*, pp. 208–9, and S. Drescher, *Econocide: British Slavery in the Era of Abolition* (Pittsburgh, 1977), pp. 76 *et seq.*, 131 *et seq.*, are less pessimistic than L. J. Ragatz in his classic book *The Fall of the Planter Class in the British Caribbean, 1763–1833* (New York, 1928), but they stress the growing dependence of British plantations on the international market – where they were confronted with American competition.

[32] In 1803–5, it supplied under ten per cent of the food imports of the British West Indies.

Newfoundland and the present maritime provinces of Canada, they suffered from French control over the Catholic countries of Southern Europe which were their chief market; a growing share of 'British-caught fish' had to be sent to American ports, in order to be re-exported on American ships toward Europe. At the same time, American fisheries, which had been the main beneficiaries of the disappearance of French fishing boats from the Newfoundland Banks, were enjoying an insolent prosperity. Lastly, the rise of American trade with India, which has been alluded to earlier, short-circuited British East Indian trade and harmed British imports and re-exports of Indian printed cottons.

On the whole, there was a crisis of the imperial economy, which developed after the renewal of the war in 1803 and became serious in 1806–7. Undoubtedly, its direct cause was American competition, including an American infiltration within the imperial economic system (for instance, British North America appeared to be on the way to being economically satellitised).[33]

No wonder, therefore, that the United States, and especially their carrying trade in colonial produce from enemy colonies, came under heavy fire not only from mercantilist die-hards like Lord Sheffield, but also from some powerful pressure groups, first of all the West India interest, but also a 'North American' lobby, the 'shipping interest' and the East India Company, which were all suffering from American competition. It was maintained that the United States were 'objective' (as one would say currently) accomplices of France and her satellites which, through their help, were able to preserve relations with their colonies and to trade almost as freely as in peace time; under such circumstances, the Royal Navy was almost neutralised as an offensive weapon, Britain's vital interests – especially her sea-power – were in jeopardy, her colonies and her re-export trade (which actually stagnated after 1803) were threatened with ruin.[34]

[33] On the contrary, the North American colonies were to prosper during the American embargo, when they exported on a large scale to the Caribbean and were a base for a smuggling trade with the US. From 1809 onwards, they benefitted greatly (as also did the shipping interest) from the rise of their timber exports to Britain, thanks to the preferential duties on colonial timber which were then established. See G. Paquet and J.-P. Wallot, 'International Circumstances of Lower Canada, 1786–1810: Prolegomenon', *The Canadian Historical Review*, LIII, 4, December 1972, pp. 371–401.

[34] F. Crouzet, 'Groupes de pression et politique de blocus: Remarques sur les origines des Ordres en Conseil de novembre 1807', *Revue Historique*, 463, July–September 1962, pp. 45–72, where more complete references to some facts mentioned in the present chapter can be found.

On the other hand, it could be pointed out that this very American carrying trade, which harmed British colonies, was most beneficial to British manufactures. The United States balance of payments had a deficit with the British Empire, but a large surplus with continental Europe, which was remitted to merchant banks in England and used eventually to pay for English manufactures which were exported to America.[35] This triangular system of international settlements had been essential to the progress of British exports to the United States.

III

In any event, the enormous American carrying trade existed only on sufferance from Britain. She tolerated it for years, but it suffered from some harassment in 1805[36] and eventually, in November 1807, the new Tory government prohibited it *de facto* altogether. The motivations for this change were complex, the main one being the necessity of countering and defeating Napoleon's Continental Blockade, but the influence of the anti-American lobbies which have just been mentioned cannot be denied, so that, in some respects, the Orders in Council were directed as much against the United States as against France.

From 1805–7, American neutral rights were therefore less and less respected by the belligerents; Napoleon, for his part, was no innocent and, on several occasions, behaved abominably with America;[37] still, occasions for incidents with Britain, as the dominant sea-power, were more frequent than with France, and there was also the burning issue of impressment and the question of the West. Confronted with the same problem as France, Britain's overwhelming sea-power and the way she was wielding it, the United States attempted to retaliate by policies which were inevitably rather similar to those followed by France. Those policies and the War of 1812 which came on top of them brought about eventually some similarities and parallelisms in the

35 Many American ships which had imported colonial produce into continental ports left them in ballast for England; it was said that three-quarters of the proceeds of American sales in these ports were remitted to London.

36 As a result of the condemnation of the ship *Essex* (July 1805), which encouraged British naval commanders and privateers to capture American ships, but not on government orders; it proved to be a false alarm and American traders carried on.

37 He suspected American ships to be used for smuggling British goods into continental ports; although this happened now and then, the US carrying trade was on the whole beneficial to France.

economic development of France and the United States during the later years of the wars.

Jefferson and Madison wanted Britain (and France) to be more respectful of American rights, but also to avoid war with her; it was obviously absurd to make war to protect American trade, which would soon be destroyed if hostilities broke out with England. So Jefferson resorted to 'peaceful coercion', that is economic sanctions. He tried, through the embargo, to deprive Britain and France of American produce, American markets and the use of American ships, which in his view they badly needed, in order to retaliate against their exactions and to force them into concessions; the embargo, therefore, was an American *self-blockade*, a refusal to trade with countries which were trampling on American rights.[38] The same calculations and the same device of self-blockade can be found in the other economic sanctions – or would-be sanctions – which were taken by the United States against the delinquent great powers, from the abortive first Non-Importation Act of 1806 to the Non-Intercourse Act of 1809 (though this was a bad joke, as nothing was easier than to violate it), and to the second – and more effective – Non-Importation Act of 1811.

Now those various measures of self-denial of trade by America were akin – though less drastic and following a native patriotic tradition of 'threats to the British pocket-book'[39] – to Napoleon's Continental Blockade, which was basically a self-blockade, the refusal to admit any ship coming from Britain and any British merchandise into France and the countries she controlled. There was, of course, the difference that Napoleon's blockade was part of a warfare system aimed at defeating England, while American 'sanctions' were diplomatic weapons, intended to bring back to its senses the British cabinet, without resorting to war: they were an 'alternative to war', as B. Perkins has called the embargo. But the two sets of measures had in common the fact that they were rather inefficient substitutes for the sea-power which neither France nor the United States had, but which would have been the only effective weapon against England. They had moreover the common fate of being violated on a grand scale: America had its

[38] Of course the embargo had also initially a defensive purpose: to save American shipping from the massive depredations that were expected from Britain and France; but, as time went on, the coercive side became dominant.

[39] B. Perkins, *Prologue to War, England and the United States, 1805–1812* (Berkeley and Los Angeles, 1961), p. 150. And the emphasis in the embargo was on preventing exports from, and not imports into, the US.

equivalents of Heligoland (the island off the north German coast which was the base for intensive smuggling of British goods), such as Amelia Island on the border between Georgia and Spanish Florida.[40] And the British Government resorted to the same devices to encourage the citizens of the United States and Napoleon's subjects to break the prohibitions against British trade which their own rulers had issued. Still, when it came to happen in 1811 and early 1812 that the American and the French self-blockades were enforced rather efficiently at the same time, the effects upon British industry were serious; so, under the pressure of manufacturers and the fear of workers' riots, the British cabinet repealed the Orders in Council on 23 June 1812; four days earlier, President Madison had proclaimed a state of war with Great Britain.

C. P. Kindleberger has written that 'war is the ultimate protective tariff',[41] but the self-blockade measures which had preceded 1812 had already afforded American industry an intermittent, but not ineffective protection. Jefferson's embargo did not affect directly the importation of British goods, and the Non-Importation Act of 1806, which was enforced during part of the embargo period, did not apply to several important British manufactures. However, many British exporters and American importers were worried by the danger of war between the two countries; they wondered also how exports to America would be paid since the embargo was preventing the United States from exporting. So, at the end of 1807 and for most of 1808, British businessmen restricted their shipments; exports of British goods to the United States fell from £11·9 million in 1807 to £5·2 million (current values) in 1808. The second Non-Importation Act, which was more comprehensive and more seriously enforced, brought about a more drastic fall of British exports to the United States: from £10·9 million in 1810 to £1·8 million in 1811. Officially, the American market was closed to British goods from April 1811 to early 1815 – though there was a good deal of smuggling.[42] This situation resulted in higher prices for manufactured goods, which made their production in the United

[40] J. A. Frankel, 'The 1807–1809 Embargo Against Great Britain', *Journal of Economic History*, XLII, 2, June 1982, pp. 291–308, maintains that the embargo was well enforced and that violations have been overestimated.

[41] C. P. Kindleberger, 'US Economic Foreign Policy, 1776–1976', *Foreign Affairs*, LV, 2, January 1977, p. 396.

[42] And the hasty but massive shipments which had been made from Britain between the repeal of the Orders in Council and the news that the US had declared war, were eventually admitted in America.

States a more economic proposition than formerly, when British goods were coming in freely and paying low duties under the tariff of 1789. On the other side of the Atlantic, the Continental Blockade was not purely an offensive weapon against England; it had also a defensive aspect, as it acted as a system of extreme protection against British competition, which fostered the growth of industry in France and some other parts of the Continent (though, at least in France, protective measures had been adopted well before the Berlin decree).

'Jefferson's embargo launched a period of Hamiltonian development in the United States', which 'entered (like France and Belgium from, say, 1800) a period of protracted industrial expansion'. One cannot but agree with those remarks by W. W. Rostow:[43] the Napoleonic period in France, the years 1808–14 in America, did see an upsurge in industrial production under the shelter of protection and war. The parallel is made closer by the fact that the most striking developments in both countries took place in the same branch – the cotton industry.

This is a well-known story and one needs only to stress that cotton was, at the time, the industry which was the most liable to grow fast, but also where British competition was the most formidable, so that its progress, on both sides of the Atlantic, was dependent on economic warfare against England. In France, machine-spinning of cotton did not develop really before the late 1790s, when the Directory tried to enforce a prohibition of English goods and when some manufacturers managed to smuggle in from England blue-prints and spare parts of 'modern' machinery. Renewed and striking progress of the cotton industry was achieved under Napoleon's rule, especially after a decree of February 1806 which prohibited the importation into France of cotton yarn and cotton grey cloth (for printing). There was a boom in machine-spinning from 1806 to 1810, with a four-fold increase in the output of machine-spun yarn. At the fall of Napoleon, France had built up a respectable cotton-spinning industry of about one million spindles (but Britain had five million of them!) and hand-spinning had disappeared. The industry's total output, as measured by its raw-cotton consumption, might have been, in its peak year, 1810, three times its 1789 figure.[44]

In the United States there had been since the 1780s a number of attempts to establish a cotton industry, but most of them had failed.

[43] Rostow, *How It All Began*, p. 202; and *The World Economy*, p. 122.
[44] See Chapter 8, pp. 303–5.

The stimulus given by the embargo was remarkable: the 'cotton craze' increased the number of mills from 15 in 1807 to 87 in 1810 (with 8,000 and 80,000 spindles respectively). Non-importation and the War of 1812 gave a further stimulus: in 1815, the United States had 213 mills with 130,000 spindles; the industry had attracted a number of men with large capital, especially the 'Boston Associates', and the factory system had taken definite roots in New England. Moreover, though weaving remained a domestic hand-loom activity, the output of cotton cloth in New England, according to R. Zevin's calculations, jumped from 84,000 yards in 1807 to 181,000 in 1808, 801,000 in 1811 and just under two million in 1814 – a fantastic rate of growth of 55 per cent per year.[45]

In other industries, the impetus from the war and the self-blockades, though widespread, is less striking – and also the similarity between France and the United States. The large French wool industry was not too exposed to British competition; still it achieved some modernisation: by 1815, most of the carding and spinning of wool was done by new machinery imitating English models. On the other hand, the United States had very little in the way of a wool industry strictly speaking, though a good deal of spinning and weaving of wool was done within households. After 1807 there was some progress, especially owing to government orders of cloth for the army during the War of 1812; in 1815, Connecticut, the main centre of the wool industry, had 25 factories employing 1,200 workers – figures which illustrate both the rise and the very modest scale of this industry in the United States. As for the iron industry, it is interesting that both in France and in America it underwent very little technical progress during the wars and started its industrial revolution after they were over (actually much later in the United States). But there was more change in the secondary metal trades, and the origins of the 'American system of manufactures' go back to the work of Eli Whitney and Simeon North for supplying firearms to government during the quasi-war with France.

On his way back from Moscow in 1812, Napoleon, who was meditating rather gloomily, suddenly said to one of his companions: 'After all, I have created French industry.' This was, of course, a gross

[45] R. B. Zevin, 'The Growth of Cotton Textile Production after 1815', in R. W. Fogel and S. L. Engerman (eds.), *The Reinterpretation of American Economic History* (New York, 1971), p. 123, Table 1.

overstatement, but with the grain of truth that his policies had helped the beginnings of the Industrial Revolution in France; indeed many scholars would maintain that modern industry was born in France during his rule. Likewise, it would be wrong to claim that the embargo, non-importation and the War of 1812 created American industry: before 1808, large quantities of manufactured goods of many varieties were already made in the United States. But those political events 'produced substantial change in the course of economic development', as C. P. Kindleberger has written, and gave to industry a strong stimulus (just what some people in Britain had feared as an indirect effect of the Orders in Council). Up to 1807, the large profits to be made in foreign trading ventures and in shipping, as well, of course, as in agriculture (owing to high farm prices), had attracted all available capital; later on, a good deal of merchants' and shipowners' capital, which was idle owing to the interruption of sea-borne trade, was shifted towards industry. So the United States had an industrial expansion 'which helped to prepare the way for the later passage of New England into sustained industrial growth',[46] *a* beginning, if not *the* beginning of the Industrial Revolution.

Both the American and the French industrial developments of the war period (especially in the cotton industry) had been 'hothouse' expansion, achieved under artificial conditions. So a last similarity between the United States and France is that, in both countries, many industrial firms, which had mushroomed during the war but which had much higher costs than their British rivals, could not stand the latter's competition when hostilities ended, inasmuch as the low-duties American tariff of 1789 was no protection against the flood of cheap British goods and the restored Bourbons announced in April 1814 a liberal trade policy. The result was an industrial 'infanticide',[47] which made the tariff question acute. In France there was such an outcry that the government had to retreat quickly; as early as December 1814, a new and strongly protectionist tariff law was passed; additional legislation during the few years that followed gave France an ultra-protectionist system which lasted, without much alleviation, until 1860. In the United States, things did not go as far, but many petitions demanded protection for the nation's infant industries and the tariff of 1816 was decidedly protectionist, especially in respect of cotton goods.

[46] Rostow, *The World Economy*, p. 122, also p. 119 and *How It All Began*, p. 203.
[47] Kindleberger, p. 396.

A lasting consequence of the Napoleonic wars was thus to create in both France and the United States a strong protectionist tradition.

IV

During the 'Second Hundred Years' War' (1689–1815), the control of North America, of the Caribbean and the glittering prizes of the carrying trade between *les deux Indes* and Europe had been major stakes in the Anglo-French struggle. Despite many set-backs – especially the loss of her North American empire in the Seven Years' War – France had managed to hold out as far as trade was concerned. However, during the final phase (1793–1815) of their long-drawn struggle, France was decisively defeated by Britain and dropped out of the race for naval, colonial and commercial supremacy. Though she started at the same time to modernise her industry and – much more slowly – her agriculture, and though she remained up to 1871 the second commercial power in the world, her role in international trade was minor in comparison with Britain, which during the war period had 'moved from a major to a dominant position in the world trading framework'.[48] Of course, Britain's economic lead had helped her win the wars (as Malthus wrote in 1820, 'in carrying on the late war, we were powerfully assisted by our steam-engines'),[49] but military victory strengthened markedly her economic position. P. O'Brien and C. Keyder have observed that the gap of about fifteen per cent between British and French per capita incomes during the nineteenth century resulted mainly from British superiority in shipping, banking and commercial services supplied to foreigners, and that 'this particular advantage was a pay-off' for earlier British 'investment in naval power and imperial conquest'.[50]

As befits a new and fast-growing country, the United States underwent at a much quicker pace an evolution which has some common features with that of France. A basically agricultural country, they came unexpectedly and without having wanted it, to be in

[48] Rostow, *The World Economy*, p. 122. C. Carrière, *Négociants marseillais au XVIIIe siècle*, (Marseilles, 1973, 2 vols.), I, pp. 147–62, has rightly stressed that there was definitely a rupture for French trade when war started in 1793, and that when it ended over twenty years later, the international trading system had completely changed.

[49] P. Sraffa (ed.), *The Works and Correspondence of David Ricardo*, vol. II (Cambridge, 1951), p. 361.

[50] P. O'Brien and C. Keyder, *Economic Growth in Britain and France, 1780–1914* (London, 1978), pp. 76, 197.

possession of the heritage of France as a great sea-trading power,[51] and therefore, willy-nilly, the rivals of England. There is no 'perfect' neutral and American neutrality was, according to circumstances, 'objectively' profitable at one time to France, at another time to Britain. For instance, the American carrying trade in colonial produce created severe competition for the British West Indies and for British re-exports of colonial produce and was helpful to France and her satellites. When Jefferson enacted the embargo, he actually sided with Napoleon in waging economic warfare against England. On the other hand, when the non-intercourse policy and still more the Macon Act of 1 May 1810 were adopted, the United States accepted to trade more or less freely with Britain (and on a massive scale in 1810), but to be deprived of any trade with France; they became indeed Britain's satellite. However, with the Non-Importation Act of 1811, they changed sides and became Napoleon's allies. During the War of 1812, they were in the boat where France had been for many years: their sea-borne trade was strangled by the British blockade, but they enjoyed an outburst of industrialisation. Anyway, because of overwhelming British sea-power, they had not been able to retain their role of *rouliers des mers* for more than a dozen years and the rise of their carrying trade was as short-lived as it had been spectacular. Though the American merchant navy remained up to the Civil War a dangerous competitor for the British, its registered tonnage in foreign trade had fallen in 1820 to 584,000 tons, against 981,000 in 1809, this latter figure not to be exceeded again before the 1840s. Roughly speaking, after 1814 the United States turned away from high-seas ventures and toward 'internal improvements', which is not too different from what took place in European countries like France, Prussia and Belgium. However, they had a continent to improve – in the long view an elementary but basic datum.

[51] And also later of Holland and Spain.

10 Western Europe and Great Britain: 'catching up' in the first half of the nineteenth century

The historical experience of today's advanced nations can be useful to the Third World, provided that hasty generalisations, from random examples, without regard to time and place, are avoided and that economists concentrate on concrete cases which can be analysed in some depth. This chapter will deal with the experience of Continental Western Europe – France, Belgium, the Netherlands, Germany and Switzerland[1] – during the period from 1815 to about 1850. This leaves aside the disturbances of the war period prior to 1815 and stops at mid-century, when there is a definite turning-point in the economic development of the area. These countries were (along with the United States) the first 'followers' or 'late-comers' who tried, during this period, to emulate Britain and to introduce the new technology which she had invented. The sample is relatively limited, homogeneous and yet varied. The study of the problems facing these countries in their attempts to catch up with the leader of the Industrial Revolution may possibly throw some light upon the questions which beset at the present day the developing nations.

However, qualification must be made from the start: there are enormous differences between the relative situation of Western Europe after the Napoleonic wars *vis-à-vis* Britain, and that of today's under-developed countries *vis-à-vis* the industrially advanced nations.

The range of current measures of per capita income in the present world shows differences of a factor of 10, 20 or more between the richest and the poorest nations.[2] But among European countries, income

[1] For brevity's sake, these five countries will henceforth be generally referred to as 'Western Europe'. This chapter was originally published in A. J. Youngson (ed.), *Economic Development in the Long Run* (London, 1972), pp. 98–125.

[2] Depending upon the conversion by specific price weights or by currency exchange rates: S. Kuznets, *Modern Economic Growth: Rate, Structure and Spread* (New Haven, 1966), pp. 360–1, 374–86; also G. Ohlin, 'Remarks on the Relevance of Western Experience in Economic Growth to Former Colonial Areas', *Journal of World History*, IX, 1 (1965), pp. 31–2.

differences between the economic leaders and the backward economies were never so pronounced. Some writers have estimated that in the early nineteenth century, per capita income in France was half that of Britain, but this is an error and it is more likely that the French figure should be put around 20 per cent below the British one;[3] income per capita may have been higher in the Low Countries than in France, and lower in Germany, but overall the gap between Britain and the Continent was undoubtedly narrower than the one presently existing between, say, the United States and Western Europe. Moreover, despite the snags inherent in such comparisons, it can be maintained that real income levels in Western Europe were markedly higher before 'modern economic growth' began than they are in many under-developed countries today.

In addition, the countries under consideration were, by 1815, in possession of a wide range of industries, the output of which was considerable. J. Marczewski has estimated that up to around 1820 the real value of industrial production was higher in France than in Britain[4] (but of course France had a larger population). Some Swiss writers assert that as early as the late eighteenth century, their country was more 'industrialised' than England – in the sense that a larger share of the labour force was employed in manufacturing activities. Belgium had also a relatively large industry, which had made some remarkable progress before 1815, to the point that some scholars maintain that the Industrial Revolution had started there in the late eighteenth century. And if Germany was more backward, it was far from destitute of manufactures. Western Europe had thus a wide basis of 'proto-industrialisation' (in a broad sense).

Thirdly, many of the 'preconditions' of the Industrial Revolution, which had been realised in eighteenth-century Britain, were also achieved (though less completely) in Western Europe by 1815; whereas they do not exist nowadays in many under-developed countries. Some of these existed thanks to the French Revolution and to its

[3] According to a calculation by the US Bureau of the Census (quoted in *The Economist*, 20 October 1966, p. 495), in 1870 the French real product per head was 80 per cent of the British, and the German 71 per cent. My own wild guess is that the relative difference between French and English incomes per capita did not change much between the late seventeenth century (when Gregory King put it at 20 per cent) and the 1950s. See also J. Marczewski, 'Le produit physique de l'économie française de 1789 à 1913 (Comparaison avec la Grande-Bretagne)', *Histoire quantitative de l'économie française*, vol. IV (Paris, 1965), p. lxxix; and below, note 55.

[4] Marczewski, p. xlv. This view was considered absurd by many scholars when it was first expressed, but it is now widely accepted.

exportation to neighbouring countries, especially by Napoleon. A whole deadwood of time-honoured institutions (such as the guilds[5] or the manorial system), which had been hampering economic progress, had been wiped out; and a bourgeois, laissez-faire social and economic system, much more akin to the British than to that of the *Ancien Régime*, had been established – and was not much tampered with by the post-Waterloo 'Restorations'. Western Europe had also rather efficient and orderly systems of government, and the short revolutionary upheavals or the limited wars recurring here and there between 1815 and 1850 cannot be considered to have seriously hampered economic growth; while there was nothing like the heavy burden of military expenditure which many underdeveloped countries of today impose on themselves.

Western Europe had also some supplies of capital of indigenous origin and was well provided with human capital: a largely (and increasingly) literate population, an industrial labour force well trained in the skills of traditional crafts, some reservoirs of entrepreneurs and managers, as well as numerous communities of scientists, many of whom were up to the best British standards.

A last contrast with the present situation of underdeveloped countries lies in the field of population. Western Europe had no population explosion,[6] with its depressing effects on per capita income levels and on savings. During the period under consideration, the rates of natural increase of population never reached the levels common today in the Third World. Between 1800 and 1850, they range from 0·54 per cent per year in France to 0·79 per cent in the Netherlands; and for the five countries taken together the population increased from 58 to 81 million, a mean rate of growth of 0·66 per cent per year, as opposed to an average rate of 2·2 per cent per year for the present underdeveloped countries, some of which (in Latin America for instance) go up to 2·5 per cent, 2·8 per cent or even 3 per cent.

On the other hand, it would be wrong to draw too optimistic a picture of the Western Continental countries' situation in the post-Waterloo era; and Maurice Lévy Leboyer has even stressed that their prospects of economic development were quite gloomy.[7] Though ahead of the rest of Europe – and of the world, in relation to Britain

[5] However, the guilds survived in Germany until after 1850.

[6] Largely because death rates, though falling, remained at high levels.

[7] M. Lévy-Leboyer, *Les Banques européennes et l'industrialisation internationale dans la première moitié du XIXe siècle* (Paris, 1964), pp. 27–32, 49 (quoted below: Lévy-Leboyer).

these countries were backward and underdeveloped; the lag behind this happy island, which had become obvious in the 1780s, had been seriously aggravated by the wars, blockades and internal upheavals of the Revolutionary and Napoleonic period. While a technical revolution was in full swing in England – not only in industry, but in agriculture and in transport – it had hardly started on the Continent, which retained an essentially eighteenth-century or *Ancien Régime* pattern of economic structures. Agriculture was archaic, with many regions living in isolation upon the produce of a quasi-subsistence economy; industry, except in a very few cases, was pursued on a handicraft and domestic-system basis; the transport networks and the banking systems were quite inadequate.

To be sure, during the Napoleonic era, the first rumblings of the Industrial Revolution had been heard, and some English innovations had been introduced in a few industries, especially cotton-spinning. Cotton mills had been set up in various parts of France and Germany, as well as in Belgium and Switzerland; and a small machine-building industry had emerged to supply them with machinery. But even these new 'advanced' industries were suffering from a considerable lag behind England. Continental cotton mills of 1815 were equipped with the type of plant that had prevailed in Britain in the 1790s, and they were driven by horse-gins or water-wheels, very rarely by steam engines. This small 'modern' sector, which had grown in the hothouse atmosphere of the Continental Blockade, was therefore quite weak, and unable to withstand British competition; and in fact many concerns which had prospered under Napoleon were wiped out when British goods flooded the Continent after the Emperor's fall.[8]

The Continental countries were thus faced with a problem of backwardness, just like that of today's underdeveloped countries; but, unlike them, they had to *transform* existing industries, to 'modernise' them by the large-scale introduction of the new techniques which had been invented and perfected in England, and did not need to build up completely new industries from scratch. This was in some ways an easier task,[9] inasmuch as the Continentals, once peace and normal

[8] See above, chapter 8, pp. 302ff.

[9] As a matter of fact, in France, traditional industries – especially wool and linen – grew at a snail's pace, and this was a major factor in the relatively slow growth of aggregate industrial output; while 'new' industries, like mining, iron, engineering, chemicals and cotton progressed much more rapidly. See F. Crouzet, 'Essai de construction d'un indice annuel de la production industrielle française au XIXe siècle', *Annales ESC*, XXV, 1, January–February 1970, p. 85.

relations with Britain had been re-established in 1815, were theoretically able to take advantage of the experience accumulated by the British during the preceding decades, to tap their reservoir of technical expertise, and to borrow straight away the best British practice. And there were powerful commercial and official influences, both in Britain and on the Continent, to encourage the diffusion of the new technology.

However, in many other respects, the process of modernisation ran into some serious obstacles. Those which were 'internal', i.e. related to conditions within the Continental countries themselves, will be discussed later; but we must mention from the outset the 'external' barrier which resulted from Britain's lead, and from the position of strength – and a constantly growing strength – which she had secured *vis-à-vis* the Continent.

Britain had superabundant supplies of cheap coal and of capital; she had a large and skilful labour-force, which moreover was already partly trained to factory work; her equipment and plant were much larger in quantity, better in quality and constantly improved by cumulating innovations; her industrial districts were provided with a full panoply of ancillary services; thanks to high productivity techniques, her costs of production were markedly lower; and she was in a position to take advantage, almost alone, of the increase in demand which was to be expected.[10] Not only could England exclude the Continentals from third markets, she threatened also to invade their own home markets, and one could well wonder in 1815 if Continental industries had much chance of survival in the face of British competition. Moreover, the threat of the overwhelming economic power of Britain, which was hovering over Continental industries, was by itself a brake upon modernisation, as it created among manufacturers an inferiority complex which crippled their initiative. Of course the British challenge could be also a stimulus, an incentive to modernise, to improve productivity in order to lower costs, but, during the early post-Waterloo period, the balance between its stimulating and discouraging effects was still not settled.

There was of course a simple parry to the British threat: protectionism – to which, for instance, France reverted after the short-lived

English translation in R. Cameron (ed.), *Essays in French Economic History* (Homewood, Ill., 1970), pp. 245–78. In Belgium and Germany, there was an absolute decline of the linen industry.

[10] Lévy-Leboyer, pp. 32 ff.

attempt at a liberal customs system under the First Restoration. The policy of protection has been strongly criticised, both by contemporary and by recent writers, who have seen it as one major factor making for slowness in the modernisation and growth of the French economy. It is more reasonable, however, to recognise that protection was absolutely necessary to the survival of most Continental industries.[11] The French mistake was to carry it to extreme lengths – to downright prohibition of most foreign manufactured goods. But even this 'Second Continental Blockade' did not allow archaic industries to lead a quiet life, owing to smuggling, to the long-term fall in industrial prices, and to a sharpening inter-regional competition, within the 'large' countries. On the other hand, Switzerland is an interesting example of industrial progress under free trade conditions, but at the price of successive and sometimes painful adaptations and of extremely low wages for labour. Belgian industry undoubtedly suffered from the low customs duties it had to labour under during the Dutch period, up to 1830. And in the 1830s and early 1840s, the German market was flooded with imported pig iron (as customs duties on this product were low), and this competition was so disastrous for German ironmasters that they were unable to modernise; they started to do so only after the duties had been raised in 1844. This is proof that a free trade policy was no sure receipt for modernisation. One must add that up to the 1840s, Britain retained a system of protection and prohibition, which would in any case have prevented the Continent from specialising in primary production, or in the few industries – such as the silk industry – in which Continental countries were able to compete on favourable terms with English manufacturers. However, protection was no complete solution, and could even make things worse as far as foreign markets were concerned; and such markets, especially in overseas countries, were those where demand was to rise the most spectacularly after 1815. To give them up to the British was to accept a slow growth, based on home markets only.

Modernisation was thus an inescapable necessity for Western Europe; she had to 'catch up' with Britain, and I shall now consider how this challenge had been taken up by the mid-nineteenth century. I shall say at once that the Continent's drive towards modernisation and

[11] Bairoch, *Révolution industrielle et sous-développement* (Paris, 1963), pp. 126 ff., 205–6, stresses that the 'isolation' of the national market allowed forward and backward linkages to play their full part, and stimulated induced growth. Protection, by high tariffs and by high transport costs, greatly helped the diffusion of the new technology.

growth had been partly successful – with an equal stress on those two words.

Western Europe had built up a 'modern' industrial sector, which used machinery and processes borrowed from England. The mechanisation of Western Europe's textile industries and the renovation of her metallurgical industries had made some remarkable progress: she had coke-burning blast-furnaces, puddling furnaces, rolling mills, textile mills equipped with spinning machinery and power-looms; she had an engineering industry, which made a wide range of machinery, including railway engines and steamships. She had extended and improved her roads and internal navigation, and had started to build a railway network. Banking facilities had been improved and some forerunners of the post-1850 Banking Revolution were already to be seen. There were a number of industrial districts with complex and diversified activities, which could be compared, on a smaller scale, with Lancashire or the Black Country.

Such qualitative changes had been accompanied by a relatively high rate of economic and especially of industrial growth – at least according to nineteenth-century standards (P. Bairoch, years ago, pointed out that the long-term growth rates of Western economies in the nineteenth century never exceeded 2 per cent per year for aggregate national product, and 1·3 per cent for real incomes per capita).[12] Unfortunately, we are rather short of good quantitative data. For France, to be sure, three indices of industrial production are now available, but they display growth rates which are markedly different. For Belgium, a major quantitative research is in progress under Pierre Lebrun,[13] but its starting point is in the 1840s. And we are quite destitute for Germany and still more for Switzerland, except for some isolated figures. However, we do not need at the moment more than very rough estimates, and in this respect all the evidence suggests that the rates of growth of industrial production, and very likely also of national product, were lower in Continental countries than in Britain, at least in the aggregate (on a per capita basis, the picture would be different, owing to the much faster increase of the population of Britain – at a rate of 1·34 per cent per year from 1801 to 1851).

[12] P. Bairoch, 'Le Mythe de la croissance économique rapide au 19e siècle', *Revue de l'Institut de Sociologie*, 1962, No. 2, pp. 307 ff.

[13] P. Lebrun, 'L'Industrialisation en Belgique au XIXe siècle. Première approche et premiers résultats', in P. Léon, F. Crouzet, R. Gascon (eds.), *L'Industrialisation en Europe au XIXe Siècle* (Paris, 1972), pp. 171–86; and see note 52 below.

In 1964, M. Lévy-Leboyer computed an index of French industrial production, which grew between 1815 and 1850 at practically the same yearly rate as Hoffmann's index of British industrial output (3·25 per cent as against 3·5 per cent).[14] But this optimistic view is not supported by other writers' calculations. For instance, a careful comparison by Jean Marczewski gives the following growth rates per year.[15]

		France 1815–24 to 1845–54 (%)	Great Britain 1811–21 to 1841–51 (%)
Agricultural product,	aggregate	1·2	1·5
Agricultural product,	per capita	0·7	0·2
Industrial product,	aggregate	2·5	3·7
Industrial product,	per capita	2·0	2·3
Material product,	aggregate	1·9	2·7
Material product,	per capita	1·4	1·3

I have also built up an index of French industrial production, which shows a still lower rate of growth: 1·6 per cent per year between 1815 and 1850; but for various reasons, this figure may be too low, and moreover, this index grows at a faster rate during the later part of the period under consideration: 2 per cent for 1830–50, 2·3 per cent for 1830–60. Undoubtedly, French industrial growth and change accelerated in the 1830s and the early 1840s to reach a peak, after the depression of the late 1840s, during the 1850s, and therefore the gap with the British growth rate narrowed (a fact which appears also from Marczewski's calculations).[16] This acceleration, which would be still more pronounced in the case of Germany (whose industries had been seriously depressed in the early part of the period, but progressed

[14] Lévy-Leboyer, p. 410; see also his 'Les Processus d'industrialisation: le cas de l'Angleterre et de la France', *Revue Historique*, CCXXXIX, 2, April–June 1968, pp. 282, 284, 297; 'La croissance économique en France au XIXe siècle. Résultats préliminaires', *Annales ESC*, XXIV, 4, July–August 1968, p. 793, with a different index and a growth rate of 2·98 per cent for French industrial output, 1815–44.

[15] Marczewski, pp. cxxxvi, cxxxviii. Products are computed at constant prices, from Deane and Cole's figures for Britain, and from Markovitch's for France; adjustments were made to take into account differences in price levels.

[16] Crouzet, 'Essai de construction', pp. 85–8, 96.

sharply later), heralded the unprecedentedly rapid growth of the post-1850 years – what David Landes has called 'Continental industry's coming of age'.[17]

The idea of a slower rate of growth in France than in Britain is supported by the available data for some major industries – an approach which can also be used for the other Continental countries, for which aggregate indices are lacking. For instance, raw cotton consumption increased between 1815–17 and 1849–51 at a mean rate of growth of 5·6 per cent per year in the United Kingdom, and 4·4 per cent in France. For Belgium, Germany and Switzerland, taken together, the available statistics plus a number of rough guesses would seem to show a rate of growth in cotton-inputs of 6·2 per cent during the same period; but for the total consumption of the four Continental countries, the rate of growth would be 5 per cent only.[18]

As for the output of pig-iron, between 1815 and 1847, it seems to have increased at a mean rate of 6 per cent per year in Britain and of 5·4 per cent in France. If one adds Belgium and Germany to France, and if one takes the years 1830–47, the rate would be 4·75 per cent as against over 6 per cent for Britain.

It seems therefore that the industrial production of Continental Western Europe grew more slowly than that of Britain between Waterloo and the mid-nineteenth century; there is of course a strong possibility that Belgium and Switzerland achieved higher growth rates than France, and perhaps also Germany at the end of the period (but on the other hand, the Netherlands obviously failed to industrialise); and average product per capita would seem to have grown at about the British rate, if not faster. But, even on the most favourable interpretation, Western Europe as a whole had, by 1850, failed to catch up with Great Britain, from the quantitative point of view; and as a result, in absolute terms, the gap between England and the Continental countries had enormously widened since 1815 and was now formidable, especially in the 'modern' sectors such as coal, iron, engineering,

17 D. S. Landes, *The Unbound Prometheus: Technological Change and Industrial Development in Western Europe from 1750 to the Present* (Cambridge, 1969), p. 193. The deep crisis of the late 1840s hastened change by devastating archaic rural/domestic industries.

18 Calculations from *ibid.*, p. 165, completed by various figures, estimates and guesses, for which I ask the reader to take my word, as full references would be too lengthy. For Switzerland, I have calculated cotton consumption from the spindleage, and its ratio to French spinning capacity. An acceleration in the growth of the cotton industry in Belgium, Germany and Switzerland in the 1830s and 1840s seems certain. Their cotton consumption would have grown from about 5,000 m.t. around 1815 to 42,000 in 1849–50; with France included, the figures would be 19,000 to 100,000 m.t. Raw wool consumption seems to have increased in Britain and in France at the same rate from 1815 to 1850 (and it was of the same order of magnitude in both countries).

cotton. Britain was responsible for over half of the world iron output, and in 1850 made 2,249,000 metric tons of pig-iron, against 763,000 for Belgium, France and Germany (in this last country, pig-iron output per capita was 6 per cent only of the British figure). Britain's steam-power capacity was 1,290,000 HP, against 700,000 for the three Continental countries.[19] Her cotton-spinning industry had 21 million spindles, and Western Europe had a little over 6 million. With a much smaller territory, her railway mileage was equal to that of the five Continental countries taken together. The scale of the British economy, and especially of its industry, had become unrivalled; British predominance seemed overwhelming (and it was still more so in international trade and shipping). As Peter Mathias puts it, there was an impressive list of collective criteria of the process of industrialisation by which Britain could claim by 1850 to be 'unique by being first';[20] she had become 'the first industrial nation', and no Continental country, not even Belgium, was approaching her level of development.

From the qualitative, technological point of view, things might look somewhat better for the Continent, owing to the widespread introduction of British technology, but this must not conceal serious persistent lags and backwardness. Very few of the Continent's most progressive concerns were up to the best British practice. Machinery was generally less advanced (for instance, in cotton-spinning, the self-actor, invented in 1825, had come into general use in Britain after 1830; it was introduced in France in 1836, but did not become common until after 1847; in Germany it appeared in the 1840s only, while some hand-spinning survived for wool and flax); steam-power was far less used than in England; the size of firms and of plant was smaller, the large-scale, power-driven factory being still the exception; the productivity of labour was lower, costs higher; industry was also more scattered and often retained rural locations. Moreover, many sectors remained deeply archaic, both in their techniques and in their modes of production. Power-loom weaving in factories was not common in France, and was very rare in Germany and Switzerland; in 1847, whereas the British cotton industry had 250,000 power-looms, the Continental countries had about 45,000,[21] and a few thousands more

[19] Landes, p. 194.

[20] P. Mathias, 'British Industrialisation: Unique or not?', in Léon *et al.*, p. 503.

[21] There were 31,000 in France, under 8,000 in the Zollverein, 4,000 in Belgium, 3,000 (or less) in Switzerland. One can estimate the total number of power-looms (for all textiles) in 1850 as 300,000 in Britain and 60,000 in Western Europe.

in their other textile industries. In the iron industry, France made just under half of her pig-iron by coke-smelting, and Germany 11 per cent only; Belgium alone had almost entirely changed to the new process.

Although Western Europe had clearly entered the stage of the Industrial Revolution, this had been belated and was still incomplete by 1850; large lumps of the economic *Ancien Régime* survived. The period 1815–50 is a *Gründerzeit*: a number of industrial centres and of industrial firms of great promise had been established; industrialisation had crossed a first threshold, but nowhere had it attained the massive character it had in Britain, and in the aggregate change remained modest; it was only after 1850 that the great structural mutation took place. Even if a number of new industries *de pointe* grew fast, at rates of 4 or 5 per cent per year, they remained heavily outnumbered within economies which in their bulk were still traditional. As a matter of fact, the development in Western Europe of a 'modern' sector had given to its economy, by the mid-nineteenth century, a dualistic character, which Britain had not known, and which is often considered as characteristic of today's underdeveloped countries. This was especially clear from a geographical point of view: a few regions – in the van were Alsace and the Sambre-et-Meuse axis in Belgium – had achieved remarkable breakthroughs, but each country had to bear the burden of large backward and stagnating areas: Western and Southern France, the eastern provinces of Germany, the Alpine uplands in Switzerland, overpopulated Flanders with its decaying linen industry. These inter-regional differences in productivity and skills – in a word in 'modernity' – were in fact much more pronounced than those between nations 'in the aggregate', which generally are the only ones to be discussed. And the elimination of this dualism was to take a long time; in France one can wonder if it has yet been completely achieved – not to speak of Italy and Spain, if we look for once outside our chosen area.

Moreover, during the 1850–1914 period, Germany was to be the only Continental country to 'catch up' with Britain, from the double point of view of the volume of industrial production and of technology, although not for incomes per capita (or foreign trade and investment). And this resulted not only from a fast growth on the German side after the mid-nineteenth century, but also from a slowing down on the British side from the 1870s (or even possibly earlier) onwards. Likewise, if several Continental countries have now achieved levels of income per capita which are somewhat higher than the British, this is due not only to their own exertions, but also to the disappointing rates of growth of Britain during the last thirty years.

These observations (implying that a long stretch of time is necessary to lay the basis for a vigorous industrialisation) might lead to some pessimistic conclusions as to the prospects for today's underdeveloped countries – especially if we keep in mind that a reasonably satisfactory constellation of preconditions had been achieved in Western Europe by 1815, and that the gap with Britain in the matter of incomes per capita was narrow. It would seem that backward countries have little chance of catching up with the leaders, and even of narrowing the gap, unless economic and technological progress in the advanced countries slows down markedly. On the other hand, one might stress more optimistically Lévy-Leboyer's view that, around 1815, the modernisation of the Western European economy appeared to face obstacles and handicaps which could be thought insuperable, and that they were nonetheless partly overcome; the de-industrialisation which could be feared had not in fact taken place, lags had stimulated progress, and a number of positive results had been achieved.[22]

However, we must now try to explain why Western Europe was not more successful in the competition with Britain during the first half of the nineteenth century, why its rate of economic growth was not higher, and why, in the field of technology, it did not adopt on a large scale the best possible practice, but rather stopped regularly at yesterday's machinery and processes.

To start with this last point, one might think that the introduction of the 'modern' British technology was, by itself, a difficult process. For instance, David Landes has stressed that the technical gap between Britain and the Continent had not only widened during the Revolutionary and Napoleonic period, but was more difficult to fill up by 1815 than in the 1780s. He points out that the 'modern' type of plant, which was in use in Britain at the time of Waterloo, was much more expensive and complex than it had been thirty years earlier, and that the size of the smallest effective unit of production had greatly increased. The introduction of such plant therefore required more capital and more specialised skills, to build it, operate it and maintain it; as such resources were not readily available, manufacturers might

[22] Lévy-Leboyer, pp. 326, 409–14.

have been condemned to a sort of 'voluntary obsolescence', always installing equipment which was less productive than what was theoretically available to them.[23]

For his part, Mathias has suggested that the problems of diffusing innovations already extant and publicised may prove as formidable as those of initiating crucial inventions. The successful utilisation of the British innovations depended upon highly specialised artisan skills, which were essentially 'learning by doing' skills. These were relatively abundant in Britain, because of a peculiarly favourable context of resources and of a long-developing tradition, but their exportation abroad was difficult and slow, for the means of institutionalising them were undeveloped compared with the means of diffusing formal knowledge.[24]

This was certainly true in the eighteenth century, but, during the period under consideration, my own feeling is that the introduction and utilisation of any given machinery or process was never a serious problem, and that they could be successfully operated after relatively short teething-troubles, which might be due, in the iron industry, for instance, to differences in the quality and chemical composition of the raw materials. After all, the complexity of early nineteenth-century machinery must not be overestimated, and the skills of traditional craftsmen could be adapted to build or repair it.[25] And the abundant references, in British sources, to the awkwardness and incompetence of the Continental workers who were put in charge of the new plants – 'They are all of a lazy turn,' said an English carder returned from France in 1824[26] – are possibly not to be taken literally.

As for the British efforts at prohibiting the export of many types of machinery (especially textile machinery, as well as models and drawings) or the emigration of skilled workers, and at preventing industrial espionage, Dr W. O. Henderson and several other writers have demonstrated that these were largely ineffective.[27] Hosts of Continental manufacturers, engineers and civil servants came to Britain after 1815 and toured her industrial districts to study the new techniques; a number of British businessmen settled on the Continent and founded

23 Landes, p. 145–7. 24 Mathias, pp. 504–7.

25 Bairoch, *Révolution industrielle*, p. 206.

26 Giving evidence before the Select Committee on Artizans and Machinery; quoted from S. Pollard and C. Holmes, *Documents of European Economic History*, vol. I, *The Process of Industrialization 1750–1870* (London, 1968), p. 288.

27 W. O. Henderson, *Britain and Industrial Europe, 1750–1870* (Leicester, 1965, 2nd edn).

there 'modern' undertakings; thousands of skilled workers, foremen and managers migrated also. Although they were not always the best England could provide, though they drank too much, demanded high wages, changed jobs too often and were unpopular with the locals, they played a decisive role in teaching to Continental workers those very techniques, like puddling, which could be learned only 'by doing'; while the British industrialists were specially useful in introducing and developing the most sophisticated of the 'new' industries – machine-building.

However, one can still wonder if the British laws against the export of machinery, which were in force up to 1842, did not hinder technological progress on the Continent: a foreign manufacturer, who wanted to set up, say, a new cotton mill, could not order straight away from Manchester a complete set of the most up-to-date machinery; he had to get hold, by hook or by crook, of some models, blueprints or spare parts, then have them smuggled out of England, and eventually have them copied by his own workmen or by some local engineering firm. Time-lags in the introduction of best practice were thus inevitable. On the other hand, P. Bairoch has maintained that the British bans on machinery exports, plus the tariff protection and the high transport costs which reinforced their effects, had beneficial long-term effects for the Continental countries, which were thus forced to create an engineering industry of their own, while today under-developed countries can take the easy path of buying abroad all the machinery they need.[28]

As a matter of fact, Western Europe was able fairly quickly to achieve a sort of technological independence, to build most of the machinery it needed, and to dispense with the help of the British migrants. New generations of engineers, technicians and skilled workers were soon trained, and in the 1830s and 1840s Belgium and France were able in their turn to supply to more backward countries – especially Germany to start with – the skilled cadres they needed. As for the engineering industry, it made undoubted progress; it was said in 1824 that British-made textile machinery was 40 per cent cheaper than French, and steam engines 30 per cent, but the gap seems to have narrowed later. Several witnesses before the 1841 committee on the exportation of tools and machinery stressed the rapid progress which had been made in Belgium and France, and the 'ingenuity' of the

[28] Bairoch, *Révolution industrielle*, pp. 130–5.

French: 'very inventive people ... they have no longer any difficulty in making any machine ... [they] make as good machines as we do'.[29] These technical achievements must not of course be overrated; if France, for instance, built all sorts of machinery, its output of each type was relatively limited. Still, it is important that within ten years of the Rainhill trials, Belgium, France and even Germany were able themselves to build practically all the locomotives they needed for their expanding railway networks, and that very few engines were in fact imported from England, except during the early years of railway construction. One can also observe that several important inventions – like the multi-tubular boiler, the steam-hammer, the wool-combing machine – were made simultaneously and independently in Britain and in France.

These technical achievements were partly due to the progress on the Continent of technical and scientific education, which was a noteworthy development of the period – from the French *Grandes Ecoles* and their imitations abroad, to the German and Swiss *Technische Hochschüle* and the numerous 'popular' evening classes in applied sciences. And this remains true, though one may readily concede that the new élite of engineers and technicians remained small in number, that education on the whole was far too 'classical', and that Continental countries could have done much more to develop its technical side.

It seems therefore that there was no *purely technical* barrier to the diffusion of British innovations. In fact, most of them were introduced fairly quickly on the Continent; the trouble was that they came into general use quite slowly, and more slowly than in Britain. For instance, coke-burning blast-furnaces and the puddling process appeared in France in 1817–18,[30] but thirty years later over half the make of pig-iron was smelted with charcoal. Likewise, power-looms were experimented with in France in the 1820s, just at the time when they were catching on in Britain; but they had not triumphed, even in the cotton industry, by mid-century. If British innovations were not adopted more quickly and more widely in Continental industry, it was because manufacturers did not want them in a very broad sense: because they did not appear profitable, or because they were not adapted to their lines of production, or because they could not be

[29] Pollard and Holmes, pp. 276–7, 285–97. The 1841 committee recommended to permit the exportation of machinery from Britain, in order to nip in the bud the nascent engineering industry of the Continent.

[30] Le Creusot had been an earlier, but isolated case.

afforded. The problem is therefore economic, much more than technical, and it is linked to the question which has been put formerly – why was economic growth not faster in Western Europe during this period; and why was structural change not more rapid and more widespread?

This is ground which has been well laboured by many writers, who have unearthed a whole complex of obstacles or 'bottlenecks', which are supposed to have hindered economic growth, especially in the case of France, the favourite whipping-boy of many scholars. The argument has been sometimes carried to the point that one is surprised that any growth took place at all. I do not intend to discuss thoroughly these obstacles, inasmuch as new economic historians have made lists of factors unfashionable, and I shall concentrate on a few points which seem to me of special importance.

I shall start with the demand side, which is often neglected, wrongly in my view, as I think that the narrowness of the markets which were available to their industries was one major factor in the Continental countries' slow growth and change.

The narrowness of the home markets is evident in the case of the smaller countries: Switzerland, which had only 2 million inhabitants by 1835 (plus, up to 1848, internal customs and tolls); Belgium, which suffered greatly from the loss of the French market in 1814, and again from the loss in 1830 of her markets in Holland and in her colonies (which had partly offset the separation from France), and which, after her independence, repeatedly sought a customs union either with France or with Germany; also the small German states up to the establishment of the Zollverein in 1834. As a matter of fact, the favourable influence which the Zollverein had upon German industries can be used to support the view I am putting forward. I know, of course, that present-day German scholars do not think, like their predecessors (who believed too much in the providential role played by the Prussian State), that the Zollverein was *the* decisive factor in the economic progress of Germany; but none the less, by creating a large 'common market' in Central Europe, it gave a strong stimulus to German industry.

In the larger countries, France and Prussia, opportunities in the home market were restricted by several factors: the inadequacy of the transport system (of which more later), the variations from province to province in consumers' habits and tastes, and the low purchasing power of a large majority of the population. This last fact was aggravated, in countries which remained predominantly agrarian, by the fall of agricultural prices from 1817 onwards, which brought about a deterioration in the terms of trade of agriculture towards industry; and some time lapsed before the rise in the volume of agricultural production had offset the fall in prices and had thus restored rural purchasing power. Anyhow, the fragmentation of landholdings which prevailed in France, in the Low Countries, and in western and southern Germany was rather unfavourable to industrial development, as small cultivators were only marginally involved in the market economy, and saved to buy land rather than manufactured goods.[31] There was a sort of vicious circle in which the narrowness of urban markets in countries which had few large towns discouraged agricultural improvements, and the sluggishness of rural demand slowed down industrial growth. That this circle was broken some time after 1820 by the beginnings of the agricultural revolution, with favourable induced effects for industrial growth, has been asserted by several writers. This is true especially of P. Bairoch, who has built a model in which increased demand from the rural sector (consequent upon higher agricultural productivity), both for textiles and for iron products (the latter required for better implements), is the mainspring of the Industrial Revolution. M. Lévy-Leboyer also sees an important engine of growth, in the prosperity of the French countryside in the 1830s and 1840s, owing to the rise in production and the improvement of its terms of trade. However, Michel Morineau has maintained that, as late as 1840, there were very few signs of an agricultural revolution in France, where in most regions agriculture remained deeply stagnant and backward, if not primitive, and where cereal yields had scarcely improved as compared with the eighteenth century.[32]

[31] This is why the 'Prussian way' of abolition of the 'feudal' system through expropriation of the peasantry is often considered as more congenial to modern economic growth than the French (or rather Western-European) system of small peasant-ownership, which pre-dated the French Revolution, but which the latter – and the Napoleonic inheritance statutes – consolidated. It must be kept in mind, however, that a good deal of French land was still owned by large landowners, though their estates were often divided into small farms for leasing.

[32] Bairoch, *Révolution industrielle*, pp. 98 ff.; Lévy-Leboyer, 'La Croissance économique', p. 794; M. Morineau, 'Y a-t-il eu une révolution agricole en France au XVIIIe siècle?', *Revue Historique*, CCXXXIX, 2, April–June 1968, pp. 299–326. This does not exclude, however, some productivity increases in the progressive areas of northern France. For Germany, W. Hoffmann, 'The Take-off in Germany', in W. W. Rostow (ed.), *The Economics of Take-off into Sustained Growth* (London, 1963), pp. 103–4, mentions an 'extensive growth' of agriculture up

The fragmentation and inadequacy of the Continental markets made them unsuitable for mass production, and this was one of the reasons for the 'voluntary obsolescence' which has been stressed earlier, of Continental industry, as marginal gains from the best kind of plant over less capital-intensive techniques were smaller than in England and economies of scale an unrealistic proposition. For instance, the few large ironworks, using coke-smelting and puddling, which were established in France around 1820, were for years a disappointment to their owners (some of whom went bankrupt), who found it quite difficult to dispose of an output which was too large for the available markets.

On the other hand, Continental countries were not in a favourable position to offset the narrowness of their home markets by developing a strong export trade. During the Napoleonic wars they had been cut off from overseas markets, and had lost practically all those they had enjoyed in the late eighteenth century. Britain had established an almost complete monopoly in these markets (especially in the United States and in Latin America) and she was very largely able to retain this after Waterloo, owing to the lower prices and better quality of her manufactured goods, to the acquired habits and tastes of overseas customers, and to the commercial infrastructure which Britain had set up in many countries. The Continentals found it very difficult to regain a foothold overseas after 1815; those industries which, in the eighteenth century, had been dependent upon sea-borne trade, and which had been badly hit during the Napoleonic wars, went on decaying or stagnating; and for some time Western Europe was not able to take advantage of the fast growth in the volume of world trade, which Kuznets has estimated at 50 per cent per decade between 1820 and 1850,[33] and which was undoubtedly faster than the expansion of demand in internal markets. The counterproof is that those Continental industries which expanded the fastest were precisely those which succeeded in recovering export markets, as we shall see later. To be sure, French exports increased at a fast rate of 4 per cent per year, but, starting from a very low level, they were between a third and a half of British exports, and equivalent to a small fraction (around 5 per cent)

to the 1860s, mostly through extension of tillage, with slow increases in yields per acre, but faster progress in labour's productivity.

33 Quoted in I. B. Kravis, 'Trade as a Handmaiden of Growth: Similarities between the Nineteenth and Twentieth Centuries', *The Economic Journal*, No. 320, December 1970, p. 861.

of national product, so that their induced effects on the economy were limited.[34]

It appears therefore that once a major 'modern' industrialising economy – Britain – had been established, the whole international trading context became unfavourable for other nations, and the mere presence of the new industrial giant restricted greatly the opportunities for them to base a major industrial impetus upon foreign markets.[35] Likewise, without sharing in any way the leftist view that under-development is a consequence of 'imperialism', we must admit that today the very existence of the advanced industrial countries is, in some respects, a barrier to the industrial progress of under-developed areas. On the other hand, the narrowness of many of these countries' home markets, due to the scanty population of many of them and to their low incomes per capita, is also an enormous obstacle to economic growth.

Anyhow, the demand factor seems to have been vital for Western European countries during the period under consideration, while the acceleration of their growth during its later part must largely be accounted for by the widening of the market, by the new opportunities which resulted from agricultural prosperity, the rise of foreign trade, the Zollverein, and, last, but not least, railway building. If the coming of the railway did not have much effect on the transport system as a whole before the 1850s – except in the few areas which were served by the first lines – it created a relatively enormous demand for all kinds of goods, and David Landes sees it as the 'most important single stimulus to industrial growth' in the 1840s.[36]

This brings us to the transport problem which is interrelated to both the demand and supply sides. The inadequacy of the transport network in Continental Europe is often mentioned as one of the major bottlenecks which hindered economic growth and change, and which was not really broken before the large-scale building of railways in the 1850s and 1860s. However, like the shortcomings of the banking

[34] Marczewski, pp. lx–lxiii.

[35] As for import substitution, there was not much opportunity in a country like France which had heavily protected its home market from the start (except for new products, like locomotives); and in non-protected, or half-protected markets, as in Germany, English competition was too strong for a long time. But import substitution was a likely factor in the spurt of German industry after 1840.

[36] Landes, p. 153; but he observes also (p. 175), that the fast-growing demand for iron products gave to many ironmasters a security of outlets which permitted them to sit back and reap good profits with obsolete equipment.

system, it is not really a 'primary' factor, in the sense that its deficiencies can be traced either to faulty government policy, or to inadequate private entrepreneurship, or to capital shortage. I wonder also if its influence has not been exaggerated. The high cost of transport was certainly an obstacle to the growth and technical progress of heavy industries, especially iron and chemicals. France is the classic example, because of the distance which separated the few coal-fields which had good coking coal from both the iron-ore deposits and the traditional charcoal-burning ironworks. Owing to the high price of coal, the change from charcoal to coal was not economical for most ironmasters, and this, much more than their supposed conservatism, was the main reason for the relatively slow introduction of English innovations in the French iron industry. High transport costs gave also geographical protection to traditional producers and restricted the outlets for the output of the 'modern' *forges à l'anglaise*, the marketing difficulties of which have been pointed out earlier.

On the other hand, transport was much less of a problem for the textile industries, the raw materials and finished goods of which were far less bulky than coal and ores. It is significant that prosperous and progressive cotton industries developed in Alsace and in Switzerland, very far from the ports which imported raw cotton (while the cotton industry of Normandy, which was close to Le Havre, is well known for its relative stagnation), and also far from any coal-field. On the other hand, the fast rise of a modern cotton-spinning industry in the Lille area (which, unlike Alsace and Switzerland, had no water-power) took place only when canals linking it to the neighbouring coal-fields had been dug; it could then turn to steam-power on a large scale. And there is no doubt that the slow but regular improvement of transport facilities, which was achieved everywhere in Western Europe during our period, was an important engine of growth.

If we now turn, more briefly, to the supply side, it is clear that, broadly speaking, factor endowment was less favourable in Continental Western Europe than in Britain, and, in addition, each country, with the exception of Belgium, was labouring under some serious deficiency in this respect.

From the point of view of natural resources, Belgium and Germany had rich coal-fields (though the richest deposits in the Ruhr basin were not discovered until 1838). But France was poorly endowed, at one and the same time as far as the quantity of reserves, the quality of the coal and the mining conditions were concerned. Switzerland and Holland had no coal whatever, although the former had plenty of water-power and the latter could import coal easily. I know it has become unfashionable to assign any importance to the scarcity of coal as a brake on industrialisation in the nineteenth century, but I think this is going too far, and that in the case of France the coal factor was important, inasmuch as the distribution of the coal resources was unsatisfactory in relation to other resources (especially iron-ore) and to established industrial districts.

As for capital, it was undoubtedly less abundant and more expensive on the Continent than in Britain. Moreover, there was a propensity to invest in land, buildings and government securities rather than in industrial ventures, or just to hoard. Also, the banking system and the capital market were in an embryonic state; they were not able and even did not try to drain savings towards industrial long-term investment. However, it would be wrong to think of a capital 'bottleneck' as a decisive obstacle to industrialisation. Even for Germany, which was undoubtedly the 'poorest' country, K. Borchardt has maintained that there was no absolute shortage of capital and that commercial interest rates were quite reasonable.[37] In France, within a few years from the end of the wars, the ability to save had been restored; and M. Lévy-Leboyer has convincingly refuted the traditional accusations levelled against the malthusianism of the Paris *Haute Banque*, by showing that it in fact supplied a lot of risk capital to the new industries, and channelled savings towards progressive sectors.[38] In Switzerland there was an abundance of capital and a willingness to invest it in industry, while the pioneer role of the *Société Générale de Belgique* in investment banking, as well as the important role it played in the rise of Belgium's heavy industries, are well known. Moreover, recent research and thinking has tended to eliminate the key role capital was formerly supposed to have played in the beginnings of modern economic growth and in industrialisation. The stock of capital and its rate of increase are no longer considered as the crucial determinants of a country's rate of progress. None the less capital remains a permissive factor, and it was not unimportant that in the 1830s and 1840s the investment proportion was probably a good deal

[37] Landes, p. 155, who, however, asserts that the supply of capital was limited in the aggregate, as was proved by the tension on capital markets during the railway boom of the 1840s.

[38] Lévy-Leboyer, pp. 699–704, 707–10.

lower in Continental countries (5 per cent or somewhat more) than in Britain (10 per cent). And at the microeconomic level, one can note the important results which occurred from relatively small investments by Basel capitalists in the Alsatian cotton industry,[39] by British capital in the French railways, by French and Belgian capital in several German industrial undertakings. The support given to the Belgian economy and state by the Paris house of Rothschild is also worth mentioning. But it must be stressed that these investments were either made in a favourable environment, or accompanied by transfer of technical and organisational skills to put them into effective use.[40]

It was in the matter of labour that the Continent had its only comparative advantage in relation to Britain, as the level of wages was everywhere inferior to the British (roughly by a third in Switzerland around 1830); and, as a matter of fact, labour became cheaper from west to east: it was cheaper in eastern France (for instance Alsace) than in western France (Normandy), and cheaper still in Switzerland and Germany.[41] Of course, this was not an unmitigated advantage: low labour costs were undoubtedly a major factor in the protracted survival of handwork in many Continental areas, especially of hand-loom weaving. Moreover, although the Continent had some large pools of labour which was both skilled and cheap, it had also a lot of workers who were poorly trained, not accustomed to and even hostile to factory work; and generally speaking, using the same kind of plant or machinery, the productivity of labour was inferior to that which prevailed in Britain.

It remains to point out that, from the point of view of the supply of entrepreneurship, of the socio-cultural environment and of the social values (which remained imbued with the anti-capitalist, anti-business tradition), the Continent was in an inferior position to Britain. In Germany, especially in its eastern parts, society remained deeply aristocratic, the middle class was weak, lived in mediocrity, and suffered from feelings of inferiority. In France, on the other hand, the bourgeoisie had been well integrated by the Revolution and by Napoleon into the system of land-ownership and of government, with the result that there was a steady drain of talent away from business; and if the timorous and conservative frame of mind of the French

[39] They invested also later in the cotton industry of the Grand Duchy of Baden.

[40] R. Cameron, 'Some Lessons of History for Developing Nations', *The American Economic Review*, LVII, 2, May 1967, pp. 313–16.

[41] Lévy-Leboyer, pp. 286–7.

business class has been exaggerated by many writers (recent research has stressed many cases of flexibility and innovating ability), this reputation is not entirely underserved. Moreover, although there was much more laissez-faire on the Continent after 1815 than in the eighteenth century, governments and bureaucracies had not completely given up the colbertist tradition, and their interventions, which used to be loudly praised by old textbooks, were in fact quite often inept and harmful. In France, for instance, civil servants, who were afraid of the power of large-scale capitalism, opposed the development of joint-stock companies, with harmful results on the progress of banking and railways. And Joseph Schumpeter has suggested that the Prussian state would hardly have followed a different policy from the one it chose, if it had wanted to prevent any sort of economic growth!

It is clear therefore that none of the Western European countries, except Belgium, had, during our period, a complete and satisfactory constellation of factors. Germany had coal and cheap labour, but lacked capital, was not united economically up to 1834, and had an unsuitable social structure. Switzerland had capital and cheap labour, but no natural resources, except water-power; her home market was very small; she was geographically isolated and surrounded by protectionist neighbours. France, despite all appearances, was in an unfavourable position; at a time when, to be able to withstand British competition, one needed either cheap coal and iron, or very cheap labour, coal was more expensive than in Britain, Belgium and Germany; and wages, though lower than in Britain, were higher than in Germany and Switzerland; her only advantages were some capital resources, and the skill of part of her labour force.[42] As for Holland, she stagnated during the whole period, owing to a mistaken policy which tried to restore her old staple trade, and owing to the sclerosis of her upper classes. In contrast, Belgium had coal and iron ore, cheap labour, capital (partly from French sources); she built very early the main lines of her railway network, and was thus the pioneer country on the Continent in industrialisation, investment banking and railways; and yet she had difficulties in finding markets, and her activity underwent sharp cyclical fluctuations. Even at the regional level, factor mixes were not quite satisfactory. For instance, Alsace had

[42] Lévy-Leboyer, pp. 157, 706; also 116–17, on the position of Paris, the largest manufacturing centre in the country, which had no water-power, where coal was imported from Belgium at high prices, and where labour, owing to the high cost of living, demanded high wages.

water-power, a cheap skilled labour force, a weberian group of first-class Protestant entrepreneurs; but she was far from any coal-field and from the sea-board. But it would be useless to look for some dominating factor of backwardness, in order to build a model around it: in fact it is the combination of factors which is less favourably oriented than in Britain. Likewise, the progressive erosion of obstacles and loosening of bottlenecks seem to explain the acceleration of growth and change in the later part of the period.

It is, however, rewarding to push the analysis somewhat more in depth, as the main achievements of Continental countries were in particular sectors of industry, where they were obtained by a successful adaptation to the available factor mix. As I stressed earlier, the only relative advantage the Continent enjoyed over Britain was in the cheapness of labour. This was not of much use in the field of common or low quality articles, which Britain could mass-produce with modern machinery more cheaply than the Continentals could by hand process.[43] But in the manufacture of high quality or fashionable, luxury or semi-luxury goods, the production of which it was difficult to mechanise, and in the cost of which, anyway, labour remained by far the main component, while machinery and fuel costs were small or nil, the Continentals could compete with Britain. Moreover, some groups of workers had a skill and a taste which was up to the British standards, if not better; for instance, in weaving mixed fabrics of cotton, wool or silk; in creating attractive figured designs and brilliant colour patterns. Industrialists who knew how to use these advantages could make goods which were more attractive and cheaper than their British competitors; they were thus able to penetrate foreign markets and to enjoy a faster expansion than those who had to be satisfied with the home market.[44] Moreover, profit margins per unit on such high-quality goods were larger than on coarse articles; capital accumulation within these branches of industry was faster, so that part of these profits was re-invested to develop and modernise the 'basic' industries which made semi-finished articles.

This is why Maurice Lévy-Leboyer has contrasted the 'up-stream' or 'backwards' industrialisation of the Continent with the 'down-stream' or 'forwards' industrialisation of Britain. The English Indus-

[43] However, up to the generalisation of the power-loom in Britain, the Continent was not in a bad competitive position as far as weaving was concerned; Lévy-Leboyer, pp. 114–15.

[44] Inasmuch as, in the 1830s, the demand for luxury goods revived on foreign markets; on French textile exports, cf. Lévy-Leboyer, pp. 145 ff., 175–6.

trial Revolution started with the 'basic' industries, making semi-finished goods such as cotton yarn or pig-iron, and later progressed downstream to the mechanisation of the consumption goods industries, such as weaving. The typical example is Lancashire, which, because of its superiority in cotton-spinning, 'integrated' progressively a whole range of more differentiated manufactures, such as cotton-printing, silk, engineering, etc. On the Continent, the successful industrial centres were those which took advantage of the cheapness and skill of labour to develop first the making of specialised and labour-intensive quality consumption goods, and then, later on, were able to move 'upstream' towards mechanised spinning or the primary iron industry.[45]

This model is attractive, but its symmetry is too perfect. True enough, at the beginning of the English Industrial Revolution, in the late eighteenth century, the most dramatic changes in technology and structure took place in industries which made semi-finished goods – mainly machine spinning and the primary iron industry. Those changes, however, were achieved from the springboard of large and prosperous consumption goods industries. In most cases, the founders of cotton mills and ironworks were leaders of the domestic textile industries or of the secondary metal trades; a large part of the capital for the new undertakings came from traditional industry. The transformation of British industry thus was achieved in an 'upstream' direction. Later only, during the second quarter of the nineteenth century, an inverse movement took place, particularly during the mechanisation of weaving, which was partly the work of master-spinners, who added to their mills some weaving sheds, equipped with power-looms. The same process was repeated many times on the Continent, with a time-lag, of course.

On the other hand, M. Lévy-Leboyer was right to point out that in cotton, the backward and relatively stagnant centres were those, like Normandy or Saxony, which made coarse articles, which only high tariff walls and/or wretched conditions for labour could save from British competition, but which could not be exported, and left narrow profit margins for reinvestment. Whereas the typical successful district was Alsace, from which quality printed-cottons were massively exported, and which progressed by upstream integration from printing to weaving, spinning, machine-building and chemicals, and which, in

[45] Lévy-Leboyer, pp. 49, 65–6, 95, 169–71, 288–92, 410.

the technical field, was the most progressive centre on the Continent. North-eastern Switzerland played also the card of quality goods, and specialised in articles with high labour inputs, which were not amenable to mechanisation: embroideries and light hand-printed cottons, with bright colours and attractive designs, which were varied indefinitely to suit the tastes of different markets. Their output increased enormously and they penetrated many overseas markets, but mechanisation was restricted to the spinning branch.[46] In the wool industry the great French success was the invention, from 1825 onwards, of the *nouveautés*, light fabrics, woven on Jacquard looms, of mixed woollen and worsted yarns, or wool and silk, with a great variety and a constant change of design. The most dynamic centres were those like Reims, Roubaix or Elbeuf, which specialised in these new products and were thus enabled later to establish a 'modern' spinning industry, especially for worsted yarn. One might also mention the artistic industries of Paris, or the silk industry of Lyons, which, despite higher labour costs than its competitors, re-established its leadership by the repeated imaginative creation of new fashionable goods, which rival centres had to imitate.[47] In the iron industry some undertakings, like Cockerill, started in machine-building and later on extended to the primary sector; others, like Le Creusot under the Schneiders, became profitable only when they had diversified towards engineering; or more frequently, especially in Germany and in *le Nord*, ironworks started by puddling imported pig-iron and later set up coke-burning blast furnaces. In Germany, anyhow, the most flourishing sector was the secondary metal industries, such as the hardware and cutlery of the Sauerland; and the greatest advance was made in the manufacture of those finished goods – steel and steel products – that demanded special skills and high inputs of labour.[48]

It appears therefore that Continental industrialisation was different, in its pattern and process, from the British, and moreover that, broadly speaking, it was successful to the extent that it was different. An interesting remark in that respect can be made about the tariff policy of Prussia, which was extended after 1834 to the whole Zollverein. Duties were high on finished articles, but low on raw materials and semi-

[46] Béatrice Veyrassat-Herren, 'Les centres de gravité de l'industrialisation en Suisse au XIXe siècle (Aspects géographiques et sectoriels): Le rôle du coton', in Léon *et al.*, pp. 481–94.

[47] Lévy-Leboyer, pp. 121 ff., 130, 137 ff.

[48] *Ibid.*, pp. 291, 375; Landes, pp. 178–9. The Germans, with the inventions of Lohage and Bremme, and of Krupp, were in the vanguard of progress, as far as steel was concerned.

finished goods, such as yarn or pig-iron; this system encouraged the 'upstream' industrialisation process, which was especially well-marked in Germany. For instance, the making of iron by puddling developed a great deal in the 1830s, using imported British or Belgian pig-iron, and it was only after the duties on pig-iron had been raised in 1844 that coke-smelting progressed in a big way. This differential customs policy seems to have been much better conceived than the French system, which prohibited or taxed heavily any kind of imports and encouraged therefore the development of high-cost and inefficient basic industries. The industrialisation of Germany was delayed, limited at first to consumption goods industries, based on cheap labour and imported semi-finished goods,[49] but she started to integrate backwards and to become less dependent on imports in the 1840s; and a strong basis for the jump forwards after 1850 had been laid.

It is clear also that the strategic decisions of manufacturers were dictated much more by the objective conditions which prevailed in each country or each district, by the market opportunities and the available factor mix, to which they tried, more or less successfully, to adapt their initiatives, than by 'social values' or 'national' aptitudes for entrepreneurship and innovation. The French, for instance, have been credited with a sort of innate preference for making luxury goods; to be sure, their production was relatively more developed in France than elsewhere, but mainly because the French well-to-do made up a large market for such goods and because foreign aristocracies had inherited from the eighteenth century a taste for French articles; in addition, France had highly skilled craftsmen. Moreover, these conditions, much more than an innate conservatism or the structure of the family firm, explain the low level of concentration in most Continental industries, the dispersion of manufacturing activities. In the making of quality and fashion goods, where short runs of production were the rule, flexibility was indispensable; work had to be divided. In addition, mechanisation had to be progressive and limited, especially in weaving, where for a long time the power-loom was unsuitable for fine fabrics. So an original character of French industrialisation was the parallel growth of 'small'-scale and 'large'-scale industry. As for growth, it was restricted by the smaller demand for luxury goods, both on the home and foreign markets. But these handicaps were more or

[49] Because of these conditions, it relied much less than France on quality articles, except for a few specialities.

less inescapable, owing to the initial lag behind England. One could perhaps say that Continental manufacturers made the best of a bad job, and after all, they were also innovators – especially the French, but in a different way from the British, because they depended upon a different constellation of factors: they invented new products and new fashions, rather than new machinery. The achievements of Continental industry may have been more creditable than was suggested earlier.[50]

Is it possible to draw from this analysis some lessons which could be applied to the industrialisation of the underdeveloped countries of today? A first point might be the necessity of widening the market, which in most underdeveloped countries, except those with very large populations, is far too narrow for absorbing the mass production of contemporary advanced industry and for achieving specialisation and economies of scale. This can be obtained by increasing rural purchasing power through higher agricultural productivity, which at present, thanks to various items of scientific and technical progress, seems more feasible than some years ago, despite the functional resistance to change of traditional agrarian systems. But a short cut might be the formation of regional customs unions, on the pattern of the Zollverein, with a reasonable level of protection – although one wonders if it is politically a practical proposition.

On the other hand, the obvious conclusion to be drawn from Western Europe's nineteenth-century history is that a successful industrialisation is not a slavish imitation of the more advanced countries and possibly that it is the most successful when it is the most original. It has to adapt to the configuration of the national or regional economies, to fit closely to the circumstances of time and place, to the available constellation of factors and especially to existing traditional skills of the labour force. Moreover, it is useful to look for the *créneaux* – or niches, the gaps in the range of products, where its factor endowment will enable the developing economy to compete successfully with established producers and to penetrate foreign markets, in order to achieve a fast growth. It is clear that in most cases this would mean, as in early nineteenth-century Western Europe, a concentration on the industries best suited to the relative abundance and cheapness of labour, and to

[50] Owing to the importance of quality goods in French production, the differences in the *volume* of output between England and France are reduced when one considers the *values* – for instance in the cotton industry.

the shortage of capital, on 'light' rather than 'heavy' industries – but keeping in mind that these industries are not inevitably the same as in the last century, and that, for instance, a number of engineering and even electronic industries are today labour-intensive.[51] This is the path which the 'new industrial countries' of the Far East, South Korea, Taiwan, Hong-Kong, Singapore, have entered, with amazing success, but I should hesitate to assert that it is open to allcomers.

Post scriptum

This chapter is derived from a paper which was presented at a conference in Edinburgh in 1971, which aimed at studying economic development in the long run, with an historical perspective which is often ignored by development economics; this explains the references to the Third World and to the lessons to be drawn from Western European experience. Since then, many important books – both general and monographic – have been devoted to the economic history of nineteenth-century Europe,[52] but I shall only mention here work which fills up some of the gaps in quantitative data, which are deplored on p. 347.

According to P. Bairoch, between 1800 and 1860, the aggregate GNP of 'Industrialised Europe' (Belgium, France, Sweden, Switzerland, UK) at constant prices grew at an average rate of 1·78 per cent per year; on a per capita basis, the rate is 1·13 per cent.[53]

[51] M. M. Postan, 'L'Expérience de l'industrialisation européenne et les problèmes actuels des pays sous-développés, in Léon *et al.*, p. 51.

[52] A. Milward and S. B. Saul, *The Economic Development of Continental Europe, 1780–1870* (London, 1973); C. M. Cipolla (ed.), *The Fontana Economic History of Europe*, vol. 4 (1 and 2), *The Emergence of Industrial Societies* (London, 1973, 2 vols.); P. Léon, *Histoire économique et sociale du monde*, tome 3, *Inerties et Révolutions 1730–1840*, edited by L. Bergeron (Paris, 1978); S. Pollard, *Peaceful Conquest: The Industrialization of Europe, 1760–1970* (Oxford, 1981); C. Trebilcock, *The Industrialization of the Continental Powers, 1780–1914* (London, 1981); also P. Bairoch, *Commerce extérieur et développement économique de l'Europe au XIXe siècle* (Paris, 1976).

On France: F. Caron, *Histoire économique de la France XIXe–XXe siècles* (Paris, 1981); F. Braudel and E. Labrousse (eds.), *Histoire économique et sociale de la France*, tome III, *L'Avènement de l'ère industrielle (1789 – années 1880)* (Paris, 1976, 2 vols.); M. Lévy-Leboyer and F. Bourguignon, *L'Economie française au XIXe siècle. Analyse Macro-économique* (Paris, 1985).

On Belgium: P. Lebrun *et al.*, *Essai sur la Révolution industrielle en Belgique, 1770–1847* (Bruxelles, 1979, 2nd edn, 1981); and the other volumes of *Histoire quantitative et développement de la Belgique au XIXe siècle*. Also J. Mokyr, *Industrialization in the Low Countries (1795–1850)* (New Haven, 1976).

On Switzerland: J. F. Bergier, *Histoire économique de la Suisse* (Lausanne, 1984); B. Veyrassat-Herren, *Négociants et fabricants dans l'industrie cotonnière suisse 1760–1840. Aux origines financières de l'industrialisation* (Lausanne, 1982).

[53] P. Bairoch, 'Europe's Gross National Product: 1800–1975', *Journal of European Economic History*, V, 2, Autumn 1976, especially pp. 279 and 281, Tables 2 and 4; *Commerce extérieur et développement économique de l'Europe au XIXe siècle*, pp. 139, 156, Tables 44 and 51.

The sum of the GNP of Belgium, France, Germany, the Netherlands and Switzerland had a rate of growth between 1830 and 1850 of 1·80 per cent per year; the UK GNP grew at 2·15 per cent. During the period 1830–60, Belgium and Switzerland had growth rates of GNP, both aggregate and per capita, slightly higher than those of the UK, but France, Germany and the Netherlands had markedly lower rates (the position is the same for the growth of industrial production).[54]

As for O'Brien and Keyder, they show, between 1815/24 and 1845/54, an increase in total material output which is markedly larger in Britain than in France (+66 per cent as against +48 per cent or 43 per cent); but on a per capita basis, France (+26 or 22 per cent) has the advantage over Britain (+12·5 per cent), so that, by 1845, she had made up for the lag which had occurred during the Napoleonic wars.[55] On the other hand, Crafts has found that the gap between the British and French products per capita had widened from 1830 to 1850.[56] Anyhow, the consensus nowadays is that the economic growth of Britain, which had been relatively slow in the late eighteenth century and during the wars, markedly accelerated after 1815.

P. Bairoch has also done a study of industrialisation levels per capita: between 1800 and 1860, this level increased by a factor of 4 in Britain, of 3 in Belgium and Switzerland, of 2 in France and Germany (and of course, it had been much higher in Britain by 1800 than on the Continent).[57] Bairoch has also estimated the share of world industrial output:

	1800 (%)	1830 (%)	1860 (%)
United Kingdom	4·3	9·5	19·3
Belgium + France + Germany + Switzerland	8·5	9·8	14·9

These various figures are orders of magnitude, but they confirm the increasingly overwhelming superiority of Britain.

[54] Bairoch has no figures for Swiss industrial production.

[55] P. O'Brien and C. Keyder, *Economic Growth in Britain and France, 1780–1914. Two Paths to the Twentieth Century* (London, 1978), pp. 58, Table 3.2, 60, 61, Table 3.3, 67, Table 3.6

[56] See N. F. R. Crafts, 'Economic Growth in France and Britain, 1830–1910: A Review of the Evidence', *Journal of Economic History*, XLIV, 1, March 1984, pp. 51, 53–4 (Tables 1, 2 and 3), 56. His view is that French national income per capita was markedly lower than the British (by at least 30 per cent) between 1830 and 1910; only in 1870 did it reach the level of the latter in 1840. By 1850, product per capita was 81 per cent of the British level in Belgium, 73 per cent in the Netherlands, 65 per cent in France, 63 per cent in Germany.

[57] P. Bairoch 'International Industrialization Levels from 1750 to 1980', *Journal of European Economic History*, XI, 2, Autumn 1982, pp. 281, 292, 294, 296, Tables 4, 8, 9, 10.

Additional remarks on Britain and France

The conceptual framework of the preceding essay was largely that of 'backwardness' and 'catching up' (mostly seen in technological terms), which had been used, in a masterly way, by David Landes in *The Unbound Prometheus*, a book which had been an inspiration to me. However, the application of those concepts to the economic history of the nineteenth century has been criticised by Patrick O'Brien, in the important and original book which he wrote, with C. Keyder, on *Economic Growth in Britain and France, 1780–1914*, and which has been several times mentioned in previous chapters.[58]

O'Brien is critical of the historiography 'which perceives European industrialisation as a diffusion process, with backward or retarded countries on the mainland of Europe slowly adopting techniques of production and forms of business organisation pioneered by the British'. Though 'full of insights into industrial development, ... history written in this vein becomes an account of mercantilist competition between nations. In the struggle for industrial supremacy there are leaders and followers, and the problem for the historian is to account for the lags in time before retarded nations catch up.' Too many textbooks are 'dominated by the diffusion model and by the British industrial revolution as a paradigm'; this is a restrictive approach to European industrialisation, which 'seems to gravitate towards adjectives like "backward" and "retarded" and, at its crudest, lapses into the mercantilist jargon of "national power"'; it is too much 'concerned with leads and lags in the diffusion of technology, which were, in any case, rather short-lived'.

Actually, O'Brien does not question 'the fact that the prior development and adaptation of certain elements of advanced technology ... meant that the British example became a factor in the industrial growth of France, Belgium, Germany and other countries'. In imitation of England, 'over time throughout Europe and America, more and more industrial processes became mechanised, capital deepening

[58] O'Brien and Keyder, especially pp. 15, 17–18, 21–3, 175–6. See also O'Brien's recent article: 'Do We Have a Typology for the Study of European Industrialization in the XIXth Century?', *Journal of European Economic History*, XV, 2, Autumn 1986, pp. 291–333; Rondo Cameron, 'A New View of European Industrialization', *The Economic History Review*, XXXVIII, 1, February 1985, pp. 1–23, also maintains that there were several patterns of industrialisation. A drawback of the present essay was that the work of Alexander Gerschenkron on backwardness had not been used; see his *Economic Backwardness in Historical Perspective: A Book of Essays* (Cambridge, Mass., 1962).

proceeded, ... enterprises grew larger, factories replaced workshops'. However, 'the comparison of British and French technology does not provide unambiguous indicators of a potential for development over the long run and still less of levels of development at particular periods of time'; it is thus a mistake to single out some elements of the industrialisation process and to make them into symptoms of relative backwardness. Indeed, rates of growth of per capita real output provide a viable statistical basis for comparison between Britain and France, but there is no 'unambiguous indicator for ranking countries along a scale of development at moments of time'. 'As economics teaches, it all depends on resource endowment, factor prices, product mix, demand and comparative advantages, which themselves change over time.' A comparison which is only based upon relative rates of growth assumes that producers in the two countries faced equal, or roughly equal, opportunities to expand production.

O'Brien thus rejects the 'assumptions, present too often in writings on French backwardness, that there is one definable and optimal path to higher per capita incomes and ... the implicit notion that this path can be identified with British industrialisation as it proceeded from 1780 to 1914'. He advocates 'an approach to industrial development in different countries through specialisation, factor supplies and comparative advantages', which 'may bring out the more important elements of diversity in the transition to industrial society'; nineteenth-century industrialisation must be seen 'as a processus of specialisation and labour absorption'.[59]

Readers are advised to go back to O'Brien's writings for more details, and I shall end this chapter with some comments which his comparison of British and French economic growth during the 'long nineteenth century' (1780–1914) had suggested to me.[60] It is likely that his views were a surprise to many readers, who had been sated by their education, by the media and by respected writers, with diatribes and lamentations on the poor performance and chronic backwardness

[59] Crafts, 'Economic Growth ... 1830–1910', pp. 53, 67, accepts that French economic growth followed, during the nineteenth century, a pattern which was markedly different from the British model; the latter must not be considered as typical; Crafts has calculated a 'European norm' of industrialisation, from which the British experience clearly deviates; France also diverges, but to a lesser degree. See also his 'Patterns of Development in Nineteenth Century Europe', *Oxford Economic Papers*, XXXVI, 1984, pp. 438–58.

[60] This is a revision of a short essay which was published in: D. Johnson, F. Bédarida, F. Crouzet (eds.), *Britain and France. Ten Centuries*, (Folkestone, 1980), pp. 187–95; it discussed a paper by O'Brien, in the same book, pp. 175–86.

of the French economy. Yet O'Brien's work marked the culmination of a 'rehabilitation process' for the French economy in the nineteenth century, which had been pioneered by certain American and French economic historians. O'Brien, however, dealt with the subject more completely and systematically, and carried the process further than his predecessors (perhaps even too far, which is the main question raised by his work).

The materials used for this task were those supplied by the existing quantitative histories, i.e. Phyllis Deane's and W. A. Cole's for Great Britain, and those of the ISEA team – J. Marczewski, T. Markovitch and J. Toutain – for France. Now figures for national income and its components in the nineteenth century are not totally reliable in spite of the care and ingenuity of their authors, for the latter could not compensate for the absence of certain basic data which would be necessary for real accuracy. Admittedly one must avoid being too critical. One could hardly hope to get better sets of statistics than those at O'Brien's disposal, and these statistics do, moreover, give orders of magnitude which are valid. Furthermore, the later series of Deane (1968) and of C. Feinstein (1972) – to which O'Brien did not have recourse, because they do not cover the whole of the nineteenth century – would only confirm his thesis, for they show a British GNP growth slower than in Deane and Cole.

O'Brien's most striking conclusion can be summed up in two propositions:

(1) From 1815 to 1914 the growth of product per capita is very little faster in Britain than in France.

(2) The difference in per capita income levels between the two countries was never wide, no more than 15–20 per cent. England's advantage rose out of invisible income supplied by her position as the leading provider of services to other countries. The difference would be insignificant as regards the domestic product per capita.[61]

These conclusions seem incontrovertible, with the one reservation relating to the statistical bases mentioned above. However, a few related comments might be useful.

61 See above, note 56, on the different view of Crafts, in an article which is critical of O'Brien–Keyder and of other 'revisionists', who have overestimated French achievements, which Crafts, taking the middle ground, considers as 'respectable but certainly not outstanding' (I had used the adjective 'honourable'!)

Firstly, the long-term growth of the British product per capita (at a rate of about 1·2 per cent per annum between the beginning of the nineteenth century and 1913) was not unusually fast. Other countries, particularly the United States, Germany and Sweden, did better from the moment that their industrialisation got under way. So if the French economy's performance was good compared with Britain's, it was markedly less good alongside other countries. Furthermore, from this standpoint there is likeness and not contrast between England and France as being 'old' industrial countries,[62] as opposed to the 'late-comers' to industrialisation. Also the mediocre long-term British growth rate was partly attributable to the slowing-down of growth at the end of the nineteenth and beginning of the twentieth century – often referred to as the 'decline' of the British economy. But France also experienced a distinct slowing-down during the 'Great Depression' in the last quarter of the nineteenth century, which was even more serious for her than it was for England because she had kept a much larger agricultural sector, and agriculture was the main victim of this depression. It appears that the difference between the British and French per capita incomes, which had widened during the Revolution and Empire, and then lessened in the middle of the nineteenth century, increased again during the Great Depression. However the French economy picked up vigorously in the *belle époque*, while British growth was very modest, so that France regained ground. So the per capita income growth rates were very similar in the long term and the gap between them hardly varied.

Nevertheless one essential fact is that, if on the per capita product front France 'held on', while her overall product was growing much less fast than Britain's,[63] this was solely because her population increased much more slowly than her island neighbour's.

This writer is not a fanatical supporter of historical demography and of explanations which make population the prime mover of historical change. But one cannot compare the history of France and Britain in the nineteenth century (let alone the eighteenth century) without stressing two factors: the striking reversal in the ratio of human resources that came about between the two countries on the one hand, and on the other hand the considerable 'change of scale' (to use Harold

[62] One of their characteristics might be this relatively slow growth in the long term.
[63] Up to the 1820s, French industrial output was higher in value than the British; then the position was reversed (see above).

Perkin's expression) which occurred in England, but of which there was no equivalent in France. Let us simply call to mind a few basic population figures (in millions of inhabitants):

	Around 1700	1801	1911
England	5		
Great Britain	6	10·7	40·9
France	21–22	27·3	39·6

Certainly the question of the causal connection between demographic expansion and economic growth remains obscure, as much on the theoretical as on the empirical research side. However, in England it seems proven that the 'demographic revolution', i.e. the fast and sustained increase in population, began about the middle of the eighteenth century, i.e. before the 'Industrial Revolution', and that the resulting demographic expansion was an important factor in overall growth (though one might well think that the per capita product would have been less slow to grow if population had not increased so fast). In France, birth control and the decline in fertility were obvious from the late eighteenth century onwards, i.e. well before what passed in France for an industrial revolution, and nearly a century before these same tendencies affected the British population. One could take the view that the lack of employment opportunities for the young, given the slow rate of economic growth, was a stimulus to family limitation – although fertility remained highest in the poorest and most backward regions.[64] On the whole, however, demographic developments seem to have preceded economic change on both sides of the Channel. The slow growth of the French population and its subsequent stagnation were thus far from negligible factors. Without launching into a counterfactual analysis, let us simply pose one question: Would not the political and *economic* history of the nineteenth and twentieth centuries have been different if the French had multiplied at the same rate as the British, i.e. if they had reached 60 million in 1870 and 100 million in 1914 (likely with a low standard of living)?

O'Brien concentrates on per capita income, and it is indeed true that its level and growth are the best simple indicators of economic progress, which is the condition of social progress. But does he not go

[64] On the other hand, the birth rate was high in the industrial *Nord*, while in South-Western France economic sluggishness seems to have worked for depopulation.

too far in his indifference to the views of 'mercantilists of all ages', who believe that you must maximise population and production, so as to assure the power of the state and the prestige of the nation on the international scene?

While he notes that in the nineteenth century France became relatively less powerful than her neighbours, he attaches little importance to this 'decadence', which has been described as one of the great facts of the nineteenth century, just as the decadence of Great Britain, the only super-power of the previous century, is one of the great facts of the twentieth century. O'Brien believes that one ought not to condemn the economic system of a country because it has not maintained the power and prestige of that country. Surely that point of view is too narrowly and exclusively economic? 'History is about power', the saying goes. Not only the survival of a nation, but also the welfare of its citizens depend on its power. The fact that France was five times invaded (and four times thoroughly trounced) between 1814 and 1940 was not without its economic consequences ... The most disastrous results were those of the two twentieth-century wars, but the loss in 1871 of Alsace, a particularly progressive industrial region, was a serious blow. It is true that France's military disasters have sometimes been attributed to the weakness of her industry; but the French army's lack of steel cannon in 1870 and the scarcity of heavy artillery in 1914 were the fault of the high command, and not because French industry was incapable of producing such weapons. Furthermore (to take examples outside France) Belgium, the model follower country of the nineteenth century, did not escape invasion in 1914 and 1940; and the solidity of the German mark cannot protect West Germany from the dangers which come from the cold.

So power is not to be ignored. Indeed O'Brien admits this when he regrets the error of the French leaders in not seeing the potential advantage of maritime supremacy and commercial expansion, from which the British were to draw substantial gain. Yet could it not be said that France's very error was to have engaged in a struggle with the British on and beyond the seas that was foredoomed to failure? Whereas modest advances on the Continent, such as would have resulted from lasting acquisition of the Sarre and Sambre coalfields, would have changed the economic destiny of the country. Furthermore it is not entirely mistaken to view the economic history of the nineteenth century as a race between the pioneer country and the 'followers' – as long as one does not insist too rigidly on this interpretation. After all it was Britain which was the 'first industrial nation', and the creator of the new industrial and urban civilisation. The countries who were not 'placed' in this nineteenth-century race found themselves left dangerously far behind, not only on the economic level, but on the social level as well. They were only able to make up for lost time by efforts that were often painful.

Another essential point in O'Brien's analysis concerns the process of industrialisation on the two sides of the Channel during the nineteenth century. He rightly rejects the overpopular idea that there was only one possible model – the English one. In his view France industrialised along lines which, though different from those followed by Britain, were not for that reason 'backward'. The differences are explained by the disparate opportunities which were available to manufacturers as regards structure of demand and endowment in factors of production. Hence there was specialisation of each country in the sectors where comparative advantages were enjoyed. Britain, very well endowed with coal, went in for products that required a lot of fuel. France, which lacked fuel but had a work-force that was both cheap compared with England and skilful, concentrated on finished articles, often of an elaborate kind, which could be most effectively manufactured by small firms. Markovitch had already emphasised that one original feature of French growth during a large part of the nineteenth century was the development of both 'small' and 'big' industry side by side; so the survival of small enterprises during that period should not be regarded as a sign of 'backwardness'. This is confirmed by one of the truly paradoxical discoveries of O'Brien: that productivity was higher in French than in English industry during most of the nineteenth century. This is controversial; still the elaborate French goods embodied a much higher labour-added value, than did the simple products of English 'heavy' industry, which contained a high proportion of raw materials and capital.[65]

Actually, the successes of French industry, as it was mentioned earlier for the second quarter of the nineteenth century, were in the

[65] These views on productivity have been criticised; see Crafts, 'Economic Growth, 1830–1910', pp. 59–67 (he considers that, in the nineteenth century, the productivity of labour was somewhat lower in France than in Britain); V. Hentschel, in W. Engels and H. Pohl (eds.), *German Yearbook on Business History, 1982* (Berlin, 1982); C. Nardinelli, 'Productivity in XIXth Century France and Britain: A Note on the Comparisons', *Journal of European Economic History*, XVII, 2, Autumn 1988, pp. 427–34.

sector of quality articles (but note that one example, the printed cottons of Alsace, was the product of large-scale industry). In a more general way one can assert that the industrialisation of the 'follower' countries in the nineteenth century was the more successful the further it diverged from the English model. Nevertheless the essential lines of this model were according to the main stream of economic development: mechanisation, a growing use of coal and steam engines, expansion of heavy industry and large undertakings. In a sense Britain's 'decline' originated from her halting mid-way, as it were, on the road she had mapped out; while the new great industrial powers, which outstripped Britain at the end of the nineteenth and the beginning of the twentieth century, pushed the logic of this model much further than she did, e.g. by line assembly of components that were standardised, interchangeable and produced by machine-tools, and by developing giant enterprises. On the other hand it does seem that the 'French way' of industrialisation led to a dead-end. From the 1880s onwards a whole slice of the 'artisan' or 'small industry' sector declined (as important a branch as the Lyons silk industry is an example) and even collapsed, as the result of competition from foreign manufacturers with cheaper labour, or of the closing of important markets by protectionism, notably in the United States.

Moreover France was far from being entirely committed to this 'niche' of highly complex goods which embodied much workmanship, as were Switzerland and later Sweden. Also, these latter countries specialised in precision machinery, which was an industry with a future, and did not, as did France, go in for high quality textiles, 'Paris goods' and other fripperies. Indeed, a particularly glaring deficiency in the French economy of the nineteenth century was that she did not succeed in developing a substantial and competitive engineering industry, and thus remained a net importer of machinery. This failure poses a problem, all the more because these industries have been little studied. Yet it appears that they suffered, except during the free-trade period, from the high cost of materials supplied by the French iron and steel industry, and also from the narrowness of the French home market for capital goods, a situation, one is bound to say, that resulted from an insufficient development of mechanised industry. As for exports, these could only develop from the springboard of a large home market, as England herself found at the end of the nineteenth century for certain new sorts of equipment. Thus the locomotive industry was prosperous under the Second Empire, thanks to a strong demand both at home and abroad. Later on, when the French railways limited their purchases, unit costs increased and exports became insignificant. There was one exception – the motor industry, where the French were pioneers but also managed, up to 1914, to keep a clear lead, both in quality and quantity, over England and Germany.

In any case one can consider French industry in the nineteenth century as being divided into three sectors. First there was the 'specialised' sector of quality and luxury products which O'Brien has stressed; then there was a traditional artisan sector, which produced everyday goods for popular consumption, e.g. the linen industry in the West which dragged out a long, but enfeebled, existence. Finally there was a 'big industry' sector – cotton-spinning, iron and steel, chemicals, etc. All evidence confirms that, with a few exceptions, this branch was technologically backward and not competitive. In particular the equipment was out of date, not only relative to the 'best practice' but even to the 'average' of British industry. It has been argued that it was 'irrational' (in the economic sense of the term) to create and develop this sector, sheltering it by tariffs favourable to vested interests and thus giving rise to perverse results; but the existence of this type of industry cannot be ignored. It reduces the contrast between the English and French models of industrialisation, revealing a whole branch of French industry as a reduced and somewhat pale replica of its equivalent beyond the Channel.[66]

Conversely it is true that contemporaries and historians (particularly on the French side) always overestimated the 'modernity' of the British economy in the nineteenth century, failing to see that mechanisation, the factory system and large-scale enterprise remained long-confined to a small number of branches. As late as 1870 the textile and iron and steel industries monopolised 86 per cent of the total steam power of British industry (mining excluded), which shows that the use of steam must have been the exception in a very large number of activities. O'Brien makes a good point that the sectors whose productivity was low or stagnant, in industry or in services, absorbed a large part of the surplus manpower produced by the population explosion. It was without doubt one of the reasons for the slow rate of growth of the per capita product in Britain, but one wonders why small British firms

[66] It is, however, a mistake to be obsessed by those basic, heavy industries, in which Britain was bound to have the advantage.

would have had a productivity that was inferior to their French equivalents.

Few British authors have shown much understanding of the problems of French agriculture. O'Brien, on the other hand, rightly gives them an important place, devoting some excellent pages to the subject, on which we can only offer a few suggestions.

There is no doubt that the origins of the profound differences between English and French agrarian systems go back a very long way, into the heart of the middle ages, as Marc Bloch rightly pointed out. In any case 'the disappearance of the English peasant', the concentration of land ownership, the working of the soil by relatively large farms (by French standards at least) are parts of a process which went on through several centuries (likewise for the improvement of agricultural techniques which began in the seventeenth century, if not earlier). On the other hand, in the face of wars, epidemics, revolutions, economic fluctuations, technical change, and in spite of the exactions to which he was subjected, the French peasant showed an astonishing capacity for survival. It was not until the third quarter of the twentieth century that the peasant population declined dramatically. The peasantry was equally successful for a long time in containing agrarian laissez-faire, in preventing the abolition of *droits collectifs*, the amalgamation of farms, the consolidation of fields and other practices of an English sort. The British agrarian institutions, which tended to drive the surplus population off the land, contrasted with a French system which encouraged people to stick to the land. A society without peasants and a society with a peasant majority, that was the most fundamental difference on the social plane between *England* (the situation would have been different in Scotland and Wales) and France for over two centuries – another difference being the absence in France of a genuine ruling class, which might have liquidated the peasantry, as happened in England.

One should not, however, underestimate the technical progress achieved by French peasants in the nineteenth century, which differed from the preceding centuries when population expansion only gave rise to a Malthusian cycle of pauperisation. Nor should one overestimate the extent to which French agriculture 'retained' its numbers. After all, from 1846 to 1911, the rural population of France (defined as the population of localities numbering less than 2,000 inhabitants) diminished by 4·7 million inhabitants, or 18 per cent.[67] From 1841 to 1911 the population of the *English* countryside (i.e. localities of less than 2,500 inhabitants) lost only 700,000 souls, or 9 per cent.[68] This may be found surprising at first sight: the rural exodus appears to have been more intense in France. And it is a fact that in Britain it was only the mountain regions of Scotland or Wales that experienced a net loss, while in France large regions suffered it. However one must remember that at the beginning of the nineteenth century already towns had a greater proportion of the total population in England than in France, accounting for one-third of the population as against a quarter. Furthermore, while the towns then absorbed all the population growth and even helped themselves to some of the rural population, the percentage living in towns in France increased only slowly owing to the modest rise in the nation's total population. Could not this state of affairs be partly responsible for the slow redistribution of labour towards industry, and for France's inability to carry out speedy structural changes? Moreover, Jean-Pierre Poussou, in his study of the developing currents of migration in the South-west during the eighteenth century, has suggested that there was a simultaneous push-and-pull action – push from the 'agricultural misery' of the regions from which people emigrated and pull by the high wages of the Bordeaux area.[69] One may wonder whether in the nineteenth century French towns did not exercise too little drawing-power, for the truly important centres were few as compared with Britain.

One is bound to agree with O'Brien when he demonstrates that the amount of land available per agricultural worker was higher in Britain than in France, which would account for at least 60 per cent of the gap (to France's disadvantage) in the productivity of rural labour in the two countries. He also rightly shows that the rest of this gap resulted from the difference in yields per acre, which in its turn derived from French agriculture's being less animal-intensive than British agriculture. French travellers in the eighteenth century had already been struck by the 'prodigious quantities' of cattle and horses they saw in the English countryside. On the other hand, Ronald Hubscher, in his

[67] The majority of migrants had been engaged in domestic industry, which competition by factories destroyed, or had been farm labourers.

[68] In addition, about four million people migrated from the countryside to the towns and to the mining districts. On both sides of the Channel rural population reached its peak around 1840.

[69] J. P. Poussou, *Bordeaux et le Sud-Ouest au XVIIIe siècle. Croissance économique et attraction urbaine* (Paris, 1983).

book on the agriculture of a 'progressive' region, the Pas-de-Calais, comes to the conclusion that in the middle of the nineteenth century stock raising still played only a 'subordinate role'; and his 'captains of agriculture', who were afterwards the prime movers of agricultural progress there, all put the accent on the development of stock farming.[70] O'Brien explains this difference, a crucial one in his view, by the incapacity of the French peasant to save and invest. However one should also probably take into account the greater density of the rural population in France, a legacy of history,[71] which forced the peasant to concentrate on cereals, the fragmentation of the land into small plots, and some geographical factors, to which works of modern economic history on different problems have given renewed importance. A large proportion of French territory was unsuitable for the animal-intensive system, which assured Britain's superiority, particularly for the cereal–forage rotation of crops. The dry Mediterranean region could support little more than extensive sheep-rearing, and the whole of southern France has had to wait until recently to have fodder plants suited to her soils and climate. France had and still has her *Mezzogiorno*; ever since the seventeenth century the regions south of the line Saint-Malo–Geneva have been backward compared with the others. The variety and lack of homogeneity of French agriculture – certainly more marked than in Britain – was indeed an important factor. This was true geographically, with France's marked regional contrasts as regards natural conditions and methods of cultivation, but it was also true from the social standpoint, reinforcing the contrast with England, where rural society was pretty uniform in its three-tier structure. Thus in France, even after the Revolution, the large estate was far from being unknown, but it could be associated with large or small farms; and big landowners could be either 'progressive' or traditional in their approach to estate management. At the other end of the social scale, the mass of small plot holding peasants, long since disappeared in England, was an original French feature and undeniably an obstacle to progress. It was, however, linked in many regions to the culture of the vine, allowing the survival of those tiny farms, which of course had no equivalent across the Channel.

[70] R. H. Hubscher, *L'Agriculture et la société rurale dans le Pas-de-Calais du milieu du XIXe siècle à 1914* (Arras, 1979, 2 vols.).

[71] The low density of population in the English countryside of the seventeenth and eighteenth centuries may have been an important advantage, and at least a 'permissive' factor of the Agricultural Revolution.

Like most nineteenth-century observers, O'Brien has not remained on the purely economic plane and has paid attention not only to the standard of living but also to the quality of life. He suggests, as has another recent author, R. Roehl, that the 'French way' towards industrial society was more humane than the English equivalent.[72] On the one hand he does not share Marx's aversion to the 'idiocy of rural life'; on the other he is aware of the deplorable conditions in which many inhabitants of British towns lived. In O'Brien's eyes the advantages of urban life were not obvious before 1914, and French families who remained in the country did not lose much in terms of standard and of quality of life. The delaying of the rural exodus up to our own times would have been a good thing.

Indeed the wretched sub-proletariat of the towns was probably less numerous, both absolutely and relatively, in France than in Britain. Furthermore, although the French countryside had been 'over-populated' at the end of the eighteenth and beginning of the nineteenth century, the gradual improvement in techniques and productivity, the departures to the towns and the limitation of families assured many French peasants of a reasonable standard of living, except in some very unfavoured areas, e.g. inland Brittany. One can also contrast, as was noted by certain English observers, the independence of the land-owning French peasant and the village democracy of the Third Republic with the degradation of the English rural proletariat, dominated as it was by the landlords. But one must beware of taking too idyllic a view of the French peasant in the nineteenth century and his way of life. To take the example of housing, rural slums can be less shocking to the eye and less concentrated than their large-town equivalent, but no more salubrious. For a mass of French peasants life remained 'nasty and brutish', and even short as well, because of alcoholism.

On a different plane one should note that an acceleration of structural change and industrialisation would have worsened France's political fragility, and would have plunged her into even more serious and frequent upheavals than those she endured in the course of two centuries, repeated and blood-stained though these upheavals were.

72 R. Roehl, 'French Industrialization: A Reconsideration', *Explorations in Economic History*, XIII, 3, July 1976, pp. 233–81; criticism by R. R. Locke, 'French Industrialization: The Roehl Thesis Reconsidered', *ibid.*, XVIII, 4, October 1981, pp. 415–33 (reply by Roehl, pp. 434–5). See also the articles by R. Cameron and C. E. Freedeman, D. R. Leet and J. A. Shaw, which have been mentioned above, Chapter 2, notes 1 and 13.

When O'Brien says that French development was more humane than England's, he forgets the state of civil war, sometimes 'cold' and sometimes 'hot', but in any case permanent and fierce, that reigned in France. Indeed the only serious criticism that one can address to him is that he is too 'Francophile' and has pressed the rehabilitation of the French economy too far...

We will add a few final words on the period after 1914. It presents a curious phenomenon: the movements of the British and French economies are not any more in synchronism. The 1920s were good for France but mediocre for England. This position was reversed in the 1930s. In the immediate post-Second World War period Britain had a clear advantage, but from the 1950s to the late 1970s France's growth was noticeably more rapid than England's, although one should stress that the latter, for all her difficulties, has known a stronger growth over the last fifty years than in the nineteenth century. So France did outstrip the United Kingdom in both total and per capita national product, which in the latter case was unprecedented. However, since 1979–81, i.e. the coming to power of Mrs Thatcher and of Mitterand, a new reversal has occurred. France has travelled a long way on the road to under-development; her enormous and inefficient public sector has made her akin to Eastern bloc rather than to Western advanced countries. On the other hand, after some difficult years, an English miracle may have been achieved; the British economy has been reconstructed upon sounder foundations; it has become fast-growing and very prosperous – at least in the South-East.

11 Trade and empire: the British experience from the establishment of free trade until the First World War*

The first British empire, in the seventeenth and eighteenth centuries, was a mercantilist empire which had been conceived and built up as an economic unit, as a trading system as exclusive as possible, strictly subjugated to the interests of the mother country. Although this mercantilist edifice was shaken by the loss of the thirteen colonies and undermined by the advance of the Industrial Revolution in England, it survived until the middle of the nineteenth century. Between 1846 and 1860, however, it was entirely dismantled and the mercantilist empire made way for the free-trade empire that was to last until 1931. Strictly speaking, this empire did not constitute an economic unit. The English market was thrown open and was equally accessible to the goods of any other country, whether a part of the empire or not. Moreover England did not insist on favoured treatment for its own goods in its colonies. From 1859 onwards the self-governing colonies enjoyed complete freedom in tariff policy, which even enabled them to erect protective tariffs against British goods. As for the Crown colonies and India, their customs tariffs had solely fiscal ends and included no preference for goods from the mother country. Throughout the free trade era, therefore, trade between the different parts of the British empire had all the usual features of international trade, and it might appear artificial to study the commercial and financial relations between Great Britain and its empire in isolation. This study is nevertheless worth undertaking if only to determine whether, as is often claimed, the possession of a far-flung empire was an essential factor in the prosperity of Victorian and Edwardian England. Hopefully, such a

* This chapter was originally published in French in *Annales ESC*, XIX, 2, March–April 1964, pp. 281–310. It was printed in English in B. M. Ratcliffe (ed.), *Great Britain and her World, 1750–1914, Essays in Honour of W. O. Henderson* (Manchester, 1975), pp. 209–35; it had been translated by the editor.

study might throw light on the nature and motivations of imperialism and show whether it 'pays'.[1]

In the middle of the nineteenth century commerce within the empire was characterised by the survival of traditional trading patterns which in many respects were still those of the eighteenth century. It should not be forgotten, indeed, that the mercantilist framework which channelled empire trade survived, in the main, right up to the mid-century; the Navigation Acts were abolished only in 1849 and colonial preference for sugar and timber – two of the mainstays of the old system – disappeared only in 1854 and 1860 respectively. Besides, trade within the empire was still carried on by the traditional means of transport – that is, by sailing ships, since steam vessels were not yet competitive on long-distance routes. Although freight rates had fallen since 1815, they were still too high for the long-distance carriage of heavy goods to be profitable, while the slowness of sailing ships prohibited the transport of perishable produce over great distances. Finally, the economies of many British possessions had barely changed since the eighteenth century. Thus India continued to export above all 'drugs, dyes and luxuries' and in 1858 such traditional articles – indigo, spices, drugs, saltpetre, etc. – still made up 61 per cent of British imports from India.[2] Undoubtedly the emergence of the settlement colonies in temperate zones – the future dominions – was a new factor, but at this time they were only just beginning to tap their considerable natural resources.

The pattern of trade between mother country and colonies had hardly changed, then, since the eighteenth century. Textiles enjoyed a very marked predominance in British exports: in 1850 cotton goods and cotton yarn represented by value 42 per cent of British exports to the empire, and altogether textile goods made up 64 per cent, while the share of metallurgical products of all kinds was only 16 per cent. As for

[1] In writing this survey paper, large use had been made of the *Cambridge History of the British Empire* (hereafter abbreviated to *CHBE*), vol. II, *The Growth of the New Empire, 1783–1870* (Cambridge, 1940), pp. 751–805, 'Free trade and commercial expansion, 1853–70', by H. J. Habakkuk; vol. III, *The Empire-Commonwealth, 1870–1919* (Cambridge, 1959), pp. 181–229, 438–89; and of the outstanding study by S. B. Saul, *Studies in British Overseas Trade, 1870–1914* (Liverpool, 1960). Most of the statistical data is taken from W. Schlote, *British Overseas Trade from 1700 to the 1930s*, translated by W. O. Henderson and W. H. Chaloner (Oxford, 1952), especially Tables 20–5 in the Appendix; also B. R. Mitchell and P. Deane, *Abstract of British Historical Statistics* (Cambridge, 1962). In the text the terms England, Great Britain and the United Kingdom have been used as synonymous and the word 'Colonies' applied to any British possession.

[2] *CHBE*, II, pp. 759–61, 764, 772.

United Kingdom imports from the empire, they were dominated by a small number of major items – the first five alone represented 59 per cent of total imports in 1854: timber (19 per cent), sugar (18 per cent), wool (13 per cent), indigo (5 per cent) and coffee (4 per cent). Out of these five items, three – sugar from the West Indies, indigo from India, coffee, which came mostly from Ceylon – were typical of the old colonial trade, while the large-scale imports of Canadian timber can also be looked upon as a survival of mercantilism, for they resulted from the preferential duties instituted during the Continental Blockade to promote timber imports from the colonies rather than from northern Europe. The only new item was Australian and New Zealand wool, imports of which had increased remarkably after about 1820. For only a small number of items – including the five just mentioned[3] – did the empire provide England with a significant proportion of its imports (rising from 55 per cent of the total for timber to 96 per cent for indigo).[4] Great Britain took from its possessions but a minute proportion of its imports of several very important articles, such as grain and flour, meat, dairy products, tea, tobacco and, above all, cotton.

As for the geographical distribution of imperial trade, during the years 1854–7, India came first, having 34 per cent of Great Britain's total trade with the empire (that is, imports plus exports). Australia was second, with 22 per cent, but this was a recent development, the consequence of the gold discoveries there in 1851. British North America came third, with 13 per cent of England's trade with the empire, and the West Indies fourth with 12 per cent. The share of Africa and the remaining colonies in British trade was nominal. Here again a survival of traditional patterns can be seen, with the important role played by India and the West Indies, although this was already declining. There was, however, a new element: the growing importance of the settlement colonies, which were responsible for exactly 40 per cent of England's total trade with the empire.[5]

Altogether the colonies of white settlement took slightly under a

[3] As well as spices, rice, cocoa, jute and tin, though imports of these were small.

[4] The range of goods exported by each part of the empire (with the exception of India) was also very limited and generally dominated by only one item: in 1854 timber made up 82 per cent of Britain's imports from the North American colonies; wool 82 per cent of those from Australasia and 72 per cent of those from the Cape and Natal, proof that the colonial economies were still very much 'undeveloped'.

[5] These colonies' share of England's imperial trade had greatly increased since 1830: they took 21 per cent of British exports to the empire in 1827–30, 31 per cent in 1837–40, 47 per cent in 1854–7 (Schlote, pp. 91–2 and 97).

third of British exports, excluding re-exports (31·5 per cent of the total for 1854–7), they provided a little under a quarter of Britain's imports (23·9 per cent), and their share of Great Britain's total foreign trade in 1854–7 was 25·4 per cent. The latter had hardly changed since 1815, and it remained relatively minor. We ought not, however, to be tempted to use this to explain the lack of interest shown by British opinion towards imperial problems in the middle of the nineteenth century, for in fact these percentages hardly altered during the following half-century, even at the height of the period of the 'new imperialism'. It is true that the situation was different from the colonies' point of view: if England had given up its legal monopoly of their trade it retained an actual monopoly, especially because of its overwhelming industrial superiority, and remained by far their principal supplier. Only Canada and India had important trading links with foreign countries – its American neighbour for the former and China for the latter. As H. J. Habakkuk has written, from the economic point of view Britain possessed the best of all possible empires in the middle of the nineteenth century: a group of pioneer or backward countries tied to a highly industrialised country, buying its manufactured goods in return for their primary products. The division of labour between mother country and colonies that the mercantilists had desired had been accomplished despite the abolition of mercantilist constraints.[6]

From the middle of the nineteenth century until the First World War Britain's trade with the empire underwent a series of fundamental changes, whereby new elements emerged to displace the traditional features just described. These changes were brought about by three principal factors. The first of these was rising demand in Britain for foodstuffs and raw materials. As a result of the increase in the British population (from 21 million in 1851 to 41 million in 1911), of the rise in the standard of living and of the progress of industrialisation, aggregate demand for primary products greatly increased, and in addition the structure of that demand altered. Thus, from the end of the nineteenth century onwards, technical advance increased the use of new commodities like rubber, petroleum and vegetable oils, whilst at the same time British agriculture was less and less capable of meeting the country's food needs. In 1907 Great Britain itself produced only 52

[6] *CHBE*, II, pp. 754 and 780.

per cent of the non-tropical foodstuffs it consumed, and for some important products its dependence on imports was considerably greater: in 1910–14 it imported 81 per cent of the wheat and cheese it consumed, 75 per cent of the butter and 42 per cent of the meat. There was therefore a great increase in foodstuff imports, which rose, at constant prices, from £46 million in 1854 to £285 million in 1913.[7]

It so happened that several areas of the empire possessed favourable natural conditions for the production on a large scale and at low cost of some of the primary products which were in rising demand in England. This was the case with the immense, fertile plains of the Canadian prairies, which were ideal for wheat cultivation, and the fine natural pastures under mild climates of Australia and New Zealand. It was the opening up of these areas in response to British demand that brought about major changes in imperial commerce. These resources, however, had only potential, and their cultivation was possible only because of the working of two other factors: the transport revolution and British investment in the empire.

In transport two vital developments affected imperial commerce: the reduction in maritime freight rates and the building of railways. The fall in freight rates was the consequence of the rapid technical changes that took place in maritime transport after 1870, particularly the gradual substitution of steel-hulled steamships for wooden sailing ships. Recent studies have confirmed that the victory of steam was speeded up by the digging of the Suez canal, which opened the Indian Ocean and Australian trade to steamers and which stimulated technical advance, especially the introduction of the compound engine. At all events, competition between steam and sail, cost cutting in shipbuilding and operation, and the reduction in the duration of voyages brought a rapid fall in freight rates from 1873 onwards. Thus the cost of transporting wool from Australia to England fell by 50 per cent between 1873 and 1896 and that of transporting jute from India to England by 75 per cent between 1873 and 1905. Moreover, long-distance freight rates fell the most. Given this, it became feasible to transport bulky goods long distances, for example cereals from India or Australia to England. The end of the nineteenth century was marked, indeed, by the growth of trade in bulky commodities and by a

[7] Saul, pp. 29, 209–10; L. D. Stamp and S. H. Beaver, *The British Isles: a Geographic and Economic Survey* (London, 3rd edn, 1947), p. 207. In 1909–13 the United Kingdom imported, on average, 6,060,000 tons of wheat and wheaten flour every year, 998,000 tons of meat and 212,000 tons of butter. See P. Lamartine Yates, *Forty Years of Foreign Trade* (London, 1959), pp. 70, 80 and 84.

tendency to operate longer routes.[8] The distant parts of the empire were thus able to exploit their natural advantages and to unload on to the British market large quantities of cheap foodstuffs and raw materials. In addition, more specific technical advances – e.g. the appearance of refrigeration in transport – enabled Australia and, above all, New Zealand to become exporters of meat and dairy produce. The revolution in maritime transport therefore played a decisive part in the economic growth of the empire and particularly of the 'countries of recent settlement' – the future dominions.

The building of railways, however, had no less powerful an impact, for this alone permitted the opening up of the vast untapped resources by greatly reducing transport costs between the areas of production and the ports. The role of the Canadian Pacific Railway in the development of the Canadian prairies is the most striking example but far from the only one. But this rapid railway construction – total mileage in the empire increased from 8,500 in 1870 to 53,000 in 1895 – was possible only because of the massive investment of British capital.

This brings us to the third factor, which was the key determinant of developments in imperial trade – as it was, moreover, of the economies of nearly all British possessions.[9] True, only a small proportion of the capital that went from England to the empire was invested directly in agriculture, industry or mining, the only important instances being investment in Australian and, above all, South African mines. The bulk of capital exported went, indeed, into the establishment of means of transport, and especially into railway building. A careful study has estimated that, from 1865 to 1894, 60 per cent of the funds for overseas investment raised by stock issues in London was intended to finance railways.[10] It was therefore indirectly that British investment had an impact on production in countries of the empire and on imperial trade, by facilitating the establishment of an infrastructure, and, above all, of

[8] See M. E. Fletcher, 'The Suez Canal and World Shipping, 1869–1914', *Journal of Economic History*, XVIII, 4, December 1958, pp. 556–73; Douglass North, 'Ocean Freight Rates and Economic Development, 1750–1913', *ibid.*, pp. 537–55; *CHBE*, II, pp. 762–5; Saul, pp. 188 and 210.

[9] Saul, pp. 208, 210; *CHBE*, II, p. 754.

[10] H. H. Segal and M. Simon, 'British Foreign Capital Issues, 1865–94', *Journal of Economic History*, XXI, 4, December 1961, pp. 566–81, 576. These investments were made mostly through colonial government loans, which absorbed 70 per cent of funds invested in the empire during this period and which were used to establish its economic infrastructure. On capital exports, see the bibliographical survey by P. L. Cottrell, *British Overseas Investment in the Nineteenth Century* (London, 1975); also M. Edelstein, *Overseas Investment in the Age of High Imperialism. The United Kingdom, 1850–1914* (London, 1982).

a modern transport system, which created the conditions for the internal accumulation of capital and for productive investment. Local entrepreneurs and capital were responsible for the development of production proper in the various territories of the empire. The chief function of British capital was the creation of the preconditions for the 'take-off' of economic growth.[11]

It had no less profound an effect – indeed, a dual effect – on imperial trade: in the medium and long term stimulating an export-orientated agriculture and mining industry in the colonies (accompanied by a fall in the price of primary produce and an improvement in England's terms of trade) and in the short term giving rise to the export of large quantities of English capital goods, especially rails and railway rolling stock. Furthermore, fluctuations in British investment largely determined fluctuations in imperial commerce.[12]

The total of these investments was indeed considerable. Before 1850, of course, investments in the empire had been very small, but they rose sharply after this date and increased fairly regularly until 1885–8, going especially to India and Australia. There was a falling off during the 1890s, despite investments in the mines of the Rand, but from 1904 to 1914 there was another powerful upswing, and this time the chief beneficiary was Canada.[13] Total investments in the empire rose from about £270 million in 1870 to £1,780 million in 1913, which represented 47 per cent of total British foreign investments. It is often claimed that after 1873 British capitalists tended increasingly to invest in the empire in preference to independent countries,[14] but this has not been confirmed by the analysis of Segal and Simon, according to which total flotations of 'imperial' securities on the London market between 1865 and 1894 reached 46 per cent of all flotations.[15] Indeed, these authors have shown that investments in the empire fluctuated less

[11] Saul, pp. 65–6, 206, 211–13.

[12] Saul, pp. 69–70; *CHBE*, II, pp. 799–801, 804; A. K. Cairncross, *Home and Foreign Investment, 1870–1913. Studies in Capital Formation* (Cambridge, 1953), especially, pp. 2, 225, 232–3. This author admits that foreign investment was made at the expense of home investment but he nevertheless considers it 'paying', the necessary concomitant of the economic development of England.

[13] *CHBE*, II, pp. 787–91; Saul, pp. 10 and 99; Segal and Simon, p. 572.

[14] Some early views were invalidated by the calculations of A. H. Imlah, *Economic Elements in the Pax Britannica, Studies in British Foreign Trade in the Nineteenth Century* (Cambridge, Mass., 1958), pp. 72–5.

[15] Segal and Simon, pp. 572, 574 and 579. See also *CHBE*, II, p. 788: as early as 1850–75 the empire took 40 per cent of foreign investments. Again, between 1910 and 1913, 'imperial' share issues on the London market constituted 43 per cent of total overseas issues (A. E. Kahn, *Great Britain in the World Economy*, New York, 1940, p. 139).

sharply than those that went to independent countries (chiefly in fact to the United States and South America). Thus, the share of the empire in total foreign investments increased at times of depression – between 1873 and 1877, for instance – and fell during times of international prosperity (from 1868 to 1872, in 1886–90).[16] In the long run, though, the empire's share of British capital exports did not change markedly.

It may be added that the bulk of these English investments in the empire went to the settlement colonies: in 1913 the five dominions had taken almost exactly three-quarters. In contrast, the tropical countries – India, Malaya and the African colonies, including the vast territories occupied at the end of the nineteenth century – had received but a quarter,[17] a relatively minor proportion.[18] Therefore, some of the most important changes affecting imperial commerce during the free trade era were in the trade between England and the 'new countries' of the empire.

The opening up of new sources of supply for primary produce in British possessions brought about considerable changes in the pattern of British imports from the empire. Of course, the exploitation of these new resources took place in a strictly liberal framework, without government intervention; the pattern of British imports changed in response to market forces, working through the price mechanism, importers and consumers turning to suppliers whose prices were the

[16] As will be seen below, this confirms Saul's thesis (pp. 110 and 112–14), according to which Great Britain succeeded in partly insulating herself and her empire from the worst effects of economic crises during the last quarter of the nineteenth century by redirecting her foreign investments.

[17] Detailed figures in Saul, p. 67; W. K. Hancock, *Survey of British Commonwealth Affairs*, vol. II, *Problems of Economic Policy, 1918–1939*, part I (London, 1940), p. 27 n. 1. The distribution of these investments was as follows (£ million):

Canada	515	India	379
Australia	332	Malaya	28
New Zealand	84	West Africa	37
South Africa	370	Other colonies	35
Total	1,301	*Total*	479

[18] This seems to invalidate the argument that the need to invest surplus capital was the motor of British expansion at the end of the nineteenth century. Moreover the returns on colonial government bonds and on shares in railways in the empire (which took the greater part of imperial investments) were only marginally higher than those on similar stock at home. See Cairncross, pp. 226–31; Imlah, p. 61; *CHBE*, II, pp. 802–3. W. J. Macpherson, 'Investment in Indian railways, 1845–75', *The Economic History Review*, VIII, 2, December 1955, pp. 177–86, shows that investors were attracted mostly by the 5 per cent guaranteed interest that Indian railway bonds enjoyed.

Table 11.1. *Share of the empire in different United Kingdom imports (%)*

	1854	1860	1870	1880	1890	1900	1913
Wheat	0·5	3·1	9·8	20·3	22·0	15·1	48·5
Total grain and flour	5·8	6·7	12·6	15·7	16·5	13·6	35·3
Coffee	76·0	86·4	73·7	62·2	33·0	22·3	18·7
Tea	0·7	3·5	11·4	26·7	71·7	91·2	87·3
Raw sugar	64·7	59·8	35·8	28·7	15·8	12·9	8·7
Meat	0·9	1·0	7·6	3·0	15·4	20·1	24·7
Butter	1·5	11·6	4·3	4·8	2·2	18·1	19·0
Cheese	—	—	5·3	15·1	39·8	58·8	81·7
Total for foodstuffs	19·1	18·2	17·5	17·4	19·1	20·9	27·0
Timber and joinery	55·2	46·1	35·2	43·1	26·7	24·9	16·2
Raw cotton	8·4	9·8	19·1	11·3	11·2	1·7	3·0
Wool	70·6	68·5	88·5	87·0	88·8	84·5	80·2
Oil seeds	26·5	47·4	37·0	42·8	42·3	34·0	53·3
Rubber	11·2	17·2	21·9	19·5	14·2	12·6	57·2
Tin	71·2	78·6	49·1	91·0	94·4	88·3	94·8
Total for raw materials	26·2	23·5	27·4	31·9	30·7	24·3	28·0
Total for British imports	22·4	20·4	21·4	22·5	22·9	21·0	24·9

Source. W. Schlote, p. 99, Table 40, and Appendix, pp. 164–5, Table 21.

lowest – forsaking, for instance, China tea for Indian, and West Indian cane sugar for the beet sugar of Continental Europe.

The most important aspect of this development was undoubtedly the growth of imports of 'temperate' foodstuffs from the empire – especially wheat, meat, butter and cheese. In the middle of the nineteenth century the colonies supplied only a tiny proportion of British imports of these products, but during the following sixty years some of them greatly increased their exports and provided a rising proportion of rapidly increasing British imports (see Table 11.1).

Thus in 1854 England took only 0·5 per cent of its total wheat imports from the empire. In the following years, however, significant quantities of Canadian wheat from Ontario began to be imported. This trade proved short-lived and soon declined in the face of competition from American wheat, Canada turning to the export of animal products. Nevertheless, imports of wheat from the empire continued to increase thanks to consignments from Australia and above all from India, whose exports grew rapidly after the opening of the Suez canal and again after the completion of a direct rail link between Bombay and the grain-growing regions of the north-west in 1881. Because of the uncertainty of the harvest, exports of Indian wheat showed great variation from year to year, but in 1904 India was the chief supplier of wheat to Great Britain, and during the years 1904–13 supplied 18 per cent of total imports. Besides, imports of Canadian wheat revived from 1890 and rose quickly after 1900, following the opening up of the prairie provinces, which in the space of a few years became one of the granaries of the world. Canadian wheat production quadrupled from 1901 to 1911, and the value of English imports of Canadian wheat actually consumed on the home market rose from £2·8 million in 1900 to £11 million in 1913, replacing US supplies and constituting 25 per cent of total wheat imports. At the same time Australia itself greatly increased its wheat output and exports, and provided 10 per cent of British imports between 1909 and 1914. Imports of wheat from the empire therefore made considerable progress and their share of total British imports showed a marked increase, rising to 48·5 per cent in 1913, which represented about 40 per cent of total British consumption.[19]

The trade in meat and dairy produce shows a similar development. Before 1860 the empire provided England with practically none of these. From this date on Canada began to send salt and corned beef, bacon and hams, then, after 1875, livestock, and later refrigerated meats. At the same time dairying developed in Quebec and Ontario, where a cheese of the Cheddar type was produced. Exports of cheese and butter to England increased markedly after 1880, replacing American produce on the English market, and for a time Canada was England's major cheese supplier. But these exports fell, after 1900 for meat, after 1904–5 for dairy produce, Canada's home market taking a growing proportion of output. On the other hand, Australia and New Zealand, which had started to supply Great Britain with animal products later, continued to increase their sales and became the major suppliers. The decisive factor was the perfection of refrigeration in transport: after long experiments, the first cargo of frozen mutton from New Zealand arrived in London in 1882. Thereafter imports of meat, butter and cheese from Australasia increased very quickly, reaching £8 million in 1900 and £19 million in 1913. The New Zealand economy was profoundly changed as a result, the wool growing practised mainly on South Island declining before the dairying and mutton production of the more humid North Island. In 1913 Great Britain took 25 per

[19] Saul, pp. 171–2, 177, 194–5, and 210; *CHBE*, III, pp. 460–1. In contrast, the empire supplied only a very tiny proportion of the large-scale imports of cheaper cereals (mostly maize from Argentina).

cent of its meat imports (worth over £56 million, as against £1·7 million in 1854), from the empire, which was roughly a tenth of its total consumption, as well as 19 per cent of its butter and 82 per cent of its cheese imports.[20]

The rise of 'temperate' foodstuff production in the empire – in fact in Canada and later in Australasia – and the export of this produce to England is an important element in the international economic history of the period 1860–1914.[21]

However, there was also an increase in the output of and trade in tropical produce, the most important of which was tea. In the middle of the nineteenth century the tea consumed in Great Britain – in rapidly growing quantities[22] – was imported almost entirely from China, in the clippers which participated in the famous annual tea races. Around 1820, though, wild tea plants had been found in Assam, and from 1840 onwards British plantations were set up there. Output quickly increased after 1870, and after 1880 Ceylon, whose coffee plantations had been ruined by disease, also turned to tea cultivation. As a result of various advantages – greater political security and the possibility of controlling output and sales – which British merchants enjoyed, Indian tea could be sold more cheaply than the Chinese, and consumers came to prefer it. Thus the share of India and Ceylon in British imports quickly rose, and in 1888 surpassed China's for the first time. By 1913 the empire was to provide the bulk – 87 per cent – of the British national drink.[23]

A further interesting trade is that in vegetable oils, which were of many different kinds – groundnuts, coconut, linseed, rape seed, cotton seed and palm oil. They were produced in many parts of the empire, but first of all in India and in British colonies in West Africa, where they played a leading role in economic life. It is true that they were to be used only partly for foodstuffs (above all for the production of margarine) and that their industrial use was considerable. At all events, the value of British imports increased fivefold between 1854 and 1913, and the proportion coming from the empire rose from 27 to 53 per cent.

Changes were less spectacular for raw materials than for foodstuffs.

20 Saul, pp. 28, 172–3 and 178; *CHBE*, III, pp. 209–10. In 1913 Australia and New Zealand provided 23 per cent of world trade in meat (Yates, p. 81).

21 This rise was particularly rapid after 1896.

22 Per capita consumption doubled between 1847 and 1866.

23 Saul, p. 197; *CHBE*, II, pp. 772–3, and III, p. 462.

The most important supplied by the empire (more than 80 per cent of total imports from 1870 onwards) was wool, coming primarily from Australia but also from New Zealand and South Africa, a trade which continued to grow throughout the period. The same was true for jute, of which India had a monopoly. Among the new raw materials entering trade the most striking was rubber, British demand for which increased rapidly from the end of the nineteenth century onwards as a result of the rise of the bicycle, motor car and electrical equipment industries. At first, wild rubber from the Amazon basin, plus small quantities from Sierra Leone and the Gold Coast, was used. In 1876, however, hevea plants were introduced into Malaya. Right up to the end of the nineteenth century output remained extremely small, but from 1900 onwards numerous plantations were established. Although these reached full production only during and after the First World War, as early as 1913 Malaya supplied 19 per cent of world rubber exports, whilst Ceylon supplied 10 per cent, as against Brazil's 24 per cent, and the empire was able to supply England with 57 per cent of its imports of this product. From Malaya too came tin, British imports of which had been insignificant at the mid-century but were worth over £9 million by 1913.[24]

These were the principal British imports of imperial produce which increased during the half century that preceded the First World War.[25] However, there were also imports which declined or even disappeared. This was the case particularly with the four basic commodities of the old colonial trade, which in the middle of the nineteenth century still dominated imperial trade: sugar, coffee, indigo and timber. In 1854 the empire (in other words, above all, the West Indies) supplied 65 per cent of British imports of unrefined sugar, but by 1913 its share had fallen to 9 per cent, and this becomes an insignificant proportion when the imports of refined sugar – which were considerable and came entirely from outside the empire – are taken into account. What is

[24] Yates, pp. 113–14 and 246; K. Stahl, *The Metropolitan Organisation of British Colonial Trade* (London, 1951), pp. 98–9, 110. Malaya became the world's leading tin producer in 1883. Large-scale smelting works were set up there from 1887 onwards. The empire also supplied England with lead and copper, though the exploitation of the Northern Rhodesian copper belt began only in the inter-war period. Australia and Canada sold almost the whole of their zinc, silver and nickel production direct to foreign countries (*CHBE*, III, pp. 463–4).

[25] The trade in cocoa, fruit, hides and leather might also be mentioned. For cocoa the proportion of British imports provided by the empire remained steady, at about a half, but at the beginning of the twentieth century the Gold Coast replaced Ceylon and the West Indies as the chief supplier.

more, imports from the West Indies had greatly fallen in absolute figures.[26] This decline can be explained by the competition of beet sugar sold by European countries – Germany, France, Belgium and Austria – which could take place without hindrance under free trade and which forced imperial producers out of the British market.[27] In the case of coffee the ruin of Ceylon's plantations after 1877 as a result of a coffee shrub disease left the field clear for Brazilian coffee. As for indigo, it disappeared from international trade after 1890 in the face of competition from synthetic dyes. Finally, timber imports from the empire – that is, from Canada – fell in absolute terms, and fell still more in percentage terms, after 1867, under the impact of competition from Russian and Scandinavian timber, which could take place because the tariff preference enjoyed by timber from the empire was abolished in 1860 and because these countries had the advantage of shorter distances and lower transport costs.[28] The examples of sugar and timber are a good illustration of the impact of the market mechanism on the pattern of imperial commerce.

In any case, this pattern changed and in particular the range of goods imported from the empire was widened and diversified.[29] If we take empire goods that represented more than 3 per cent of total British imports from the colonies, we find only five in the middle of the nineteenth century (1854): timber, sugar, wool, indigo and coffee, in that order of importance. In 1913, however, we find nine: wool (14 per cent of the total), wheat (11 per cent), meat (7 per cent), tea (6 per cent), rubber (6 per cent), dairy products (5 per cent), tin (5 per cent) and vegetable oils (4 per cent).[30] Thus, of the five principal items in 1854, four have disappeared from the leading group (and the imports of three of these have become unimportant). Inversely, in the leading group of 1913, four items – wheat, meat, tea and dairy products – were newcomers, only negligible imports of which came from the empire in 1854. This development demonstrates some of the basic characteristics

[26] £4,635,000 in 1876 (the peak) and £698,000 in 1913.

[27] *CHBE*, III, pp. 214–15. There was also competition from foreign cane sugar – chiefly from Cuba and Java. S. B. Saul, 'The Economic Significance of "Constructive Imperialism"', *Journal of Economic History*, XVII, 2, June 1957, pp. 176–9, describes the vain efforts of Joseph Chamberlain to revive West Indian exports to England.

[28] Saul, p. 174; *CHBE*, II, p. 767.

[29] Schlote, p. 94. At the same time the export structure of several colonies changed radically. The clearest case is that of India, with the decline of indigo, sugar and spices and the rise of wheat, tea, jute, vegetable oils, etc.

[30] These nine items made up 64 per cent of imports from the empire (the percentages given above are rounded numbers).

Table 11.2. *Share of the principal areas in British imports from the empire (%)*

	1854–7	1877–9	1898–1901	1909–13
Australia and New Zealand	13	26	31	33
South Africa	3	5	5	6
Canada and Newfoundland	16	13	20	16
Total for the five dominions	32	45	56	55
India	38	34	26	26
British Asia (excluding India)	6	10	11	13
British Africa (excluding South Africa)	6	2	2	3
West Indies	16	8	2	2
Other British possessions	2	1	2	1

Source. W. Schlote, p. 168, Table 23.

of the economic development of the empire, particularly the rise of agriculture and stock rearing in Canada and Australia and the first steps in the opening up of Malaya and the west African colonies.

At the same time, the geographical distribution of British imports from the empire altered significantly, as is shown by Table 11.2.

The most remarkable change was the considerable increase in the proportion of imports from the settlement colonies, the five dominions, which rose from a third to more than a half. Australasia, supplying wool, wheat, meat, butter and cheese, was responsible for this increase, and the value of English imports from Australia and New Zealand rose more than tenfold. Imports from Canada, on the other hand, increased less spectacularly, and her share of the total remained unchanged at the end of the period. As for India, her share of British imports fell appreciably,[31] while that of the other possessions in Asia greatly increased, as a result of the rise of the trade in rubber and tin from Malaya. In contrast, imports from the African colonies barely increased, and their share of the total declined to 3 per cent in 1909–13.[32] Finally, imports from the British West Indies collapsed as a consequence of the decline of the sugar trade.

Altogether, Great Britain's imports from the empire increased considerably, rising from an annual average of £39 million in 1854–7 to £173 million in 1909–13; their value therefore more than quadrupled.

[31] As a result of the growth of direct exports to foreign countries. In 1913 only 24 per cent of India's exports went to Great Britain.

[32] Although the first plantations were set up before 1914, only during the inter-war period did British East Africa begin to export significant quantities of coffee, sisal, cotton, etc.

They did not, however, grow at a faster rate than imports from foreign countries, so the proportion of total imports that came from the empire changed only slightly. It was 24 per cent in 1854–7; during the years 1861–5 it suddenly increased as a result of the American Civil War and the cutting off of supplies of American cotton, which were partly made up for by imports from India; in 1864 the empire supplied as much as 34 per cent of total imports. However, its share very quickly fell again to 22 per cent for 1870–4, and until the end of the century quinquennial averages remained at between 22 and 24 per cent. After 1900 a slight increase can be seen, linked with the growth of the trade in foodstuffs and rubber, though the percentage of total imports for 1909–13 was only 25 per cent.

If the analysis is extended, we find that the greatest increase took place in foodstuffs from the empire, its share in total foodstuff imports rising from 19 per cent in 1854 to 27 per cent in 1913 (This increase, however, took place after 1900).[33] In contrast, the empire's share of raw material imports increased only very slightly. Since, besides, British imports of manufactured goods increased faster than those of primary products, and since the empire did not supply such goods, it can be understood why the empire's share of total imports remained almost unchanged.[34]

This share, then, remained small and was smaller still in reality, because an appreciable proportion of imports from the empire were re-exported to other countries – 29 per cent in 1913 (above all, wool, jute, rubber and tin), and in consequence the empire supplied only 20·5 per cent of net British imports at that date.[35] Moreover, for only a small number of important items did the empire, even at the end of the period, provide a high percentage of total British imports. In 1913 its share was more than 80 per cent for jute, tin, tea, cheese and wool. For vegetable oils and rubber it was slightly more than 50 per cent and

[33] It is estimated that the empire provided about 14 per cent of Great Britain's total foodstuff requirements at this time. If non-tropical foodstuffs only are considered, the empire supplied 36 per cent of imports in 1907, which was 19 per cent of consumption as against 33 per cent from countries outside the empire and 48 per cent from home production (Stamp and Beaver, *The British Isles*, p. 207).

[34] Saul, pp. 222–3.

[35] The re-export trade in produce from the empire, considerable in the middle of the nineteenth century, had suffered from the opening of the Suez Canal which enabled European countries to open up direct trading links with the Far East. It had a brisk expansion after 1900, however, especially to the United States which took a great deal of tin and rubber from England. From this there resulted an intensification of multilateral settlements (see below). Saul, pp. 59 and 225; *CHBE*, II, pp. 761–2.

nearly 50 per cent for wheat (though only 34 per cent for all grains and flour). Appreciable percentages were also to be found with meat, butter and timber. On the other hand, the empire supplied England with relatively insignificant quantities of a number of essential items, particularly sugar, cotton, tobacco, iron ore and petroleum. Any attempt at imperial autarchy would thus have been chimerical, and even the plans for the re-introduction of imperial preference put forward from the late nineteenth century onwards would have meant imposing tariffs on the greater proportion of British imports and therefore increasing the cost of living and production costs in industry. Free trade remained the best policy for England, at any rate until the First World War.

The pattern of Great Britain's exports to its overseas possessions did not undergo as radical a transformation as did that of its imports. The principal change was the decline in the proportion of total exports to the empire made up of textiles: in the middle of the nineteenth century this was nearly two-thirds (64 per cent in 1850), but in 1913 it was only 51 per cent, the proportion of cotton yarn and piece goods having fallen from 42 to 33 per cent. In contrast, the share of the various metallurgical products, a rising proportion of which consisted of capital goods, had increased appreciably, having risen from 16 to 32 per cent of total exports to the empire. This increase partly explains the relative decline in textile exports, but it ought to be added that from 1885 the growth of the latter slowed down, chiefly as a result of the advance of the cotton industry in India, the leading market for English cotton goods. This slowing down heralded the sharp crisis that Lancashire exports were to face after the First World War.

Nor did the geographical distribution of British exports among the various imperial markets undergo spectacular changes (Table 11.3). The share of the future dominions, which had greatly increased between 1820 and 1850 to reach 47 per cent of the total in 1854–7, fluctuated thereafter at a slightly lower level, rising slightly from 1895 onwards to reach exactly 50 per cent in 1909–13. This preponderance, despite the small size of their population, resulted from their rapid economic growth and their relatively high standards of living. As with imports, Australia came first; its share of exports to the empire fell slightly, but the figures for 1854–7 were abnormally

Table 11.3. *Share of the principal areas in the export of British goods to the empire (%)*

	1854–7	1877–9	1898–1901	1909–13
Australia and New Zealand	30	28	26	25
South Africa	4	8	14	12
Canada and Newfoundland	13	10	8	13
Total for the five dominions	47	46	48	50
India	32	35	34	33
British Asia (excluding India)	6	9	8	8
British Africa (excluding South Africa)	2	2	3	5
West Indies	6	4	3	2
Other British possessions	6	3	3	2

Source. W. Schlote, p. 169, Table 23. Re-exports are not included in this table.

swollen by the boom following the gold discoveries.[36] Canada's share fell markedly at the end of the nineteenth century but rose again afterwards, to return to the same level in 1909–13 as in 1854–7. Exports to South Africa, then, showed the greatest increase. India, on the other hand, remained the most important imperial market for England, its share of total exports – very nearly one-third – being unchanged. The remaining possessions in Asia and the African colonies increased their share, but it remained very small. The West Indies' share, of course, was reduced to insignificance.

The most difficult and interesting problem, though, concerns the changes in total British exports to the empire. From 1850 to 1913 these rose from £19 million to £161 million, and this increase took place gradually, without the rather wide fluctuations that occurred in British exports to independent countries and in British exports as a whole.

This being so, the proportion of total exports that went to the empire showed quite marked fluctuations which even had a cyclical character. Thus its share increased perceptibly (if irregularly) from 1852 to 1863 – from 26 to 35 per cent of the total, falling thereafter until 1871, when it was only 23 per cent, rising up to 35 per cent in 1877, falling to 32 per cent in 1879, reaching 37 per cent in 1885, and falling to 31 per cent in 1895. There was a renewed increase to 38·5 per cent in 1902, which was the peak for the entire 1850–1913 period, a fall to 32 per cent in 1906–7, and finally a rise to 37 per cent in 1913.[37]

[36] In fact there was a marked reduction in its share in the 1860s, then a strong recovery after 1874.

[37] Figures from Schlote, Table 20b, pp. 161–3; see also Saul, pp. 213–15.

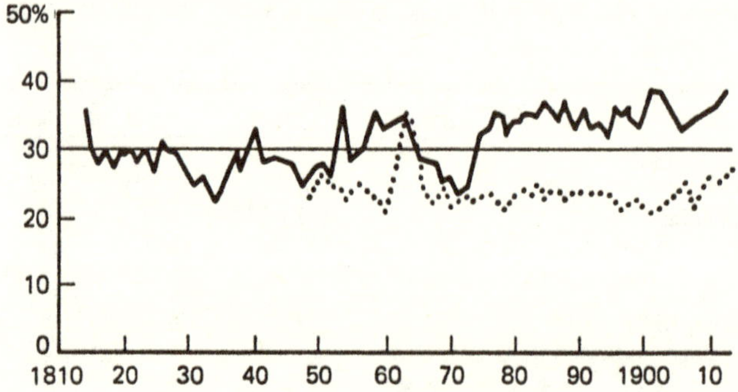

Fig. 11.1. The share of the British empire in UK trade, 1814–1914. Percentage of trade based on current values. The solid line represents exports and the dotted line imports.

S. B. Saul has linked these fluctuations with those of British investments in the empire, investments which stimulated British exports, especially of capital goods.[38] When there was a marked upswing in investments in the empire – as, for example, in the 1850s, following the gold discoveries in Australia, or between 1909 and 1913 – there was a comparable increase in imperial trade. It also grew, however, when there was a sharp fall in capital invested outside the empire, which brought about an increase in the empire's share of total foreign investment; at the same time sales of British goods outside the empire fell off, whilst those to the empire increased, or at least remained stable. This is what happened between 1873 and 1877 and between 1882 and 1885.

In contrast, when there was a rapid increase in British investment in, or exports to independent countries, the Empire's share in total exports fell, the best instance being the years 1864–72. The fluctuations in imperial commerce were therefore in large part countercyclical, at least during the period 1860–90. The empire's share in Great Britain's exports fell during years of expansion and general prosperity (especially in the 1868–72 boom and the upswing of 1878–9), but it increased during depressions (1873–7 and 1882–5). Indeed, when a crisis struck the world economy British investors forsook foreign investment, especially in the United States, and turned to the empire, where colonial government bonds offered gilt-edged

[38] Saul, pp. 98–9, 101 and 103–5. However, he also notes the impact of harvests, especially on exports to India and Australia (p. 210); and Cairncross (p. 197) asserts that India's demand for textiles depended more on harvests than on investment.

investments. This redirection of funds helped sustain merchandise, and particularly capital-goods, exports. The working of this mechanism to some extent insulated Great Britain and its empire from the worst effects of general economic crises. Thus the empire played a stabilising role in the British economy.[39] This, however, was because the latter then held a dominant position in the world economy.[40]

After 1890 the situation seems to have changed. Fluctuations in the proportion of total English exports that went to the empire were no longer counter-cyclical: its share increased during years of general prosperity – from 1897 to 1902 and from 1909 to 1913, for example – and fell during years of depression, such as 1893–5 and 1906–7. In short, imperial trade tended thereafter to move in unison with the fluctuations in world trade, and the empire was deeply affected by international depressions.[41]

This phenomenon is to be explained by the fundamental change that took place in the international position of the British economy, which lost some of its predominance and as a result was no longer able to insulate the empire from fluctuations in the world economy. In particular – and this is a point we shall return to – the United States and the new industrial powers in Europe became major purchasers of primary produce from the British empire, and in consequence when a crisis hit those powers it was passed on directly to primary producers in the empire, whose exports fell; the latter in turn reduced their purchases of English goods. And British investments were no longer capable of playing their previous role of shock absorbers, especially because the primary producing countries no longer attracted British capital when they were struck by a crisis coming from outside. In short, from the end of the nineteenth century the engine of fluctuations in imperial commerce was no longer British investment but the demand for primary produce from all the industrial countries.[42]

At all events, these fluctuations were not very great, with the exception of that between 1863 and 1873, and on the whole the empire's share in Great Britain's exports did not increase markedly in

39 Saul, pp. 110 and 112–14. This mechanism operated to the full during the 'great depression', after 1873, because the opening of the Suez Canal had improved the economic prospects of India and Australia, thus stimulating investment in these countries.

40 At the time this was divided into several autonomous circuits of multilateral settlements which were linked only through England. By redirecting their investments British capitalists could prevent a crisis from spreading from one circuit to another.

41 Saul, pp. 107, 109, 114–15, 117 and 120–1.

42 *Ibid.*, pp. 129–31.

the long run: it stood at 31·5 per cent in 1854–7 and reached 35·4 per cent in 1909–13. It might also be noted, however, that after 1875 it settled at a slightly higher level than during the preceding decades, never falling below 31 per cent.[43] It is also true that the tendency to increase was definitely more marked for textile goods – for which the share taken by the empire rose from 31 per cent of exports in 1860 to 44 per cent in 1913 – and for most metallurgical products and capital goods.[44] But if, finally, we consider British trade in its entirety – that is, the sum of exports, re-exports and imports – the headway made by the empire remained very modest: 25·4 per cent of total commerce in 1854–7 and 27·5 per cent in 1909–13.[45]

This absence of change might appear surprising, for throughout this period the empire went through considerable territorial expansion,[46] massive investments were made, and its natural resources were exploited with vigour and success. In view of this, one might even talk of a stagnation (relative, of course) in imperial trade and note that the economic results of the great imperial expansion of the late nineteenth century were meagre. This stagnation naturally distressed the 'imperialists', who blamed foreign competition in British colonies – a charge that was not without foundation.

In the middle of the nineteenth century, as we have seen, Britain retained a quasi-monopoly of the foreign trade of its colonies. This monopoly was maintained until 1870 and even beyond for some areas. During the last quarter of the century, however, foreign manufacturers – American, German, Belgian, etc. – began to infiltrate imperial markets, and competition from them went on increasing until the first World War, with the result that England's share in its colonies' imports tended to decline – sharply in certain instances. The intensity

[43] Schlote, pp. 89–91. Saul points out that the increase in the empire's share on the eve of the first World War resulted solely from very high – and abnormal – cotton goods exports to India in 1912–13, without which this share would in fact have fallen.

[44] Schlote, pp. 166–7, Table 22 and p. 104. For iron and steel products the empire's share rose from a third in the middle of the nineteenth century to nearly half in 1913. On the other hand, a marked reduction in cotton yarns, a consequence of the rise of the Indian cotton industry, should be noted. The rapid growth of British coal exports between 1860 and 1913, of which the empire took but an insignificant proportion, is the chief explanation for the relatively small increase in total exports to British possessions.

[45] See Hancock, p. 81, n. 1, for a series of quinquennial averages which shows that the empire's share in Great Britain's total trade reached a peak, at 28·3 per cent, in 1861–3 (as a result of imports of Indian cotton during the American civil war), and a low, at 22·7 per cent, in 1871–5; in 1906–10 it was 26 per cent. These figures show a remarkable stability.

[46] It was increased by over two million square miles between 1880 and 1900.

of competition, indeed, varied considerably from one territory to another.

In this respect Canada and India are the two extreme cases. It was in Canada that foreign competition was most serious – in this instance from the United States because of its rapid industrialisation, the geographical advantages it enjoyed (especially in western Canada) and its technical superiority, above all in capital goods, whose share of Canadian imports greatly increased at the expense of textiles. In consequence England's share of Canada's imports fell from 54 per cent in 1872–4 to 27 per cent in 1895–7, and to 21 per cent in 1913, whilst the United States' share moved in the opposite direction, rising from 38 per cent in 1872–4 to 57 per cent in 1895–9, and this despite the high level of British investment in Canada and the latter's return to a policy of imperial preference in 1897.[47]

The situation in India was quite different. In 1870 England supplied 85 per cent of the country's imports; her share fell slowly but it was still 70 per cent in 1890 and 66 per cent in 1913. The inroads made by foreign competitors – Germany, Belgium and later Japan – were therefore limited, and the British defended their position well. This was because of the predominance of textiles in India's exports, in which Lancashire enjoyed a clear superiority, and because British firms benefited from a quasi-monopoly of the very considerable government orders for capital equipment.[48]

The other colonies stood between these two extremes. In New Zealand, where the market was so small that foreign firms had no interest in establishing themselves, there was little competition and England still supplied 60 per cent of imports in 1913. Her share of South Africa's imports, however, fell from 83 per cent in 1881 to 56 per cent in 1913, and of Australia's from 73 per cent to 52 per cent. Altogether the five dominions took 38 per cent of their imports from Great Britain in 1913, while for the empire as a whole the percentage was 44 per cent.[49]

Foreign competition thus made real progress in imperial markets, but, except in Canada, it was not as severe as the protectionists claimed. And it was not the sole cause of the relative stagnation in English exports to the empire. This – at least at the beginning of the

[47] Saul, pp. 174–6 and 180–3. After 1872, there was a stagnation and even a fall in English exports to Canada.

[48] *Ibid.*, pp. 198–200 and 203.

[49] *Ibid.*, pp. 215–17; *CHBE*, III, p. 483; Hancock, pp. 306–11.

twentieth century – can also be explained by the rapid expansion of British exports to Latin America and the Far East. It can be explained equally by the fact that British superiority was concentrated in the textile sector, which was where demand was growing most slowly. Competition was most intense in capital goods, world trade in which greatly increased after 1890, and it was in this sector that England's ability to compete had weakened.[50]

This shows the fallacious nature of the propaganda of protectionists and advocates of imperial preference, for the remedies they were proposing would in no way have improved the position of British industry in this critical sector. It might even be maintained, indeed, that the dominant position which England retained in imperial markets had adverse consequences. The ease of access to such outlets, and especially to the unprotected market for textiles in India, dulled the sense of many exporters and turned them away from markets where there was competition. England was encouraged to continue to concentrate on its traditional export lines – textiles and railway material – where expansion was relatively slow, and to neglect new dynamic sectors – machine tools, motor cars, and the electrical equipment industry.[51]

This competition, finally, had a corollary: Britain's industrial competitors did not restrict themselves to selling manufactures to British colonies; they spent far more than they earned in purchasing primary produce, and the development of this multilateral system of trade and payments brought considerable advantages to England.

From about 1890 and especially at the beginning of the twentieth century the pattern of international trade was changing markedly. In particular, in the industrial countries of Continental Europe, in the United States and later in Japan there was a rapidly growing need for raw materials, and more and more of these were bought from the British empire, whose production of various primary products had grown faster than the absorptive capacity of the English market: wool from Australia, rubber and tin from Malaya, rice, rape seed, groundnuts, jute sacking, hides, leathers and cotton from India, palm oil from west Africa. Despite their increased sales of manufactures to these areas, the balances of trade of the industrial countries went into a large (and growing) deficit, especially with India and Australia, and

[50] Saul, pp. 218–19. In 1913, however, US exports of machinery to the empire, excluding Canada, were only a quarter of those from Britain (*ibid.*, p. 36).

[51] Saul, pp. 220 and 229.

also with Malaya, Ceylon and British West Africa. European countries, though, easily made good their deficit with the primary producers by means of the surpluses they enjoyed in their balance of payments with the United States and Great Britain. For its part, the United States made up its deficit with Continental Europe, India and Australia by means of the growing surpluses in its transactions with England and Canada. The latter squared its deficit with the United States through the surplus it enjoyed in trade with Great Britain.

As for Britain, she had deficits in her balance of trade with Continental Europe and the United States, as well as with many areas in the empire: South Africa, east Africa, Ceylon, Malaya, New Zealand and Canada. However, Britain enjoyed large and growing surpluses in her transactions with west Africa, Australia and, most of all, India. It was as a result of these surpluses and of her considerable invisible earnings that Britain's total balance of payments was not in deficit and was even in surplus, and the circle thereby closed.[52]

England was therefore at the centre of this system of multilateral settlements which developed from 1890 onwards[53] and which she found extremely valuable. It had been possible to establish this system, moreover, only because of Britain's policy of free trade, which made her a major importer of manufactures from Europe and the United States, giving them the surpluses with which they could finance their growing imports of primary products without being obliged to increase their direct exports to primary producing countries. This system, then, clearly reduced the competition England might have faced in overseas markets. Had Britain repudiated free trade the other industrial powers would have been forced to look for new sources of supply – in their own colonies, for example – or else to increase their exports to the British empire. Again, by opening her markets to the free importation of primary produce, Great Britain encouraged the growth of a number of primary producing countries and thus secured expanding markets for her own manufactured goods. British free-trade policy was therefore essential for the smooth working of the international economy, and in an apparently paradoxical way it protected England from foreign competition in overseas markets.[54]

52 This summarises drastically the analysis in Saul, chapters III and IV, pp. 43–89, 171, 186 and his very useful diagram, p. 58. This schema is described as it functioned *c.* 1910.

53 Saul considers that previously only a series of multilateral 'schemas', each rather isolated from the others, had existed (see above).

54 Saul, pp. 63 and 221; W. Ashworth, *A Short History of the International Economy, 1850–1950* (London, 1952), pp. 166–7.

The advocates of imperial preference, and still more those of an imperial *Zollverein*, overlooked these basic facts. They were also unaware that on the eve of the First World War the British empire was no longer a group of pioneer or underdeveloped areas, heavily dependent on an industrial mother country; from then on its different parts maintained important trading links with foreign countries, which it would have been disastrous for them to sever. The idea of even a partial isolation of the empire was chimerical.[55]

Plans for imperial preference, however, were naturally attractive for those countries in the empire which were developing foodstuff exports, the sole market for which was in England – a market which seemed nearly boundless. This was the case with Canada,[56] and even more so with New Zealand, and naturally this small antipodean dominion was particularly empire-minded. Such projects were already less attractive for Australia, whose foodstuff exports were certainly heavily dependent on the British market but which sent very large quantities of wool and metals to France and the United States as well. The same was true for South Africa, whose wool and gold exports to England were in large part re-exported. And finally these projects were without interest for India or for Great Britain herself, dependent far more on foreign markets than on imperial ones.[57]

The smooth working of free trade and the system of multilateral settlements was dependent, however, on at least two conditions, neither of which was to survive the World War. The first was the proven strength of Great Britain's balance of payments, thanks to the considerable invisible earnings which made up the growing deficit on current account. After 1918 the British balance of payments became fragile, and this put everything in jeopardy. The second condition was the continuing existence of a large surplus in the balance of payments with India; on the eve of 1914, indeed, Great Britain was more and more dependent on this surplus to make up the increasing deficit in her

[55] In 1913 total exports from empire countries (including precious metals) stood at £575 million; of this Great Britain took £238 million, but as she re-exported almost all the precious metals and 29 per cent of the merchandise, her net imports of imperial goods were no more than a quarter of total imports and 20·5 per cent of her retained imports (Saul, p. 225). She took 90 per cent of the exports of the Union of South Africa (though almost all the gold and all the wool were re-exported), 80 per cent of New Zealand's exports, 50 per cent of Canada's, 45 per cent of Australia's and only 24 per cent of India's.

[56] Besides, Canadians saw in such a system a means of ensuring their independence from the United States. Consequently, this dominion was the driving force behind the campaign for imperial preference.

[57] Saul, pp. 185–6 and 226–9.

transactions with other countries (in fact India alone made up two-fifths of this deficit). India had thus become the keystone of the British system of payments and of the entire world network of multilateral settlements. Trade with her was thus of considerable advantage to England, all the more so as Indian exports consisted, above all, of raw materials which were in wide demand and freely admitted into most countries. This limited the vexatious effects on Great Britain of the protective tariffs which had been imposed in a number of States at the end of the nineteenth century. As for the Indian market, it was wide open to England's exports, especially her cotton goods – it was indeed the only large market in the world (outside Britain) where there was no tariff protection. This absence of protection is to be explained, of course, by Britain's political control over India. And it is here that one of the principal economic advantages which the possession of the empire conferred on England is to be found. (It is true that in the long run the effects were deleterious because of the over-concentration on cotton goods exports.) In this instance, too, the First World War, by stimulating the rise of the cotton industries of India and Japan, was to be harmful to the British economy.[58]

At all events, the empire was a source of wealth for Great Britain as an open, dynamic system, integrated into the main current of the international economy, and not as a defensive mechanism that would shelter Britain from foreign competition, as the protectionists thought.[59]

This, moreover, was the tendency of all economic changes in the empire between the introduction of free trade and the First World War, the countries of the empire carrying on more and more of their trade with foreign countries and integrating into the international economy. Thus the tendency to decentralisation which dominated the political evolution of the empire was to be seen equally in the economic sphere.[60]

58 *Ibid.*, pp. 61–3, 88–9, 188, 203–6, 221 and 228. Saul considers that the growth of industry in the dominions had hardly any effect on England's trade.

59 Saul (pp. 228–9) finds that, all things considered, the empire was a source of great strength for Great Britain and that France suffered from not having a similar outlet. The greatest advantages were of an indirect kind, linked with the sale throughout the world of primary produce from the empire, which ensured the smooth working of international trade, including Britain's.

60 True, as a result of the large-scale investments of British capital in the colonies, their economies were in large part controlled from offices in the City where the railway, banking, plantation, mining and other companies had their headquarters.

It is true that the World War and the storm of 1929–31 brought a reversal in this centrifugal tendency and enabled the protectionists to impose their views. The experience, however, showed that the dreams of imperial autarchy and isolation were chimerical. Certainly, during the inter-war period and especially after the Ottawa agreements every Commonwealth country saw a marked increase in the proportion of its foreign trade with other members of the empire. This relative increase resulted, however, from the fall in trade with foreign countries, and the practical results of the Ottawa system were disappointing. As W. K. Hancock has written, the major theme at Ottawa had been imperial *self-sufficiency*; the experience of a few years provided the *self-insufficiency* of the empire.[61]

Is it possible, finally, to perceive some causal relationships between the economic changes just sketched out and changes in British policy towards the empire? There can be no question here of an extensive analysis of this problem, and we shall restrict ourselves to a few remarks, which, however, seem to indicate that the answer is negative.

Much importance has often been attached to the fact that the proportion of British exports that went to the empire increased appreciably at the beginning of the 'Great Depression' – from 23 per cent in 1871 to 35 per cent in 1877. From this it has been concluded that British businessmen, driven out of foreign markets by the 1873 crisis and the revival of protection, and finding alternative markets in the empire, were promptly converted to a belief in colonial expansion, abandoning the anti-imperialist principles of Cobden and Gladstone (whose first Ministry, from 1868 to 1874, came just at the time when imperial trade was least important for Britain) for the imperialism of Disraeli and later of Chamberlain. But is not this to overestimate the importance of short-term changes in the ratio of imperial to England's total foreign trade that took place around 1870? It overlooks the fact that the ratio goes through a series of fluctuations of a cyclical kind, of which the latter is merely the most marked; that during the years 1853–63 the empire's share of British exports had already reached percentages close to 33 per cent (and even 35 per cent in 1863); that after a maximum in 1886 it fell again until 1895 at the very moment when the tide of imperialist sentiment was rising strongly.

[61] Hancock, p. 266; see also my *Economie du Commonwealth* (Paris, 1950), pp. 124–9.

Admittedly, the proportion of total exports that went to the empire stood at a higher level after 1875 than during the preceding half century, but the difference was still small. It would be rash to maintain that a change of a few percentage points could have determined or even seriously influenced the state of opinion, let alone British government attitudes. The very widely held view according to which the great depression launched Britain along the road to imperialism is in no way proved, especially since the economic difficulties of the period may not have been as serious for England as has often been maintained.

Far sounder seems the viewpoint defended by Gallagher and Robinson, two scholars whose studies greatly altered traditional views of British imperialism, and according to whom it is useless to try to link changes in British imperial policy with fluctuations in the British economy, and in exports and terms of trade in particular.[62] Roughly speaking, the analysis we have attempted seems to reinforce the arguments of these two historians.

That trade with the empire always constituted a relatively small part of Britain's total commerce confirms the view that colonial expansion proper, the increase of what Gallagher and Robinson call the 'formal empire', was but one aspect, a function, of a much wider and multi-faceted imperialism, whereby England, the dominant economy in the nineteenth century, extended her ascendancy over, developed for her own benefit and integrated into the international economy overseas underdeveloped countries, some of which were annexed to the 'formal empire', but many of which were only part of an 'informal empire' – the rulers in London invariably showing a preference for methods of informal expansion and only reluctantly having recourse to annexation when it appeared absolutely necessary for the defence of British interests. This being so, a basic continuity can be ascertained in British imperialism all through the nineteenth century, and the traditional division into two major periods – liberal and imperialist – with a sharp break after 1870 seems no longer tenable.[63] All that can be discerned are short-term changes in imperial policy, especially in the policy followed in the various regions of British

62 R. Robinson and J. Gallagher, 'The Imperialism of Free Trade', *The Economic History Review*, VI, 1, August 1953, p. 6. See also their subsequent book, *Africa and the Victorians* (London, 1961).

63 O. Macdonagh, 'The Anti-Imperialism of Free Trade', *The Economic History Review*, XIV, 3, April 1962, pp. 489–501, suggests some modifications to this, for, while he admits there were clear manifestations of imperialism during the Palmerston era in the middle of the nineteenth century, he emphasises the hostility of authentic free-traders to this policy. On the other hand, Robinson and Gallagher themselves recognise changes in imperial policy after 1870.

expansion, which were much more a response to local and international developments than to economic factors in Britain itself or to the promptings of pressure groups. The lack of change in trade and investment in the empire in relation to total British trade and capital exports seems to fit in with Robinson and Gallagher's arguments, as well as with other recent studies which have emphasised the decisive role played by strictly political and strategic factors in British expansion in Africa during the last quarter of the nineteenth century.[64]

Several scholars have pointed out that the territories Britain annexed at this time (with the exception of the Transvaal) had but slight economic value and attracted but little investment, and that their trade constituted but an insignificant proportion of imperial trade. Gallagher and Robinson have written that in the competition between colonial powers the best finds and prizes had already been made before the end of the nineteenth century, and in Africa the imperialists 'were scraping the bottom of the barrel'.[65] For his part D. K. Fieldhouse has shown that the supposed need investors had to find outlets for their surplus capital had little to do with the partition of Africa and that the enthusiasm for imperial expansion shown by a large section of British opinion was not determined by economic factors. At the end of the nineteenth century, as during the preceding half century, financiers continued to invest their funds in profitable economic projects, generally in settlement colonies in temperate zones or in the independent 'new countries'. Statesmen, however, spurred on by a public opinion for which the possession of colonies had become a psychological necessity, continued 'to scrape the bottom of the barrel for yet more colonial burdens for the white man to carry'.[66]

[64] Especially D. K. Fieldhouse, 'Imperialism: an Historiographical Revision', *The Economic History Review*, XIV, 2, December 1961, pp. 187–209; D. S. Landes, 'Some Thoughts on the Nature of Economic Imperialism', *Journal of Economic History*, XXI, 4, December 1961, pp. 496–512; R. J. Hammond, 'Economic Imperialism: Sidelights on a Stereotype', *ibid.*, pp. 582–98. According to Robinson and Gallagher the English government was compelled to undertake large-scale intervention in Africa as a result of the crises that broke out in Egypt and South Africa and which it was feared would endanger the safety of the route to India. It sought, therefore, not to build a new African empire or to grab Africa's trade, but simply to defend the long-standing Indian empire. Fieldhouse, in contrast, stresses the importance of international rivalries in Europe and of Bismarck's decision to annex African territories.

[65] 'The Imperialism of Free Trade', p. 15.

[66] Fieldhouse, pp. 207–8 and also pp. 189–90, where he points out J. A. Hobson's conjuring trick (in his famous work of 1902, *Imperialism: A Study*, frequently used afterwards, notably by Lenin), where a list of territories England annexed after 1870 is placed side by side with a table showing the increase in foreign investment, without any analysis of its distribution. Fieldhouse's views have been criticised by Eric Stokes, 'Late Nineteenth-Century Colonial

Too frequently the 'extensive' annexations of marginal areas of illusory value – desert, steppe, and savanna – which took place at the end of the nineteenth century, over which English opinion enthused and which gave rise to so many disputes with rival powers, make us forget the much more important and lasting achievement of British imperialism at the time: the speeding up of development in the old colonies – Canada, Australasia and India – and of South America in the 'informal' empire.[67] It was this development, greatly stimulated by British capital, which led to a major change in imperial trade and contributed to England's growing wealth. Anyhow, the debate on the economic factors of imperialism is far from closed . . .[68]

Expansion and the Attack on the Theory of Economic Imperialism: A Case of Mistaken Identity?', *Historical Journal*, XII, 2, 1969, pp. 285–301; see also P. J. Cain, 'J. A. Hobson, Cobdenism and the Radical Theory of Economic Imperialism, 1898–1914', *The Economic History Review*, XXXI, 4, November 1978, pp. 564–84; plus criticisms by P. F. Clarke and an answer by Cain, *ibid.*, XXXIV, 2, May 1981, pp. 308–16.

67 Gallagher and Robinson, 'The Imperialism of Free Trade', p. 15.

68 This essay, first published in 1964, would need much revision to be updated, especially its last part, as many contributions to the debate on 'imperialism' and its relationship with trade and investment have been made since then. They are surveyed in an excellent small book by P. J. Cain, *Economic Foundations of British Overseas Expansion 1815–1914* (London, 1980). Only a few will be mentioned here. For instance, the posthumous book of J. Gallagher († 1980): *The Decline, Revival and Fall of the British Empire, The Ford Lectures and other Essays.* Edited by Anil Seal (Cambridge, 1982); and D. K. Fieldhouse's *Economics and Empire 1830–1914* (London, 1973), where he qualifies his earlier views. The Gallagher and Robinson thesis has been criticised by many writers; among them: Jean Stengers, 'L'Impérialisme colonial de la fin du 19e siècle, mythe ou réalité?', *Journal of African History*, III, 1962, pp. 469–91; D. C. M. Platt, 'Economic Factors in British Policy during the "New Imperialism"', *Past and Present*, XXXIX, April 1968, pp. 120–38; 'The Imperialism of Free Trade: Some Reservations', *The Economic History Review*, XXI, 2, August 1968, pp. 296–306; 'Further Objections to an "Imperialism of Free Trade"', *The Economic History Review*, XXVI, 1, February 1973, pp. 77–91; and his important book: *Finance, Trade and Politics in British Foreign Policy, 1814–1914* (Oxford, 1968).

A number of contributions to this debate have been reprinted in W. R. Louis (ed.), *Imperialism: The Robinson and Gallagher Controversy* (New York, 1976). One can also read: W. G. Hynes, *The Economics of Empire: Britain, Africa and the New Imperialism 1870–95* (London, 1979); B. Semmel, *The Rise of Free Trade Imperialism. Classical Political Economy, the Empire of Free Trade and Imperialism, 1750–1850* (Cambridge, 1970); C. C. Eldridge (ed.), *British Imperialism in the Nineteenth Century* (London, 1984). The major recent contributions are: L. E. Davis and R. A. Huttenback, *Mammon and the Pursuit of Empire, The Political Economy of British Imperialism, 1860–1912* (Cambridge, 1987); P. J. Cain and A. G. Hopkins, 'The Political Economy of British Expansion Overseas, 1750–1914', *The Economic History Review*, XXXIII, 4, November 1980, pp. 463–90; 'Gentlemanly Capitalism and British Expansion Overseas', *The Economic History Review*, XXXIX, 4, November 1986, pp. 501–25, and XL, 1, February 1987, pp. 1–26; P. K. O'Brien, 'The Costs and Benefits of British Imperialism 1846–1914', *Past and Present*, 120, August 1988, pp. 163–200. The present writer is inclined, nowadays, to give more weight to economic factors, in the history of the British Empire, than when he wrote the article which is reprinted as Chapter 11.

12 ❧ British coal in France in the nineteenth century*

Some years ago, as I was passing through a town in Brittany, my attention was caught by a faded, virtually obliterated inscription, which was displayed on the walls of an abandoned yard; just below the name of the firm, one could read 'Importers of English coal'. This seemed to me a kind of archaeological monument, and one which evoked a trade which has now all but disappeared, but which had its moment of glory, and which represented an important episode in the history of coal in France and in Britain.

The importation of English coal into France developed thanks to geographical conditions which greatly favoured it. The coastal areas of west and south-west France were far away from the French coal fields, while English and Welsh coal, which came from rich 'maritime' coal-fields and was transported by sea, was cheaper there than French coal, which had to be carried great distances overland. One author has quite justifiably observed that France 'offered itself to imports' and that English coals were blockading the French coasts.[1]

However, imports of English coal only gained real momentum relatively late in the nineteenth century. Certainly, from the sixteenth century, England had exported coal to France and, at the end of the *Ancien Régime*, these exports were considerable for the period, for example, 185,000 tons in 1788. But this trade was interrupted by the Revolutionary and Napoleonic wars and, during the following twenty years, it continued to be very small, with only 35,000 tons on average being imported from Britain each year between 1816 and 1834.[2]

* This text first appeared in L. Trenard (ed.), *Charbon et Sciences humaines. Actes du colloque organisé par la Faculté des Lettres de l'Université de Lille en mai 1963* (Paris–The Hague, 1966), pp. 173–205; I have made cuts, especially in the notes; interested readers may refer to the original.

1 R. Lafitte-Laplace, *L'Economie charbonnière de la France* (Paris, 1933), pp. 450, 466.

2 *Statistique de l'Industrie minérale*, 1838, p. 22. Most of my figures are taken from this official publication (referred to from now on as SIM), and notably from the *Volume du Centenaire* (Paris,

The trade had in fact been paralysed by crushing customs duties. The law of 28 April 1816 saddled coal imported by sea – which meant, in effect, coal from England, against whom this measure was clearly directed – with a duty of 10 francs per ton if it was transported on French ships and 15 francs per ton if it was carried by foreign vessels; conversely, coals imported by land, from Belgium or the Prussian Rhineland, were taxed much more lightly: 6 francs, 3 francs or 1·50 francs per ton, depending upon the frontier 'zones' through which they passed.[3] On the other hand, pit-coal, as it left England, was still saddled with a fairly high export duty.[4] Under these conditions, English coal could only reach consumers at almost prohibitive prices, and coals which arrived from Belgium and from Valenciennes, along canals to Dunkirk, from where they were offloaded into coasters, were able to compete successfully with them in the Channel and Atlantic ports. Whereas the importation of Belgian coal increased rapidly after 1815, amounting to as much as 620,000 tons in 1834, France only imported 49,000 tons of English coal in this same year.[5]

However, in 1834, England cut export duties on coal drastically; admittedly, a higher duty was reimposed in 1842, but only for a short period, since it was scrapped in 1845 and finally, in 1850, all export duties on coal were definitively abolished.[6]

In France, on the other hand, an order of 8 July 1834 admitted

1936, 4°), in which, unfortunately, figures for imports from Britain do not include those for bunker coal, which are in fact important. We have therefore used throughout this study the following figures for French imports:
- for the period 1815–1900, those from graph no. 3 (inset), in SIM, 1900;
- for the years 1901–12, those from the diagram in SIM, 1912, p. 15;
- for 1913, those in SIM, 1913, p. 15, corrected so as to include bunker coals.

Our figures for imports from Britain and for total imports therefore always include bunker coals, with the exception of those which were loaded by foreign ships in French ports (the quantities were not large). Imported cokes and briquettes were replaced 'by the corresponding weight in raw coal'; but again, quantities were small.

[3] L. Amé, *Etude sur les tarifs de douanes et sur les traités de commerce* (Paris, 1876, 2 vols.), vol. 1, p. 197. Useful summaries of customs legislation regarding coal may be found in SIM, 1870–2, pp. xxv–xxvi, and in J.-L. Gras, *Histoire de la Chambre de Commerce de Saint-Etienne depuis sa création en 1833 jusqu'en 1898* (Saint-Etienne, 1913), pp. 183–6.

[4] D. A. Thomas, 'The Growth and Direction of our Foreign Trade in Coal during the Last Half Century', *Journal of the Royal Statistical Society*, LXVI, part III, September 1903, p. 445; J. H. Clapham, *An Economic History of Modern Britain*, I, *The Early Railway Age. 1820–1850* (Cambridge, 1939, 2nd edn.), pp. 322, 484, note 2; *Parliamentary Papers* (abbreviated from here on as PP), 1871, XVIII, p. 1164.

[5] SIM, 1838, pp. 19–20, 60, 121, note; PP, 1871, XVIII, pp. 1027–8. Belgian coals entered by the canal from Mons to Condé, which had been completed in 1814.

[6] J. H. Morris and L. T. Williams, *The South Wales Coal Industry, 1841–1875* (Cardiff, 1958), p. 30; Thomas, p. 445; Clapham, pp. 484, note 2, 497–8; PP, 1871, XVIII, p. 1164.

duty-free foreign coals intended for use by French steamships, whether naval or merchant; then a number of measures passed between 1835 and 1837 ended up by lowering duties to 5 francs per ton for coals imported into ports from Dunkirk to Sables-d'Olonne, and to 3 francs for the ports lying to the south of Sables-d'Olonne. It is true that duties on overland imports were also cut, roughly by half, so that the discrimination against English coal persisted.[7] Nevertheless, these measures combined to lessen the burden imposed upon the importation of English coal, which had been paralysed since 1815 by excessive customs duties, as its sudden and rapid increase after 1834 demonstrates. Indeed, imports of English coal doubled from 1834 to 1835, and then tripled from 1835 to 1838. The *Statistique de l'Industrie minérale* was therefore able to record in 1838 that these reforms 'brought about a genuine revolution in the importation of coal by sea ... Nowadays, we find that the coals of Great Britain have almost wholly driven out the Belgian coals which had dominated virtually in all our Atlantic ports prior to 1834'.[8]

Subsequently, a decree of 1853 lowered entry duties again, with 3·60 francs being levied on imports by sea from Dunkirk to Sables-d'Olonne, and 1·80 francs for ports further south. Finally, the 1860 trade treaty with England committed France to abolishing all forms of discrimination against English coal within four years; in fact, a decree of 18 July 1860 brought duties levied on imports by sea down to 1·50 francs per ton and on 27 January 1863 duties on coal were fixed definitively at 1·20 francs per ton, regardless of the origin of the coal involved.[9] These last measures do not actually seem to have had an appreciable effect upon the Anglo-French coal trade, whose rate of growth did not alter after 1860. It was therefore the customs reductions of 1834–7 which enabled this trade to flourish.

The ultra-protectionist policies pursued during the Restoration probably had a damaging effect upon Western France, whose economy, smothered by twenty years of war at sea, would perhaps have benefited from unrestricted imports of English coal. However,

[7] The industrialists of Normandy and of Northern France protested against the excessively high duties on coal, so that the government organised in 1832–3 an enquiry, which resulted in the measures mentioned.

[8] SIM, 1838, pp. 20, 121, note. Only 9,000 tons of Belgian and French coal were shipped from Dunkirk in 1837.

[9] Amé, vol. II, p. 386; Gras, p. 188. The English government, for its part, had bound itself not to prohibit the export of coal and not to impose any duty on it.

after 1860, one can not say that France protected her high cost mines to the detriment of her industries, and thus produced too *much* coal, that is, more than would have been economically desirable,[10] since the duty of 1·20 francs was low, and never came to 10 per cent of the average price of imported coals.[11]

There were of course other factors besides custom reforms which contributed after 1834 to the rise in imports of English coal. First of all, there was an increase in coal consumption in France, owing to the Industrial Revolution, to the building of railways and to the development of steamships, whose need for bunker coal played an important part. This was all the more so given that, from 1830, and still more from 1840, the working in South Wales of seams of smokeless coal, which had previously been neglected and which were well adapted to the requirements of steamers, was started. A number of Welsh coal-owners also made special efforts to break into the French market. John Nixon, an engineer from Durham, who had worked in France, played a key part in this. He was to recall in later years that, in 1840, while on board a steamer on the Thames, he had been struck by the quality of the coal used, which did not make any smoke. This coal came from the area around Merthyr-Tydfil. Nixon went to Wales and proposed to Thomas Powell, who was working some mines in the Aberdare valley, that they introduce his coal on to the French market. The two men agreed to deliver coal free of charge to the first French consumers who would be prepared to use it and to adapt their plant to it. Nixon set up in business at Nantes and converted the refiners of sugar there, and then the owners of steamships on the Loire, to the use of Welsh coal. This coal was also adopted by the French navy, in preference to the coal of north-eastern England.[12]

Given these circumstances, imports of English coal into France increased rapidly and continued to increase up until the First World

10 R. Cameron, 'Profit, croissance et stagnation en France au XIXe siècle', *Economie Appliquée*, X, 1957, pp. 336, 443.

11 The duty of 1·20 francs remained unchanged up until 1926.

12 Morris and Williams, pp. 18, 31; A. H. John, *The Industrial Development of South Wales, 1750–1850* (Cardiff, 1950), pp. 121–2. On the French side, Hypolite Worms was later to play an important role. He was a merchant in Rouen and, from around 1842, he planned to import English coal and to drive Belgian coal out of the Seine-Inférieure; the opening in 1848 of the Dieppe–Rouen railway seemed to him to be the long-awaited opportunity, because it enabled him to import coal to Rouen at better terms than before; but he realised that it was necessary to avoid middlemen and to buy directly from mineowners, if one was to undercut the Belgians; he therefore set up agents in Newcastle (December 1848) and Cardiff (1851), and his affairs made rapid progress. See *Un Centenaire (1848–1948): Worms et Cie* (Paris, 1949), pp. 15–16, 18, 21, 29.

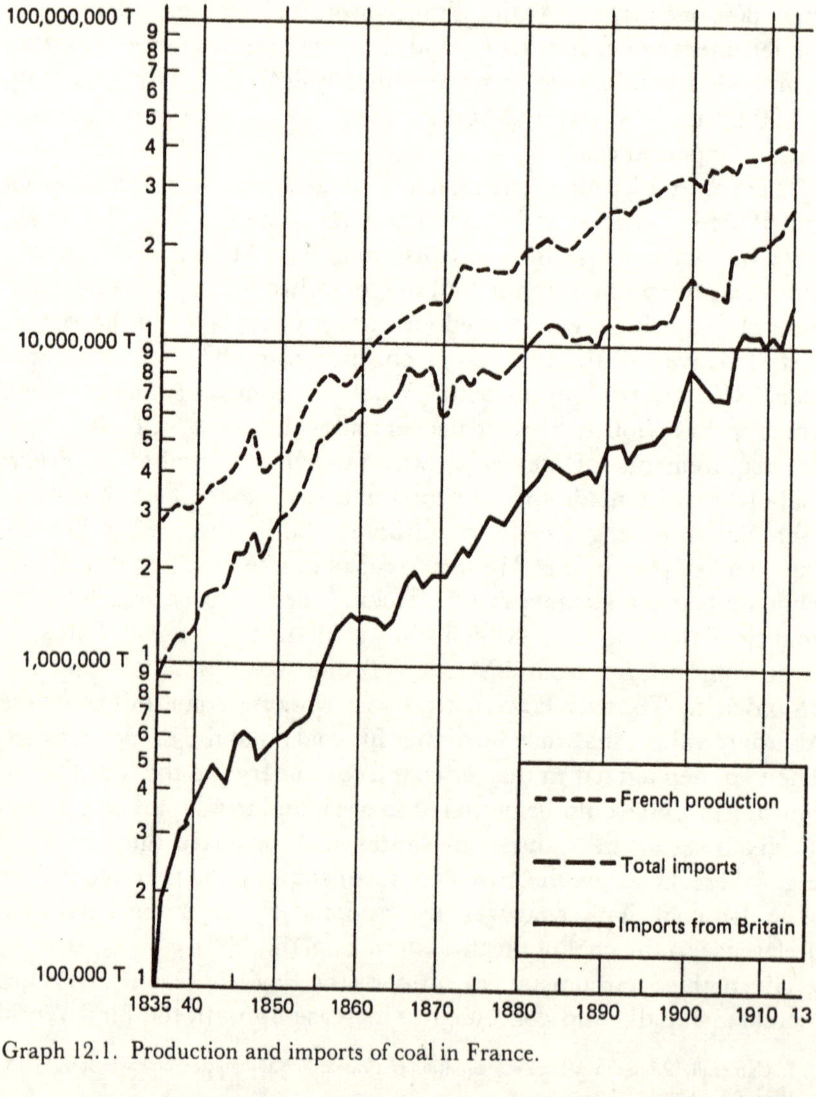

Graph 12.1. Production and imports of coal in France.

War. They exceeded 500,000 tons by 1845, 1 million tons in 1856, 2 million in 1872, 4 million in 1883, 8 million in 1900 and, finally, 12 million in 1913.[13] This trade was thus marked by a high rate of growth:

[13] Statistics for British coal exports to France (in 'long' tons of 1,016 kg) do of course give slightly different figures – a little higher as a rule, for they include all the bunker coals; but their fluctuations closely parallel those of imports into France. Some useful tables may be found in the appendices to the reports of the Royal Commissions of 1871 and 1905 into problems regarding coal: PP, 1871, XVIII, vol. III, p. 989; PP, 1905, XVI, part XI, pp. 786–91.

Table 12.1.

	Imports of British coal in France (5-years averages) 000-Tons	Share of British coal in total imports of coal by France %	in total consumption of coal in France %
1841–1845	476	24	9
1846–1850	576	24	8
1851–1855	702	19	7
1856–1860	1,236	22	9
1861–1865	1,392	21	8
1866–1870	1,854	24	9
1871–1875	2,240	30	10
1876–1880	3,012	35	12
1881–1885	4,032	37	14
1886–1890	4,156	40	13
1891–1895	4,805	42	13
1896–1900	6,232	48	16
1901–1905	7,181	49	15
1906–1910	10,235	53	19
1911–1913	11,107	49	18

Source. See note 2, pp. 414–15. Bunker-coal used by French ships is included in French consumption.

5·15 per cent per year, for the period 1838–1913 (starting after the customs measures which had made its increase possible). Imports of English coal not only increased faster than production of French coal, whose average rate of growth during the same period was only 3·5 per cent, but also outstripped total coal imports, whose rate of growth was 4·2 per cent (see Graph 12.1).

As a consequence, English coals represented an increasing share, not only of total imports, but also of the total consumption of coal in France. Table 12.1 shows that, by the years 1841–50, English coal constituted almost a quarter of French coal imports and provided almost a tenth of the country's total consumption. During the next fifteen years, these percentages dipped slightly[14] but, after 1865, they rose appreciably and, by 1876–80, Britain provided over a third of all imports and 12 per cent of the total amount consumed. English coals

[14] On account of a rapid increase in imports from Germany, which, however, were not in competition with English coal, and on account of the latter's loss of its outlets on the Mediterranean coast (see below, pp. 432–3).

made slightly less headway, it is true, between 1885 and 1898, but there was a leap forward in 1899–1901, when they reached and even, for the first time, exceeded 50 per cent of total imports. The peak occurred in 1905–10, with 53 per cent of imports and 19 per cent of French coal consumption; the last years of the pre-war period were marked by a slight drop in percentage.

There were therefore two main stages in the penetration of English coal into the French market: the first, at the end of the 1830s, was sudden and rapid, but it only secured a relatively small share of this market, a share which remained stable for the following quarter of a century; the second, which only began after 1865, was longer and slower, with a gradual increase of the British share in the French market. This increase was achieved at the expense of coals imported from other countries rather than of French coal.[15] In fact, after 1866, imports from England continued to increase rapidly,[16] whereas the rate of growth of total imports was clearly slowing down (see Graph 12.1), with those of German coals falling sharply after 1870, as a consequence of the loss of Alsace–Lorraine, which was one of their main outlets, and those of Belgian coals having levelled out after 1866, and then declined after 1883.

However, the main cause of this relative, and then absolute decline of Belgian coal imports was the competition not of English coal but of the new French mines in the Pas-de-Calais, which successfully made their mark in the traditional Belgian fiefdom of northern France.[17] From the late 1830s, English coal had, as we have seen, eliminated Belgian coals from the French Atlantic ports; under the Second Empire, they drove them out of the Lower Seine area, and even out of Calais and Boulogne. Finally, in the last third of the nineteenth century, the zones for the sale of Belgian and English coals were completely

[15] The ratio between French production and total consumption of coal only suffered short term and small fluctuations after 1865 (a maximum of 75 per cent in 1898, a minimum of 61 per cent in 1866); it stood at the same level in 1913 as in 1864, namely, 64 per cent.

[16] The rapid fall in the price of English coal and in ocean freight charges after 1873 undoubtedly played a part. Thus, freight from Cardiff to Bordeaux fell from 11 francs per ton on average in 1873–5 to 7·25 francs in 1883–5 (H. S. Jevons, *The British Coal Trade*, London, 1915, p. 692).

[17] From 1866 to 1883, imports from Belgium increased only 12 per cent, reaching 5,756,000 tons, a maximum which they were never again to touch (4,987,000 tons in 1913). The share of Belgian coals in total imports, which had been 83 per cent in 1834, 60 per cent in 1866, and still as high as 50 per cent in 1889, fell to 36 per cent in 1901 and to 20 per cent in 1913. See F. Lentacker, 'Les Charbons belges sur le marché français au cours du XIXe siècle', Académie royale des sciences d'outre-mer, *Bulletin des Sciences*, 1964, no. 6, pp. 1392–1431.

different; they only competed in the Paris area where, indeed, the latter made progress at the expense of the former.[18]

However, England only won first place on the French market quite late; it was in fact in 1894 that imports of English coal definitively overtook those of Belgian coal. Yet, after 1901, they were no longer gaining ground within the French market as a whole, whereas the importation of German coal was increasing very rapidly, rising from 2,021,000 tons in 1900 to 6,846,000 tons in 1913, so that their proportion of total imports rose from 12 per cent to 27 per cent. Admittedly, the greater part of these coals, which were intended for the steel industry of Lorraine in particular, were not in direct competition with English coal; but the latter were nevertheless under threat in their fiefdoms of Western and South-western France. Thanks to its forceful commercial methods, the Kohlensyndikat of the Rhineland and Westphalia succeeded, from 1902 on, in selling significant quantities of coal, which were exported by way of the Rhine and Rotterdam, to ports such as Boulogne, Rouen, Saint-Nazaire, La Rochelle and Bayonne; its main clients were in fact some steel works which were located on the coast, in places such as Outreau, Trignac and Le Boucau.[19] Some of these gains were merely temporary but, in 1911, in seven of the coastal departments,[20] which consumed large quantities of English coal (some 2,641,000 tons), sales of German coals reached 580,000 tons. German coal did not, however, make any inroads into the other departments on the Channel and Atlantic coasts. All in all, Germany did not pose a serious threat to British coal interests.

Be this as it may, imports of English coals into France rose rapidly and regularly. However, their curve naturally features cyclical fluc-

18 In 1911, the Seine consumed 1,303,000 tons of English coal and 698,000 tons of Belgian coal.

19 This traffic began quite suddenly in 1902; it increased dramatically in 1903. There is a great deal of information about this problem in Final Report of the Royal Commission on Coal Supplies, part XIII, Replies of HM Consular Officers in Answer to a Series of Questions upon the Maintenance of the British Coal Trade in Foreign Countries, PP, 1905, XVI, Cd. 2365, especially pp. 848–53, 857–9, 872–3, 877, 879, where the reports of consuls stationed in French ports are to be found. Some of them were anxious about German competition and its methods (a single agent in each town, the paying of great attention to the desires of clients, even a certain amount of dumping); but, in other ports, such as Cherbourg, Saint-Malo and Brest, it had not yet started. See also H. S. Jevons, *Foreign Trade in Coal* (London and Cardiff, 1909), pp. 4–5, who claims that transport costs up to Rouen for coal from the Ruhr were higher (by 18 per cent) than for those from Wales. But the Germans were still able to compete, thanks to the cheapness of their labour and the lower profits levied by mineowners. From 1901 to 1906, an export tax of one shilling per ton was imposed in England. The complaint often was that it favoured German exports, especially as regards lower quality coals.

20 Seine-Inférieure, Loire-Inférieure, Vendée, Charente-Inférieure, Calvados, Ille-et-Vilaine and Bouches-du-Rhône.

tuations, so that years of growth alternate with others in which imports stagnate or fall (see the graph on p. 418). There is a very strong correlation between imports from England and total imports of coal, with both increasing or receding at one and the same time; the only significant exception is located in 1870–1, when the halting of imports from Germany brought down total imports sharply, whereas those from England increased a little. There is also a clear correlation between imports of English coal and French production of coal; most maxima and minima are located for both in the same years; but, in some cases, a time-lag is evident, the turning points of imports from England occurring a little later than those of French output.[21]

These movements are of course related to the cyclical fluctuations of French economic activity: it is by and large during years of expansion and prosperity that imports of English coal increase, whereas setbacks tend to correspond with periods of depression.

Such correlations are commonplace enough but, more interestingly, there are some obvious discrepancies between the changes in imports of English coal and the overall cyclical fluctuations. In the first place, a number of the latter, although sharp ones, had scarcely any effect upon purchases of English coal, which, for instance, increased uninterruptedly between 1849 and 1861, without even the 1857 crisis slowing them down; during the Great Depression, which began in 1873, imports go on rising, with only slight and short setbacks in 1874 and in 1878.

On the other hand, in several instances there is a time-lag between imports and the overall conjuncture. Thus, the years of maxima for imports are often situated after the peaks of activity, and may even be years of recession. Conversely, several of the years in which imports from England fall were years of economic recovery.

These differences may be explained by the lack of elasticity peculiar to coal production, and by the fact that prices of imported coals, whose movements are determined by external forces and reflect conditions on the international market, are ahead of those of French coal and tend to fluctuate more sharply.[22]

[21] There are also instances of such time-lags between the production of British mines (see A. J. Taylor, 'Labour Productivity and Technological Innovation in the British Coal Industry, 1850–1914', *The Economic History Review*, XIV, 1, August 1961, p. 51) and exports to France, with English producers turning towards the latter at the beginning of a recession.

[22] F. Simiand, 'Essai sur le prix du charbon en France au XIXe siècle', *Année Sociologique*, V, 1900–1, pp. 1–81; especially pp. 33–45, 75–9.

At the start of a phase of expansion, prices of imported coal were the first to rise, so that consumers turned towards French coals, all the more so given that mining companies had cut their costs during the depression. French mines therefore profited from the recovery and increased their share of the market, whereas imports remained at a low level. However, after a period of time, the demand for coal increased more rapidly than French extraction, so that French mines could no longer keep pace with demand, prices rose sharply, and sometimes there was a 'panic rise', as Simiand has written, 'a coal famine' (for example, in 1872–3 and in 1900). Hence a boom in imports, not only in absolute terms but also relatively, for example from 1879 to 1883, when English coal increased its share of the market, especially in those regions where it was in competition with French or Belgian coals. The increase in imports is sometimes quite startling, as for example in 1890 (when they were 27 per cent higher than in 1889), in 1899–1900, in 1906 and in 1913. The price rises also stimulated orders during the final phase of expansion, as did the fact that English coal prices were the first to fall. One can thus understand why imports maximum should often be situated after peaks of the business cycle. Moreover, during some recessions, price rebates by English exporters had the result of making imports diminish less than did French output and regain their upward movement fairly quickly. When, however, the slump was a prolonged one, imports only got going again some time after recovery had started.

All in all, the phases during which imports rose corresponded to spurts in coal prices and freights, while drops in imports are correlated with falling prices. However, there are at least two significant exceptions, with a growth in trade occurring in years when prices were falling; namely, between 1856 and 1859, and between 1874 and 1879.

Fluctuations in imports thus shed some light upon the workings of the coal market, but they were not so sharp as to alter significantly the rising long-term trend, at any rate until 1883, as subsequently it became more irregular. There was never a time, moreover, when a maximum failed to attain a higher level than the one immediately preceding it, and the same is true of the minima. Phases of regression are, on the other hand, short-lived, one or two years at most, save for two of them, namely, 1884–9 and 1901–5. In addition, there were only two cases when the difference between a maximum and the minimum which followed it was higher than 15 per cent of the volume of imports

Table 12.2. *Share of British ports (by groups) in exports of coal to France*

	Bristol Channel %	North-East %	Humber %	Scotland %	Others %
1850	26	63	6	1·5	3·5
1868	47	44	4	4	1
1895	65	23	4	7	1
1900	62	23	5	10	—
1905	64	24	3	8	1
1910	55	30	4	9	2
1913	57	30	6	7	—

Source. See note 24, p. 424.

during the peak year: a drop of 17 per cent is apparent between 1846 and 1848 and a drop of 20 per cent between 1900 and 1905. There was in fact some crisis in the Anglo-French coal trade after 1900, whose main aspect was the emergence of German competition, but it was a temporary one and was followed by a vigorous recovery.

All in all, the rapid growth of imports of British coal into France was only slightly affected by business cycles,[23] which may be explained by the fact that their main markets were in regions that were not much industrialised.

Two of the main British coalfields – of Northumberland–Durham (or North-eastern), and of South Wales – together supplied France with the greater part of the coals which she imported from Britain. Much smaller quantities came from Yorkshire, by way of the ports on the Humber, and from Scotland (see Table 12.2).[24]

In the middle of the nineteenth century, it was the north-eastern coalfield which was France's main supplier. However, from 1860 on, exports from South Wales rapidly increased (they more than doubled in the space of ten years), for both its geographical situation, being closer to several French ports which were large-scale importers (Cardiff to Bordeaux was 540 miles, as against 905 miles from the Tyne), and the nature of the coal it produced were in its favour.[25] Its

[23] Thomas, p. 467, also notes that, from 1870 to 1900, total exports of British coal increased almost continuously, without being clearly affected by business cycles.

[24] According to PP, 1871, XVIII, pp. 1202, 1204, 1207, 1211, 1214–15; F. A. Gibson, *A Compilation of Statistics of the Coal Mining Industry of the United Kingdom, of the Various Coalfields thereof, and the Principal Foreign Countries of the World* (Cardiff, 1922), p. 100.

[25] E. D. Lewis, *The Rhondda Valleys. A Study in Industrial Development from 1800 to the Present Day* (London, 1959), pp. 137–8.

share grew quite steadily, amounting to 65 per cent of total exports to France in 1895, as compared with only 23 per cent for the North-east coalfield. Wales did lose some ground after 1905; nevertheless, in 1913, it shipped 7,246,000 tons of coal to France, as compared with the 3,823,000 sent from the North-east. Cardiff was the leading port for exports, with 2,923,000 tons, followed by the Tyneside ports (2,735,000 tons), Swansea (1,915,000 tons), Port Talbot (1,124,000 tons), Newport (1,037,000 tons), and Sunderland (688,000 tons).[26]

Wales was almost the sole supplier of ports to the west of the Seine, to which it sent bituminous coal for household and industrial use, steam coal and anthracite; Northumberland exported mainly gas-coal, and Durham, coking coal, to the ports to the north of the Seine.[27]

France was far and away the largest foreign customer for British coal. According to an English statistical source, between 1870 and 1904, Britain exported in toto 155 million tons of coal to France, that is, 17 per cent of its total exports, which amounted to 902 million; to Germany, its second largest customer, it only exported 118 million tons.[28] France's share in this trade remained remarkably constant during the whole of the period under consideration, hovering around the 17 per cent mark. Thus, it stood at 20 per cent in 1840–1, and 18 per cent for the years 1856–60 and 1871–5; it reached 19 per cent in 1881–5 and then fell a little; in 1911–13, it stood at 16·4 per cent (but it was 17·4 per cent in 1913). The French market was therefore of great importance for the export of British coal. During the half-century before 1914, these exports increased far faster than did British consumption and production themselves, so that they absorbed a growing share of output, which rose gradually from 10 per cent in 1852–60 to 28 per cent in 1901–5, and to 34 per cent in 1913.[29] Exports to France therefore represented 1·9 per cent of Britain's total production in 1856–60, 2·8 per cent in 1900–4 and 4·5 per cent in 1913. This overall percentage remained low, but the ratio was of course much higher for

26 PP, 1914, LXXVIII, pp. 393–427. For the 1860s, see *Question des houilles. Mission de M. de Ruolz en France et en Angleterre* (Paris, 1872–5, 3 tomes in 4 volumes), t. III, p. 305. This monumental report contains a mass of useful information.

27 Lafitte-Laplace, p. 451; PP, 1905, XVI, p. 410, gives detailed figures regarding the destination of Welsh coal within France.

28 PP, 1905, XVI, p. 771. 536,000 tons of coke and 4,018,000 tons of briquettes must be added to total exports; France imported very little of these two products. Bunker coals of ships sailing from Britain are not included in these totals.

29 Bunker coals included; Jevons, *The British Coal Trade*, p. 676. From 1850 to 1900, total exports of coal were multiplied by 15, British domestic consumption by more than 3, and extraction by 4.

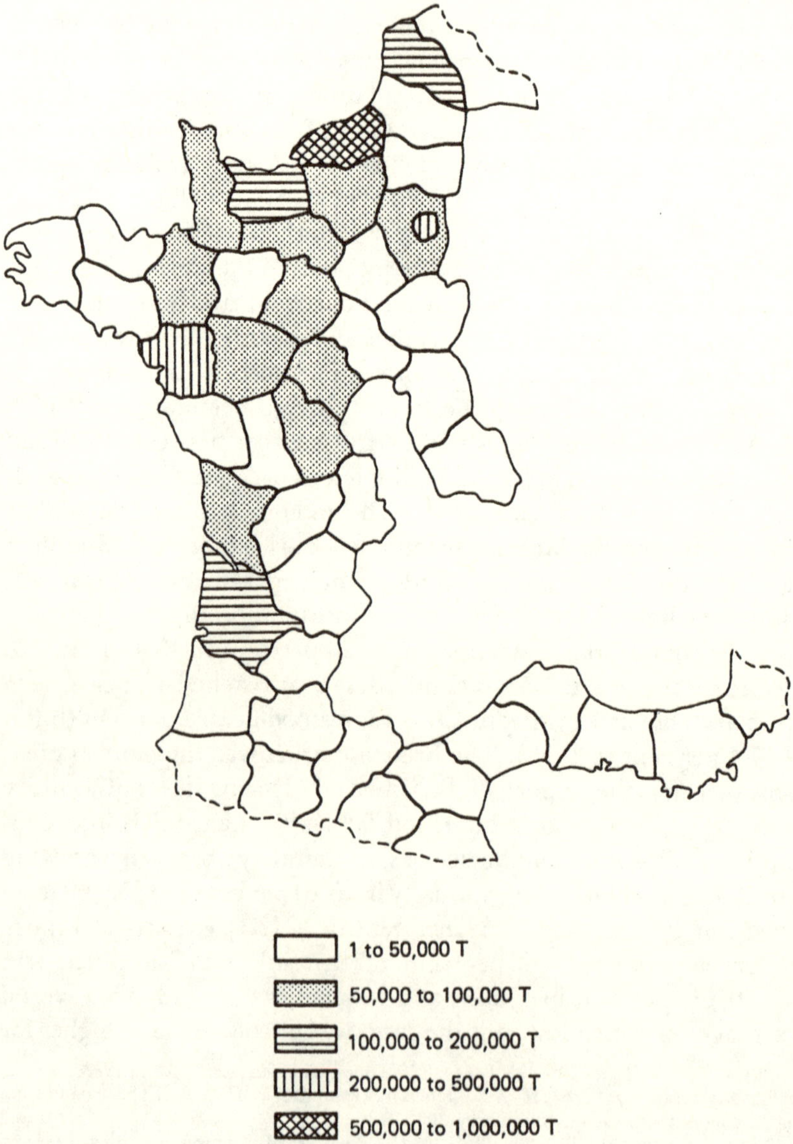

Map 12.1. Consumption of British coal by *département* in 1879.
N.B. Consumption of British coal was nil or minimal in the *départements* which do not feature on this map.

the South Wales coalfield, which exported overseas 53 per cent of its production in 1913 and sent 24 per cent of its exports to France; the latter therefore absorbed 10 per cent of that coalfield's production in 1895 and 13 per cent in 1913.[30]

The distribution of British coal imports among French ports and the main sections of the French coast also deserves consideration (see map on p. 426).[31] During the whole of the period 1838–1913, Normandy was in the lead, but its share of imports fell appreciably, from 55 per cent to 38 per cent. This primacy is of course explicable in terms of the large coal requirements of the industrial region around Rouen, together with the hinterland of the Norman ports, which supplied Paris and the inland areas of Western France with English coals.

The ports of Brittany (including those at the mouth of the Loire, which accounted for almost two thirds of the trade in this sector), and the Atlantic ports south of the Loire tied for second place. The former group's share rose appreciably from 1838 to 1867, and then stabilised at around 20 per cent of total imports; that of the second increased steadily, moving from 16 per cent to 24 per cent.

The ports to the north of the Somme trailed a long way behind. In this sector, consumption of English coal was insubstantial, limited to the requirements of Calais, Boulogne and their neighbourhoods,[32] with the penetration inland of imported coals being quickly halted by competition from the coals of the Pas-de-Calais, a competition which intensified.[33] Under the Second Empire, moreover, the greater part of the coals imported in Dunkirk and Calais were sent to Paris by rail. This through traffic continued up until the beginning of the twentieth century, but declined in importance with respect to that passing through Rouen.[34] This sector only took 7 per cent of English coal imports in 1892 and in 1913, as against 14 per cent in 1867.

The Mediterranean ports' share of total imports fluctuated sharply;

30 Gibson, p. 78; PP, 1919, XII, Cmd. 360, p. 795. In 1895, Wales exported 44 per cent of its production and sent 22 per cent of its exports to France. Bunker coals of ships sailing from Welsh ports are not included in exports. If they were, France's share in Welsh exports would be a little lower: 18 per cent in 1895, 20 per cent in 1913.

31 See SIM, 1839, p. 19; 1881, map h.t. pp. 18–19; 1892, map h.t.; 1913, table 6, pp. 98–100; Ruolz, *La Question des houilles*, t. I, pp. 640–1, t. III, pp. 280–94.

32 Especially the ironworks of Marquise and Outreau.

33 PP, 1905, XVI, pp. 850, 852. In 1904, the English consuls at Boulogne, Calais and Dunkirk noted that imports were tending to stagnate or even to fall. The consul at Boulogne, for example, stated that the steam-trawlers of this port were only using French coal, whereas two years earlier English coal ruled supreme.

34 Ruolz, *La Question des houilles*, t. I, pp. 93, 95, 410, 425; PP, 1905, XVI, p. 855.

it was by no means negligible in the 1830s and 40s, fell badly in the 1860s – as English coals were eliminated by those from French pits in Gard and Hérault; but it rallied well after 1870 and reached the 10 per cent mark in 1913.

All things considered, there was a general tendency for outlets for English coal to shift southwards, so that the share of ports to the west of Mont Saint-Michel increased from 35 per cent in 1838 to 47 per cent in 1881 and to 54 per cent in 1913. This was attributable to the competition by French coal in the north of the country, and to an increased level of consumption in the fiefdoms of English coal, namely, the West and the South-west.

Some interesting changes are also evident in the ranking of the importing ports. In the 1860s, Dieppe, Le Havre and Bordeaux were competing for first place. In 1866–8, Dieppe prevailed briefly over its rivals; the cheapness of freight and handling charges worked in its favour, as did the good railway links; this port was therefore receiving a large part of the coal used by the Compagnie de l'Ouest (Western Railway Co.) and by the industries of Rouen and Elbeuf; it also sent some by rail to Paris. Saint-Nazaire, Nantes and Rouen trailed a good way behind these ports, with this latter merely in sixth place, although it had been in the lead in 1838.[35]

During the following decades, Le Havre, Dieppe and Dunkirk's coal traffic increased at a slower rate than did total imports, and these ports lost ground. In other ports, on the other hand, the rate of growth of this traffic was higher than that of the total imports of English coals into France, and their share of the market increased. This was true of La Rochelle, Marseilles, Bayonne, and above all of Rouen and Bordeaux. Rouen was favoured by the growing demand for English coals in the Paris region and by the cheapness of river transportation along the Seine; its imports multiplied six times over between 1892 and 1913. Bordeaux's traffic did not increase quite so rapidly but nevertheless it was ten times larger in 1913 than it had been in 1863; its hinterland's coal requirements were, admittedly, limited, but those of local industry and of the railways – especially those of the Compagnie d'Orléans, which used Bordeaux as its main importing port – account for this expansion.[36] By the closing years of the nineteenth century, Rouen and

[35] Ruolz, *La Question des Houilles*, t. I, pp. 441, 492–3; t. III, pp. 185–257 (detailed statistics), 304.

[36] E. Huyard, *Le Port de Bordeaux* (Bordeaux and Paris, 1909), pp. 101–6.

Bordeaux had become the two leading French coal ports.[37] Ranked behind them, in order, were – in 1913 – Marseilles, Saint-Nazaire, La Rochelle, Caen and Nantes.

Importing tended also to concentrate in a small number of large ports. In the 1850s and 1860s, it had been relatively scattered. Thus, in 1869, shipments of coal were being made from Britain to almost 130 different French ports, and small coasters would offload a few hundred or even a few dozen tons at insignificant harbours in Normandy, Brittany and the Vendée. M. Le Lannou has shown that English coal had played a key role in the 'modest prosperity' enjoyed by Breton ports in the years between 1860 and 1880. However, after this date, three quarters of these ports effectively died, falling victim to the railways, which worked to the advantage of the main ports, which were better equipped and had lower import costs.[38]

This restructuring of the coal trade was of great importance for the French Atlantic and Channel ports for, from the mid nineteenth century, imports of coal, for the most part English, constituted an increasing and dominant share of their total imports in volume, being always more than a half and sometimes two thirds, as was for instance the case in La Rochelle–La Pallice and Caen. These ports thus depended more and more upon English coal.[39]

Precise information regarding the consumption of English coals in France is not available, except regarding two aspects, namely, consumption by the French merchant navy and by railways.

Bunker coals represented a significant share of total imports at the beginning of the period during which the traffic in English coals rose sharply, being 15 per cent in 1835–9 and 22 per cent in 1841–5; but this percentage fell appreciably later on, dropping to 4 per cent in 1871–5. After 1860, these imports actually suffered a fall in absolute terms, because the French navy deliberately stopped using English coals, so as to avoid running short in case of war.[40] Imports of bunker coal

37 They really took off during these years. By 1900, Rouen received over one million tons of British coals, and Bordeaux 800,000.

38 PP, 1871, XVIII, pp. 1216–17; M. Le Lannou, 'Ports et Havres de Bretagne', in Association Guillaume Budé, Breton section, *Conférences universitaires de Bretagne (1942–1943)* (Paris, 1943), pp. 191–6.

39 Share of coal in the total volume of imports in 1907: La Rochelle–La Pallice, 70 per cent; Bordeaux, 63 per cent; Rouen, 60 per cent; Saint-Nazaire, 58 per cent; Nantes, 50 per cent. At Bordeaux, in 1881–90, the percentage had only been 33 per cent.

40 Amé, t. II, p. 388, note 1; Ruolz, *La Question des houilles*, t. I, pp. 85, 148, 529, 548, 551, 597, 700; t. III, p. 177, état XII, 245, état XVIII.

picked up again after 1880, when steamships became more numerous in the French merchant navy; during the thirty years up to 1910, bunker coal represented 10 to 12 per cent of the total amount of imports. Originating, as one would expect, in South Wales, these bunker coals satisfied almost all the requirements of the French merchant navy.[41] As far as the railways were concerned, the Paris–Orléans, Midi and Ouest-État companies used large quantities of English coal (in 1910–11, it accounted for around half their consumption, in the case of the first two companies, and two thirds in the case of the last). British coal accounted for 31 per cent of the total consumption of the major railway companies in 1900–1, and 28 per cent in 1910–11. The railways absorbed 17 per cent of the imports of English coal in 1879 and 21 per cent in 1900–1, as also in 1910–11.[42] This is a high figure and, all things considered, the maritime and railway transport systems consumed a third of imported British coal at the beginning of the twentieth century.

The other two thirds were shared out between 'domestic' and 'industrial' usages, but in proportions that are not known. In the late 1860s, in ten large coal-consuming towns, the proportions were as follows: industry, 50 per cent; households, 33 per cent; gas-works, 17 per cent.[43] This structure may barely have changed during later years, but these figures are averages and conceal large variations from one region to the next.[44]

We are better informed as to the geographical distribution of British coal consumption.[45] Moreover, broadly speaking, it remained remarkably stable from the 1840s to the First World War. British coals enjoyed a dominant position, indeed a monopoly, in all those regions which were both near to the sea and removed from the French

[41] 80 per cent in 1910, 73 per cent in 1911.

[42] 513,000 tons in 1879, 1,758,000 in 1900, 2,119,000 in 1910. See SIM, 1879, p. 24; 1900, Table 5, p. 35, and Table 6, p. 49; 1901, Table 5, p. 87, and Table 6, p. 101; 1910, Table 6, p. 117; 1911, Table 6, p. 117. The Paris–Lyon–Méditerranée railway also consumed a good deal of British coal but this was only a small part of its total consumption.

[43] According to Ruolz, *La Question des houilles*, t. III, état X, pp. 88 ff.

[44] The English consuls' reports mention that, around 1904, domestic consumption absorbed two thirds of British coals imported in the 'consular district' of Boulogne, a sixth in that of Nantes and a quarter in that of Bordeaux. On the other hand, consuls at Cherbourg and Saint-Malo noted that domestic consumption was low in their districts, because wood was still the main fuel used in the countryside (PP, 1905, XVI, pp. 848, 850, 853, 872, 879).

[45] Up until 1911, the *Statistique de l'Industrie minérale* published each year a table of the consumption of mineral fuels in each department, specifying the origin of the coals used. These statistics are fairly reliable as far as orders of magnitude are concerned.

coalfields,[46] that is, by and large in Western France. However, there were a number of changes, as a consequence of developments in the French coal industry, in the transport system[47] and in the industrial, or even domestic, demand in the various regions.[48]

'The coals of Great Britain', wrote the anonymous author of the *Statistique de l'Industrie minérale* in 1839, 'today supply, to the exclusion of virtually every other mineral fuel, the littoral of the Channel and of the Atlantic Ocean';[49] generally speaking, this judgement continued to be valid up until 1914, the preferred area for English coals having always been the coastal region between the Somme and the Spanish border. It was along this long coastal strip that English coals were most firmly entrenched, enjoying what amounted to monopolies; there too the greater part of the coals imported from Britain were consumed, over two thirds in the middle of the nineteenth century, around 60 per cent later, and still 48 per cent in 1911.

If one considers the fourteen departments in this zone as one unit, one finds that English coals accounted in 1838 for 66 per cent of their coal requirements;[50] in fact, in Calvados, Manche, Loire-Inférieure and Vendée, small local coalfields were able to cover a substantial part of a still tiny consumption.[51] However, in the third quarter of the

46 It was there that the difference between the costs of British and of French coals was the greatest. In 1860, according to Ruolz, *La question des houilles* (t. I, pp. 88, 167, 444–7, 471–3, 484–5, 537–8; t. II, p. 630), the French navy could buy British coals delivered to Atlantic ports at 28 francs a ton, whereas French coals, transported by railway, would have cost 45 to 48 francs (i.e. 66 per cent more). In 1869, English coals were sold at Dieppe, Fécamp and Le Havre, 20 to 30 per cent cheaper than the same kinds of French coals; at Rouen, the difference was less (10 to 20 per cent), but at Nantes, British coals were 30 per cent cheaper than those from the Loire coalfield. There is also the important question of quality; in general, French coals had less calorific power than British coals classified within the same category, left more cinders and clinker etc., so that the real difference in price was greater than the nominal one.

47 The construction of railways aided the diffusion of coals from small fields on the west and south of the Massif Central; during the last third of the nineteenth century, they stole some ground from British coals in the Loire valley, in Aquitaine and in the Mediterranean region. Conversely, railways facilitated the penetration of British coals into the *Ouest intérieur*.

48 See SIM, 1839, pp. 80 ff.; 1865–9, pp. 116–17; 1879, map h.t.; 1892, Tables 5 and 6, pp. 32, 34–43; 1900, map h.t., pp. 35, 38–48; 1911, map h.t., pp. 103, 106–16.

49 SIM, 1839, p. 18.

50 These needs were then very limited, save in Seine-Inférieure. British coal did not penetrate at all into the interior of Brittany; in 1838, in the Côtes-du-Nord, it was only used by blacksmiths and locksmiths; in Finistère, the dockyard at Brest and the navy were the sole consumers. Demand was slight in the Gironde also, and here wood from Les Landes was a serious competitor for English coal, which was used mainly by the glassworks of Bordeaux (SIM, 1838, pp. 40, 46, 48–9; 1839, map h.t.).

51 Coal from these small deposits (for instance at Littry, Le Plessis, Vouvant-Chantonnay) was low quality, expensive, and mainly used in lime kilns (Ruolz, *La Question des Houilles*, t. I, pp. 516, 520, 575; SIM, 1838, pp. 35, 59, 64–5). The production of these coalfields which had reached 180,000 tons in 1879, fell away in subsequent years (110,000 tons in 1911).

nineteenth century, British coals substantially improved their position, for local production was not able to keep step with demand; their share in total consumption reached 80 per cent in 1867, 88 per cent in 1883 and 1900 – when English coals accounted for over 90 per cent of requirements in ten departments.[52] It was only after 1900 that British positions were undermined by competition from German, Belgian and French coals, especially in the Seine, Loire-Inférieure, Vendée and Gironde, so that, by 1911, England's share in consumption along the coastal sector had fallen to 75 per cent. She had nevertheless long enjoyed a quasi-monopoly in the larger part of this zone,[53] in particular in Brittany and Aquitaine, where the consumption of coal actually increased more rapidly than in Normandy.[54]

There were two other coastal sectors, on either side of this great fiefdom of British coals, where they did not enjoy so dominating a position, because of competition from French mines nearby, but where consumption did nevertheless reach significant levels. The first was the coast to the north of the Somme or, more exactly, the ports of Boulogne and Calais, together with their vicinity, where English coals dominated the market,[55] and where industrial and domestic demand was sufficiently strong for the Pas-de-Calais to be regularly classed among the group of departments which were large consumers of English coals; however, the latter only represented a small part of its total consumption – slightly less than one tenth.

The other sector was the Mediterranean coast of France. In the 1840s and 1850s, English coals were used at various points along this coast and, in particular, at Marseilles; only modest quantities were involved, although in 1847 they accounted for 15 per cent of the consumption of Bouches-du-Rhône. However, after 1858, fierce competition arose on the part of the coals from mines in Gard and Hérault, as the building of railways had helped their transport to the ports, so that English coals were from then on imported in insignificant quantities only. 'English coals', wrote the *Statistique de l'Industrie*

[52] Calvados, Manche, Côtes-du-Nord, Ille-et-Vilaine, Morbihan, Loire-Inférieure, Vendée, Charente-Inférieure, Landes, Basses-Pyrénées.

[53] See the map appended to SIM, 1880, which shows that the consumption of French coal was either nil or insignificant in all the coastal departments to the west of the Seine-Inférieure, and in Sarthe and Orne also.

[54] Seine-Inférieure was the leading department as far as consumption was concerned, but it was also nearest to the mines of Nord-Pas-de-Calais and of Belgium; in 1911, the share of English coals fell to 63 per cent.

[55] But they lost ground; see above note 33.

minérale, 'which in former times had ruled supreme over the market along the Mediterranean coasts, have now been almost wholly driven out'.[56] But, after 1870 and still more 1880, thanks to the lowering of sea freight charges, imports picked up again. In 1911, English coals accounted for 25 per cent of total coal consumption in the eight Mediterranean departments. Yet it was only in Bouches-du-Rhône[57] and Alpes-Maritimes that they were used in significant quantities.

To summarise, all of the departments of the French littoral consumed, in 1838, 86 per cent of imported British coals; this percentage then dropped, falling to 73 per cent in 1867 and 70 per cent in 1879, but climbing again to 76 per cent in 1900. However, it dropped again appreciably after this date, falling to 62 per cent in 1911.[58] It is thus clear that, before 1850, English coals were hardly used except in the coastal regions, because the high cost of transport meant that they could only penetrate inland in tiny quantities.[59] Under the Second Empire, the building of railways helped to spread English coals further, but it did as much for coals from French mines,[60] so that, during the last third of the nineteenth century, the former did not gain much ground. At the beginning of the twentieth century, there was some progress, in the Paris region especially, thanks to which the share of inland departments in the total consumption of English coals became of real significance.

At any rate, from the 1850s on, English coals were sold in inland France in significant quantities, throughout a vast, crescent-shaped zone (see map on p. 426). They met with some competition, however, from French (and sometimes Belgian) coals, and it was only in two of these sectors that they clearly enjoyed a dominant position. These sectors were *Ouest intérieur* and *Centre-Ouest*, i.e. eight departments of Western France, both north of the Loire and south of it, which are not

56 SIM, 1860–4, p. xxvii; also 1869, p. xxviii and Ruolz, *La Question des Houilles*, t. I, pp. 186, 626.

57 Ranking fifth among consumers of English coals, with 388,000 tons, which represented 33 per cent of its consumption.

58 The recovery after 1879 derived largely from the reappearance of British coals on the Mediterranean coast. On the other hand, the fall after 1900 could be over-estimated because of the exclusion of bunker coals (and also of coal used by railways) from the consumption statistics by department.

59 See the map appended to SIM, 1839. When they penetrated fairly far inland, for example as far as Limoges, Périgueux or Agen, it was only along rivers.

60 In 1867, Ruolz, *La Question des Houilles* (t. I, pp. 640–1), reckoned that, out of 1,921,000 tons of British coal imported, 1,070,000 tons, that is 56 per cent, were used in the ports and in their immediate environs; only 822,000 tons penetrated inland. Their average penetration was not in excess of 150 kilometres (t. I, p. 632).

too far from importing ports and which were not well served by main-line railways, so that French coal could not possibly compete in most of those areas.[61]

In three other sectors, the market share of English coal was much lower, although the Paris region (the Seine and Seine-et-Oise departments) constituted an important outlet, actually the largest in inland France. Admittedly, in the mid-nineteenth century, English coal only reached Paris fairly irregularly,[62] but after 1860 it accounted for a by no means negligible share of the market, and one which held steady up until the end of the century, namely, over a tenth of the total coal consumption of the Paris region (which, on the other hand, also absorbed a tenth of British coals consumed in France). However, after 1900, sales of English coals suddenly leapt forward; in 1911, they were almost three times higher than they had been in 1900, and accounted for a quarter of the requirements of a region which absorbed one fifth of English coals consumed in France. On the other hand, neither the region of the middle Loire valley nor inland Aquitaine were important outlets for English coals. Moreover, these coals did not penetrate at all beyond a line which ran from Toulouse to Paris, except sporadically and in tiny quantities.[63] They were kept out of Central, Eastern and most of South-eastern France, and also from Northern parts (save for the Pas-de-Calais), by the distance from the sea and by the proximity of French, or else Belgian and German, coalfields.[64] The zone in which they were consumed was nevertheless an extensive one, which grew larger in the course of the period under consideration, with 36 departments involved in 1838, 45 in 1869, 49 in 1884 and 62 in 1911. It was, however, only close to the coast and in a few departments of the *Ouest Intérieur* and the *Centre-Ouest* that English coals ruled supreme.

It is also clear that in many departments the consumption of English

[61] *Ouest intérieur*: Orne, Sarthe, Mayenne, Maine-et-Loire; *Centre-Ouest*: Vienne, Deux-Sèvres, Charente, Haute-Vienne.

[62] It was then Belgian coal which supplied the Paris region: 55 per cent of consumption in 1847, 84 per cent in 1855. In 1867, according to Ruolz, *La Question des Houilles* (t. I, p. 412), Belgium was still cornering 7/10 of the Parisian market against the 2/10 which went to French coals, and 1/10 to British coals. After 1870, the Nord and Pas-de-Calais coals took the lead.

[63] In 1900, a year of 'coal famine', British coals penetrated much further, for instance up to Rhône, Côte d'Or, Yonne, even Meurthe-et-Moselle and Vosges.

[64] In the *département du Nord*, Dunkirk imported substantial quantities of English coal, as we have seen, but the greater part was dispatched by rail to Paris, and local consumption was insignificant. In the northern sector as a whole, English coal in fact lost ground during the period under consideration. In 1904, the British consul at Lille noted that English coal only penetrated into this region when French miners were on strike (PP, 1905, XVI, p. 863).

coal – along with the total consumption of coal – was relatively low, which was only to be expected given that most parts of Western France had hardly industrialised. In 1838, there were only ten departments that consumed over 10,000 tons of English coal; in 1879, while imports had increased by a multiple of ten, only six departments used more than 100,000 tons (see map on p. 426), and in 1911, out of a total consumption of 7,500,000 tons (excluding that by the railways and the merchant navy), ten departments consumed over 200,000 tons of British coal.[65]

This group of leaders always included Seine-Inférieure, which was first up until the eve of the first World War,[66] Loire-Inférieure, Gironde, Pas-de-Calais and Calvados; Seine (i.e. Paris) began to feature after 1860 and captured first place at the beginning of the twentieth century; Bouches-du-Rhône also numbered among the leaders, save during the 1860–80 period. In short, the regions where there was high consumption of English coal were relatively few and, if the Seine is set aside, they were those harbouring the handful of industrial and urban centres of importance along French coasts: Calais, Boulogne, the estuaries of the Seine and of the Loire, Caen, Bordeaux and Marseilles.[67]

It is also worth noting that, throughout the period under consideration, the six departments that were the biggest consumers of English coals absorbed over half the imports of such coals. Their dominance tended, however, to lessen, with their share of total consumption falling from two thirds in the mid nineteenth century to just over 50 per cent at the beginning of the twentieth. This suggests that the use of English coals became more widespread, especially in several departments of Brittany, the *Ouest intérieur* and the *Centre-Ouest*; consumption there was minute in the late 1840s, but the use of coal developed faster there than in the large centres, and by the end of the nineteenth century they had become substantial consumers. It would be interesting to make a detailed study of the way in which coal penetrated into such areas, not only because of the information it might give regarding

65 Out of sixty-two departments into which English coal had penetrated, thirty-two used less than 50,000 tons.

66 It had long had a very substantial lead over the other departments; in 1838, it consumed almost a third of all imported English coal; and, again in 1883, a quarter.

67 Ruolz, *La Question des Houilles* (t. I, pp. 421, 425, 479, 509, 511, 535, 560, 567, 571, 589 etc., and t. II, état X, pp. 88 ff.) gives detailed data on the consumption of English coal in different towns in 1867; only Rouen and Paris used over 100,000 tons.

the economic progress of those French regions, but also as an analysis of a significant sociological fact, namely, the replacement of woodfires in open chimneys or charcoal-pans with kitchen ranges or stoves, which used coal or briquettes.

A final problem is that of the commercial organisation of the Anglo-French coal trade. It was fairly rudimentary in its early days, when sea captains, commissioned by French importers, would dock in Welsh ports and deal directly with the mineowners' agents; but it gradually became more sophisticated, with the development, in Britain, of firms which specialised in exporting and, in France, of similar firms concerned with imports. It would seem that an increasing, and in the end a dominant, share of the trade passed through the hands of such intermediaries. However, major consumers, namely steamship companies, railway companies and steel firms, tended to deal directly with British mining companies.[68]

A study of coal trading would be of interest, especially because of the links which clearly existed between French and British firms.[69] A number of companies involved in the mining or export of coal from Wales set up subsidiaries in France in order to market their coal. To take one important example, the Powell Duffryn group, which dated back to 1864, and which was the giant of the Welsh mining industry, founded in 1913 the Compagnie française Powell Duffryn, which set up offices in Rouen, Paris, Nantes and Bordeaux.[70] It was also English capital which launched the Société française Graigola-Merthyr, which set up depots at Dieppe and Saint-Brieuc and factories for making briquettes at Saint-Malo and La Rochelle; it was in fact a subsidiary of an important concern involved in the export of Welsh coal, Llewellyn, Merrett and Price, which had links with the Graigola Mining Company.[71] Another curious case is that of Louis Gueret, a Frenchman, who

[68] John, p. 127; Morris and Williams, pp. 165–6; Jevons, *The British Coal Trade*, pp. 295–6, 303–5; Lafitte-Laplace, pp. 446–7. In the mid nineteenth century, the large Welsh producers of coal sent commercial travellers to France.

[69] The next paragraph owes much to information generously made available to me by the Compagnie française Powell Duffryn, the Société de combustibles Delmas-Vieljeux, the Société commerciale d'affrètements et de combustibles, and by Paul Aicard.

[70] It had previously (from 1895) been represented in Bordeaux by an exclusive agent. It is also worth mentioning the Sociéte française William Cory et fils, which was the offshoot of a large British firm interested in shipping and in the exporting of coal.

[71] This would seem to have been the same business as the Compagnie houillère de Graigola-Merthyr, a French limited company with a capital of 7 million francs, founded in Paris in 1875. Cf. R. E. Cameron, *France and the Economic Development of Europe, 1800–1914* (Princeton, 1961), p. 98. In 1928, the Société française Graigola-Merthyr, the Société des houilles et agglomérés and the Compagnie Delmas-Vieljeux set up a joint management for their coal enterprises; the

was one of the pioneers in the coal-dust briquette industry in South Wales, and who, once he had made his fortune, returned to France and set himself up in business once again, founding the Société générale des houilles et agglomérés (in which there was a British interest until the Second World War). British participation in French import concerns was thus significant: 'Several of these firms', wrote Lafitte-Laplace, 'are in personal contact of some kind or other with English exporters, who are represented on their boards.'[72]

On the other hand, French import firms do not seem to have invested in British coal mines.[73] This is in contrast to the large investment by Frenchmen, and especially by steel companies, in the Belgian, Dutch and German coalfields. Admittedly, during the inter-war period, the Compagnie des forges de Châtillon, Commentry et Neuves-Maisons acquired a coal mine near Durham, in order to improve her supplies of coke,[74] but this was an exception and, fundamentally, in the case of coal, as with other branches of industry, commercial relations between England and France did not bring about the creation of durable and organic links between the two economies.[75]

I shall make no attempt here to pursue the history of the Anglo-French coal trade beyond 1913.[76] Some glorious days still lay ahead, so that upon several occasions the volume achieved in 1913 was actually exceeded: during the First World War in particular (over 20 million

former, being put in charge, assumed the trade name of Société des houilles Delmas, Vieljeux, Graigola. This association came to an end in 1943.

72 Lafitte-Laplace, p. 448. A number of Welsh exporters, who had some difficulty in selling their smaller coals, set up briquette factories in France, or gave their French clients financial assistance in installing them (PP, 1919, XII, Cmd. 360, pp. 795–6, 994).

73 However, D. S. Landes, *Bankers and Pashas* (London, 1958), p. 312, mentions that, in the 1870s, the Dervieu bank gave financial assistance in the setting up of industrial concerns in South Wales.

74 Lafitte-Laplace, p. 636.

75 Among the firms trading in coal, a special but interesting case is that of Worms et Cie, the founder of which, Hypolite Worms, and his successor, Henri Goudchaux, developed, from 1848 on (see above, note 12), not only the large-scale import of British coal into France (the leading one up until 1914), but a multinational business, which distributed coal throughout the Mediterranean and owned huge depots in Suez and Port-Said; it became involved early on in shipping and later in the distribution of petroleum, in shipbuilding and finally in banking (though it remained a family concern). In 1871, Worms et Cie handled 7 per cent of British coal exports throughout the world and, in 1872, they delivered 75 per cent of the coal loaded by ships using the Suez Canal. In 1856, moreover, H. Worms established a business association with the Manchester, Sheffield and Lincoln Railway (which sought to develop the port of Grimsby), in order to create the Société anglo-française de Navigation, which linked this port to France and to Dieppe in particular. See *Un Centenaire*, especially pp. 38–9.

76 See Lafitte-Laplace, especially pp. 20–31, 437–71; J. Lajugie, *L'Industrie et le marché britannique du charbon* (Bordeaux, 1939), especially book III.

tons in 1916), and in 1923. There were, however, violent fluctuations, with alternating peaks and troughs (in 1921 and, still more, in 1926); these fluctuations, which contrasted with the steady growth of the nineteenth century, show quite clearly that a phase of disorder in international economic relations, and a period of crisis for the British coal industry, had begun. Nor did this trade outlive the Second World War.

I would like instead, by way of conclusion, to try and evaluate the role played by British coal in the French nineteenth-century economy, and especially in those regions which depended upon imports from Britain for fuel supplies. There can be no doubt that English coal was a necessary condition for the industrial development which occurred during the nineteenth century along the estuaries of the Seine and the Loire, and, to a lesser extent, on the Gironde and the Adour. These industries could in fact only have obtained French coal at prices appreciably higher than those charged for imported British coal.[77]

	Averages for the years	
	1847–1850–1853	1892–1895–1898
Nord	71	67
Loire	47	75
Seine-Inférieure	151	97
Loire-Inférieure	129	120
Gironde	147	128
Finistère	168	155

However, the latter was relatively expensive by the time it reached France, which runs counter to what one might suppose, given its low price at the pit-head (about one third lower, on average, than that of French coals)[78] and the cheapness of bulk transport by sea as against rail. Indeed, the maps drawn up by Francois Simiand, on the basis of data in the *Statistique de l'Industrie minérale*, show that in the mid nineteenth century coal prices for consumers were much higher in the coastal departments of the *Ouest* than in producer departments which

[77] In his conclusion to *La Question des Houilles* (t. I, pp. 634, 642), Ruolz acknowledged in 1872 that, in all regions on the Atlantic and Channel coasts, French coals could only have competed with British ones by adopting out-and-out protectionist measures, which would have been disastrous for industry.

[78] R. Cameron, 'Economic Growth and Stagnation in France, 1815–1914', *Journal of Modern History*, XXX, 1, March 1958, p. 8.

had coal-mines, such as Nord and Loire. The difference had lessened by the end of the century, but it was still considerable. If one posits an average price for the whole of France as 100, price indices in various departments were as shown in the table on p. 438.[79] High prices can be accounted for in terms of the cost of maritime transport,[80] which, as the following figures show,[81] was expensive:

	Freight from Cardiff to Bordeaux (Francs per ton)	Ratio between this freight and the average price of British exported coals (%)
1867	14	110
1873–5	11	53
1883–5	7·25	64
1893–5	5·32	42
1903–5	4·74	35
1911–13	7·20	46

In the 1860s, freight alone brought about a doubling of the price of coal as it was transported from its British port of export to its French port of import.[82] After 1873, ocean freights fell fast, and this fall continued up until the beginning of the twentieth century, with a recovery starting on the eve of the First World War. The relative cost of maritime transportation was therefore reduced, as the FOB prices of British coal did not change much in the long term, throughout the period

79 Simiand, pp. 47–59.

80 One should set aside the notion that the British imposed monopoly prices upon French buyers. That would be to suppose rigorous agreements between exporters when, in fact, the nineteenth-century British coal market was very competitive. Nor can one claim that British coals were sold in French ports at prices just below those that would have allowed French coals to compete; all the information we have suggests that there was a clear and sometimes a substantial difference between the selling price of British coals and the cost price of French coals on the markets dominated by the former.

81 According to data in Jevons, *The British Coal Trade*, p. 692; PP, 1919, XIII, p. 31; Ruolz, *La Question des Houilles*, t. III, p. 373. The Cardiff-Bordeaux freights charges may be regarded as representative of coal freightages from Britain to France.

82 Of course, the difference between the price at the pit-head in Britain and the price for French consumers was still greater, especially in the early period. According to the *Statistique de l'Industrie minérale*, the ratio between these two prices (averaging out the three departments of Seine-Inférieure, Loire-Inférieure and Gironde) changed as follows:

1838	1 to 3·86
1850	1 to 3·50
1872	1 to 2·16

But, according to Ruolz, *La Question des Houilles*, t. I, p. 630, in the late 1860s average transport costs for French coal to the Channel ports stood at 30 francs per ton, whereas the average freight from England to France was 13 francs.

1860–1910.[83] Nevertheless, in the early twentieth century, transportation costs still represented a significant fraction of the FOB prices of British coals, which was thus increased upon arrival in France by 25 per cent to 50 per cent, depending upon the quality involved.[84] Although industrial consumers on the French coast were able to get excellent coal from Britain, they paid quite dearly for it, and this factor undoubtedly checked the growth of industries 'by the water's edge'.[85]

This may well be one of the reasons why factory industry developed to a much greater extent beside the French coalfields of the North and the Centre, rather than in the ports which imported British coal, whose industrialisation remained limited, even along the estuaries of the Seine and the Loire, and weak or non-existent in the South-West and in Brittany. Whilst no one would dispute that other factors played a part in the industrial underdevelopment of Western France, the coal question was by no means a negligible one.

It was for a long time received wisdom that the deciding factor which would account for the gaps and lags in France's economic growth was the insufficiency of its coal resources or, more precisely, the high cost of extraction and the scarcity of some varieties of coal on the one hand, the inconvenient location of the coal-fields and the high transportation costs on the other. This explanation has long been discredited, under the influence of American economic historians, who have placed the emphasis on the impact of socio-cultural factors upon what is called, with a degree of exaggeration, the stagnation of the French economy in the nineteenth century. But the coal factor has undoubtedly been given short shrift, and we would do well to acknowledge again its importance in the economic history of France.[86]

[83] Thomas, pp. 473–4, notes that, freight charges having fallen by over 50 per cent between 1872 and 1901, while FOB prices had barely changed, prices for foreign consumers had fallen by a third on average.

[84] In 1909–13, the freightage from Wales to Rouen represented on average 32 per cent of the price of the higher quality 'large' coals and 54 per cent of that of the 'small' ones (PP, 1919, XII, p. 794). Freightage costs having risen after 1908, this percentage had been lower prior to this date – 25 per cent for the better Cardiff coal dispatched to Bordeaux in 1900 or 1903 (PP, 1905, XVI, p. 849).

[85] A negative factor was the sharpness of the fluctuations in the prices of British coal; Ruolz, *La Question des Houilles*, t. I, p. 713, asserts that the rise of 1872–3 was a catastrophe for many industrialists.

[86] See E. A. Wrigley, *Industrial Growth and Population Change* (Cambridge, 1961). Wrigley compares the economic development of the different parts of the 'Austrasian Basin', from the Ruhr to the Pas-de-Calais, between 1850 and 1914. He concludes that the geological factor (that is, the distribution of coal reserves and the conditions for their exploitation) was crucial for the uneven growth of its various sectors. See also above, pp. 98, 360–1.

Although English coal cannot be said to have compensated Western France for the lack of a large coalfield on the Welsh mode, it did nevertheless allow it a degree of economic growth, and I therefore cannot agree with those who have described the importing of it as 'a necessary evil' or with M. Le Lannou when he described the 'small, black but sovereign tramp-steamer, blowing its whistle for the pilot at the mouth of our estuaries', into which it brought its coal, as a symbol of Brittany's underdevelopment.[87] This is a sight which is anyway no longer to be seen, which returns me to my starting-point, to the faded inscription on a wall in Brittany. Like the steamer, it is an image of the 'age of coal', during which England was the dominant economy, while France could only play second fiddle – and not too well.

87 Lafitte-Laplace, p. 466; Le Lannou, p. 197.

13 The core and the periphery of the core: Franco-British trade in the *belle époque**

There has been no lack of interest in relations between the 'core' and the 'periphery' of the world-economy, between the advanced and industrialised countries on the one hand, the rest of the world on the other. However, relations within the 'core' itself, between industrial countries, also pose a problem, which I shall tackle here in connection with trade between Britain and France during the Indian Summer of free trade, the twenty years prior to the First World War (the starting point is justified, from the French point of view, by the imposition of the Méline tariff in 1892).[1] The two partners were not, in fact, equal, for the industrial, commercial and financial power, and the level of industrialisation of Britain were much higher than was the case in France, and her per capita income was higher also. The question then arises whether France was not in a 'peripheral' position *vis-à-vis* England, which was indeed the centre of the industrialised world, and whether its trade with her was not of the same kind as links the industrial West and the Third World. Britain's position as dominant economy, which, in spite of a decline in relative terms, she enjoyed up until 1914, may have distorted France's economic development, and rendered her dependent upon, and complementary to, the British

* An earlier English version of this essay was presented to a conference on 'The British and the French', organised by the University of Wales, at Swansea, in May 1982.

[1] Except where I specify otherwise, the series used in this study cover the years 1893 to 1913. The growth rates have all been calculated by exponential adjustment. Figures for total trade were drawn from the following compilations: For the UK's trade with France: B. R. Mitchell and P. Deane, *Abstract of British Historical Statistics* (Cambridge, 1962), pp. 325–6; for France's trade with the UK: INSEE, *Annuaire statistique de la France. 1966. Résumé rétrospectif* (Paris, 1966), pp. 350, 353. The more detailed statistics regarding French trade derive from the annual and ten-yearly tables for France's foreign trade, as published by the Direction générale des douanes. The French consuls' reports quoted here have been studied in the archives of the Ministry of Foreign Affairs, by Mlle Monique Bongrand, who was then Ingénieur de recherches at the CNRS.

economy. Indeed, Jean Périer,[2] the French Consul in London, maintained in his reports for 1901 and for subsequent years – and without intending to be pejorative – that the French economy was 'complementary ... to a remarkable extent' to that of Britain; while the USA, Germany and Belgium had outputs which were 'more and more antagonistic' towards that of England (because they made the same commodities), the latter and France were involved in very little competition with each other, whether in their home markets or in third countries, because of dissimilarities in their climates and their soil, as well as the [particular] 'aptitudes of the two races'. It is possible, in fact, that trade between developed countries stimulated specialisation, the exploitation of comparative advantages, and a better utilisation of factors of production, thereby ensuring a maximisation of incomes on both sides.

British and French customs statistics are detailed, but present certain divergences;[3] notably, up until 1905, British customs included, in the category of imports from France, commodities which had passed through the latter and which came in the main from Switzerland and Italy (silk goods, clocks and watches, condensed milk); this trade may have accounted for around 10 per cent of goods arriving in Britain from French ports. Conversely, French exports to the United Kingdom included commodities which were to be trans-shipped (from one ship to another, in an English port) or re-exported to another country, mainly within the British empire. Consumption of French products in the United Kingdom was probably therefore 15 per cent less, in rough figures, than the French export figures would suggest.[4]

I

Confirmation of the hypothesis that France was dependent upon Britain would seem to be provided by the fact that the latter was France's best foreign customer, whereas the reverse was not the case:

[2] He became commercial attaché in 1905, the year in which this post was created.

[3] The coefficient of correlation between exports from the UK to France and imports in France from the UK is close to +1, which is excellent; conversely, the coefficient is close to 0 for the correlation between French exports to the UK and British imports from France, which is worrying and hard to explain. Of course, there are also differences in the labelling and classification of commodities.

[4] This study mainly uses French customs statistics and reports by French consuls in Britain. A more extended use of English sources would usefully complete it.

Percentage of France's total exports which went to the United Kingdom	
1893–5	29·8
1902–4	28·5
1911–13	20·5

Admittedly, figures for the 1890s (reaching a peak of 31·6 per cent in 1897) were particularly high, a little above those for the previous three decades. It is also true that a change occurred after 1902: England's share of French exports fell steadily and perceptibly, dropping to one fifth upon the eve of war, but this was still a high percentage. In fact, during this decade, exports to the United Kingdom made slower progress than did France's total exports, and especially those to its second- and third-ranking customers, Belgium and Germany; these two countries trailed far behind Britain in the 1890s, but they drew closer in subsequent years (in 1911–13, they received respectively 17 per cent and 13 per cent of French exports). Moreover, as far as purchases from France per inhabitant were concerned, the United Kingdom only came third, far behind Belgium and Switzerland, which perhaps goes to show that the French were not exploiting all the possibilities offered by the market of a country which was rich and wide open, thanks to free trade, to foreign products.

With the relation between French exports and French physical product standing at around 20 per cent during our period, exports to the United Kingdom represented 6 per cent of France's physical product in the 1890s and 4 per cent in 1913, which suggests a dependence which was not negligible but which was not overwhelming either.

As for imports to France from the United Kingdom, they were of much lower value than were French exports to the latter (roughly one half, up until 1905; then the gap lessened). As a consequence, Britain's share in the total imports of France was much lower than her share in French exports; what is more, it remained stable during the whole period under consideration:

	(%)
1893–95	12·9
1902–04	12·0
1911–13	12·8

This resulted in a balance of trade which was very much in France's favour, although her surplus clearly fell after 1905. This is a familiar phenomenon: France and the other industrialised countries on the Continent sold around two-thirds of their exports in Europe, whereas the Continent received only one-third of British exports, with the other two-thirds going to non-European countries. It was their surplus *vis-à-vis* England that enabled France and her neighbours to cover their substantial trade deficit with distant countries, in the British empire in particular, such as India. The United Kingdom was nevertheless France's first supplier, but Germany was hard on its heels by the end of the period.

From the British point of view, commercial relations with France were clearly less important (without being negligible).[5]

France's share in the United Kingdom's trade (%).

	Imports	Exports of British goods	Re-exports of foreign goods	Total exports
1893–95	11·0	6·2	10·8	7·2
1902–04	9·3	5·3	9·9	6·2
1911–13	6·1	5·4	10·8	6·4

The most striking feature is the drop in the French share of British imports (the French share of world exports fell to the same extent). France had been Britain's second most important supplier, after the United States, in the 1890s, but she was overtaken by Germany in 1900 and, later on, by India; she thus dropped to fourth place (and, in 1913, Russia was on her heels). The setback is less marked as far as British exports are concerned, with France continuing to be England's fourth most important customer, but, as we shall see, a fair proportion of commodities sold to her were raw materials, so that the French market was not very important for British industry (nevertheless, in 1913, it was absorbing almost as many *British* goods – strictly speaking – as did the USA).

Actually, the various components of the trade between the two countries evolved quite differently:

[5] If one adds up imports and exports, the trade of each country with the other represents the following shares of their total trade (%):

	France with the UK	The UK with France
1893–1895	20·6	9·4
1902–1904	20·0	8·1
1911–1913	16·2	6·2

Average rates of growth per year from 1893 to 1913 (%).

Imports from France in the United Kingdom 0·37 (a)	Exports from France to the United Kingdom 1·67
Exports from the United Kingdom to France 3·64	Imports from the United Kingdom in France 4·32

Even if rate (a) is inaccurate, the slowness of the growth of French exports remains striking. Admittedly, it accords with a general slowing-down of growth in Anglo-French trade, which had become obvious at the end of the 1870s, after rapid progress in the 1860s and in the early 1870s. The peak figure, one billion francs, which French exports to England had reached in 1875, was not exceeded until 1897 (although prices had admittedly fallen in the meantime). Nevertheless, there was a recovery from the late 1880s and new records were achieved in 1899 and 1900. These were boom and high prices years, however, which inflated the value of the traffic. Subsequently, exports to Britain all but stagnated, even during the prosperous years after 1905, whereas total exports from France were accelerating; from 1905 to 1913, the rate of growth of the latter was 4·2 per cent per year, whereas exports to England only advanced by 0·96 per cent per year.[6]

The situation was still worse in terms of the volume of trade, since prices were rising on trend after 1896.[7] At constant prices, French sales to Britain peaked in 1902 and declined subsequently. However, at the same time, the volume of France's total exports was expanding fairly rapidly. Since the growth of United Kingdom's total imports also accelerated in this period, French products would seem to have lost their competitive edge on the British market in particular, unless exporters had deserted the latter for more attractive outlets. At any rate, in 1907 and again in 1908, the commercial attaché in London wrote that the progress of French exports to England was not 'what it should be'.

The growth rate of the United Kingdom's imports into France, on

[6] For the whole of the period 1893–1913, the growth rates were 1·67 per cent for exports by France to the UK, and over 3 per cent for her total exports.

[7] By deflating the current values by A. H. Imlah's price indexes for the English series, and by M. Lévy-Leboyer's for the French series, one obtains the following average annual growth rates of volumes, for the period 1893–1913 (%):

Imports from France into the UK	−0·52	Exports from France to the UK	0·16
Exports from the UK to France	2·36	Imports from the UK into France	2·38

the other hand, was close to that of France's total imports, with fluctuations matching those of the French industrial conjuncture, which is what one would expect given that they largely consisted of raw materials and semi-finished goods. They tended to fall between 1882 and 1897 (their figure for the first of these years was not exceeded before 1906); they then underwent a vigorous but short-lived recovery, due in part to the rise in prices, which peaked in 1900; finally, they benefited from a rapid and sustained growth spurt from 1905 to 1913 (at a rate of 6·8 per cent per year). At constant prices, growth was slower but still substantial.

Some of the fluctuations in traffic may be explained in terms of political events. Thus, the Boer War was one of the causes of the high prices prevalent in 1900, which inflated the value of trade; but there were reports that, on account of the increasing tax burden, the war reduced Britain's consumption of French luxury articles; on the other hand, it occasioned the export to England of several thousand French stallions, which were mainly Percherons. It is also said that demand for French articles of fashion was affected by the death of Queen Victoria, and later by that of King Edward VII. Conversely, during the preparations for the Coronation of the latter, some Birmingham firms sent out batches of rough precious stones to workshops in the Jura, to be cut. However, it is the analysis of the structure of trade which enables us to understand its long-term development.

II

In the treatment of French exports to the United Kingdom, agricultural commodities will be first considered. In the 1880s and 1890s, they accounted for around one-third of the total, but in later years their share fell appreciably, to one quarter. Indeed, sales of several of these products stagnated or even regressed to a significant degree.[8]

This was even the case with French products that the British Isles could, for climatic reasons, 'in no sense provide themselves', and which therefore constituted, according to J. Périer, 'the most complementary and the most stable part' of French exports, for example, cognacs, wines, early vegetables and various fruits. Common opinion, however,

[8] P. O'Brien and C. Keyder, *Economic Growth in Britain and France, 1780–1914. Two Paths to the Twentieth Century* (London, 1978), p. 161, Table 6.6. Raw and processed foodstuffs formed 35 per cent of British imports from France in 1865, 33 per cent in 1888, 27 per cent in 1905.

overestimates the part played by wines and spirits in French trade; although wine was the only primary product in the world trade of which France was the leader, her share in it had much declined after the phylloxera epidemic. At any rate, sales of French wines and spirits to the United Kingdom, which had respectively peaked in 1894 and 1897, fell away subsequently; for the whole of the period 1893–1913, they presented high negative rates of growth, namely, −3·5 per cent and −4·1 per cent per year. As a consequence, in 1911–13, wines, brandies and liqueurs only represented 4 per cent of French exports across the Channel, compared with 9·7 per cent in 1893–5.

How is one to account for this decline? Some have invoked the change in British methods of calculating customs duties, in 1899, which would in fact have increased them; others have noted the impact of the Boer War on the purchasing power of the middle classes, but this effect was only temporary. The crucial factor was a change in the consumption habits of the British, which brought about a sharp reduction in the level of wine consumption per head of population: 2 litres a year in 1898, 1·31 litres in 1907. During this same year, the French commercial attaché wrote that the English were gradually losing the habit of drinking wine; he praised them for being 'true connoisseurs' of cognac, but this latter, like wine, suffered from the competition from whisky, which was the preferred drink of 'the younger generation' and benefited from an 'enormous advertising campaign'.[9] It is worth noting that champagne accounted for over two-thirds – in value – of wine exports: in 1902, the British drank six million bottles of it, which matches the traditional image of upper class life in the Edwardian period.[10] Conversely, the sales of bottled vintage wines were low and tending to decline still more. In 1913, the British consul at Bordeaux noted that Germany had become the main customer for wines exported from the port (accounting for 32 per cent of shipments) and he added:

> Some 25 to 30 years ago the United Kingdom used to be the best market for the Bordeaux wine merchants, as regards fine wines. Its place has now been taken by Germany. This state of affairs is entirely due to the complete change in our social habits and customs, the after-dinner sitting, which used to be dedicated to tasting and

[9] However, France virtually had a monopoly of the British market as far as brandies were concerned (and this market absorbed half of French exports of the latter at the beginning of the twentieth century). In the case of wines, France supplied half (in value) of Britain's total imports.

[10] The figures for 1910–12 are approximately the same.

enjoying clarets, having practically disappeared. Again, the present habit of smoking immediately after meals has ruined the palate for appreciating the most delicate flavours of good clarets, and further, the increased cost of living has caused a general decline throughout the country in the consumption of foreign wines, whose places have been supplanted by whisky.[11]

Exportations of three other French agricultural products were also declining, namely, butter, eggs and sugar. Périer noted that France enjoyed some advantages in such labour-intensive products, thanks to the strenuous and meticulous labours of her small farmers, but he had to admit that these virtues were not sufficient to prevail against foreign competition, mainly from Denmark, but also from the Low Countries, Russia (actually, Siberia) and New Zealand. It was estimated that in 1907 Denmark supplied Great Britain with 400 million francs' worth of butter, eggs and meat, whereas French sales of these articles only amounted to 70 million. The fall was especially spectacular as regards eggs, for which France had been the main foreign supplier during the 1880s, but whose exports to England fell from 29 million francs in 1893 to 9 million in 1913. Sales of butter, which came mainly from Normandy, held steadier (61 million in 1897 and again in 1903, 36 million in 1911–13); but as early as 1891 the vice-consul in Newport, in Monmouthshire, was pointing out that French butter was no longer to be seen in the county. This was also the case, two years later, in Manchester and in the north of England as a whole.

It was sugar, however, which suffered the most serious collapse. Exports of French sugar to England had been much encouraged at the end of the nineteenth century by a system of export bounties and, in 1900, they reached a value of 125 million francs (10 per cent of total French exports to the United Kindgom). But the abolition of bounties at the Conference of Brussels (1903) and competition from the German sugar industry, which was more efficient, dealt a fatal blow: in 1911–13, exports of French sugar were almost negligible (7 million francs). Butter, eggs and sugar had represented 12 per cent of French exports to Britain in 1893–5, but by 1911–13 they accounted for less than 4 per cent.

Conversely, French exports of vegetables and fruit had made some progress. Varieties of fruit featured were plums, pears, cherries and nuts, but no grapes or apples – the Golden Delicious had not yet been

[11] PP, 1913, LXX, pp. 14–15. Exports of Bordeaux wines to the UK had fallen by two-thirds in twenty or twenty-five years.

invented, and English customers did not much like French apples. New potatoes, from Brittany, shipped by way of Saint-Malo, were the dynamic element (enjoying a growth rate of 7·7 per cent per year from 1893 to 1913). If sales of fruit and vegetables held steady, it was mainly because their shipment dates differed from those of competing produce from other countries or else because, in the case of fruit, 'delicate varieties' were involved, which would never have borne long distance transportation (from Spain or Italy, for example). However, all kinds of fruit, vegetables and seeds only accounted for a small part of France's total exports to England (around 4 per cent).

France only supplied Britain with small amounts of cereals, cheeses (mainly camembert), meat and poultry; but she sold her an average of a million francs' worth of *pâtés de foie gras* per year, and about the same amount of truffles. I ought, finally, to mention the fairly substantial exports of wood, that is, pit-props, which came from the Landes by way of Bordeaux or Bayonne, or from Morbihan also. These pit-props were destined for South Wales, and served as return freight for the coalers; this traffic amounted to over a million tons a year, but it declined gradually, as a result of competition from cheaper Norwegian and Russian wood.

In 1904, Jean Périer wrote that French agricultural exports to Britain were neither what they had been previously nor what they might be, given the size of the English market. He added that the competition which was proving damaging to French agricultural products was not that of the 'new countries', which were sending cheap foodstuffs for low income customers, but rather that of other European countries; these latter had in fact increased their sales of foodstuffs to England and had profited from the sharp increase in this country's needs, in spite of competition from overseas, whereas French exports were stagnating or regressing. These countries, and Denmark in particular, had a superior commercial organisation (thanks to farmers' cooperatives and exporters' syndicates), lower transport costs (even though Brittany and Normandy were closer to England), and they were managing to offer, at lower prices, products which were standardised and which appealed to the taste of British consumers. According to Périer, French agriculture was not sufficiently 'industrialised and commercialised'; some of its products were too expensive: for instance, the table-fowls of Houdan (near Paris) were prestige articles, which were only consumed by 'society' during the London 'season';

others were badly packaged and presented (for example, eggs from Brittany arrived in damp straw, which gave them a nasty taste).

The decline in cross-Channel sales of agricultural products and foodstuffs was largely responsible for the slow growth of French exports to the United Kingdom, and it also reflected the fact that agriculture was the genuinely backward sector within the French economy.

French exports to Britain also included a few raw materials,[12] but, at the beginning of the twentieth century, two-thirds consisted of manufactured articles (almost all of which were finished goods, moreover).[13] There was plainly a radical difference between the position of France and that of genuinely peripheral countries – which only export primary products; and also a tendency, during the period under consideration, for trade in manufactured articles between industrialised countries to intensify. Moreover, these French exports, though being varied, were clearly specialised, and therefore occupied 'niches', that is, they were products which did not have to be manufactured on a large scale, so that a small country or small producers could successfully penetrate international markets – thanks to natural resources, historical traditions, innovations in fashion or in technology (I shall give the examples below of the silk and automobile industries) and, above all, a skilled workforce.

This was the case with France's two main traditional exports, namely, silks and quality worsteds. Free trade had enabled these goods to penetrate the English market, and the silk manufacturers of Lyons had virtually dominated it for a period; admittedly, they had suffered a crisis from 1876 to 1888 and been hard hit by foreign competition, but they had managed to adjust and so continued to dictate fashions. In

12 7 per cent of British imports from France in 1888, 8 per cent in 1905, according to O'Brien and Keyder, p. 161, Table 6.6. These commodities included raw silk, hides and skins. Britain also dispatched some of these to France, but different varieties or qualities were probably involved; likewise, there was traffic in both directions of dressed hides and skins, which are intermediate goods, wool and wool waste; these latter exports can be explained by the fact that the small French town of Mazamet had become the 'world capital for skin wools'. Curiously enough, copper and ostrich feathers feature among both French exports and French imports, which is surprising, since France had neither copper mines nor ostrich farms. This fact is related to the complexity of exchanges between industrial countries, a point to which I shall return below.

13 According to O'Brien and Keyder, pp. 161, Table 6.6, 162, manufactured articles (including intermediate goods) constituted some 41 per cent of British imports from France in 1865, 51 per cent in 1888 and 63 per cent in 1905. Furthermore, if one adds on finished industrial products and processed foodstuffs one comes up with the figure of 60 per cent in 1888 and 69 per cent in 1905. According to French consuls, net consumption of French industrial products in the UK stood at the beginning of the twentieth century at 700 million francs a year.

spite of a falling off at the turn of the century, French exports of silks to the United Kingdom rose at the respectable rate of 2·2 per cent per year between 1893 and 1913. France supplied 40 per cent of silks imports to Great Britain which, because of the decline of its own silk industry, was the 'international regulator' of demand and 'the great world market' for silks. However, France was also the main foreign buyer of English silks. Silk articles made up 11 per cent of French exports to Britain in 1893–5 and 12 per cent in 1911–13.

Silks had thus overtaken woollens and worsteds, which had been in the lead at the beginning of the 1890s. After the treaty of 1860, French manufacturers, especially in Roubaix and Rheims, had made remarkable inroads into the British market, at the expense of the oldest English industry; they had launched a range of high quality textiles, of pure worsted, which had won over English women and competed successfully with the mixed fabrics from the West Riding. This traffic had, however, reached its absolute and relative apogee around 1890, and had fallen off in subsequent years, for new shifts in fashion had been unfavourable to French worsteds and Bradford industrialists had counterattacked with some success. Admittedly, Roubaix continued to be the leader of fashion in worsted fabrics used in women's clothes, but the growth rate of exports to Britain by the French wool industry was negative for the period 1893–1913, and their share in France's total exports to England fell from 14 per cent in 1893–5 to less than 7 per cent in 1911–13 (although France was virtually the only foreign country to sell woollens and worsteds in Britain).

Silks and worsteds were by far the most important French exports, but other textile articles, which had been exported in negligible quantities in the early 1890s, afterwards enjoyed high growth rates and eventually accounted for a significant share of total exports: linen, cottons, lace and embroideries, clothes and lingerie. Given England's supremacy in the cotton industry, it is a little surprising to find exports of French cottons to its neighbour growing at a rate of 11 per cent per year between 1893 and 1913, reaching 52 million francs in 1913; these were high quality textiles, which had been dyed or printed with special care.[14]

All in all, textiles (including clothes) accounted for 29 per cent of French exports to the United Kingdom in 1893–5 and 31 per cent in

[14] The growth rate was 9 per cent for cotton yarn and 6 per cent for clothes and lingerie; in 1902, 84,470 corsets were dispatched across the Channel.

1911–13; but these percentages probably underestimate the role of the textile industries and of their ancillary or complementary activities, for a number of their products were classified by customs under other headings, such as 'fashion goods' or 'Paris goods'. It is quite possible that the products of all the industries which worked to 'clothe', in the broadest sense of the term, their customers, accounted for anything up to 45 per cent of French exports to Britain.

According to J. Périer, the bulk of this trade consisted of 'articles for women and children';[15] he wrote in 1907 that, for the previous fifteen years, 'English women had more and more become fond of dress'; this had resulted in a massive increase in the demand for articles 'of fashion'. France had benefited greatly from this, given that her exports were largely composed of luxury articles, that were 'well finished', 'special' and 'in good taste'. We know that this was a tradition of the French textile industry which, for various reasons, but mainly because of the relative cost of the factors of production, had concentrated upon the fabrication of quality articles, which were skilled labour-intensive. The wealth of the British upper and middle classes, their 'extravagant' habits, as Périer put it, their 'preference' for French articles, and of course free trade all served to open up major outlets across the Channel for French quality products. This was all the more so given that the British textile industry's strong point was mass production, necessarily involving 'current' or medium quality articles (although Périer acknowledged that the British were capable of making 'special' articles, for example, by creating Liberty fabrics). This is a very clear instance of complementarity and international division of labour.

There were, moreover, several other French industries which exported 'special', highly finished or, at any rate, labour-intensive products to Britain. This was the case, for example, with gloves (for which France was the leading foreign supplier), luxury shoes for women, porcelain from Limoges and crystal glass from Baccarat, a number of delicate chemical products and, above all, 'articles whose manufacture depends in the main upon the aptitudes of French craftsmen', upon their ingenuity and their skill. These were 'articles from Paris' and 'articles from the Jura', that is, all kinds of small objects worked in wood, metal, mother of pearl or in other materials, and also fans, paintings, drawings, *objets d'art*, plus pipes, made in Saint-Claude, of which the British bought 15 million in 1902, i.e. over one for every adult male.

[15] This may have helped to reinforce France's 'feminine' image; see below, Chapter 14, p. 483.

If one adds to the above items the by no means negligible entries for ornamental feathers, for 'fashions' (hats etc.) and for artificial flowers,[16] these French craft products accounted for nearly 20 per cent of France's total exports to Britain, and in this Périer identified yet another instance of complementarity between the two countries, since England, according to him, had but a few craftsmen. These products did, admittedly, meet with fierce foreign competition, especially on the part of Germany, which, in addition to its heavy industry, had an extensive but less well-known artisanal sector. The Germans clearly enjoyed an advantage in the British market with respect not only to children's toys or musical instruments, but also in the case of fancy goods, such as cheap jewellery, which had for long been a French speciality but which were now copied in Germany (or this, at any rate, was the gist of French complaints) and sold for less, because German wages were lower. Indeed, many articles that customs classified under the heading 'Paris goods' were in fact 'made in Germany'![17]

Indeed, from the 1880s or 1890s, almost all of these traditional French exports were on the defensive – and not just on the British market – and were not an engine of growth. France's share of the world market, in all important manufactured articles, diminished between 1899 and 1913. There was one exception, however, namely, automobiles, which were the most dynamic element among French exports to the United Kingdom, whose purchases of French motor vehicles climbed vertiginously, from 2·6 million francs in 1899 to 10 million in 1901, 34 million in 1903 and 61 million in 1906; these did, admittedly, level out in subsequent years and even fell back a little, after a peak of 65 million in 1910.[18] The French automobile industry had greatly benefited from Britain's lateness in entering this field, but its exports to England were checked as the latter set about catching up, in the last years prior to the First World War. In the meantime, the French had been delighted by their success. In 1903, J. Périer wrote as follows: 'I very much doubt if one could find in the whole of our economic history [an interestingly early use of this term, by a non-specialist] another example of such a rapid development' as automobile exports under-

[16] Exports of perfumes and jewellery were minimal; it is reported that English tourists used to buy jewellery direct in Paris, and in 1900 that they were very taken with the *Art Nouveau* styles.

[17] There were also complaints about American competition in gloves, shoes and other leather articles (probably mass-produced by machinery, in America).

[18] 55 millions in 1913. Statistics for the first half-year of 1914 show that 2 million francs' worth of 'aircrafts' (spare parts included) were exported.

went in these years; in 1908, he added: 'It was in the nick of time that our marvellous automobile industry succeeded in plugging the gaps in our sales to England', which was a somewhat optimistic assessment, given that the highest share enjoyed by motor vehicles in French exports to the United Kingdom was 5 per cent, in 1910. On the other hand, up until 1914, the automobile remained in Europe a luxury item, which was constructed by craftsmen, and only bought by rich people, plus a few professional men (doctors, in particular). Intensive in skilled labour, these machines were produced by the traditional methods employed in the engineering industry and not on mass production lines. The success enjoyed by French automobiles in England was therefore still within the tradition of 'French quality'.[19]

All in all, it would not seem way off the mark to regard French industrial exports to the United Kingdom as belonging to the 'niche' category. Thus, those which mattered were concentrated in branches that the British had neglected (such as 'Paris goods' and other fancy articles or, in the early years, automobiles), or that had been lost to French competition in an earlier period (this was the case with silks). Indeed, the 'complementarity' of the two economies had been established before the beginning of the period being studied here (save, of course, in the case of automobiles, which were wholly new products). One can therefore understand J. Périer's observation that there were no complaints in England with respect to French economic rivalry, since it did not harm any British industry, whereas there were howls of rage against that of Germany (which may also mean, admittedly, that France was a lightweight as far as industry was concerned). This analysis also confirms that niches have a somewhat random character, that they are the product of particular resources, of an accumulation of skills, of historical traditions. We find, moreover, that the development of niches for exporting generally requires a fairly extensive domestic market; this is just how it was for France where luxury articles were concerned, because of the aristocratic and bourgeois traditions of conspicuous consumption. However, the structure of exports to Britain was more biassed in favour of a small number of niches than was that of France's total exports.

[19] See in PP, 1913, LXX, no. 5137, p. 40, a British consular report which points out that, in the automobile industry, 'France once had a virtual monopoly, but now it has to struggle against intense foreign competition', even in France itself, to which Americans, in 1912, had sold more cars than they had bought. 'Theirs are cheap machines, whereas it is of so-called *de luxe*

The counter-proof for this is supplied by France's absence from the British market, and from the world market too, for the products of industries where economies of scale were large. Her exports to England of metals, articles made of metal, machines, tools and other capital goods (save, curiously enough, a few merchant ships and, in 1903–5, three locomotives of the new, Atlantic type) were insignificant. As far as machinery was concerned, France did far less well than genuinely 'small countries', such as Switzerland and Sweden. It is striking, also, that the rapid growth of the French steel industry during the pre-war period had no impact upon exports to Britain, in a period when the latter's market was being invaded by Belgian and German steel, which suggests that French steel was not competitive.[20]

III

The value of imports into France from the United Kingdom was, as already indicated, much inferior, especially prior to 1905, to that of French exports to Britain. Moreover, they included non-British goods, which had been re-exported from Britain. Fortunately, English statistics enable us to distinguish them from 'domestic' exports. The ratio between the two groups remained steady, with re-exports accounting for just under a third of the United Kingdom's total exports to France: 32 per cent in 1893–5, 31 per cent in 1911–13. Britain's role as the warehouse of world trade had, admittedly, declined in the course of the nineteenth century, but France continued to use the facilities of this emporium, especially given that her merchant navy and her commercial networks were insufficient to maintain regular relations with many distant countries, in the British empire in particular.

Raw wool, coming mainly from Australia, but also from South Africa, was far and away the most substantial item among those re-exported, but it lost ground in relative terms; another textile raw material, jute, was significant, although the trade in it was an irregular one and was also stagnating in the long term. Conversely, France got her raw cotton from the United States and from other producer countries, and did not import any from England. Two articles enjoyed a rapid growth and represented, at the end of the period under

vehicles, that is, the highest category with costly accessories, that French exports mainly consist.'

[20] It is true that the steel-works of Lorraine were a long distance away from England.

consideration, a significant share of France's total imports, namely, rubber, whose growing importance was obviously linked to the rise of the French automobile industry, and 'ornamental feathers' – mainly ostrich feathers from South Africa – which France bought in increasing quantities, amounting to some 40 million francs worth on the eve of the First World War, because of the peculiar fashions in women's hats during the *belle époque*. Copper and tin should also be mentioned among re-exports, since England was no longer extracting their ores.[21] Minor re-exports were as numerous and as various as were the territories within the empire and their productions: namely, raw silk, sponges, whalebone, elephants' tusks, tortoise shells, pearls and mother-of-pearl, wax and gum, etc. Tea, however, was only re-exported to France in tiny quantities.

After this hors-d'oeuvre, let us consider the first and most dynamic of British exports to France, namely coal. I will, however, deal summarily with this mineral, since it is the focus of Chapter 12. French imports of British coal rose from 4 million tons in 1893 to 7·5 million in 1900 and to 12 million in 1913, i.e. at an average rate of growth of 5·4 per cent per year; the total value of these imports rose from 67 million francs in 1891–3 to 238 million in 1911–13 (281 million in 1913), with a still higher rate of growth, of 6·9 per cent per year. They accounted for 14 per cent of total French imports from the United Kingdom in 1891–3 and 23 per cent in 1911–13; they were responsible for 44 per cent of the increase in the value of those total imports between these two dates (which explains, to a large extent, why imports from Britain increased more quickly than exports from France to Britain). Indeed, their progress was interrupted but once, from 1901 to 1905, owing to recession in France and to German competition; but, although this latter grew more intense, it did no serious harm to British positions on the French market.

There is something paradoxical about the most industrialised nation effecting these massive sales of a raw mineral to a less industrialised country (although this phenomenon has been repeated recently, with the rise in coal exports by the United States . . .). Yet the causes are too obvious to need reiterating: France was simply producing less coal than she was consuming; furthermore, her mines were situated in her northern and central areas, whereas several of the British coalfields

21 But it had smelting works for imported copper and tin ores, and the non-ferrous metals sent into France could have come to some extent from such works.

were close to the sea. English coal therefore had a virtual monopoly in all those parts of France which were near to the coast and distant from French coalfields, i.e., the whole of western and south-western France. Still it was only in 1894 that Britain ousted Belgium as the first supplier of coal to France, but from 1899 its share in French total imports of coal amounted to over half.[22] As for the share of France's total consumption which was supplied by Britain, it rose from 13 per cent in 1891–5 to 18 per cent in 1911–13.

Furthermore, France was the leading foreign client for the British coal industry, regularly consuming 16 or 17 per cent of its total exports; since these latter outpaced extraction in the pre-war period, France consumed 2·8 per cent of British coal output in 1900–4 and 4·5 per cent in 1913; the percentage was much higher, however, for the South Wales coalfield which, in 1913, sent 13 per cent of its production to France. At any rate, the rapid growth of imports of British coal during the period under consideration is a very clear proof of the industrialisation and modernisation that France was then undergoing.

Since re-exports from Britain to France were almost entirely primary products, since 'domestic' exports comprised, apart from coal, other raw materials or semi-finished articles (cotton and woollen yarn, pig-iron, iron and steel, dressed hides, etc.), raw materials and intermediate goods represented, on the eve of 1914, well over half of the imports into France from the United Kingdom, and a small part only consisted of finished manufactured articles. This was precisely the reverse structure to that observable for French exports to England.[23]

One explanation for this surprising contrast that immediately springs to mind is that France was protecting her industries, whereas England was a free trade country. Indeed, J. Périer noted in 1904 that, without the 'artificial supports' of protectionism, a number of French industries would not have been able to hold out against British competition. One should, however, bear in mind that French protec-

[22] A maximum of 53 per cent in 1906–10, followed by a downward turn to 49 per cent in 1911–13.

[23] Table 6.6 in O'Brien and Keyder, p. 161, is solely concerned with the export of *British* goods to France; it therefore underestimates the part played by raw materials, since they constituted most of the re-exports; moreover this study classifies wool and cotton fabrics and linen among intermediate goods exported to France. Be this as it may, the table gives the following percentages:

	1888	1905
Raw materials	12	26
Intermediate goods	55	35
Finished industrial goods	20	28

tionism was of a fairly moderate kind, even after the tariffs of 1892 and 1910; the average rate of customs duties was lower than in many other countries (for example, the United States) and only just above the German level. It is true that the 1881 tariff, although mild, was succeeded by a sharp fall in French imports of British cottons (which continued up until 1897), and of iron and steel also. Conversely, the Méline tariff of 1892, which is often denounced as ultra-protectionist, seems to have had no effect upon imports from Britain, save, perhaps, with regard to jute textiles; and, in spite of this tariff, French imports of British manufactures rose during the two succeeding decades, but with very different paces according to products.

French purchases of British textiles underwent a much lower than average growth, and their share in total imports from England fell from 20 per cent to 10 per cent. Woollens and worsteds, which had been the most important item in the 1890s, had almost zero growth.[24] Should one conclude from this that the French textile industry was becoming more competitive? Or that British exporters 'failed' as entrepreneurs? Or else that they were hardly interested in a market whose accessible sector was too narrow?

On the other hand, the rates of growth of exports by the metal and engineering industries were in general high, although some articles were not of much significance (such as iron and steel, or merchant ships).[25] At the head of this group was machinery, imports of which increased quickly and steadily; they represented, in 1911–13, 6 per cent of total imports from the United Kingdom. This serves as a further sign of France's industrialisation, but it would be of some interest to compare these imports with those from Germany and from the United States, which are generally held to have been in a better position than England to supply other countries with the sophisticated equipment that was increasingly in demand (electrical plant and machine-tools, in particular).

There is one last point that must be emphasised, namely, the sheer complexity of exchanges, such that the simplistic view of things, with wine and silks being traded against coal and machinery, just will not

24 This matches the decline in French exports of worsteds.

25 In 1911–13, France imported 194,000 tons of pig-iron, iron and steel from Britain. As for merchant vessels, the tonnage bought in Britain (partly new and partly second-hand) only exceeded 50,000 tons for 5 out of the 21 years considered. In 1913, the British shipyards having too many orders, a British shipping company ordered three steamships from the shipyards at Dunkirk; PP, 1913, LXX, no. 5137, p. 11.

do.[26] The traffic in either direction involved a wide range of textiles, plus, among other things, paper, leather, glass and porcelain goods. One can thus see emerging, in the commercial relations between Britain and France prior to the First World War, the typical pattern for trade between industrialised countries in the present day, which mainly involve manufactured articles which are, very broadly speaking, the same, such as automobiles or electronic equipment. Anyhow, for reasons of quality, price or fashion, significant quantities of British manufactured goods managed to cross the French customs barriers, while a number of specialities of French industry made real inroads into the English market, in spite of the global superiority of British industry. Furthermore, if there was specialisation, it existed at the level of particular branches of industry rather than at the level of whole industries. The most striking instance of this is that of France selling England worsted goods for women's clothes, while at the same time buying from England fabrics for men's clothes.[27] There were therefore exchanges within branches and a degree of complementarity as well: the English would sell worsted tops to the manufacturers of Roubaix, who would spin them, weave them and export the finished cloth to England.

IV

Coming back now, to conclude, to the question which was raised at the start of this chapter, it is plain that commercial relations between Britain and France did not fit with the prevailing pattern of trade between countries of the 'core' and of the 'periphery', according to which the former export manufactured articles to the latter and, conversely, import raw materials from them. From another perspective, France was unilaterally dependent upon England, which was its leading foreign customer (and also its leading supplier of energy); the surplus which France enjoyed in its balance of trade with Britain was crucial from the point of view of its balance of payments. Moreover, the British market absorbed a considerable part of France's total exports in several of its leading products: around a half, for example, for

[26] A point already noted above in relation to raw materials (note 13).

[27] Smart English ladies had dresses of French silks and worsteds; Frenchmen who pretended to elegance wore English materials and the very chic had their clothes tailored in London!

cognacs, silk goods, woollen and worsted fabrics.[28] Admittedly, we know little of the ratio between exports and production as regards these different articles. However, in 1908, the commercial attaché at the French Embassy in London estimated the exports by the various French regions to Britain; according to these calculations, 75 per cent of France's exports to this country originated in five regions: 31 per cent from Paris and its suburbs, 16 per cent from the *Nord*, 13 per cent from Lyons and roundabout, 8 per cent from the valley of the Garonne and 7 per cent from Normandy. Cliometricians have taught us to be chary of the epithet 'important' but, for want of a better one, let me assert that the British market was important for the Paris fashion and automobile industries, for the worsted industry of Roubaix, for the Lyons silk industry, and for the champagne and cognac producers also. It is true that wine and spirits exports, which were falling and had few backward or forward linkages, were not an engine of industrialisation, although they contributed to the prosperity of the wine-growing regions. Conversely, the export of large numbers of automobiles to England was a factor in the rapid growth of the automobile industry, and therefore in the beginnings of a deep structural change in French industry.

Indeed, of the various 'niches' occupied by French exports, there was only one, that of automobiles, which was 'progressive' in relation to world demand; all the others were 'regressive', i.e. they involved products for which demand was increasing more slowly than was international trade as a whole. Thus, the study of French exports to England would seem to confirm the idea that the reconversion of the French economy during the Great Depression and after had been insufficient and, more particularly, that concentration upon traditional products, mainly luxury articles, had continued to be excessive. Admittedly, an informed observer like Périer was recommending French exporters to concentrate upon up-market, prestige products, intended for the wealthy classes, which were very expensive, but which offered high profit margins, and to leave it to other countries to supply 'the people'. At any rate, the existence of the British market, which was a large one as far as luxury goods were concerned and, thanks to free trade, wide open, may have helped, through the dominant role it played, to ensure the survival of traditional structures of production

28 Britain had also been the leading foreign buyer of French butter, eggs and sugar, before their exports declined drastically.

and trade, and to delay the reconversion of the French economy (just as the possession of vast captive markets within its empire probably did harm, in the long run, to British industry). Conversely, France's specialisation implied a successful adaptation to its endowment in factors of production and therefore had a positive effect on incomes.

Be this as it may, the above analysis cannot be used to revive the jeremiads regarding the French industrialists' supposed lack of entrepreneurial qualities. The French consuls' reports do, admittedly, contain criticisms of French exporters; for example, they bewail the fact that all merchandise intended for the British market (save pit-props!) was sent to London, from where wholesalers would redistribute them to the rest of the country, whereas a more decentralised system of marketing seemed preferable to them. But, as we have seen, a major reason for the slow growth of French exports to Britain was the decline in sales of foodstuffs, whereas sales of manufactured articles did much better; if the surplus in the balance of trade enjoyed by France over Britain tended to diminish, this was largely because of the dramatic rise in exports of British coal, which is in itself a positive sign. Besides, France's exports to other countries made faster progress than did those to England, which is why her dependence on the British market diminished. The present study in no way invalidates the notion that the French economy was very dynamic during the *belle époque*. Indeed, it is worth quoting O'Brien and Keyder's observations on this subject:

> Apart from the absence of machinery in French exports to Britain, there seems to be little in the patterns of trade to suggest that French industry lagged far behind British industry ... Our classification ... reveals two developed economies trading on the basis of their relatively abundant natural resources and specialised along lines of comparative advantage.[29]

It is, however, possible to argue that France should be considered, with respect to Britain, as 'a small country', in the sense in which economists use this expression, that is, a country which pursues a strategy of specialisation, but which does not control the international market in its specialities. In fact, there are major differences between France and the classical cases of industrialised 'small countries' in Northern Europe, such as Belgium and Sweden. These countries depended far more than did France upon foreign trade and upon trade with England

[29] O'Brien and Keyder, p. 162.

in particular. Besides, France had more 'niches' and could call upon more numerous and more varied specialisations; she also had, of course, a larger domestic market, which enabled her, for example, to develop a national automobile industry. Thirdly, her industrialisation, which had been started under the shelter of strong protectionist policies, was far from being purely complementary to that of Britain and had even been 'antagonistic' to it, to echo the phrase from consul Périer quoted above. Yet one must also acknowledge that France did not display the same flexibility as the small northern countries, which were able to take advantage of new opportunities and to abandon traditional forms of production. One could put it that France was 'a big small country', if this does not seem a poor jest – or an assemblage of small countries – Paris, the Bordeaux and Lyons areas, Champagne, etc. One therefore arrives at the somewhat banal conclusion that Anglo-French commercial relations had a special character, on account of the precocious industrialisation of both countries, and because of the mixture of divergences and similarities in the 'paths to the twentieth century' which they had each taken.[30]

[30] Franco-British trade during the period which precedes that considered in this chapter has been studied in an important article: Gabrielle Cadier, 'Les Conséquences du traité de 1860 sur le commerce franco-britannique', *Histoire, Economie, Société*, VII, 3, 1988, pp. 355–80.

14 ❧ Problems of communication between Britain and France in the nineteenth and twentieth centuries*

Before I tackle the huge problem of communication between Britain and France from 1815 to the present, which I can only hope to touch upon here, it is worth asking whether the question of England's image in France and of France's image in England, which has been a kind of hobby of mine for a long time, is of real importance to historians.

Specialists in international relations regard collective representations as among the underlying forces which influence the foreign policies of governments. Yet my own impression, in the case of England and France, is that these representations have in fact been influenced by the vicissitudes of political relations between the two countries, as I shall attempt to delineate at the end of this chapter. These representations are probably most interesting in so far as they reveal aspects of collective mentalities. While the knowledge one people has of another is invariably biassed and incomplete, while it rarely teaches us very much about the realities of the country which is the object of such knowledge, it nevertheless serves as a test, a reagent of the mental structures of the 'subject'-people, of the representation it has of itself, of its system of values. It enables one to sound out its national consciousness. This is all the more so given that the image of another people tends by and large to be the reverse of the one a nation has of itself.[1] If, therefore, the French declared in the nineteenth century that the English were hypocrites and egoists, this meant that they regarded themselves as upright and generous; when the English saw the French as frivolous and immoral, that meant that they judged

* From a paper delivered at the Franco-British conference of historians, which was held at Lyons in October 1974. The text was originally published in *Revue Historique*, CCLIV, No. 515, July–September 1975, pp. 105–34. Only minor changes and additions have been made in the present translation, but a postscript was added in 1985 and a second one in 1989.

[1] P. Reboul, *Le Mythe Anglais dans la littérature française sous la Restauration* (Lille, 1962), pp. 1–2, also pp. 8, 329.

themselves to be serious and virtuous. On a different plane, nineteenth-century English observers regarded France as the country of egalitarianism, which most of them also disapproved of; in the 1940s and 1950s, however, the British did often criticise France for the social inequality believed to prevail there. This change reflected a reversal of values in English public opinion with regard to the problem of equality. The present topic is also of interest because of the special relationship which has existed, up until recently, between France and England, each country occupying a special place in the consciousness of the other, and serving to represent the quintessential foreigner, in relation to which one's own identity would be defined.[2]

A study of this nature cannot help but encounter serious methodological difficulties, as regards choice of primary sources, use of quantitative or linguistic methods, and one's assessment of the influence and representativeness of information and value-judgements.[3] I am not unaware of these problems, but I have chosen here to disregard them. Furthermore, given the present state of research, I will concern myself in the main with representations within educated public opinion, although I will also advance a few tentative observations regarding 'popular' views on the subject.

Let me begin by a few observations regarding the sources of knowledge and information. Travel, which involves direct contact with foreign countries, was the basis of any knowledge, for three main reasons. First, the traveller brought back with him an image of the country he had visited; second, he spread this image around, through his conversation, his letters and the publication of travel narratives, which were very common in the nineteenth century;[4] third, he left the natives of the country he had visited some kind of impression (which was rarely a favourable one) of himself and, by extension, of his compatriots. This third factor was of some significance, especially in the case of the popular image of the Englishman in nineteenth-century France, for its only real basis was, together with memories of the

[2] *Ibid.*, p. 2. Admittedly, from 1870 to the morrow of the Second World War, this relation became a *ménage à trois*, which included Germany, and it was in relation to the latter that many French people defined themselves.

[3] For these questions, I would refer to René Rémond, *Les États-Unis devant l'opinion française (1815–1852)* (Paris, 1962, 2 vols.), vol. I, pp. v–vii, 1–11; S. Marandon, *L'Image de la France dans l'Angleterre victorienne (1848–1900)* (Paris, 1967), pp. 121–39.

[4] See, for example, Ethel Jones, *Les Voyageurs français en Angleterre de 1815 à 1830* (Paris, 1930); M. Moraud, *La France de la Restauration d'après les visiteurs anglais (de la première abdication de Napoléon à sa mort), 1814–1821* (Paris, 1932).

Napoleonic wars, contact with British tourists. However, the history of English tourism in France – and of French tourism in England (which was less extensive a phenomenon) – has yet to be written in full.[5] Both its volume greatly increased and its social nature and quality changed: the rich traveller of the early nineteenth century made long stays and was received into 'society'; the holiday-maker on a package tour sees a handful of monuments in haste and has contacts only with hotel staff.[6] There has thus been a steady decline in personal contacts, and especially in 'drawing-room conversations', as a source of information about countries abroad. There has also been a change in the geography of knowledge of those countries. For a long period, the English were familiar only with Paris, the roads from the Channel ports to the capital and from the latter to Switzerland or Italy; this is why they had the notion that France was not picturesque (the expression 'la belle France' being employed then in an ironical sense), a view which altered at the end of the nineteenth century, when regions such as Brittany, the Pyrenees and the Massif Central were discovered.[7] The French, in the early nineteenth century, visited Scotland, the homeland of Sir Walter Scott, in fairly large numbers; a visit to Manchester was likewise for a long time obligatory for every serious traveller. Conversely, M.-F. Guyard has noted that, in the inter-war period, French writers who went to England rarely strayed from a circuit consisting of Dover, London and Oxford; this accounts for their very fragmentary knowledge of Britain, and for a number of unwarranted extrapolations made on the basis of it.[8] The huge English armies in France during two world wars constituted a particular kind of mass tourism, and one which undoubtedly influenced collective representations. This influence would be worth studying,[9] as would be that of exchange visits by school-children and students.[10]

[5] P. Gerbod, 'Voyageurs et résidents britanniques en France au XIXe siècle. Une approche statistique', *Acta Geographica*, IV, 76, December 1988, pp. 19–35.

[6] Between these two extremes there arose, from the mid nineteenth century, a tourism of the middle classes, whose influence on collective representations is still unclear.

[7] Marandon, pp. 74, 97, 155–81.

[8] M.-F. Guyard, *L'Image de la Grande-Bretagne dans le roman français (1914–1940)* (Paris, 1954), pp. 47–72.

[9] However, C. Campos, *The View of France. From Arnold to Bloomsbury* (London, 1965), pp. 239–40, reckons that the First World War had hardly any influence upon the English image of France, especially as regards the literature produced in England.

[10] The problem of languages has been neglected in this essay; cf. P. Gerbod, 'La Langue anglaise en France au XIXe siècle (1800–1871)', *Revue Historique*, CCLXXV, no. 557, January–March 1986, pp. 109–27.

In addition to travellers, there were those who lived abroad, whether they were idle rich, modest wage-earners or political refugees. The English colonies in nineteenth-century France, whether in Paris, on the Riviera, or in various provincial towns, undoubtedly played a by no means negligible role in the process we are considering here;[11] P. Reboul has emphasised the influence, during the French Restoration, of the rich English who settled in Paris, who mingled with the French upper class and 'anglicised' it.[12] Foreign residents are not necessarily 'representative', especially as regards their social origin, of their homeland. Thus, the French living in England included many cooks, hairdressers and prostitutes, while the English residing in France counted among their number many eccentric 'Milords', remittance men, merchants and engineers, not to mention governesses. In either case, such imbalances helped to perpetuate conventional stereotypes.[13]

However, the main means of communication, up until recently (when new audiovisual media invaded the field), was the printed word.[14] It was produced in huge and remarkably diverse quantities, even if one excludes newspapers, which yet were the sole source of information for uneducated and low-income milieux. Much was written in England about France, and vice versa, and translations were plentiful also,[15] although there were occasional time-lags, especially in the first decades of the nineteenth century (thus, none of Balzac's novels had been translated into English prior to 1859).[16] Of course, it was not necessarily the most famous or the most perceptive works which did most to influence the image that was formed of the other country. Thus, S. Marandon reckons that, at the end of the nineteenth century, two now all but forgotten books served as breviaries for the English as regards France, namely, P. G. Hamerton's *Round my House* (1876), which described provincial life in the area around Autun, in

11 There are several clues in Marandon, pp. 101–5, 159; Guyard, pp. 73–83; also Simona Pakenham, *Sixty Miles from England. The English at Dieppe, 1814–1914* (London, 1967); Dieppe was at one time a meeting-place for writers and artists from both sides of the Channel.

12 Reboul, pp. 24–6, 130–1, 227; M. E. Elkington, *Les Relations de société entre l'Angleterre et la France sous la Restauration (1814–1830)* (Paris, 1929). Relations between the cosmopolitan fractions of the English and French aristocracies, which met not only in drawing-rooms, but also on the racetracks, out hunting, around the gaming tables, and which were linked by marriage ties, deserve to be studied in detail.

13 Guyard, p. 85; see also below, note 67.

14 Marandon, p. 21.

15 See the Appendix in C. Campos, pp. 242–5; from 1903 to 1913, out of 4,000 works published each year in Britain, 160 on average were concerned with France or were translations of French works.

16 Marandon, pp. 28–33; also Reboul, pp. 327–8.

Burgundy, where the author himself had settled, and a book by the historian J. E. C. Bodley.[17] More recently, P. Bourdan's *Perplexités et grandeur de l'Angleterre* (1945) has remained virtually unknown, while Daninos' pitiful clowning has given a new lease of life to the stereotype of the English gentleman, with his moustache, bowler hat and umbrella. In addition, there are some particular categories of works which can exert a significant influence. This is the case with children's books, which are liable to have a deep and lasting effect upon their readers; it is of some significance that, for a long time in France, countless children read (in translation) some of Dickens' novels; on the other hand, several of the British characters in Jules Verne are quite unattractive, and some other famous French novels for the young in the nineteenth century were very anti-English, for example, *The Adventures of Captain Corcoran*, by A. Assollant. School textbooks, especially in the field of history,[18] are also important, as is history writing in general; its most widely read section, intended for the general public, almost invariably has a strong emphasis on military history and a heavy nationalistic bias. Thus, in England, the flood of biographies of Nelson and Wellington shows no sign of abating. Nor does in France writing about the Napoleonic period, which rarely has a good word for the British ...

I believe, however, the opinion of some specialists notwithstanding, that literature, in the narrow sense of the term, has been the most powerful factor in the formation of collective representations in educated milieux and, by osmosis, in those that are less so. This has worked on two different planes, firstly through those works which the writers of one country have devoted to the other (P. Reboul reckons that it was the French writers who, during the Restoration, gave life to some *membra disjecta* in order to create an 'English myth'), and, secondly, by the diffusion in a country of foreign books (M. F. Guyard has stressed that, during the inter-war period, it was literature that constituted the true presence of England in France, rather than personal encounters, economists' statistics or politicians' speeches).[19]

[17] Marandon, p. 134.

[18] According to Marandon, pp. 92–4, English textbooks of the late nineteenth century are little more than chronologies and do not present any clearly characterised 'vision' of French history. On the French side, the series of *Malet–Isaac–Alba* textbooks, which secondary school pupils used for half a century, presented the history of England with objectivity and sympathy.

[19] Reboul, p. 77; Guyard, pp. 86, 106. However, Campos, pp. 5–6, maintains that French writers contributed to the formation of the image of France only indirectly, inasmuch as they were the source or inspiration for British authors. But he also makes the point (p. 4) that the

More particularly, novels are for many the sole means they have of arriving at some knowledge of the familiar, everyday reality of the country where they have been written. Indeed, it seems to me that a number, albeit a fairly small one, of writers and their works have wielded, whether in their native country or across the Channel, a considerable influence upon collective representations.

Thus, P. Reboul ascribes to Lord Byron, and to *Don Juan* and his *Memoirs* in particular, a crucial role in the formation of an 'English myth' which was to last for generations. This enabled the French to give a coherent and unifying explanation, in terms of the notion of hypocrisy, of the contradictory qualities of English civilisation. Before Lord Byron, England had had two countenances, one perfidious and the other noble; he united these two aspects and gave to England a masked face.[20] Much later, Oscar Wilde (the public figure rather than the writer), and then the translations of James Joyce and D. H. Lawrence (*Lady Chatterley's Lover*, 1932) did much to modify accepted ideas of British morality.[21] Of the French authors, Hippolyte Taine had a deep and lasting influence; in particular, he introduced into France an image of the 'gentleman' which ruled uncontested for around half a century;[22] in the inter-war period, an entire generation came to know England through André Siegfried, if they were fairly sophisticated, through André Maurois and his characters – Colonel Bramble and Major O'Grady, if they were less so.[23]

On the English side, *A Tale of Two Cities* had a strong influence on people's minds,[24] and many English travellers were out to identify among French peasants of their own time the wretched living conditions which Dickens had represented as being theirs under the *Ancien Régime*. Thackeray's chronicles in *Punch* did much to perpetuate the stereotypes of the French as dancers and swashbucklers, excitable and boastful, whereas Matthew Arnold gave currency to the idea that they were intelligent, educated (but always according to the uniform norms

view of France of the average Englishman is conditioned by the ideas of the writers of two or three generations before.

20 Reboul, pp. 149–53, 256–8, 328.   21 Guyard, pp. 87, 200.

22 F. C. Roe, *Taine et l'Angleterre* (Paris, 1923), pp. vii, 166–72; Guyard, pp. 5, 27, 115. Roe claims that Taine's views on England were more popular than those of any other author who had attempted to explain to Frenchmen their neighbours; up until 1914, his successors adopted his views, which made up a powerful and coherent system. It was only in 1900 that a serious criticism was advanced of it, by P. Mantoux, in his *A travers l'Angleterre contemporaine*.

23 Guyard, pp. 28–9, 161, 289–94.

24 And also Carlyle's *The French Revolution* (1837), with a not dissimilar outlook.

imposed in the *Lycées*), sociable and sensual. At the end of the nineteenth century, fashionable French novels did much to spread the idea that all French *ménages* were *ménages à trois* and carried to its pitch the notion, already firmly anchored in English public opinion, that the French were fundamentally immoral.[25]

Finally, it may be worth mentioning a number of other, secondary sources of information, such as oral tradition (memories of wartime, whether in the Napoleonic period or more recently, and anecdotes regarding 'national characters'), caricature, theatre, and later, cinema (in which foreign characters are almost invariably marionettes of the most conventional kind) and, finally, those dumb travellers, as P. Reboul terms the objects imported from the other country, which allow one to form some image of it. At the time of the French Restoration, English commodities helped to spread the idea of England as a rich country and the very pinnacle of progress, but a utilitarian and inhuman one. For her part, S. Marandon notes that French products sold in Victorian England, which were mainly foodstuffs and luxury articles, reinforced the traditional image of France as an agricultural country on the one hand, and as a land of elegance and easy living, gifted for the arts but not for industry, on the other.[26] In the present day, advertising, whether touristic or commercial, tends to present England or France under their most traditional guises, with Beefeaters and Rolls Royces on the one hand, haute cuisine, haute couture and cancan on the other.

Long before the rise of mass media, communication between Great Britain and France had therefore been intense, with a considerable volume of information available in each country respecting the other, and the quality of this information was often quite high. Thus, P. Reboul asserts that France has never had a better instrument for diffusing knowledge about England than the *Revue Britannique*, which, from 1825 on, published translations of the better articles which had appeared in British reviews.[27]

We still need to know whether information on the neighbouring country was more plentiful or of higher quality on the one side of the Channel than on the other. The British have often been conscious of

[25] Marandon, pp. 39, 44–9; Campos, pp. 13 ff., 48, 63–89.

[26] Reboul, pp. 34–6; Marandon, pp. 113–15.

[27] Reboul, p. 187; K. Jones, *La Revue britannique, son histoire et son action littéraire (1825–1840)* (Paris, 1939).

having a better knowledge of France than the French have had of England. S. Marandon believes that there was justification for this belief in the nineteenth century and M.-F. Guyard has pointed to the number of important French writers who never even set foot in England, whereas, from the middle of the nineteenth century at least, there have been very few educated English people who have not travelled in France.[28] At the present time, many more good studies of France are undoubtedly published in England, and especially in the field of history works, than vice versa.[29] However, France redeemed herself to some degree through the sheer quality of some of her interpreters of England, writers such as Hippolyte Taine, Elie Halévy and André Siegfried. Nowadays, however, thanks to Richard Cobb, Douglas Johnson, Theodore Zeldin, and others, Britain has no basis for jealousy.

Nevertheless, Anglo-French collective representations have been misleading, offering only an incomplete and distorted view of reality abroad, which reverts at times to the most vulgar caricature.

As a consequence of the actual sources of information, these representations are inevitably selective and tend to lapse into unwarranted generalisation. Since Descartes mentioned the story of the red-haired woman of Calais, we have known that travellers are liable to resort to generalisations just as soon as they have left their country. He will judge a whole country on the basis of his experience of customs, transportation or inns; he will be quite prepared, either in all seriousness or to amuse himself, to give a lot of importance to chance episodes or encounters.[30] S. Marandon has also noted that the English in the nineteenth century tended to eliminate from their vision of France every aspect which reminded them of England or else which was more forcefully represented elsewhere – for example, the Alps, which were regarded as typical of Switzerland.[31] As for popular papers, they are only interested in a foreign country when there are political crises, general strikes, bloody riots or spectacular crimes.

On the other hand, observers, even the most thoughtful among them, make choices as a consequence of their previous, bookish acquaintance with the country they are visiting. As Taine expressed it,

28 Marandon, p. 670; Guyard, pp. 28, 44–5.

29 *The Times Literary Supplement* regularly has reviews of recent French books. None of the French weeklies for 'intellectuals' does the same for English books.

30 Reboul, pp. 30–2. 31 Marandon, pp. 144–5.

one goes to 'check' one's ideas abroad,[32] knowing the moment one sets out what it is that one will find there. Travel narratives are therefore relentlessly involved in observing the same things, again and again, because it is the same things that their authors expect to encounter. So it is that images become not only selective but exclusive as well. P. Reboul notes how the French of the Restoration period neglected various aspects of English life, because they did not conform to the 'English myth', for example, radicalism, philanthropy, religious dissent, because everybody *knew* that the English were conservative, selfish and formed a closely united nation.[33] Foreign literature is itself a distorting mirror, indeed a screen, for the novel reveals not so much the real country as the one imagined by novelists, whereas readers abroad tend to see it as a faithful reflection of the life in the other country. Becoming mixed up with its literature, the real identity of the country comes in part to be hidden behind it.[34]

Finally, as René Rémond has shown with respect to the French image of the United States, observers see, think and form judgements in terms of the problems that dominate the domestic politics of their own country; they will tend to look abroad for answers to the questions which are raised at home, and for weapons that may be used in domestic polemics. The neighbouring country is used as a living lesson, as a model or as a foil.[35] Setting aside the more obvious examples, I shall merely mention the lively and continuing interest the English showed in the nineteenth century – in connection with the debates on landed property – in the question of the equal sharing of inheritances in France – a factor which many believed could by itself account for every aspect of French life.[36]

[32] Taine had asked a young man, who was about to set out for Italy, which ideas he was going to check there; see Roe, p. viii, and also pp. 17, 81–2, 144, which emphasise that Taine had thus defined his own method. The three journeys he made, prior to the publication of his *Notes*, lasted only ten weeks in all, but he prepared for them by undertaking a huge course of reading, so that his on-the-spot investigations served simply to confirm conclusions to which he had already come.

[33] Reboul, pp. 31, 328–9. Likewise Marandon, pp. 603–4, observes that commonplace views in England on the intellectual capacities of the French presented whoever differed from the norm – for example, Hugo or Balzac – as not really belonging to France's genuine literary heritage, and therefore neglected them. See also, M. Moraud, *Le Romantisme français en Angleterre de 1814 à 1848* (Paris, 1933), pp. 32–7.

[34] Guyard, p. 357; Reboul, p. 37; Campos, pp. 168, 176, 235; the idea that French art and literature are pagan and sensual is often applied to French life as a whole.

[35] Rémond, pp. 861–7, and *passim*; Campos, p. 241, also notes that English writers have 'explored' France in order to find answers to their own problems.

[36] Marandon, pp. 412–22.

Collective representations also have the attribute of stability, indeed, of virtual permanence. For example, the 'English myth', whose formation under the Restoration Reboul has described, survived almost intact up until the end of the nineteenth century; Taine's views regarding the admirable equilibrium enjoyed by English society and its institutions were prevalent up until 1914, if not later.[37]

Admittedly, it happens that reality develops slowly and that each country therefore preserves much the same features for a long period of time, but there is frequently a serious time-lag between the images and the actual development of a foreign society: they tend to represent its past rather than its present,[38] and they find it difficult to integrate change. Such images are often nourished by isolated observations wholly lacking in historical depth, by time-honoured authors and out-of-date books, by old recollections presented as current testimonies. Guyard, for example, has shown that many French writers of the inter-war period described England as they had known it twenty or thirty years before, prior to the First World War; as for André Maurois, he remained a prisoner of his own experience as an interpreter with the British Army during the war, when he had dealings exclusively with 'gentlemen in uniform'.[39] The tendency of such images to persist for a long time, and therefore to become anachronistic, was reinforced by the vision of England as a country of tradition and of fidelity to the past,[40] so much so that serious specialists have often proved blind to the transformations that it was undergoing, and have gone on seeing it as it was in the Edwardian, nay the Victorian period. Likewise, from the English side of things, public opinion has always failed to appreciate France's economic progress,[41] including the spectacular advances of the third quarter of the twentieth century, and serious writers frequently describe French agriculture as 'medieval'.

37 Reboul, pp. 153, 325; Guyard, pp. 5, 8. For an example of the way in which Taine's perspective endured, see E. Boutmy, *Essai d'une psychologie politique du peuple anglais au XIXe siècle* (Paris, 1901).

38 Reboul, p. 2. Thus, a number of Taine's views, to which I have alluded, were already anachronistic at the time he wrote; Roe, *Taine et l'Angleterre*, pp. 90, 100–4, 109, 140.

39 Guyard, pp. 85, 143–51, 287–9, 346–51. Likewise, Campos, pp. 222 ff., shows that the Bloomsbury set's ideas on France were largely derived from Matthew Arnold's conceptions – one of the 'Eminent Victorians' whom they abhorred – which were about fifty years old. Campos also maintains (pp. 8, 10) that the English image of France which had crystallised between the 1890s and the end of the First World War has largely survived up until the 1960s.

40 Which corresponds, on the English side, to the commonly held idea (often expressed, for example, in 1968) that French history is involved in an unceasing repetition or restaging of the psychodrama of the French Revolution.

41 Marandon, pp. 185–6, 363.

The blindness of journalists and writers is compounded by the reluctance of the general public to accept novelty. The most successful works from, or concerning abroad, are those which accord with traditional images and which serve to reinforce their hold on the popular imagination. Hence, in the 1930s and 1940s, the vogue in France, which seemed somewhat surprising in Britain, for the works of the English novelist, Charles Morgan.[42] Besides, when it finally dawns on people that a change has occurred, there may be unease or irritation, and their admiration for a country they feel has become different may be modified. This is the case with those English people who were enamoured of the France of *Clochemerle* and who felt disconcerted by, if not hostile towards, a France which has industrialised ... Likewise, Frenchmen who used to admire Britain as a 'Welfare State', have been upset by Thatcherism.[43]

Because they are both selective and stable, collective representations also have a tendency to become impoverished, and to turn into stereotypes, into ready-made and simplistic formulas, which are automatically associated with a foreign country. They become the *idées reçues* recorded by Flaubert in his *Dictionary*, which has this excellent entry: 'Englishmen – All rich.'[44] These stereotypes are wholly immune to any attempt at bringing them into line with reality, and they are therefore remarkably long-lasting.[45] They play an important part, at every level of public opinion, in the formation of images of other countries, and, as one descends the IQ scale, they gradually become the sole knowledge. Furthermore, stereotypes are assiduously hawked around by the media, which, whether out of intellectual poverty or for demagogic purposes, rarely presents any image of foreigners other than the one their public expects.

Among the most characteristic, influential and long-lasting stereotypes are those which refer to 'national characteristics'. In the nineteenth century, they were lent credence by the racist myths which were then in vogue and by speculations concerning the supposed psychology of the original peoples of Europe, the Celts, Latins, Teutons, Normans and so on[46] (there is still a trace of this in the frequent use in England of the name 'Gaul' and of the disparaging epithet 'Gallic'). It also used to

[42] Guyard, p. 358; Campos, p. 229. [43] This last sentence is, of course, a 1989 addition.

[44] G. Flaubert, *Bouvard et Pécuchet* (Paris, 1966 edn.), p. 335. [45] Marandon, pp. 125–6.

[46] See Roe, p. 128, on the idea of race as the cornerstone of all of Taine's views on England and the English; see also Campos, pp. 35–40, on the same idea in Matthew Arnold's work.

be believed in England that, since French society was codified and constraining, all the French resembled each other.[47] Even in the present day, a belief in national characters or temperaments is deeply rooted in popular belief, and is not foreign to the best minds, despite its racist undertones.

One should, however, banish the notion that images have ever been wholly fixed, for in fact they adapt themselves and are renewed, with new stereotypes replacing old ones, generally fairly slowly but sometimes rapidly.

Thus, the Revolutionary and Napoleonic wars had successfully demolished the image of England and the English which had prevailed during the eighteenth century in France and, in the space of a few years, between 1818 and 1827, a new myth was formed and established itself. England was no longer represented as populated by rationalist philosophers and had become instead Old England, a country of conservatism and empiricism, dominated by aristocracy and plutocracy.[48] Sometimes one can even identify the precise moment, as P. Reboul has done, when a new stereotype, such as that of English hypocrisy, arises. This stereotype did not form part of the traditional ideas respecting the English character and it was born quite suddenly in 1815, when the Allies seized a large number of pictures from the Louvre and when Wellington declared that this action should be taken by the French as a moral lesson. Applied first to British foreign policy, this stereotype came to be regarded, under Byron's influence, as a principle that would explain the whole of English civilisation.[49] Later on, an author as serious as Taine would seem to have originated the idea that English women have long teeth and big feet, which he explained quite seriously in terms of the cold climate, which required a meat diet – which strengthened the jaws, and the practice of physical exercise.[50]

Anyhow, stereotypes are tough and it may happen that those which seem to have been obliterated in fact live on somewhere in the collective memory, ready to re-emerge when circumstances, and international disputes in particular, are congenial. Thus, the idea, which was formulated by Barère during the Revolution, that English diplomacy was perfidious and Machiavellian, has resurfaced period-

[47] Marandon, p. 675. [48] Reboul, pp. 3–4, 6–9, 66, 243, 318–19.
[49] *Ibid.*, pp. 15, 149–53.
[50] H. Taine, *Notes sur l'Angleterre* (Paris, 1928 edn.), pp. 22, 25, 59.

ically in France. Likewise, in England, the stereotype of a chauvinistic, militaristic, glory-loving France was revived after 1918, then again at the time of General de Gaulle, and commentators then invoked Louis XIV, Napoleon and, indeed, the Continental Blockade, with respect to the Common Market.

Of course, the stereotypes which last the longest and change most slowly are those respecting national characteristics. S. Marandon has observed that the majority of the character traits which the British used to attribute to the French in the eighteenth century continued to dominate their consciousness throughout the nineteenth century also. These traits would include a lively, superficial and unpractical mind, displays by men of gallantry towards the other sex, and coquettishness – moral laxity even – among the women, a tendency to emotional behaviour, wild gesturing and volubility (all typical of an essentially 'histrionic' people), and, above all, the superficiality and frivolity of a people concerned only with amusing themselves. On the other hand, a number of traditional images grew blurred, for example, the vision of a combative, turbulent, indeed bellicose people, a people that was also full of high spirits and *joie de vivre*; these attributes were effectively swept away by the disasters of 1870. Conversely, the image of the typical Frenchman was enriched with new elements at the end of the nineteenth century, such as a passion for work, frugality, an eager concern to save and to be independent, and, in addition, the closeness of family ties, which previously were thought to have been destroyed by universal debauchery.[51]

These are interesting developments, which can in part be explained by the discovery of new social strata. For, fundamentally, stereotypes of national characters are caricatures of particular social types. The Frenchman, as he was seen by the English for the greater part of the nineteenth century, was elegant, accomplished, gallant, witty, sceptical, frivolous and pleasure-seeking, all attributes of the *habitué* of eighteenth-century salons, who was kept alive in the degraded version of the original, namely, the Parisian *boulevardier* of the nineteenth century. Similarly, the Englishman, as seen by the French in the eighteenth and the first part of the nineteenth century, was rich, phlegmatic, arrogant, sometimes coarse, sometimes eccentric and morose, and later often a dandy; in short, he was nothing other than a Milord doing the Grand Tour. Thanks to the influence of Taine, in

[51] Marandon, pp. 193–333; Campos, p. 240.

particular, he was replaced by the 'Christian gentleman', of the kind that was being fashioned in the public schools. Thus, the characteristics, more or less accurately observed, of the upper class, or indeed of a minority within it, were extended to a whole nation. However, as British tourists discovered both the French provinces and the more lowly social classes – the middle and the petty bourgeoisie and the peasantry – they began to introduce into the stereotype new elements, of the kind mentioned above, which were found in such milieux. So it was that, under the Third Republic, a new 'typical Frenchman' was born, who can be called the man with the beret: hard-working, thrifty, stingy even, and with him there came the notion that Frenchmen are profoundly conservative (and not revolutionary, as one used to suppose). However, this view of things only permeated a minority of British public opinion, and the popular conception remained what it had been almost since time immemorial, namely, that of the frivolous and immoral Frenchman.[52]

In France, by contrast, the notion of the gentleman continued right into the twentieth century to encapsulate the essence of the popular notion of the Englishman. The nineteenth century had been aware that poverty was widespread in England, but the lower middle class and the working class had somehow been left outside of the French popular image of what the English character was, and later on these social groups almost disappeared from this image of Britain. During the inter-war period, the age, social origin, literary and political ideas of the majority of French writers led them to depict almost exclusively the English upper classes; the Yahoo, as Paul Dottin called the inhabitants of the East End, only made fleeting and almost unnoticed appearances.[53] It is only recently that the stereotype of the English worker, passing his day in tea breaks, or being on strike most of the time, has become a feature of French popular opinion, as well, of course, as the football hooligan.

It may be worth pointing out, in passing, the way in which, under the Third Republic, a number of differences in social structure and social mobility, namely, the rise of *nouvelles couches* in France, served to

[52] Marandon, pp. 225–6, 451–4, 669; see also J. R. Rabier, 'Comment les peuples européens se voient et voient les autres', *Revue de psychologie des peuples*, 19th year, no. 1, 1964, pp. 22–32, about an opinion poll which reveals that, for the British in the early 1960s, the four main attributes of the French were of being passionate, romantic, light-hearted and 'Don Juans'.

[53] Guyard, pp. 162 ff., 182 ff., 193–4, 354–5; P. Dottin, *John Bull à la découverte de son île* (Paris, 1925), pp. 7–47.

inhibit Anglo-French communication. I shall restrict myself to two quotations. In 1914, Sir John French wrote to Lord Kitchener with regard to French military commanders: '*Au fond*, they are a low lot and one should always bear in mind the class from which the majority of these French generals have come.'[54] Likewise, Harold Nicolson, after a grand dinner given in honour of the French Prime Minister, E. Daladier in 1937, noted: 'I was not impressed by the latter's appearance: compared to our own Ministers, who were resplendent in stars and ribbons, he looked like some Iberian merchant visiting the Roman Senate.'[55]

I will now try a brief analysis of the content of these collective representations and of their positive or negative meaning. Indeed, the image of another people is never neutral; it always bears, depending upon the values of those presenting it or carrying it, some favourable or disapproving nuance.

Throughout the nineteenth century, the French image of England was that of a country of contrasts, even of extremes,[56] where, as Taine wrote, 'the bad and the good are ... greater than in France',[57] and in every field. The countryside was green, but the towns were blackish and smoky; the rich were wealthy and comfortable, while the lower classes lived in appalling poverty, such that the French tended to think that they were more wretched than were the poor of their own country;[58] every citizen enjoyed liberty and self-government prevailed everywhere, yet social life was governed by the strictest formalism; there was free speech but a unanimous respect for fundamental principles; the parliamentary régime had reached a point of perfection, and yet the aristocracy was still dominant; the constitution was stable but the system was open to reforms; religious sentiments ran deep, yet materialism prevailed in a nation athirst for gold; moral principles were a powerful force, family life was austere and pure (Taine, ever keen to quantify, stated that *ménages* which lived in sin were three times

[54] B. W. Tuchman, *August 1914* (London, 1962), p. 241. Actually, Joffre, the French commander-in-chief, was the son of a country baker.

[55] H. Nicolson, *Diaries and Letters, 1930–1939*, edited by Nigel Nicolson (London, 1969), pp. 291–2. Daladier had started as a schoolteacher. See also F. Crouzet, 'Réactions françaises devant les *Conséquences économiques de la paix* de Keynes', in *Revue d'histoire moderne et contemporaine*, XIX, January–March 1972, pp. 25–6.

[56] This vision is captured remarkably in Gustave Doré's famous engravings on wood for Louis Enault's *Londres* (Paris, 1876, 2 vols.). See also Reboul, pp. 5, 43 ff., 155 ff., 188, 227–8, 237 ff., 327–9.

[57] Taine, p. 49.

[58] *Ibid.*, pp. 35–9, 41–2, 292 ff., 322, 374.

less common than in France, and that, at Oxford, 'one half of the students are chaste'),[59] but prostitution was openly paraded in the streets, there was shamelessness later in public parks, and there was the 'English vice' – i.e. homosexuality (the French, a little irked at being considered immoral by their neighbours, have periodically been delighted to discover a few tears in the mantle of British virtue).[60] This antinomy recurs in the last avatar of the English myth in France, during the 1930s and 1940s, when the English were seen as an indolent, sluggish people, eccentric and treating everything as if it were a game, and yet disciplined, stubborn, courageous and always winners of the last battle.[61]

This Manichean vision lent itself as readily to admiration as to condemnation, to anglomania and to anglophobia alike, depending upon the aspects that the system of values of each Frenchman led him to stress or to disregard. Hence the division in French public opinion regarding England, a topic I shall return to below.[62] Hence, also, the notion of an 'English mystery', which tended to disconcert the French, who were in general unable to attribute to their neighbours a dominant quality which would resolve those contradictions, except when the explanation for all these antinomies was found to be hypocrisy.[63] Admittedly, as time passed, these antinomic images underwent simplification and polarisation. For a fairly long period, during the nineteenth century, the views of French authors regarding England were complex and nuanced; this is true of the writings of Chateaubriand, Stendhal or even Taine, just to take three examples. However, gradually, the anglophiles opted for the positive aspects alone, whereas the anglophobes focused on the offensive ones; on either side of the divide, the myth was emptied of contradictions, simplified and impoverished.[64] One could perhaps put it that there was a fall from

59 *Ibid.*, pp. 131, 135.

60 Reboul, pp. 49, 143–4; Guyard, pp. 215–8; Taine, pp. 47, 126 ff., 131–4. The theme of English immorality had first emerged in 1815 in the book by maréchal de camp Pillet, *L'Angleterre à Londres et dans ses provinces pendant un séjour de dix années, dont six comme prisonnier de guerre* (Paris, 1815), who has no less than six chapters on this subject, including this remarkable passage (p. 206), about the use of churchyards for assignations by 'working-class girls': 'This is where many young women, yielding to libertinage, have been made pregnant, on the very grave of their own mothers.'

61 See Jean Queval, *De l'Angleterre* (Paris, 1956), and earlier, L. Cazamian, *Ce qu'il faut connaître de l'âme anglaise* (Paris, 1927).

62 Cazamian, p. 8, also notes that England inspired mixed feelings in everyone, namely, distrust and admiration, esteem and envy.

63 Guyard, p. 195.

64 Reboul, pp. 109, 230–1, 330.

Taine to André Maurois or, at the other extreme, to Céline. Furthermore, this process of idealisation drew strength from the actual progress that England was making, for example, in proceeding down the path of democracy or in reducing pauperism. Considered overall, if one exempts a few 'wild men' (whose hatred was itself mingled with a secret admiration and envy of, for example, the sacred egoism they tended to ascribe to English foreign policy), and if one sets to one side a popular anglophobia which drew sustenance from memories of the Revolutionary and Napoleonic wars and which, although little is known of it, lasted for a long time, the average judgement of the French respecting England has tended to be positive, or 'by and large favourable', to use the language of opinion polls. 'One can not love the English, but it is impossible not to feel esteem for them', Lamartine had written,[65] an aphorism which well describes a widespread response.[66]

However, not every aspect of English civilisation was admired. Taine, a convinced anglophile, concluded his *Notes on England* by asserting that three things were superior on the other side of the Channel, namely, the political system, religion, and the capacity to produce wealth; in addition, he regarded English education as better by far than the French. Three things, however, were better in France, and these were climate, the less unequal distribution of wealth and the more pleasant and relaxed family and social life (along with the brilliance of intellectual life in France, in comparison with which the English mind was to him similar to a travel guide, which contains a large quantity of facts but few ideas!).[67] This was a representative enough opinion, for what the French have admired in England has been above all else its institutions; what they have rejected (with the exception of a handful of fashionable 'anglomanes') is the quality or,

[65] A quotation that Guyard chose as the epigraph of his book.

[66] The development of the stereotype of the 'Englishman' is typical. Thus, during the Restoration, although he was allowed to have serious qualities deep down, he was often a fairly unsympathetic lout; later Taine himself observed that, alongside gentlemen, there existed an average, very John Bullish type; but finally, came the triumph of the gentleman, a man of heart and conscience, with only a few ridiculous ways. Yet one should not forget that many Frenchmen for long maintained a feeling of superiority, and that – conversely – there was often a strong sense of jealousy with regard to the wealth, stability and civic virtues of the British (Reboul, p. 329), hence forms of banter which were often an expression of an inferiority complex.

[67] Taine, pp. 390–4; also p. 235; on education, see p. 135 ff.; on the quality of life, see pp. 9, 15–17, 24, 62, 73.

rather, what seemed to them to be the lack of a quality of life, involving fog, cooking, English Sundays, women's toilette, the excessive formality, the sheer boredom (the English attitude to France, as we shall see, was almost the exact reverse).

The British image of France was simpler, because all its constituent elements in the nineteenth century were negative, with the additional proviso that, before 1850, they were almost uniformly pejorative, whereas, in subsequent years, they became less monolithic, thanks to an increasing awareness of the diversity of France.[68] Things have changed in the course of the twentieth century, but only in part, so that one could still quote recent judgements, taken from quite serious sources, which closely resemble those current a century before, along the lines of what S. Marandon has reconstituted for the second half of the nineteenth century.[69] In broad outline, what we see is an economically backward, poor, dirty country; a society without a head, as the upper classes and the nobility in particular stood aside, and where egalitarianism is rampant; an intrusive, oppressive bureaucracy, an ubiquitous police force, a system of justice which presumed that the defendant was guilty, and therefore no genuine liberty; a uniform educational system, which was stifling and which did not succeed in forming pupils morally; politics regarding which the most generous judgement was that it was surprising that a people that was so gifted in many respects was unable to manage its own affairs any better. France, in this view, continually oscillated between revolution and Caesarism, with instability the only constant factor; its parliamentary procedures were a poor parody of the British system, its political life was a farce, sometimes a tragedy. As far as foreign policy was concerned, the hypertrophy of its ego made France the paranoiac of Europe; regarded up until 1870 as a firebrand ever liable to attack its neighbours, it was subsequently seen as a decadent country which, through false pride and lack of realism, refused to accept its decline; the narrow-minded patriotism of the French kept them in ignorance of

68 Marandon, p. 11; Campos, pp. 13–14, 240; also Enid Starkie, *From Gautier to Eliot. The Influence of France on English Literature, 1851–1939* (London, 1960), pp. 10–20; R. Heppenstall, *The Fourfold Tradition. Notes on the French and English Literatures, with some Ethnological and Historical Asides* (London, 1961), pp. 105–8. The last two authors emphasise the hostility that prevailed towards France, and the slight intellectual influence she had in England during the first half of the nineteenth century, and even beyond.

69 See, in particular, Chapters V, VI, VII, VIII.

foreign countries and led them to believe that the rest of the world were nothing but barbarians.[70]

It was, however, on the moral plane that the British image of the French was most thoroughly negative, and the condemnation by the Victorians the most categorical. Living in a country which was blamed for being both catholic and irreligious, the Frenchman was held to have undergone no moral training and to have no moral principles, so that he believed in nothing, respected nothing and laughed at everything; he was prone to think only of his own pleasures, debauch was the national sport, which was responsible, moreover, for the decadence of France, which, according to Matthew Arnold, writing in 1885, was devoured by 'the great goddess Lubricity'. Sexual immorality constituted the most fundamental notion, the one that was most automatically associated with France and the French in English popular opinion. As S. Marandon has written, morality is the most impregnable citadel of British superiority, and the need that was endlessly felt to reassert this superiority over the vice which prevailed on the other side of the Channel would seem to be a significant characteristic of the collective mentality of Victorian and post-Victorian England.[71]

However, the English image of France also contained a number of positive elements and even some decorative flourishes, such as the bizarre idea that the French have an artistic temperament and that taste, indeed a taste for art, is a widespread feature of all classes. It is true that such qualities, although they might be admired in certain educated milieux, could be scorned in others. Thus, it was very commonly said that the French were intelligent, but it was also reckoned that they made poor use of this quality, in so far as they tended to become intoxicated by logic; indeed, English empiricists came very close to seeing the intelligence of the French as a poisoned present. Likewise, the French were seen as having the art of enjoying life, and aesthetes praised them for being pagans and sensualists, but these were hardly the most glowing of references as far as the Non-conformist conscience was concerned.[72]

Considered overall, the English representation of France was tinged

[70] The British are rightly exasperated by the ignorance of other countries, the Gallocentrism, and the conviction of cultural superiority, all of which are still common in France.

[71] Marandon, ch. IX, pp. 527 ff., 566–86; Campos, pp. 147–53, 207.

[72] Marandon, pp. 587–602; Campos, p. 240. The stale cliché regarding the sweetness of the French way of life is far from having disappeared; see for example, Starkie, p. 211; E. Powell, 'An Englishman's Dordogne', *The Independent*, 19 September 1987.

with contempt,[73] and rested upon the notion that the Frenchman was inferior as a man. Thackeray, for example, had written in *Punch* in 1845: 'Whatever one does ... one cannot respect these Frenchmen.'[74] A psychoanalyst might find it of some interest that, in the nineteenth century, the Frenchman was often compared to a child or a woman, whereas the British would reserve the qualities of maturity and virility for themselves.[75] At the level of popular opinion, the smallest common denominator of the stereotype of the Frenchman seems to have involved, along with immorality, the featherweight quality, the fundamental lack of seriousness of a puppet-man, who is garrulous, argumentative and prone to wild gestures.[76]

I shall not try to explain why it was that, very crudely, the French image of England has been 'somewhat favourable', while the English image of France has been quite clearly unfavourable. I shall simply note that the main factor was the balance of power. From 1815 on, England had been more stable and better governed than was France, and up until a very recent date she has been richer and more powerful. The British never saw much to admire in France, save, to some extent, on the cultural plane, and undoubtedly their contempt was wholly justified. Many French, on the other hand, admired and envied the wealth and stability of their neighbour. Actually, when the gap between the two countries seemed to be closing, when France appeared, rightly or wrongly, to be powerful, as under the Second Empire or on the morrow of the First World War (or, more recently, under De Gaulle's presidency), the contempt diminished and at times disappeared, but only to be replaced, because of political disputes, by animosity.[77] Changes in the respective strength of the two countries, combined with the persuasive myths of new great powers (such as the United States), also account for the weakening of the English myth in

[73] I trust the reader will bear in mind that I am not adopting here one of the standard tactics of French anglophobes, which was to inform their compatriots that the English despised them (see, for instance, Pillet, pp. 487–92; also Guyard, p. 241, on Henri Béraud, who wrote that, in the eyes of Englishmen, 'niggers started at Calais,' i.e., that the French were considered as an inferior breed).

[74] Quoted by Marandon, p. 675, note 15. [75] *Ibid.*, pp. 228–30.

[76] Guyard, pp. 171, 241; Campos, p. 68; this latter reckons that this image can be traced back to the Frenchmen whom one saw in England in the eighteenth century, and who were predominantly actors, dancing and fencing teachers, valets, and cooks, and that it was further reinforced by the behaviour of the émigrés during the French Revolution.

[77] Marandon, p. 526, observes that France earned a little sympathy in those periods when her pride was brought low by defeat, as in the post-1871 period.

France: England was not any more a country where everything was, according to Taine, on a gigantic scale, and 'the mirror of our future', as Stendhal put it, in which the French had contemplated the scenes of life in times to come.[78]

However, to arrive at a true understanding of the need of the British to feel superior, one should also plumb the depths of their collective mentality, taking into account the inheritance of a distant past, which involved England in long struggles with a much more heavily populated France: confronted with so redoubtable an enemy, it was imperative for the English to despise it and, what is more, their many victories, from Crécy to Waterloo, lent credence to the popular conviction that an Englishman was worth at least two Frenchmen. Perhaps one should also follow S. Marandon in thinking that, in the nineteenth century, the English wanted to defend themselves against the attraction exerted by France, a forbidden fruit against which they protected themselves by means of anathema and the assertion of their own moral superiority. The repressions and suppressions, which were characteristic of a moralising civilisation, may well have contributed to the success of so negative a myth.[79] One should also, of course, take into account the insularity of the British and their distrust of everything foreign,[80] the Frenchman suffering from the handicap of being, as I have already observed, the foreigner *par excellence*, the super-foreigner. It is true that a large section of educated English public opinion set aside their distrust of foreigners, to the benefit of Germany, during the nineteenth century and in the 1920s, but germanophilia was invariably accompanied by francophobia.[81] One only has to recall how Carlyle justified the annexation of Alsace by Germany in 1871 by contrasting noble, patient, deep, pious, strong, tender, loyal and solid Germany with fickle, superficial, vain and turbulent France, or, later on, the pro-German and anti-French attitude of John Maynard Keynes.[82] Finally, in the post Second World War period, negative stereotypes of France would seem to have served as tranquillisers. A journalist asked ironically, in 1960, 'How could we put up with

[78] Reboul, pp. 230, 236, 330; Taine, p. 18. [79] Marandon, p. 624.

[80] Reliable English observers admit that, overall, their compatriots are unable to take foreigners seriously and that they find everything French especially funny.

[81] The inverse was also often true. French politicians who favoured a rapprochement with Germany were generally reticent about England

[82] A. A. W. Ramsay, *Idealism and Foreign Policy. A Study of the Relations of Great Britain with Germany and France, 1860–78* (London, 1925).

ourselves if the French did not exist?'[83] It is as if people will more readily accept an unsatisfactory situation if they are able to persuade themselves that things are going even worse in the neighbouring country. Thus, during the late 1940s, the iniquities of the French black market helped to put up with British rationing.

Up until this point, I have placed the emphasis upon the stability of collective representations; however, they are neither immutable nor uniform; they are subject to variations over time and, at a given moment, public opinion in each country is rarely unanimous in its attitudes towards the other.

I will survey the short- and medium-term fluctuations very cursorily, for they are fairly well known, and the part they have played in the renewal of images seems to me to have affected not so much the content of the representations as their affective aura, that is, the sentiments of sympathy or hostility surrounding them.[84] These fluctuations have been largely dictated by the vicissitudes of political relations between England and France,[85] and wars or threats of war are the high points for these.

Thus, the Revolutionary and Napoleonic wars – and the hatred they had created – cast a long shadow, which lasted well beyond 1815; the latent hostility between the two countries was moreover periodically reawakened in subsequent decades.[86] This accounts for the relentlessly negative image of France that prevailed in England. In France, although Britain seemed then to be very much the model to imitate, even the most anglophile were not without their reservations,[87] and the English myth therefore incorporated frankly negative elements, such as hypocrisy.

The war of 1870 brought about a change. In England, fear of France almost disappeared once and for all and, while on the one hand the war

[83] I have not managed to find again the precise reference for this quotation, which was taken from a review entitled 'Perfidious Marieanne' (*sic*), of J. Fauvet's book, *The Cockpit of France*, which was published in *The Guardian* in 1960(?).

[84] Although I would not deny that these fluctuations may be violent and rapid and may give rise to a sudden reversal of feelings towards the other country; but these are mere arabesques when compared with the permanence of the basic images.

[85] Even judgements regarding the literature of the neighbouring country, and its influence, fluctuate as a function of the political conjuncture; see M. Moraud, *Le Romantisme*, pp. 56–8, 156 ff., 232 ff.

[86] It is worth recalling the bizarre 'invasion scares' in England in 1847 and 1859.

[87] Especially with regard to British foreign policy, which was judged very harshly by such avowed anglophiles as Montalembert and de Tocqueville; Comte de Montalembert, *De l'avenir politique de l'Angleterre* (Paris, 1856), pp. 5–6, 10–11, 268–9; S. Drescher, *Tocqueville and England* (Cambridge, Mass., 1964), pp. 152 ff.

provided an occasion for invective, such as Carlyle's famous letter to *The Times*, a remarkable case of fair play in kicking a fallen victim, on the other, there was a current of public opinion that felt some sympathy for the defeated country and this opened the way to a recasting of the dominant stereotypes.[88] On the French side, Germany took the place of England as the hereditary enemy, and the latter's image tended to shed its negative characteristics, so that the 'gentleman' as depicted by Taine came to be regarded as the typical Englishman.

However, at the end of the century, colonial rivalries led to the unleashing of mutual phobias. The most virulent of the English anathemas against French immorality date from this period, and France's decadence became a byeword.[89] Likewise, on the French side, new heights of anglophobia were attained, for example, in Captain Danrit's *La Guerre fatale*, a war-fiction novel which described the invasion of England by the French army, after the Royal Navy had been put out of action by flotillas of submarines, and which contained passages of great violence directed against the British.[90]

With the advent of the Entente Cordiale and the brotherhood-in-arms of the First World War, all or almost all of this past would seem to have been forgotten; perfidious Albion became dear and loyal England, France became the valiant ally, although the propaganda machines had to work hard to conceal the reservations that existed, both in public opinion and in the minds of the combatants; Marshal Haig's acerbic notes on the lack of fighting spirit in the French soldiers are an eloquent reminder of this.[91] *The Economist* wrote recently that 'the experience of two wars has inspired in the English neither sympathy nor respect for the French'; but the assertion might be not completely accurate as regards the First World War.

The political disagreements of the inter-war period were later to

[88] Marandon, pp. 496–505; Campos, pp. 49 ff.

[89] Yet, at the same time, cultural francophilia developed (see below), and Paris became a Mecca for artists and writers; cf. Starkie, pp. 129–31; Marandon, p. 587; but Heppenstall, p. 108, notes that, from this time on, francophilia was tinged with 'fashionable smartness'.

[90] Even an anglophile such as Boutmy (p. 414 ff.) was very harsh, in 1901, in his judgements of English colonial and foreign policies. The Boer war was the occasion for a number of scurrilous and obscene songs, about Queen Victoria and the Prince of Wales; see the appendix to H. Lorblanchet's unpublished thesis presented at the *Ecole des Chartes*, March 1989.

[91] R. Blacke (ed.), *Les Carnets secrets du maréchal Douglas Haig (1914–1919)* (Paris, 1964), pp. 114, 221, 258, 317, 348, 352–3, 410, 420, 428–9, 431. Conversely, in the inter-war period, a number of French ex-servicemen recalled with bitterness that they had to come to the rescue of the English army in the Spring of 1918.

create a troubled climate, in which positive and negative images co-existed or alternated in the two countries, and in which a sense of irritation and disillusionment regarding the ex-ally's behaviour was mingled with a confused feeling of unavoidable solidarity.[92] Finally, the Second World War brought about a new and savage breach, with the events of 1940 having launched the two countries upon radically different trajectories; the contrast lasted into the post-war period, when England seemed to recover rapidly and France to sink into ever deeper trouble. I hardly dare to say too much of the English image of France that these events occasioned, save to say that it was at best informed by pity.[93] On the French side, there arose, in a large section of public opinion, a new myth of Britain, involving heartfelt admiration and gratitude; but the economic and political circumstances of the 1960s and 1970s were to dispel this myth, so that in time it was to live on only in a generation which by now had grown old, and in their memories of the Battle of Britain and of the voice of the BBC.[94]

P. Reboul has written of the English myth in France during the Restoration that it was one and indivisible, i.e., that all educated French people, of whatever class or party, had the same image of England.[95] I am not sure of this and, anyway, there are invariably differences of opinion and nuances of light and shade; each country always has its opposed currents, francophiles and gallophobes, anglophiles and anglophobes. The 'philes', so to speak, have a generally favourable image of the other country and feel sympathy for it, whereas

92 So much so that anglophobia in France and francophobia in England may have been less widespread and less vigorous than at first seemed the case, given the hostility of English politicians towards France in the 1920s, or the imprecations of certain notorious French anglophobes. An interesting article is J. C. Cairns', 'A Nation of Shopkeepers in Search of a Suitable France: 1919–1940', *American Historical Review*, 79, June 1974, pp. 710–43, which stresses British exasperation at the intractableness of their ex-ally, ignorance of French realities and propensity to make harsh judgements of the neighbouring country, along with the final satisfaction, in June 1940, at being rid of their 'bloody allies' – a phrase quoted by T. Barker (ed.), *The Long March of Everyman* (London, 1975), p. 219.

93 See Starkie, p. 212, on the notion, after 1940, that France was a 'morally degenerate' country and that it was 'finished'. However, a poll conducted by UNESCO in 1948 showed that British judgements of France were not excessively pejorative, culminating in a 'friendship score' of +9 on a scale running from −100 to +100 (with the United States getting +26); see W. Buchanan, 'Stéréotypes et tension que révèle le sondage international de l'Unesco', *Bulletin international des sciences sociales*, III, 3, Autumn 1951, pp. 565, 568–9.

94 The poll analysed by J. R. Rabier, pp. 27, 29, shows that, as far as the French were concerned, the paramount quality of the British was their 'reliability'. Conversely, some later polls show that the great majority of Britons have no confidence in France and the French, especially at times of crisis (no doubt there are memories here of 1940!). See below, pp. 496, 499.

95 Reboul, pp. 228–9, 305 ff., 328–9.

the 'phobes' have a negative image, tinged with hostility; moreover, the former want to reach an *entente* with their partners on the other side of the Channel, whereas the latter tend to be indifferent or even hostile. Admittedly, individual opinions will tend to cover a wide spectrum. For example, French admirers of British institutions have often condemned English foreign policy, whereas British addicts of French culture have detested Poincaré or de Gaulle, and followers of Charles Maurras have been anglomanes in dress and manners.[96] In spite of such variations, these attitudes do by and large display, in the long term, a kind of pattern, especially in France, where anglophobe and anglophile tendencies constitute enduring currents of opinion, corresponding to quite precise political divisions.

Indeed, ever since 1815, the French far right and far left, irrespective of their successive labellings, have been anglophobe,[97] whereas the moderate groupings in between have been anglophile. According to Frances Acomb's study of eighteenth-century anglophobia, this division dates back to the end of the *Ancien Régime*, when the most conservative elements and the advanced wing of the *philosophe* movement both tended to denounce the vices of the English political system.[98]

Subsequently, the Ultras of the Restoration period, forgetful of the hospitality they had so often received as émigrés on the other side of the Channel, regarded England as the country from which revolutionary ideas had first come, whose gold and plotting had undermined the monarchy, and whose political system had inspired the constitutional Charter of 1814, which they rejected. While some of them allowed that this system had its good side in England, for it was native there, they claimed that it could only be an artifice, and therefore, damaging, in France, unless one set about re-establishing the domination of the aristocracy that still prevailed in its country of origin. Moreover, anglophobia gave the Ultras a way of defending themselves against the accusation of having returned to power through the aid of foreign countries.[99]

The most traditionalist wing of French public opinion has been marked by this hostility towards the homeland of liberalism and parliamentary government up until our own day. This feeling was

96 Guyard, pp. 237–8.
97 *Ibid.*, pp. 238 ff., brings out very well this 'union of extremes' in the inter-war period.
98 F. Acomb, *Anglophobia in France, 1763–1789* (Durham, NC, 1950).
99 Reboul, pp. 7, 12, 22, 115.

further strengthened by the religious factor, French catholics being very distrustful of a protestant country, and by an agrarian anticapitalism, which was hostile towards industrialisation and regarded an economic system based upon industry and trade as responsible for the misery of the people.[100] As the far right gravitated towards nationalism, this tendency was further reinforced by the colonial disputes of the end of the nineteenth century, then, after 1919, by England's relatively mild attitude towards Germany; it culminated in the anglophobia of the *Action Française*, of the fascistic movements of the 1930s and of Vichy; in many cases, it served as a kind of school for pro-German collaborators during the Second World War.[101] One also cannot rule out the possibility that certain aspects of this right-wing anglophobia were to resurface in Gaullist attitudes towards England.

At the other end of the political spectrum, the 'Independents' of the Restoration period execrated England for being the builder of coalitions and the conqueror who had deprived France of her natural frontiers and who had forced the Bourbons upon her. While some aspects of her political system seemed of value to them, they judged it to be on the whole out of date, corrupted, overrespectful of tradition, and they wished for France a more radical régime; they also denounced the continuing despotism of the aristocracy, the social inequality and the poverty which prevailed on the other side of the Channel.[102]

Although the more nationalistic of such themes were in time to disappear, the French far left never had much love for England.[103] It denounced the liberal and democratic camouflage – which was, moreover, so well done that it was liable to deceive the onlooker – of a capitalist society and of an imperialism which did not only exploit the English workers but also the peoples of the whole world.[104] More

100 *Ibid.*, pp. 312–16, 437.

101 See Guyard, pp. 154–7, 161, 247 ff., 255–8, 275, especially as regards the original contribution of the two last prophets of anglophobia, Louis-Ferdinand Céline and Henri Béraud (the latter, a former fellow-traveller, is a link with leftist anglophobia), who argued for a connection between the perfidy of English policy and that of individuals.

102 Reboul, pp. 17, 67–8, 115, 310–11.

103 There are virulent examples of this, at the mid nineteenth century, in Ledru-Rollin, *De la décadence de l'Angleterre* (Paris, 1850, 2 vols.); he regarded the corruption and misery prevailing in England as decisive proof of the iniquity of feudal society, government by the aristocracy and laissez-faire, all of which made decadence inevitable. In Book III, Ledru-Rollin translated and summarised (acknowledging his sources) articles published by H. Mayhew in the *Morning Chronicle* in 1849–50, on the poverty of workers in London; they have been reprinted by E. P. Thompson and E. Yeo, in their *The Unknown Mayhew* (London, 1971).

104 The oppression of Ireland, which also moved the Catholics, and of India, were two themes dear to anglophobes. For the inter-war period, see Guyard, pp. 251 ff.

recently, the left has seen England as the faithful servant of American imperialism. It is worth adding that the left has also tended to look down with some scorn upon a country which, since the seventeenth century, has not proved capable of carrying out the smallest of revolutions, and that it has felt a profound distaste for the moralism of English life and for the religious imprint with which it was marked.[105]

If one wishes to find French anglophiles, one must therefore look to the centre; it is there that one can identify, from the time of the *Doctrinaires* of the Restoration up until the pre-Mitterand socialist party, the uninterrupted existence of a current of opinion favourable to England and, more particularly, full of admiration for British political institutions. For this current, England has been the classic land of liberty, the homeland of parliamentary government and then of democracy, of reasonable and gradual reforms, of a civilised and tolerant political life. Furthermore, in the twentieth century, England also became the necessary ally, the country with which France had to have a good understanding if her security was to be guaranteed, even if she had to obey her *gouvernante anglaise*.

True enough perceptible nuances separate the anglophilia of the centre right from that of the centre left. French conservatives, for example, have tended to be especially appreciative of the cult of tradition that has prevailed in England, of the solidity which the monarchy and the social hierarchy enjoyed, of the enduring power retained by the traditional ruling classes, of the absence of centralisation, in short, of a system which, as Taine put it, gave power to the 'natural representatives', to the 'born leaders' among the population; they admired a régime in which there was 'aristocratic liberty' (Chateaubriand) and a 'living feudalism' (Montalembert).[106] The intellectual and moral qualities of the English were also admired: their common sense, their pragmatism, their disciplined and active individualism, their moral seriousness and their religiosity. In short, what was so much loved was a Burkean England, with its marvellous continuity, its slow coming to maturity, which had been so natural and intuitive, the organic growth of its institutions and the cohesion of its society (which the Labour Party and the Trade Unions, thanks to their sense of 'moderation' and their 'realism', had done nothing to undermine). Which is effectively to say that this brand of anglophilia was

[105] *Ibid.*, pp. 311 ff. [106] Taine, pp. 215–25; Reboul, pp. 72, 91–7, 298.

nostalgic:[107] England was everything that France was not, everything that she might have been if the Revolution had been halted in 1790, and yet people were painfully aware that British customs and institutions could not be transplanted to the other side of the Channel. Thus, this anglophilia was often accompanied by pessimistic views of French history and politics and, in its most extreme version, it became a form of francophobia. Thus, Taine, when visiting Oxford, compared the colleges and the fine houses of the Dons with the mediocre establishments of the Sorbonne and the Collège de France, and with the 'cages on the third floor' where Parisian professors lived. His highly characteristic observation went as follows:

> How wretched the French are, how wretched, and without a fixed abode too! We were born yesterday; from father to son, we have been ruined, by Louis XIV, by Louis XV, by the Revolution and by Napoleon. We had demolished everything, and we have had to start out all over again. Here, the new generation does not break with the previous one; reforms are superimposed upon institutions, and the present, leaning upon the past, continues it.[108]

On the centre left, anglophilia had fewer complexes, especially under the Third and Fourth Republics, when it reckoned that French democracy was not in every respect inferior to that on the other side of the Channel; it was also, of course, less enamoured of the monarchical pomp and aristocratic survivals to be found in England. What the centre left appreciated was, first and foremost, the extent and solidity of the established liberties, the unanimous adherence to parliamentary government, the sense of realism of the ruling class and its readiness to grant timely concessions and, increasingly, the importance of social reforms. This anglophilia reached one of its peaks during the 1945 Labour Government, with its welfare programmes and egalitarian policies, and its successful decolonisation.[109]

This anglophile current has been a continuous and powerful one, although the deliberate moderation of its spokesmen, intent upon imitating British understatement, has led to its being frequently

107 Taine, p. 329.

108 *Ibid.*, pp. 168–9; see also A. Thibaudet, *Histoire de la littérature française de 1789 à nos jours* (Paris, 1936), pp. 349–51; Roe, *Taine et l'Angleterre* (pp. 7–9, 14, 93–5. The same nostalgia would be evident in Tocqueville (see Drescher, pp. 193 ff., 222–3) or in Montalembert (*De l'avenir politique*); for both of them, under the Second Empire, England had become the sole hope for liberty, the sole refuge from Caesarism and from revolutionary democracy. Roe, p. 82, points out that Taine expressed for the first time his ideas on English politics in a review of Montalembert's book.

109 See, for example, J. Lequiller, *Retour de Londres* (Paris, *Le Monde*, 1961).

eclipsed by those who sing in more strident, anglophobic tones. It did, however, suffer from certain weaknesses. First of all, anglophilia was often permeated by nostalgia; secondly, it was undermined by the marginal position of some of its most fervent representatives; Guyard has made the pertinent point that, from Guizot to Taine and to André Siegfried, French authorities on English affairs have often been protestant in education, faith or general inclination. The crucial point, however, is that anglophilia has tended to become ever more impoverished, to become sclerotic and ritualised, as Guyard has shown for the inter-war period: blinded by the maintenance of traditional forms, it failed to perceive the changes which were occurring in Britain; it endlessly reiterated the same tired formulas, it presented its memories or desires as if they were realities, and it was often an England of the past that it quite simplistically venerated.

Finally, one ought perhaps to judge, as Guyard has done, that England's prestige in France was tied up with that of liberalism, of which it was the incarnation, so that when the latter went into decline, so did the former.[110]

On the British side, the situation was of course appreciably different and attitudes towards the neighbouring country are not so closely correlated with currents in political thought as was the case in France. Besides, since the 1790s, since the age of Burke and Paine, there has never been in Britain a major debate on France, comparable to the one in France which aligned the admirers and adversaries of English institutions on opposing sides, for the simple reason that the overwhelming majority of the British public reckoned that it had nothing to learn from France.[111] The latter has served, rather, as a foil, especially during the nineteenth century, for everyone who was conservative in the broad sense of the term, and who saw the country of the French Revolution as supplying a terrifying proof of the danger of rising up against the establishment and of breaking with tradition.[112] Conversely, there long survived, within a small minority of radicals (John Stuart Mill was the prominent example), the English 'Jacobin' tradition, a current which was in sympathy with France, the mother of

[110] Guyard, pp. 44, 46, 276–7, 302–5, 357. The present socialist party, which wants to be further to the left than the defunct SFIO, does not share the latter's anglophilia. Conversely, the Thatcher experience has aroused much interest on the French right.

[111] Save, very rarely, on specific points, as in the 1960s, when people used to talk in England of imitating 'French economic planning'.

[112] Marandon, p. 17.

revolutions, the land of liberty, of equality and of experimentation in political matters.[113] A section of the English 'left' felt very sympathetic towards France during the Franco-Prussian war (at least after the collapse of the Second Empire) and some among its ranks defended the Third Republic, which was seen by them as a kind of régime best suited to France.[114] Besides, radicals were often in favour of the 'liberal alliance', that is, an understanding with France, to oppose the absolutist powers of Eastern Europe.

The most interesting point to note, however, is the reversal of these positions that occurred in the twentieth century. Admittedly the debate since the beginning of the latter has been mainly concerned with the problem of England's relations with France, involving an alignment on opposite sides of opinions favourably disposed or hostile to a close understanding with her, but, for obvious reasons, it was tinged with sympathy or antipathy towards the partner on the other side of the Channel. Broadly speaking, and taking account of many exceptions and various fluctuations, it tends to be the conservatives who supported agreement with France, and who expressed a degree of sympathy or at any rate a condescending kind of understanding towards her. One should not forget, of course, that this position was mainly based upon their conception of Britain's national interests (this was the meaning of Winston Churchill's 1933 speech, 'Thank God for the French Army'), nor that there persisted in the most traditionalist and insular elements a solid fund of xenophobia, for example, that of Nancy Mitford's Uncle Matthew, for whom 'abroad is unutterably bloody and foreigners are fiends'.[115] On the other hand, a significant part, if not the majority of the British 'left', that is, the radicals, and then the Labour Party, has constantly proved, if not hostile, at any rate reticent towards the idea of entente with France, and has displayed an evident lack of sympathy towards her. Little is known of this change of attitude – in comparison with the nineteenth century; according to

113 Some nineteenth-century English democrats admired the smallholding system prevalent in France and would have liked to transplant it to Britain; Marandon, p. 384. The last representatives of this Jacobin, francophile tradition were some communist or fellow-traveller intellectuals in the post-1945 years.

114 See, for example, M. Betham-Edwards, *France of To-Day. A Survey Comparative and Retrospective* (London, 1892).

115 N. Mitford, *The Pursuit of Love* (Harmondsworth, 1949), p. 129. Nevertheless, Lord Radlett considered 'Frogs' as somewhat better than 'Huns' or 'Wops'. A good example of non-fictional francophobia is provided by Sir Henry Channon, an ultra-conservative and Chamberlainite politician; see *Chips. The Diaries of Sir Henry Channon*, edited by R. R. James (Harmondsworth, 1970), pp. 39, 187, 232–6, 319–20, 324, 465.

A. J. P. Taylor, it began during the years prior to the First World War or, more particularly, at the time of the Agadir crisis, and was completed during the aftermath of the war. I wonder, however, whether this tendency was not manifest somewhat earlier, especially in non-conformist milieux, who were prejudiced against a country that was both popish and immoral, or among intellectuals attracted by German culture. At any rate, after 1911 and above all 1919, France appeared as the quintessential imperialist and militarist country, the one responsible for all of Europe's troubles. It was held that France's alliance with Russia, then her *entente* with England (though it had been hailed at the time by the radicals), were the main causes of the war; her blind, egoistic and chauvinistic policy, which had imposed on Europe that monument of hypocrisy and folly, the Treaty of Versailles, and which had blocked any revision of it, and the enormous stockpile of armaments she maintained were the sole threat to peace.[116] Although this extreme hostility did later evaporate, sympathy towards France was never exactly effusive, and, after the Second World War, for example, her political instability, the black market, the colonial wars, the weakness of the Socialist Party and the power of the Communists were looked at by Labour Party members with distrust.[117] More recently, the authoritarian aspect, whether real or supposed, of the Fifth Republic, the unfriendly attitude of General de Gaulle towards Britain, hostility towards the Common Market and the tactical possibilities the debate around it offered for exploiting the old, popular xenophobic reflexes together created in many Labour Party members a curious francophobic complex.

It should, however, be emphasised that the most powerful and most lasting of the francophile currents in England has been cultural, in the wide sense of the term, based upon an appreciation of French literature, French arts and certain French ways of life. This current developed at the end of the nineteenth century, in connection with the reactions of writers and artists against the most constraining and

[116] A. J. P. Taylor, *The Trouble Makers. Dissent over Foreign Policy 1792–1939* (London, 1969 edn), pp. 101–3, 107–15, 160–4.

[117] It is worth recalling the famous conversation of 1949 between Sir Stafford Cripps and Averell Harriman, when the latter complained about England's reluctance to 'go into Europe'. Sir Stafford then asked what Harriman's attitude would be if the United States were asked 'to go into bed with Brazil'. The American replied 'that he would object'. 'Well, that's how we feel about France', replied the austere Chancellor; N. Beloff, *The General Says No. Britain's Exclusion from Europe* (Harmondsworth, 1963), p. 53.

philistine aspects of Victorian culture,[118] and it has persisted, although recently in a more diluted form, up until our own time. Yet this current had, of course, to be a minority one, restricted to certain upper class milieux and to intellectuals (although, in their case, it could co-exist with a political francophobia, as in the Bloomsbury set). Moreover, it carried with it, especially in what I shall call its Nancy Mitford variety, a whiff of snobbery and an association with the upper classes. These aspects were to prove counterproductive and led to francophilia being rejected by people of more modest origin, such as the hero of Kingsley Amis' *Lucky Jim*.[119] This is also true of another form of francophilia, the kind which has populist and picaresque nuances, which has a taste for the lewd and shady aspects of French life, and which is hardly likely to arouse sympathy for France on the part of the conventional Englishman.[120]

Altogether, the divisions between 'philes' and 'phobes' have almost always been appreciably different on the two sides of the Channel, both through their nature and through their positions on the political chessboard; this distortion has proved a real obstacle to serious communication and to an authentic understanding between the two countries.

Where, then, do we now stand (1974)? This is the question that I would like to pose, by way of conclusion. However, I do not hope to resolve it, for to do so one would have to take account of the massive influence of television upon collective representations, a problem which has not yet been explored.

On the French side, it would seem that the last fifteen or twenty years have seen the dispelling of the English myth. Weakened and suffering from chronic economic difficulties, England no longer counts for much in the French national consciousness; it is not detested, as many English imagine, but simply ignored; it no longer serves as a model and is no longer a real concern, a fact that is wounding to the

118 The first intimations of this new francophilia, which was a 'quest for a new morality', as well as for new literary and artistic techniques, involving the notion that France should be judged in terms of her art and not her politics, are well treated in Campos, pp. 9–10, 90–105, 164 ff., 241; he ascribes the improvement in France's image to a loss of confidence in purely English, that is, Victorian, values.

119 These francophiles have been reproached with being fanatical and intolerant, hostile towards other cultures, locked in the past and prone to mix indiscriminately a worship of Proust or Monet with an enthusiasm for good wines and expensive perfumes; see *The Times Literary Supplement*, 4 May 1962, editorial; also 31 May 1961; Starkie, p. 136; Campos, pp. 160–1.

120 This tendency was evident in the 1890s for instance in George Moore's writings (see Campos, pp. 138–47, 153 ff., 183).

most francophile British. All that remained was the fairly vague image of a people which, in spite of all their oddities and archaisms, have great qualities, but which flounder in a sea of monetary crises and strikes.[121]

On the British side, the press frequently claims that francophobia is virtually the rule. Thus, *The Observer* noted in 1967: 'Universal and astonishingly fierce anti-French feelings, even in intellectual circles ... This kind of profound national aversion is incurable in the short term.'[122] Perhaps one ought not to exaggerate, for these sentiments are certainly more widespread among politicians or in the media[123] than among historians, who, to my knowledge, are not prone to them! However, at the time of a poll conducted in 1966, which asked the British which was the foreign country in which 'they would have complete confidence', 9 per cent only of those questioned chose France (and Germany likewise), as against 67 per cent for Australia, 38 per cent for Sweden and the United States, 15 per cent for India and 10 per cent for Italy.[124] Possibly the discourtesies of Gaullist diplomacy gave rise to a crystallisation, a transfer on to, or rather against France of some of the bitterness and resentment generated by the decline of British power. Moreover, it is clear that cultural francophilia is in retreat, among the younger generation in particular, because of its counterproductive aspect (which I mentioned above), because of the rarity of truly important and original works in France, and because of the attraction of the United States.[125] Another reason may be that the France of the Fifth Republic was no longer, for many of its traditional admirers, the France they had loved, and because the narcissistic insularity of the Parisian intelligentsia ended up by exasperating even the most francophile English.[126]

[121] In the late 1970s, Britain's economic difficulties had led to the expression 'these poor English' ('*ces pauvres Anglais*') becoming current in France.

[122] The *Observer*, 17 September 1967; also *The Times Literary Supplement*, 8 April 1960.

[123] It is a fact that major British papers, such as *The Observer* and *The Economist*, without being openly francophobe, never show much sympathy for France and their comments on her are often sour. See, for instance, in the latter's issue of 22–28 August 1987, an article which starts: 'Are the French a nation of informers?'; but also, see below, p. 501. From their articles, the Paris correspondents, in recent years, of some leading British newspapers obviously felt a strong dislike of France and the French (addition made in 1989).

[124] The *Observer*, 26 June 1966.

[125] According to Campos, pp. 8, 10, 209, 241, the interest in France by English intellectual milieux reached its peak at the beginning of the twentieth century, declined from the beginning of the First World War and was virtually extinguished in the 1930s.

[126] See, for example, the front article and the editorial of *The Times Literary Supplement*, 4 May 1962, and the editorial of the same journal, 1 June 1962. Interestingly, some later articles have

This would seem to be a fairly depressing situation for the last brigade of anglophiles and francophiles. Yet is it really so new? Intellectual and affective communication between England and France has always been determined by the balance of power; particularly, when forces (or, as nowadays, weaknesses) balance each other out, political disputes give rise to incomprehension and irritation.[127] Furthermore, as *The Times Literary Supplement* wrote some years ago: 'Rarely have the relations between two civilised countries suffered more from a reciprocal *Schadenfreude*'.[128] Ever since 1815, there have been periodic announcements in each country that the irremediable decadence of the other is at hand; and more or less concealed amusement has been had from observing the crises which struck one's neighbour on the other side of the Channel, although it is usually mixed with some anxiety regarding their possible repercussions. This is a fairly friendly and, in the circumstance, inevitable form of sadism, and one can merely hope that the predictions will remain unfulfilled. On this note I will end this exposition which, owing to its simplificatory and selective schematism, is undoubtedly too close to the stereotypes that I have considered above, and which shows yet again the superficial character of the French mind and the drawbacks of Gallic logic.

Postscript

What can I add in 1985, so as to bring the above account up to date?

At first glance, the revival of the phobias which I had noted ten years ago has continued and even accelerated. Britain's entrance into the European Economic Community has multiplied inexorably the occasions for 'diplomatic' friction between London and Paris, but now this involves economic problems, which affect not only interest groups, but sometimes millions of consumers and producers, which makes it easier for the media to exploit these disputes.

It was inevitable that the current of francophobia already evident in Britain prior to 1972 should have developed further, all the more so given that membership of the EEC was still contested by a sector of British public opinion and given that 'anti-European' and insularist

poured ridicule on the French intelligentsia, especially its radical chic variety; see R. Scruton, in *The Times*, 12 August 1986, R. W. Johnson in *The Times Literary Supplement*, 31 July 1987.

127 See above, pp. 483, 485–7.

128 *The Times Literary Supplement*, 9 August 1957.

sentiments crystallised around France. The latter seemed to be the profiteer of the Common Market, as if it had grown rich at England's expense, in order to ensure the survival of 'inefficient' and 'medieval' peasants. Admittedly, various incidents, for example, acts of violence committed on French territory against British citizens, by fishermen and farmers, have given rise to legitimate indignation in British opinion and have done nothing to improve France's image. The tabloid press has exploited such a situation for all it is worth. Thus, in 1984, the anniversary of the Entente Cordiale, the *Sun* organised a competition for anti-French jokes (or, as they put it, for 'Frog jokes'), of the same kind as the paper had levelled at the Argentinians at the time of the Falklands War; it also mounted a symbolic recapture of the town of Calais. In television, BBC 1 has broadcast a long serial which ridiculed the French Resistance.[129] Admittedly BBC 2 did broadcast two documentaries which presented the Resistance in the most favourable light, but they had far fewer watchers. This contrast is undoubtedly symbolic of an ambivalence in attitude. But it is significant that *The Times* editorial, on the anniversary of the signature of the agreement of 1904 judged it necessary to recall that 'France is, in fact, the friend, ally and partner of Great Britain and not her enemy.'[130]

Although it is less powerful, less evident and, in general, less crude, a kind of anglophobia has indisputably re-emerged in France also. French seamen, and naval officers in particular, were for long the quintessential anglophobe group; now farmers have taken over this role instead! Yet, more broadly, many French people, though they are not concerned about the price of milk, now tend to see England as the filibusterer who puts spokes in the wheels of Europe and who only came into the EEC in order to sabotage it.

In short, on either side of the Channel, the other country has been presented as a selfish and greedy Shylock, in a hurry to obtain his pound of flesh, and has served as a scapegoat for many of the difficulties which western Europe has undergone.

Several polls would seem to confirm this progress of unfavourable images. Thus, in 1984, a Parisian weekly published the results of a poll in which those interviewed were requested to classify fourteen coun-

[129] *The Sunday Times*, 9 September 1984, published a strong criticism of the bad taste of this serial ('Allo' Allo'').

[130] *The Times*, 9 April 1984.

tries in order of decreasing sympathy towards them; Britain came twelfth. *The Sunday Times* replied with a similar enquiry on the other side of the Channel; France came eleventh.[131] It is therefore a little surprising to see the results of a detailed poll, which was carried out on both sides of the Channel in September 1984, under the auspices of the French services of the BBC and of the Franco-British Council; it used a sample of 2,000 people in each country.[132] It appears that 72 per cent of the French who were interviewed thought that the English were '*sympathique*'; 61 per cent of the British thought that the French were 'nice'. It is true that by no means negligible minorities (15 per cent in France, 18 per cent in England) were of a different opinion. On the other hand, if one considers only the adults under thirty years old, the percentages of favourable judgements climb to 77 per cent in France and 72 per cent in Britain. In the answers given to questions in this poll, the youth of the two countries always have a better image of the neighbouring country than do their elders. In addition, a relative, but clear majority (45 per cent in England, 48 per cent in France) of the persons interviewed in each country reject the proposition that one cannot place any confidence in the nationals of the other country. Conversely, a big, absolute majority of British and French do not accept the idea that in a period of crisis the two countries are always on the same side. A majority of the same order reckon that at the present moment Britain and France disagree on most problems. Above all 74 per cent of Britons who were polled thought that France benefits more from the EEC than does Britain; 51 per cent of French people reckon, on the other hand, that it is Britain that obtains the more. A comparison between these different percentages suggests, although the hypothesis is a fragile one, that conflicts between governments have less influence on public opinion than one would suppose.

Some of the other results are just as interesting:[133] 80 per cent of French people have never set foot in Britain (only 71 per cent of the 'young'), whereas 55 per cent of British people have visited France (including, it is true, those who have simply passed through on their

131 *The Times*, 6 July 1984.

132 *Franco-British Attitudes. Attitudes Franco-Britanniques. A Survey by the BBC French Service and the Franco-British Council*, November 1984.

133 It is a pity that some stereotypes were not tested in this survey. One might suppose that the spread of permissiveness has undermined the theme of French 'immorality'. In the 1970s, on the other hand, traditionally-minded French families refused to send their children to England, deeming it a place where they would be corrupted.

way to reach another country); 56 per cent of French people have the feeling that they do not know England at all, whereas only 30 per cent of Britons have the same impression with respect to France. I cannot think of a better way of concluding than to quote the words of James Hadley, the director of the British section of the Council, who observed that 'the tendencies observable in this poll are encouraging, but there are still huge gaps in our mutual understanding of our two countries.'

Postscript II (1989)

During the last four years, the role of the EEC as a factor of francophobia in Britain has decreased; after all, British public opinion has become used to membership of the Community, and some British claims as regards its working and finances have been satisfied. The recent outcry, in some conservative and business circles, against federalism, 'social' and 'cultural' Europe, has been directed against the Brussels bureaucracy and not against France, despite the citizenship of Jacques Delors.

On the other hand, the Channel Tunnel has met with a good deal of hostility, which some observers consider as resulting more from 'anti-French feelings' than from sheer insularity,[134] inasmuch as the project has been made to appear as inspired by France. However, the impact of this new adverse factor appears to be limited, mainly to inhabitants of Kent.

Admittedly the economic recovery which Britain has enjoyed and her higher standing in international affairs have made again some Britons arrogant, contemptuous, patronising towards foreigners. There has been a revival of jingoism and xenophobia in some quarters; for instance on the occasion of the 400th anniversary of the defeat of the Spanish Armada, there were complaints that the celebrations were ecumenical and not patriotic, that the Spanish ambassador was included among the organisers, and that an effort was made not to give offence to the Spaniards, not to stress 'the good thrashing' they had got.[135] Moreover, the King of Spain having criticised the behaviour of some British holiday-makers, the *Sun* wrote: 'We hope that in future British tourists will go anywhere in the world but Spain. We hope that

[134] *Modern and Contemporary France*, no. 34, July 1988, p. 51, in a review article by Clive Church.
[135] *The Times*, 17 September 1987.

they will tell the high and mighty Juan Carlos just what he can do with his sunshine, his beaches, his sour wine and his mouldy paella.'[136]

It has been suggested earlier that the balance of power between Britain and France has had in the past a strong influence upon British attitudes to the country across the Channel; recent developments bear out this schema. The weakening and decay of France under Mitterand's rule have undoubtedly reduced animosity towards her and enabled an improvement in Anglo-French relations. Anglophobes will find here an opportunity to revive the cliché of 'perfidious Albion', who prefers to have a banana republic on the other side of the Channel; one might also suggest that an incompetent, inefficient, corrupt, boastful government in Paris, with an elderly *roué* as its head, fits well with conventional views of France and the French. In any case, the amount of indulgence which British media and British commentators (including persons of quite conservative opinions) have displayed toward the Mitterand régime is amazing, as is their indifference to its illiberal and authoritarian characters, which would have shocked British public opinion if it had been correctly informed. Shortly before the French presidential election of 1988, *The Economist* described Mitterand as 'the best of a good bunch' of candidates and concluded: 'This newspaper ... would ... welcome another spell for Mr Mitterand.'[137]

Still, on the French side, the government–run radio and television channels and the pro-socialist press have been constant in their attacks against the conservative government and specially against the person of the Prime Minister. This campaign has included a particularly vile song, composed by a pop-singer who is a quasi-official bard of the French régime and has played a role in Mitterand's re-election campaign.

Anyhow, the ambivalence about France which has been previously observed, has continued. Malicious attacks have by no means disappeared. At the start of the holiday season in 1987, *The Times* rang the alarm against drunken driving in France; 'Watch out! There's a drunk about – though you may not see him until his Peugeot comes round the bend. Our *chers amis* have a drink problem ... The French Disease in *The Times* tomorrow.'[138] Terrorism and hostages have also been the occasion of harsh judgements.

It is easy, however, to find comments which are quite different, for

[136] Quoted by *The Times*, 26 August 1987. [137] *The Economist*, 16 April 1988, pp 17–18.
[138] Advertisement in *The Sunday Times*, 26 July 1987.

instance in the 'Survey of France', which *The Economist* published in 1988 and which is wildly and mistakenly optimistic about the present and future of the French economy, politics and culture, as is shown by its first words: 'France, by most standards, is a rich and successful country.'[139] Indeed, the interest in things French has been maintained and even increased. It is striking that a Society for French History was founded in 1987 and that it publishes an excellent scholarly journal, *French History*;[140] its annual conferences are attended by scores of participants. One does not dare to wonder how many persons would come to a colloquium on British history in France! One hopeful note, however, is the publication, in 1989, of *Les Anglais*, by Philippe Daudy, the first writer for many years to explain England to the French general public.[141]

Two opinion polls, which have been published late in 1988, can be finally mentioned. In the first, people in nine Western countries were asked whether France was, in their eyes, *sympathique* or *antipathique*; in Britain, 29 per cent of people polled said *sympathique* (the second lowest percentage among the nine countries) and 17 per cent answered *antipathique* (the second highest percentage); but the most significant figure may be that 54 per cent of the British gave no answer to the question. The second poll was done in France, where a sample of the population was asked which countries were the best friends of France; 54 per cent put Western Germany ahead; Britain came fourth, with only 21 per cent – after the USA and Belgium.[142]

If these polls give a good image of public opinion, the conclusion would be that the long history of the love–hate relationship between Britain and France has reached its end, as indifference has become the dominant feeling.

139 *The Economist*, 12 March 1988.

140 It also publishes a bulletin *The French Historian*; and there is a different journal, *Modern and Contemporary France*, which, admittedly, is inter-disciplinary and not purely historical.

141 However, new British interpretations of France keep on being published; for instance: Christopher Sinclair-Stevenson, *That Sweet Enemy: A personal view of France and the French* (London, 1988); John Ardagh, *France Today* (London, 1982; new revised edition, 1988).

142 *Figaro Magazine* 22 October (pp. 168–9) and 12 November (p. 108) 1988. In a later poll (17 June 1989, pp. 90–1), Frenchmen were asked for what EEC countries they felt sympathy; 59 per cent answered England, as against 60 per cent for Germany, while Belgium led with 76 per cent. Another question on the country which was the surest friend of France was so answered: 43 per cent Belgium, 42 per cent Germany, 34 per cent England.

On the British side, the bally-hoo and extravagance of the French Revolution bi-centenary have reawakened, among many conservatives, an obvious dislike and distrust towards France, as the country of the guillotine and the motherland of revolution and terror.

Index

www.ingramcontent.com/pod-product-compliance
Lightning Source LLC
LaVergne TN
LVHW102006210926
848483LV00009B/114
9780521344340